The Porter Sargent Handbook Series

SCHOOLS ABROAD
OF INTEREST TO AMERICANS

PUBLISHER'S STATEMENT

Esteemed educational and social critic Porter Sargent established *The Handbook of Private Schools* in 1914, with the aim "to present a comprehensive and composite view of the private school situation as it is today. No attempt has been made at completeness. The effort on the contrary has been to include only the best, drawing the line somewhat above the average."

Today, **The Porter Sargent Handbook Series** continues its founder's mission: to serve parents, educators and others concerned with the independent and critical evaluation of primary and secondary educational options, leading to a suitable choice for each student.

The Handbook of Private Schools, Guide to Summer Camps and Summer Schools (1924) and *Schools Abroad of Interest to Americans* (1959) provide the tools for objective comparison of programs in their respective fields. *The Directory for Exceptional Children,* first published in 1954, broadens that mission and service to parents and professionals seeking the optimal educational, therapeutic or clinical environment for special-needs children.

SCHOOLS ABROAD
OF INTEREST TO AMERICANS

A SURVEY OF INTERNATIONAL PRIMARY
AND PREPARATORY EDUCATION

2006/2007
11th Edition

PORTER SARGENT PUBLISHERS, INC.
Editorial Office:
11 Beacon Street, Suite 1400
Boston, Massachusetts 02108
Tel. 617-523-1670   Fax: 617-523-1021
info@portersargent.com   www.portersargent.com

PRINTED IN CANADA

LIBRARY OF CONGRESS CATALOG CARD NUMBER 67-18844

ISBN-10 0-87558-155-2
ISBN-13 978-0-87558-155-2
ISSN 0899-2002

All information as reported to Porter Sargent Publishers, Inc., as of 4/7/2006. Schools and organizations should be contacted for updated information.

Cost: US$45.00 + $7.00 shipping and handling in the USA. Additional copies are available from booksellers, or from the Publisher's customer service center: 400 Bedford St., Ste. 322, Manchester, NH 03101. Tel: 800-342-7470. Fax: 603-669-7945. orders@portersargent.com. www.portersargent.com.

TABLE OF CONTENTS

ASIA & PACIFIC ISLANDS

ILLUSTRATED ANNOUNCEMENTS

This section is provided as a supplement to the basic descriptions. Schools have paid for this space to portray—in their own words and pictures—their programs, objectives and ideals.

(includes Accrediting Associations, Advocacy Organizations, Professional Associations, School Membership Associations and Student Exchange Organizations)

SCHOOLS ABROAD
OF INTEREST TO AMERICANS

Senior Editor   Daniel P. McKeever

Production Manager   Leslie A. Weston

Editor   James S. Martinho

PORTER SARGENT PUBLISHERS, INC.

Publisher   Cornelia E. Sargent

President   John P. Yonce

Director   Keith L. Hughes

Publishers

1914-1950	Porter E. Sargent
1951-1975	F. Porter Sargent
1976-1999	J. Kathryn Sargent

PREFACE

Completely revised and updated, the 11th edition of *Schools Abroad* has resulted from data solicited by this office through thousands of E-mail, fax and postal communications, as well as with assistance from international educational associations, consultants, and agencies of the United States and foreign governments. The book's primary purpose is to objectively describe more than 750 English-medium elementary and secondary schools in roughly 150 countries

Some noteworthy format changes and additions are evident in this edition. Information pertaining to International Baccalaureate programming is now more detailed: Listings specify which of the three IB programs—Primary Years Program, Middle Years Program or Diploma Program—a school offers, if any. For the first time, we will include lists of available activities and varsity interscholastic sports. Finally, listing entry numbers have been eliminated; readers may now more easily locate schools of interest by referencing page numbers provided in the Index of Schools.

The resulting roster of schools will appeal to those parents, students, educational advisors and corporate relocation specialists who have an interest in primary and secondary schooling outside of the 50 United States. While not all listed schools enroll a substantial percentage of American students (or, for that matter, employ many instructors from the US), the schools do display a willingness to enroll American applicants. In addition, the curricula employed at listed schools facilitate a smooth transition to another international school or back to an American school.

In the editorial section of the book, we present—at no cost or obligation to the schools—the information parents and advisors want and ought to know. Data was compiled based upon responses given on our questionnaire. The accuracy and completeness of the school's description depend greatly on the thoroughness of the school's response. In preparing the descriptive text at the end of the listing, all suggestions are carefully reviewed, but our editorial staff reserves the right to determine what information is pertinent and significant in keeping with our long tradition of impartial reporting of facts.

In an effort to provide the reader with a more comprehensive listing of schools abroad, we have included abbreviated listings for many schools that failed to respond to our questionnaire by our production deadline. These listings are evident by their relative brevity: They typically contain only contact information and basic facts about their programs. The truncated nature of these listings is not a reflection of the quality of these schools, but instead indicates that further data was not available from the institutions. Our editors have independently verified information found in these listings.

Schools Abroad does not seek to evaluate differences among schools, although careful study of school descriptions may reveal varying approaches and attitudes. From an aggregate of information, we chose those aspects that seemed to most effectively characterize a school in the limited space available.

When searching for a school, final selection should come only after careful thought and planning—involving direct contact with prospective schools—as well as advice from reputable educational consultants and associations. Selecting a program solely on the basis of the school's own literature is unwise and may have unfortunate consequences.

The editorial section is alphabetically organized first by world region, then by country, city name and program name. There are two exceptions to this organizing structure: In the cases of Australia and Canada, schools are presented first by province, then by city and school name.

Preceding each country is a short geographical sketch that presents pertinent statistical information about the country. Our editors utilized two sources in compiling this data: the US Department of State Web site (www.state.gov) and the Central Intelligence Agency World Factbook (www.odci.gov).

Some schools authorize Illustrated Announcements in a separate advertising section. Through these individualized statements, schools are able to emphasize the features they consider most significant in describing their programs and aims. Those concerned with international education welcome the opportunity to read these distinctive statements, and a school thereby furthers not only recruitment, but public relations in general. A school's purchase of space in the autonomous Illustrated Announcements section, however, does not affect the length or content of its free listing.

The editors wish to thank the hundreds of school officials in all parts of the world who supplied information to make this edition possible. We are also grateful to the many educational associations—in the US and abroad—whose assistance in one form or another contributed to the completion of this book.

EDUCATIONAL SYSTEMS
OF OTHER NATIONS

WHAT KINDS OF SCHOOLS ARE AVAILABLE?

Variety is one of the basic characteristics of independent schools abroad. Countless variables exist from country to country and from school to school. Nevertheless, to aid in gaining an overall perspective, most schools may be classified in one of three general groups.

The first group consists of privately operated American-sponsored schools, often referred to as "community schools." They have been founded by members of English-speaking business and diplomatic communities abroad in response to the need for an English-language school program for their children. Many such schools are missionary founded and sponsored; some are sponsored by corporations; others are operated by individuals of diverse backgrounds.

The American community school constitutes the nearest overseas parallel to a typical school in the United States. The curricula, teaching methods and materials are American, as are a substantial percentage of faculty members and students. The basic objective of the academic program is to facilitate transfer back to schools in the US and to provide preparation for the US College Boards. Most of these schools offer courses in the language and culture of the host country and encourage enrollment from a variety of nationalities.

The second group of schools, variously referred to as binational, multinational or international, includes many American schools. They offer curricula adapted from more than one country's system of education and often enroll highly cosmopolitan students. Frequently, instruction is in more than one language. Some schools offer a program leading to the International Baccalaureate, the first international university entrance examination.

Most of these schools, however, provide different national sections or divisions (for example, English speaking, French speaking, German speaking) that fulfill curriculum and college preparation requirements of specific countries. Private schools in Switzerland probably best exemplify this kind of school, although schools of a multinational nature are located in many other parts of the world. American- and foreign-sponsored international schools may include as many as 20 to 30 nationalities among their students and often have at least half a dozen countries represented on the faculty.

The third category of schools are those native to the host country. Here is the greatest opportunity to enter thoroughly into another culture. There are, of course, many inherent obstacles to enrolling in an entirely native program, but the potential rewards are great. *Schools Abroad* contains a number of these schools throughout the world that indicate a willingness to accept American students.

While a comprehensive comparison of differing national systems is beyond the scope of *Schools Abroad,* we provide the following capsules of the educational systems of a few key countries represented in this volume.

Familiarization with the British system of education should help in understanding the concept of education elsewhere in Europe. The British influence, especially on the secondary level, is evident in many other parts of the world.

UNITED KINGDOM

Although the two countries share a common heritage and language, the school systems of Great Britain and the US differ widely. In England, independent secondary schools are called "Public Schools" and are usually boarding programs. Also private, a "Preparatory School" prepares for Public School, not for college or university. The school year is traditionally divided into three terms running from mid September to mid July, with a month's vacation in both winter and spring.

Grade Levels. An essential difference in the structures of the two systems is the concept of grade levels. A four-year secondary program, found almost universally in the US, does not exist as such in England. Boys and girls in English schools do not progress automatically from grade to grade (the term "grade" is not part of the English school lexicon). Nor do pupils accumulate "credits" for having covered work at a certain grade level. Depending entirely on ability, a student may be placed in one of several basic "forms" and in different "sets" for mathematics and languages. Once ability has been demonstrated, a pupil may be promoted during the year, sometimes more than once. There is no automatic promotion at year's end.

The National Curriculum. In 1988, England and Wales instituted a standardized national curriculum that was designed to result in a more balanced and broader program. The curriculum comprises four Key Stages: Key Stage 1 (ages 5-7), Key Stage 2 (ages 7-11), Key Stage 3 (ages 11-14) and Key Stage 4 (ages 14-16). There is no legally prescribed national curriculum in Scotland, and Northern Ireland conducts a somewhat similar curriculum.

Examinations. Required for admission to most Public Schools is successful passage of the Common Entrance Examinations (CEE), taken before age 14. After two to three years in a Public School, the student may begin taking the General Certificate of Secondary Education (GCSE), and later the General Certificate of Education (GCE) Advanced (A) levels, the British equivalents of national examinations. The Advanced Supplementary (AS) levels enable students to complement their intensive A level courses with less demanding AS levels. A typical pupils takes three courses at A level and three at AS level each term.

The GCSE, taken around age 16, usually covers six to eight subjects (with a maximum of 12) spread over several terms. Once these are behind him or her, the student moves into the Sixth Form to begin in-depth study and specialization in preparation for university entrance. Most work during the next two years is concentrated on a continuous course in two or three subjects, typically in the same general field. At the end of this period (ages 17 and 18), the student takes the GCE 'A' levels in his or her chosen subjects only.

Students who go on to college usually stay another term or two and take University Scholarship Exams. Six GCSE and two GCE subjects are generally required for university entrance, but even further study may be necessary as competition for admission increases.

British schools do not hold graduation ceremonies. A student remains as long as necessary and then departs. The British use the term "leaver" to designate a graduate.

Age and Grade Equivalencies. Passage of the British GCSE roughly corresponds to graduation from an American secondary school. By age 15 or 16, the average British student has covered the same ground as a 17- or 18-year-old in the US. British children, however, begin school at age five and have a slightly longer school year calendar. The American student who has graduated from a secondary school before going to England is usually fitted into a second-year Sixth Form with his own age group. Successful results in the GCE 'A' levels are regarded as the equivalent of having completed at least the first year of an American college course.

College Preparation and Entry. Only about one-third of the students who "leave" a British Public School go on to university. Several factors account for this. Until recently, the concept of a liberal arts college was unknown in Britain. Many young people choose higher education only if a degree is required for an intended career such as law or medicine. Often, firms and industries actually prefer to take students directly from school to conduct their own training.

The examination and selection procedures in British schools tend to screen university candidates rather thoroughly. Despite the "new universities" founded in recent years and a growing number of colleges of technology, commerce, business studies and the creative arts, competition for entrance is even keener than in the US because there are comparatively fewer places available.

OTHER NOTEWORTHY NATIONAL CURRICULA

CANADA

As in the US, there is no single national plan of education in Canada. Rather, each of the ten provinces exercises autonomous control over its own public school system. Accordingly, each provincial system should be inspected on an individual basis. Private schools usually follow the same general curriculum as the public schools, preparing for university matriculation examinations. These exams are drawn up by faculty members of certain Canadian universities or by the provincial departments of education. Influences of British, American and French education practices are found in both public and private schools throughout the country.

FRANCE

Programming begins with pre-elementary level (ages 2-6), which prepares children for elementary school. *Ecole primaire* (ages 6-11) emphasizes basic academic skills,

French secondary schools, or lycées, provide a seven-year course of study leading to the French Baccalaureate examination. The youngest class, called *sixième,* is roughly equivalent to sixth or seventh grade in the US and consists of 11- and 12-year-olds. The *cinquième, quatrième, troisième, deuxième* and *première* follow. The Brevet Etudes Première Cycle (BEPC) is an academic diploma awarded to students of about age 14 or 15. During the *première* (the sixth secondary year, equivalent to 12th grade in the US), students 16 or older may prepare for the first part of the Baccalaureate. The seventh secondary year, or *année philosophie,* is open to French students who have passed the first Baccalaureate exam or to foreign students of similar level. At the end of this final year, equivalent to the first year of college in the US, the second part of the Baccalaureate is required for admission to a French university.

GERMANY

The German curriculum follows the European model of free public education leading to various types of secondary school for academic or vocational training, rather than the US approach, in which pupils attend a single comprehensive high school. Secondary classes begin in grade 5 and continue until grade 10, at which time students choose from vocational training, technical or business school, or an academically oriented course of studies that leads to the *Abitur* diploma and college entrance.

SWITZERLAND

Switzerland is well known for its many private boarding schools, which draw upon French, German, British, American and Swiss curricula and enroll children from all over the world. It is not uncommon for a school with 50 students to have 20 nationalities represented among those enrolled. Most Swiss children go to state schools, with private schools most often operated for foreign students.

The Swiss Maturite, the national examination of Switzerland, corresponds to the French Baccalaureate. Examinations for the Maturite consist of eight to 12 subjects and include at least two foreign languages. Successful candidates are immediately admitted to the faculties of medicine, law, philosophy or science at Swiss universities.

HOW TO READ THE
SCHOOL DESCRIPTIONS

Following the concept utilized in the annual *Handbook of Private Schools,* the editors have employed a standardized, abbreviated format that presents numerous statistics in a concise manner. Although the appeal of this volume is international, the intent has been to provide information in a form understandable to the American reader.

To this end, certain liberties in terminology have been taken in the interest of clarity. In listings for schools that do not follow US programs, age spans may be listed instead of grade ranges. Americanizations appear throughout the text with the use of terms such as "Graduates" ("Leavers" is the common designation in British schools), "College Prep," "Boarding," "Day" and "Tuition"—which may have different meanings in a foreign setting.

For further clarification of the terminology used in *Schools Abroad,* consult the Key to Abbreviations, the Key to Examinations and the Key to Educational Associations. Brief notes on systems of education in selected countries appear in the section entitled "Educational Systems of Other Nations."

1.   **WESTON INTERNATIONAL SCHOOL**

        Bdg — Coed Gr 6-12; Day — Coed PS-12

2. **1004 Lausanne, Switzerland. 65 rue Pasteur. Tel: 41-22-29-29-31. Fax: 41-22-29-29-46. EST+6.**
   www.modelschool.ch.   E-mail: info@modelschool.ch.

3. **Paul Davis, Head.** BA, MEd. **Dave Yarrington, Adm.**

4. **Col Prep. Gen Acad. IB PYP. IB MYP. IB Diploma. Curr:** US Intl. **Exams:** A-level AS-level CEEB. **Bilingual:** Fr. **AP**—Eng Calc. **Feat**—Span Ger Photog Studio_Art Drama. **Supp**—Rem_Read Tut. **Sports**—Soccer. **Activities**—Acad Media.

5. **Enr 320.** B 90/110. G 110/10. Elem 150. Sec 170. US 150. Host 80. Other 90. Accepted: 90%. Yield: 80%. Avg class size: 17.

6. **Fac 45.** M 36/3. F 3/3. US 10. Host 5. Other 30. Adv Deg: 40%.

7. **Grad '05—60. Col—58. US Col—20** (Cornell 4, Brown 3, Yale 3, Stanford 2, Trinity Col-CT 2, Marist 1). Avg SAT: M/V—1150, Essay—620.

8. Tui '05-'06: Bdg SwF22,000 (+SwF3000). **Day SwF9200-12,400** (+SwF1500). **Aid:** 5 pupils (SwF100,000).

9. Summer: Acad Enrich. Tui Bdg SwF1000/2-wk ses. Tui Day SwF500/ 2-wk ses. 8 wks.

10. Endow SwF500,000. Plant val SwF1,000,000. Bldgs 5. Dorms 4. Class rms 24. Lib 10,000 vols. Labs 3. Auds 1. Courts 2. Fields 1. Swimming pools 1.

11. Est 1956. Nonprofit. Roman Catholic. Sem (Sept-Je). Assoc: CIS MSA.

12.   With an enrollment drawn chiefly from Switzerland and the US, this school prepares students for the US College Boards, as well as for the British A levels and the International Baccalaureate Diploma. The study of French is required from grade 5. Pupils choose from a variety of liberal arts electives and a small number of Advanced Placement courses.

   The active extracurricular and sports program, which is similar to that found in American secondary schools, includes joint activities with students from surrounding Swiss schools. High schoolers fulfill a 20-hour annual service commitment. There are frequent excursions to cultural events and sightseeing/study trips to various parts of Europe.

13.   **See Also Page 500**

---

   1.   SCHOOL NAME AND TYPE. Boarding, day, gender, and age or grade range information is provided. If the school conducts both boys' and girls' single-gender programs, "Coord" (Coordinate) appears prior to the grade range to distinguish the school from coeducational institutions.

   2.   CONTACT INFORMATION. City or town (province, county or canton follows, where applicable), street or mailing address, postal code, telephone and fax numbers, Web site and E-mail address are listed. Time zone information is indicated in relation to Eastern Standard Time (EST). In some cases, a separate contact address follows.

   3.   ACADEMIC HEAD OF SCHOOL. An active president or superintendent may be listed for larger schools, followed in many cases by the head of school or the principal. The director of admissions (or the administrator who fills this role) immediately follows, unless the academic head serves in this capacity.

   4.   GRADES OFFERED, CURRICULUM, EXAMINATIONS FOR WHICH STUDENTS ARE PREPARED, and COURSE OFFERINGS. The grade range incorporates preschool through postgraduate

programs, where applicable. The basic curriculum is defined as college preparatory, pre-preparatory or general academic. Availability of one or more of the curricula designed by the International Baccalaureate Organization is indicated next. The Primary Years Program (PYP) serves children ages 3-12, the Middle Years Program (MYP) runs from age 11 through age 16, and the Diploma Program is offered to pupils ages 16-19. Schools that prepare students for the French Baccalaureate are so designated. The type or types of curriculum a school follows are denoted after the heading "Curr." "Nat" indicates a native or national curriculum, "Intl" an international curriculum. Examinations and college admissions tests for which graduates are prepared are cited next. For the Key to Examinations, see page 33. If the school conducts a bilingual program, the second language of instruction will be indicated. Schools that employ English as the primary language of instruction but teach some nonlanguage classes in another language have such information after the heading "Supp Lang." A sampling of courses offered is often reported. "AP" indicates regularly offered Advanced Placement courses; "Feat" denotes courses of interest that the school does not offer at the AP level; and "Supp" refers to supplemental areas of instruction. "Sports" indicates which interscholastic sports the school offers at a varsity level. "Activities" are divided into seven broad categories: "Acad" (Academic), "Arts," "Cultural/Relig" (Cultural/Religious), "Govt/Pol" (Government/Politics) "Media," "Rec" (Games/Recreation) and "Service" (Service/Activism).

5.   ENROLLMENT. The total number of students enrolled is reported with the following breakdown: Number of boys boarding/day. Girls boarding/day. Elementary, secondary and postgraduate pupils. Number of US, host and other students enrolled. Listings may also include percentage of applicants accepted, the percentage of accepted students who enroll ("Yield") and average class size.

6.   FACULTY. Faculty figures are detailed as follows: Total number. Number of males full/part-time. Females full/part-time. Number of US, host and other teachers on faculty. The percentage of teaching faculty members who have earned advanced degrees follows.

7.   GRADUATE RECORD. These figures specify the total number of students in the previous academic year's graduating class, the number entering college or preparatory school, and the number entering US colleges or preparatory schools. As many as six US schools entered by the largest number of class members are cited. Secondary school listings may include average ACT Assessment results, in addition to average combined math and verbal Scholastic Aptitude Test (SAT) scores. Some listings also include average SAT essay scores.

8. TUITION AND SCHOLARSHIP AID. When both boarding and day divisions are maintained, both tuitions are given. Fees are reported in either US dollars or native currency (abbreviations of foreign monetary units appear in the geographical description preceding each country's listings). Grouped tuition figures (for example, SwF9200-12,400) typically give the fee span from the lowest to the highest grade. Extra expenses are indicated in parentheses. Note: Reference year for listed tuition figure(s) precedes this data. Because of fluctuating international equivalency rates, parents are urged to contact the schools directly regarding fees. Scholarship aid, if available, is designated by "Aid," with total dollar amount provided listed after number of recipients.

9. SUMMER SESSION. The type, orientation, tuition and duration may be given for schools with summer programs.

10. ESTABLISHMENT, CALENDAR and ASSOCIATION MEMBERSHIP. The establishment date, organizational structure (if school is incorporated or incorporated nonprofit), and religious or other affiliation are cited. The school calendar (typically semester, trimester or quarter) and months of operation follow. Each school's American educational association membership is listed, as provided by the associations. For a list of Educational Associations, see page 35.

11. PLANT EVALUATION and ENDOWMENT. Following the dollar values of the endowment and the physical plant is a list of the school's facilities.

12. PARAGRAPH DESCRIPTIONS. Comments are provided to amplify or supplement data reported in the statistics. They are written by the Porter Sargent Staff, based upon questionnaires and supplementary literature received from school officials. Material is not presented when it does not serve to objectively define a school. Frequently, information is provided on a school's curriculum, setting, location and history.

13. PAGE CROSS-REFERENCE TO ILLUSTRATED ANNOUNCEMENT. Some schools supply their own appraisals of ideals and objectives in paid advertisements in the "Illustrated Announcements" section. Page cross-references are appended to the paragraph descriptions of sponsoring schools.

GLOSSARY

advanced degree: Regarding teaching faculty members, this figure designates the percentage of teachers who hold any degree more advanced than a bachelor's degree.

Advanced Placement: "AP" courses, which comprise advanced material and follow the syllabi set forth by the College Board in Princeton, NJ, are listed after the AP designation in the statistical portion of the editorial listing. Upon completing each AP course, students may sit for the standardized Advanced Placement examination. Favorable scores in these examinations may lead to advanced standing at the college level.

coordinate: Used to describe schools that share some key administrators and admit both boys and girls, yet operate separate boys' and girls' divisions. Classes at such schools are not typically coeducational, although there are exceptions. Some schools operate coeducationally at certain grade levels and coordinately at others.

country day school: This concept became popular in the 1930s, when day schools (with boarding school aspirations in terms of academic rigor) flourished in rustic settings and placed importance on physical education as a complement to academics. The term lives on in many school names, although it now has no concrete meaning.

developmental reading: Instruction that focuses upon fundamental reading skills.

endowment: Funds or property donated to a school as a source of income.

enrichment: Supplemental instruction (such as a field trip) intended to amplify or extend classroom learning.

elementary: When used in the statistical portion of the editorial listing, "Elem" refers to grades preschool through eight.

honors: Many high schools designate certain advanced courses with this label. Unlike Advanced Placement courses, however, honors courses meet no specific curricular requirements and thus gain the honors distinction at the discretion of the school.

independent school: An institution of this type does not rely upon local or federal government funding, but instead operates on the basis of tuition fees, donations and, in many instances, the investment yield gained from the school's endowment.

International Baccalaureate: The International Baccalaureate Organization (IBO) is a nonprofit, international foundation that works with more than 1500 schools (in 120 countries) to oversee three distinct programs. The Primary Years Program (PYP), for students ages 3-12, is a comprehensive international curriculum that comprises learning guidelines, a teaching methodology and assessment strategies. The Middle Years Program (MYP) is a five-year program for students ages 11-16 that is flexible enough to encompass other subjects not determined by the IBO but required by local authorities. The Diploma Program, the most commonly utilized IB program in the United States, is a two-year, precollege course of study that leads to standardized examinations. It is designed for highly motivated students ages 16-19. While these programs form a continuous sequence, each may be offered independently.

learning disabilities: Comprising such conditions as dyslexia, dysgraphia and dyscalculia, learning disabilities are a group of neurological disorders that affect the brain's ability to receive, process, store and respond to information and stimuli.

makeup: An opportunity for the student to retake a course in which mastery was not previously displayed.

Montessori: Developed in the early 1900s by Maria Montessori, Italy's first female physician, the Montessori method of education incorporates manipulative materials with which children essentially teach themselves. Multi-age groupings are commonly found in Montessori settings, and the Montessori approach is usually employed during the elementary years.

nonprofit: Refers to schools that are legally categorized as Section 501(c)(3) organizations, and thus not designed to be profit-making businesses.

plant: The physical facilities and land owned by the school.

postgraduate: Typically a year in duration, "PG" offers course work to high school graduates who wish to bolster their academic credentials, improve their readiness for college, or both.

preschool: For reasons of standardization, "PS" in the statistical portion of the editorial listings refers to any schooling prior to five-year-old kindergarten (for example, nursery, transitional kindergarten or pre-kindergarten), regardless of how the school itself refers to such grade level(s).

remedial: Intended to remedy a deficit, often in the areas of math or reading.

review: Reinforcement of previously covered material.

secondary: When used in the statistical portion of the editorial listing, "Sec" refers to grades nine through 12.

tutoring: One-on-one or small-group instruction for students requiring extra assistance in a subject.

underachiever: Underachieving students, who are typically of average or above-average intelligence, have failed to learn to potential due to motivational, emotional, behavioral or learning problems.

Waldorf: Developed by Austrian intellectual Rudolf Steiner in 1919, Waldorf education typically incorporates play and toys as important learning tools for children. Instructors follow a developmental approach that seeks to address the changing needs of the child as he grows and matures.

yield: The percentage of accepted students who matriculate at the school.

KEY TO ABBREVIATIONS

Commonly accepted abbreviations do not appear on this list. For further clarification, refer to How to Read the Program Descriptions.

ACT	American College Test
Actg	Acting
Adm	Director of Admission(s)
Anat	Anatomy
Anthro	Anthropology
AP	Advanced Placement (College Board)
Arch	Archery
Architect	Architecture
ASL	American Sign Language
Aud	Auditorium
B	Boys
Bac	Baccalaureate
Basket	Basketball
Bdg	Boarding
Bio	Biology
Bowl	Bowling
CC	Community College
Cheer	Cheerleading
Chrm	Chairman
Co Day	Country Day
Comp	Computer
Coord	Coordinate, Coordinator
Crew	Crew/Rowing
Crse	Course
Curr	Curriculum
Dev	Development, Developmental
Ec, Econ	Economics
Ed, Educ	Education
EFL	English as a Foreign Language
Elem	Elementary (Preschool–Grade 8)

Endow	Endowment
Enr	Enrollment
Enrich	Enrichment
Environ	Environmental
ESL	English as a Second Language
EST	Eastern Standard Time
F	Females
F_Hockey	Field Hockey
Feat	Featured Courses
Fr	French
G	Girls
Hand	Handball
Head	Head of School, Headmaster, Headmistress
IB	International Baccalaureate
Japan	Japanese
JC	Junior College
Journ	Journalism
LI	Language of Instruction
M	Males
Milit	Military
MYP	Middle Years Program
PG	Postgraduate
Pol	Political, Politics
Port	Portuguese
Prgm	Program
PS	Preschool
PYP	Primary Years Program
Racquet	Racquetball
Rem	Remedial
Sail	Sailing
Sculpt	Sculpture
Sec	Secondary (grades 9-12)

Sem	Semester
Ses	Session
Ski	Skiing
Sociol	Sociology
Speak	Speaking
Stud	Studies
Swim	Swimming
Tech	Technical, Technology
Track	Track and Field
Tri	Trimester
Trng	Training
Tui	Tuition
Tut	Tutorial, Tutoring
Volley	Volleyball
W_Polo	Water Polo
X-country	Cross-country Running

KEY TO EXAMINATIONS

ACT
The **American College Test** examination assesses high school students' general educational development and their ability to complete college-level work in four skill areas: English, math, reading and science reasoning. Many US colleges review ACT scores as part of the admission process.

CEE
The **Common Entrance Examination** is required for admission to most Public Schools in Great Britain and is usually taken before age 14.

CEEB
College Entrance Examination Board tests are taken by many students applying to college in the United States. Commonly referred to as "College Boards," they include the **Scholastic Aptitude Test (SAT)**, the **Preliminary Scholastic Aptitute Test/National Merit Scholarship Qualifying Test (PSAT/NMSQT)** and **Achievement Tests** in various subjects.

Fr Bac
The national examination in France, the **French Baccalaureate** is divided into two parts: the first portion usually taken after age 16, the second after age 17 or 18.

GCE
Usually taken at age 17 or 18, the **General Certificate of Education** Advanced ('A') levels are the British equivalent of a national examination system. This exam provides the foundation for higher education, employment and training. The Advanced Supplementary ('AS') levels provide less intensive instruction in courses the student is not pursuing at 'A' level.

GCSE
Introduced to completely replace the GCE Ordinary ('O') levels in Britain, the **General Certificate of Secondary Education** is a series of qualifying exams. Normally taken at the end of the Fifth Form (age 15 or 16), the **GCSE** is generally thought to be comparable to a high school diploma.

IB   After two years of preparation, usually at the age of 17 or 18, students sit for the **International Baccalaureate,** which is recognized at most universities throughout the world as an acceptable entrance examination.

IGCSE   Based on the British GCSE, the **International General Certificate of Secondary Education** is tailored to international needs. The **IGCSE** is designed as a two-year common curriculum, for students ages 14 to 16 of all ability levels, leading to an internationally recognized certificate. It may lead to further education, training or employment.

SSAT   The **Secondary School Admission Test** measures the scholastic ability of students applying to secondary schools. The exam consists of two parts: the General School Ability Test and the Reading Test.

Sw Mat   In preparation for the **Swiss Maturite,** the national examination of Switzerland, students study eight to 12 subjects, including at least two foreign languages.

TOEFL   The **Test of English as a Foreign Language** uses a multiple-choice format to measure English proficiency. The test consists of three sections: Listening Comprehension, Structure and Written Expression, and Vocabulary and Reading Comprehension.

KEY TO
EDUCATIONAL ASSOCIATIONS

Association accreditation and membership data are supplied by the following associations and recorded in each editorial school listing, using the abbreviations indicated in boldface.

Listed below are accrediting associations that serve international schools at the elementary, secondary and college levels.

CIS	Council of International Schools
MSA	Middle States Association of Colleges and Schools *Accredits schools abroad that are American or American international in nature.*
NEASC	New England Association of Schools and Colleges *Accredits American and international schools abroad that employ English as the primary language of instruction.*
SACS	Southern Association of Colleges and Schools *Accredits American and international schools in Latin America.*
WASC	Western Association of Schools and Colleges *Accredits American and international schools in South and Southeast Asia, the Far East and the Pacific Islands.*

Listed below are nonaccrediting associations for which school membership or affiliation is reported in the editorial school listings.

AASCA	Association of American Schools of Central America
AASSA	Association of American Schools in South America
ACCAS	Association of Colombian-Caribbean American Schools
AISA	Association of International Schools in Africa
A/OPR/OS	US Department of State, Office of Overseas Schools
ASOMEX	Association of American Schools in Mexico
EARCOS	East Asia Regional Council of Overseas Schools
MAIS	Mediterranean Association of International Schools

For more information about the above associations—as well as other organizations that serve independent schools, parents and educational professionals—refer to the list of Associations and Organizations beginning on page 559.

SCHOOL FEATURE INDEXES

School	City	Girls' Grade Range Bdg	Girls' Grade Range Day	Boys' Grade Range Bdg	Boys' Grade Range Day	Enr	Curriculum	IB	Bilingual	Page
			ALBANIA							
TIRANA INTL	Tirana		3-13[A]		3-13[A]	75	US			299
			ANGOLA							
LUANDA INTL SCH	Luanda		PS-12		PS-12	300	Intl	PYP DP		93
			ARGENTINA							
BELGRANO DAY	Buenos Aires		K-12		K-12	847	Intl Nat		Span	509
BUENOS AIRES INTL	Buenos Aires		PS-12		PS-12	67	US			510
NORTHLANDS	Buenos Aires		PS-12		PS-12	1531	Intl Nat	DP	Span	510
LINCOLN ARGENTINA	La Lucila		PS-12		PS-12	705	US Intl	DP		511
ST ANDREW'S-ARGENTIN	Olivos		PS-12		PS-12	1899	UK Intl Nat	DP	Span	511
ST GEORGE'S-ARGENTIN	Quilmes	6-12	PS-12	6-12	PS-12	650	Intl Nat	DP	Span	512
			ARMENIA							
QSI INTL YEREVAN	Yerevan		3-17[A]		3-17[A]	84	US			459
			ARUBA							
INTL ARUBA	Wayaca		PS-12		PS-12	135	US			279
			AUSTRALIA							
NEW ENGLAND GIRLS'	Armidale	5-12	K-12				Intl Nat	DP		248
ST LEONARD'S-AUSTRAL	Brighton East		PS-12		PS-12	1700	US Intl Nat	PYP DP		250
GEELONG GRAMMAR	Corio	5-12	PS-12	5-12	PS-12	1500	Intl Nat	DP		250
GLENUNGA INTL	Glenunga		8-12		8-12	1250	Intl Nat	MYP DP		248

School	City	Girls' Grade Range Bdg	Girls' Grade Range Day	Boys' Grade Range Bdg	Boys' Grade Range Day	Enr	Curriculum	IB	Bilingual	Page
BAHRAIN SCH	Juffair	9-12	K-12	9-12	K-12	400	US Intl	DP		461
BANGLADESH										
AMER INTL DHAKA	Dhaka		PS-12		PS-12	647	US Intl	DP		145
BELARUS										
QSI INTL-MINSK	Minsk		5-15 A		5-15 A	20	US			302
BELGIUM										
BRIT INTL BRUSSELS	Brussels		PS-5		PS-5		UK			303
BRIT JR BRUSSELS	Brussels		PS-5		PS-5	120	UK			303
BRUSSELS ENG	Brussels		2.5-11 A		2.5-11 A	240	Intl			304
EUROPEAN SCH-BRUSSEL	Brussels		PS-12		PS-12		Intl			304
INTL BRUSSELS	Brussels		PS-PG		PS-PG	1397	Intl	DP		304
ANTWERP INTL	Ekeren		PS-12		PS-12	572	Intl	DP		305
WORLD INTL	Rhode St Genese		PS-10		PS-10		Intl	MYP		305
BRIT-TURVUREN	Tervuren		PS-5		PS-5	250	UK			305
BRIT BRUSSELS	Tervuren		PS-12		PS-12		Intl	DP		306
INTL MONTESSORI	Tervuren		PS-10		PS-10	230	Intl	MYP	Fr	306
ST JOHN'S-BELGIUM	Waterloo		PS-13		PS-13	930	US UK Intl	DP		307
BERMUDA										
MT ST AGNES	Hamilton		K-12		K-12	600	US			282
SALTUS GRAMMAR	Hamilton		K-12		K-12	1066	UK			282

School	City	Girls' Grade Range Bdg	Day	Boys' Grade Range Bdg	Day	Enr	Curriculum	IB	Bilingual	Page
ESCUOLA AMER DO RIO	Rio de Janeiro		PS-12		PS-12	776	US Intl Nat	DP		518
PAN AMER BAHIA	Salvador		PS-12		PS-12		US Nat			519
ASSOCIACAO ESCOLA	Sao Paulo		PS-12		PS-12	1119	US Intl	DP		519
CHAPEL	Sao Paulo		PS-12		PS-12	700	Intl	DP		520
PAN AMER CHRISTI	Sao Paulo		K-12		K-12	316	US			520
ST PAUL'S-SAO PAULO	Sao Paulo		PS-12		PS-12	1001	UK Intl Nat	DP		521
BRITISH VIRGIN ISLANDS										
CEDAR SCH	Cruz Bay		PS-12		PS-12		US Intl	MYP		283
BRUNEI										
JERUDONG INTL	Bandar Seri Begawan	9-12	PS-12	9-12	PS-12	1152	UK Intl			146
INTL BRUNEI	Berakas		PS-12		PS-12	935	UK Intl	DP		147
BULGARIA										
AMER COL SOFIA	Sofia		8-12		8-12	635	US Intl Nat	DP		308
ANGLO-AMER SOFIA	Sofia		PS-9		PS-9	190	Intl			309
BURKINA FASO										
INTL OUAGADOUGOU	Ouagadougou		PS-12		PS-12	139	US			96
CAMBODIA										
INTL PHNOM PENH	Phnom Penh		PS-12		PS-12	335	Intl	PYP MYP DP		148
NORTHBRIDGE INTL	Phnom Penh		PS-12		PS-12	273	US Intl			148
ZAMAN INTL SCH	Phnom Penh		PS-12		PS-12		UK Intl			149

School	City	Girls' Grade Range Bdg	Girls' Grade Range Day	Boys' Grade Range Bdg	Boys' Grade Range Day	Enr	Curriculum	IB	Bilingual	Page
YORK SCH	Toronto		PS-13		PS-13	600	Intl	PYP MYP DP		269
ST GEORGE'S-VANCVR	Vancouver			6-12	1-12	1130	Nat			260
YORK HOUSE	Vancouver		K-12		K-12	600	US Nat			260
GLENLYON NORFOLK	Victoria		K-12		K-12		Intl Nat	DP		261
LESTER B. PEARSON	Victoria	11-12		11-12		203	Intl	DP		261
SELWYN HOUSE	Westmount		K-11		K-11	565	Nat		Fr	273
BALMORAL HALL	Winnipeg	6-12	PS-12			500	Nat			262
ST JOHN'S-RAVENSCOUR	Winnipeg	7-12	1-12	7-12	1-12		US Nat			262
CHAD										
AMER INTL N'DJAMENA	N'Djamena		PS-8		PS-8	57	US			98
CHILE										
ANTOFAGASTA INTL	Antofagasta		PS-12		PS-12	50	Intl			522
GRANGE SCH-CHILE	Santiago		PS-12		PS-12	1740	Intl Nat	DP	Span	522
INTL PREP-SANTIAGO	Santiago		PS-12		PS-12	141	UK			523
INTL NIDO DE AGUILAS	Santiago		PS-12		PS-12	1199	US Intl	DP		523
LINCOLN INTL-SANTIAG	Santiago		PS-12		PS-12	465	US Nat		Span	524
SANTIAGO COL	Santiago		PS-12		PS-12	1813	US Intl Nat	PYP MYP DP	Span	524
CHINA										
BEIJING BISS INTL	Beijing		K-12		K-12	377	Intl	PYP MYP DP		150
BEIJING YEW CHUNG	Beijing		PS-12		PS-12	328	UK Intl	DP	Chin	150

School	Girls' Grade Range Bdg	Girls' Grade Range Day	Boys' Grade Range Bdg	Boys' Grade Range Day	Enr	Curriculum	IB	Bilingual	Page
COLUMBUS		PS-12		PS-12	1460	US Nat		Span	530
DEMOCRATIC REPUBLIC OF THE CONGO									
AMER KINSHASA		PS-12		PS-12	180	US			99
LITTLE JEWELS INTL		PS-7		PS-7		US			99
ENG LUBUMBASHI		PS-8		PS-8	32	US UK			99
COSTA RICA									
CO DAY COSTA RICA		PS-12		PS-12	840	US Nat			439
AMER INTL COSTA RICA		PS-12		PS-12	210	US Nat			440
LINCOLN-COSTA RICA		PS-12		PS-12	1148	US Intl	DP	Span	440
MARIAN BAKER		PS-12		PS-12	201	US Nat			441
COTE D'IVOIRE									
INTL COMM ABIDJAN		K-12		K-12	66	US			100
CROATIA									
AMER ZAGREB		PS-12		PS-12	165	US Intl	DP		310
CUBA									
INTL HAVANA		PS-12		PS-12	190	US UK Intl	DP		284
CYPRUS									
AMER ACAD-LARNACA		1-13		1-13	1000	UK Nat			462
MEDITERRANEAN HS		1-12		1-12	310	UK			462
AMER ACAD-LIMASSOL		PS-12		PS-12		UK			463

School	City	Girls' Grade Range Bdg	Girls' Grade Range Day	Boys' Grade Range Bdg	Boys' Grade Range Day	Enr	Curriculum	IB	Bilingual	Page
INTER-AMER	Guayaquil		PS-12		PS-12	208	US			531
ACADEMIA COTOPAXI	Quito		PS-12		PS-12	475	US Intl Nat	PYP DP		531
ALLIANCE ACAD	Quito	1-12	PS-12	1-12	PS-12	400	US			532
AMER QUITO	Quito		PS-12		PS-12	2240	US Intl Nat	MYP DP	Span	532
BRIT QUITO	Quito		PS-12		PS-12	240	UK Intl	DP		533
EGYPT										
SCHUTZ AMER	Alexandria		PS-12		PS-12	236	US			101
AMER INTL EGYPT	Cairo		PS-12		PS-12	987	US Intl	DP		101
BRIT INTL SCH-CAIRO	Cairo		PS-12		PS-12		UK Intl	DP		102
INTL CHOUEIFAT-CAIRO	Cairo		K-12		K-12	93	US UK			102
MAADI BRIT INTL	Cairo		PS-5		PS-5	290	UK			102
MODERN ENG SCH	Cairo		PS-12		PS-12		US UK Intl	DP		103
NEW CAIRO BRIT	Cairo		PS-12		PS-12		UK			103
CAIRO AMER COL	Maadi		K-12		K-12	1331	US Intl	DP		103
NEW HORIZON INTL SCH	Maadi		K-12		K-12		UK			104
EL GOUNA INTL SCH	Red Sea		PS-12		PS-12		UK			104
EL SALVADOR										
INTL SAN SALVADOR	San Salvador		PS-12		PS-12	310	US Nat			441
AMER-SAN SALVAD	San Salvador		PS-12		PS-12	1720	US Nat			442
ACAD BRIT CUSCATLECA	Santa Tecla		PS-12		PS-12	1299	UK Intl	DP		442

School	City	Girls' Grade Range Bdg	Girls' Grade Range Day	Boys' Grade Range Bdg	Boys' Grade Range Day	Enr	Curriculum	IB	Bilingual	Page
HELSINGIN SUOMALAINE	Helsinki		10-12		10-12	75	Intl	DP	Finnish	322
INTL HELSINKI	Helsinki		K-12		K-12	331	Intl	PYP MYP DP		322
FRANCE										
GREENFIELD BILINGUAL	Collonges-au-Mont-d'Or		PS-5		PS-5	160	Nat		Fr	323
INTL TOULOUSE	Colomiers		PS-12		PS-12	307	UK Intl	DP		324
BRIT PARIS	Croissy-sur-Seine		K-12		K-12	830	UK			324
COL INTL FONTAINEBLE	Fontainebleau		1-12		1-12	400	UK		Fr	325
EAB-MARCQ-EN-BAROEUU	Marcq-en-Baroeul	6-12	6-12	6-12	6-12	546	Intl Nat	DP	Fr	326
MOUGINS	Mougins		PS-12		PS-12	400	UK			326
MARYMOUNT-FRANCE	Neuilly sur Seine		PS-8		PS-8	400	US			326
INTL NICE	Nice		K-12		K-12	303	Intl	DP		327
EAB-PARIS	Paris		9-12		9-12		US UK Intl Nat	DP		328
EAB-PARIS JEANNINE	Paris		PS-12		PS-12	2900	Intl Nat	DP	Fr	328
INTL PARIS	Paris		PS-12		PS-12	500	Intl	PYP MYP DP		328
LENNEN BILINGUAL	Paris		PS-5		PS-5	120	US Nat		Fr	329
UN NURSERY-PARIS	Paris		2-5A		2-5A	59	US Nat		Fr	329
SCHOOL YEAR-FRANCE	Rennes	11-12		11-12		60	US			330
AMER PARIS	Saint Cloud		PS-12		PS-12	751	US Intl	DP	Fr	330
LYCEE INTL	Saint-Germain-en-Laye		PS-12		PS-12	680	US		Fr	331
SECT INTL DE SEVRES	Sevres		K-12		K-12	1063	Intl Nat	DP	Fr	332

School	City	Girls' Grade Range Bdg	Day	Boys' Grade Range Bdg	Day	Enr	Curriculum	IB	Bilingual	Page
BERLIN BRANDENBURG	Kleinmachnow		PS-12		PS-12	425	Intl	PYP MYP DP		340
LEIPZIG INTL	Leipzig		PS-12		PS-12	353	Intl	DP		341
FRANKFURT INTL	Oberursel		PS-12		PS-12	1750	Intl	DP		342
ERASMUS INTL	Potsdam	11-12	PS-12	11-12	PS-12	80	US Intl Nat			342
SCHULE SCHLOSS SALEM	Salem	5-13	5-13	5-13	5-13	700	Intl Nat	DP	Ger	343
MUNICH INTL	Starnberg		PS-12		PS-12	1281	Intl	PYP MYP DP		344
INTL STUTTGAR	Stuttgart		PS-12		PS-12	455	Intl	DP		344
THURINGIA INTL	Weimar	K-7	K-7	K-7	K-7	66	Intl			345
GHANA										
GHANA INTL	Accra		PS-12		PS-12	1130	UK			109
LINCOLN COMM	Accra		PS-12		PS-12	540	US Intl	PYP MYP DP		109
GREECE										
AMER COMM ATHENS	Halandri		PS-12		PS-12		US Intl	MYP DP		346
TASIS HELLENIC INTL	Kifissia		PS-12		PS-12	196	US Intl	PYP MYP DP		346
CAMPION	Pallini		PS-12		PS-12		UK Intl	DP		347
PINEWOOD INTL SCH	Pilea	9-12	PS-12	9-12	PS-12		US Intl	MYP DP		347
ANATOLIA COL	Pylea	7-12	7-12	7-12	7-12	1299	Intl Nat	DP		348
ST LAWRENCE-GREECE	Varkiza		PS-12		PS-12	800	UK			348
GUAM										
ST JOHN'S-GUAM	Tumon Bay	9-12	PS-12	9-12	PS-12	505	US Intl	DP		158

School	City	Girls' Grade Range Bdg	Girls' Grade Range Day	Boys' Grade Range Bdg	Boys' Grade Range Day	Enr	Curriculum	IB	Bilingual	Page
GERMAN SWISS INTL	Hong Kong		K-12		K-12	1185	UK Intl			162
HONG KONG ACAD	Hong Kong		PS-8		PS-8	250	Intl	PYP		163
ISLAND	Hong Kong		11-18^A		11-18^A		UK			163
AMER INTL-KOWLOON	Kowloon		PS-12		PS-12		US			163
INTL CHRIST-KOWLOON	Kowloon		K-12		K-12	800	US			164
CHRISTIAN ALLIANCE	Kowloon City		K-12		K-12	500			164	164
LI PO CHUN UNITED WO	Sha Tin	11-12		11-12		252	Intl	DP		164
SHA TIN COL	Sha Tin		6-12		6-12	1150	UK Intl	DP		165
HONG LOK YUEN INTL	Tai Po		PS-6		PS-6	338	UK			165
HONG KONG INTL	Tai Tam		PS-12		PS-12	2630	US			166
HUNGARY										
AMER INTL BUDAPEST	Budapest		PS-12		PS-12	678	Intl	DP		349
INTL BUDAPEST	Budapest		PS-8		PS-8	52	US Intl			349
INTL CHRIST BUDAPEST	Diosd		1-12		1-12	204	US			350
ICELAND										
AMER EMB REYKJAVIK	Reykjavik		K-6		K-6	11	US			350
INDIA										
CANADIAN INTL-INDIA	Bangalore	7-12	PS-12	7-12	PS-12	320	Intl	DP		167
INTL BANGALORE	Bangalore	2-12	PS-12	2-12	PS-12	389	Intl	DP		167
MALLYA ADITI INTL	Bangalore		K-12		K-12	465	UK Nat			168

School	City	Girls' Grade Range Bdg	Girls' Grade Range Day	Boys' Grade Range Bdg	Boys' Grade Range Day	Enr	Curriculum	IB	Bilingual	Page
MOUNTAINVIEW INTL	Salatiga	7-12	K-12	7-12	K-12	141	US			180
SEMARANG INTL	Semarang		PS-8		PS-8	69	UK			181
HILLCREST INTL	Sentani	6-12	K-12	6-12	K-12	175	US			181
SEKOLAH CIPUTRA	Surabaya		PS-12		PS-12	1080	Intl	PYP MYP DP		182
SURABAYA INTL	Surabaya		PS-12		PS-12	235	US			182
YOGYAKARTA INTL	Yogyakarta		PS-7		PS-7	30	Intl			183
IRAQ										
BAGHDAD INTL	Baghdad		PS-12		PS-12	47	UK			466
IRELAND										
ST ANDREW'S-IRELAND	Blackrock		PS-12		PS-12	1184	US Intl	DP		351
ISRAEL										
ANGLICAN JERUSALEM	Jerusalem		PS-12		PS-12	203	Intl	DP		467
WALWORTH BARBOUR	Kfar Shmaryahu		K-12		K-12	450	US			467
ITALY										
INTL NAPLES	Bagnoli		PS-12		PS-12	237	US			352
UNITED WORLD ADRIATI	Duino	11-12		11-12		196	Intl	DP		353
INTL SCH OF FLORENCE	Florence		PS-12		PS-12	368	US Intl Nat	PYP MYP DP		353
AMER INTL GENOA	Genoa		PS-12		PS-12	241	US Intl Nat	DP		354
CASTELLI INTL	Grottaferrata		1-8		1-8	110	Intl		Ital	354
AMER MILAN	Milan		PS-12		PS-12	496	US Intl	MYP DP		355

JAPAN

School	City	Girls' Grade Range Bdg	Girls' Grade Range Day	Boys' Grade Range Bdg	Boys' Grade Range Day	Enr	Curriculum	IB	Bilingual	Page
FUKUOKA INTL	Fukuoka	7-12	PS-12	7-12	PS-12	221	US Intl			183
HIROSHIMA INTL	Hiroshima		PS-12		PS-12	127	Intl	PYP MYP DP		184
CANADIAN ACAD	Kobe	8-12	PS-12	8-12	PS-12	703	US Intl	DP		184
MARIST BROTHERS INTL	Kobe		PS-12		PS-12	250	US			185
ST MICHAEL'S-KOBE	Kobe		PS-6		PS-6	158	UK			186
KYOTO INTL	Kyoto		PS-8		PS-8	90	Intl			186
NAGOYA INTL	Nagoya		PS-12		PS-12	305	US			187
KANSAI CHRISTIAN	Nara Ken		1-12		1-12	44	US			187
OSAKA INTL SCH	Osaka		PS-12		PS-12	240	Intl	PYP MYP DP		188
OSAKA YMCA INTL	Osaka		PS-7		PS-7	84	Intl			189
HOKKAIDO INTL	Sapporo	7-12	PS-12	7-12	PS-12	182	US			189
TOHOKU INTL	Sendai		PS-12		PS-12	105	US			190
AMER JAPAN	Tokyo		PS-12		PS-12	1400	US			191
AOBA-JAPAN INTL	Tokyo		PS-9		PS-9	580	Intl			191
BRIT SCH IN TOKYO	Tokyo		PS-7		PS-7	500	UK			191
CHRISTIAN ACAD JAPAN	Tokyo	6-12	K-12	6-12	K-12	426	US			192
INTL SACRED HEART	Tokyo		PS-12		PS-K	518	Intl			192
K INTL SCH-TOKYO	Tokyo		PS-12		PS-12		Intl	PYP MYP DP		193
NISHIMACHI INTL	Tokyo		K-9		K-9	400	Intl Nat		Japan	193

School	City	Girls' Grade Range Bdg	Day	Boys' Grade Range Bdg	Day	Enr	Curriculum	IB	Bilingual	Page
HILLCREST SEC	Nairobi	6-12	7-12	6-12	7-12	440	UK			111
INTL KENYA	Nairobi		PS-13		PS-13	574	US Intl	DP		112
KENTON COL PREP	Nairobi		6-13^A		6-13^A	240	UK			112
ROSSLYN ACAD	Nairobi		K-12		K-12	459	US			113
KUWAIT										
DASMAN MODEL SCH	Dasman		PS-12		PS-12		US Nat		Arabic	472
AMER KUWAIT	Hawalli		PS-12		PS-12	1379	US			473
NEW ENG SCH-KUWAIT	Hawalli		PS-12		PS-12		UK			473
UNIVERSAL AMER	Khaldiya		PS-12		PS-12	1063	US			474
AMER CREATIVITY ACAD	Kuwait		PS-12^C		PS-12^C	1813	US			474
ENG SCH FAHAHEEL	Kuwait		PS-12		PS-12	800	UK			474
KUWAIT ENG SCH	Kuwait		PS-12		PS-12	2000	UK			475
KUWAIT NATL ENG	Kuwait		PS-12		PS-12		UK			475
AL-BAYAN BILINGUAL	Safat		PS-12		PS-12	1700	US Nat		Arabic	475
BRIT SCH-KUWAIT	Safat		PS-12		PS-12	1450	UK			476
ENG-KUWAIT	Safat		PS-8		PS-8		UK			476
KYRGYZSTAN										
BISHKEK INTL	Bishkek		PS-12		PS-12		US			198
SILK RD INTL SCH	Bishkek		K-10		K-10	110	UK			199
LAOS										

School	City		Grades	Enrollment	Type	Program	Page
VIENTIANE INTL	Vientiane		PS-12		Intl		199
LATVIA							
INTL LATVIA	Jurmala		PS-12	172	Intl	PYP MYP DP	365
LEBANON							
AMER COMM BEIRUT	Beirut		PS-12	997	US Intl Nat	DP	477
INTL COL-BEIRUT	Beirut		PS-12	3407	US Intl Nat	DP	477
EASTWOOD COL	Mansourieh		PS-12	800	US Nat		478
SAGESSE HIGH	Metn	5-12	PS-12	1157	US Intl Nat	DP	478
LESOTHO							
MACHABENG COL	Maseru	6-12	6-12	114	Intl	DP	114
MASERU ENG	Maseru	3-12A	3-12A	286	Intl	PYP	114
NATL UNIVERSITY	Roma	K-12	K-12	428	Intl Nat		114
LITHUANIA							
AMER INTL-VILNIUS	Vilnius		PS-10	84	US		366
LUXEMBOURG							
INTL LUXEMBOURG	Luxembourg		PS-12	598	Intl	DP	366
ST GEORGE'S-LUXEMBOU	Weimershof		PS-8		UK		367
MACEDONIA							
AMER MACEDONIA	Skopje		PS-12	63	US		367
QSI INTL SCH-SKOPJE	Skopje		PS-8	144	US		368
MADAGASCAR							
AMER ANTANANARIVO	Antananarivo		PS-12	144	US		115

School	City	Girls' Grade Range Bdg	Girls' Grade Range Day	Boys' Grade Range Bdg	Boys' Grade Range Day	Enr	Curriculum	IB	Bilingual	Page
				MALAWI						
BISHOP MACKENZIE	Lilongwe		PS-12		PS-12		UK Intl	DP		116
KAMUZU	Mtunthama	6-12		6-12		517	UK			116
				MALAYSIA						
KINABALU INTL	Kota Kinabalu		PS-10		PS-10	135	UK			200
GARDEN INTL	Kuala Lumpur		3-18^A		3-18^A	1790	UK			200
INTL KUALA LUMPUR	Kuala Lumpur		PS-12		PS-12	1240	US Intl	DP		201
MONT'KIARA INTL	Kuala Lumpur		PS-12		PS-12	700	US Intl	DP		202
DALAT	Penang	1-12	PS-12	1-12	PS-12	311	US			202
INTL PENANG UPLANDS	Penang	3-12	PS-12	3-12	PS-12		UK Intl	DP		203
ST CHRISTOPHER-MALAY	Penang		PS-5		PS-5	500	UK			203
ALICE SMITH SCH	Seri Kembangan		PS-12		PS-12		UK			203
				MALI						
AMER INTL BAMAKO	Bamako		PS-12		PS-12	115	US			117
				MALTA						
VERDALA INTL	St Andrews	7-12	PS-12	7-12	PS-12	230	US UK Intl	DP		369
ST EDWARD'S MALTA	Vittoriosa				K-10	600	UK Nat			369
				MARSHALL ISLANDS						
KWAJALEIN	Kwajalein		PS-12		PS-12	400	US			204
				MAURITIUS						

School	City	Girls' Grade Range Bdg	Girls' Grade Range Day	Boys' Grade Range Bdg	Boys' Grade Range Day	Enr	Curriculum	IB	Bilingual	Page
GEO WASH-MOROCCO	Casablanca		PS-12		PS-12		US		Arabic Fr	120
RABAT AMER	Rabat		PS-12		PS-12	388	US Intl	DP		120
AMER TANGIER	Tangier	7-12	PS-12	7-12	PS-12	330	US			120
MOZAMBIQUE										
AMER INTL-MOZAMBIQUE	Maputo		PS-12		PS-12	260	US Intl	DP		121
MAPUTO INTL SCH	Maputo		PS-12		PS-12		UK			122
MYANMAR										
INTL YANGON	Yangon		PS-12		PS-12		US			205
NAMIBIA										
WINDHOEK INTL	Windhoek		PS-12		PS-12	296	Intl	PYP DP		122
NEPAL										
BRIT-KATHMANDU	Kathmandu		K-12		K-12	280	UK			206
BUDHANILKANTHA SCH	Kathmandu	4-12		4-12		928	UK Nat			206
KATHMANDU INTL	Kathmandu	6-12		6-12		75	UK			207
LINCOLN-NEPAL	Kathmandu		PS-12		PS-12	260	US			207
THE NETHERLANDS										
INTL AMSTERDAM	Amstelveen		PS-12		PS-12	870	Intl	PYP MYP DP		371
BRIT AMSTERDAM	Amsterdam		2-11A		2-11A		UK			371
ARNHEM INTL SCH	Arnhem		PS-12		PS-12	225	Intl	MYP DP		372
AFNORTH INTL	Brunssum		PS-12		PS-12	1200	US Intl			372

School	City		Grades	Grades	No.	Type	Programs	Page
INTL EINDHOVEN	Eindhoven		11-18[A]	11-18[A]	305	Intl	MYP DP	373
REGIONAL INTL	Eindhoven		PS-6	PS-6	441	UK Intl		373
INTL THE HAGUE	The Hague		11-18[A]	11-18[A]	600	Intl	DP	374
INTL HILVERSUM	Hilversum		1-12	1-12	400	Intl	PYP MYP DP	374
VIOLENSCHOOL INTL	Hilversum		PS-5	PS-6	280	Intl	PYP	374
INTL MAASTRICHT	Maastricht		11-19[A]	11-19[A]	215	UK Intl	DP	375
HET RIJNLANDS	Oegstgeest		6-12	6-12	250	Intl	DP	375
INTL SCH EERDE	Ommen	2-12	PS-12	2-12	130	Intl	DP	376
AMER INTL ROTTERDAM	Rotterdam		PS-12	PS-12	226	Intl	DP	376
ROTTERDAM INTL	Rotterdam		7-12	7-12	165	UK Intl	DP	376
BRIT NETHERLANDS	Voorschoten		PS-13	PS-13	1600	UK		377
AMER THE HAGUE	Wassenaar		PS-12	PS-12	1050	US Intl	DP	378
NETHERLANDS ANTILLES								
INTL CURACAO	Curacao		K-12	K-12	287	US Intl	DP	287
INTL ST MAARTEN	St Maarten		4-12	4-12	287	US		287
NEW ZEALAND								
AUCKLAND INTL COL	Auckland	10-12	10-12	10-12	253	Intl	DP	253
KRISTIN SCH	Auckland		PS-12	PS-12	1400	Intl Nat	PYP DP	253
NICARAGUA								
AMER-NICARAGUAN	Managua		PS-12	PS-12	1021	US Nat		452
NIGER								
AMER INTL NIAMEY	Niamey		K-12	K-12	56	US		123

School	City	Girls' Grade Range Bdg	Girls' Grade Range Day	Boys' Grade Range Bdg	Boys' Grade Range Day	Enr	Curriculum	IB	Bilingual	Page
				NIGERIA						
HILLCREST SCH	Jos		1-12		1-12	250	US			124
AMER INTL LAGOS	Lagos		PS-9		PS-9	479	US			124
BRIT INTL-LAGOS	Lagos	6-12	6-12	6-12	6-12	250	UK Intl			124
GRANGE SCH-NIGERIA	Lagos		K-10		K-10	595				125
GREENSPRINGS	Lagos	6-13	PS-13	6-13	PS-13	951	UK Intl	PYP		126
				NORWAY						
OSLO INTL	Bekkestua		K-12		K-12	500	UK Intl	DP		378
INTL BERGEN	Bergen		PS-10		PS-10	210	Intl	MYP		379
RED CROSS NORDIC UWC	Flekke	11-12		11-12		200	Intl	DP		379
INTL STAVANGER	Hafrsfjord		PS-12		PS-12	462	Intl	DP		380
SKAGERAK INTL SCH	Sandefjord		PS-12		PS-12		Intl	DP		380
BRIT INTL-STAVANGER	Stavanger		PS-7		PS-7	150	UK			380
BIRRALEE INTL	Trondheim		4-13A		4-13A	175	UK Intl Nat			381
				OMAN						
AMER INTL MUSCAT	Azaiba		PS-12		PS-12	430	US Intl			479
AMER-BRIT-MUSCAT	Muscat		PS-12		PS-12	743	US UK Intl PYP MYP DP			480
BRIT SCH MUSCAT	Ruwi		PS-12		PS-12	800	UK			481
MUSCAT PRIVATE SCH	Ruwi		PS-12		PS-12	700	UK Nat			481
				PAKISTAN						

School	City	Girls' Grade Range Bdg	Girls' Grade Range Day	Boys' Grade Range Bdg	Boys' Grade Range Day	Enr	Curriculum	IB	Bilingual	Page
AMER WARSAW	Konstancin-Jeziorna		PS-12		PS-12	824	US Intl	DP		382
BRIT INTL CRAKOW	Krakow		3-19A		3-19A	144	UK Intl	DP		382
INTL SCH OF KRAKOW	Krakow		PS-12		PS-12	72	US Intl Nat			383
BRIT SCH-WARSAW	Warsaw		PS-12		PS-12	500	UK Intl	DP		383
			PORTUGAL							
INTL SAO LOURENCO	Almancil		PS-12		PS-12	266	UK			384
INTL PREP-CARCAVELOS	Carcavelos		PS-6		PS-6	160	UK			385
ST JULIAN'S-PORTUGAL	Carcavelos		PS-12		PS-12	900	UK Intl Nat	DP		385
ST DOMINIC'S-PORTUGA	Sao Domingos de Rana		PS-12		PS-12	650	Intl	PYP MYP DP		385
CARLUCCI AM INTL SCH	Sintra		PS-12		PS-12	435	US Intl	DP		386
			PUERTO RICO							
BALDWIN	Bayamon		PS-12		PS-12		US			288
TASIS DORADO	Dorado		PS-8		PS-8		US			288
CARIBBEAN SCH	Ponce		PS-12		PS-12	610	US			289
ACADEMIA DEL PERPETU	San Juan		K-12		K-12	1360	US			289
CARIBBEAN PREP	San Juan		PS-12		PS-12	741	US			289
ROBINSON	San Juan		PS-12		PS-12		US			290
SAINT JOHN'S-PR	San Juan		PS-12		PS-12	750	US			290
			QATAR							
DOHA COL	Doha		6-12		6-12	740	UK			482

School	City	Girls' Grade Range Bdg	Girls' Grade Range Day	Boys' Grade Range Bdg	Boys' Grade Range Day	Enr	Curriculum	IB	Bilingual	Page
DAKAR ACAD	Dakar	6-12	K-12	6-12	K-12	331	US			127
INTL DAKAR	Dakar		PS-12		PS-12	193	US			127
SERBIA AND MONTENEGRO										
ANGLO-AMER BELGRADE	Belgrade		6-12		6-12	20	US UK Intl			392
BRIT INTL BELGRADE	Belgrade		PS-12		PS-12	96	US UK			393
INTL SCH BELGRADE	Belgrade		PS-12		PS-12	223	US Intl	PYP MYP DP		393
SEYCHELLES										
INTL-VICTORIA	Victoria		PS-13		PS-13	398	UK			127
SINGAPORE										
AUSTRALIAN-SINGAPORE	Singapore		PS-12		PS-12	1200			214	214
CANADIAN-SINGAPORE	Singapore		PS-12		PS-12	1200	Intl	PYP MYP DP		214
CHATSWORTH INTL	Singapore		PS-12		PS-12	630	US UK			214
DOVER COURT PREP	Singapore		PS-9		PS-9	650	UK			214
ETON HOUSE INTL	Singapore		PS-6		PS-6	440	UK Intl	PYP	Chin	215
INTL COMM-SINGAPORE	Singapore		PS-12		PS-12	200	US			215
ISS INTL SINGAPORE	Singapore		PS-12		PS-12	502	Intl	PYP MYP DP		216
OVERSEAS FAMILY	Singapore		K-JC		K-JC	2363	US UK Intl	PYP MYP DP		216
SINGAPORE AMER	Singapore		PS-12		PS-12	2900	US			217
TANGLIN TRUST	Singapore		3-18^A		3-18^A	1950	UK			217
UNITED WORLD-SING	Singapore	6-12	PS-12	6-12	PS-12	2855	Intl	DP		218

School	City	Girls' Grade Range		Boys' Grade Range		Enr	Curriculum	IB	Bilingual	Page
		Bdg	Day	Bdg	Day					
INTL COL SPAIN	Alcobendas		PS-12		PS-12	602	Intl Nat	PYP MYP DP		397
SIERRA BERNIA	Alfaz del Pi		3-18[A]		3-18[A]	200	UK Nat			397
BENJAMIN FRANKLIN	Barcelona		PS-12		PS-12	378	US			398
KENSINGTON	Barcelona		4-18[A]		4-18[A]	250	UK			398
AMER BILBAO	Berango		PS-12		PS-12	313	US Intl Nat			399
ENG CENTRE	El Puerto de Santa Maria		PS-12		PS-12	820	UK Nat		Span	399
AMER BARCELONA	Esplugues de Llobregat		PS-12		PS-12	500	US Nat			400
XABIA INTL	Javea		PS-12		PS-12	300	UK			400
RUNNYMEDE COL	La Moraleja		PS-12		PS-12	540	UK			401
BRIT GRAN CANARIA	Las Palmas de Gran Canaria	PS-12		PS-12		476	UK Nat			401
OAKLEY COL	Las Palmas de Gran Canaria	PS-12		PS-12		350	UK			402
AMER MADRID	Madrid		PS-12		PS-12	730	US Intl Nat	DP		402
BRIT-POZUELO	Madrid		PS-12		PS-12	1892	UK Nat		Span	403
EVANGELICAL CHRIST	Madrid		1-12		1-12	90	US			403
HASTINGS	Madrid		PS-12		PS-12	400	UK			404
INTL MADRID	Madrid		PS-12		PS-12	550	UK Nat			404
ALOHA COL	Marbella		PS-12		PS-12	700	UK Intl Nat	DP		405
ENG-MARBELLA	Marbella		PS-12		PS-12	500	UK			405
ACAD INTL-SPAIN	Marratxi		PS-12		PS-12	226	UK Nat		Span	405
SUNLAND INTL	Nueva Aljaima		PS-9		PS-9	212	UK Intl Nat	PYP		406

School	City	Girls' Grade Range Bdg	Girls' Grade Range Day	Boys' Grade Range Bdg	Boys' Grade Range Day	Enr	Curriculum	IB	Bilingual	Page
INTL HELSINGBORG	Helsingborg		K-12		K-12	333	Intl Nat	PYP MYP DP		410
BLADIN'S INTL	Malmo		PS-10		PS-10	238	Intl	PYP MYP		410
SODERKULLA INTL	Malmo		PS-8		PS-8	125	Nat		Swedish	411
INTL NACKA	Saltsjobaden		PS-10		PS-10	350	Intl Nat	PYP MYP DP		411
SIGTUNASKOLAN HUMANI	Sigtuna	9-12	9-12	9-12	9-12	590	Intl Nat	MYP DP		411
STOCKHOLM INTL SCH	Stockholm		PS-12		PS-12	357	Intl	PYP MYP DP		412
UPPSALA INTL SCH	Uppsala		PS-9		PS-9	160	Nat		Swedish	412
SWITZERLAND										
INTL ZUG	Baar		PS-8		PS-8	522	Intl	PYP MYP		413
INTL RHEINTAL	Buchs		1-11		1-11	90	Intl	PYP MYP		413
AIGLON COL	Chesieres-Villars	9-18A	9-18A	9-18A	9-18A	350	UK			414
ST GEORGE'S-SWITZ	Clarens	6-12	PS-12		PS-9	158	UK			415
INTL GENEVA	Geneva		PS-13		PS-13	3749	Intl	PYP MYP DP	Fr	415
GENEVA ENG	Genthod		PS-6		PS-6	170	UK			416
GSTAAD INTL	Gstaad	8-12		8-12			US UK			417
BRIT BERN	Gumligen		PS-6		PS-6	68	UK Intl			417
INTL BERNE	Gumligen		PS-12		PS-12	236	Intl	PYP MYP DP		418
ECOLE D'HUMANITE	Hasliberg-Goldern	5-12	1-12	5-12	1-12	146	US UK Nat		Ger	418
BILINGUAL-TERRA NOVA	Kusnacht		PS-6		PS-6	116	Intl Nat		Ger	419
LAKESIDE BILINGUAL	Kusnacht		PS-7		PS-7	135	Intl Nat		Ger	419

School	City	13-19^A	13-19^A	13-19^A	13-19^A	Enr	Affiliation	Program	Lang	Page
BRILLANTMONT INTL	Lausanne					150	US UK			420
ECOLE NOUVELLE	Lausanne	7-12	PS-12	7-12	PS-12	476	Intl Nat		Fr	420
INTL LAUSANNE	Le Mont-sur-Lausanne		PS-12		PS-12	557	UK Intl	PYP DP		421
LEYSIN AMER	Leysin	9-PG		9-PG		330	US Intl	DP		422
TASIS-SWITZ	Montagnola-Lugano	7-PG	K-PG	7-PG	K-PG	384	US Intl	DP		422
INSTITUT MONTE ROSA	Montreux	6-PG	6-PG	6-PG	5-PG	65	US			423
NEUCHATEL JR COL	Neuchatel	12-12		12-12		90				424
INTL SCH BASEL	Reinach	PS-12	PS-12	PS-12	FS-12	940	Intl	PYP MYP DP		425
INSTITUT LE ROSEY	Rolle	1-12	1-12	3-6	3-6	340	Intl	DP	Fr	425
JFK-SWITZ	Saanen	K-8	K-8	K-8	K-8	60	Intl			426
INSTITUT AUF DEM ROS	St Gallen	1-13	1-13	1-13	1-13	170	US UK Nat			427
COL DU LEMAN INTL	Versoix	7-13	PS-13	7-13	PS-13	1752	US UK Intl	DP	Fr	427
COL ALPIN BEAU	Villars-sur-Ollon	6-12		6-12		163	US UK Intl	DP	Fr	428
ZURICH INTL	Wadenswil	FS-12	FS-12	FS-12	FS-12	928	US Intl	PYP DP		428
RIVERSIDE-ZUG	Zug	7-12	7-12		7-12	115	Intl	MYP		429
INSTITUT MONTANA	Zugerberg	5-12	5-12	5-12	5-12	145	US Intl	DP		430
INTER-COMM ZURICH	Zumikon	PS-12	PS-12		FS-12	683	Intl	PYP MYP DP		430
SYRIA										
ICARDA INTL	Aleppo	PS-12	PS-12	PS-12	PS-12	263	US UK Intl	PYP DP		486
DAMASCUS COMM	Damascus	PS-12	PS-12	PS-12	PS-12		US			487
TAIWAN										
NATL EXPERIMENTAL	Hsinchu	1-12	1-12	1-12	1-12	537	US		Chin	224

School	City	Girls' Grade Range Bdg	Girls' Grade Range Day	Boys' Grade Range Bdg	Boys' Grade Range Day	Enr	Curriculum	IB	Bilingual	Page
AMER SCH-TAICHUNG	Taichung	9-12	PS-12	9-12	PS-12	185	US			225
MORRISON CHRISTIAN	Taichung	9-12	K-12	9-12	K-12	916	US			226
DOMINICAN INTL	Taipei		K-12		K-12	386	US			226
TAIPEI AMER	Taipei		K-12		K-12	2200	US Intl	DP		227
TAIPEI EURO SCH	Taipei		PS-12		PS-12	920	UK Intl Nat	DP		227
TAJIKISTAN										
DUSHANBE INTL	Dushanbe		K-11		K-11	228	UK			487
TANZANIA										
INTL TANGANYIKA	Dar es Salaam		PS-12		PS-12		Intl	PYP MYP DP		133
INTL MOSHI	Moshi	2-12	PS-12	2-12	PS-12	490	Intl	PYP MYP DP		133
TANGA INTL SCH	Tanga	PS-6	PS-6	PS-6	PS-6		Intl			134
THAILAND										
BANGKOK PATANA	Bangkok		PS-12		PS-12	2145	UK Intl	DP		228
CONCORDIAN INTL	Bangkok		PS-8		PS-8	120	Intl	MYP	Mandarin Thai	228
HARROW INTL	Bangkok		PS-12		PS-12	730	UK			229
INTL COMM-BANGKOK	Bangkok		PS-12		PS-12	661	US			230
KIS INTL SCH	Bangkok		PS-9		PS-9	301	Intl	PYP MYP		231
NEW INTL-THAILAND	Bangkok		PS-12		PS-12	1346	UK Intl	PYP MYP DP		231
RUAMRUDEE INTL	Bangkok		K-12		K-12	1649	US Intl	DP		232
ST JOHN'S-BANGKOK	Bangkok		PS-12		PS-12	393	UK			232

School	City				Enroll	Affiliation	Programs	Page
ST STEPHEN'S-BANGKOK	Bangkok		PS-5	PS-5	402	UK		233
AMER PAC-THAILAND	Chiang Mai	6-12	1-12	1-12		US		233
CHIANG MAI INTL	Chiang Mai		K-12	K-12	400	US		234
NAKORN PAYAP INTL	Chiang Mai		PS-12	PS-12		US		234
PREM TINSULANONDA	Chiang Mai	4-12	K-12	K-12	414	Intl	PYP MYP DP	234
INTL EASTERN	Chonburi		PS-12	PS-12	375	US Intl	DP	235
REGENTS-THAILAND	Chonbury	3-12	PS-12	PS-12	780	UK Intl	DP	235
ST STEPHEN'S-KHAO Y	Nakhorn Ratchasima	3-12	3-12	3-12	108	UK		236
INTL BANGKOK	Nonthaburi		K-12	K-12	1878	US Intl	DP	237
BRIT CURR INTL	Phuket	2-12	PS-12	PS-12	800	UK Intl	DP	237
QSI INTL PHUKET	Phuket		PS-12	PS-12	97	US		238
ST ANDREWS RAYONG	Rayong		PS-10	PS-10	235	UK Intl		238
TOGO								
AMER INTL LOME	Lome		PS-12	FS-12	55	US		134
BRIT SCH OF LOME	Lome	3-12	PS-12	FS-12	135	Intl	PYP MYP DP	135
TRINIDAD AND TOBAGO								
INTL PORT OF SPAIN	Westmoorings		PS-12	FS-12	379	US		291
TUNISIA								
AMER COOP TUNIS	Tunis		PS-12	FS-12	530	US Intl	DP	135
TURKEY								
ROBERT COL	Arnavutkoy	9-12	9-12	9-12	954	US Nat	Turkish	488
ISTANBUL INTL	Bebek		PS-12	FS-12	422	US Intl	PYP MYP DP	489

School	City	Girls' Grade Range Bdg	Girls' Grade Range Day	Boys' Grade Range Bdg	Boys' Grade Range Day	Enr	Curriculum	IB	Bilingual	Page
BILKENT U PREP	Bilkent		PS-12		PS-12	560	US UK Intl Nat	DP		490
BRIT INTL ISTANBUL	Istanbul		PS-12		PS-12	350	UK Intl	DP		490
ENKA SCHS	Istanbul		PS-12		PS-12	1000	Intl	DP		491
EYUBOGLU	Istanbul		PS-12		PS-12	2050	Intl Nat	PYP MYP DP	Turkish	491
IRMAK	Istanbul		PS-12		PS-12	585	Intl Nat	DP	Turkish	492
MEF INTL	Istanbul		PS-12		PS-12	100	Intl	PYP DP		492
ISIKKENT	Izmir		PS-9		PS-9	323			493	
IZMIR OZEL TURK KOLE	Izmir	6-12	PS-12	6-12	PS-12	2750	Nat		Turkish	494
TARSUS AMER COL	Tarsus		1-12	9-12	1-12	522	US Nat		Turkish	494
TURKMENISTAN										
ASHGABAT INTL SCH	Ashgabat		PS-12		PS-12	69	US			495
TURKS AND CAICOS ISLANDS										
ASHCROFT	Providenciales		PS-8		PS-8	120	Intl			292
UGANDA										
INTL UGANDA	Kampala		PS-12		PS-12	425	Intl	PYP MYP DP		136
KABIRA INTL	Kampala		PS-12		PS-12		UK Intl	MYP		136
RAINBOW INTL	Kampala	2-13	PS-13	2-13	PS-13	670	UK			136
UKRAINE										
KIEV INTL SCH	Kiev		PS-12		PS-12	186	US Intl	DP		431
PECHERSK INTL	Kiev		PS-12		PS-12	320	Intl	PYP MYP DP		431

School	City	Girls' Grade Range Bdg	Girls' Grade Range Day	Boys' Grade Range Bdg	Boys' Grade Range Day	Enr	Curriculum	IB	Bilingual	Page
ANTILLES	St Thomas		PS-12		PS-12	520	US			294
UZBEKISTAN										
TASHKENT INTL	Tashkent		K-12		K-12	196	US Intl	DP		503
TASHKENT ULUGBEK	Tashkent		K-12		K-12	245	UK			503
VENEZUELA										
ESCUELA CAMPO ALEGRE	Caracas		PS-12		PS-12	635	US Intl	DP		540
INTL CARACAS	Caracas		PS-12		PS-12	225	US Intl	MYP DP		540
ESCUELA BELLA VISTA	Maracaibo		K-12		K-12	430	US Intl	DP		541
INTL MONAGAS	Maturin		PS-12		PS-12	110	US			541
MORROCOY INTL	Puerto Ordaz		PS-10		PS-10		Intl			542
COLEGIO INTL CARABOB	Valencia		PS-12		PS-12	322	US			542
VIETNAM										
HANOI INTL SCH	Hanoi		K-12		K-12	240	Intl	DP		239
UN INTL-HANOI	Hanoi		PS-12		PS-12	700	Intl	PYP MYP DP		240
INTL HO CHI MINH	Ho Chi Minh City		PS-12		PS-12	589	Intl	DP		240
SAIGON S INTL	Ho Chi Minh City		PS-12		PS-12	382	US			241
WALES										
ATLANTIC COLLEGE	Vale of Glamorgan	11-12		11-12		330	Intl	DP		432
YEMEN										
SANAA INTL	Sanaa		PS-12		PS-12	119	US			504

ZAMBIA

AMER INTL-LUSAKA	Lusaka	PS-12	PS-12	425	Intl	PYP MYP DP	137
BANANI INTL	Lusaka	8-12		130	Intl Nat		138
INTL LUSAKA	Lusaka	PS-12	PS-12	379	UK Intl	DP	138
LUSAKA INTL	Lusaka	PS-10	PS-10	350	UK		139

ZIMBABWE

HARARE INTL SCH	Harare	PS-12	PS-12		Intl	PYP DP	140
PETERHOUSE BOYS'	Marondera	12-18[A]		480	UK		140

Schools with More Than 33% US Students

Schools with More Than 66% US Faculty

Southern Hemisphere Schools on a
Northern Hemisphere Academic Schedule

SCHOOL LISTINGS

Statistical details are provided for each country. Within each country, schools are arranged alphabetically by city or town, then program name.

AFRICA

INDEX TO COUNTRIES IN AFRICA

AFRICA

ANGOLA

Sq. Miles: 481,400 (Slightly less than twice the size of Texas). **Country Pop:** 11,190,786 (2005). **Capital:** Luanda, pop. 4,000,000 (2005). **Terrain:** Well-watered agricultural highlands; savanna in the far east and south; and rainforest in the north and Cabinda. **Ethnic Group(s):** Ovimbundu Kimbundu Bakongo European. **Religion(s):** Roman_Catholic Protestant Indigenous_Beliefs. **Official Language(s):** Portuguese. **Other Language(s):** Ovimbundu Kimbundu Bakongo. **Government:** Republic. **Independence:** 1975 (from Portugal). **Per Capita Income:** $951 (2005). **GDP:** $21.6 billion (2005). Agriculture 8%. Industry 67%. Services 25%. **Currency:** Angolan Kwanza (Kz).

LUANDA INTERNATIONAL SCHOOL
Day — Coed Gr PS-12

Luanda, Angola. Rua da Talatona, Caixa 1566, Barrio da Talatona. Tel: 244-222-46-07-52. Fax: 244-222-46-07-82. EST+6.
www.lisluanda.com   E-mail: enrollment@lisluanda.com
  Col Prep. IB PYP. IB Diploma. Curr—Intl. Feat—Humanities Port Span Comp_Sci Econ Performing_Arts Visual_Arts. Supp—LD.
  Enr 300.
  Fac 38.
  Tui '05-'06: Day $13,000-14,000.
  Est 1996. Nonprofit. Tri (Aug-June). Assoc: A/OPR/OS CIS NEASC.

BOTSWANA

Sq. Miles: 224,710 (About the size of Texas). **Country Pop:** 1,690,000 (2001). **Capital:** Gaborone, pop. 186,007 (2001). **Terrain:** Desert and savanna. **Ethnic Group(s):** Tswana Kalanga Kgalagadi Herero Bayeyi Himbukush Basarwa Khoi. **Religion(s):** Christian Indigenous_Beliefs. **Official Language(s):** English. **Other Language(s):** Setswana Ikalanga. **Government:** Parliamentary Republic. **Independence:** 1966 (from France). **Per Capita Income:** $4736 (4736). **GDP:** $8.33 billion (2005). Agriculture 2%. Mining 35%. **Currency:** Botswanan Pula (P).

MARU A PULA SCHOOL
Bdg and Day — Coed Ages 12-19

Gaborone, Botswana. Private Bag 0045. Tel: 267-3912953. Fax: 267-3973338. EST+7.
www.map.ac.bw   E-mail: principal.map@info.bw
A. S. Taylor, Prin.

Col Prep. Curr—UK. **Exams**—IGCSE A-level. **Feat**—Fr Setswana Comp_Sci Studio_Art Drama Music.

Enr 588. B 74/219. G 70/225. US 3. Host 346. Other 239. Accepted: 75%. Avg class size: 26.

Fac 57. Adv Deg: 28%.

Grad '05—103.

Tui '05-'06: Bdg P42,000-45,000 (+P1000). **Day P25,500** (+P1000). **Aid:** 124 pupils.

Summer: Acad Enrich. 12 wks.

Endow P5,000,000. Plant val P10,000,000. Dorm rms 50. Class rms 42. Lib 20,000 vols. Sci labs 7. Lang labs 4. Comp labs 2. Auds 1. Theaters 1. Art studios 2. Music studios 2. Fields 2. Courts 2. Pools 1.

Est 1972. Nonprofit. Tri (Jan-Dec).

Maru a Pula School's British-style curriculum prepares students for the A-level and IGCSE examinations. The lower forms focus on basic courses, including English, history, geography, math and sciences, supplemented by French, Setswana, art and commerce. Students in the upper forms concentrate on English, history, geography, economics, math, physics, chemistry and biology.

Approximately half of the students are from Botswana, with the other half representing roughly 40 nations. Leisure and cultural activities occupy four afternoons each week. Boys' and girls' team and individual sports are available.

NORTHSIDE PRIMARY SCHOOL
Day — Coed Gr K-7

Gaborone, Botswana. PO Box 897. Tel: 267-352440. Fax: 267-353573. EST+7.
www.northsideschool.net   E-mail: administration@northsideschool.net
Mark McCarthy, Head.

Gen Acad. Curr—Intl Nat UK. **Feat**—Fr Setswana Computers Studio_Art Music. **Supp**—ESL Rem_Math Rem_Read.

Enr 433. B 213. G 220. Avg class size: 29.

Fac 33. M 4. F 25/4. Adv Deg: 6%.

Grad '05—34.

Tui '06-'07: Day P7350-7900 (+P1500).

Bldgs 5. Class rms 17. Lib 6000 vols. Sci labs 1. Comp labs 1. Music studios 1. Gyms 1. Fields 1. Courts 1. Pools 1.

Est 1974. Nonprofit. Anglican. Tri (Jan-Dec). Assoc: AISA ECIS.

Although the curriculum at Northside is British oriented, it does prepare students for US secondary school exams and for the Botswana Primary Leaving Examination. The program includes English, history and literature, arts and crafts, social studies, sciences, and traditional and modern mathematics.

Students participate in various sports and extracurricular activities.

WESTWOOD INTERNATIONAL SCHOOL
Day — Coed Gr K-12

Gaborone, Botswana. PO Box 2446. Tel: 267-306736. Fax: 267-306734. EST+7.
www.westwood.ac.bw   E-mail: westwood@info.bw
Michael J. Thompson, Prin. BEd, MA. **Chantal McAllister, Adm.**
   Col Prep. Gen Acad. IB Diploma. Curr—Intl. **Exams**—IGCSE. **Feat**—Fr Span
   Setswana. **Supp**—EFL ESL LD Rem_Math Rem_Read.
   Enr 624. Elem 491. Sec 133. US 20. Host 117. Other 487. Accepted: 50%. Avg
   class size: 23.
   Fac 61. M 19/1. F 38/3. US 4. Host 4. Other 53. Adv Deg: 19%.
   Grad '05—43.
   Tui '05-'06: Day P21,705-35,712.
   Bldgs 15. Class rms 32. 2 Libs 15,000 vols. Sci labs 3. Lang labs 2. Comp labs 1.
   Theaters 1. Art studios 2. Fields 2. Courts 3. Pools 2.
   Est 1988. Nonprofit. Tri (Jan-Dec). Assoc: AISA A/OPR/OS CIS NEASC.

Westwood originally served as a primary school on the Maru a Pula School
campus. In 1993, the school moved to its present site in Gaborone West and has
since become a full primary and secondary school. The school community includes
children from more than 40 different countries. Program emphasis is on preparing
boys and girls to reenter their home systems, or, in many instances, to move on to
an educational system elsewhere in the world.

Students prepare for the IGCSE examinations and then work toward the IB
Diploma. Aside from English, pupils may study French, Spanish or Setswana, and
both ESL and EFL are also available.

Community service trips, athletics, rock climbing, drama and music complement academics.

LEGAE ACADEMY
Day — Coed Gr 6-12

Mogoditshane, Botswana. PO Box 750. Tel: 267-3924-313. Fax: 267-3924-333.
   EST+7.
www.info.bw/~legae   E-mail: legae@info.bw
E. Oommen, Prin.
   Col Prep. Curr—Intl UK. **Exams**—IGCSE. **Feat**—Setswana Comp_Sci Econ
   Studio_Art Bus. **Supp**—ESL.
   Tui '05-'06: Day P16,500-20,000 (+P100).
   Est 1992. Tri.

BURKINA FASO

Sq. Miles: 106,000 (About the size of Colorado). **Country Pop:**
13,925,313 (2005). **Capital:** Ouagadougou, pop. 1,000,000. **Terrain:** Savanna, brushy plains and scattered hills. **Ethnic Group(s):**
Mossi Bobo Mande Lobi Fulani Gurunsi Senufo. **Religion(s):** Muslim

Christian Indigenous_Beliefs. **Official Language(s):** French. **Other Language(s):** Moore Dioula. **Government:** Republic. **Independence:** 1960 (from France). **Per Capita Income:** $300 (2003). **GDP:** $4.5 billion (2003). Agriculture 32%. Industry 18%. **Currency:** African Coalition Franc (CFAF).

INTERNATIONAL SCHOOL OF OUAGADOUGOU
Day — Coed Gr PS-12

Ouagadougou, Burkina Faso. c/o US Embassy, 01 BP 35. Tel: 226-50-36-21-43. Fax: 226-50-36-22-28. EST+5.
www.iso.bf   E-mail: iso@iso.bf
Larry Ethier, Dir. BS, MEd.
  Col Prep. Curr—US. **Exams**—ACT AP CEEB. **AP**—Eng Fr Calc US_Hist. **Feat**—Comp_Sci African_Stud Studio_Art Drama Music. **Supp**—ESL Tut.
  Sports—Basket Ice_Hockey Soccer Softball Squash Swim Tennis Track Volley. **Activities**—Arts Govt/Pol Media Rec Service.
  Enr 139. Elem 95. Sec 44. US 43. Host 20. Other 76. Accepted: 98%. Avg class size: 10.
  Fac 29. M 6/2. F 13/8. US 12. Host 6. Other 11. Adv Deg: 37%.
  Grad '05—9. **Col**—6. **US Col**—3. (Wm & Mary, KS St). Avg SAT: M/V—1053, Essay—513.
  Tui '05-'06: Day €8940-12,070 (+€5000).
  Bldgs 10. Class rms 17. Lib 8000 vols. Sci labs 1. Comp labs 1. Fields 1. Courts 3. Pools 1.
  Est 1976. Nonprofit. Quar (Aug-June). Assoc: AISA A/OPR/OS MSA.

Serving the needs of the American community and children of other diplomatic and development mission representatives from more than 25 nations seeking an English-language education, the school offers a US curriculum at the elementary and secondary levels. ISO administers a test each February to gauge basic skill improvement, and boys and girls may take the PSAT, SAT, ACT and Advanced Placement examinations during the high school years. Math and reading are individualized by level. Other subjects are grouped according to grade; offerings include science, math, French, humanities and literature classes.

Frequent overnight and local field trips complement academic work. ISO also conducts a student-exchange program and an active extracurricular program.

CAMEROON

Sq. Miles: 184,000 (About the size of California). **Country Pop:** 16,380,005 (2005). **Capital:** Yaounde, pop. 1,111,641 (2005). **Largest City:** Douala, pop. 1,300,000 (2005). **Terrain:** Northern plains, central and western highlands, southern and coastal tropical forests. **Ethnic Group(s):** Cameroon_Highlanders Equatorial_Bantu Kirdi Fulani Northwestern_Bantu Eastern_Nigritic. **Religion(s):** Christian Indigenous_Beliefs Muslim. **Official Language(s):** French English. **Other Language(s):** Pidgin Fulfulde Ewondo. **Government:** Republic. **Independence:** 1961. **GDP:** $10.1 billion (2002). Agriculture 44%. Manufacturing 20%. Services 36%. **Currency:** African Coalition Franc (CFAF).

AMERICAN SCHOOL OF YAOUNDE
Bdg — Coed Gr 2-12; Day — Coed PS-12

Yaounde, Cameroon. BP 7475. Tel: 237-223-0421. Fax: 237-223-6011. EST+6.
www.asoy.org   E-mail: school@asoy.org
Nanci Shaw, Dir. PhD.
    Col Prep. Curr—US. **Exams**—AP CEEB. **AP**—Eng Fr Bio Chem US_Hist Comp_ Govt & Pol Econ Art_Hist. **Feat**—Comp_Sci. **Supp**—ESL Rem_Read.
    Sports—Basket Soccer Volley. **Activities**—Acad Govt/Pol Rec.
    Enr 180. B 5/85. G 3/87. US 45. Host 45. Other 90. Accepted: 99%. Yield: 98%. Avg class size: 14.
    Fac 24. M 4/1. F 17/2. US 11. Host 3. Other 10.
    Grad '05—13. Col—13. US Col—9.
    Tui '05-'06: Bdg $19,800-20,900 (+$1500-3300). **Day $8600-11,900** (+$1500-3300). **Aid:** 18 pupils ($57,000).
    Bldgs 6. Class rms 20. Lib 15,000 vols. Sci labs 1. Comp labs 2. Art studios 1. Fields 1. Basketball courts 1. Tennis courts 4. Pools 1.
    Est 1964. Nonprofit. Quar (Sept-June). Assoc: AISA A/OPR/OS CIS MSA.

Founded to serve children of American diplomats, this US-style school now provides an early childhood (age 2½) through high school program for a varied student body. All boys and girls take core courses in the following areas: English/language arts, math, science, social studies, French and physical education. Work in the computer lab on keyboarding and computer skills is integral to the program.

ASOY's extracurricular activities program enables pupils to engage in new or familiar pursuits. Certain activities, among them swimming, tae kwon do and tennis lessons, incur an additional fee. The school also emphasizes community service: All high schoolers engage in a two-year project prior to graduation.

RAIN FOREST INTERNATIONAL SCHOOL
Day — Coed Gr 7-12

Yaounde, Cameroon. c/o SIL Intl, BP 1299. Tel: 237-230-56-21. Fax: 237-230-24-09. EST+6.
www.rfis.org   E-mail: rfis-admin@sil.org
Vincent Griffis, Dir. BA, MA, MBA. Mary LeBeuf, Adm.
    Col Prep. Gen Acad. Curr—UK US. **Exams**—AP CEEB TOEFL IGCSE. **AP**—Eng Fr Calc Bio Chem Physics Econ. **Feat**—Comp_Sci Bible. **Supp**—EFL.
    Sports—Basket Soccer Volley. **Activities**—Arts Rec.
    Enr 103. B 49. G 54. Elem 20. Sec 83. US 52. Host 32. Other 19. Accepted: 90%. Avg class size: 13.
    Fac 19. M 6/2. F 10/1. US 11. Host 4. Other 4. Adv Deg: 10%.
    Grad '05—23. Col—18. US Col—9. (Wartburg, VA Polytech, U of MN-Twin Cities,

LA St-Baton Rouge, John Brown, IL Inst of Tech). Avg SAT: M/V—1114.
Tui '05-'06: Day $8300. Aid: 54 pupils ($68,800).
Bldgs 4. Class rms 14. Libs 1. Sci labs 1. Comp labs 1. Auds 1. Art studios 1. Music studios 1. Courts 1.
Est 1991. Nonprofit. Evangelical. Sem (Aug-June). Assoc: AISA.

This multimission Evangelical school provides middle school and high school programming with a strong Christian worldview. The curriculum incorporates elements from the American and British systems. In grades 11 and 12, students choose from general and Advanced Placement courses that lead to a general studies, college preparatory or honors diploma.

Boys and girls enroll from more than a dozen countries in North and South America, Africa, Asia, Australia and Europe. Hostelling is available to pupils whose parents reside outside of Yaounde.

CHAD

Sq. Miles: 496,000 (About twice the size of Texas). **Country Pop:** 9,826,419 (2002). **Capital:** N'Djamena, pop. 1,000,000 (2005). **Terrain:** Desert, mountainous north, large arid central plain, fertile lowlands in extreme southern region. **Ethnic Group(s):** Gorane Zaghawa Kanembou Ouaddai Arab Baguirmi Hadjerai Fulbe Kotoko Hausa Boulala Maba Sara Moudang Moussei Massa French. **Religion(s):** Muslim Christian Indigenous_Beliefs. **Official Language(s):** French Arabic. **Other Language(s):** Sara. **Government:** Republic. **Independence:** 1960 (from France). **Per Capita Income:** $237 (2003). **GDP:** $2.65 billion (2003). Agriculture 38%. Industry 13%. Services 49%. **Currency:** African Coalition Franc (CFAF).

AMERICAN INTERNATIONAL SCHOOL OF N'DJAMENA
Day — Coed Gr PS-8

N'Djamena, Chad. BP 413. Tel: 235-52-21-03. Fax: 235-51-56-54. EST+6.
Contact: c/o US State Dept, 2410 N'Djamena Pl, Washington, DC 20521.
www.aisn.org   E-mail: aisn@aisn.org
Bradford Barnhardt, Dir.
  Gen Acad. Curr—US. **Feat**—Fr.
  Enr 57. Elem 57. US 15. Host 4. Other 38.
  Fac 10. US 2. Host 2. Other 6.
  Tui '05-'06: Day $8000-10,000 (+$1125).
  Nonprofit. Quar (Aug-June). Assoc: AISA A/OPR/OS MSA.

DEMOCRATIC REPUBLIC OF THE CONGO

Sq. Miles: 905,063 (Slightly less than one-quarter the size of the US). **Country Pop:** 60,085,804 (2000). **Capital:** Kinshasa, pop. 6,500,000 (2005). **Terrain:** Varies from tropical rainforests to mountainous terraces, plateau, savannas, dense grasslands, and mountains. **Ethnic Group(s):** Luba Kongo Anamongo. **Religion(s):** Roman_Catholic Protestant Traditional_Beliefs Kimbanguist Muslim. **Official Language(s):** French. **Other Language(s):** Lingala Swahili Kikongo Tshiluba. **Government:** Republic. **Independence:** 1960 (from Belgium). **GDP:** $5.6 billion (2003). Agriculture 55%. Industry 11%. Services 44%. **Currency:** Congolese Franc (CDF).

THE AMERICAN SCHOOL OF KINSHASA
Day — Coed Gr PS-12

Kinshasa, Democratic Republic of the Congo. Tel: 243-81-8846619. EST+6.
Contact: c/o American Embassy, Unit 31550, APO, AE 09828.
www.tasok.cd   E-mail: tasokinquiries@yahoo.com
Rob Leveillee, Supt.
  Col Prep. Curr—US. Exams—AP CEEB. AP—Eng Fr Calc Physics US_Hist Econ Psych Music_Theory. Feat—Comp_Sci African_Stud Fine Arts.
  Enr 180.
  Fac 27. M 5. F 17/5.
  Tul '05-'06: Day $2800-10,200.
  Est 1961. Sem (Aug-June). Assoc: AISA A/OPR/OS MSA.

LITTLE JEWELS INTERNATIONAL SCHOOL OF KINSHASA
Day — Coed Gr PS-7

Kinshasa, Democratic Republic of the Congo. 7475 Ave OUA, Ngaliema. Tel: 243-8844735. EST+7.
http://littlejewelskinshasa.tripod.com   E-mail: littlejewels@ic.cd
Najma Munshi, Head.
  Gen Acad. Curr—US. Feat—Fr Computers Studio_Art Music.
  Est 1972. Sem (Sept-June). Assoc: AISA.

THE ENGLISH-SPEAKING SCHOOL OF LUBUMBASHI
Day — Coed Gr PS-8

Lubumbashi, Democratic Republic of the Congo. Tel: 243-88-98405. EST+7.
Contact: c/o United Methodist Church, PO Box 22037, Kitwe, Zambia.
www.gbgm-umc.org/apumc/tesol   E-mail: fameth@aol.com
Ellen Hoover, Dir. BA, MPhil, PhD.
  Pre-Prep. Curr—UK US. Feat—Fr Relig Studio_Art Music. Supp—ESL Makeup

Rem_Math Rem_Read Tut.
Enr 32. B 11. G 21. Elem 32. US 1. Host 4. Other 27. Accepted: 100%. Avg class size: 5.
Fac 12. M 5/2. F 3/2. US 2. Adv Deg: 16%.
Grad '05—5. Prep—5.
Tui '02-'03: Day $2100 (+$150). **Aid:** 18 pupils ($14,850).
Summer: Acad Enrich Rev Rec. Tui Day $30. 2 wks.
Plant val $300,000. Bldgs 6. Class rms 9. Lib 5000 vols. Sci labs 1. Comp labs 1. Fields 2. Courts 2.
Est 1987. Nonprofit. United Methodist. Tri (Sept-July). Assoc: AISA.

An interdenominational Christian school, TESOL serves missionary children and other pupils who are interested in receiving an English-medium elementary education. Students learn in a small-class setting similar in structure to a Christian school in the US. Each day begins with religious education or an all-school assembly, after which boys and girls follow a curriculum that incorporates elements of the British and American systems.

COTE D'IVOIRE

Sq. Miles: 124,500 (Slightly larger than New Mexico). **Country Pop:** 17,298,040 (2005). **Capital:** Yamoussoukro, pop. 110,013. **Largest City:** Abidjan, pop. 1,934,342. **Terrain:** Forested, undulating, hilly in the west. **Ethnic Group(s):** Akan Voltaiques Gur Northern Mandes Krous Southern_Mandes Lebanese French. **Religion(s):** Muslim Christian Indigenous_Beliefs. **Official Language(s):** French. **Government:** Republic. **Independence:** 1960 (from France). **GDP:** $17.4 billion (2004). Agriculture 27%. Industry 21%. Services 52%. **Currency:** African Coalition Franc (CFAF).

INTERNATIONAL COMMUNITY SCHOOL OF ABIDJAN
Day — Coed Gr K-12

Abidjan 06, Cote d'Ivoire. BP 544. Tel: 225-2247-1152. Fax: 225-2247-1996. EST+5.
www.icsa.ac.ci   E-mail: office@icsa.ac.ci
Robert Walbridge, Dir.
    Col Prep. Curr—US. Exams—CEEB. AP—Eng Fr Calc Bio Physics. Feat—Comp_ Sci African_Hist Studio_Art Music. Supp—ESL.
    Enr 66.
    Fac 10.
    Tui '05-'06: Day $5600-11,500.
    Est 1972. Nonprofit. Sem (Aug-June). Assoc: AISA A/OPR/OS CIS MSA.

EGYPT

Sq. Miles: 386,000 (Approximately the size of Texas and New Mexico combined). **Country Pop:** 77,505,756 (2005). **Capital:** Cairo, pop. 16,000,000. **Terrain:** Desert, except Nile Valley and delta. **Ethnic Group(s):** Egyptian Bedouin_Arab Nubian. **Religion(s):** Muslim Coptic_Christian. **Official Language(s):** Arabic. **Other Language(s):** English French. **Government:** Republic. **Independence:** 1922 (from United Kingdom). **GDP:** $91.7 billion (2003). Agriculture 17%. Industry 33%. Services 50%. **Currency:** Egyptian Pound (£E).

SCHUTZ AMERICAN SCHOOL
Day — Coed Gr PS-12

Alexandria 21111, Egypt. 51 Schutz St, Raml, PO Box 1000. Tel: 20-3-576-2205. Fax: 20-3-576-0229. EST+7.
www.schutzschool.org.eg   E-mail: schutz@schutzschool.org.eg
Anthony Spencer, Head. PhD. Omneya El Naggar, Adm.
   Col Prep. Curr—US. Exams—CEEB. AP—Eng Fr Calc Bio Physics World_Hist Econ. Feat—Arabic Comp_Sci Studio_Art Drama Music Journ. Supp—Tut.
   Sports—Basket Soccer Swim Tennis Track. Activities—Arts Govt/Pol Media.
   Enr 236. B 123. G 113. Avg class size: 16.
   Fac 32. M 9. F 22/1. US 17. Host 8. Other 7. Adv Deg: 46%.
   Grad '05—11. Col—11. US Col—4. (Eastern U, Pepperdine, Geo Wash, U of CA-Riverside). Avg SAT: M/V—1064.
   Tui '05-'06: Day $3500-10,750 (+$2000). Aid: 14 pupils ($75,145).
   Bldgs 7. Class rms 29. 2 Libs 15,000 vols. Sci labs 1. Comp labs 2. Auds 1. Art studios 2. Music studios 1. Gyms 1. Fields 1. Courts 2. Pools 1.
   Est 1924. Nonprofit. Sem (Aug-June). Assoc: A/OPR/OS CIS NEASC.

Schutz provides a US-style program that runs from early childhood through high school for students from approximately 20 countries, with the US and Egypt represented most prominently. Science and math programs are traditional, while English and social studies courses meet two days a week for 12 weeks to study a specific facet of a subject. Qualified pupils choose from an array of Advanced Placement courses. Electives include music, arts, crafts, sewing, cooking, typing and photography. The curriculum also features Middle Eastern cultural studies.

AMERICAN INTERNATIONAL SCHOOL IN EGYPT
Day — Coed Gr PS-12

Cairo, Egypt. 5th Settlement, E Mubarak Police Academy, New Cairo City. Tel: 20-2-617-4001. Fax: 20-2-617-4002. EST+7.
www.aisegypt.com   E-mail: info@esolonline.com
Walid Abushakra, Supt.
   Col Prep. IB Diploma. Curr—Intl US. Exams—CEEB. Feat—Arabic Fr Comp_Sci Studio_Art Music. Supp—LD.

Enr 987. Elem 582. Sec 405. US 79. Host 671. Other 237.
Tui '05-'06: Day €4200-7400.
Est 1990. Assoc: MAIS MSA.

BRITISH INTERNATIONAL SCHOOL
CAIRO

Day — Coed Gr PS-12

Cairo, Egypt. PO Box 137, Gezira. Tel: 20-2-736-5959. Fax: 20-2-736-4168. EST+7.
www.bisc.edu.eg   E-mail: info@bisc.edu.eg
Hugh Pullan, Prin. BA, DipEd.
   Col Prep. IB Diploma. Curr—Intl UK. **Exams**—GCSE. **Feat**—Arabic Fr Ger Environ_Sci Studio_Art Bus.
   Tui '05-'06: Day £3114-7578 (+£100-3526).
   Est 1976. Tri (Sept-June).

INTERNATIONAL SCHOOL OF CHOUEIFAT
CAIRO

Day — Coed Gr K-12

Cairo, Egypt. PO Box 2760, El Horreya, Heliopolis. Tel: 20-2-7580001. Fax: 20-2-7580006. EST+7.
www.isccairo-sabis.net   E-mail: isccairo@sabis.net
   Col Prep. Curr—UK US. **Exams**—AP CEEB TOEFL GCSE IGCSE O-level AS-level A-level. **Feat**—Arabic Fr.
   Enr 93.
   Fac 26.
   Est 1995. Tri.

MAADI BRITISH INTERNATIONAL SCHOOL

Day — Coed Gr PS-5

Cairo 84, Egypt. 4th District, Zahraa El Maadi. Tel: 20-2-705-8671. Fax: 20-2-705-8679. EST+7.
www.mbisegypt.com   E-mail: mbis@mbisegypt.com
Gerard L. Flynn, Head. BPhil.
   Gen Acad. Curr—UK. **Feat**—Arabic Fr Comp_Sci Relig Studio_Art Music. **Supp**—ESL Rem_Math Rem_Read.
   Enr 290. Accepted: 98%. Avg class size: 19.
   Fac 20. M 4. F 14/2.
   Grad '05—20.
   Tui '05-'06: Day £6114.
   Est 1995. Nonprofit. Tri (Sept-June).

MBIS enrolls students from approximately 40 countries, with only a limited number of pupils coming from Egypt. Following the English national curriculum, the school offers distinct academic programs for children of all ages. The nursery school (ages 2-4) places a strong focus on learning through play. In the primary school (ages 4-11), academics combine the core subjects of English, math and science with such foundation courses as music, art and design technology. The curriculum features four years of both French and Arabic.

Among extracurriculars are computers, riding, soccer, art, music, Scottish country dance, drama, pottery and tae kwon do.

MODERN ENGLISH SCHOOL
CAIRO

Day — Coed Gr PS-12

Cairo 11712, Egypt. PO Box 92, Serai Al Kubba. Tel: 20-12-226-1646. Fax: 20-12-617-0020. EST+7.
www.mescairo.com   E-mail: mescairo@mescairo.com
Peter T. Godfrey, Prin.

> Col Prep. IB Diploma. Curr—Intl UK US. Exams—CEEB IGCSE. Feat—Arabic Fr Econ Relig Art_Hist Graphic_Arts Sculpt Studio_Art Drama Music Bus.
> Tui '06-'07: Day $7500-8450.
> Est 1990. Tri (Sept-June). Assoc: MSA.

NEW CAIRO BRITISH INTERNATIONAL SCHOOL

Day — Coed Gr PS-12

Cairo, Egypt. PO Box 9057, Nasr City. Tel: 20-2-758-2881. Fax: 20-2-758-1390. EST+7.
www.ncbis.org   E-mail: info@ncbis.org
Frank Esser, Actg Prin.

> Col Prep. Curr—UK. Exams—GCSE AS-level A-level. Feat—Fr Comp_Sci Econ Music.
> Est 1978. Tri (Aug-June).

CAIRO AMERICAN COLLEGE

Day — Coed Gr K-12

Maadi 11431, Cairo, Egypt. PO Box 39. Tel: 20-2-755-5555. Fax: 20-2-519-6584. EST+7.
www.cacegypt.org   E-mail: support@cacegypt.org
Monica N. Greeley, Supt. MEd. Amina O'Kane, Adm.

> Col Prep. IB Diploma. Curr—Intl US. Exams—AP CEEB. AP—Calc US_Hist Studio_Art. Feat—Arabic Fr Span Astron Egyptian_Culture. Supp—ESL.
> Sports—Basket Baseball X-country Soccer Softball Swim Tennis Track Volley W_Polo Wrestling. Activities—Acad Arts Govt/Pol.
> Enr 1331. Elem 829. Sec 502. US 648. Host 189. Other 494. Avg class size: 18.
> Fac 137. M 39. F 98. US 73. Host 33. Other 31. Adv Deg: 59%.
> Grad '05—116. Col—116. US Col—10. (U of VA, Earlham, Emory, Geo Mason, Wm & Mary).
> Tui '05-'06: Day $12,150-12,450.

Summer: Enrich Rec. Tui Day $200-315. 2 wks.
Bldgs 12. Class rms 126. Lib 65,000 vols. Sci labs 13. Lang labs 2. Comp labs 10.
   Theaters 1. Art studios 1. Music studios 1. Gyms 2. Fields 2. Courts 3. Pools 1.
   Weight rms 1.
Est 1945. Nonprofit. Sem (Aug-June). Assoc: A/OPR/OS MSA.

Originally founded by the business and missionary community in Cairo as an elementary school, CAC has since expanded to include secondary grades. There are more than 70 different nationalities represented among the students, many of whom are American. A US-style college preparatory curriculum is followed, and graduates have attended universities in Europe, Asia, Africa and the Americas. Some background in English is required for admission, but ESL is offered to those who lack proficiency. Spanish, French and Arabic are available from grade 3.

NEW HORIZON INTERNATIONAL SCHOOL
Day — Coed Gr K-12

Maadi, Cairo, Egypt. PO Box 1079. Tel: 20-2-516-2685. Fax: 20-2-516-2685. EST+7.
www.newhorizon-eg.com   E-mail: newhorizon01@hotmail.com
Aicha Wassef, Dir.
   Col Prep. Curr—UK. **Exams**—IGCSE. **Feat**—Arabic Fr Relig.
   Est 1993. (Sept-June).

EL GOUNA INTERNATIONAL SCHOOL
Day — Coed Gr PS-12

Red Sea, Egypt. El Gouna. Tel: 20-65-580080. Fax: 20-65-580081. EST+7.
www.elgounaschool.com   E-mail: elgounais@yahoo.co.uk
   Col Prep. Curr—UK. **Exams**—IGCSE AS-level. **Feat**—Arabic Fr Ger Comp_Sci
      Studio_Art Music Bus. **Supp**—ESL.
   Tui '05-'06: Day $2570-4540 (+$1000).
   Est 1998. Tri. Assoc: ECIS.

ERITREA

Sq. Miles: 48,000 (About the size of Pennsylvania). **Country Pop:** 4,561,599 (2005). **Capital:** Asmara, pop. 435,000. **Terrain:** Central highlands straddle escarpment associated with Rift Valley, dry coastal plains and western lowlands. **Ethnic Group(s):** Tigrinya Tigre Saho Afar Beja Bilen Kunama Nara Rashaida. **Religion(s):** Christian Muslim Indigenous_Beliefs. **Other Language(s):** Afar Arabic Tigre Kunama Tigrinya. **Government:** Transitional. **Independence:** 1993 (from Ethiopia). **Per Capita Income:** $900 (2004). **GDP:** $700 million (2004). Agriculture 12%. Industry 26%. Services 62%. **Currency:** Eritrean Nafka (Nfa).

ASMARA INTERNATIONAL COMMUNITY SCHOOL
Day — Coed Gr PS-11

Asmara, Eritrea. PO Box 4941. Tel: 291-1-161-705. Fax: 291-1-161-705. EST+8.
www.aics.org.er   E-mail: aics@aics.org.er
Sean Goudie, Dir.

>**Gen Acad. IB PYP. Curr**—Intl UK US. **Feat**—Arabic Fr Tigrinya Comp_Sci Studio_
> Art Music. **Supp**—ESL.
>**Enr 134.** Accepted: 90%. Avg class size: 14.
>**Fac 17.** Adv Deg: 29%.
>**Tui '05-'06: Day $5000-13,500** (+$2500). **Aid:** 25 pupils ($75,000).
>**Summer:** Rec. Tui Day $300. 4 wks.
>Bldgs 3. Class rms 12. Lib 2500 vols. Sci labs 1. Lang labs 1. Comp labs 1. Auds
> 1. Fields 1.
>**Est 1994.** Nonprofit. Tri (Aug-June). Assoc: AISA A/OPR/OS MSA.

This elementary and secondary school combines elements from the US, UK and international educational systems. Instruction is in English, and AICS conducts an ESL program for students lacking fluency in the language. Foreign language options include French and Arabic, both of which pupils may take from grade 1 on.

Extracurricular activities comprise sports, interest clubs, fitness opportunities and drama. A month-long summer recreational program is also available.

ETHIOPIA

Sq. Miles: 472,000 (About the size of Texas, Oklahoma and New Mexico combined). **Country Pop:** 73,053,286 (1997). **Capital:** Addis Ababa, pop. 2,600,000. **Terrain:** High plateau, mountains and dry lowland plains. **Ethnic Group(s):** Oromo Amhara Tigre Somali. **Religion(s):** Orthodox_Christian Sunni_Muslim Protestant Indigenous_Beliefs. **Official Language(s):** Amharic. **Other Language(s):** Tigrinya Oromifa English Somali. **Government:** Federal Republic. **Per Capita Income:** $116 (2004). **GDP:** $8.1 billion (2004). Agriculture 47%. Industry 12%. **Currency:** Ethiopian Birr (Br).

BINGHAM ACADEMY
Bdg — Coed Gr 6-12; Day — Coed K-12

Addis Ababa, Ethiopia. PO Box 4937. Tel: 251-1-279-1791. Fax: 251-1-279-1783.
EST+8.
www.binghamacademy.net   E-mail: info@binghamacademy.net
Steve Mosman, Dir. BSc, MEd.

>**Gen Acad. Curr**—Intl US. **Exams**—IGCSE. **Feat**—Fr Comp_Sci Bible Studio_Art
> Music. **Supp**—ESL LD.
>**Sports**—Basket Soccer Tennis Volley. **Activities**—Arts.
>**Enr 210.** Accepted: 50%. Avg class size: 20.
>**Fac 30.** US 20. Host 3. Other 7.

Tui '05-'06: Day $3900-4200. Aid: 5 pupils ($10,000).
Bldgs 9. Dorms 1. Class rms 15. Lib 13,000 vols. Chapels 1. Sci labs 1. Lang labs 1. Comp labs 1. Art studios 1. Music studios 1. Gyms 1. Fields 1.
Est 1946. Nonprofit. Evangelical. Sem (Sept-June). Assoc: AISA.

Situated near downtown Addis Ababa, BA offers a typical elementary and secondary curriculum that includes international social studies courses. All students follow a program assigned to their grade level, and all take part in Bible study. Participation in the Scripture Memory Program, offered in all Bible classes, is encouraged.

INTERNATIONAL COMMUNITY SCHOOL OF ADDIS ABABA
Day — Coed Gr PS-12

Addis Ababa, Ethiopia. PO Box 70282. Tel: 251-11-371-1544. Fax: 251-11-371-0722. EST+8.
http://addis.ecis.org   E-mail: ics@ethionet.et
Stephen Plisinski, Dir. MEd, MBA. **Michael Archbold, Adm.**
    Col Prep. IB Diploma. Curr—Intl US. **Exams**—CEEB. **Feat**—Fr. **Supp**—ESL LD.
    Sports—Basket Soccer Tennis Track Volley. **Activities**—Arts Govt/Pol Media Rec Service.
    Enr 434. Elem 286. Sec 148. US 115. Host 51. Other 268. Accepted: 95%. Yield: 95%. Avg class size: 16.
    Fac 45. M 13/2. F 26/4. US 23. Host 4. Other 18. Adv Deg: 55%.
    Grad '05—21. US Col—7. (Ithaca 2, MIT 1, York U-Canada 1, U of PA 1, Yale 1, NYU 1). Avg SAT: M/V—1133.
    Tui '05-'06: Day $11,770-13,665 (+$595-2395). **Aid:** 16 pupils ($208,000).
    Summer: Acad Enrich Rec. $115/ses. 2 wks.
    Endow $331,000. Bldgs 20. Libs 2. Sci labs 5. Comp labs 3. Art studios 2. Gyms 1. Fields 2. Courts 2.
    Est 1966. Nonprofit. Quar (Aug-June). Assoc: AISA A/OPR/OS MSA.

Students from more than 50 countries attend ICS. The American-based curriculum and the International Baccalaureate Diploma Program prepare boys and girls for both American and international universities.

SANDFORD INTERNATIONAL SCHOOL
Day — Coed Gr PS-12

Addis Ababa, Ethiopia. PO Box 30056MA. Tel: 251-1552275. Fax: 251-1551945. EST+8.
http://sandford.ecis.org   E-mail: sandford@telecom.net.et
John Stow, Head.
    Col Prep. IB Diploma. Curr—Intl UK. **Exams**—IGCSE. **Feat**—Fr Ger Ital Amharic Environ_Sci Econ Psych Studio_Art Drama Music Dance.
    Enr 600.
    Tui '05-'06: Day £3414-5439.
    Est 1946. Tri (Sept-June). Assoc: AISA.

GABON

Sq. Miles: 103,347 (About the size of Colorado). **Country Pop:** 1,389,201 (2005). **Capital:** Libreville, pop. 673,995 (2005). **Terrain:** Narrow coastal plain; hilly, heavily forested interior; some savanna regions in the east and the south. **Ethnic Group(s):** Fang Myene Bapounou Eshira Bandjabi Bateke Obamba. **Religion(s):** Christian Muslim Indigenous_Beliefs. **Official Language(s):** French. **Other Language(s):** Fang Myene Bateke Bapounou. **Government:** Republic. **Independence:** 1960 (from France). **Per Capita Income:** $4579 (2004). **GDP:** $4.8 billion (2003). Agriculture 7%. Industry 9%. **Currency:** African Coalition Franc (CFAF).

AMERICAN INTERNATIONAL SCHOOL OF LIBREVILLE
Day — Coed Gr PS-8

Libreville, Gabon. BP 4000, Blvd du Bord de Mer. Tel: 241-72-45-56. Fax: 241-74-52-40. EST+6.
Contact: Dept of State, 2270 Libreville Pl, Washington, DC 20521.
E-mail: librevilleschool@yahoo.com
Gary Eubank, Dir.
  Pre-Prep. Gen Acad. Curr—US. **Feat**—Fr Comp_Sci Studio_Art Drama. **Supp**— EFL ESL Tut.
  Enr 51. B 24. G 27. Accepted: 100%. Avg class size: 8.
  Fac 8. M 1. F 4/3. US 6. Other 2. Adv Deg: 25%.
  Grad '05—4. Prep—4.
  Tui '05-'06: Day $3190-15,000.
  Plant val $750,000. Bldgs 1. Class rms 5. Lib 5000 vols. Sci labs 1. Comp labs 1. Art studios 1. Music studios 1. Fields 1. Courts 1.
  Est 1975. Nonprofit. Quar (Aug-June). Assoc: AISA A/OPR/OS MSA.

The school provides an English-medium education for boys and girls of all nationalities. The student body comprises children of the local US business community, Gabon natives and pupils from approximately a dozen other nations. AISL follows a traditional US-style curriculum. French is taught daily as a foreign language.

THE GAMBIA

Sq. Miles: 4361 (About the size of Maryland). **Country Pop:** 1,328,000 (2003). **Capital:** Banjul, pop. 34,828 (2003). **Terrain:** Flood plain of the Gambia River flanked by low hills. **Ethnic Group(s):** Mandinka Fula Wolof Jola Serahule Serere Krio Manjago Bambara. **Religion(s):** Muslim Christian. **Official Language(s):** English. **Other Language(s):** Mandinka Wolof Fula. **Government:** Civilian. **Independence:** 1965 (from United Kingdom). **Per Capita Income:** $330 (2002). **GDP:** $360 billion (2002). Agriculture 29%. Industry 12%. **Currency:** Gambian Dalasi (GD).

BANJUL AMERICAN EMBASSY SCHOOL
Day — Coed Gr PS-8

Serrekunda, The Gambia. PO Box 2596. Tel: 220-449-5920. Fax: 220-449-7181. EST+5.
Contact: Dept of State, 270 Banjul Pl, Washington, DC 20521.
www.baes.gm   E-mail: baes@qanet.gm
Earl J. Ballard, Head. BS, MS, MA.

> **Gen Acad. Curr**—Intl US. **Feat**—Fr Computers Studio_Art Music. **Supp**—ESL Rem_Read Tut.
> **Sports**—Basket Soccer Volley.
> **Enr 66.** B 32. G 34. Elem 64. Sec 2. US 15. Host 7. Other 44. Accepted: 95%. Yield: 95%. Avg class size: 9.
> **Fac 9.** M 1/2. F 6. US 3. Host 3. Other 3. Adv Deg: 33%.
> **Grad '05—8.**
> **Tui '05-'06: Day $2800-8750** (+$1750).
> Bldgs 4. Lib 6000 vols. Sci labs 1. Comp labs 1. Fields 1. Courts 1.
> **Est 1984.** Nonprofit. Quar (Sept-June). Assoc: AISA A/OPR/OS MSA.

The academic program at BAES serves English-speaking students of all nationalities. A US curriculum is followed, with fluency in English required at all grade levels. Social studies features the social and cultural history of The Gambia, and local field trips provide enrichment.

While the school's program runs only through grade 8, BAES helps pupils in grades 9-12 arrange correspondence courses through the University of Nebraska-Lincoln.

GHANA

Sq. Miles: 92,100 (About the size of Illinois and Indiana combined). **Country Pop:** 21,029,853 (2005). **Capital:** Accra, pop. 3,000,000 (2005). **Terrain:** Plains and scrubland, rainforest, savanna. **Ethnic Group(s):** Akan Ewe Ga Moshi-Dagomba. **Religion(s):** Christian Muslim Indigenous_Beliefs. **Official Language(s):** English. **Other Language(s):** Akan Mole-Dagbani Ewe Ga-Adangbe. **Government:** Democracy. **Independence:** 1957 (from United Kingdom). **Per Capita Income:** $365 (2004). **GDP:** $7.5 billion (2004). Agriculture 34%. Industry 24%. Services 42%. **Currency:** Ghanaian New Cedi (¢).

GHANA INTERNATIONAL SCHOOL

Day — Coed Gr PS-12

Accra, Ghana. PO Box 2856. Tel: 233-21-777163. Fax: 233-21-774379. EST+5.
www.gis.edu.gh   E-mail: prinoffice@gisedu.com
Diana Nyatepe-Coo, Prin.
Col Prep. Curr—UK. Exams—CEEB IGCSE A-level. Feat—Fr Comp_Sci Geog
Studio_Art Music. Supp—ESL.
Enr 1130. B 540. G 590.
Fac 149. M 47/1. F 54/47.
Est 1955. Nonprofit. Tri (Sept-June). Assoc: AISA.

LINCOLN COMMUNITY SCHOOL

Day — Coed Gr PS-12

Accra, Ghana. c/o US Embassy, PO Box 194. Tel: 233-21-774-018. Fax: 233-21-
780-985. EST+5.
www.lincoln.edu.gh   E-mail: lincoln@lincoln.edu.gh
John S. Roberts, Supt. BA, MEd. **Yvonne Tetteh, Adm.**
Col Prep. IB PYP. IB MYP. IB Diploma. Curr—Intl US. Exams—CEEB. Feat—Fr
Span Twi Intl_Relations Psych Studio_Art Theater. Supp—ESL LD.
Sports—Basket Soccer Swim Volley. Activities—Acad Arts Govt/Pol Rec Service.
Enr 540. B 276. G 264. Elem 375. Sec 165. US 108. Host 73. Other 359. Accepted:
98%. Yield: 100%. Avg class size: 19.
Fac 64. M 13/2. F 44/5. US 25. Host 10. Other 29. Adv Deg: 62%.
Grad '05—38. Col—31. US Col—12.
Tui '05-'06: Day $5000-11,600. Aid: 2 pupils ($20,000).
Plant val $1,700,000. Bldgs 13. Class rms 59. 2 Libs 15,000 vols. Sci labs 3. Comp
labs 3. Auds 1. Art studios 3. Music studios 2. Gyms 1. Fields 2. Courts 1. Pools
1.
Est 1968. Nonprofit. Quar (Aug-June). Assoc: AISA A/OPR/OS MSA.

The enrollment of LCS consists of pupils from the United States, Ghana, the Netherlands, Korea, South Africa and some 40 other countries. The curriculum is comparable to that found in internationally oriented elementary and secondary schools around the world. The school makes a commitment to community service at all grade levels, as evidenced by student participation in projects ranging from medical personnel assistance to home building with Habitat for Humanity.

GUINEA

Sq. Miles: 95,000 (About the size of Oregon). **Country Pop:** 9,467,866 (2005). **Capital:** Conakry, pop. 2,000,000 (2003). **Terrain:** Generally flat along the coast and mountainous in the interior. The country's four geographic regions are a narrow coastal belt, pastoral highlands, the northern savanna and the southeastern rainforest. **Ethnic Group(s):** Peuhl Malinke Soussou. **Religion(s):** Muslim Christian Indigenous_Beliefs.

Official Language(s): French. **Government:** Republic. **Independence:** 1958. **Per Capita Income:** $376 (2003). **GDP:** $4.7 billion (2003). Agriculture 33%. Industry 18%. **Currency:** Guinean Franc (GNF).

INTERNATIONAL SCHOOL OF CONAKRY
Day — Coed Gr PS-12

Conakry, Guinea. BP 603, Corniche Sud, Matam Lido. Tel: 224-661535. Fax: 224-411522. EST+5.
Contact: Dept of State, 210 Conakry Pl, Washington, DC 20521.
E-mail: thomasbgilbert@hotmail.com
Bruce Gilbert, Dir. Camilla Asp-Schussheim, Adm.

> Col Prep. Curr—US. Exams—CEEB. Feat—Fr Comp_Sci Studio_Art Music. Supp—ESL.
> Enr 92. B 49. G 43. Accepted: 85%. Avg class size: 7.
> Fac 12. M 2/1. F 7/2.
> Grad '05—3. Col—3. US Col—3. (GA St, Emporia St, E Carolina).
> Tui '05-'06: Day $3400-11,400 (+$2000). Aid: 20 pupils ($100,000).
> Plant val $500,000. Bldgs 2. Class rms 9. Libs 1. Sci labs 1. Comp labs 1. Art studios 1. Music studios 1. Fields 1. Pools 1.
> Est 1964. Nonprofit. Sem (Aug-June). Assoc: AISA A/OPR/OS MSA.

Students of approximately 10 nationalities attend this small day school, which follows an American elementary curriculum featuring individualized classes in math and language arts. Instruction is in English, with French taught as a foreign language. The capital city, Conakry is situated on a small island, linked to the mainland by a bridge.

KENYA

Sq. Miles: 224,960 (Slightly smaller than Texas). **Country Pop:** 33,829,590 (2005). **Capital:** Nairobi, pop. 2,100,000. **Terrain:** Kenya rises from a low coastal plain on the Indian Ocean in a series of mountain ridges and plateaus. **Ethnic Group(s):** Kikuyu Luhya Luo Kalenjin Kamba Kisii Meru Asian European Arab. **Religion(s):** Protestant Roman_Catholic Muslim Indigenous_Beliefs. **Official Language(s):** English Swahili. **Other Language(s):** Tribal_Languages. **Government:** Republic. **Independence:** 1963 (from United Kingdom). **Per Capita Income:** $271 (2003). **GDP:** $12.7 billion (2003). Agriculture 19%. Industry 19%. Services 62%. **Currency:** Kenyan Shilling (KSh).

ST. ANDREW'S SCHOOL
Bdg — Coed Gr K-10

Molo 20106, Kenya. Private Bag. Tel: 254-51-721283. Fax: 254-51-721061. EST+8.

www.standrewsturi.com   E-mail: headseniorschool@turimail.co.ke
David Bryson, Co-Head. Ian Bateman, Co-Head. Kate Patterson, Adm.
  Pre-Prep. Gen Acad. Curr—Intl UK. Exams—GCSE IGCSE. Feat—Fr Ger Relig
    Studio_Art Drama Music. Supp—Tut.
  Sports—Badminton Basket X-country F_Hockey Gymnastics Rugby Soccer Swim
    Tennis Volley. Activities—Arts.
  Enr 348. B 187. G 161. Avg class size: 18.
  Fac 62. M 27/3. F 24/8. Host 9. Other 53.
  Grad '05—55.
  Tui '05-'06: Bdg $9500-12,500 (+$1500). Aid: 20 pupils ($25,000).
  Dorms 8. Sci labs 5. Comp labs 2. Art studios 2. Music studios 2. Perf arts ctrs 1.
    Gyms 1. Fields 8. Courts 6. Pools 1.
  Est 1931. Nonprofit. Nondenom Christian. Tri (Sept-July).

Located in the Rift Valley region, St. Andrew's prepares students for the GCSE
and IGCSE examinations in an international setting. The school follows a British
National Curriculum at all levels. Religion is emphasized through Bible study,
group worship and community service. Extracurricular pursuits range from music
lessons, art and drama to camping and mountain climbing.

HILLCREST SECONDARY SCHOOL

Bdg — Coed Gr 6-12; Day — Coed 7-12

Nairobi, Kenya. PO Box 24819. Tel: 254-20-882-222. Fax: 254-20-882-350. EST+8.
www.hillcrest.ac.ke   E-mail: admin@hillcrest.ac.ke
Christopher N. J. Drew, Head. BSc, MA.
  Col Prep. Gen Acad. Curr—UK. Exams—CEEB IGCSE O-level AS-level A-level.
    Feat—Fr Ger Lat Span Kiswahili Comp_Sci Econ Psych Sociol Studio_Art
    Drama Music Bus. Supp—LD.
  Sports—Badminton Basket X-country F_Hockey Golf Gymnastics Rugby Soccer
    Squash Swim Tennis Volley. Activities—Acad Arts Govt/Pol Media Service.
  Enr 440. B 15/185. G 25/215. US 5. Host 180. Other 255. Accepted: 90%. Yield:
    90%. Avg class size: 22.
  Fac 55. M 30/5. F 18/2. US 1. Host 20. Other 34. Adv Deg: 40%.
  Grad '05—95. Col—95. US Col—30. (Harvard, U of PA, U of Tulsa, Yale, Brown).
  Tui '05-'06: Bdg $4050. Day $3000.
  Bldgs 30. Dorms 3. Dorm rms 30. Class rms 35. Libs 1. Sci labs 6. Comp labs 2.
    Theaters 1. Art studios 2. Music studios 1. Dance studios 1. Gyms 1. Fields 6.
    Courts 6. Pools 1.
  Est 1975. Inc. Tri (Sept-July).

Catering to the international, professional and local business communities,
Hillcrest conducts a UK-style program that accommodates students from more than
35 countries. In grades 6-8, boys and girls take a broad range of subjects. Middle
schoolers (grades 9 and 10) typically take 10 subjects (including electives). Boys
and girls in the senior school (grades 11 and 12) generally take four subjects the first
year at AS level, then three courses at A level their final year.

Learning support is available for pupils with specific learning disabilities such
as dyslexia, as well as for those to whom English is a second language. An exten-

sive field trip program features social and educational excursions within Kenya, throughout the East African region and overseas.

INTERNATIONAL SCHOOL OF KENYA
Day — Coed Gr PS-13

Nairobi 00800, Kenya. PO Box 14103. Tel: 254-20-418-3622. Fax: 254-20-418-3272. EST+8.
www.isk.ac.ke   E-mail: admin@isk.ac.ke
Areta Williams, Supt.

> **Col Prep. IB Diploma. Curr**—Intl US. **Exams**—ACT CEEB. **Feat**—Fr Span Kiswahili Comp_Sci Anthro Econ African_Stud Studio_Art Music.
> **Enr 574.** US 79. Host 42. Other 443.
> **Fac 61.**
> **Grad '05—53. US Col—6.** (Lewis & Clark, Brown, Tufts, Princeton, Stanford, Wm & Mary).
> **Tui '05-'06: Day $4120-13,520** (+$1000).
> **Summer:** Rec. 4 wks.
> Bldgs 15. Lib 15,000 vols. Theaters 1. Gyms 1. Courts 1. Pools 1.
> **Est 1976.** Nonprofit. Sem (Aug-June). Assoc: AISA A/OPR/OS CIS MSA.

Both the curriculum and the school organization of ISK reflect conditions found at college preparatory schools in North America. Students who wish to do so may pursue the International Baccalaureate Diploma. An intercultural program exposes students to the people, the culture and the environment of East Africa. Campus activities, reading and research prepare students for a variety of field trips, including visits to Kenyan tribal societies, a climb of Mount Kenya, and the study of Indian Ocean marine life and the ecosystem of a national park.

Team sports include basketball, soccer, field hockey, netball, rugby, volleyball, softball and handball. Extracurricular activities, which vary according to student interest, include such options as choir, jewelry making, modern dance, ballet, golf and swimming.

KENTON COLLEGE PREPARATORY SCHOOL
Day — Coed Ages 6-13

00100 Nairobi, Kenya. PO Box 30017. Tel: 254-20-4347000. Fax: 254-20-4347332. EST+8.
www.kentoncollege.com   E-mail: admin@kenton.ac.ke
Maureen Cussans, Head. BA, MA.

> **Pre-Prep. Gen Acad. Curr**—UK. **Exams**—CEE. **Feat**—Fr Ger Lat Kiswahili Relig Studio_Art Drama Music.
> **Sports**—F_Hockey Rugby Swim Tennis. **Activities**—Arts Rec.
> **Enr 240.** B 120. G 120. Avg class size: 16.
> **Fac 24.** Host 8. Other 16.
> **Grad '05—32.**
> **Tui '05-'06: Day KSh645,000.**
> **Est 1924.** Nonprofit. Anglican. Tri (Sept-Aug).

Moved in 1935 from its original hilltop site at Kijabe to its present location at

Kileleshwa, which was enveloped by Nairobi over the years, the school provides a traditional education leading to the British Common Entrance Examination. French and classical background are introduced in the early grades, and computer studies are taught from year 2. Concentration on secondary school preparation is supplemented by art, music, speech, drama and physical education.

Frequent excursions are made into the city and the surrounding countryside, and Kenton College offers a variety of extracurricular activities, clubs, sports and games.

ROSSLYN ACADEMY
Day — Coed Gr K-12

00800 Nairobi, Kenya. PO Box 14146, Westlands. Tel: 254-20-7122407. Fax: 254-20-7121306. EST+8.
www.rosslynacademy.com E-mail: rosslyn@rosslyn.iconnect.co.ke
Dena Brent, Supt. BA, MEd.
  Col Prep. Curr—US. **Exams**—ACT AP CEEB. **AP**—Eng Fr Span Calc Bio Physics Eur_Hist US_Hist. **Feat**—Kiswahili Comp_Sci Econ Studio_Art Drama Music. **Supp**—LD.
  Sports—Basket F_Hockey Rugby Soccer Track Volley. **Activities**—Arts Service.
  Enr 459. B 213. G 246. Elem 252. Sec 207. US 221. Host 55. Other 183. Avg class size: 22.
  Fac 43. M 20. F 17/6. US 35. Host 2. Other 6.
  Grad '05—45. Col—43. **US Col**—41. (Wheaton-MA 2, Harding 2, Union Col-NY 2, LeTourneau 2, John Brown 2). Avg SAT: M/V—1153, Essay—592.
  Tui '05-'06: Day $4592-8270 (+$300).
  Bldgs 11. Class rms 28. 2 Libs 14,000 vols. Sci labs 3. Auds 1. Art studios 2. Music studios 5. Gyms 1. Fields 3. Courts 3.
  Est 1948. Nonprofit. Sem (Aug-May). Assoc: AISA MSA.

Originally located in Tanzania, the academy was established to provide an American education for the children of Mennonite missionaries in East Africa. Today, approximately 70 percent of the students enroll from North America, with the remainder coming from some 30 countries. The US-based curriculum is supplemented by the study of African history and culture. Kiswahili is available as a foreign language, as are French and Spanish.

The school occupies 40 acres in a residential area on the outskirts of the city.

LESOTHO

Sq. Miles: 11,718 (About the size of Maryland). **Country Pop:** 1,867,035 (2005). **Capital:** Maseru, pop. 173,700 (2005). **Terrain:** High veld, plateau and mountains. **Ethnic Group(s):** Basotho European Asian. **Religion(s):** Roman_Catholic Evangelical Anglican Muslim Hindu. **Official Language(s):** Sesotho English. **Other Language(s):** Zulu Xhosa. **Government:** Constitutional Monarchy. **Independence:** 1966 (from United Kingdom). **Per Capita Income:** $550 (2003). **GDP:** $1.43 billion (2003). Agriculture 16%. Industry 43%. Services 41%. **Currency:** Lesothan Loti (plural, Maloti) (M).

MACHABENG COLLEGE
THE INTERNATIONAL SCHOOL OF LESOTHO
Bdg and Day — Coed Gr 6-12

Maseru 100, Lesotho. PO Box 1570. Tel: 266-313224. Fax: 266-316109. EST+7.
www.machcoll.co.ls   E-mail: machabhm@lesoff.co.za
Christopher Philip, Head.
> **Col Prep. IB Diploma. Curr**—Intl. **Exams**—IGCSE. **Feat**—Fr Span Geog Visual_ Arts Music Bus.
> **Fac 48.** M 13/1. F 21/13.
> **Tui '05-'06: Bdg M38,440-74,910. Day M17,230-63,700.**
> **Est 1977.** Nonprofit. Tri (Sept-July). Assoc: AISA CIS NEASC.

MASERU ENGLISH MEDIUM PREPARATORY SCHOOL
Day — Coed Ages 3-12

Maseru 100, Lesotho. PO Box 34. Tel: 266-22-312-276. Fax: 266-22-312-276. EST+7.
www.maseruprep.co.ls   E-mail: office@maseruprep.co.ls
Ken Jarman, Head.
> **Gen Acad. IB PYP. Curr**—Intl. **Feat**—Fr Computers Studio_Art Music. **Supp**— ESL.
> **Enr 286.** B 138. G 148.
> **Fac 28.** M 5. F 18/5.
> **Tui '05-'06: Day M14,541-29,079.**
> **Est 1890.** Tri (Sept-July). Assoc: AISA ECIS.

NATIONAL UNIVERSITY OF LESOTHO
INTERNATIONAL SCHOOL
Day — Coed Gr K-12

Roma, Lesotho. PO Roma 180. Tel: 266-22340601. Fax: 266-22340000. EST+7.
E-mail: rs.fitter@nul.ls
Roshan Savakshaw Fitter, Head. MEd.
> **Col Prep. Gen Acad. Curr**—Intl Nat. **Exams**—IGCSE. **Feat**—Fr Sesotho Comp_ Sci World_Relig Studio_Art Music Accounting Bus. **Supp**—Dev_Read Tut.
> **Sports**—Basket Soccer Tennis Volley. **Activities**—Acad Arts Cultural/Relig.
> **Enr 428.** B 226. G 202. US 1. Host 370. Other 57. Avg class size: 34.
> **Fac 20.** M 2. F 18. Host 14. Other 6. Adv Deg: 40%.
> **Grad '05—34.**
> **Tui '03-'04: Day M3080-6180** (+M2000).
> **Summer:** Acad Rev. 4 wks.
> Bldgs 10. Class rms 14. Libs 1. Sci labs 1. Comp labs 1.

Est 1962. Nonprofit. Quar (Jan-Dec). Assoc: AISA.

This elementary and secondary school maintains a broad curriculum that emphasizes the basic skills of literacy and numeracy in the lower grades and provides opportunities for advanced study in all subject areas at the secondary level. NULIS' program combines elements of the national curriculum with those of other English-medium systems of education, and boys and girls take both national and international examinations. Pupils acquire the knowledge and skills necessary to continue their studies at institutions around the world. Parental involvement in both academic and nonacademic areas is integral to the program.

MADAGASCAR

Sq. Miles: 228,880 (Slightly less than twice the size of Arizona). **Country Pop:** 18,040,341 (2005). **Capital:** Antananarivo, pop. 1,300,000 (2005). **Terrain:** Mountainous central plateau, coastal plain. **Ethnic Group(s):** Malagasy Comorian French Indian Chinese. **Religion(s):** Indigenous_Beliefs Christian Muslim. **Official Language(s):** Malagasy. **Other Language(s):** French. **Government:** Republic. **Independence:** 1960 (from France). **Per Capita Income:** $240 (2003). **GDP:** $5.5 billion (2003). Agriculture 29%. Industry 15%. **Currency:** Madagascan Franc (FMG).

AMERICAN SCHOOL OF ANTANANARIVO
Day — Coed Gr PS-12

Antananarivo 101, Madagascar. BP 1717. Tel: 261-20-22420-39. Fax: 261-20-22345-39. EST+8.
Contact: Dept of State Antananarivo, Washington, DC 20521.
www.asamadagascar.org   E-mail: asamad@wanadoo.mg
Jay Long, Dir.
    Col Prep. Curr—US. **Exams**—CEEB TOEFL. **AP**—Fr Calc Comp_Govt & Pol.
        Feat—Environ_Sci Computers Studio_Art Music. **Supp**—ESL.
    Enr 144.
    Fac 28.
    Tui '05-'06: Day $7250-11,354 (+$2250).
    Est 1969. Nonprofit. Quar (Sept-June). Assoc: AISA A/OPR/OS MSA.

MALAWI

Sq. Miles: 45,747 (Land the size of Pennsylvania, with a lake the size of Vermont). **Country Pop:** 12,158,924 (2005). **Capital:** Lilongwe, pop. 440,471 (1998). **Largest City:** Blantyre, pop. 502,053 (1998). **Terrain:** Plateaus, highlands, and valleys. **Ethnic Group(s):** Chewa Nyanja

Tumbuka Yao Lomwe Sena Tonga Ngoni Ngonde Asian European. **Religion(s):** Protestant Roman_Catholic Muslim Indigenous_Beliefs. **Official Language(s):** English Chichewa. **Other Language(s):** Chitumbuka Chiyao Chilomwe. **Government:** Democracy. **Independence:** 1964 (from United Kingdom). **Per Capita Income:** $151 (2005). **GDP:** $1.87 billion (2005). Agriculture 39%. Industry 16%. **Currency:** Malawian Kwacha (MK).

BISHOP MACKENZIE INTERNATIONAL SCHOOL
Day — Coed Gr PS-12

Lilongwe, Malawi. PO Box 102. Tel: 265-1756364. Fax: 265-1751374. EST+7.
www.bmis.cois.org   E-mail: info@bmismw.com
Peter Todd, Dir.
  Col Prep. IB Diploma. Curr—Intl UK. Exams—IGCSE. Feat—Fr Comp_Sci Studio_Art Drama Music Bus.
  Tui '05-'06: Day $7293-12,000 (+$50).
  Tri (Aug-June). Assoc: AISA A/OPR/OS CIS NEASC.

KAMUZU ACADEMY
Bdg — Coed Gr 6-12

Mtunthama, Malawi. Private Bag 1. Tel: 265-1253-488. Fax: 265-1253-586. EST+7.
www.geocities.com/kamuzuacademy   E-mail: academic@ka.ac.mw
Francis J. Cooke, Head. BSc.
  Col Prep. Gen Acad. Curr—UK. Exams—CEEB GCSE IGCSE O-level AS-level A-level. Feat—Fr Greek Lat Comp_Sci Econ Law Relig Studio_Art Drama Music. Supp—ESL Rev Tut.
  Activities—Arts.
  Enr 517. B 243. G 274. Elem 410. Sec 107. US 3. Host 494. Other 20. Accepted: 60%. Yield: 80%. Avg class size: 24.
  Fac 44. M 30. F 13/1. US 1. Host 33. Other 10. Adv Deg: 15%.
  Grad '05—89.
  Tui '05-'06: Bdg $6900 (+$150).
  Class rms 36. 2 Libs 29,000 vols. Sci labs 6. Lang labs 1. Comp labs 2. Auds 1. Theaters 1. Art studios 1. Music studios 1. Dance studios 1. Fields 3. Courts 2. Pools 1.
  Est 1981. Nonprofit. Ecumenical. Tri.

Founded by Dr. H. Kamuzu Banda, first president of Malawi, this school in southern Africa combines full boarding with a classical, UK-style curriculum. Latin and Greek courses form part of the core curriculum, and French is another foreign language option. After preparing for the GCSE or IGCSE examinations, students choose from an array of AS-level and A-level courses. Graduates typically matriculate at universities in the UK, the US, South Africa and Malawi.

The arts play an important role at the academy. A well-developed drama program features both indoor productions and smaller ones that are staged in an outdoor theater. Visits with local artists and craftsmen enhance the study of art and enable pupils to view pottery, wood carvings and cane furniture. Kamuzu's school choir performs both in the chapel and at area functions.

MALI

Sq. Miles: 474,764 (About the size of Texas and California combined). **Country Pop:** 12,291,529 (2005). **Capital:** Bamako, pop. 1,000,000 (2005). **Terrain:** Savannah and desert. **Ethnic Group(s):** Manding Fulani Saracole Mianka Songhai Tuareg Maur. **Religion(s):** Muslim Indigenous_Beliefs Christian. **Official Language(s):** French. **Other Language(s):** Bambara. **Government:** Republic. **Independence:** 1960 (from France). **Per Capita Income:** $250 (2003). **GDP:** $4.8 billion (2003). Agriculture 36%. Industry 22%. **Currency:** African Coalition Franc (CFAF).

AMERICAN INTERNATIONAL SCHOOL OF BAMAKO
Day — Coed Gr PS-12

Bamako, Mali. BP 34. Tel: 223-22-47-38. Fax: 223-22-08-53. EST+5.
Contact: Dept of State, 2050 Bamako Pl, Washington, DC 20521.
www.aisbmali.org   E-mail: aisb@aisbmali.org
James Workman, Dir.
    Col Prep. Curr—US. Feat—Fr Environ_Sci Comp_Sci Econ Studio_Art Drama
        Music. Supp—ESL Tut.
    Enr 115. Accepted: 98%. Avg class size: 8.
    Fac 21.
    Tui '05-'06: Day $13,400 (+$2000). Aid: 6 pupils ($30,000).
    Plant val $500,000. Bldgs 8. Class rms 13. Lib 6000 vols. Sci labs 1. Lang labs 1.
        Comp labs 1. Auds 1. Art studios 1. Music studios 1. Gyms 1. Fields 1.
    Est 1977. Nonprofit. Tri (Aug-June). Assoc: AISA A/OPR/OS MSA.

AISB, located on the banks of the Niger River, offers an American-style elementary education. The prekindergarten program enrolls children from age 3. Class size remains small at all grade levels, thereby facilitating individualized instruction. The school's student body consists of pupils from approximately 20 countries.

MAURITIUS

Sq. Miles: 720 (About the size of Rhode Island). **Country Pop:** 1,230,602 (2005). **Capital:** Port Louis, pop. 146,319 (2005). **Terrain:** Volcanic island surrounded by coral reefs. A central plateau is rimmed by mountains. **Ethnic Group(s):** Indo-Mauritian Creole Sino-Mauritian Franco-Mauritian. **Religion(s):** Hindu Roman_Catholic Muslim. **Official **Language(s):** English French. **Other Language(s):** Creole Hindi Urdu Hakka Bhojpuri. **Government:** Republic. **Independence:** 1968 (from United Kingdom). **Per Capita Income:** $4900 (2004). **GDP:** $6 billion (2004). Agriculture 6%. Financial Services 10%. Manufacturing 21%. Tourism 6%. **Currency:** Mauritian Rupee (MauRs).

ALEXANDRA HOUSE SCHOOL
Day — Coed Gr K-6

Floreal, Mauritius. King George V Ave. Tel: 230-696-4108. Fax: 230-696-4108. EST+9.
www.alexandrahouseschool.com   E-mail: admin@alexandrahouseschool.com
B. Langlois, Head. BEd. **Martina Beejadhur, Dir.** BA, DipEd.

> **Gen Acad. Curr**—Intl UK. **Feat**—Fr Computers Studio_Art Drama Music Study_ Skills.
> **Activities**—Arts Rec.
> **Enr 90.** B 45. G 45. Elem 90. US 1. Host 24. Other 65. Accepted: 90%. Yield: 99%. Avg class size: 15.
> **Fac 9.** F 6/3. Host 1. Other 8.
> **Grad '05—10.**
> **Tui '05-'06: Day $2900. Aid:** 16 pupils ($40,600).
> Bldgs 1. Class rms 6. Lib 2000 vols. Comp labs 1. Fields 1.
> **Est 1975.** Inc. Tri (Aug-July).

Alexandra House conducts an English-style primary school with a strong international component. Both expatriate and local children enroll, although all are fluent in English. The school follows the British curriculum closely in the core subjects of English, math and science, while instruction takes a more international approach in the other disciplines.

LE BOCAGE INTERNATIONAL SCHOOL
Day — Coed Gr 6-12

Moka, Mauritius. Mount Ory. Tel: 230-433-1159. Fax: 230-433-4914. EST+9.
www.lebocage.net   E-mail: lbis@intnet.mu
David Muddle, Head. BSc, MEd.

> **Col Prep. Gen Acad. IB Diploma. Curr**—Intl. **Exams**—IGCSE. **Feat**—Fr Span Comp_Sci Econ Psych Sociol Studio_Art Chorus Accounting Bus. **Supp**—EFL ESL.
> **Sports**—Badminton Basket Rugby Soccer Volley. **Activities**—Arts Govt/Pol Media Service.
> **Enr 615.** B 390. G 225. Elem 218. Sec 397. Host 563. Other 52. Avg class size: 20.
> **Fac 70.** M 28. F 42. Host 63. Other 7. Adv Deg: 17%.
> **Grad '05—74.**
> **Tui   '05-'06:   Day   MauRs165,000** (+MauRs40,000). **Aid:** 20 pupils (MauRs500,000).
> Bldgs 4. Class rms 37. Libs 7000. Sci labs 3. Comp labs 3. Auds 1. Theaters 1. Fields 2.
> **Est 1990.** Nonprofit. Tri (Jan-Nov). Assoc: AISA ECIS.

The program at this English-medium school features small classes and specialized instruction. Children in grades 6-8 follow a typical middle school curriculum, while pupils in grades 9 and 10 work towards the IGCSE. The school conducts the IB Diploma program in the final two grades.

MOROCCO

Sq. Miles: 172,413 (Slightly larger than California). **Country Pop:** 29,891,708 (2004). **Capital:** Rabat, pop. 1,622,860 (2004). **Largest City:** Casablanca, pop. 2,933,684 (2004). **Terrain:** Coastal plains, mountains, and desert. **Ethnic Group(s):** Arab-Berber. **Religion(s):** Muslim Jewish Christian. **Official Language(s):** Arabic. **Other Language(s):** Berber French. **Government:** Constitutional Monarchy. **Independence:** 1956 (from France). **Per Capita Income:** $1678 (2004). **GDP:** $50 billion (2004). Agriculture 16%. Industry 32%. **Currency:** Moroccan Dirham (DH).

CASABLANCA AMERICAN SCHOOL
Day — Coed Gr PS-12

20150 Casablanca, Morocco. Rte de la Mecque, Lotissement Ougoug, Quartier Californie 20150. Tel: 212-22-21-41-15. Fax: 212-22-21-24-88. EST+5.
www.cas.ac.ma   E-mail: cas@cas.ac.ma
Jack F. Shepherd, Jr., Dir. Gilbert Armenta, Adm.
  Col Prep.Exams—AP CEEB TOEFL. Feat—Arabic Fr Span Environ_Sci Comp_ Sci. Supp—Dev_Read ESL LD Rem_Math Rem_Read Rev Tut.
  Sports—Badminton Basket Soccer Softball Track Volley. Activities—Acad Govt/Pol Service.
  Enr 513. B 264. G 249. US 64. Host 301. Other 148. Accepted: 85%. Yield: 90%. Avg class size: 17.
  Fac 69. US 40. Host 14. Other 15. Adv Deg: 56%.
  Grad '05—23. Col—23. US Col—9. (Worcester Polytech, Geo Wash). Avg SAT: M/V—1117, Essay—551.
  Tui '05-'06: Day $4590-11,180.
  Plant val $4,600,000. Bldgs 4. Class rms 33. Libs 2. Sci labs 2. Comp labs 2. Auds 1. Theaters 1. Art studios 2. Music studios 1. Gyms 1. Fields 1. Courts 1.
  Est 1973. Tri (Sept-June). Assoc: A/OPR/OS MAIS NEASC.

CAS conducts an American-based academic program with advanced courses and French, Spanish and Arabic offered as foreign languages. Language arts and the fine arts, as well as music and drama, enrich the curriculum. Activities include sports and arts and crafts.

GEORGE WASHINGTON ACADEMY

Day — Coed Gr PS-12

20220 Casablanca, Morocco. Km 5.6 Rte d'Azemmour, Dar Bouazza. Tel: 212-22-95-30-00. Fax: 212-22-93-56-68. EST+5.
www.gwa.ac.ma   E-mail: info@gwa.ac.ma
Andrew A. Dias, Dir.

> **Col Prep. Curr**—US. **Bilingual**—Arabic Fr. **Exams**—AP CEEB. **Feat**—Span Programming Web_Design Moroccan_Hist Photog Studio_Art Theater Music.
> **Tui '05-'06: Day DH42,600-60,000** (+DH15,400).
> **Est 1998.** Nonprofit. (Sept-June). Assoc: MAIS.

RABAT AMERICAN SCHOOL

Day — Coed Gr PS-12

10000 Rabat, Morocco. c/o American Embassy, BP 120. Tel: 212-37-671-476. Fax: 212-37-670-963. EST+5.
www.ras.ma   E-mail: info@ras.ma
Paul Johnson, Dir. BAEd, EdD. **Btissam Touijer, Adm.**

> **Col Prep. Gen Acad. IB Diploma. Curr**—Intl US. **Exams**—CEEB. **Feat**—Arabic Fr Comp_Sci Web_Design Geog Moroccan_Stud Studio_Art Chorus Music Journ. **Supp**—Dev_Read ESL LD Tut.
> **Sports**—Badminton Basket Soccer Swim Track Volley. **Activities**—Acad Arts Rec.
> **Enr 388.** B 168. G 220. Elem 262. Sec 126. US 75. Host 146. Other 167. Accepted: 99%. Avg class size: 15.
> **Fac 54.** M 13/3. F 30/8. US 23. Host 9. Other 22. Adv Deg: 61%.
> **Grad '05—32. Col—27. US Col—6.** (Am U, Geo Wash, Boston U, Boston Col, Fairleigh Dickinson, Rochester Inst of Tech). Avg SAT: M/V—1190.
> **Tui '05-'06: Day $6975-14,340** (+$5000).
> **Summer:** Acad Enrich Rec. Tui Day $300. 5 wks.
> Bldgs 11. Class rms 38. 2 Libs 21,000 vols. Sci labs 3. Comp labs 3. Auds 1. Theaters 1. Art studios 2. Music studios 3. Dance studios 2. Gyms 1. Fields 3. Courts 1. Pools 2.
> **Est 1962.** Nonprofit. Tri (Aug-June). Assoc: A/OPR/OS MAIS MSA.

Serving the international community of Rabat, RAS has an enrollment that is roughly one-fifth American, with children from Europe and Morocco making up the balance. The curriculum follows American guidelines. French and Arabic are taught throughout the school, and music, art and physical education are integrated into the academic program.

AMERICAN SCHOOL OF TANGIER

Bdg — Coed Gr 7-12; Day — Coed PS-12

90000 Tangier, Morocco. Rue Christophe Colomb. Tel: 212-39-93-98-27. Fax: 212-39-94-75-35. EST+5.
www.as-t.org   E-mail: astcompu@menara.ma
Joseph A. McPhillips III, Head. BA.

> **Col Prep. Curr**—US. **Feat**—Arabic Fr Comp_Sci Islamic_Hist Studio_Art.

Enr 330. Accepted: 90%. Avg class size: 20.
Fac 43.
Grad '05—13. Col—11. US Col—9. (S VT, Bryn Mawr, Gettysburg, Earlham, U of ME-Orono, Col of Wooster).
Tui '02-'03: Bdg $17,400 (+$60). **Day $3000-12,570** (+$60).
Bldgs 3. Dorm rms 14. Class rms 19. Libs 2. Labs 2. Fields 1. Courts 2.
Est 1950. Nonprofit. Tri (Sept-June). Assoc: A/OPR/OS MAIS.

Located on an 11-acre campus outside of Tangier, this school offers an American college preparatory curriculum to students from Morocco, the US and approximately 20 other countries. Boarding students enroll primarily from southern Morocco, Algeria, the Middle East and West Africa. Instruction in Arabic begins in grade 1, and French courses commence in grade 5. Graduates matriculate at competitive universities in the US and Europe.

Student activities are an integral part of the school program and include annual dramatic productions. Basketball and soccer are the chief competitive sports, although pupils may also take part in tennis, riding, karate, volleyball, weightlifting and golf. Situated on the Straits of Gibraltar, the cosmopolitan city of Tangier has a long history as a commercial and cultural link between Europe and Africa.

MOZAMBIQUE

Sq. Miles: 308,642 (About twice the size of California). **Country Pop:** 19,400,000 (2005). **Capital:** Maputo, pop. 1,200,000 (2005). **Terrain:** Varies from lowlands to high plateau. **Ethnic Group(s):** Makua Tsonga Makonde Shangaan Shona Sena Ndau. **Religion(s):** Indigenous_ Beliefs Christian Muslim. **Official Language(s):** Portuguese. **Other Language(s):** Tribal_Languages. **Government:** Democracy. **Independence:** 1975 (from Portugal). **Per Capita Income:** $250 (2004). **GDP:** $5.5 billion (2005). Agriculture 25%. Industry 35%. Services 40%. **Currency:** Mozambican Metical (Mt).

AMERICAN INTERNATIONAL SCHOOL OF MOZAMBIQUE
Day — Coed Gr PS-12

Maputo, Mozambique. Caixa Postal 2026, Costa do Sol. Tel: 258-21-491-994. Fax: 258-21-490-596. EST+7.
www.aism-moz.com   E-mail: aism@aism-moz.com
Mary Jo Heatherington, Dir. PhD.
    Col Prep. IB Diploma. Curr—Intl US. Exams—CEEB. Feat—Fr Port Environ_Sci Comp_Sci Econ Studio_Art Drama Music Journ. Supp—ESL.
    Enr 260.
    Fac 38. US 14. Host 12. Other 12.
    Tui '05-'06: Day $7600-10,800 (+$2650-3400).
    Est 1990. Sem (Aug-June). Assoc: AISA A/OPR/OS MSA.

MAPUTO INTERNATIONAL SCHOOL
Day — Coed Gr PS-12

Maputo, Mozambique. 389 Rua da Nachingwea, Caixa Postal 4152. Tel: 258-21-492195. Fax: 258-21-492382. EST+7.
www.mis.ac.mz   E-mail: mis@virconn.com
Samuel Mondlane, Dir.

> Col Prep. Curr—UK. Exams—IGCSE AS-level A-level. Feat—Fr Port Comp_Sci Studio_Art Music Bus.
> Tui '05-'06: Day $4650-7020 (+$250-500).
> Est 1975. Tri (Jan-Dec). Assoc: AISA.

NAMIBIA

Sq. Miles: 320,827 (About the size of Texas and Louisiana combined). **Country Pop:** 2,030,692 (2005). **Capital:** Windhoek, pop. 233,529 (2001). **Terrain:** Varies from coastal desert to semiarid mountains and plateau. **Ethnic Group(s):** Ovambo Kavango Herero Damara Nama Caprivian. **Religion(s):** Christian Indigenous_Beliefs. **Official Language(s):** English. **Other Language(s):** Afrikaans German. **Government:** Republic. **Independence:** 1990. **Per Capita Income:** $2370 (2004). **GDP:** $5.5 billion (2004). Agriculture 10%. Mining 7%. **Currency:** Namibian Dollar (N$).

WINDHOEK INTERNATIONAL SCHOOL
Day — Coed Gr PS-12

Windhoek, Namibia. Scheppman St, Private Bag 16007. Tel: 264-61-24-1783. Fax: 264-61-24-3127. EST+6.
www.wis.edu.na   E-mail: cheimstadt@wis.edu.na
Helen Birkbeck, Dir.

> Col Prep. IB PYP. IB Diploma. Curr—Intl. Exams—IGCSE. Feat—Fr Ger Port Environ_Sci Comp_Sci Anthro Psych Philos Visual_Arts Music. Supp—ESL.
> Enr 296. B 159. G 137. Elem 217. Sec 79. US 16. Host 163. Other 117. Avg class size: 15.
> Fac 51. M 10/1. F 38/2. US 5. Host 20. Other 26. Adv Deg: 17%.
> Tui '05-'06: Day N$18,170-118,050 (+N$21,000).
> Bldgs 10. Class rms 43. Lib 10,500 vols. Sci labs 2. Comp labs 1. Auds 1. Art studios 2. Gyms 1. Fields 1. Courts 1.
> Est 1990. Nonprofit. Quar (Aug-June). Assoc: AISA A/OPR/OS CIS NEASC.

WIS offers the International Baccalaureate Primary Years and Diploma programs. The primary school curriculum is organized around large concepts, with subject-specific skills added as they become relevant. The middle school follows a curriculum that draws upon curricula from around the world. Preparation for a broad range of IGCSE examinations begins in grade 9, and students pursue the IB

Diploma in grades 11 and 12. A learning support center provides academic help to students in English as a Second Language and other subjects.

Windhoek, the capital of Namibia, is located in a basin between the Khomas Highland and the Auas and Eros mountains. It has the country's only international airport, and the city center features European cafe culture and German cuisine.

NIGER

Sq. Miles: 490,000 (About three times the size of California). **Country Pop:** 11,665,937 (2005). **Capital:** Niamey, pop. 723,200 (2002). **Terrain:** About two-thirds desert and mountains, one-third savanna. **Ethnic Group(s):** Hausa Djerma Fulani Tuareg Beri_Beri Arab Toubou Gourmantche. **Religion(s):** Muslim Christian. **Official Language(s):** French. **Other Language(s):** Hausa Djerma. **Government:** Republic. **Independence:** 1960 (from France). **Per Capita Income:** $232 (2003). **GDP:** $2.8 billion (2003). Agriculture 40%. Industry 18%. **Currency:** African Coalition Franc (CFAF).

AMERICAN INTERNATIONAL SCHOOL OF NIAMEY
Day — Coed Gr K-12

Niamey, Niger. Tel: 227-72-39-42. Fax: 227-72-34-57. EST+6.
Contact: c/o Dept of State Niamey, 2420 Naimey Pl, Dulles, VA 20189.
www.geocities.com/asniamey   E-mail: asniger@intnet.ne
Frank Walsh, Dir.
   Pre-Prep. Curr—US.
   Enr 56. B 29. G 27.
   Fac 11.
   Tui '05-'06: Day $10,404-12,485 (+$1876).
   Est 1982. Sem (Aug-May). Assoc: AISA A/OPR/OS MSA.

NIGERIA

Sq. Miles: 356,700 (About the size of California, Nevada and Arizona combined). **Country Pop:** 128,771,988 (2005). **Capital:** Abuja, pop. 100,000. **Largest City:** Lagos, pop. 12,000,000. **Terrain:** Ranges from southern coastal swamps to tropical forests, open woodlands, grasslands and semidesert conditions in the far north. **Ethnic Group(s):** Hausa-Fulani Igbo Yoruba. **Religion(s):** Muslim Christian Indigenous_Beliefs. **Official Language(s):** English. **Other Language(s):** Hausa Igbo Yoruba. **Government:** Republic. **Independence:** 1960 (from United

Kingdom). **Per Capita Income:** $290 (2002). **GDP:** $72 billion (2004). **Currency:** Nigerian Naira (N).

HILLCREST SCHOOL

Day — Coed Gr 1-12

Jos, Nigeria. 13 Old Bukuru Rd, Box 652. Tel: 234-73-465410. Fax: 234-73-465410. EST+6.
www.hillcrestschool.net   E-mail: hillcrestschool@yahoo.com
Dick Seinen, Supt. BRE, MAT.

> **Col Prep. Gen Acad. Curr**—US. **Exams**—ACT AP CEEB. **AP**—Eng Fr Calc Comp_Sci Bio Chem World_Hist Psych Studio_Art. **Feat**—Hausa Bible. **Supp**—Rem_Read Tut.
>
> **Sports**—Basket Soccer Tennis Volley. **Activities**—Service.
>
> **Enr 250.** US 50. Host 100. Other 100. Accepted: 50%. Avg class size: 21.
>
> **Fac 38.** M 15/1. F 18/4. US 15. Host 19. Other 4. Adv Deg: 23%.
>
> **Grad '05**—24. **Col**—22. **US Col**—2. (LeTourneau 2). Avg SAT: M/V—1110. Avg ACT: 22.
>
> **Tui '05-'06: Day $3790-6315.**
>
> **Est 1942.** Nonprofit. Nondenom Christian. Quar (Aug-May). Assoc: AISA MSA.

Hillcrest gives admission preference to the children of sponsoring groups, although other children are welcomed if space permits. Chapel services, morning prayer and Bible study are part of the Christian-centered program. The US-style curriculum features AP courses.

AMERICAN INTERNATIONAL SCHOOL OF LAGOS

Day — Coed Gr PS-9

Lagos, Nigeria. 1004 Federal Estates, Victoria Island. Tel: 234-1-261-7793. Fax: 234-1-261-7794. EST+6.
www.aislagos.com   E-mail: information@aislagos.com
Mary Wilson, Supt.

> **Gen Acad. Curr**—US. **Feat**—Fr Comp_Sci Studio_Art Drama Music.
>
> **Enr 479.**
>
> **Fac 63.** M 15/2. F 31/15.
>
> **Tui '05-'06: Day $7380-14,490** (+$100).
>
> **Est 1964.** Nonprofit. Tri (Aug-June). Assoc: AISA A/OPR/OS MSA.

BRITISH INTERNATIONAL SCHOOL

Bdg and Day — Coed Gr 6-12

Lagos, Nigeria. 1 Landbridge Ave, Oniru Estate, PO Box 75133. Tel: 234-1-774-8066. Fax: 234-1-270-6437. EST+6.
www.bis-lagos.org.uk   E-mail: bisnigeria@yahoo.co.uk
Kenneth John Baines, Prin. BEd. **Cheryl Williams, Adm.**

> **Gen Acad. Curr**—Intl UK. **Exams**—GCSE IGCSE O-level AS-level A-level. **Feat**—Fr Hausa Igbo Yoruba. **Supp**—EFL ESL.

Sports—Basket Rugby Soccer Track. **Activities**—Arts Rec Service.
Enr 250. B 60/65. G 40/85. Elem 140. Sec 110. US 5. Host 170. Other 75. Accepted: 60%. Yield: 50%. Avg class size: 20.
Fac 26. M 11. F 15. Host 9. Other 17. Adv Deg: 61%.
Grad '05—23.
Tui '06-'07: Bdg $20,000 (+$800). **Day $11,000** (+$800). **Aid:** 1 pupil ($20,000).
Endow N400,000,000. Plant val N1,000,000,000. Bldgs 9. Dorms 5. Dorm rms 20. Class rms 20. Lib 6976 vols. Sci labs 3. Lang labs 1. Comp labs 2. Art studios 1. Music studios 1. Dance studios 1. Gyms 1. Fields 1. Courts 2. Pools 1.
Est 2001. Inc. Tri (Sept-June). Assoc: AISA.

BIS' academic program meets the requirements of the English national curriculum. As students progress, they prepare for the IGCSE examinations, then the AS and A levels. Boys and girls follow a compulsory curriculum in grades 6-8, then choose which IGCSE courses they wish to take in grades 9 and 10. Extra IGCSE classes are available in grades 11 and 12, during which time BIS provides an array of AS- and A-level courses.

Career education is an integral element of the program.

GRANGE SCHOOL

Day — Coed Gr K-10

Lagos, Nigeria. 6 Harold Shodipo Crescent, PO Box 22, Ikeja. Tel: 234-1-2706046. Fax: 234-1-2713886. EST+6.
www.grangeschool.com   **E-mail:** info@grangeschool.com
William Pope, Prin. BA.
  Gen Acad.Exams—IGCSE. **Feat**—Fr Comp_Sci Studio_Art Music. **Supp**—LD Rem_Math Tut.
  Sports—Basket Gymnastics Soccer Swim Volley. **Activities**—Acad Arts Rec.
  Enr 595. B 302. G 293. Host 554. Other 41. Avg class size: 20.
  Fac 62. M 25. F 37. Host 60. Other 2.
  Grad '05—36. Col—32. US Col—9. (Harvard, Princeton, Johns Hopkins, Boston U).
  Tui '05-'06: Day N637,500-750,000 (+N209,500).
  Endow N60,940,000. Plant val N11,326,000. Bldgs 4. Libs 1. Sci labs 4. Lang labs 1. Comp labs 3. Auds 2. Art studios 2. Music studios 2.
  Est 1958. Nonprofit. Tri (Sept-July). Assoc: AISA.

Founded by a group of British expatriates interested in an English-medium education for their children equivalent to that found in the United Kingdom, Grange follows the English National Curriculum from age 5 through the IGCSE examinations. The youngest children develop basic skills in English (speaking, listening, reading and writing), math, science, design and technology, computers, history, geography, art and design, music and physical education. Hands-on learning gains increasing prominence as students progress, with field trips employed as a supplement to classroom activities.

During the first three years of the secondary school (grades 6-8), pupils engage in a full range of subjects, while also taking part in creative pursuits and athletics. The school places considerable emphasis on independent learning and research skills during these years. Grange's program culminates in the two years leading up to the IGCSE exams. Boys and girls at this level continue taking the compulsory subjects of English, math and foreign language, then add courses in their chosen subjects. Students typically sit for eight or nine IGCSEs.

GREENSPRINGS SCHOOL

Bdg — Coed Gr 6-13; Day — Coed PS-13

Lagos, Nigeria. 32 Olatunde Ayoola Ave. Tel: 234-1-4930679. Fax: 234-1-4926190. EST+6.
www.greenspringsschool.com   E-mail: info@greenspringsschool.com
John A. Todd, Head. BSc, MAEd.
> **Col Prep. Gen Acad. IB PYP. Curr**—Intl UK. **Exams**—CEE IGCSE AS-level A-level. **Feat**—Fr Yoruba Comp_Sci Econ Studio_Art Drama Music Accounting. **Supp**—Dev_Read LD Rem_Math Rem_Read Rev Tut.
> **Enr 951.** B 53/447. G 42/409. Elem 711. Sec 240. US 120. Host 701. Other 130. Accepted: 75%. Yield: 80%. Avg class size: 25.
> **Fac 120.** M 50. F 70. Host 115. Other 5. Adv Deg: 25%.
> **Grad '05—98.**
> **Tui '05-'06: Bdg N1,400,000. Day N790,000.**
> Sci labs 3. Comp labs 2. Auds 1. Art studios 2. Music studios 2. Fields 1.
> **Est 1985.** Sem (Sept-June). Assoc: AISA.

Founded as a Montessori preschool, Greensprings now conducts a full program for students ages 18mos-18. The preschool, which serves children through age 4, continues to employ adapted Montessori principles. Pupils ages 5-10 follow the International Baccalaureate PYP and may also prepare for the British CEE. During the secondary years (ages 11-15), students take part in the UK National Curriculum for Key Stage 3, then engage in the IGCSE program in years 10 and 11. In the Sixth Form, boys and girls work toward the AS- and A-level exams. The foreign language program consists of Yoruba at the elementary level and French at the elementary and secondary levels.

SENEGAL

Sq. Miles: 76,000 (About the size of South Dakota). **Country Pop:** 11,126,832 (2005). **Capital:** Dakar, pop. 1,905,000 (1998). **Terrain:** Flat or rising to foothills. **Ethnic Group(s):** Wolof Fulani Toucouleur Serer Diola Mandingo. **Religion(s):** Muslim Christian. **Official Language(s):** French. **Other Language(s):** Wolof Pulaar Serer Diola Mandingo Soninke. **Government:** Republic. **Independence:** 1960 (from France). **Per Capita Income:** $700 (2002). **GDP:** $4.9 billion (2002). Agriculture 19%. Industry 21%. Services 40%. **Currency:** African Coalition Franc (CFAF).

DAKAR ACADEMY
Bdg — Coed Gr 6-12; Day — Coed K-12

Dakar, Senegal. BP 3189, 69 Route des Peres Maristes. Tel: 221-832-0682. Fax: 221-832-1721. EST+5.
www.dakar-academy.org E-mail: office@dakar-academy.org
Bruce Evans, Dir.
  Col Prep. Curr—US. Exams—ACT AP CEEB. AP—Eng Fr Span Calc Comp_Sci World_Hist Music_Theory. Feat—Astron Environ_Sci Econ Pol_Sci Psych Sociol Bible Studio_Art. Supp—ESL.
  Enr 331.
  Tui '05-'06: Bdg $9210-9825. Day $6950-7565.
  Est 1961. Nonprofit. Quar (Aug-June). Assoc: AISA MSA.

ˮ INTERNATIONAL SCHOOL OF DAKAR
Day — Coed Gr PS-12

Dakar, Senegal. PO Box 5136. Tel: 221-825-08-71. Fax: 221-825-50-30. EST+5.
www.isd.sn E-mail: isd@enda.sn
Judith Fenton, Dir.
  Col Prep. Curr—US. Exams—ACT AP CEEB. AP—Eng Fr Calc Bio Physics. Feat—Comp_Sci Studio_Art Music. Supp—ESL.
  Enr 193. B 104. G 89.
  Fac 28. M 5/1. F 17/5.
  Tui '05-'06: Day $2950-12,680 (+$35-3590).
  Est 1983. Nonprofit. Quar (Aug-June). Assoc: AISA A/OPR/OS MSA.

SEYCHELLES

Sq. Miles: 171 (Approximately two and a half times the size of Washington, DC). **Country Pop:** 81,188 (2005). **Capital:** Victoria, pop. 22,800 (2002). **Terrain:** About half of the islands are granitic in origin, with narrow coastal strips and central ranges of hills. The other half are coral atolls, many uninhabitable. **Ethnic Group(s):** Creole. **Religion(s):** Catholic Anglican Christian. **Official Language(s):** Creole English French. **Government:** Republic. **Independence:** 1976 (from United Kingdom). **Per Capita Income:** $7600 (2001). **GDP:** $603.9 million (2001). **Currency:** Seychelles Rupee (SR).

THE INTERNATIONAL SCHOOL
Day — Coed Gr PS-13

Victoria, Seychelles. PO Box 315, Mahe. Tel: 248-610444. Fax: 248-610460. EST+9.
www.internationalschool.sc E-mail: admin@internationalschool.sc

Martin Kennedy, Head. BEd. **Carole Emille, Adm.**
  Col Prep. Gen Acad. Curr—UK. Exams—IGCSE A-level. Feat—Chin Fr Span
  Drama Bus. Supp—Dev_Read EFL LD Rem_Math Rem_Read Tut.
  Sports—Swim. **Activities**—Acad Arts Govt/Pol Rec.
  Enr 398. B 182. G 216. Elem 273. Sec 125. US 9. Host 262. Other 127. Avg class
  size: 25.
  Fac 48. M 7. F 35/6. Host 27. Other 21. Adv Deg: 8%.
  Grad '05—52. US Col—1. (Boston U).
  Tui '05-'06: Day SR11,400-25,050 (+SR3070).
  Bldgs 4. Class rms 22. 2 Libs 1500 vols. Sci labs 2. Comp labs 3. Theaters 1. Art
  studios 1. Gyms 1.
  Est 1969. Nonprofit. Tri (Sept-July).

This school enrolls students from Seychelles, Great Britain, India, South Africa,
Australia, the United States and approximately 20 other nations. Serving children
from early childhood through Sixth Form, the school conducts a UK-based curriculum at all age levels. Older students prepare for the IGCSE and the A levels.

SOUTH AFRICA

Sq. Miles: 470,462 (Slightly less than twice the size of Texas). **Coun-
try Pop:** 44,344,136 (2005). **Capital:** Pretoria, pop. 1,104,479 (1996).
Largest City: Cape Town, pop. 2,415,408 (1996). **Terrain:** Plateau,
savanna, desert, mountains, coastal plains. **Religion(s):** Christian Hindu
Muslim Jewish. **Official Language(s):** Afrikaans English isiNdebele
Sepedi Sesotho SiSwati Xitsonga Setswana Tshivenda isiXhosa isiZulu.
Government: Parliamentary Democracy. **Independence:** 1910 (from
United Kingdom). **Per Capita Income:** $3480 (2004). **GDP:** $213 bil-
lion (2004). Agriculture 11%. Industry 24%. Services 65%. **Currency:**
South African Rand (R).

AMERICAN INTERNATIONAL SCHOOL
OF JOHANNESBURG
Day — Coed Gr PS-12

**Bryanston 2021, Johannesburg, South Africa. Private Bag X4. Tel: 27-11-464-
1505. Fax: 27-11-464-1327. EST+7.**
www.aisj-jhb.com   E-mail: info@aisj-jhb.com
Robert Ambrogi, Dir. EdD. **Elinor Parkes, Adm.**
  Col Prep. IB Diploma. Curr—Intl US. Exams—CEEB TOEFL. Feat—Fr Span
  Environ_Sci Comp_Sci S_African_Hist Econ Psych Sociol Studio_Art Drama
  Music. Supp—ESL LD.
  Sports—Basket Soccer Volley. **Activities**—Acad Arts Govt/Pol Rec.
  Enr 559. B 283. G 276. Elem 394. Sec 165. US 227. Host 35. Other 297. Avg class
  size: 15.
  Fac 78. M 28/1. F 43/6. US 36. Host 23. Other 19. Adv Deg: 47%.
  Grad '05—43. Col—43. US Col—43. (U of CA-Berkeley 4, Drexel 4, Am U 3,

Purdue 3, U of VA 2, U of Chicago 1). Avg SAT: M/V—1171, Essay—615.
Tui '05-'06: Day $7400-19,082 (+$4200).
Bldgs 10. Class rms 75. Libs 2. Sci labs 6. Comp labs 6. Auds 1. Theaters 1. Art stu-
dios 3. Music studios 1. Dance studios 1. Gyms 1. Fields 3. Courts 6. Pools 1.
Est 1982. Nonprofit. Sem (Aug-June). Assoc: AISA A/OPR/OS MSA.

Located on 235 acres of rolling hills, AISJ provides a US-style academic curriculum that includes both college preparatory and general education programs. An
ESL program assists students wishing to improve their English language skills. The
academic program is complemented by instruction in art, music, physical education
and computer science. Field trips exploring South African culture, history, ecology
and industry enrich the curriculum.

AMERICAN INTERNATIONAL SCHOOL OF CAPE TOWN
Day — Coed Gr PS-12

**Constantia 7806, Cape Town, South Africa. 42 Soetvlei Ave. Tel: 27-21-713-2220.
Fax: 27-21-713-2240. EST+7.**
www.aisct.org.za E-mail: info@aisct.org.za
Ryan Blanton, Head. BEd, MEd.
 Col Prep. Gen Acad. Curr—US. **Exams**—CEEB. **Feat**—Lib_Skills Fr Span Comp_
 Sci Anthro Psych African_Stud World_Relig Studio_Art Music. **Supp**—ESL Tut.
 Sports—Basket Soccer Swim Tennis. **Activities**—Govt/Pol Rec.
 Enr 110. B 60. G 50. Elem 85. Sec 25. US 30. Host 32. Other 48. Accepted: 90%.
 Avg class size. 14.
 Fac 18. M 3. F 13/2. US 12. Host 4. Other 2. Adv Deg: 55%.
 Tui '05-'06: Day R21,000-52,000. Aid: 5 pupils.
 Summer: Acad Enrich Rev. 4 wks.
 Plant val $2,000,000. Bldgs 5. Class rms 30. Lib 5000 vols. Sci labs 1. Comp labs
 1. Auds 1. Theaters 1. Art studios 1. Music studios 1. Dance studios 1. Gyms 1.
 Fields 2. Courts 2. Pools 2.
 Est 2001. Nonprofit. Spons: International School Development Foundation. Sem
 (Aug-June). Assoc: WASC.

Providing a US-based international program for pupils as young as age 4, AISCT
places considerable emphasis on the global and cultural aspects of its student body.
The curriculum incorporates a theory of multiple intelligences and employs schoolwide thematic units. All units of study integrate technology and the fine arts, and
foreign language instruction begins in prekindergarten. Specialists teach foreign
language, computer, music, visual and fine arts, and physical education courses.

INTERNATIONAL SCHOOL OF SOUTH AFRICA
Bdg — Coed Gr 2-12; Day — Coed PS-12

**Mafikeng 2745, South Africa. Private Bag X2114. Tel: 27-18-381-1102. Fax: 27-18-
381-1187. EST+7.**
www.issa.co.za E-mail: admin@issa.co.za
James Haupt, Head. BA.
 Col Prep. Curr—UK. **Exams**—CEEB GCSE IGCSE A-level. **Feat**—Fr Ger Afrikaans Comp_Sci Econ Studio_Art Drama Music Bus Home_Ec. **Supp**—Rem_

Math Rem_Read Tut.

Sports—Badminton Basket F_Hockey Gymnastics Soccer Squash Swim Tennis Volley. **Activities**—Acad Arts Cultural/Relig Rec.

Enr 689. B 96/253. G 40/300. Elem 470. Sec 219. Host 563. Other 126. Avg class size: 20.

Fac 52. M 15/1. F 36. Host 44. Other 8. Adv Deg: 9%.

Tui '05-'06: Bdg R48,375-70,347. Day R6078-33,135. Aid: 10 pupils (R50,000).

Plant val R150,000,000. Bldgs 62. Dorms 9. Dorm rms 207. Class rms 50. Libs 2. Sci labs 11. Comp labs 2. Theaters 1. Art studios 3. Music studios 2. Dance studios 1. Gyms 1. Fields 8. Tennis courts 7. Squash courts 4. Pools 1.

Est 1990. Nonprofit. Tri (Jan-Dec).

With students drawn mainly from South Africa, other African countries and, in smaller numbers, from Europe, the Far East and the US, ISSA conducts a UK-style curriculum at the elementary and secondary levels. The primary school curriculum emphasizes the acquisition of skills and concepts through the core subjects of English, math and social studies. Additional electives at this level include information technology, art, music and physical education.

Pupils enrolled in the secondary school prepare for IGCSE and A-level examinations. An array of business and technology classes supplements the curriculum.

As part of their extracurricular program, ISSA assigns specific community service projects each year. Choices include visits to a local children's hospital ward, work at a children's shelter and meal preparation for street children.

ST. BARNABAS COLLEGE

Bdg and Day — Coed Gr 7-12

Newclare 2112, South Africa. PO Box 88188. Tel: 27-11-474-2055. Fax: 27-11-474-2249. EST+7.

www.stbarnabas.co.za   E-mail: sbc2@cybertrade.co.za

Glynn Blignaut, Head.

Gen Acad. Curr—Nat. **Feat**—Afrikaans Comp_Sci Studio_Art Drama Music.

Enr 400.

Tui '06-'07: Bdg R13,900. Day R5900.

Quar (Jan-Dec).

SUDAN

Sq. Miles: 967,500 (Slightly more than one-quarter the size of the US). **Country Pop:** 40,187,486 (2005). **Capital:** Khartoum, pop. 1,400,000 (2005). **Largest City:** Omdurman, pop. 2,100,000 (2005). **Terrain:** Generally flat with mountains in east and west. **Ethnic Group(s):** African Arab Beja. **Religion(s):** Sunni_Muslim Indigenous_Beliefs Christian. **Official Language(s):** Arab. **Other Language(s):** English Tribal_Languages. **Government:** Military Dictatorship. **Independence:** 1956 (from United Kingdom). **Per Capita Income:** $490 (2004). **GDP:** $19 billion

(2004). Agriculture 39%. Industry 20%. Services 41%. **Currency:** Sudanese Dinar (SDD).

KHARTOUM AMERICAN SCHOOL
Day — Coed Gr PS-12

Khartoum, Sudan. c/o US Embassy, PO Box 699. Tel: 249-183-512042. Fax: 249-183-427592. EST+8.
Contact: c/o US Embassy, 2200 Khartoum Pl, Washington, DC 20521.
www.krtams.org   E-mail: kas@krtams.org
Phil Clinton, Supt. BA, MDiv.
  Col Prep. Curr—US. Exams—CEEB TOEFL. Feat—Arabic Fr Comp_Sci Studio_Art Music. Supp—ESL.
  Enr 175.
  Fac 24.
  Tui '05-'06: Day $4000-11,000 (+$610).
  Est 1957. Nonprofit. Quar (Aug-May). Assoc: AISA A/OPR/OS MSA.

SWAZILAND

Sq. Miles: 6704 (Slightly smaller than New Jersey). **Country Pop:** 1,173,900 (2005). **Capital:** Mbabane, pop. 60,000 (2004). **Largest City:** Manzini, pop. 65,000 (2004). **Terrain:** Mountainous plateau to savanna. **Ethnic Group(s):** Swazi. **Religion(s):** Zionist Roman_Catholic Muslim. **Official Language(s):** Siswati English. **Government:** Monarchy. **Independence:** 1968 (from United Kingdom). **Per Capita Income:** $1891 (2003). **GDP:** $2.8 billion (2004). Agriculture 16%. Manufacturing 35%. **Currency:** Swaziland Emalangeni (E).

SIFUNDZANI SCHOOL
Day — Coed Ages 5-17

Mbabane, Swaziland. Swazi Plz, PO Box A286. Tel: 268-404-2465. Fax: 268-404-0320. EST+7.
E-mail: sifundzani@realnet.co.sz
Ella Magonga, Prin.
  Gen Acad. Curr—UK. Supp Lang—Fr. Exams—IGCSE. Feat—Fr Siswati Afrikaans Comp_Sci Relig Music. Supp—ESL.
  Enr 615. Accepted: 20%. Avg class size: 27.
  Fac 48.
  Grad '05—19.
  Tui '05-'06: Day $1204-2605.
  Bldgs 10. Class rms 26. Libs 1. Fields 1. Pools 1.
  Est 1981. Tri (Jan-Dec). Assoc: AISA A/OPR/OS.

The curriculum at this school, which is similar to that found in the UK, includes five years of French and Siswati. Visits to game reserves, museums, houses of Parliament, industrial areas and agricultural projects are part of the program. The primary and secondary schools occupy two separate campuses in the Mbabane area.

WATERFORD KAMHLABA UNITED WORLD COLLEGE OF SOUTHERN AFRICA

Bdg and Day — Coed Gr 9-12

Mbabane, Swaziland. Box 52. Tel: 268-42-20866. Fax: 268-42-20088. EST+7.
www.waterford.sz   E-mail: admissions@waterford.sz
Laurence Nodder, Prin.

Col Prep. IB Diploma. Curr—Intl UK. Exams—IGCSE O-level. Feat—Fr Span Afrikaans Siswati Comp_Sci Studio_Art Drama Theater Music.
Enr 500.
Fac 45.
Tui '05-'06: Bdg E50,515-71,890. Day E32,140-42,810.
Est 1963. Tri (Jan-Dec).

Waterford is one of 10 related UWC international schools dedicated to promoting international understanding through education. The organization has campuses in Britain, Canada, Hong Kong, India, Italy, Norway, Singapore, Swaziland, the US and Venezuela, and each school is a community representing more than 70 countries. In grades 11 and 12, all students follow the International Baccalaureate curriculum in preparation for the IB Diploma.

Community service, outdoor programs and events pertaining to global issues supplement the academic offerings.

USUTU FORESTS PRIMARY SCHOOL

Day — Coed Gr PS-7

Mhlambanyatsi H115, Swaziland. PO Box 264. Tel: 268-46-74134. Fax: 268-46-74192. EST+7.
www.usutuprimary.ac.sz   E-mail: ufps@africaonline.co.sz
Malcolm Kennedy, Head.

Gen Acad. Curr—Intl.
Enr 350. Elem 350.
Fac 20.
Est 1963. Tri (Jan-Dec).

TANZANIA

Sq. Miles: 378,640 (Slightly smaller than New Mexico and Texas combined). **Country Pop:** 36,766,356 (2005). **Capital:** Dar es Salaam, pop. 2,497,940 (2002). **Terrain:** Varied. **Religion(s):** Muslim Christian Indigenous_Beliefs. **Official Language(s):** Kiswahili. **Other Language(s):** English. **Government:** Republic. **Independence:** 1964 (from United

Kingdom). **Per Capita Income:** $300 (2004). **GDP:** $10 billion (2004). Agriculture 46%. Industry 9%. **Currency:** Tanzanian Shilling (TSh).

INTERNATIONAL SCHOOL OF TANGANYIKA
Day — Coed Gr PS-12

Dar es Salaam, Tanzania. United Nations Rd, PO Box 2651. Tel: 255-22-2151817. Fax: 255-22-2152077. EST+8.
www.istafrica.com   E-mail: fjstucker@istafrica.com
F. Joseph Stucker, Dir.

Col Prep. IB PYP. IB MYP. IB Diploma. Curr—Intl. Feat—Humanities Fr Span Kiswahili Environ_Sci Comp_Sci Visual_Arts Theater_Arts Music.
Tui '05-'06: Day $5885-14,930 (+$3100).
Est 1963. Nonprofit. Quar (Aug-June). Assoc: AISA A/OPR/OS CIS MSA.

INTERNATIONAL SCHOOL MOSHI
Bdg — Coed Gr 2-12; Day — Coed PS-12

Moshi, Kilimanjaro, Tanzania. PO Box 733. Tel: 255-27-275-5004. Fax: 255-27-275-2877. EST+8.
www.ismoshi.org   E-mail: school@ismoshi.org
Barry Sutherland, CEO. Keiron White, Adm.

Col Prep. IB PYP. IB MYP. IB Diploma. Curr—Intl. Exams—CEEB IGCSE. Feat— Fr Swahili Comp_Sci Econ Visual_Arts Theater_Arts Bus. Supp—EFL ESL LD.
Sports—Basket Soccer Volley. Activities—Acad Arts Govt/Pol Rec Service.
Enr 490. B 30/210. G 30/220. Elem 345. Sec 145. US 45. Host 105. Other 340. Accepted: 95%. Yield: 90%. Avg class size: 18.
Fac 59. M 21/3. F 24/11. US 6. Host 7. Other 46. Adv Deg: 30%.
Grad '05—43. Col—38. US Col—19.
Tui '05-'06: Bdg $15,875-20,875 (+$2000). Day $3000-11,600 (+$2000). Aid: 41 pupils ($90,000).
Dorms 7. Dorm rms 60. Class rms 60. Libs 2. Sci labs 6. Comp labs 2. Auds 1. Art studios 2. Music studios 2. Gyms 1. Fields 3. Courts 2. Pools 2. Stables 1.
Est 1969. Nonprofit. Tri (Aug-June). Assoc: AISA CIS MSA.

Founded to provide education for the children of expatriate personnel working in Tanzania, the school has grown to occupy two sites: the Moshi campus accommodates day and boarding students in grades pre-K-12, while the Arusha campus serves day pupils in grades pre-K-8. Children in grades K-8 follow an English-medium curriculum with African and international perspectives; ninth and tenth graders take IGCSE courses; and students in grades 11 and 12 take part in the school's IB program. Special needs and ESL and EFL assistance is available as needed.

At all levels, there is an emphasis on environmental education and practical service, and music, drama and computers are noteworthy elements of the program. Pupils engage in various outdoor pursuits, as the school makes use of Mount Kilimanjaro and the environment of northern Tanzania. In addition, ISM operates a field studies center on the Indian Ocean coast.

TANGA INTERNATIONAL SCHOOL
Bdg and Day — Coed Gr PS-6

Tanga, Tanzania. PO Box 1178. Tel: 255-27-264-2979. Fax: 255-27-264-2979. EST+8.
www.tistanzania.com   E-mail: info@tistanzania.com
Simon McCloskey, Prin.
> Gen Acad. Curr—Intl. Feat—Comp_Sci Studio_Art Music.
> Nonprofit. Tri (Aug-July). Assoc: AISA.

TOGO

Sq. Miles: 21,853 (Slightly smaller than West Virginia). **Country Pop:** 5,681,519 (2005). **Capital:** Lome, pop. 850,000 (2004). **Terrain:** Savannah and hills and coastal plain. **Ethnic Group(s):** Ewe Mina Kabye Cotocoli Moba. **Religion(s):** Indigenous_Beliefs Christian Muslim. **Official Language(s):** French. **Other Language(s):** Ewe Mina Kabye. **Government:** Republic. **Independence:** 1960. **Per Capita Income:** $270 (2002). **GDP:** $1.4 billion (2002). Agriculture 40%. Industry 21%. Services 38%. **Currency:** African Coalition Franc (CFAF).

AMERICAN INTERNATIONAL SCHOOL OF LOME
Day — Coed Gr PS-12

Lome, Togo. 35 Rue Kayigan Lawson, BP 852. Tel: 228-221-30-00. Fax: 228-222-73-58. EST+5.
Contact: 2300 Lome Pl, Dulles, VA 20891.
www.multimania.com/aisl   E-mail: aisl@laposte.tg
Ruth Kramer-Sackett, Dir. PhD.
> Col Prep. Curr—US. Exams—CEEB. Feat—Fr Comp_Sci Govt Studio_Art Drama Music. Supp—ESL Tut.
> Activities—Rec.
> Enr 55. B 29. G 26. Elem 38. Sec 17. US 4. Host 12. Other 39. Accepted: 100%. Avg class size: 10.
> Fac 10. M 3/4. F 2/1. US 2. Host 2. Other 4. Adv Deg: 30%.
> Grad '05—10. Col—10. US Col—9. (Edmonds CC 6, U of WA 1, SUNY 1, Black Hawk 1).
> Tui '05-'06: Day $3000-9000 (+$500-2200). Aid: 12 pupils.
> Class rms 7. Lib 4000 vols. Sci labs 1. Lang labs 1. Comp labs 1. Art studios 1. Music studios 1. Dance studios 2. Gyms 2. Courts 1.
> Est 1967. Nonprofit. Quar (Aug-June). Assoc: AISA A/OPR/OS MSA.

The school was started by American missionary parents who wanted an American curriculum to meet the needs of their children in a French-speaking country. Individually guided education is stressed, and every child may pursue independent study. Physical education activities include fundamental rhythm, gymnastics and team sports.

AISL also supervises supplementary correspondence course work for students in grades 9-12.

THE BRITISH SCHOOL OF LOME
Bdg — Coed Gr 3-12; Day — Coed PS-12

Lome, Togo. Residence du Benin, BP 20050. Tel: 228-226-46-06. Fax: 228-226-49-89. EST+5.
www.bsl.tg   E-mail: admin@bsl.tg
Ian A. Sayer, Head.
   Col Prep. IB PYP. IB MYP. IB Diploma. Curr—Intl. Exams—GCSE IGCSE. Feat—Lib_Skills Fr Ger Comp_Sci Studio_Art Drama Music.
   Tui '05-'06: Bdg €16,540-19,055 (+€153). Day €7165-11,130 (+€153).
   Est 1983. Tri (Aug-June).

TUNISIA

Sq. Miles: 63,378 (Slightly larger than Georgia). Country Pop: 10,074,951 (2005). Capital: Tunis, pop. 2,225,900. Terrain: Arable land in north and along central coast; south is mostly semiarid or desert. Ethnic Group(s): Arab-Berber European. Religion(s): Muslim Christian Jewish. Official Language(s): Arabic. Other Language(s): French. Government: Republic. Independence: 1956 (from United Kingdom). Per Capita Income: $2667 (2004). GDP: $16.2 billion (2004). Agriculture 13%. Industry 28%. Services 39%. Currency: Tunisian Dinar (TD).

AMERICAN COOPERATIVE SCHOOL OF TUNIS
Day — Coed Gr PS-12

2045 Tunis, Tunisia. Route de la Marsa, Cite Taieb Mhiri. Tel: 216-71-760-905. Fax: 216-71-761-412. EST+6.
Contact: c/o Dept of State, 6360 Tunis Pl, Washington, DC 20520.
www.acst.net   E-mail: american.school@acst.intl.tn
Patrick Meyer, Dir.
   Gen Acad. IB Diploma. Curr—Intl US. Exams—CEEB. Feat—Arabic Fr Comp_Sci Tunisian_Stud Studio_Art Music. Supp—ESL.
   Enr 530. Elem 407. Sec 123.
   Fac 56.
   Tui '05-'06: Day $5460-12,340 (+$600-3530).
   Est 1959. Nonprofit. Sem (Aug-June). Assoc: A/OPR/OS MAIS MSA.

UGANDA

Sq. Miles: 93,070 (About the size of Oregon). **Country Pop:** 27,269,482 (2005). **Capital:** Kampala, pop. 1,200,000 (2002). **Terrain:** 18% inland water and swamp; 12% national parks, forest, and game reserves; 70% forest, woodland, grassland. **Ethnic Group(s):** African European Asian Arab. **Religion(s):** Christian Muslim. **Official Language(s):** English. **Other Language(s):** Luganda Swahili Bantu Nilotic. **Government:** Republic. **Independence:** 1962 (from United Kingdom). **Per Capita Income:** $1500 (2004). **GDP:** $39.4 billion (2004). Agriculture 36%. Industry 21%. Services 43%. **Currency:** Ugandan Shilling (USh).

THE INTERNATIONAL SCHOOL OF UGANDA
Day — Coed Gr PS-12

Kampala, Uganda. PO Box 4200. Tel: 256-41-200374. Fax: 256-41-200303. EST+8. www.isu.ac.ug   E-mail: gmail@isu.ac.ug
Donald Groves, Head.
  Col Prep. IB PYP. IB MYP. IB Diploma. Curr—Intl. Exams—CEEB IGCSE.
  Enr 425. B 258. G 167.
  Fac 47.
  Tui '05-'06: Day $2493-14,112.
  Est 1966. Nonprofit. Tri (Aug-June). Assoc: AISA A/OPR/OS CIS MSA.

KABIRA INTERNATIONAL SCHOOL
Day — Coed Gr PS-12

Kampala, Uganda. PO Box 2020, Bukoto. Tel: 256-41-530-472. Fax: 256-41-543-444. EST+8.
www.kabiraschool.com   E-mail: office@kabiraschool.com
Elaine Whelen, Prin. BA, MA.
  Col Prep. IB MYP. Curr—Intl UK. Feat—Humanities Fr Environ_Sci Comp_Sci Econ Studio_Art Theater_Arts Music.
  Fac 32.
  Tui '05-'06: Day $4670-11,361 (+$483-609).
  Est 1993. Tri (Sept-July). Assoc: AISA CIS NEASC.

RAINBOW INTERNATIONAL SCHOOL
Bdg — Coed Gr 2-13; Day — Coed PS-13

Kampala, Uganda. PO Box 7632. Tel: 256-41-268003. Fax: 256-41-269697. EST+8.
www.risk.sc.ug   E-mail: admin@risk.sc.ug
C. A. Green, Co-Head. BSc. **P. R. Arnold, Co-Head.** BA.
  Col Prep. Gen Acad. Curr—UK. Exams—IGCSE AS-level A-level. Feat—Fr Comp_Sci Econ Sociol Studio_Art Drama Music Accounting Bus. Supp—Dev_

Read ESL LD Rem_Math Rem_Read.
Sports—Basket Gymnastics Soccer Swim Volley. **Activities**—Arts Govt/Pol Media Rec Service.
Enr 670. B 12/311. G 8/339. Elem 484. Sec 186. US 10. Host 214. Other 446. Accepted: 100%. Yield: 90%. Avg class size: 19.
Fac 60. M 22. F 38. Host 42. Other 18. Adv Deg: 10%.
Grad '05—24. Col—18. US Col—6.
Tui '05-'06: Bdg $6490-9210. Day $1760-4860 (+$500).
Plant val $1,500,000. Bldgs 13. Class rms 47. Libs 1. Sci labs 3. Comp labs 3. Art studios 2. Fields 2. Courts 1. Pools 1.
Est 1991. Inc. Tri (Aug-July).

Founded as an English-medium elementary school, Rainbow expanded its UK-style curriculum into the secondary years in 1993. At the primary level, differentiated teaching in math, English and science allows instructors to address varying learning needs. Pupils remain with their homeroom teacher for most classes, but specialists teach French, music, swimming and physical education. The secondary program follows the British national curriculum: Students prepare for the IGCSE examinations in grades 10 and 11, then take A-level courses in grades 12 and 13.

Interest club participation begins in grade 2. Interscholastic athletic teams are also available.

ZAMBIA

Sq. Miles: 290,585 (Slightly larger than Texas). **Country Pop:** 11,261,795 (2005). **Capital:** Lusaka, pop. 1,000,000. **Terrain:** Varies; mostly plateau savanna. **Ethnic Group(s):** African European. **Religion(s):** Christian Indigenous_Beliefs Muslim Hindu. **Official Language(s):** English. **Other Language(s):** Bemba Lozi Kaounde Lundu Luvale Tonga Nyanja. **Government:** Republic. **Independence:** 1964 (from United Kingdom). **Per Capita Income:** $478 (2004). **GDP:** $4.3 billion (2004). **Currency:** Zambian Kwacha (ZK).

AMERICAN INTERNATIONAL SCHOOL
Day — Coed Gr PS-12

Lusaka, Zambia. Leopards Hill Rd, PO Box 31617. Tel: 260-1-260509. Fax: 260-1-252225. EST+7.
Contact: Dept of State, 2310 Lusaka Pl, Washington, DC 20521.
www.aislusaka.org   E-mail: aesl@zamnet.zm
Irene Epp, Dir. PhD.
  Col Prep. Gen Acad. IB PYP. IB MYP. IB Diploma. Curr—Intl. **Exams**—CEEB SSAT. **Feat**—Fr Span Comp_Sci Zambian_Stud Studio_Art Drama Music. **Supp**—EFL ESL LD Tut.
  Sports—Basket X-country F_Hockey Rugby Soccer Swim Tennis W_Polo. **Activities**—Acad Arts Govt/Pol Rec.
  Enr 425. B 199. G 226. Elem 334. Sec 91. US 102. Host 39. Other 284. Accepted:

99%. Yield: 100%. Avg class size: 15.
Fac 59. US 24. Host 5. Other 30. Adv Deg: 28%.
Grad '05—4.
Tui '05-'06: Day $3000-10,500 (+$2000).
Plant val $3,630,000. Bldgs 11. Class rms 33. Lib 10,000 vols. Sci labs 3. Lang labs 2. Comp labs 2. Art studios 2. Music studios 2. Fields 3. Tennis courts 2. Pools 2.
Est 1986. Nonprofit. Tri (Aug-June). Assoc: AISA ECIS.

AIS conducts an international program that emphasizes the traditional subjects and integrates computer technology. Foreign language study is an important aspect of the curriculum: All children receive daily French instruction beginning at age 5. Specialist teachers conduct regularly scheduled art, music and physical education courses. The school seeks to ensure a smooth transition for students who either return to their home country or move on to another international school.

BANANI INTERNATIONAL SECONDARY SCHOOL
Bdg — Girls Gr 8-12

Lusaka, Zambia. Private Bag RW 199X, Ridgeway 15102. Tel: 260-1-213821. Fax: 260-1-214785. EST+7.
www.banani.sch.zm   E-mail: schooladmin@banani.sch.zm
Amy Davis, Prin.
   Col Prep. Gen Acad. Curr—Intl Nat. **Exams**—IGCSE. **Feat**—Fr Comp_Sci World_Relig Studio_Art Music. **Supp**—Dev_Read ESL Rem_Math Rem_Read Rev Tut.
   Enr 130. G 130. Sec 130. US 1. Host 115. Other 14. Avg class size: 25.
   Fac 12. M 5/1. F 3/3. Host 4. Other 8. Adv Deg: 25%.
   Grad '05—24. Col—18. US Col—3. (Old Dominion, Middlebury, Seattle U).
   Tui '01-'02: Bdg $4950 (+$300).
   Bldgs 19. Dorms 5. Dorm rms 50. Class rms 7. Lib 5000 vols. Sci labs 2. Comp labs 1. Theaters 1. Art studios 1. Music studios 1. Dance studios 1. Fields 1. Courts 1. Pools 1.
   Est 1993. Nonprofit. Tri (Jan-Nov). Assoc: AISA.

In grades 8 and 9, girls at Banani follow the Zambian syllabus. Grade 10 is spent in preparation for the IGCSE, which students work toward in grades 11 and 12. Program emphasis is on the sciences and agricultural education, in addition to the arts. Computer studies are part of the curriculum, as is a course in world religions. Instruction is in English, with French language classes offered all five years.

Music and drama, an environmental awareness group and sports are among the school's extracurricular options. Girls devote time to community service projects each week.

INTERNATIONAL SCHOOL OF LUSAKA
Day — Coed Gr PS-12

Lusaka, Zambia. 6945 Nangwenya Rd, PO Box 50121. Tel: 260-1-252291. Fax: 260-1-252865. EST+7.

E-mail: isl@zamnet.zm
Anthony Lindoe, Head.
  Col Prep. IB Diploma. Curr—Intl UK. **Exams**—CEEB TOEFL IGCSE. **Supp**—ESL.
  Enr 379. B 186. G 193.
  Fac 42.
  Tui '05-'06: Day $2100-8250.
  Est 1963. Nonprofit. Tri (Aug-June). Assoc: AISA A/OPR/OS CIS NEASC.

LUSAKA INTERNATIONAL COMMUNITY SCHOOL
Day — Coed Gr PS-10

Lusaka, Zambia. 242B Kakola Rd, PO Box 30528. Tel: 260-1-292447. Fax: 260-1-290048. EST+7.
www.lics.sch.zm   E-mail: lics@coppernet.zm
Steve Weatherall, Head. BSc, MA.
  Gen Acad. Curr—UK. **Exams**—IGCSE. **Feat**—Fr Comp_Sci Geog Studio_Art Music Bus. **Supp**—ESL Rem_Math Rem Read Rev.
  Enr 350. Accepted: 99%. Avg class size: 14.
  Fac 27. M 6. F 21. Host 8. Other 19. Adv Deg: 18%.
  Grad '05—6.
  Tui '02-'03: Day $5550 (+$200).
  Plant val $675,000. Bldgs 11. Class rms 30. 2 Libs 5000 vols. Sci labs 1. Comp labs 1. Art studios 2. Music studios 1. Dance studios 1. Fields 2. Courts 3. Pools 2.
  Est 1993. Nonprofit. Tri (Aug-June). Assoc: ECIS.

Founded to serve Lusaka's expatriate community, the school occupies an 11-acre campus in the residential suburb of Roma. LICS provides English-language instruction in an international environment and features an early learning center program for children ages 2-4. Emphasis is placed upon community service, and the school also maintains a strong athletic tradition, particularly in swimming and soccer.

ZIMBABWE

Sq. Miles: 150,760 (Slightly larger than Montana). **Country Pop:** 12,746,990 (2005). **Capital:** Harare, pop. 1,500,000 (2005). **Terrain:** Desert and savanna. **Ethnic Group(s):** Shona Ndebele. **Religion(s):** Christian Muslim. **Official Language(s):** English. **Other Language(s):** Shona Sindebele. **Government:** Parliamentary. **Independence:** 1980 (from United Kingdom). **Per Capita Income:** $327 (2003). **GDP:** $3.6 billion (2003). Agriculture 20%. Manufacturing 25%. Mining 8%. Public Administration 9%. Transport & Communications 6%. **Currency:** Zimbabwean Dollar (Z$).

HARARE INTERNATIONAL SCHOOL
Day — Coed Gr PS-12

Harare, Zimbabwe. 66 Pendennis Rd, Mount Pleasant. Tel: 263-4-301682. Fax: 263-4-883371. EST+7.
www.his-zim.com   E-mail: his@his.ac.zw
Paul Poore, Dir.

Col Prep. IB PYP. IB Diploma. Curr—Intl. Feat—Fr Span Comp_Sci Econ Visual_ Arts Theater_Arts Music. Supp—ESL LD.

Tui '05-'06: Day $10,720-15,220 (+$3000-4000).

Est 1992. Nonprofit. Sem (Aug-June). Assoc: AISA A/OPR/OS CIS NEASC.

PETERHOUSE BOYS' SCHOOL
Bdg — Boys Ages 12-18

Marondera, Zimbabwe. Private Bag 3741. Tel: 263-79-24951. Fax: 263-79-24200. EST+7.
http://home.vicnet.net.au/~petrean   E-mail: peterrec@mweb.co.zw
J. B. Calderwood, Rector.

Col Prep. Curr—UK. Exams—IGCSE O-level A-level. Feat—Fr Shona Stats Comp_Sci Relig Studio_Art Drama Music.

Enr 480. B 480.

Est 1955. Anglican. Tri (Jan-Dec).

ASIA & PACIFIC ISLANDS

INDEX TO COUNTRIES IN
ASIA & PACIFIC ISLANDS

ASIA & PACIFIC ISLANDS

BANGLADESH

Sq. Miles: 55,813 (About the size of Wisconsin). **Country Pop:** 144,319,628 (2005). **Capital:** Dhaka, pop. 10,000,000. **Terrain:** Mainly flat alluvial plain, with hills in the northeast and the southeast. **Ethnic Group(s):** Bengali. **Religion(s):** Muslim Hindu Christian Buddhist. **Official Language(s):** Bangla. **Other Language(s):** English. **Government:** Parliamentary Democracy. **Independence:** 1971 (from Pakistan). **Per Capita Income:** $421 (2004). **GDP:** $276 billion (2004). Agriculture 21%. Industry 27%. Services 52%. **Currency:** Bangladeshi Taka (Tk).

AMERICAN INTERNATIONAL SCHOOL-DHAKA
Day — Coed Gr PS-12

Dhaka, Bangladesh. United Nations Rd, Baridhara. Tel: 880-2-882-2452. Fax: 880-2-882-3175. EST+11.
www.ais-dhaka.net   E-mail: info@ais-dhaka.net
Walter Plotkin, Supt.

Col Prep. IB Diploma. Curr—Intl US. **Exams**—AP CEEB. **AP**—Eng Fr Span Stats Comp_Sci Bio Chem Human_Geog Eur_Hist Econ Studio_Art. **Feat**—Bangla Theater_Arts Journ Speech. **Supp**—ESL Tut.

Sports—Basket F_Hockey Soccer Swim Track Volley. **Activities**—Arts Govt/Pol Media Service.

Enr 647. B 354. G 293. Elem 464. Sec 183. US 149. Host 70. Other 428. Avg class size: 16.

Fac 81. US 67. Host 3. Other 11.

Grad '05—38.

Tui '06-'07: Day $6500-16,660 (+$5450).

Summer: Rec. 4 wks.

Bldgs 4. Class rms 70. Lib 30,000 vols. Sci labs 6. Lang labs 4. Comp labs 4. Theaters 1. Art studios 3. Music studios 2. Gyms 1. Fields 1. Pools 1.

Est 1972. Nonprofit. Quar (Aug-June). Assoc: A/OPR/OS CIS NEASC.

Successor to the former Dhaka American Society School (founded in 1963), AIS/D serves the expatriate community of Dhaka. During the elementary years (grades PS-5), children follow a core curriculum of language arts, math, science and social studies, which are all taught by a homeroom teacher. Specialists teach music, art, computer, library, South Asian studies and physical education classes. The program, which incorporates American curricular standards, also includes service learning, student support services and extracurricular activities.

The thematic middle school program (grades 6-8) is similar to that conducted in the US. The core curriculum incorporates both service learning and information technology. AIS/D's college preparatory high school (grades 9-12) offers both Advanced Placement course work and the two-year IB Diploma Program.

Elementary school and middle school students choose from an array of after-school activities, while high schoolers may take part in any of a number of interest clubs and interscholastic sports.

BRUNEI

Sq. Miles: 2226 (Slightly larger than Delaware). **Country Pop:** 372,361 (2005). **Capital:** Bandar Seri Begawan, pop. 74,700. **Terrain:** East: flat coastal plains with beaches; west: hilly with a few mountain ridges. **Ethnic Group(s):** Malay Chinese. **Religion(s):** Muslim. **Other Language(s):** Malay English Chinese Iban. **Government:** Constitutional Sultanate. **Independence:** 1984 (from United Kingdom). **GDP:** $4.71 billion (2003). Agriculture 5%. Industry 45%. Services 50%. **Currency:** Bruneian Dollar (Br$).

JERUDONG INTERNATIONAL SCHOOL
Bdg — Coed Gr 9-12; Day — Coed PS-12

Bandar Seri Begawan BS 8672, Brunei. PO Box 1408. Tel: 673-241-1000. Fax: 673-241-1010. EST+13.
www.jis.edu.bn   E-mail: office@jis.edu.bn
John Price, Prin. MA. Lynn Payne, Adm.
   Col Prep. Curr—Intl UK. Exams—GCSE IGCSE AS-level A-level. Feat—Chin Fr Span Bahasa_Melayu Malay Comp_Sci Econ Psych Studio_Art Drama Music Accounting Bus. Supp—ESL Rem_Math Rem_Read.
   Sports—Basket Swim. Activities—Arts Rec.
   Enr 1152. B 82/540. G 61/469. Elem 570. Sec 582. US 6. Host 403. Other 743. Accepted: 90%. Yield: 95%. Avg class size: 25.
   Fac 121. M 67. F 54. Host 8. Other 113. Adv Deg: 16%.
   Grad '05—95. US Col—1. (Harvard).
   Tui '05-'06: Bdg Br$26,436 (+Br$1000). Day Br$13,236 (+Br$1000).
   Summer: Rec. Tui Day Br$250/wk. 2 wks.
   Bldgs 13. Dorms 8. Dorm rms 32. Libs 1. Sci labs 14. Lang labs 8. Comp labs 12. Art studios 6. Music studios 12. Dance studios 1. Gyms 1. Fields 1. Courts 3. Pools 1.
   Est 1997. Nonprofit. Sem (Aug-July).

Located on a 64-acre site overlooking the South China Sea on Brunei's northwest coastline, JIS conducts a UK-style program that runs from age 4 through A levels. The primary school program follows the National Curriculum of England and Wales while stressing the acquisition of basic skills (particularly reading). Foreign languages and information technology are integral to the primary curriculum.

The secondary school places particular emphasis on college preparation: Course work provides preparation for the GCSE and IGCSE examinations at the end of grade 11, and the A and AS levels at the conclusion of grade 13. Secondary pupils progress from a broad curriculum to a more focused one.

As a complement to academics, boys and girls may take part in such extracurricular activities as sports, music, drama, societies and cultural pursuits. The boarding department features five- and seven-day options.

INTERNATIONAL SCHOOL OF BRUNEI
Day — Coed Gr PS-12

Berakas BB3577, Brunei. MPC Old Airport, PO Box 192. Tel: 673-2-330608. Fax: 673-2-337446. EST+13.
www.isb.edu.bn E-mail: isbadmin@brunet.bn
David G. Taylor, Dir.
Col Prep. **IB Diploma. Curr**—Intl UK. **Exams**—CEEB GCSE IGCSE. **Feat**—Fr Malay Comp_Sci Studio_Art Drama Music. **Supp**—ESL LD.
Enr 935. B 485. G 450. Avg class size: 26.
Fac 51. Adv Deg: 11%.
Tui '05-'06: Day Br$6050-9900.
Libs 2. Sci labs 4. Comp labs 2. Fields 1. Courts 2. Pools 1.
Est 1991. Nonprofit. Tri (Aug-July). Assoc: ECIS.

Due to the diverse student body enrolled at ISB, one that comprises pupils of varying ability levels and facility with the English language, the school builds some flexibility into its curriculum. The academic program's general framework is that employed in the United Kingdom, with course work leading to the GCSE and the IGCSE, then culminating with the IB Diploma. Intensive ESL support is available as required, and ISB also addresses the needs of both gifted students and those with specific learning difficulties.

An extensive extracurricular program allows interested boys and girls to participate in athletics, music, art, drama and vocational training courses. In addition, pupils lacking fluency in the language may receive after-school English instruction.

CAMBODIA

Sq. Miles: 69,900 (About the size of Missouri). **Country Pop:** 13,607,069 (2005). **Capital:** Phnom Penh, pop. 1,200,000 (2005). **Terrain:** Heavy forests away from the rivers and the lake, mountains in the southwest and north along the border with Thailand. **Ethnic Group(s):** Cambodian Vietnamese Chinese. **Religion(s):** Buddhist Muslim Christian. **Official Language(s):** Khmer. **Other Language(s):** French English. **Government:** Constitutional Monarchy. **Independence:** 1953 (from France). **GDP:** $4.2 billion (1995). Agriculture 35%. Industry 30%. Services 35%. **Currency:** Cambodian Riel (CR).

INTERNATIONAL SCHOOL OF PHNOM PENH
Day — Coed Gr PS-12

Phnom Penh, Cambodia. PO Box 138. Tel: 855-23-213-103. Fax: 855-23-361-002. EST+12.
www.ispp.edu.kh   E-mail: ispp@ispp.edu.kh
Rob Mockrish, Dir. PhD.

> **Col Prep. Gen Acad. IB PYP. IB MYP. IB Diploma. Curr**—Intl. **Exams**—CEEB. **Feat**—Lib_Skills Fr Khmer Comp_Sci Khmer_Culture Studio_Art Study_Skills. **Supp**—Dev_Read EFL ESL LD Rem_Math Rem_Read.
> **Enr 335.** B 155. G 180. US 37. Host 54. Other 244. Accepted: 100%. Avg class size: 17.
> **Fac 50.** M 17. F 31/2. US 3. Adv Deg: 30%.
> **Grad '05—12. Col—10. US Col—3.** (U of MI, Calvin, Swarthmore).
> **Tui '05-'06: Day $4180-10,450. Aid:** 14 pupils ($80,000).
> **Summer:** Enrich. 3 wks.
> Bldgs 4. Class rms 35. 2 Libs 8000 vols. Sci labs 2. Comp labs 2. Auds 1. Art studios 2. Music studios 1. Gyms 1. Fields 1. Courts 2. Pools 1.
> **Est 1989.** Nonprofit. Sem (Aug-June). Assoc: A/OPR/OS CIS WASC.

Offering comprehensive elementary and secondary programs on two distinct campuses, ISPP enrolls students from more than 30 countries, with highest representation coming from Europe, North America, Cambodia, other parts of Asia and Australasia. During the early years, instructors particularly emphasize the acquisition of basic skills within the framework of the International Baccalaureate Primary Years Program. The social studies curriculum focuses on Cambodia, Thailand, Vietnam and the US, and art, music and computer classes supplement work in the standard disciplines.

Pupils in grades 6-10 follow the IB Middle Years Program. All boys and girls learn a second language (French or Khmer) at this time. In grades 11 and 12, students pursue the internationally recognized IB Diploma. ISPP makes provisions for older pupils wishing to take the PSAT and SAT examinations. ESL and learning support programs are strong at all grade levels.

Community service is an integral aspect of the school's activities program. Other offerings include cultural pursuits and athletics.

NORTHBRIDGE INTERNATIONAL SCHOOL CAMBODIA
Day — Coed Gr PS-12

3 Phnom Penh, Cambodia. PO Box 2042. Tel: 855-23-886-000. Fax: 855-23-886-009. EST+12.
www.niscambodia.com   E-mail: info@niscambodia.com
David E. Eaton, Head. MEd.

> **Col Prep. Curr**—Intl US. **Exams**—AP CEEB TOEFL. **AP**—Eng Calc Bio Physics Eur_Hist Comp_Govt & Pol Studio_Art. **Feat**—Chin Fr Span Khmer Environ_Sci Comp_Sci Theater_Arts Music. **Supp**—Dev_Read ESL Tut.
> **Sports**—Basket Soccer Softball Volley. **Activities**—Arts Govt/Pol Rec.
> **Enr 273.** B 131. G 142. Elem 197. Sec 76. US 74. Host 63. Other 136. Accepted: 85%. Yield: 95%. Avg class size: 16.
> **Fac 34.** M 10/2. F 16/6. US 17. Host 1. Other 16. Adv Deg: 50%.

Grad '05—9. Col—9. US Col—3. (HI Pacific, Northwest U). Avg SAT: M/V—1020, Essay—580.
Tui '05-'06: Day $6600-9200 (+$4000-4500). **Aid:** 3 pupils ($28,000).
Summer: Rec. Tui Day $300. 3 wks.
Plant val $5,000,000. Bldgs 4. Sci labs 2. Comp labs 2. Auds 1. Art studios 2. Music studios 2. Gyms 1. Fields 2. Courts 2. Pools 1.
Est 1997. Nonprofit. Spons: Northbridge Communities. Sem (Aug-June). Assoc: EARCOS WASC.

This American-style school offers an array of Advanced Placement courses as part of its college preparatory curriculum. The elementary program at NISC accommodates children of varying ability levels. Students take French from kindergarten and Khmer from grade 2, and they also make weekly visits to the library and the computer lab. Activity days, after-school programming, performances and field trips complement academics. An elective program at the high school level enables boys and girls to sample many areas of potential interest early in high school, then specialize in areas of particular interest by senior year.

ZAMAN INTERNATIONAL SCHOOL
Day — Coed Gr PS-12

Phnom Penh, Cambodia. PO Box 2508. Tel: 855-23-214040. Fax: 855-23-210036. EST+12.
www.zamanisc.org   E-mail: info@zamanisc.org
Atilla Yusuf Guleker, Dir.
  Col Prep. Curr—Intl UK. Supp Lang—Khmer. Feat—Khmer_Lit Khmer Turkish Geol Comp_Sci Civics Studio_Art Music. Supp—ESL.
  Tui '05-'06: Day $1900-4500 (+$850-1100).
  Est 1997. Sem (Sept-June).

CHINA

Sq. Miles: 3,700,000 (Slightly smaller than the US). **Country Pop:** 1,306,313,812 (2005). **Capital:** Beijing, pop. 11,490,000 (2003). **Largest City:** Shanghai, pop. 17,110,000 (2003). **Terrain:** Plains, deltas, and hills in east; mountains, high plateaus, deserts in west. **Ethnic Group(s):** Han_Chinese Zhuang Manchu Hui Miao Uygur Yi Mongolian Tibetan Buyi Korean. **Religion(s):** Taoist Buddhist Muslim Christian. **Official Language(s):** Mandarin. **Government:** Communist. **Per Capita Income:** $1200 (2004). **GDP:** $1.65 trillion (2004). Agriculture 14%. Industry 53%. Services 33%. **Currency:** Chinese Yuan Renminbi (Y).

BEIJING BISS INTERNATIONAL SCHOOL
Day — Coed Gr K-12

Beijing 100029, China. 17 Area 4, An Zhen Xi Li, Chaoyang District. Tel: 86-10-6443-3151. Fax: 86-10-6443-3156. EST+13.
www.biss.com.cn   E-mail: admissions@biss.com.cn
Iain Stirling, Head. MA. Regis Hlawka, Adm.

> **Col Prep. IB PYP. IB MYP. IB Diploma. Curr**—Intl. **Exams**—CEEB. **Feat**—Chin Fr Span Korean Comp_Sci Econ Studio_Art Theater_Arts Music Design. **Supp**—EFL ESL.
> **Sports**—Basket Soccer Volley. **Activities**—Govt/Pol.
> **Enr 377.** B 193. G 184. Elem 268. Sec 109. US 25. Host 18. Other 334. Accepted: 95%. Yield: 95%. Avg class size: 18.
> **Fac 56.** M 28. F 28. US 22. Host 3. Other 31. Adv Deg: 48%.
> **Grad '05—49. Col—30. US Col—6.** (Carleton, MI St, Johns Hopkins, U of CA-Berkeley, Purdue, Am U).
> **Tui '05-'06: Day $9900-19,800** (+$500).
> **Summer:** Acad Rec. Tui Day $900/2-wk ses. 4 wks.
> Bldgs 3. Libs 2. Sci labs 3. Comp labs 3. Art studios 2. Music studios 2. Dance studios 1. Courts 4. Tracks 1.
> **Est 1994.** Sem (Aug-June). Assoc: EARCOS WASC.

Employing faculty members from Africa, Australia, Asia, Europe and North America, BISS conducts a full kindergarten through high school program for the area's expatriate community. The transdisciplinary International Baccalaureate Primary Years Program serves as the basis for the curriculum in grades K-6. During these years, specialist teachers conduct courses in Chinese studies, music, English for Speakers of Other Languages, and physical education, all of which are integral to the program. The middle school (grades 7 and 8) at BISS, which follows the IB Middle Years Program, serves as a transition between the lower grades and the high school years. Particular emphasis falls on the development of oral and practical skills, investigation, problem solving, skill application and knowledge acquisition, and individual and cooperative work skills.

College preparation becomes increasingly important in grades 9 and 10. During these years, pupils study languages, math, the sciences, humanities, social studies and the creative arts. Two distinct programs operate in grades 11 and 12: The IB Diploma Program, which features course work at two levels, and the Alternative Academic Program, into which students for whom the IB curriculum is not appropriate are assigned by BISS.

A learning center assists pupils with specific learning needs, those participating in enrichment programs and those enrolled in gifted classes.

BEIJING YEW CHUNG INTERNATIONAL SCHOOL
Day — Coed Gr PS-12

Beijing 100025, China. Honglingjin Park, 5 Houbalizhuang. Tel: 86-10-8583-3731. Fax: 86-10-8583-2734. EST+13.
www.ycef.com   E-mail: imeldal@ycef.com
Betty Chan Po-King, Dir. Nick Combes, Prin. Robyn Combes, Adm.

> **Col Prep. IB Diploma. Curr**—Intl UK. **Bilingual**—Chin. **Exams**—IGCSE O-level

A-level. **Feat**—Comp_Sci Studio_Art Music Design. **Supp**—Tut.
Enr 328. B 150. G 178. US 100. Other 228. Accepted: 100%. Avg class size: 15.
Fac 50. M 10. F 40. US 10. Host 20. Other 20.
Grad '05—2. Col—2.
Tui '05-'06: Day Y141,100-157,700. **Aid:** 3 pupils ($4590).
Bldgs 4. Class rms 40. Lib 4000 vols. Sci labs 2. Lang labs 4. Comp labs 1. Art studios 1. Music studios 1. Dance studios 1. Gyms 1. Fields 1. Courts 1.
Est 1995. Nonprofit. Nondenom Christian. Tri (Aug-July). Assoc: NEASC.

Part of a network of Christian schools that includes other institutions in Shanghai, Hong Kong and the United States, BIS conducts a structured bilingual program in Beijing from early childhood through high school. The curriculum combines an English-language, UK-style component with a Chinese program that meets national requirements. The school provides intensive ESL and Chinese as a Second Language for pupils needing to improve their English or Chinese language ability.

During the elementary years, BIS emphasizes basic skills, critical thinking, and the ability to work both independently and with others. In grades 9 and 10, students pursue an IGCSE program of study. Instruction in grades 11 and 12 combines in-depth work in the standard subjects with various electives.

Interested boys and girls may take part in BIS' World Classroom Program, which allows them to experience different cultures and interact with their people. Relevant course work precedes and follows each tour. Tours may include visits to Italy, England, France, Asia, China, or locations in the Americas.

INTERNATIONAL SCHOOL OF BEIJING

Day — Coed Gr PS-12

Beijing 101300, China. 10 An Hua St, Shunyi District. Tel: 86-10-8149-2345. Fax: 86-10-8046-2001. EST+13.
www.isb.bj.edu.cn E-mail: admissions@isb.bj.edu.cn
Tom Hawkins, Dir.
Col Prep. IB Diploma. Curr—Intl US. Exams—CEEB. Supp—EFL.
Enr 1775. Elem 1183. Sec 592.
Fac 62.
Tui '05-'06: Day $14,050-21,300 (+$1450-3800).
Est 1980. Nonprofit. Quar (Aug-June). Assoc: A/OPR/OS EARCOS NEASC.

SCHOOL YEAR ABROAD

Bdg — Coed Gr 11-12

Beijing 100088, China. 12 Xinjiekouwai. Tel: 86-10-6235-4503. Fax: 86-10-6235-4505. EST+13.
Contact: 439 S Union St, Lawrence, MA 01843. Tel: 978-725-6828. Fax: 978-725-6833.
www.sya.org E-mail: mail@sya.org
Woodruff W. Halsey II, Exec Dir. AB, MA. **Whitney Hermann, Adm.**
Col Prep. Curr—US. Exams—AP CEEB. **AP**—Calc. **Feat**—Chin Chin_Hist Chin_Stud.

Sports—Basket Track. **Activities**—Service.
Enr 50. Sec 50. Accepted: 66%. Yield: 85%. Avg class size: 15.
Fac 12. M 4/2. F 5/1. US 4. Host 8. Adv Deg: 83%.
Avg SAT: M/V—1315, Essay—668.
Tui '05-'06: Bdg $36,000 (+$2000). **Aid:** 25 pupils ($639,942).
Est 1994. Nonprofit. Quar (Sept-June).

School Year Abroad was established by Phillips Academy and is now a consortium of 26 independent schools. SYA China provides a fully accredited year of study for high school students in Beijing. Pupils may enroll with or without prior knowledge of Mandarin.

Students live with native families and travel during vacation periods. English is the medium of instruction in all nonlanguage courses. Program participants learn about the culture and customs of the host country. Educational trips are organized to different historical and cultural landmarks each year. Students prepare for the US College Boards and for certain Advanced Placement exams.

Similar programs operate in France, Italy and Spain (see separate listings).

WESTERN ACADEMY OF BEIJING

Day — Coed Gr PS-12

Beijing 100103, China. 10 Lai Guang Ying Dong Lu, Chao Yang District, PO Box 8547. Tel: 86-10-8456-4155. Fax: 86-10-6432-2440. EST+13.
www.wab.edu   E-mail: wabinfo@westernacademy.com
John McBryde, Dir. Sinead Collins, Adm.

Col Prep. Gen Acad. IB PYP. IB MYP. IB Diploma. Curr—Intl. **Feat**—Chin Fr Span Environ_Sci Comp_Sci Econ Performing_Arts Visual_Arts Drama Music Dance. **Supp**—Dev_Read ESL LD Rem_Math Rem_Read.
Sports—Basket X-country Gymnastics Soccer Tennis Volley. **Activities**—Acad Arts Govt/Pol Media Rec.
Enr 1227. B 618. G 609. Elem 1017. Sec 210. US 233. Host 17. Other 977. Accepted: 98%. Yield: 98%. Avg class size: 19.
Fac 145. M 54. F 84/7. US 17. Host 9. Other 119. Adv Deg: 20%.
Tui '05-'06: Day Y77,480-173,470. Aid: 29 pupils ($410,000).
Plant val $50,000,000. Class rms 90. Lib 40,000 vols. Sci labs 8. Lang labs 20. Comp labs 7. Auds 2. Theaters 4. Art studios 6. Music studios 14. Dance studios 1. Gyms 3. Fields 1. Courts 6. Pools 1.
Est 1994. Nonprofit. Tri (Aug-June). Assoc: CIS EARCOS NEASC.

This English-medium school places particular importance on information technology, with computers employed extensively in specialist subject areas such as foreign language, science, art and music, as well as in such support services as English as a Second Language. WAB's international syllabus follows the International Baccalaureate curriculum, as pupils progress from the Primary Years Program to the Middle Years Program. Course work comprises eight subject areas: English, foreign language, math, science, social studies, technology, physical education and the arts. Transdisciplinary themes run through the curriculum, and instructors place considerable emphasis on the development of transferable research, communication and critical-thinking skills. High school students may pursue the standard Chinese diploma or the IB Diploma.

An early childhood center provides half-day instruction for three- and four-year-olds, while the prekindergarten serves four- and five-year-olds. Chinese language courses begin in kindergarten, then expand to three levels (including one for native speakers).

AMERICAN INTERNATIONAL SCHOOL
OF GUANGZHOU

Day — Coed Gr PS-12

Guangzhou 510105, China. 3 Yan Yu St S, Ersha Island, Dongshan District. Tel: 86-20-8735-3392. Fax: 86-20-8735-3339. EST+13.
www.aisgz.edu.cn   E-mail: info@aisgz.edu.cn
David Shawver, Dir.

Col Prep. Gen Acad. IB PYP. IB Diploma. Curr—Intl US. Exams—CEEB. Supp—ESL.

Enr 710.

Fac 66.

Tui '05-'06: Day $4950-16,900 (+$950).

Est 1981. Sem (Aug-June). Assoc: A/OPR/OS EARCOS WASC.

UTAHLOY INTERNATIONAL SCHOOL
GUANGZHOU

Day — Coed Ages 2-18

Guangzhou 510515, China. 6 Km Sha Tai Hwy, Jin Bao Gang, Tong He. Tel: 86-20-87200702. Fax: 86-20-87044296. EST+15.
www.utahloy.com   E-mail: uis@utahloy.com
Lester Waud, Head. BA, MLitt. Tina Lin, Adm.

Col Prep. Gen Acad. IB MYP. IB Diploma. Curr—Intl. Exams—CEEB IGCSE. Feat—Humanities Chin Fr Korean Comp_Sci Chin_Stud Studio_Art Music. Supp—ESL.

Sports—Basket Soccer Volley.

Enr 670. US 36. Other 634. Accepted: 85%. Yield: 95%. Avg class size: 18.

Fac 66. M 29/1. F 30/6. US 2. Host 6. Other 58. Adv Deg: 100%.

Grad '05—18.

Tui '05-'06: Day $13,000. Aid: 6 pupils.

Summer: Enrich Rec. ESL. Tui Day $4000. 4 wks.

Endow $10,000,000. Plant val $60,000,000. Bldgs 5. Class rms 60. Lib 20,000 vols. Sci labs 2. Comp labs 1. Theaters 1. Art studios 2. Music studios 1. Fields 1.

Est 1998. Nonprofit. Sem (Aug-June).

While English is the language of instruction, all students at UIS receive daily Putonghua instruction. The school's international curriculum draws elements from the English and Australian educational systems for its kindergarten and primary classes. Middle schoolers follow the International Baccalaureate Middle Years Program. Information technology is integral to the middle school program. Boys and girls share in the Chinese culture through cultural activities and language study.

Field trips and athletic competitions with area schools are among the school's special activities.

HANGZHOU INTERNATIONAL SCHOOL
Day — Coed Gr PS-12

Hangzhou City, Bi Jiang 310053, China. 80 Dongxin St, Binjiang District. Tel: 86-571-8669-0045. Fax: 86-571-8669-0044. EST+13.
www.scischina.org/hangzhou   E-mail: info@scischina.org
William Parker, Prin. BA, MEd, PhD. **Richard Bird, Adm.**

> **Col Prep. Curr**—Intl US. **Exams**—AP CEEB TOEFL. **Feat**—Chin Comp_Sci Web_Design E_Asian_Stud Studio_Art Music. **Supp**—ESL.
>
> **Enr 185.** B 90. G 95. Elem 150. Sec 35. US 20. Other 165. Accepted: 80%. Yield: 95%. Avg class size: 13.
>
> **Fac 25.** M 12. F 12/1. US 8. Host 2. Other 15. Adv Deg: 48%.
>
> **Tui '05-'06: Day $8000-10,000** (+$1800-2800). **Aid:** 10 pupils ($8500).
>
> Plant val $3,000,000. Bldgs 8. Class rms 32. Lib 12,000 vols. Sci labs 2. Comp labs 3. Auds 1. Theaters 1. Art studios 1. Music studios 1. Dance studios 1. Fields 1. Courts 2.
>
> **Est 2002.** Nonprofit. Spons: International School Development Foundation. Sem (Aug-June). Assoc: WASC.

HIS provides a US-based international curriculum for children from expatriate families. The curriculum uses primarily American, Australian and New Zealand texts and materials. Specialist classes in Mandarin, computer, music and physical education complement work in the core subjects. Field trips and local cultural activities enrich classroom instruction.

Affiliated schools operate in Shanghai; Jakarta, Indonesia; and Cape Town, South Africa.

NANJING INTERNATIONAL SCHOOL
Day — Coed Gr PS-12

Nanjing 210046, China. Xian Lin College & University Town, Qi Xia District. Tel: 86-25-8589-9111. Fax: 86-25-8589-9222. EST+13.
www.nanjing-school.com   E-mail: enquiries@nanjing-school.com
Gez Hayden, Dir. BA, MEd.

> **Col Prep. IB PYP. IB MYP. IB Diploma. Curr**—Intl. **Exams**—CEEB TOEFL. **Feat**—Humanities Chin Fr Comp_Sci Econ Performing_Arts Visual_Arts. **Supp**—EFL ESL Rem_Math Rem_Read.
>
> **Sports**—Basket Soccer Volley. **Activities**—Rec.
>
> **Enr 340.** B 170. G 170. Elem 276. Sec 64. US 33. Other 307. Accepted: 100%. Yield: 100%. Avg class size: 12.
>
> **Fac 57.** M 23. F 34. US 5. Host 7. Other 45.
>
> **Tui '05-'06: Day Y93,375-133,630** (+Y830).
>
> Lib 24,000 vols. Sci labs 4. Comp labs 3. Auds 1. Theaters 1. Gyms 1. Fields 1. Courts 1.
>
> **Est 1990.** Nonprofit. Sem (Aug-June). Assoc: EARCOS.

NIS offers all three elements of the International Baccalaureate Program: the

Primary Years Program for children ages 3-10, the Middle Years Program for boys and girls ages 11-16, and the Diploma Program for students ages 16-18. As all instruction is in English, the school maintains an ESL department to enable non-English-speaking pupils to be mainstreamed as quickly as possible. Staff specialists assist boys and girls with learning difficulties; gifted students also receive special support.

NIS conducts an optional after-school activities program that comprises a range of cultural, recreational and athletic activities.

CONCORDIA INTERNATIONAL SCHOOL SHANGHAI
Day — Coed Gr PS-12

Shanghai 201206, China. 999 Mingyue Rd, JinQiao. Tel: 86-21-5899-0380. Fax: 86-21-5899-1685. EST+13.
www.ciss.com.cn   E-mail: registrar@ciss.com.cn
David Rittmann, Head. MA, PhD. **Solveig Kettinger, Adm.**
    Col Prep. Curr—US. **Exams**—ACT AP CEEB. **AP**—Eng Calc Bio Chem Physics US_Hist World Hist Econ Studio_Art. **Feat**—Humanities Chin Span Comp_Sci Relig Fine_Arts Drama Band Chorus.
    Sports—Basket F_Hockey Rugby Soccer Volley. **Activities**—Acad Arts Govt/Pol Service.
    Enr 694. B 350. G 344. Elem 569. Sec 125. US 418. Host 2. Other 274. Accepted: 69%. Yield: 70%. Avg class size: 15.
    Fac 66. M 22/1. F 40/3. US 41. Host 4. Other 21. Adv Deg: 53%.
    Grad '05—16. Col—16. US Col—7. (Pomona, Boston U, Hope, Emory, U of MI, Calvin). Avg SAT: M/V—1370, Essay—700.
    Tui '06-'07: Day Y138,850-185,300 (+Y9650).
    Summer: Acad Enrich Rev Rem Rec. Tui Day $500/crse. 3 wks.
    Plant val $12,500,000. Bldgs 3. Class rms 51. Lib 16,000 vols. Sci labs 3. Art studios 3. Music studios 3. Gyms 3. Fields 2.
    Est 1998. Nonprofit. Lutheran. Sem (Aug-June). Assoc: EARCOS WASC.

Offering English-medium instruction at all grade levels, CISS conducts a flexible program that moves gradually from concrete to abstract concepts as pupils progress. The high school curriculum places particular emphasis on college preparation. Various electives complement course work in the traditional disciplines, and Advanced Placement classes are available for qualified students. The school operates a family center that serves the needs of international families living in Shanghai.

SHANGHAI AMERICAN SCHOOL
Day — Coed Gr PS-12

Shanghai 201107, China. 258 Jin Feng Lu, Zhudi Town, Minhang District. Tel: 86-21-6221-1445. Fax: 86-21-6221-1269. EST+13.
www.saschina.org   E-mail: info@saschina.org
Dennis Larkin, Supt. EdD. **Barbara Brogoch, Adm.**
    Col Prep. Gen Acad. IB Diploma. Curr—Intl US. **Exams**—ACT AP CEEB. **Feat**—Chin Fr Span Comp_Sci Studio_Art Drama Music. **Supp**—ESL.
    Sports—Badminton Basket X-country F_Hockey Soccer Swim Track Volley. **Activi-**

ties—Acad Arts Media Service.
Enr 2300. Avg class size: 18.
Fac 265.
Tui '05-'06: Day $11,500-20,000.
Summer: Enrich. 4 wks.
Bldgs 4. Class rms 76. Lib 3000 vols.
Est 1980. Nonprofit. Sem (Aug-June). Assoc: A/OPR/OS EARCOS WASC.

Sponsored by the US Consulate in Shanghai, SAS conducts its American-style program on two suburban campuses: The 25-acre Pudong location (Shanghai Links, San Jia Gang, Pudong New Area, Postal Code 201201) enrolls children in grades pre-K-10, while the 29-acre Puxi campus in Zhudi Town serves pupils in grades pre-K-12.

During the high school years, the curriculum features Advanced Placement courses, in addition to the IB Diploma program in grades 11 and 12. English is the language of instruction in all classes. Students at both campuses have access to the Internet (in all classrooms), English-language libraries and computer labs.

SHANGHAI COMMUNITY INTERNATIONAL SCHOOLS
Day — Coed Gr PS-12

Shanghai 200050, China. 79 Ln 261, Jiangsu Rd, Changning. Tel: 86-21-6252-3688.
Fax: 86-21-6212-2330. EST+13.
www.scischina.com   E-mail: info@scischina.org
Michael D. Williams, Head. BA, MEd. **Laurie Williams, Adm.**
  Col Prep. Gen Acad. Curr—US. **Exams**—AP CEEB. **AP**—Eng Calc Stats
    Comp_Sci Bio Chem Environ_Sci Physics Comp_Govt & Pol Econ Studio_Art
    Music_Theory. **Feat**—British_Lit Chin Fr Span Web_Design E_Asian_Stud
    Drama Music Journ. **Supp**—ESL LD.
  Sports—Basket X-country Soccer Swim Volley. **Activities**—Acad Arts Govt/Pol
    Rec.
  Enr 1121. B 574. G 547. Elem 1017. Sec 104. US 270. Host 3. Other 848. Accepted:
    80%. Yield: 95%. Avg class size: 16.
  Fac 131. M 44/1. F 86. US 69. Host 12. Other 50. Adv Deg: 34%.
  Avg SAT: M/V—965.
  Tui '05-'06: Day $10,500-20,000. Aid: 124 pupils ($550,893).
  Summer: Acad Enrich Rec. Tui Day $600/3-wk ses. 6 wks.
  Plant val $8,100,000. Bldgs 9. Class rms 96. 3 Libs 26,000 vols. Sci labs 4. Comp
    labs 6. Auds 2. Theaters 1. Art studios 3. Music studios 6. Gyms 3. Fields 3.
    Courts 3. Pools 1.
  Est 1996. Nonprofit. Spons: International School Development Foundation. Quar
    (Aug-June). Assoc: EARCOS WASC.

On four separate campuses, SCIS serves expatriate children who are temporarily dwelling in the area and are interested in a US-based international program. Serving students from Pudong, Puxi, Hongqiao and Minhang, the Pudong location comprises grades PS-12. Hongqiao, the smallest of the campuses, serves boys and girls in grades PS-8, while the Changning campus enrolls children in grades PS-6. A second preschool through grade 12 location, Hangzhou International School, operates in Hangzhou (see separate listing).

Specialists teach music and drama, computers, library skills, art, physical education and Mandarin. Instructors come from many nations, with Chinese staff teaching Mandarin and Chinese culture. A well-developed technology program enables students to develop their skills through lab work and regularly scheduled computer classes. Upperclassmen choose from an array of Advanced Placement courses while preparing for both the AP exams and the College Boards.

Field trips are integral to the program at all grade levels. Lower schoolers go on excursions throughout Shanghai. Upper school students embark on a cultural trip to a location within or outside of China; this annual trip often incorporates community service work. After-school and weekend activities round out the SCIS' program.

SHEKOU INTERNATIONAL SCHOOL

Day — Coed Gr PS-11

Shenzhen, Guangdong 518067, China. Tai Zi Rd, Shekou Industrial Zone. Tel: 86-755-6693669. Fax: 86-755-6674099. EST+13.
www.sis.org.cn   E-mail: sis@sis.org.cn
Robert Dunseth, Dir.
  Pre-Prep. Gen Acad. Curr—US.
  Enr 300.
  Fac 40.
  Tui '05-'06: Day $16,500-18,500 (+$3500-4500).
  Est 1988. Tri (Aug-June). Assoc: EARCOS WASC.

INTERNATIONAL SCHOOL OF TIANJIN

Day — Coed Gr K-12

Tianjin 300350, China. Weishan Rd, Shuanggang, Jinnan District. Tel: 86-22-2859-2001. Fax: 86-22-2859-2007. EST+13.
www.istianjin.org   E-mail: info@istianjin.net
Nick Bowley, Dir.
  Col Prep. IB PYP. IB MYP. IB Diploma. Curr—Intl. Feat—Chin Fr Japan Span Korean Comp_Sci Geog Drama Music. Supp—ESL.
  Activities—Govt/Pol.
  Enr 370. Elem 176. Sec 94. US 19. Other 351. Avg class size: 18.
  Fac 50. M 15. F 35. US 20. Other 30.
  Grad '05—7. Col—7. US Col—4. (Bowdoin, Purdue, CA St U-Long Beach, AZ St).
  Tui '05-'06: Day $17,712.
  Est 1994. Nonprofit. Sem (Aug-June). Assoc: CIS EARCOS WASC.

IST offers an international education preparing students for higher education in the US, Europe and Asia. Students follow the three International Baccalaureate programs: Primary Years, for students ages 3-11; Middle Years, for students ages 11-16; and Diploma, for students ages 17-19. High school students may also pursue the standard IST diploma.

FIJI

Sq. Miles: 7056 (Slightly smaller than New Jersey). **Country Pop:** 893,354 (2005). **Capital:** Suva, pop. 167,000. **Terrain:** Mountainous or varied. **Ethnic Group(s):** Indigenous_Fijian Indo-Fijian. **Religion(s):** Methodist Roman_Catholic Hindu Muslim. **Official Language(s):** English. **Other Language(s):** Fijian Hindi. **Government:** Parliamentary Democracy. **Independence:** 1970 (from United Kingdom). **Per Capita Income:** $3436 (2004). **GDP:** $2.9 billion (2004). Agriculture 17%. Industry 22%. Services 61%. **Currency:** Fijian Dollar (F$).

INTERNATIONAL SCHOOL SUVA
Day — Coed Gr PS-12

Suva, Fiji. PO Box 10828, Laucala Beach Estate. Tel: 679-393-300. Fax: 679-340-017. EST+17.
www.international.school.fj   E-mail: info@international.school.fj
Dianne Korare, Prin.
   Col Prep. IB PYP. IB MYP. IB Diploma. Curr—Intl Aus. **Exams**—IGCSE. **Feat**—Fr
   Japan Geog Visual_Arts Bus.
   Enr 572.
   Fac 50.
   Tui '05-'06: Day F$7683-13,918 (+F$1500).
   Est 1973. Quar (Jan-Dec). Assoc: A/OPR/OS WASC.

GUAM

Sq. Miles: 212 (About three times the size of Washington, DC). **Country Pop:** 168,564 (2005). **Capital:** Agana, pop. 40,877. **Terrain:** Volcanic origin, surrounded by coral reefs; relatively flat coralline limestone plateau with steep coastal cliffs and narrow coastal plains in north, low-rising hills in center, mountains in south. **Ethnic Group(s):** Chamorro Filipino Chinese Japanese Korean. **Religion(s):** Roman_Catholic. **Other Language(s):** English Chamorro Japanese. **Governed By:** United States. **GDP:** $3.2 billion (2000). Agriculture 7%. Industry 15%. Natural Resources 78%. **Currency:** US Dollar ($).

ST. JOHN'S SCHOOL
Bdg — Coed Gr 9-12; Day — Coed Gr PS-12

Tumon Bay, GU 96913. 911 N Marine Corps Dr. Tel: 671-646-8080. Fax: 671-649-1055. EST+15. (Dial 1+ from US).
www.stjohnsguam.com   E-mail: info@stjohnsguam.com

Jorge O. Nelson, Head.
   Col Prep. IB Diploma. Curr—Intl US. **Exams**—CEEB. **Feat**—Japan Span Environ_Sci Econ Philos Relig Studio_Art Drama. **Supp**—Tut.
   Enr 505. Elem 361. Sec 144. Accepted: 70%. Avg class size: 13.
   Fac 59. M 19. F 39/1. US 51. Other 8. Adv Deg: 42%.
   Grad '05—21. Col—21. US Col—21. (USC, Seattle U, U of PA, MI St, U of CA-Santa Barbara, Middlebury). Avg SAT: M/V—1220.
   Tui '02-'03: Bdg $26,308-26,776. **Day** $7190-10,766. **Aid:** 95 pupils ($400,000).
   Summer: Acad Enrich Rev Rem Rec. Tui Day $500. 4 wks.
   Bldgs 7. Dorms 1. Dorm rms 10. Libs 1. Sci labs 5. Comp labs 3. Art studios 2. Music studios 2. Dance studios 1. Gyms 1. Fields 1. Courts 1.
   Est 1962. Episcopal. Quar. Assoc: EARCOS.

St. John's offers an American college preparatory curriculum that features Advanced Placement classes in several disciplines. International Baccalaureate course work is also available. A varied curriculum includes selections related to Guam and other early American settlements. Attendance at weekly chapel services is compulsory, although participation is optional.

School activities include student council, interest clubs, and such interscholastic sports as track and field, basketball, soccer, golf, tennis, cross-country and softball.

HONG KONG

Sq. Miles: 422 (Six times the size of Washington, DC). **Country Pop:** 6,898,686 (2005). **Terrain:** Hilly to mountainous, with steep slopes and natural harbor. **Ethnic Group(s):** Chinese. **Official Language(s):** Cantonese English. **Government:** Limited Democracy. **Governed By:** China. **GDP:** $164 billion (2004). Industry 11%. Services 89%. **Currency:** Hong Kong Dollar (HK$).

CANADIAN INTERNATIONAL SCHOOL
OF HONG KONG
Day — Coed Gr PS-12

Aberdeen, Hong Kong. 36 Nam Long Shan Rd. Tel: 852-2525-7088. Fax: 852-2525-7579. EST+13.
www.cdnis.edu.hk   E-mail: schoolinfo@cdnis.edu.hk
David S. McMaster, Head. Emily Pong, Adm.
   Col Prep. Gen Acad. Curr—Can. **Exams**—AP. **AP**—Eng Bio Chem Physics Eur_Hist Econ Music_Theory. **Feat**—Chin Fr Comp_Sci Studio_Art.
   Sports—Badminton Basket X-country Golf Soccer Squash Swim Track Volley. **Activities**—Acad Arts Media Rec.
   Enr 1578. B 852. G 726. Elem 1275. Sec 303. US 146. Host 295. Other 1137. Avg class size: 23.
   Fac 118.
   Grad '05—62. Col—62. US Col—7. (AZ St, Boston U, U of HI-Manoa, IN U, NYU, U of San Francisco).

Tui '05-'06: Day HK$55,100-82,700.
Summer: Rec. 1-4 wks.
Sci labs 5. Lang labs 2. Comp labs 3. Art studios 2. Music studios 4. Dance studios 2. Gyms 2. Courts 3. Pools 1.
Est 1991. Nonprofit. Sem (Aug-June).

Founded to address a perceived shortage of Hong Kong international schools employing a North American curricular model, CDNIS offers a rigorous academic program that includes a strong technology component and an emphasis on the performing arts. Starting in the early years (pre-reception and reception), children take specialist-taught Mandarin, library skills and music classes. Boys and girls develop a foundation in the basic skills in language arts, math, Mandarin, the social sciences, art, science, music and physical education through grade 4, then begin the study of French in grade 5.

The transitional middle school takes students from the self-contained classroom approach of the junior school to the curriculum-based, departmental focus of the high school. A Chinese Studies program in the middle school and high school reinforces Mandarin instruction. The high school division, which leads to the Ontario (Canada) Secondary School Diploma, includes Advanced Placement course work and incorporates enriching field trips that provide opportunities for off-site learning. In grades 9 and 10, pupils choose from two course levels; in grades 11 and 12, the selection expands to four tracks. Saturday classes are available to interested students.

BRADBURY SCHOOL

Day — Coed Gr K-5

Hong Kong, Hong Kong. 43C Stubbs Rd. Tel: 852-2574-8249. Fax: 852-2834-7880. EST+13.
www.bradbury.edu.hk   E-mail: enquiries@bs.esf.edu.hk
Anne Wilkinson, Prin.
   Gen Acad. Curr—UK. **Feat**—Chin Comp_Sci Relig Studio_Art Music. **Supp**—Dev_Read EFL ESL LD Rem_Read.
   Enr 750. B 375. G 375. Elem 750.
   Fac 40. M 8. F 30/2. Host 1. Other 39.
   Grad '05—120.
   Tui '05-'06: Day HK$47,300 (+HK$10,000).
   Bldgs 1. Class rms 25.
   Est 1993. Nonprofit. Tri (Sept-Apr).

Bradbury follows the UK national curriculum and employs English as its sole language of instruction. The early years department exposes children to a range of activities in an effort to encourage independence and promote an interest in learning. The middle years continue to focus on developing independent learning skills. Programming integrates collaborative group work and extracurricular activities. The upper school curriculum builds on previous learning steps and includes investigative work and sustained projects.

Activities in the arts—among them choir, orchestra, instrumental music, dramatic productions, compulsory dance workshops, sketching and painting—form an important component of school life. A well-developed athletic program includes netball, cricket, soccer, rugby, judo and roller hockey.

CARMEL SCHOOL OF HONG KONG
Day — Coed Gr PS-8

Hong Kong, Hong Kong. 10 Borrett Rd, Mid-levels. Tel: 852-2964-1600. Fax: 852-2813-4121. EST+13.
www.carmel.edu.hk   E-mail: admin@carmel.edu.hk
Edwin Epstein, Head.
  Gen Acad. Curr—US. **Supp**—EFL.
  Enr 250.
  Fac 57.
  Tui '05-'06: Day HK$91,500-107,500 (+HK$2000).
  Est 1991. Jewish. Sem (Aug-June). Assoc: EARCOS WASC.

CHINESE INTERNATIONAL SCHOOL
Day — Coed Gr PS-12

Hong Kong, Hong Kong. 1 Hau Yuen Path, Braemar Hill. Tel: 852-2510-7288. Fax: 852-2510-7378. EST+13.
www.cis.edu.hk   E-mail: cis_info@cis.edu.hk
Richard Blumenthal, Head. BA, MA, PhD. **Bonnie Chan, Adm.**
  Col Prep. Gen Acad. IB MYP. IB Diploma. Curr—Intl. **Bilingual**—Chin. **Exams**—CEEB. **Feat**—Fr Comp_Sci Econ Drama Music. **Supp**—ESL.
  Sports—Basket X-country Rugby Soccer Track. **Activities**—Arts Cultural/Relig Govt/Pol Media Rec Service.
  Enr 1369. B 685. G 684. Elem 974. Sec 395. US 305. Host 242. Other 822. Accepted: 31%. Yield: 77%. Avg class size: 22.
  Fac 142. US 14. Host 11. Other 117. Adv Deg: 46%.
  Grad '05—95. Col—95. **US Col**—36. (USC 5, Tufts 3, Stanford 2, U of Chicago 2, Brown 2, U of PA 2). Avg SAT: M/V—1260.
  Tui '05-'06: Day HK$76,000-120,500 (+HK$4310-7700). **Aid:** 20 pupils (HK$2,000,000).
  Summer: Enrich. Tui Day HK$425/wk. 4 wks.
  Bldgs 7. Class rms 112. 2 Libs 50,000 vols. Sci labs 8. Comp labs 6. Auds 1. Art studios 4. Music studios 2. Dance studios 1. Drama studios 2. Gyms 4. Courts 1. Pools 1.
  Est 1983. Nonprofit. Tri (Aug-June). Assoc: EARCOS ECIS.

CIS provides a bilingual and bicultural atmosphere in which English-speaking children study Chinese culture as well as Mandarin. Beginning Mandarin is offered at many grade levels. During the secondary school years, students follow the International Baccalaureate Middle Years and Diploma curricula. Graduates matriculate predominantly at institutions in the United States, Canada and the United Kingdom.

The school's residential location atop Braemar Hill is easily accessible to Hong Kong's cultural and educational resources.

FRENCH INTERNATIONAL SCHOOL
Day — Coed Ages 3-18

Hong Kong, Hong Kong. 165 Blue Pool Rd, Happy Valley, GPO Box 9814. Tel: 852-2577-6217. Fax: 852-2577-9658. EST+13.
www.lfis.edu.hk   E-mail: lfi@lfis.edu.hk
Francois Genu, Head.

> Col Prep. Gen Acad. IB Diploma. Fr Bac. Curr—Intl. Supp Lang—Fr. Exams—IGCSE. Feat—Chin Lat Comp_Sci Studio_Art Drama Music.
> Enr 1200.
> Fac 107.
> Tui '05-'06: Day HK$67,100-108,150 (+HK$3600).
> Est 1984. Nonprofit. Tri (Sept-June).

GERMAN SWISS INTERNATIONAL SCHOOL
Day — Coed Gr K-12

Hong Kong, Hong Kong. 11 Guildford Rd, The Peak. Tel: 852-2849-6216. Fax: 852-2849-6347. EST+13.
www.gsis.edu.hk   E-mail: gsis@gsis.edu.hk
Jens-Peter Green, Prin. Eva Geisslreither-Moog, Adm.

> Col Prep. Gen Acad. Curr—Intl UK. Supp Lang—Ger. Exams—GCSE A-level. Feat—Chin Fr Ger Lat Comp_Sci Studio_Art Drama Music. Supp—LD.
> Enr 1185. B 576. G 609. US 125. Host 40. Other 1020. Avg class size: 23.
> Fac 112. M 40. F 72.
> Grad '05—95. US Col—7. (NYU, Brown, Yale, Stanford, Carnegie Mellon, Northwestern).
> Tui '05-'06: Day HK$81,600-105,000 (+HK$1200).
> Summer: Acad Enrich Rec. Tui Day HK$3500/1½-wk ses. 4 wks.
> Bldgs 3. Class rms 72. Libs 2. Sci labs 8. Lang labs 2. Comp labs 6. Theater/auds 1. Art studios 2. Music studios 3. Dance studios 1. Gyms 2. Courts 2. Pools 1.
> Est 1969. Tri (Aug-June).

Enrolling a student body that represents more than 30 nations, GSIS conducts both English- and German-speaking streams at the kindergarten, primary and secondary levels. German speakers work toward the German Abitur diploma, while English-speaking pupils engage in a British-style system that leads to the GCSE, AS- and A-level examinations.

As GSIS is a German school, the program places significant emphasis on the German language, even in the international stream. Students may take French or Mandarin as a second foreign language. The secondary department, which is characterized by small classes and the incorporation of technology into the curriculum, seeks to develop such abilities as presentation and communicational skills. Local and overseas field trips enrich classroom work. School graduates typically matriculate at competitive colleges in Europe, North America, Australia and Asia.

Balancing academics are many extracurricular activities, including interest clubs, athletics, art, drama, music and community service.

HONG KONG ACADEMY
PRIMARY SCHOOL
Day — Coed Gr PS-8

Hong Kong, Hong Kong. 4F Chung On Hall, 15 Stubbs Rd. Tel: 852-2575-8282. Fax: 852-2891-4460. EST+13.
www.hkacademy.edu.hk   E-mail: admin@hkacademy.edu.hk
Teresa A. Richman, Prin. BS, MS. **Benjamin L. Frankel, Adm.**
> **Gen Acad. IB PYP. Curr**—Intl. **Feat**—Chin Comp_Sci. **Supp**—Dev_Read ESL LD Rem_Math Rem_Read Tut.
> **Activities**—Acad Arts Rec.
> **Enr 250.** B 120. G 130. Elem 250. US 75. Host 14. Other 161. Avg class size: 18.
> **Fac 22.** M 2. F 20. US 8. Host 3. Other 11. Adv Deg: 22%.
> **Tui '05-'06: Day HK$83,250** (+HK$13,500).
> Bldgs 1. Class rms 13. Lib 3500 vols. Auds 1. Art studios 1. Music studios 1. Courts 1.
> **Est 2000.** Nonprofit. Tri (Aug-June). Assoc: EARCOS WASC.

Providing an English-medium program for young children of expatriate families, the academy conducts a transdisciplinary, Western-style curriculum that borrows elements from various national systems. Course work integrates both local and global perspectives, and the school places particular emphasis on Mandarin instruction and the incorporation of information technology into all aspects of the curriculum.

Faculty members come predominantly from Asia, Australia, North America and Europe.

ISLAND SCHOOL
Day — Coed Ages 11-18

Hong Kong, Hong Kong. 20 Borrett Rd. Tel: 825-2524-7135. Fax: 825-2840-1673. EST+13.
www.Island.edu.hk   E-mail: school@mail.island.edu.hk
David J. James, Head. BEd, MEd.
> **Col Prep. Curr**—UK. **Exams**—GCSE A-level. **Feat**—Chin Fr Japan Span Econ Geog Psych Visual_Arts Drama Music Bus.
> **Fac 90.**
> **Est 1967.** Nonprofit. Tri (Sept-June).

AMERICAN INTERNATIONAL SCHOOL
Day — Coed Gr PS-12

Kowloon, Hong Kong. 125 Waterloo Rd. Tel: 852-2336-3812. Fax: 852-2336-5276. EST+13.
www.ais.edu.hk   E-mail: aisadmin@ais.edu.hk
Cameron Fox, Head.
> **Col Prep. Curr**—US. **Exams**—AP CEEB. **AP**—Eng Physics Psych. **Feat**—Chin Fr Comp_Sci Geog Film Drama.
> **Tui '05-'06: Day HK$50,000-93,600.**

Est 1986. Nonprofit. Sem (Aug-June). Assoc: EARCOS WASC.

INTERNATIONAL CHRISTIAN SCHOOL
Day — Coed Gr K-12

Kowloon, Hong Kong. 45-47 Grampian Rd. Tel: 852-2338-9606. Fax: 852-2338-9517. EST+13.
www.ics.edu.hk   E-mail: ics@ics.edu.hk
Ben Norton, Head.
> **Col Prep. Gen Acad. Curr**—US. **Exams**—AP. **AP**—Eng Calc Comp_Sci Bio Chem US_Hist Studio_Art. **Feat**—Humanities Chin Bible Drama Music.
> **Enr 800.**
> **Fac 65.**
> **Tui '05-'06: Day $64,000-87,000.**
> **Est 1992.** Nonprofit. Nondenom Christian. Quar. Assoc: EARCOS WASC.

CHRISTIAN ALLIANCE P.C. LAU MEMORIAL INTERNATIONAL SCHOOL
Day — Coed Gr K-12

Kowloon City, Hong Kong. 2 Fu Ning St. Tel: 852-2713-3733. Fax: 852-2760-4324. EST+13.
www.cais.edu.hk   E-mail: info@cais.edu.hk
Arthur Enns, Head.
> **Col Prep. Curr**—Can. **Exams**—CEEB TOEFL. **AP**—Eng Calc Chem. **Feat**—Comp_Sci Econ Geog Law Psych Visual_Arts Drama Music Dance.
> **Enr 500.**
> **Fac 42.**
> **Tui '05-'06: Day HK$56,000-80,000** (+HK$3285-6260).
> **Est 1992.** Nondenom Christian. (Aug-June).

LI PO CHUN UNITED WORLD COLLEGE OF HONG KONG
Bdg — Coed Gr 11-12

Sha Tin, New Territories, Hong Kong. 10 Lok Wo Sha Ln, Sai Sha Rd. Tel: 852-2640-0441. Fax: 852-2643-4088. EST+13.
www.lpcuwc.edu.hk   E-mail: office@lpcuwc.edu.hk
Stephen Codrington, Prin.
> **Col Prep. IB Diploma. Curr**—Intl. **Feat**—Chin Fr Span Environ_Sci Econ Chin_Stud Visual_Arts Theater_Arts. **Supp**—Tut.
> **Enr 252.** B 116. G 136.
> **Fac 25.** M 14. F 11. US 1. Host 2. Other 22. Adv Deg: 60%.
> **Grad '05—123. Col—120. US Col—53.** (Macalester, U of MI, U of TX-Austin, U of PA, Harvard, Bates).
> **Tui '05-'06: Bdg HK$171,000. Aid:** 212 pupils.
> Bldgs 6. Dorms 4. Dorm rms 64. Libs 1. Sci labs 5. Art studios 1. Music studios 1.

Gyms 1. Fields 1. Courts 4. Pools 1.
Est 1992. Nonprofit. Sem (Aug-May).

Enrolling pupils from approximately 60 countries, LPCUWC conducts the two-year International Baccalaureate Diploma program for able, highly motivated students. All boys and girls take six courses, with three typically being at the higher level and three at the standard level. Students elect course work from each of the following areas: literature, foreign language, math, experimental sciences, and individuals and societies.

Community and environmental service are integral to school life: Pupils may work with the elderly, with special-needs or disadvantaged young people, or on environmental projects. A wide selection of athletic and recreational options includes basketball, badminton, swimming, climbing, kayaking, squash, tennis, football and volleyball. The school's location adjacent to the parks and islands of the New Territories enables interested boys and girls to hike, camp and embark on informal excursions. Art, music, drama and assorted student-run activities complete the extracurricular program.

SHA TIN COLLEGE
Day — Coed Gr 6-12

Sha Tin, New Territories, Hong Kong. 3 Lai Wo Ln, Sui Wo Rd, Fo Tan. Tel: 852-2699-1811. Fax: 852-2695-0592. EST+13.
www.shatincollege.edu.hk   E-mail: info@shatincollege.edu.hk
Col Prep. IB Diploma. **Curr**—Intl UK. **Exams**—GCSE IGCSE A-level.
Enr 1150.
Fac 88.
Est 1982. Nonprofit. Tri (Sept-July).

HONG LOK YUEN INTERNATIONAL SCHOOL
Day — Coed Gr PS-6

Tai Po, New Territories, Hong Kong. 3 20th St, Hong Lok Yuen. Tel: 852-2658-6935. Fax: 852-2651-0836. EST+13.
www.hlyis.edu.hk   E-mail: info@hlyis.edu.hk
Elaine Goddard-Tame, Prin. BA, MEd.
Gen Acad. **Curr**—UK. **Feat**—Chin Computers Chin_Stud Studio_Art Music. **Supp**—ESL LD.
Sports—Gymnastics Soccer. **Activities**—Arts Govt/Pol Rec.
Enr 338. B 172. G 166. Elem 338. US 33. Host 84. Other 221. Avg class size: 25.
Fac 25. M 7. F 18. Adv Deg: 44%.
Grad '05—23.
Tui '05-'06: Day HK$68,650-78,800.
Est 1982. Nonprofit. Trl (Sept-July). Assoc: ECIS.

HLYIS follows the British National Curriculum while also emphasizing the Chinese language and Chinese traditions. More than half of the students have a Chinese background; the rest enroll from the US, the UK, The Netherlands, Australia and

South Africa. Instruction is in English, but all students learn to read, write and speak Chinese and gain class placement according to their initial proficiency.

All subjects integrate information technology through networked computers and interactive white boards. The curriculum includes a number of educational outings and a residential outdoor education excursion.

HONG KONG INTERNATIONAL SCHOOL

Day — Coed Gr PS-12

Tai Tam, Hong Kong. 1 Red Hill Rd. Tel: 852-2812-5000. Fax: 852-2813-4293. EST+13.

www.hkis.edu.hk   E-mail: admiss@hkis.edu.hk

Richard Mueller, Head. Vicky G. Sparrow, Adm.

> **Col Prep. Gen Acad. Curr**—US. **Feat**—Chin Fr Span Comp_Sci Asian_Stud Relig Studio_Art Music. **Supp**—EFL LD.
>
> **Enr 2630.** Elem 1894. Sec 736. US 1394. Host 160. Other 1076. Avg class size: 20.
>
> **Fac 240.**
>
> **Grad '05—179. Col—177. US Col—174.** (USC, Carnegie Mellon, Boston U, Duke, Marymount Col-NY, NYU).
>
> **Tui '05-'06: Day HK$117,900-148,700** (+HK$15,000).
>
> **Summer:** Acad Enrich. Tui Day $580/3-wk ses. 6 wks.
>
> Bldgs 4. Class rms 120. Libs 4. Sci labs 6. Comp labs 4. Auds 1. Theaters 1. Art studios 5. Music studios 3. Dance studios 2. Gyms 4. Fields 1. Courts 4. Pools 1.
>
> **Est 1966.** Nonprofit. Lutheran-Missouri Synod. Quar (Aug-June). Assoc: A/OPR/OS EARCOS WASC.

This American school operates under the auspices of the Missouri Synod of the Lutheran Church. Students of approximately 40 nationalities attend, with the vast majority coming from the US. The college preparatory curriculum is supplemented by courses in Asian studies and languages and includes religion classes. Students pursue independent projects during interim week and may also undertake independent study during terms. Pupils choose from an extensive list of elective offerings.

Various extracurricular activities and sports provide balance to academics.

INDIA

Sq. Miles: 1,300,000 (About one-third the size of the US). **Country Pop:** 1,080,264,388 (2005). **Capital:** New Delhi, pop. 12,800,000 (2001). **Largest City:** Mumbai, pop. 16,400,000 (2001). **Terrain:** Varies from Himalayas to flat river valleys. **Ethnic Group(s):** Indo-Aryan Dravidian Mongoloid. **Religion(s):** Hindu Muslim Christian Sikh Buddhist Jain Parsi. **Official Language(s):** Hindi English. **Government:** Federal Republic. **Independence:** 1947 (from United Kingdom). **Per Capita Income:** $640 (2004). **GDP:** $691 billion (2004). Agriculture 23%. Industry 26%. Services 51%. **Currency:** Indian Rupee (Rs).

THE CANADIAN INTERNATIONAL SCHOOL

Bdg — Coed Gr 7-12; Day — Coed PS-12

Bangalore 560 092, India. 14/1 Kodigehalli Main Rd, Sahakar Nagar. Tel: 91-80-2343-8414. Fax: 91-80-2343-6488. EST+9.5.
www.canschoolindia.org   E-mail: csib@vsnl.com
Brian Tinker, Prin. BSc, MA. Penelope Abraham, Adm.

   Col Prep. IB Diploma. Curr—Intl Can. Exams—CEEB TOEFL. Feat—Fr Ger Span Hindi Comp_Sci Anthro World_Relig Drama Bus. Supp—ESL.
   Sports—Basket Soccer. Activities—Arts Rec.
   Enr 320. B 20/140. G 15/145. Elem 230. Sec 90. US 67. Host 41. Other 212. Accepted: 90%. Yield: 99%. Avg class size: 15.
   Fac 45. M 15. F 30. US 2. Host 5. Other 38. Adv Deg: 51%.
   Grad '05—26. Col—26. US Col—15.
   Tui '05-'06: Bdg Rs533,950. Day Rs228,900-385,450.
   Bldgs 1. Dorms 1. Dorm rms 55. Class rms 30. Lib 11,000 vols. Sci labs 3. Comp labs 2. Auds 1. Art studios 1. Music studios 1. Fields 1. Courts 1.
   Est 1997. Inc. Sem (Aug-June).

CIS prepares students for admission to colleges and universities in the United States, Canada and elsewhere. The elementary and middle school curricula, which follow the guidelines set by the Ontario Ministry of Education, include an instructional music program that begins in kindergarten. High school students, who perform compulsory community service, may pursue either the Canadian diploma or the International Baccalaureate Diploma.

THE INTERNATIONAL SCHOOL BANGALORE

Bdg — Coed Gr 2-12; Day — Coed PS-12

Bangalore 562 125, Karnataka, India. NAFL Valley, Whitefield-Sarjapur Rd, Near Dommasandra Cir. Tel: 91-80-782-2550. Fax: 91-80-782-2553. EST+10.5.
www.tisb.org   E-mail: admission@tisb.ac.in
Hector S. MacDonald, Prin. BSc, MA. Priya Swamy, Adm.

   Col Prep. IB Diploma. Curr—Intl. Exams—CEEB IGCSE. Feat—Fr Ger Span Comp_Sci Anthro Psych Islamic_Hist Philos Studio_Art Drama Music. Supp—Dev_Read EFL ESL LD Rem_Math Rev Tut.
   Enr 389. B 131/97. G 76/85. Elem 201. Sec 188. US 292. Host 97. Accepted: 80%.
   Fac 44. M 12. F 29/3. US 2. Host 39. Other 3. Adv Deg: 52%.
   Grad '05—34.
   Tui '05-'06: Bdg $9000-12,000 (+$500). Day $5300-5700 (+$200).
   Bldgs 6. Dorms 2. Libs 1. Sci labs 3. Comp labs 1. Theaters 1. Art studios 1. Music studios 1. Dance studios 1. Gyms 1. Fields 1. Courts 2. Pools 1.
   Est 2000. Sem (Aug-June).

TISB's international program is designed to provide children with greater flexibility in their future endeavors. Children ages 3-10 follow the IB Primary Years Program, a comprehensive, inquiry-based approach to learning. In the early secondary years (ages 11-15), increasingly structured course work offers preparation for the IGCSE examination in Grade 10. Students work toward the IB Diploma in grades

11 and 12. After fulfilling requirements in music, art and drama in the primary school, pupils then pursue one of these subjects in depth at the secondary level.

Compulsory sports classes introduce students to various games and activities during the school day. For the benefit of boarders, TISB also conducts an after-school program that features such enrichment options as debates, quizzes, art contests, craft shows, cooking contests, fashion shows and social events.

MALLYA ADITI INTERNATIONAL SCHOOL
Day — Coed Gr K-12

Bangalore 560 064, India. PO Box 6427, Yelahanka. Tel: 91-80-846-2508. Fax: 91-80-846-3058. EST+10.5.
E-mail: mais@aditiblr.org
Geetha Narayanan, Dir. BSc, BEd, MA.

   Col Prep. Curr—Nat UK. **Exams**—IGCSE. **Feat**—Fr Ger Comp_Sci Indian_Stud Music Dance. **Supp**—EFL ESL LD Rem_Math Rem_Read Tut.
   Enr 465. B 243. G 222. Elem 260. Sec 205. US 35. Host 388. Other 42. Avg class size: 28.
   Fac 78. M 12/4. F 49/13. Host 74. Other 4.
   Grad '05—73. **US Col**—12. (OH Wesleyan, Bryn Mawr, U of MI, Brandeis, Columbia, U of PA). Avg SAT: M/V—1350.
   Tui '05-'06: Day $10,000-11,250.
   3 Libs 40,000 vols. Sci labs 4. Lang labs 2. Comp labs 2. Theaters 1. Art studios 1. Music studios 2. Dance studios 1. Fields 1. Courts 1.
   Est 1984. Nonprofit. Sem (June-Apr).

MAIS provides both a British preparatory curriculum preparing students for the IGCSE and AICE examinations and a national preparatory course that leads to the Indian certificate. Pupils study both Indian culture and traditions at all grade levels.

Guest speakers and performers, in addition to seminars, supplement these culture and history courses. Field trips throughout the region enrich class work. Students may participate in such physical activities as basketball, cricket, volleyball, swimming and Indian dance.

CALCUTTA INTERNATIONAL SCHOOL
Day — Coed Gr PS-12

Calcutta 700 020, West Bengal, India. 18 Lee Rd. Tel: 91-33-2247-9131. Fax: 91-33-2280-3258. EST+10.5.
www.calcuttainternationalschool.in
E-mail: admissions@calcuttainternationalschool.in
Anuradha Das, Prin. PhD.

   Col Prep. Curr—UK. **Exams**—O-level A-level. **Feat**—Fr Ger Bengali Hindi Korean Comp_Sci Econ Geog Sociol Studio_Art Drama Accounting Bus.
   Sports—Basket Soccer Swim. **Activities**—Acad Arts Rec.
   Enr 471. Elem 321. Sec 150. US 61. Host 308. Other 102. Avg class size: 24.
   Fac 61. M 6/4. F 45/6.
   Tui '06-'07: Day Rs24,200-28,400 (+Rs150,000).

Libs 1. Sci labs 1. Comp labs 1.
Est 1970. Nonprofit. Quar (June-May).

Founded to serve a small number of British expatriates living in Calcutta, CIS now welcomes the children of expatriates, foreign passport holders, nonresident Indians and the local community. The school follows the British National Curriculum up through the GCE examinations. An emphasis on foreign languages begins in the middle school, with instruction in Hindi, Bengali, French, and, for foreign students, German and Korean. Students choose an academic track in the humanities, business studies or science while preparing for the O- and A-level examinations.

AMERICAN INTERNATIONAL SCHOOL
CHENNAI
Day — Coed Gr PS-12

Chennai 600 113, Tamil Nadu, India. 100 Feet Rd, Taramani. Tel: 91-44-2254-9000. Fax: 91-44-2254-9001. EST+11.
www.aisch.org   E-mail: officemanager@aisch.org
Barry Clough, Head. BEd, MA, MEd.

  Col Prep. **Curr**—US. **Exams**—AP CEEB. **AP**—Eng Fr Calc Comp_Sci Bio Chem Environ_Sci Physics US_Hist World_Hist Econ. **Feat**—Indian_Stud Studio_Art Music. **Supp**—ESL LD.
  Sports—Basket Soccer Swim Volley. **Activities**—Acad Arts Govt/Pol Media Rec Service.
  Enr 314. Elem 229. Sec 85. US 71. Host 26. Other 217.
  Fac 52. US 16. Host 29. Other 7.
  Grad '05—4. Col—1. US Col—1. (GA Inst of Tech). Avg SAT: M/V—1250, Essay—610.
  Tui '05-'06: Day $14,250-16,250 (+$4135).
  Plant val $7,500,000. Bldgs 3. Class rms 30. Lib 18,000 vols. Sci labs 3. Lang labs 2. Comp labs 2. Art studios 2. Music studios 2. Gyms 1. Fields 1. Basketball courts 1. Tennis courts 4. Pools 1.
  Est 1995. Nonprofit. Sem (Aug-June). Assoc: A/OPR/OS.

Founded to provide English-speaking students in the area with an education comparable to that found in the US, AISC offers an American-style curriculum with an unusually extensive Advanced Placement component. The hands-on preschool and kindergarten lead into an elementary program in which specialists teach athletics, art, music, foreign language and ESL. Middle schoolers spend an increasing amount of their time with specialist teachers as they ready themselves for the college preparatory high school division.

The high school program combines course requirements with elective options. Qualified boys and girls may earn the Advanced Placement International Diploma upon graduation. Pupils fulfill a 10-year annual community service requirement during the high school years. Among other service options are visits to orphanages and homes for the needy.

INTERNATIONAL SCHOOL OF HYDERABAD

Day — Coed Gr PS-12

Hyderabad 500 034, Andhra Pradesh, India. 6-3-346 Rd 1, Banjara Hills. Tel: 91-40-2335-1110. Fax: 91-40-2339-5065. EST+10.5.

www.ishhyd.com   E-mail: ish@ishhyd.com

Helge Gallinger, Prin.

   Col Prep. Curr—UK. Exams—IGCSE. Feat—Fr Span Comp_Sci Indian_Culture Studio_Art Music. Supp—EFL ESL LD.

   Enr 56. B 20. G 36. Elem 42. Sec 14. US 14. Host 18. Other 24. Accepted: 90%. Avg class size: 8.

   Fac 18. M 1/3. F 12/2. Host 16. Other 2. Adv Deg: 11%.

   Tui '05-'06: Day Rs240,000-390,000 (+Rs65,000).

   Bldgs 2. Lib 6000 vols. Sci labs 1. Comp labs 1. Art studios 1. Music studios 1. Gyms 1. Courts 1.

   Est 1981. Nonprofit. Tri (Aug-June). Assoc: ECIS.

The broad curriculum at ISH approximates that found in the UK. Students prepare for the IGCSE exam, and the school also conducts a US high school diploma program in conjunction with the University of Nebraska at Lincoln. In many courses, pupils further develop their individual research skills through projects and thematic studies. Educational field trips to places of interest in the area provide enrichment in various subjects.

Each term, ISH offers an array of activities and clubs in which students may participate as space permits. In addition, boys and girls have access to on-campus swimming and athletic facilities on Saturday mornings during the school year.

INDIA INTERNATIONAL SCHOOL

Day — Coed Gr 1-12

Jaipur 302020, India. Gurukul Marg, SFS, Mansarovar. Tel: 91-141-2397906. Fax: 91-141-2395494. EST+10.5.

www.icfia.org   E-mail: iis@icfia.org

Ashok Gupta, Dir. MA, PhD.

   Col Prep. Gen Acad. Curr—Intl Nat. Exams—IGCSE O-level A-level. Feat—Fr Ger Hindi Sanskrit Environ_Sci Comp_Sci Econ Psych Studio_Art Music Accounting Bus. Supp—Dev_Read Rem_Math Rem_Read Rev Tut.

   Activities—Acad Arts Service.

   Enr 2306. B 1350. G 956. Host 2300. Other 6. Avg class size: 45.

   Fac 90. M 15. F 75. Adv Deg: 61%.

   Tui '06-'07: Day Rs24,500-26,100.

   Summer: Acad Enrich Rem Rec. 2 wks.

   Endow Rs18,238,000. Bldgs 2. Class rms 60. 2 Libs 18,000 vols. Sci labs 2. Comp labs 3. Auds 2. Art studios 2. Music studios 1. Dance studios 1. Fields 1. Courts 2. Pools 1.

   Est 1990. Nonprofit. (Apr-Mar).

With a particular emphasis on fostering international understanding among its students, IIS conducts a program that combines Indian and international elements. The varied curriculum features a particularly strong computer literacy program and includes a selection of business courses. Student clubs address such interests as science, stamp collecting, debate and computers.

KODAIKANAL INTERNATIONAL SCHOOL
Bdg — Coed Gr 4-12; Day — Coed PS-12

Kodaikanal 624-101, Tamil Nadu, India. Seven Roads Jct, PO Box 25. Tel: 91-4542-241-104. Fax: 91-4542-241-109. EST+10.5.
www.kis.in   E-mail: contact@kis.in
Geoffrey Fisher, Prin. Sarah Ann Lockwood, Adm.
   Col Prep. IB Diploma. Curr—Intl US. Exams—ACT CEEB. Feat—Fr Ger Japan Span Hindi Tamil Bengali Environ_Sci Biotech Comp_Sci Ethics Studio_Art Music. Supp—ESL Rem_Math Rem_Read.
   Enr 490. B 209/63. G 155/63. Elem 176. Sec 314. US 45. Host 292. Other 153. Accepted: 80%. Avg class size: 15.
   Fac 85. M 39. F 46. Adv Deg: 58%.
   Grad '05—50.
   Tui '02-'03: Bdg $15,000 (+$50). Day $8000-10,000 (+$50). Aid: 100 pupils ($84,600).
   Bldgs 22. Dorms 15. Class rms 50. 4 Libs 40,000 vols. Sci labs 6. Comp labs 5. Auds 1. Art studios 3. Music studios 2. Dance studios 1. Gyms 1. Fields 3. Courts 13.
   Est 1901. Nonprofit. Nondenom Christian. (July-May). Assoc: MSA.

KIS' curriculum parallels that of the American school system, although it includes adaptations to the Indian environment and to the needs of non-American students. Preparation is offered for the US College Boards and the International Baccalaureate.

The school is located on an extensive plateau in the hill station of Kodaikanal, about 125 miles above the southern tip of India. Surrounded by rolling hills and bordering a lake, the school enjoys a natural setting for hiking, camping and other outdoor activities. The 7000-foot elevation ensures a temperate climate.

AMERICAN SCHOOL OF BOMBAY
Day — Coed Gr PS-12

Mumbai 400 098, India. SF 2, G Block, Bandra Kurla Complex Rd, Bandra E. Tel: 91-22-2652-1111. Fax: 91-22-2652-1234. EST+10.5.
www.asbindia.org   E-mail: asb@asbindia.org
Paul Fochtman, Supt.
   Col Prep. IB PYP. IB MYP. IB Diploma. Curr—Intl US. Exams—CEEB TOEFL. Feat—Humanities Fr Comp_Sci Psych Fine_Arts Performing_Arts.
   Enr 426. B 229. G 197. Elem 301. Sec 125. US 68.
   Fac 56. M 17. F 39.
   Tui '05-'06: Day $3900-23,000.
   Est 1981. Nonprofit. Sem (Aug-June). Assoc: A/OPR/OS MSA.

WOODSTOCK SCHOOL

Bdg — Coed Gr 2-12; Day — Coed K-12

Mussoorie 248 179, Uttaranchal, India. Tel: 91-135-2635-900. Fax: 91-135-2632-885. EST+10.5.
www.woodstock.ac.in   E-mail: mail@woodstock.ac.in
David Jeffery, Prin. BA, MA. **Cathy Holmes, Adm.**

Col Prep. Curr—Intl. **Exams**—AP CEEB IGCSE. **AP**—Eng Fr Calc Stats Comp_
Sci Bio Chem Environ_Sci Physics US_Hist Comp_Govt & Pol Econ US_Govt &
Pol Studio_Art Music_Theory. **Feat**—Shakespeare Indian_Lit Hindi Relig Journ.
Supp—ESL LD Tut.

Sports—Basket Soccer. **Activities**—Media Service.

Enr 444. B 202/29. G 178/35. US 39. Host 197. Other 208.

Fac 62. M 27. F 33/2. US 25. Host 19. Other 18. Adv Deg: 37%.

Grad '05—74. Col—68. US Col—42. Avg SAT: M/V—1102. Avg ACT: 23.

Tui '05-'06: Bdg Rs510,000-598,000. Day Rs210,000-270,000. Aid: 177 pupils
($625,000).

Summer: Acad Rem. ESL. 3½ wks.

Bldgs 11. Dorms 5. Dorm rms 200. Class rms 40. 2 Libs 30,000 vols. Sci labs 4.
Comp labs 3. Auds 2. Theaters 2. Art studios 2. Music studios 3. Dance studios
1. Fields 1. Courts 3. Pools 1.

Est 1854. Nonprofit. Nondenom Christian. Sem (July-June). Assoc: MSA.

This long-established international Christian school's enrollment reflects a
mix of North Americans, Indians, other Southeast Asians and students of other
nationalities. The curriculum, which is college preparatory, offers US College
Board and IGCSE exam preparation. Electives include such offerings as drama and
art. Woodstock also maintains a strong music program. Emphasis is placed on the
intercultural program, which features course work in Hindi and special instruction
in Indian music and dance. Students have made many field trips to noted cultural
and tourist centers in India.

Set on a hillside on the first range of the Himalayas at an altitude of 6500 feet, the
school offers ample opportunities for outdoor pursuits. The academic year begins
in late July and ends the following June, with a two-and-a-half-month vacation
taken during the Himalayan winter from December to February. Woodstock was
until 1976 under cooperative missionary management. Now it is a registered Indian
Society whose members are chosen from the parent body to represent American and
Indian interests, in addition to those of other nations represented at the school.

THE BRITISH SCHOOL

Day — Coed Gr PS-12

**New Delhi 110021, India. San Martin Marg, Chanakyapuri. Tel: 91-11-4102183.
Fax: 91-11-6112363. EST+10.5.**
www.british-school.org   E-mail: principal@british-school.org
Ian Bayly, Dir.

Col Prep. Curr—UK. **Exams**—GCSE IGCSE A-level. **Feat**—Fr Ger Hindi Envi-
ron_Sci Comp_Sci Econ Studio_Art Drama Music Accounting Bus. **Supp**—EFL
ESL LD Rem_Math Tut.

Enr 508. B 270. G 238.

Fac 78. M 4. F 64. Adv Deg: 58%.
Grad '05—32. US Col—7. (Macalester, NYU, Mt Holyoke, Smith, Brandeis, U of MI). Avg SAT: M/V—1163.
Tui '05-'06: Day Rs321,355-371,335.
Endow Rs39,504,000. Bldgs 2. Class rms 27. Libs 2. Sci labs 4. Comp labs 3. Auds 1. Theaters 2. Art studios 4. Music studios 2. Fields 3. Courts 4.
Est 1963. Nonprofit. Sem (Aug-May). Assoc: ECIS.

Founded by a group of area British parents in cooperation with the British High Commissioner, the school continues to base its curriculum on England's national program. While British and Indian pupils constitute over half of the student body, boys and girls enroll from more than 50 nations. The modified international program, which enables the school's transient population to move easily from one school to another, emphasizes college preparation and stresses the visual and performing arts.

Instruction in grades PS-8 mirrors that found in England, with environmental studies and computer complementing traditional course work. The foreign language department features a choice between French and Hindi in grades 4 and 5; in grades 6-8, German is added as a third language option, and children take two of the three. Boys and girls in grades 9 and 10 prepare for either the GCSE or the IGCSE, typically enrolling in nine subjects during each of these years. In grades 11 and 12, schedules combine three or four A-level courses with a general course of studies that involves the arts, health education, sports and games, and community service.

For an additional tuition fee, remedial teachers provide support for pupils requiring assistance in English, math or both.

HEBRON SCHOOL

Bdg and Day — Coed Gr 1-13

Ootacamund 643 001, Nilgiris, India. Lushington Hall. Tel: 91-423-2442372. Fax: 91-423-2441295. EST+10.5.
www.hebronooty.org E-mail: admin@hebronooty.org
Alastair J. Reid, Prin. MA. **Sushila Marshal, Adm.**
   Col Prep. Curr—UK. **Exams**—GCSE IGCSE AS-level A-level. **Feat**—Fr Ger Hindi Comp_Sci Relig Studio_Art Drama Music. **Supp**—ESL Rem_Math Rem_Read.
   Sports—Badminton Basket X-country F_Hockey Gymnastics Soccer Softball Squash Swim Tennis Volley. **Activities**—Arts Media Rec.
   Enr 356. B 144/44. G 133/35. US 38. Host 167. Other 151. Avg class size: 20.
   Fac 61.
   Grad '05—32. Avg SAT: M/V—1100.
   Tui '05-'06: Bdg Rs195,000-336,000 (+Rs12,000-26,000). **Day Rs99,000-198,000** (+Rs6000-20,000).
   Bldgs 8. Dorms 8. Class rms 20. Libs 2. Sci labs 3. Comp labs 2. Fields 2. Pools 1.
   Est 1899. Nonprofit. Nondenom Christian. Sem (Aug-June).

Located on a 23-acre, wooded estate overlooking the Government Botanical Gardens, Hebron prepares students for the GCSE, IGCSE and A-level examinations. AS-level courses are also available. All pupils complete course work in such subjects as English, math and religious studies.

Hebron offers instrumental music lessons for an additional fee, and drama productions are popular. A mandatory extracurricular program emphasizes camping and other outdoor activities.

THE MAHINDRA UNITED WORLD COLLEGE
OF INDIA

Bdg and Day — Coed Gr 11-12

Pune 412 108, India. Post Office Paud. Tel: 91-2029-43263. Fax: 91-2029-43260. EST+10.5.
www.muwci.net   E-mail: dwilkinson@muwci.net
David Wilkinson, Head.
  Col Prep. IB Diploma. Curr—Intl. **Feat**—Environ_Sci Econ Pol_Sci Psych Peace_ Stud World_Relig Film Studio_Art Music.
  Fac 22.
  Est 1997.

MUWCI is one of 10 related UWC international schools dedicated to promoting international understanding through education. The organization has campuses in Britain, Canada, Hong Kong, India, Italy, Norway, Singapore, Swaziland, the US and Venezuela, and each school is a community representing more than 70 countries. All students follow the International Baccalaureate curriculum in preparation for the IB exams.

Community service, outdoor programs and events pertaining to global issues supplement the academic offerings.

MERCEDES-BENZ INTERNATIONAL SCHOOL

Bdg — Coed Gr 5-11; Day — Coed PS-11

Pune 411057, India. P-26 Rajiv Gandhi Infotech Park, Hinjiwadi. Tel: 91-20-2293-4420. Fax: 91-20-2293-2762. EST+10.5.
www.mbis.org   E-mail: mbisch@pn2.vsnl.net.in
Michael Thompson, Dir. BEd, MA.
  Col Prep. Gen Acad. IB PYP. IB MYP. Curr—Intl. **Feat**—Fr Ger Environ_Sci Comp_Sci Performing_Arts Visual_Arts Drama. **Supp**—Dev_Read ESL LD Rem_Math Rem_Read.
  Sports—Soccer. **Activities**—Arts Govt/Pol Service.
  Enr 164. B 22/72. G 4/66. Elem 126. Sec 38. US 18. Host 81. Other 65. Avg class size: 14.
  Fac 25. M 4/2. F 16/3. US 1. Host 16. Other 8. Adv Deg: 48%.
  Tui '06-'07: Bdg Rs730,000. Day Rs530,000 (+Rs2500).
  Bldgs 1. Dorms 2. Dorm rms 14. Class rms 11. 2 Libs 20,000 vols. Sci labs 2. Lang labs 3. Comp labs 1. Theaters 1. Art studios 1. Music studios 1. Dance studios 1. Fields 2. Courts 1. Pools 2.
  Est 1998. Nonprofit. Quar (Aug-June). Assoc: ECIS.

MBIS was founded to serve the children of the multinational expatriate community in Pune and surrounding areas. Instruction is in English, and elements of Indian culture are integrated into the curriculum and activities. German language instruction begins in grade 2 as part of the International Baccalaureate Primary Years Program. French, environmental studies and community service are introduced in the IB Middle Years Program.

The school maintains an academic relationship with Mahindra United World College, where eligible students may pursue the IB Diploma.

INDONESIA

Sq. Miles: 736,000 (Slightly less than three times the size of Texas). **Country Pop:** 241,973,879 (2005). **Capital:** Jakarta, pop. 8,800,000. **Terrain:** Large islands consist of coastal plains with mountainous interiors. **Ethnic Group(s):** Javanese Sundanese Madurese Coastal_Malay. **Religion(s):** Muslim Protestant Catholic Hindu Buddhist. **Official Language(s):** Bahasa_Indonesia. **Other Language(s):** Javanese. **Government:** Independent Republic. **Independence:** 1945. **Per Capita Income:** $1143 (2004). **GDP:** $255.9 billion (2004). Agriculture 14%. Manufacturing 45%. Services 40%. **Currency:** Indonesian Rupiah (Rp).

BALI INTERNATIONAL SCHOOL
Day — Coed Gr PS-12

Bali, Indonesia. PO Box 3259, Denpasar. Tel: 62-361-288770. Fax: 62-361-285103. EST+13.
www.baliinternationalschool.com   E-mail: info@baliis.net
Jeanie Forde, Dir.
  Gen Acad. Curr—Intl. Exams—CEEB.
  Fac 24.
  Tui '05-'06: Day $4825-9330.
  Est 1986. Nonprofit. Quar (Aug-June). Assoc: EARCOS WASC.

BANDUNG ALLIANCE INTERNATIONAL SCHOOL
Bdg — Boys Gr 6-12; Day — Coed PS-12

Bandung 40142, West Java, Indonesia. Jalan Gunung Agung 14. Tel: 62-22-203-18-44. Fax: 62-22-203-42-02. EST+12.
www.baisedu.org   E-mail: info@baisedu.org
Joseph Beeson II, Dir. BA, MS. John Driscoll, Adm.
  Col Prep. Curr—US. Exams—AP CEEB TOEFL. AP—Eng Fr Calc Bio Physics Eur_Hist US_Hist. Feat—Bahasa_Indonesia Environ_Sci Comp_Sci Econ Psych Bible Studio_Art Bus. Supp—ESL Tut.
  Sports—Basket Soccer Swim Volley. Activities—Acad Arts Media.
  Enr 202. Elem 155. Sec 47. US 58. Host 52. Other 92. Accepted: 90%. Avg class size: 14.
  Fac 27. M 11. F 16. US 22. Host 3. Other 2. Adv Deg: 11%.

Grad '05—12. Col—11. US Col—6. (OH St, Boston U, HI Pacific, U of CA-Davis, SUNY-Buffalo). Avg SAT: M/V—1164.

Tui '05-'06: Bdg $12,840-12,940. Day $7256-7940. Aid: 8 pupils ($7063).

Bldgs 3. Dorms 1. Dorm rms 3. Class rms 13. Lib 14,400 vols. Sci labs 1. Comp labs 1. Auds 1. Art studios 1. Music studios 1. Dance studios 1. Fields 1. Courts 1.

Est 1956. Nonprofit. Nondenom Christian. Sem (Aug-June). Assoc: EARCOS WASC.

The school offers a well-rounded program for elementary and middle school children in an international setting. The general academic disciplines of reading and language arts, social studies, math and science are supplemented by regular instruction from specialist teachers in Bahasa Indonesia language, music, art, computer, Bible and physical education. The school is affiliated with the Network of International Community Schools.

In addition to the core curriculum, course work in the middle school includes various electives, among them journalism, drama and sign language. Beginning in grade 4, students may engage in various after-school activities.

BANDUNG INTERNATIONAL SCHOOL
Day — Coed Gr PS-12

Bandung 40011, West Java, Indonesia. Jl Drg Suria Sumantri 61, PO Box 1167. Tel: 62-22-201-4995. Fax: 62-22-201-2688. EST+12.

www.bisdragons.com   E-mail: bisadmin@bisdragons.com

Oscar Nilsson, Head. Mary Gilleece, Adm.

Col Prep. IB Diploma. Curr—Intl. **Exams**—ACT AP CEEB. **AP**—Eng Bio Chem Physics Eur_Hist Studio_Art. **Feat**—Bahasa_Indonesia. **Supp**—ESL Tut.

Enr 169. B 82. G 87. Elem 136. Sec 33. US 11. Host 34. Other 124. Accepted: 14%.

Fac 26. M 7/4. F 9/6. US 5. Host 2. Other 19. Adv Deg: 19%.

Grad '05—8. Col—8.

Tui '05-'06: Day $3500-10,200 (+$1250).

Bldgs 8. Class rms 31. Lib 12,000 vols. Sci labs 2. Comp labs 2. Gyms 1. Fields 1. Pools 1.

Est 1972. Nonprofit. Sem (Aug-June). Assoc: CIS EARCOS NEASC.

BIS provides a comprehensive, English-medium liberal arts program for children of expatriates who are temporarily residing in Indonesia. The curriculum, which draws upon Western educational methods, encourages creative thinking and emphasizes the development of pupil's problem-solving skills. Instructors employ US teaching materials and prepares boys and girls for a return to the US for further schooling or for college admission.

THE INTERNATIONAL SCHOOL OF BOGOR
Day — Coed Gr PS-9

Bogor 16151, West Java, Indonesia. Jalan Papandayan 7, PO Box 258. Tel: 62-251-324360. Fax: 62-251-328512. EST+13.

www.isbogor.org   E-mail: isb@isbogor.org

Chris Rawlins, Prin.
    Gen Acad. IB PYP. Curr—Intl.
    Enr 75.
    Est 1974. Nonprofit. Quar (Aug-June). Assoc: EARCOS.

CILEGON INTERNATIONAL SCHOOL
Day — Coed Gr PS-7

Cilegon 42414, Banten, Indonesia. Jalan Raya Merak 49. Tel: 62-254-396552. Fax: 62-254-394335. EST+12.
E-mail: cisind@indosat.net.id
Peter King, Prin. BEd.
    Gen Acad. Curr—Intl UK. **Feat**—Bahasa_Indonesia Studio_Art Music. **Supp**— ESL.
    Enr 41. B 22. G 19. Accepted: 100%. Avg class size: 6.
    Fac 6. M 2. F 4. Host 1. Other 5.
    Tui '02-'03: Day $4800-8850.
    Bldgs 1. Libs 1. Sci labs 1. Comp labs 1. Gyms 1. Fields 1. Courts 1. Pools 1.
    Est 1994. Nonprofit. Tri (Sept-July).

Conducting an English-language program for expatriate children from Australia, North America, and various Asian and European countries, this school places emphasis on the development of literacy and math skills. Class sizes remain small and instructors utilize computers in the classroom.

The preschool program (ages 3 and 4) promotes the child's social development within a structured environment. Integrating Australian and British curricular elements, the primary program (grades K-7) reflects the multicultural nature of the school and accommodates children requiring assistance with the English language. Beginning at the primary level, students take Bahasa Indonesia classes, and faculty integrate Indonesian culture into the school program whenever possible.

BRITISH INTERNATIONAL SCHOOL
Bdg — Coed Gr 6-12; Day — Coed PS-12

Jakarta 12041, Indonesia. PO Box 4120. Tel: 62-21-745-1670. Fax: 62-21-745-1671. EST+12.
www.bis.or.id   E-mail: enquiries@bis.or.id
Peter Derby-Crook, Prin. BEd. **Laura Smith, Adm.**
    Col Prep. IB Diploma. Curr—Intl UK. **Feat**—Fr Ger Environ_Sci Econ Studio_Art Drama Music Bus.
    Sports—Badminton Basket F_Hockey Golf Rugby Soccer Swim Tennis. **Activities**—Acad Arts Media Rec Service.
    Enr 1094. B 3/572. G 2/517. Elem 868. Sec 226. US 26. Host 269. Other 799. Avg class size: 22.
    Fac 95. M 40. F 50/5. Host 5. Other 90. Adv Deg: 7%.
    Tui '05-'06: Bdg $24,610 (+$650-1090). **Day $6100-13,900** (+$650-1090).
    Summer: Ages 6-13. Acad Enrich. 2 wks.
    Class rms 51. Libs 2. Sci labs 12. Lang labs 1. Comp labs 8. Auds 1. Theaters 1. Art studios 1. Music studios 2. Gyms 1. Fields 4. Courts 3. Pools 2.

Est 1973. Nonprofit. Tri (Aug-July).

Offering a program that follows the British national curriculum, BIS comprises three divisions: infant (ages 3-7), junior (ages 7-11) and senior (ages 11-18). The curriculum extends through the GCSE and concludes with the two-year International Baccalaureate program. A predominantly British faculty instructs a large number of British expatriate children, as well as students from Australia, Malaysia, New Zealand, the US and other nations.

BIS provides pupils with ample opportunities to develop interest and talents in the visual and performing arts. A full extracurricular program complements academics.

JAKARTA INTERNATIONAL SCHOOL
Day — Coed Gr PS-12

Jakarta 12010, Indonesia. PO Box 1078 JKS. Tel: 62-21-769-2555. Fax: 62-21-750-7650. EST+12.

www.jisedu.org   E-mail: admissions@jisedu.or.id

Niall C. W. Nelson, Head. BEd, MEd, EdD. Steven R. Money, Adm.

   Col Prep. IB Diploma. Curr—Intl US. Exams—ACT AP CEEB. AP—Eng Fr Span Calc Stats Bio Chem Environ_Sci Physics US_Hist Econ Psych Music_Theory. Feat—Dutch Ger Japan Bahasa_Indonesia Korean Asian_Stud Studio_Art Drama Theater Music. Supp—ESL.

   Sports—Badminton Rugby Soccer Softball Swim Tennis Track Volley. Activities—Acad Arts Govt/Pol Rec Service.

   Enr 2543. B 1297. G 1246. Elem 1614. Sec 929. US 532. Host 437. Other 1574. Accepted: 99%. Avg class size: 18.

   Fac 270. M 105/4. F 140/21. US 130. Host 12. Other 128. Adv Deg: 41%.

   Grad '05—195. US Col—91. (Boston Col 3, Kalamazoo 3, U of IL-Urbana 3, Dartmouth 2, U of CA-Berkeley 2, U of MI 2). Avg SAT: M/V—1125. Avg ACT: 25.

   Tui '05-'06: Day $9550-15,500 (+$10,000). Aid: 17 pupils ($61,085).

   Summer: Enrich Rem. Tui Day $420-560. 3-4 wks.

   Bldgs 46. Class rms 206. 4 Libs 120,000 vols. Sci labs 19. Comp labs 7. Photog labs 1. Theaters 4. Gyms 4. Fields 5. Courts 3. Pools 2.

   Est 1951. Nonprofit. Sem (Aug-June). Assoc: A/OPR/OS CIS EARCOS WASC.

JIS' student body enrolls from more than 60 nations; although the curriculum is American based, it reflects the school's international composition. Students may prepare for the US College Boards, and the two-year International Baccalaureate Diploma program is available in grades 11 and 12. Advanced Placement courses are offered in most disciplines in preparation for the International Advanced Placement Diploma. Annual Project Week trips for high school students combine environmental and cultural elements with social service.

A second elementary division occupies quarters in the Pattimura neighborhood, near central Jakarta.

NORTH JAKARTA INTERNATIONAL SCHOOL
Day — Coed Gr PS-10

Jakarta 14250, Indonesia. PO Box 6759-JKUKP, Kelapa Gading Permai. Tel: 62-21-450-0683. Fax: 62-21-450-0682. EST+12.
www.njis.org   E-mail: info@njis.or.id
Allan R. Forslund, Head. MSEd. Anna Rangkuti, Adm.
> Gen Acad. Curr—Intl US. Feat—Chin Fr Bahasa_Indonesia Comp_Sci Studio_Art. Supp—ESL.
> Sports—Basket Golf Soccer Track Volley. Activities—Acad Arts Media Service.
> Enr 282. B 150. G 132. Elem 266. Sec 16. US 17. Host 155. Other 110. Accepted: 90%. Yield: 95%. Avg class size: 16.
> Fac 32. M 16. F 16. US 19. Host 2. Other 11. Adv Deg: 40%.
> Grad '05—29.
> Tui '05-'06: Day $6525-10,895 (+$2500-3500).
> Summer: Acad Enrich Rec. Tui Day $300-600. 4 wks.
> Plant val $4,000,000. Bldgs 8. Class rms 40. Lib 14,000 vols. Sci labs 2. Lang labs 2. Comp labs 2. Theaters 1. Art studios 1. Music studios 1. Dance studios 1. Gyms 1. Fields 1. Pools 1. Weight rms 1.
> Est 1990. Nonprofit. Spons: International School Development Foundation. Tri (Aug-June). Assoc: EARCOS ECIS.

NJIS operates an international program based on the US model but enhanced by strategies and materials from throughout the English-speaking world. Designed to meet the needs of expatriate families living in Indonesia, the school enrolls boys and girls from many different countries. Two-thirds of the pupils speak English proficiently, while the remaining students spend part of the day enrolled in the school's ESL program. Instruction by specialist teachers in Bahasa Indonesia, French, Mandarin, art, music, computers and physical education supplements course work in the core subjects of English, math, social studies and science.

Located in the Kelapa Gading area, NJIS is accessible to Kuningan, Menteng, Kebayoran Baru, and south and central Jakarta.

SEKOLAH PELITA HARAPAN
LIPPO KARAWACI
Day — Coed Gr PS-12

Lippo Karawaci 15811, Tangerang, Indonesia. Bulevar Palem Raya 2500. Tel: 62-21-546-0243. Fax: 62-21-546-0242. EST+12.
www.sph.edu   E-mail: info@sph.ac.id
Brian Cox, Head.
> Col Prep. IB PYP. IB MYP. IB Diploma. Curr—Intl. Supp Lang—Bahasa_Indonesia.
> Enr 1010. B 530. G 480.
> Fac 115. M 43/1. F 71.
> Tui '05-'06: Day $5000.
> Est 1992. Nonprofit. Assoc: CIS NEASC.

WESLEY INTERNATIONAL SCHOOL

Day — Coed Gr K-12

Malang 65101, East Java, Indonesia. Jalan Simpang Kwoka 1, Kotak Pos 275.
Tel: 62-341-586-410. Fax: 62-341-586-413. EST+12.
www.wesleyinterschool.org   E-mail: wesley@wesleyinterschool.org
Paul Richardson, Prin. MEd.

   Col Prep. Curr—US. Exams—SSAT. Feat—Chin Span Bahasa_Indonesia Comp_
   Sci Bible Studio_Art Music. Supp—ESL.
   Enr 82. Elem 58. Sec 24. US 19. Host 8. Other 55.
   Fac 16. M 5/3. F 5/3. US 10. Host 4. Other 2. Adv Deg: 31%.
   Grad '05—7. Col—7. US Col—3.
   Tui '05-'06: Day $3750-5600 (+$4200-5200).
   Bldgs 2. Class rms 12. Lib 13,000 vols. Sci labs 1. Comp labs 1. Gyms 1. Fields 1.
   Est 1971. Nonprofit. Evangelical. Sem (Aug-May). Assoc: WASC.

WIS, founded by an evangelical Christian organization for the education of missionary children, enrolls students from the expatriate business community. Among students' home countries are Australia, New Zealand, India, Korea, Germany, Norway, Switzerland, The Netherlands, the US and the UK.

A variety of activities, including plays, an international bazaar, Christmas and spring programs, student-teacher parties and a sports day, complements the academic program.

MOUNTAINVIEW INTERNATIONAL CHRISTIAN SCHOOL

Bdg — Coed Gr 7-12; Day — Coed K-12

Salatiga 50711, Jateng, Indonesia. Jalan Nakula Sadewa 55, PO Box 142. Tel: 62-
298-311673. Fax: 62-298-321609. EST+12.
www.mountainviewics.org   E-mail: office@mountainviewics.org
William J. Webb III, Supt. BS. Heather Webb, Adm.

   Col Prep. Curr—US. Exams—ACT CEEB. Feat—Span Bahasa_Indonesia Comp_
   Sci Bible Studio_Art Music. Supp—ESL LD Tut.
   Sports—Basket Soccer Volley. Activities—Arts Govt/Pol Media Service.
   Enr 141. Elem 85. Sec 56.
   Fac 35. M 16. F 19. US 30. Host 3. Other 2.
   Grad '05—20.
   Tui '05-'06: Bdg $9000-10,000. Day $5000-6000.
   Bldgs 6. Dorms 2. Dorm rms 30. Class rms 20. Lib 7500 vols. Sci labs 1. Comp labs
   1. Auds 1. Fields 3. Courts 1.
   Est 1981. Nonprofit. Nondenom Christian. Sem (Aug-May).

MICS conducts a US-based program from a Christian perspective. Indonesian language instruction runs throughout the program. Students, who enroll from approximately a dozen countries, must be proficient in English to enroll in the regular MICS program; an intensive ESL program aids those lacking fluency in the language. Graduates typically matriculate at universities in the US, Australia, New Zealand, the United Kingdom, Canada and Korea.

SEMARANG INTERNATIONAL SCHOOL

Day — Coed Gr PS-8

Semarang 50254, Central Java, Indonesia. Jalan Jangli 37, Candi Lama. Tel: 62-24-8311-424. Fax: 62-24-8311-994. EST+12.
www.semarangis.or.id   E-mail: info@smg.bit.net.id
Barry Burns, Prin.

  Pre-Prep. Curr—UK. **Feat**—Bahasa_Indonesia Comp_Sci Studio_Art Music Dance. **Supp**—ESL Rem_Math Rem_Read.

  Enr 69. B 35. G 34. Elem 69. Host 23. Other 46. Accepted: 100%. Avg class size: 15.

  Fac 5. M 1. F 4. Host 1. Other 4.

  Grad '05—3. Prep—2.

  Tui '02-'03: Day $740-5940.

  Bldgs 1. Class rms 5. Lib 2000 vols. Comp labs 1. Art studios 1. Fields 1.

  Est 1982. Nonprofit. Sem (Aug-June).

Located in a house in a residential area of Semarang, this school welcomes expatriate children of all nationalities. SIS conducts a basic UK-style curriculum that includes classes in Indonesian language, culture and geography. Regular use of computers begins at age 2. The school schedules field trips to local sites of interest and students attend cultural exhibitions. Most teachers come from English-speaking countries.

HILLCREST INTERNATIONAL SCHOOL

Bdg — Coed Gr 6-12; Day — Coed K-12

Sentani 99352, Papua, Indonesia. Box 249. Tel: 62-967-591460. Fax: 62-967-591673. EST+13.
www.hismk.org   E-mail: hisdirector@hismk.org
Margaret Hartzler, Dir.

  Col Prep. Curr—US. **Exams**—ACT AP CEEB. **AP**—Eng Calc Comp Sci Physics Eur_Hist. **Feat**—Fr Bahasa_Indonesia Anthro Psych Bible Studio_Art Music Outdoor_Ed. **Supp**—Dev_Read ESL LD Rem_Math Rem_Read.

  Sports—Basket Soccer Volley. **Activities**—Service.

  Enr 175. B 6/84. G 13/72. Elem 114. Sec 61. US 111. Host 6. Other 58. Accepted: 100%. Yield: 100%. Avg class size: 11.

  Fac 28. M 12. F 11/5. Adv Deg: 10%.

  Tui '05-'06: Bdg $10,400 (+$200). **Day $6000-8000** (+$200).

  Bldgs 16. Dorms 2. Dorm rms 14. Class rms 24. 2 Libs 4000 vols. Sci labs 2. Comp labs 2. Auds 1. Art studios 2. Music studios 1. Gyms 2. Fields 2. Courts 2. Pools 1.

  Est 1987. Nonprofit. Nondenom Christian. Sem (Aug-May). Assoc: EARCOS WASC.

This college preparatory school, which follows a US curriculum, offers preparation for the American college-entrance examinations. Advanced Placement courses are part of the high school program. Students complete one compulsory year of Indonesian language, culture and geography. Applied anthropology and biology classes utilize the school's unique surroundings in the remote region of Papua.

SEKOLAH CIPUTRA
SURABAYA

Day — Coed Gr PS-12

Surabaya 60213, East Java, Indonesia. Karasan Puri Widya Kencana, Kota Mandiri CitraRaya. Tel: 62-31-741-5018. Fax: 62-31-741-5016. EST+12.
www.ciputra-sby.sch.id   E-mail: sekolah@ciputra-sby.sch.id
Barbara Cock, Exec Dir. BA, DipEd. **Susan Mellina Wijaya, Adm.**

    Col Prep. IB PYP. IB MYP. IB Diploma. Curr—Intl. **Feat**—Chin Bahasa_Indonesia Comp_Sci Civics Econ Geog Sociol Relig Accounting.

    Sports—Basket Soccer Swim Volley. **Activities**—Arts.

    Enr 1080. B 556. G 524. Host 1055. Other 25. Accepted: 90%. Yield: 70%. Avg class size: 22.

    Fac 171. M 56/2. F 112/1. US 1. Host 154. Other 16. Adv Deg: 6%.

    Grad '05—55. US Col—4. (U of Portland 4).

    Tui '05-'06: Day Rp4,000,000.

    Plant val Rp100,000,000,000. Class rms 72. 2 Libs 25,000 vols. Sci labs 6. Comp labs 4. Art studios 1. Music studios 1. Dance studios 1. Gyms 1. Fields 1.

    Est 1996. Nonprofit. Sem (July-June).

English is the language of instruction at this international school for expatriate and Indonesian children. The elementary school follows the IB Primary Years Program and incorporates elements from the Indonesian curriculum. As the native language of most pupils, Bahasa Indonesia language study is integrated into the curriculum; in addition, boys and girls take compulsory Mandarin classes in grades 1-6. Religion is another course requirement, with specialist teachers leading instruction for Christian, Catholic, Buddhist and Muslim students.

Junior high schoolers fulfill the requirements of the IB Middle Years Program and prepare for the Indonesian national examinations at the end of grade 9. Starting in grade 11, boys and girls either pursue the IB Diploma or prepare for national examinations in English, Indonesian and mathematics.

SURABAYA INTERNATIONAL SCHOOL

Day — Coed Gr PS-12

Surabaya 60225, East Java, Indonesia. CitraRaya International Village, Lakarsantri, Tromol Pos 2/SBDK. Tel: 62-31-741-4300. Fax: 62-31-741-4334. EST+12.
www.sisedu.net   E-mail: sisadmin@sisedu.net
Larry Jones, Supt.

    Col Prep. Curr—US. **Feat**—Humanities Chin Fr Bahasa_Indonesia Comp_Sci Studio_Art Drama Music.

    Enr 235. B 115. G 120.

    Fac 28.

    Tui '05-'06: Day $4963-10,666 (+$6600).

    Est 1971. Nonprofit. Sem (Aug-June). Assoc: A/OPR/OS EARCOS WASC.

YOGYAKARTA INTERNATIONAL SCHOOL
Day — Coed Gr PS-7

Yogyakarta 55284, Indonesia. Pogung Baru Blok A-18, Jl Kaliurang Km 5. Tel: 62-274-586067. Fax: 62-274-586067. EST+12.
www.yisedu.org   E-mail: info@yisedu.org
Lee Stafford, Prin.
  Gen Acad. Curr—Intl. Feat—Bahasa_Indonesia Comp_Sci Studio_Art Drama Music.
  Enr 30. Elem 30. US 3. Host 4. Other 23.
  Fac 15.
  Grad '05—1.
  Tui '05-'06: Day $6000-6600. Aid: 11 pupils ($17,500).
  Bldgs 2. Class rms 3. Lib 3000 vols. Fields 2.
  Est 1989. Nonprofit. Sem (Aug-June). Assoc: EARCOS.

Established to provide an English-language education for expatriate children, YIS conducts a standard elementary program. Curricular offerings include English literature, in addition to Indonesian language and culture courses.

JAPAN

Sq. Miles: 145,902 (Slightly smaller than California). **Country Pop:** 127,417,244 (2005). **Capital:** Tokyo, pop. 8,340,000 (2003). **Terrain:** Rugged, mountainous islands. **Ethnic Group(s):** Japanese Korean. **Religion(s):** Shinto Buddhist Christian. **Official Language(s):** Japanese. **Government:** Constitutional Monarchy with Parliamentary Government. **GDP:** $4.7 trillion (2004). Agriculture 1%. Industry 25%. Services 74%. **Currency:** Japanese Yen (¥).

FUKUOKA INTERNATIONAL SCHOOL
Bdg — Coed Gr 7-12; Day — Coed PS-12

Fukuoka 814-0006, Japan. 18-50 Momochi 3-chome, Sawara-ku. Tel: 81-92-841-7601. Fax: 81-92-841-7602. EST+14.
www.fis.ed.jp   E-mail: administration@fis.ed.jp
Michael Saffarewich, Head.
  Col Prep. Curr—Intl US. Exams—ACT AP CEEB TOEFL. AP—Eng Calc Stats Comp_Sci Chem World_Hist Econ. Feat—Fr Japan Span Korean Japan_Stud. Supp—ESL.
  Sports—Basket Volley. Activities—Govt/Pol.
  Enr 221. B 2/103. G 4/112. Elem 176. Sec 45. US 58. Host 78. Other 85. Avg class size: 13.
  Fac 38. M 11/4. F 14/9. US 17. Host 7. Other 14.
  Grad '05—12. US Col—2. (Brigham Young, CA St U-Sacramento). Avg SAT: M/V—1131. Avg ACT: 23.
  Tui '05-'06: Bdg ¥2,023,540-2,103,540. Day ¥1,160,000-1,360,000. Aid: 35 pupils (¥24,200,000).

Summer: Rev Rem Rec. 4 wks.
Est 1972. Nonprofit. (Aug-June). Assoc: A/OPR/OS EARCOS WASC.

Located on Hakata Bay in the northern part of the island of Kyushu, Fukuoka offers an international program that leads to an American-style diploma. Students of all nationalities may apply; an extensive English as a Second Language program assists pupils who require help with the language, as all instruction is in English. A well-developed Advanced Placement program features courses in most disciplines.

One year of community service is required for graduation; a variety of on- and off-campus options are available. A selection of sports and other extracurricular offerings balances the academic program.

HIROSHIMA INTERNATIONAL SCHOOL
Day — Coed Gr PS-12

Hiroshima 739-1743, Japan. 3-49-1 Kurakake, Asakita-ku. Tel: 81-82-843-4111. Fax: 81-82-843-6399. EST+14.
www.hiroshima-is.ac.jp   E-mail: hisadmin@hiroshima-is.ac.jp
Philip Armstrong, Prin.
   Col Prep. Gen Acad. IB PYP. IB MYP. IB Diploma. Curr—Intl. **Feat**—Japan Studio_Art Music. **Supp**—ESL.
   Enr 127. B 64. G 63. Elem 107. Sec 20. US 36. Host 42. Other 49. Accepted: 95%. Yield: 100%. Avg class size: 15.
   Fac 20. M 8/2. F 7/3. US 6. Host 8. Other 6. Adv Deg: 30%.
   Tui '05-'06: Day ¥700,000-800,000 (+¥250,000-620,000).
   Summer: Enrich Rec. Tui Day ¥35,000/wk. 4 wks.
   Plant val ¥892,859,000. Bldgs 1. Class rms 10. Lib 15,000 vols. Sci labs 1. Lang labs 1. Comp labs 1. Gyms 1. Fields 1. Tennis courts 2.
   Est 1962. Nonprofit. Tri (Aug-June). Assoc: A/OPR/OS CIS EARCOS NEASC.

Courses in Japanese language and culture, as well as a variety of electives in the social sciences, art and music, enrich the internationally oriented curriculum at the school. Originally an elementary school, HIS gradually expanded its program through high school, culminating with the addition of grade 12 in August 2006. The school utilizes all three components of the International Baccalaureate Program.

HIS maintains two campuses: The main building is located on the outskirts of the city in Koyo, while the smaller second campus—used primary for early childhood classes—is in Ushita.

CANADIAN ACADEMY
Bdg — Coed Gr 8-12; Day — Coed PS-12

Kobe 658-0032, Japan. 4-1 Koyo-cho Naka, Higashinada-ku. Tel: 81-78-857-0100. Fax: 81-78-857-3250. EST+14.
www.canacad.ac.jp   E-mail: hdmaster@canacad.ac.jp
Fred Wesson, Head. Charles A. Kite, Adm.
   Col Prep. IB Diploma. Curr—Intl US. **Exams**—CEEB. **Feat**—Ger Econ Psych Studio_Art Music. **Supp**—Dev_Read ESL Rem_Math.
   Enr 703. Elem 500. Sec 203. US 195. Host 187. Other 321. Accepted: 95%. Avg

class size: 14.
Fac 85. M 30. F 55. US 48. Host 9. Other 28.
Grad '05—56. Col—56. US Col—50. (Haverford, Stanford, Tufts, Purdue, UCLA, U of VA). Avg SAT: M/V—1260.
Tui '05-'06: Bdg ¥2,939,000-2,956,000. Day ¥1,195,000-1,616,000. Aid: 50 pupils ($350,000).
Bldgs 2. Dorm rms 12. Class rms 80. Lib 37,000 vols. Sci labs 5. Comp labs 3. Theaters 1. Art studios 2. Music studios 3. Gyms 2. Fields 2. Courts 2.
Est 1913. Nonprofit. Sem (Aug-June). Assoc: A/OPR/OS EARCOS WASC.

Situated in the southeast corner of Rokko Island, the school requires proficiency in English for admission. The elementary school follows an American curriculum that emphasizes learning about Japan. Self-contained classrooms provide a base for free-flowing groupings and individualized instruction. In addition to core courses, CA offers specialist-taught classes in music, art, physical education, computer and Japanese. The college preparatory secondary school curriculum includes electives in the social sciences, languages and the arts. The academy also serves as a testing center for the Educational Testing Service and the American College Testing Program.

Student activities include drama, choral, concert band and Model UN, as well as such sports as volleyball, soccer, basketball, track and field, and baseball.

MARIST BROTHERS INTERNATIONAL SCHOOL
Day — Coed Gr PS-12

Kobe 654-0072, Japan. 1-2-1 Chimori-cho, Suma-ku. Tel: 81-78-732-6266. Fax: 81-78-732-6268. EST+13.
www.marist.ac.jp   E-mail: headmaster@marist.ac.jp
Ian A. M. Robinson, Head.
  Col Prep. Curr—US. **Exams**—ACT CEEB SSAT. **Feat**—Creative_Writing Fr Japan Econ Intl_Relations Psych Sociol Asian_Stud Relig Accounting Bus. **Supp**—ESL.
  Enr 250. B 130. G 120. Elem 170. Sec 80. US 25. Host 95. Other 130. Avg class size: 17.
  Fac 34. M 14/1. F 12/7. US 13. Host 6. Other 15. Adv Deg: 26%.
  Grad '05—14.
  Tui '02-'03: Day $9700-10,300.
  Summer: Enrich Rem Rec. 5 wks.
  Bldgs 2. Class rms 23. Sci labs 2. Comp labs 1.
  Est 1951. Nonprofit. Roman Catholic. Sem (Sept-June). Assoc: EARCOS WASC.

The school enrolls students from approximately two dozen nations, among them India, Korea, Japan, China, the US, Indonesia and a number of European countries. Aside from the regular academic curriculum, field trips to historical buildings, the zoo, the aquarium, a botanical garden, the planetarium, mountain and beach ecosystems, and government offices and agencies play an important role in the students' education. Many electives and independent study projects are available to students at the high school level. Boys and girls may prepare for the US College Boards, the Advanced Placement exams and the TOEFL.

Extracurricular activities include intramural sports, yearbook, newspaper and student council. Baseball, basketball, soccer, volleyball, badminton and softball are the interscholastic sports. An annual international food fair and bazaar are among Marist's special events.

ST. MICHAEL'S INTERNATIONAL SCHOOL
Day — Coed Gr PS-6

Kobe 650-0004, Japan. 17-2 Nakayamate-Dori, 3-Chome, Chuo-ku. Tel: 81-78-231-8885. Fax: 81-78-231-8899. EST+14.
www.smis.org   E-mail: head@smis.org
Hugh Mawby, Head.
>   **Gen Acad. Curr**—UK. **Feat**—Lib_Skills Fr Japan Comp_Sci Relig Studio_Art Music. **Supp**—EFL ESL LD Rem_Math Rem_Read Tut.
>   **Activities**—Arts Rec.
>   **Enr 158.** B 76. G 82. Elem 158. US 20. Host 28. Other 110. Avg class size: 20.
>   **Fac 31.** M 5/2. F 16/8. US 3. Host 12. Other 16.
>   **Tui '05-'06: Day ¥950,000** (+¥250,000). **Aid:** 20 pupils (¥8,500,000).
>   **Summer:** Acad Enrich Rev Rem Rec. 4 wks.
>   Bldgs 2. Class rms 14. Libs 1. Lang labs 5. Comp labs 1. Art studios 1. Music studios 1. Gyms 1. Courts 1. Pools 1.
>   **Est 1946.** Nonprofit. Anglican. Tri (Sept-June). Assoc: EARCOS WASC.

Sponsored by the Anglican Church of Japan, St. Michael's provides an English-medium education for children of the international community. The school's curriculum and methods are based on those employed in British schools, with an emphasis placed on individual and small-group instruction. Students who lack English fluency are divided into groups for English as a Second Language instruction.

KYOTO INTERNATIONAL SCHOOL
Day — Coed Gr PS-8

Kyoto 602-8247, Japan. 317 Kitatawara-cho, Nakadachiuri-sagaru, Yoshiyamachi-dori, Kamigyo-ku. Tel: 81-75-451-1022. Fax: 81-75-451-1023. EST+14.
www.kyoto-is.org   E-mail: kis@kyoto-is.org
Annette Levy, Co-Prin. Colin Duff, Co-Prin.
>   **Pre-Prep. Curr**—Intl. **Feat**—Japan Comp_Sci Studio_Art Music. **Supp**—Dev_Read Rev Tut.
>   **Activities**—Rec.
>   **Enr 90.** Elem 90. US 20. Host 33. Other 37. Accepted: 91%. Avg class size: 6.
>   **Fac 12.** M 3/1. F 3/5. US 2. Host 4. Other 6. Adv Deg: 8%.
>   **Grad '05**—2.
>   **Tui '05-'06: Day ¥1,160,000** (+¥360,000).
>   **Summer:** Enrich. Tui Day ¥40,000. 2 wks.
>   Endow ¥21,827,000. Plant val ¥1,000,000. Bldgs 1. Class rms 6. Lib 5000 vols. Sci labs 1. Comp labs 1. Gyms 1. Fields 1.
>   **Est 1957.** Nonprofit. Tri (Sept-June). Assoc: EARCOS WASC.

Enrolling children of many nationalities, KIS is supported by a Western community of visiting professors, businessmen and long-term foreign residents. The international curriculum features both individualized instruction and courses in Japanese language and culture.

Kyoto is a cultural center of Japan, noted for its temples, shrines, palaces and universities. After-school activities include interest clubs, sports and cultural exchanges with neighboring Japanese schools, and field trips to museums and other sites of interest.

NAGOYA INTERNATIONAL SCHOOL

Day — Coed Gr PS-12

Nagoya 463-0002, Japan. 2686 Minamihara, Nakashidami, Moriyama-ku. Tel: 81-52-736-2025. Fax: 81-52-736-3883. EST+14.
www.nisjapan.net   E-mail: info@nis.ac.jp
Charles Barton, Head. AB, MEd. **John Gaylord, Prin.** BA, MEd. **Erik Olson-Kikuchi, Adm.**

Col Prep. Curr—US. **Exams**—ACT AP CEEB TOEFL. **AP**—Eng Calc Comp_Sci Human_Geog. **Feat**—Creative_Writing Japan Span Web_Design Econ Ceramics Drawing Painting Photog Studio_Art Drama Music Journ. **Supp**—ESL Tut.

Sports—Badminton Basket Baseball Soccer Softball Volley. **Activities**—Acad Arts Govt/Pol Service.

Enr 305. B 138. G 167. Elem 227. Sec 78. US 74. Host 127. Other 104. Accepted: 95%. Yield: 100%. Avg class size: 15.

Fac 36. M 14/1. F 17/4. US 13. Host 8. Other 15. Adv Deg: 58%.

Grad '05—16. Col—16. **US Col**—15. (Yale, Worcester Polytech, Carleton, Clark U, Hiram, U of HI-Manoa). Avg SAT: M/V—1098, Essay—500. Avg ACT: 19.

Tui '05-'06: Day ¥1,279,000-1,441,000 (+¥20,000). **Aid:** 42 pupils (¥16,664,813). Endow ¥55,475,000. Plant val ¥1,164,373,000. Bldgs 3. Class rms 23. Lib 20,600 vols. Sci labs 2. Comp labs 1. Art studios 1. Music studios 2. Dark rms 1. Gyms 1. Fields 1. Courts 1.

Est 1964. Nonprofit. Quar (Aug-June). Assoc: A/OPR/OS EARCOS WASC.

Students from Japan constitute nearly one-third of the enrollment at this school, with smaller numbers coming from the US, Korea, Britain and other countries. The American-style curriculum, which includes Advanced Placement course work in grades 11 and 12, features College Board preparation and courses in Japanese language and culture.

One of Japan's principal ports, Nagoya is located at the head of Ise Bay in the central part of Honshu, about 200 miles west of Tokyo.

KANSAI CHRISTIAN SCHOOL

Day — Coed Gr 1-12

Nara Ken 630-0243, Japan. 951 Tawaraguchi Cho, Ikoma Shi. Tel: 81-743-74-1781. Fax: 81-743-74-1781. EST+14.
www3.kcn.ne.jp/~kcsjapan   E-mail: kcsjapan@yahoo.com
Dawn Winter, Prin. BA, MEd.

Col Prep. Curr—US. **Feat**—Japan Bible Studio_Art Drama Music. **Activities**—Arts Rec.

Enr 44. B 20. G 24. Elem 31. Sec 13. US 15. Host 18. Other 11. Accepted: 90%.

Avg class size: 8.

Fac 9. M 1/1. F 5/2. US 4. Host 3. Other 2. Adv Deg: 11%.

Grad '05—3. Col—2. US Col—1. (Northwestern Col-MN).

Tui '05-'06: Day ¥840,000-1,025,000 (+¥30,000-90,000). **Aid:** 26 pupils (¥10,122,000).

Summer: Acad Enrich Rev. Tui Day ¥60,000. 4 wks.

Bldgs 2. Class rms 6. Lib 7000 vols. Sci labs 1. Comp labs 1. Fields 1. Courts 1.

Est 1970. Nonprofit. Nondenom Christian. Sem (Sept-June).

An English-language Christian school, KCS does admit a limited number of children from non-Christian families; however, more than half of the students enrolled typically come from evangelical missionary families. Instructors present all subjects from a biblical perspective.

Field trips throughout the Kansai region enrich classroom instruction. Pupils from missionary families receive a tuition discount.

OSAKA INTERNATIONAL SCHOOL

Day — Coed Gr PS-12

Osaka 562-0032, Japan. 4-16 Onohara Nishi 4-chome, Mino. Tel: 81-72-727-5050. Fax: 81-72-727-5055. EST+14.

www.senri.ed.jp   E-mail: admissions@senri.ed.jp

Col Prep. IB PYP. IB MYP. IB Diploma. Curr—Intl. **Exams**—CEEB. **Feat**—Chin Ger Japan Korean Comp_Sci Econ Studio_Art Music. **Supp**—ESL.

Enr 240. B 115. G 125. Elem 175. Sec 65. US 58. Host 76. Other 106. Accepted: 80%. Avg class size: 15.

Fac 45. M 19/3. F 19/4. US 15. Host 11. Other 19. Adv Deg: 51%.

Grad '05—15. Col—15. US Col—8. (W WA).

Tui '05-'06: Day ¥1,110,000-1,630,000 (+¥200,000). **Aid:** 24 pupils (¥6,306,250).

Bldgs 1. Class rms 16. Lib 50,000 vols. Sci labs 4. Lang labs 1. Comp labs 2. Planetariums 1. Theaters 1. Art studios 4. Music studios 2. Gyms 2. Fields 2. Courts 1. Pools 2. Weight rms 1.

Est 1991. Nonprofit. Tri (Sept-June). Assoc: EARCOS WASC.

Offering an English-language program beginning at age 4 and running through high school, OIS prepares its students primarily for universities outside of Japan. The school is affiliated with Senri International School, a Japanese-medium institution that serves pupils who have returned to Japan after time spent abroad. The relationship between these two schools allows for jointly conducted music, art and physical education courses, as well as sports and other after-school activities.

The elementary school (grades PS-5) commences with an early childhood program for four- and five-year-olds that incorporates movement and play. Multi-age groupings designed to address specific developmental needs combine children in grades 1 and 2, as well as those in grades 3 and 4. Single-grade instruction begins in grade 5. Focusing on the transition from elementary school to high school, the middle school (grades 6-8) features a varied academic program, small classes, individual and group guidance, an advisor program and activities. When dictated by individual need and ability level, boys and girls may cross grade levels in certain subjects, among them music and Japanese. The high school program blends elements of different educational systems. Of particular note is the International Baccalaureate Diploma Program, which OIS conducts in grades 11 and 12.

OSAKA YMCA INTERNATIONAL SCHOOL

Day — Coed Gr PS-7

Osaka 552-0007, Japan. 1-2-2-800 Benten, Minato-ku. Tel: 81-6-4395-1002. Fax: 81-6-4395-1004. EST+14.
www.oyis.org   E-mail: general-inquiry@oyis.org
John Murphy, Prin. BEd.

   Gen Acad. Curr—Intl. Feat—Japan Comp_Sci Studio_Art Music. Supp—ESL.
   Enr 84. B 44. G 40. Elem 84. US 3. Host 46. Other 35. Accepted: 90%. Yield: 90%. Avg class size: 10.
   Fac 12. M 5/1. F 6. US 5. Other 7. Adv Deg: 25%.
   Grad '05—10.
   Tui '05-'06: Day ¥1,000,000-1,250,000 (+¥20,000-80,000).
   Summer: Acad Enrich Rev. Tui Day ¥30,000/wk. 2 wks.
   Class rms 9. Libs 1. Music studios 1. Gyms 1. Pools 1.
   Est 2001. Nonprofit. Tri (Sept-June). Assoc: WASC.

Operated in the tradition of the YMCA, OYIS conducts an English-medium program for children as young as age 3. During homeroom sessions, children in grades 1-7 study English, language arts, social studies, math, and science and technology while following a structured model that makes interconnected themes and ideas apparent. Due to its importance, writing is an aspect of course work in each subject. Specialists teach music, physical education and Japanese as a Second Language (a course that also examines aspects of Japanese culture). With guidance from their instructors, pupils learn to research various topics independently. Speech and debate training assists older children with their presentational skills.

OYIS reserves time at the conclusion of the academic day for daily extracurricular activities.

HOKKAIDO INTERNATIONAL SCHOOL

Bdg — Coed Gr 7-12; Day — Coed PS-12

Sapporo, Hokkaido 062-0935, Japan. 1-55 5-jo 19-chome, Hiragishi, Toyohira-ku. Tel: 81-11-816-5000. Fax: 81-11-816-2500. EST+14.
www.his.ac.jp   E-mail: his@his.ac.jp
Wayne Rutherford, Head. BA, MA.

   Col Prep. Curr—US. Exams—AP CEEB TOEFL. AP—Eng Calc Physics World_ Hist Studio_Art. Feat—Japan Span Asian_Stud Jazz_Band Drama Music Speech. Supp—ESL Tut.
   Sports—Basket Soccer Volley. Activities—Govt/Pol Media Rec.
   Enr 182. B 11/80. G 10/81. Elem 127. Sec 55. US 25. Host 60. Other 97. Accepted: 80%. Yield: 90%. Avg class size: 14.
   Fac 23. M 10/1. F 9/3. US 13. Host 3. Other 7. Adv Deg: 52%.
   Grad '05—14. Col—10. US Col—4. (Clark U 2, Middlebury 1, Notre Dame 1, Hamilton 1). Avg SAT: M/V—1043.
   Tui '05-'06: Bdg ¥1,700,000 (+¥150,000). Day ¥934,000-1,052,000 (+¥50,000).

Aid: ¥6,600,000.
Summer: Day. Acad Rec. Tui Day ¥60,000. 5 wks.
Endow $10,000,000. Plant val $6,000,000. Bldgs 2. Dorms 1. Dorm rms 10. Class rms 13. Lib 9000 vols. Sci labs 1. Comp labs 1. Art studios 1. Music studios 1. Gyms 1. Fields 1. Courts 1. Tracks 1.
Est 1958. Nonprofit. Tri (Aug-June). Assoc: A/OPR/OS EARCOS WASC.

HIS opened as Hokkaido American School after the closing of a local US military school to educate the remaining American missionary pupils who had been left without a school to attend. The school assumed its current name in 1961 as a reflection of its growth, and the present-day school serves the entire international community of Sapporo.

Students follow a primarily American curriculum, with Advanced Placement courses part of the high school program. The core curriculum comprises language arts, math, science and social studies. Japanese becomes part of the course of studies in grade 3 and is available as an elective (along with Spanish) from grade 7 on. The college preparatory program readies graduates for entrance into universities throughout the world: Many matriculate at American colleges, and Canadian and Australian institutions are also popular destinations.

In addition to HIS' athletic and extracurricular offerings, students take part in a well-established outdoor program that features skiing and camping trips and wilderness hikes.

TOHOKU INTERNATIONAL SCHOOL
Day — Coed Gr PS-12

Sendai 981-3214, Japan. 7-101-1 Yakarta, Izumi-ku. Tel: 81-22-348-2468. Fax: 81-22-348-2467. EST+14.
www.tisweb.net   E-mail: admin@tisweb.net
Matthew Farwell, Head.
    Col Prep. Curr—US. **Exams**—CEEB. **Feat**—Japan Comp_Sci Studio_Art Music.
      Supp—ESL Makeup Rem_Math Rem_Read Tut.
    Enr 105. B 55. G 50. Elem 85. Sec 20. Accepted: 90%. Avg class size: 10.
    Fac 19. M 6. F 6/7. US 5. Host 5. Other 9. Adv Deg: 21%.
    Grad '05—6. Col—6. US Col—2. (U of HI-Manoa, U of MN-Twin Cities).
    Tui '05-'06: Day ¥610,000-1,080,000. Aid: 19 pupils ($50,000).
    Summer: Enrich Rem. 6 wks.
Bldgs 2. Class rms 12. Lib 5000 vols. Sci labs 1. Comp labs 1. Gyms 1. Fields 1.
Est 1989. Inc. Sem (Aug-June). Assoc: EARCOS WASC.

With origins dating back to the 1950s, the school was reestablished in its present form in 1989. Maintaining a low student-teacher ratio at all grade levels, TIS provides an American-based curriculum in an English-language setting. The experiential preschool program precedes elementary and middle school instruction in the traditional subject areas and in Japanese language, art, music and cultural enrichment. High schoolers follow a typical college preparatory program that enables pupils to take Japanese courses through the School Festina's International Program. Students at the high school level may also enroll in correspondence courses offered by the University of Nebraska.

TIS operates a language institute for middle and high school pupils who lack English proficiency, thereby allowing students to develop their language skills enough to participate fully in academics and school life. Field trips, which consist of exchange days with nearby Japanese schools and hiking, skiing and museum excursions, augment classroom instruction and promote greater awareness of Japanese culture.

AMERICAN SCHOOL IN JAPAN
Day — Coed Gr PS-12

Tokyo 182-0031, Japan. 1-1-1 Nomizu, Chofu-shi. Tel: 81-422-34-5300. Fax: 81-422-34-5303. EST+14.
www.asij.ac.jp   E-mail: info@asij.ac.jp
Tim Carr, Head.
   Col Prep. Curr—US. Exams—CEEB. Feat—Fr Japan Span Comp_Sci Studio_Art Theater_Arts Music Communications. **Supp**—EFL.
   Enr 1400.
   Fac 140.
   Tul '05-'06: Day ¥1,922,000 (+¥820,000).
   Est 1902. Nonprofit. Sem (Sept-June). Assoc: A/OPR/OS EARCOS WASC.

AOBA-JAPAN INTERNATIONAL SCHOOL
Day — Coed Gr PS-9

Tokyo 168-0081, Japan. 2-10-7 Miyamae, Suginami-ku. Tel: 81-3-3335-6620. Fax: 81-3-3332-6928. EST+14.
www.a-jis.com   E-mail: leey@a-jis.com
Allen Huies, Dir.
   Pre-Prep. Curr—Intl. Supp—ESL.
   Enr 580.
   Fac 120.
   Tui '05-'06: Day ¥1,530,000-2,557,000 (+¥570,000).
   Est 1976. Tri (Sept-June). Assoc: CIS EARCOS NEASC.

THE BRITISH SCHOOL IN TOKYO
Day — Coed Gr PS-7

Tokyo 150-0002, Japan. 21-18 Shibuya 1-chome, Shibuya-ku. Tel: 81-243-6534. Fax: 81-2536-8384. EST+14.
www.bst.ac.jp   E-mail: admissions@bst.ac.jp
Michael Farley, Head.
   Pre-Prep. Curr—UK. Exams—CEE. Feat—Fr Japan Computers Relig Studio Art Music. **Supp**—ESL.
   Enr 500.
   Tui '05-'06: Day ¥1,400,000-1,990,000 (+¥670,000).
   Est 1989. Nonprofit. Tri (Aug-June).

CHRISTIAN ACADEMY IN JAPAN

Bdg — Coed Gr 6-12; Day — Coed K-12

Tokyo 203-0013, Japan. 1-2-14 Shinkawa Cho, Higashi Kurume-shi. Tel: 81-424-71-0022. Fax: 81-424-76-2200. EST+14.
www.caj.or.jp   E-mail: infodesk@caj.or.jp
John Nelson, Head. BS, MA.
  Col Prep. Gen Acad. Curr—US. Exams—CEEB TOEFL. Feat—Fr Japan Span Global_Issues Bible Indus_Arts Home_Ec. Supp—Dev_Read ESL LD.
  Enr 426. B 8/189. G 7/222. Elem 243. Sec 183. US 212. Host 108. Other 106. Accepted: 72%.
  Fac 56. M 15/1. F 18/22. US 34. Host 10. Other 12. Adv Deg: 19%.
  Grad '05—37. Col—29. US Col—22. (Calvin, Biola, Wheaton-MA). Avg SAT: M/V—1096.
  Tui '05-'06: Bdg ¥2,304,500-2,414,500 (+¥45,000-130,000). Day ¥945,000-1,415,000 (+¥45,000-360,000). Aid: 30 pupils ($25,000).
  Plant val $11,000,000. Bldgs 7. Dorms 1. Dorm rms 8. Class rms 30. Lib 21,698 vols. Sci labs 2. Comp labs 1. Auds 1. Art studios 1. Music studios 5. Gyms 1. Fields 1. Basketball courts 1. Tennis courts 3. Volleyball courts 2. Badminton courts 6.
  Est 1950. Inc. Quar (Aug-June). Assoc: EARCOS WASC.

Most of the children at this school are of missionary families from the United States, South Korea or Northern Europe. The academic program prepares students for the College Boards, and many graduates enter American colleges. A full range of fine arts activities and extracurricular sports rounds out the program.

INTERNATIONAL SCHOOL OF THE SACRED HEART

Day — Boys PS-K, Girls Gr PS-12

Tokyo 150-0012, Japan. 4-3-1 Hiroo, Shibuya-ku. Tel: 81-3-3400-3951. Fax: 81-3-3400-3496. EST+14.
www.issh.ac.jp   E-mail: info@issh.ac.jp
Sr. Masako Egawa, Head.
  Col Prep. Curr—Intl. Exams—CEEB.
  Enr 518.
  Fac 83. M 16/3. F 48/16.
  Tui '05-'06: Day ¥1,800,000-1,980,000 (+¥70,000-720,000).
  Summer: Acad Rec. 3 wks.
  Bldgs 3. 2 Libs 27,000 vols. Gyms 1. Fields 2. Tennis courts 2.
  Est 1908. Nonprofit. Roman Catholic. Tri (Aug-June). Assoc: CIS EARCOS WASC.

The Catholic Sisters of the Society of the Sacred Heart offer a college preparatory program in a Christian setting at ISSH. Students may receive preparation for the American College Boards. Boys and girls choose from a wide variety of extracurricular activities.

K INTERNATIONAL SCHOOL
TOKYO

Day — Coed Gr PS-12

Tokyo 136-0074, Japan. 3-31-5 Higashisuna, Koto-Ku. Tel: 81-3-5632-8714. Fax: 81-3-5632-8715. EST+14.
www.kist.ed.jp   E-mail: Info@kist.ed.jp
Sasha Marshall, Prin.

  Col Prep. IB PYP. IB MYP. IB Diploma. Curr—Intl. Feat—Humanities Japan Comp_Sci Studio_Art Music. Supp—ESL.
  Tui '05-'06: Day ¥960,000-1,350,000 (+¥518,000-618,000).
  Bldgs 2.
  Est 1997. Tri (Aug-June).

NISHIMACHI INTERNATIONAL SCHOOL

Day — Coed Gr K-9

Tokyo 106-0046, Japan. 2-14-7 Moto Azabu, Minato-ku. Tel: 81-3-3451-5520. Fax: 81-3-3456-0197. EST+14.
www.nishimachi.ac.jp   E-mail: info@nishimachi.org
Terence M. Christian, Head. MA.

  Gen Acad. Curr—Intl Nat. Bilingual—Japan. Feat—Comp_Sci Studio_Art Music.
  Enr 400.
  Tui '06-'07: Day ¥1,912,000 (+¥100,000-900,000).
  Est 1949. Nonprofit. Sem (Aug-June). Assoc: A/OPR/OS CIS EARCOS WASC.

ST. MARY'S INTERNATIONAL SCHOOL

Day — Boys Gr K-12

Tokyo 158-8668, Japan. 6-19 Seta 1-chome, Setagaya-ku. Tel: 81-3-3709-3411. Fax: 81-3-3707-1950. EST+14.
www.smis.ac.jp   E-mail: uhaku@smis.ac.jp
Br. Michel Jutras, Head. BA, MS.

  Col Prep. IB Diploma. Curr—Intl US. Exams—CEEB. Feat—Chin Ger Lat Span Asian_Stud Relig Studio_Art Music. Supp—ESL.
  Enr 912. B 912. Elem 661. Sec 251. US 254. Host 177. Other 481. Avg class size: 25.
  Fac 99. M 48/3. F 31/17. US 37. Host 21. Other 41. Adv Deg: 33%.
  Grad '05—52. Col—52. US Col—38. (Temple, Wash U, U of PA, U of IL-Urbana, Lewis & Clark).
  Tui '05-'06: Day ¥1,940,000 (+¥350,000-750,000).
  Summer: Acad Enrich Rec. Tui Day ¥40,000. 3 wks.
  Bldgs 2. Lib 30,000 vols. Gyms 1. Fields 1. Courts 2. Pools 1.
  Est 1954. Nonprofit. Roman Catholic. Sem (Aug-June). Assoc: CIS EARCOS WASC.

Although operated by the Brothers of Christian Instruction, St. Mary's accepts boys of all creeds. The school follows an American-style curriculum, but pupils have the option to work towards the International Baccalaureate Diploma in grades

11 and 12. Featured classes include computer science, religion, Japanese, Asian studies and calculus.

A full sports program allows boys to take part in such activities as judo, swimming, ice hockey and soccer. Situated in a residential section of Tokyo, the school draws its enrollment from Great Britain, Japan, Korea, China, the US and more than 60 other nations.

SEISEN INTERNATIONAL SCHOOL
Day — Boys PS-K, Girls Gr PS-12

Tokyo 158, Japan. 12-15 Yoga 1-chome, Setagaya-ku. Tel: 81-3-3704-2661. Fax: 81-3-3701-1033. EST+14.
www.seisen.com   E-mail: sisinfo@seisen.com
Virginia Villegas, Head.

    Col Prep. IB Diploma. Curr—Intl US. **Exams**—CEEB TOEFL. **Feat**—Fr Japan Span Relig Studio_Art Drama Music Dance Bus. **Supp**—ESL.

    Enr 700. Elem 580. Sec 120.

    Fac 63. M 14. F 49. Adv Deg: 30%.

    Tui '05-'06: Day ¥1,035,000-1,940,000.

    Est 1949. Roman Catholic. Sem (Aug-June). Assoc: CIS EARCOS NEASC.

TOKYO INTERNATIONAL SCHOOL
Day — Coed Gr PS-8

Tokyo 108-0073, Japan. 3-4-22 Mita, Minato-ku. Tel: 81-3-5484-1160. Fax: 81-3-5484-1139. EST+14.
www.tokyois.com   E-mail: tis@tokyois.com
Darren Laverick, Prin. BEd, MEd. **Cathy Marti & Miyuki Jessee, Adms.**

    Pre-Prep. IB PYP. IB MYP. Curr—Intl. **Feat**—Japan Computers Studio_Art Music. **Supp**—Dev_Read ESL.

    Sports—Basket X-country Swim. **Activities**—Acad Arts Rec.

    Enr 320. Elem 320. Accepted: 80%. Yield: 90%. Avg class size: 16.

    Fac 38. M 15/1. F 21/1. US 5. Host 4. Other 29. Adv Deg: 15%.

    Grad '05—5. Prep—5.

    Tui '05-'06: Day ¥1,800,000 (+¥150,000-575,000).

    Summer: Rec. Tui Day ¥35,000/wk. 3 wks.

    Bldgs 1. Class rms 28. Libs 1. Sci labs 1. Lang labs 2. Comp labs 3. Art studios 1. Music studios 1. Gyms 1. Fields 1. Pools 1.

    Est 1994. Inc. Tri (Aug-June). Assoc: EARCOS ECIS.

Founded as a preschool by international parents, TIS added an elementary school division three years after the founding. With its student body representative of more than 40 countries, the school employs English as its language of instruction. Children may enter the preschool with limited or nonexistent English skills, but at least one of each such child's parents must be fluent in English. The hands-on preschool curriculum incorporates elements from approaches in the US, England, Canada and Australia, while the traditional elementary program consists of the following main subject areas: language arts; social sciences; math and science; visual arts; music and drama; technology; and physical education.

Various after-school clubs provide students with enrichment and social opportunities. Clubs meet for an hour per session.

SAINT MAUR INTERNATIONAL SCHOOL

Day — Coed Gr PS-12

Yokohama 231-8654, Japan. 83 Yamate-cho, Naka-ku. Tel: 81-45-641-5751. Fax: 81-45-641-6688. EST+14.

www.stmaur.ac.jp   E-mail: office@stmaur.ac.jp

Jeanette K. Thomas, Head. MEd, MBE.

> Col Prep. Gen Acad. IB Diploma. Curr—Intl UK US. Exams—AP CEEB SSAT TOEFL IGCSE. AP—Eng Fr Span Calc Bio Chem Physics Econ Psych Studio_Art. Feat—Japan Comp_Sci Japan_Hist Visual_Arts Music. Supp—Dev_Read ESL Rem_Math Rem_Read Tut.
>
> Sports—Basket Baseball X-country Soccer Track Volley. Activities—Acad Arts Rec.
>
> Enr 440. B 194. G 246. Elem 309. Sec 131. US 108. Host 182. Other 150.
>
> Fac 62. M 18. F 35/9. US 12. Host 9. Other 41. Adv Deg: 59%.
>
> Grad '05—30. Col—29. US Col—16. (Brown, Notre Dame, Rochester Inst of Tech, U of Rochester, OH Wesleyan, Embry-Riddle). Avg SAT: M/V—1131.
>
> Tui '05-'06: Day ¥1,050,000-1,900,000 (+¥165,000-465,000).
>
> Summer: Acad Enrich Rev Rem Rec. Tui Day ¥25,000-100,000. 3 wks.
>
> Bldgs 5. Class rms 31. Lib 23,000 vols. Chapels 1. Sci labs 3. Lang labs 1. Comp labs 3. Auds 1. Art studios 2. Music studios 5. Gyms 1. Fields 1. Tennis courts 1.
>
> Est 1872. Nonprofit. Roman Catholic. Tri (Aug-June). Assoc: CIS EARCOS NEASC.

The oldest international school in Japan, Saint Maur conducts a Montessori program for children of ages 2½-5, traditional elementary and middle schools, and a college preparatory course of study at the high school level. Children in the elementary school pursue the International Primary Curriculum, a specialized course of studies that is implemented in state and international systems around the world. High schoolers prepare for the IGCSE, IB and AP examinations, with college preparation being the primary emphasis.   **See Also Page 550**

YOKOHAMA INTERNATIONAL SCHOOL

Day — Coed Gr PS-12

Yokohama 231-0862, Japan. 258 Yamate-cho, Naka-ku. Tel: 81-45-622-0084. Fax: 81-45-621-0379. EST+14.

www.yis.ac.jp   E-mail: yis@yis.ac.jp

Neil Richards, Head. BA, MPhil. Edward B. Bernard, Adm.

> Col Prep. IB PYP. IB Diploma. Curr—Intl. Exams—CEEB IGCSE. Feat—Fr Ger Japan Span Comp_Sci Studio_Art Theater_Arts Music.
>
> Enr 700. Avg class size: 20.
>
> Fac 89. M 29/1. F 41/18. US 12. Host 15. Other 62. Adv Deg: 23%.

Grad '05—27. Col—27. US Col—3. (Dartmouth, Brown, Cornell). Avg SAT: M/
V—1100.
Tui '05-'06: Day ¥1,975,000 (+¥680,000).
Summer: Acad. Tui Day ¥15,000-30,000/wk. 3 wks.
Bldgs 7. Class rms 45. Lib 20,000 vols. Sci labs 4. Comp labs 2. Auds 1. Art studios
2. Music studios 2. Gyms 1. Courts 1.
Est 1924. Nonprofit. Quar (Aug-June). Assoc: CIS EARCOS NEASC.

The school combines ideals of the American, British and Continental European educational systems, preparing students for the US College Boards and the Advanced Placement tests, as well as the International Baccalaureate Diploma and the IGCSE examinations. Major sports include cross-country, field hockey, soccer, and track and field; minor sports are tennis, basketball and volleyball. Students also participate in strong intramural programs. After-school activities play an important part in the student's education.

OKINAWA CHRISTIAN SCHOOL INTERNATIONAL
Day — Coed Gr K-12

Yomitan-Son, Okinawa 904-0391, Japan. PO Box 6. Tel: 81-98-958-3000. Fax: 81-98-958-6279. EST+14.
www.ocsi.org   E-mail: ocschool@ii-okinawa.ne.jp
Randal J. Hadley, Supt. BA, MA.
Gen Acad. Curr—US. **Exams**—ACT AP CEEB TOEFL. **AP**—Eng Calc. **Feat**—Japan Span Bible Studio_Art. **Supp**—ESL.
Sports—Basket Soccer Volley.
Enr 342. Elem 254. Sec 88. US 92. Host 122. Other 128.
Fac 35. M 6. F 28/1. US 24. Host 4. Other 7. Adv Deg: 31%.
Grad '05—23. **Col**—13. **US Col**—10. (CA St U 3, Baylor 2, U of Chicago 1, U of San Diego 1, LeTourneau 1, Pepperdine 1). Avg SAT: M/V—1050.
Tui '05-'06: Day ¥523,800-584,200 (+¥25,000-53,000).
Summer: Acad Enrich Rem. 5 wks.
Bldgs 2. Class rms 39. Libs 2. Sci labs 1. Comp labs 2. Gyms 1. Fields 1.
Est 1957. Nonprofit. Nondenom Christian. Sem (Aug-June). Assoc: WASC.

The school offers an American curriculum in a Christian atmosphere to an international student body. OCSI's US-style curriculum includes several Advanced Placement courses, and the school offers preparation for American college entrance examinations. Bible courses are an important element of the academic program. Students enroll from the US, Japan, China, The Philippines, India and Korea, among other countries.

KAZAKHSTAN

Sq. Miles: 1,042,476 (About the size of Western Europe). **Country Pop:** 16,700,000 (2001). **Capital:** Astana, pop. 313,000. **Largest City:** Almaty, pop. 1,129,400. **Terrain:** Extends from the Volga to the Altai Mountains and from the plains in western Siberia to oases and desert in Central Asia. **Ethnic Group(s):** Kazakh Russian Ukrainian Uzbek German Uyghur. **Religion(s):** Sunni_Muslim Russian_Orthodox Protestant. **Official Language(s):** Kazakh Russian. **Government:** Republic. **Independence:** 1991 (from Soviet Union). **GDP:** $29.7 billion (2003). Agriculture 7%. Industry 38%. Services 55%. **Currency:** Kazakhstan Tenge (KZT).

ALMATY INTERNATIONAL SCHOOL
Day — Coed Gr PS-12

Almaty 050000, Kazakhstan. 185 Auezov St, Kalkaman Village. Tel: 7-3272-50-45-61. Fax: 7-3272-50-45-64. EST+11.
www.qsi.org/kaz   E-mail: almaty@qsi.org
David Pera, Dir.

Col Prep. Curr—US. **Exams**—AP CEEB. **AP**—Eng Physics US_Hist. **Feat**—Fr Russ Comp_Sci Studio_Art Music.
Enr 160.
Fac 28.
Est 1993. Nonprofit. Tri (Aug-June). Assoc: A/OPR/OS MSA.

MIRAS INTERNATIONAL SCHOOL
Day — Coed Gr PS-12

Almaty 050043, Kazakhstan. 190 Al Farabi St. Tel: 7-3272-551025. Fax: 7-3272-551151. EST+11.
www.miras.kz   E-mail: secretary@miras.kz
Wayne McCullar, Supt. PhD. Irina Loginova, Dir.

Col Prep. IB PYP. IB MYP. IB Diploma. Curr—Intl Nat UK. **Bilingual**—Russ. **Exams**—IGCSE. **Feat**—Humanities Fr Ger Comp_Sci Econ Studio_Art Music Bus. **Supp**—EFL.
Activities—Acad Arts Media Rec Service.
Enr 490. B 240. G 250. Elem 387. Sec 103. US 25. Host 375. Other 90. Avg class size: 18.
Fac 105. M 14/2. F 77/12. Adv Deg: 4%.
Grad '05—35.
Tui '05-'06: Day $7000-14,500.
Bldgs 5. Class rms 45. Libs 2. Sci labs 3. Lang labs 3. Comp labs 2. Theaters 1. Art studios 2. Music studios 2. Dance studios 1. Gyms 2. Fields 1. Courts 1. Pools 1.
Est 1999. Tri (Aug-June). Assoc: CIS NEASC.

This bilingual school offers the International Baccalaureate Primary Years, Middle Years and Diploma programs. Students in grades PS-8 receive instruction in English and Russian, with elements of Kazakh language and culture integrated into the curriculum. Nonnative speakers receive additional instruction in English or Russian.

Students in grades 6-10 may supplement IB programming with preparation for national examinations and the Kazakh diploma. Pupils who follow the international track prepare for a selection of IGCSE examinations and the IB diploma in classes conducted exclusively in English. A large greenhouse on campus provides opportunities for the study of ecology and conservation.

MIRAS SCHOOL IN ASTANA
Bdg — Coed Gr 6-12; Day — Coed PS-12

Astana 010009, Kazakhstan. 30 Abylaikhan Ave. Tel: 7-3172-36-98-67. Fax: 7-3172-36-98-68. EST+11.
www.miras-astana.kz   E-mail: info@miras-astana.kz
Elena Khamitova, Dir.
  Col Prep. IB PYP. IB MYP. Curr—Intl. Exams—IGCSE. Feat—Fr Russ Kazakh Comp_Sci Kazakh_Hist Visual_Arts Drama Music Dance. Supp—EFL.
  Enr 225.
  Est 1999. Sem (Sept-June). Assoc: CIS NEASC.

KYRGYZSTAN

Sq. Miles: 199,000 (Slightly smaller than South Dakota). **Country Pop:** 5,146,281 (2005). **Capital:** Bishkek, pop. 631,300. **Terrain:** Mountainous, with some desert regions. **Ethnic Group(s):** Kyrgyz Russian Uzbek Dungan Uighurs Tatars German. **Religion(s):** Muslim Russian_Orthodox. **Official Language(s):** Kyrgyz Russian. **Government:** Republic. **Independence:** 1991 (from Soviet Union). **Per Capita Income:** $380 (2003). **GDP:** $1.9 billion (2003). Agriculture 38%. Manufacturing 23%. Services 39%. **Currency:** Kyrgyzstani Som (KGS).

BISHKEK INTERNATIONAL SCHOOL
Day — Coed Gr PS-12

Bishkek 720055, Kyrgyzstan. 14A Tynystanova St. Tel: 996-312-543890. Fax: 996-312-441178. EST+11.
www.qsi.org/kgz   E-mail: bishkek@qsi.org
Roy Douthitt, Dir. BA, MA, PhD.
  Col Prep. Gen Acad. Curr—US. Exams—CEEB. Feat—Comp_Sci Studio_Art Drama Music.
  Tui '05-'06: Day $13,000 (+$1700).
  Est 1994. Nonprofit. Spons: Quality Schools International. Tri (Sept-June). Assoc: A/OPR/OS MSA.

SILK ROAD INTERNATIONAL SCHOOL
Day — Coed Gr K-10

Bishkek, Kyrgyzstan. 11 Mikroregion, Aytieva 7A. Tel: 966-312-520290. Fax: 966-312-520490. EST+11.
www.sris.com.kg   E-mail: silkschool@hotmail.com
    Pre-Prep. Curr—UK. Exams—GCSE. **Feat**—Fr Ger Russ Kyrgyz Turkish Comp_
    Sci Econ Studio_Art Music. **Supp**—ESL.
    Enr 110.
    Fac 30.
    Est 1999. Tri (Sept-May).

LAOS

Sq. Miles: 91,430 (Slightly larger than Utah). **Country Pop:** 6,217,141 (2005). **Capital:** Vientiane, pop. 633,000 (2003). **Terrain:** Rugged mountains, plateaus, alluvial plains. **Ethnic Group(s):** Lao_Loum Lao_Theung Lao_Sung Hmong Yao Vietnamese Chinese. **Religion(s):** Buddhism. **Official Language(s):** Lao. **Other Language(s):** French English. **Government:** Communist. **Independence:** 1949 (from France). **Per Capita Income:** $320 (2002). **GDP:** $2 billion (2004). Agriculture 53%. Industry 23%. Services 24%. **Currency:** Laotian Kip (KN).

VIENTIANE INTERNATIONAL SCHOOL
Day — Coed Gr PS-12

Vientiane, Laos. PO Box 3180. Tel: 856-21-313-606. Fax: 856-21-315-008. EST+12.
www.vis.laopdr.com   E-mail: dragon@laotel.com
John Ritter, Dir.
    Col Prep. Curr—Intl. **Feat**—Lib_Skills Fr Comp_Sci Lao_Hist Lao_Stud Studio_Art
    Music. **Supp**—ESL.
    Fac 33.
    Tui '05-'06: Day $4185-9900 (+$2750).
    Plant val $96,000. Bldgs 6. Class rms 15. Libs 1. Sci labs 1. Comp labs 1. Art studios
    1. Music studios 1. Fields 2. Courts 1.
    Est 1991. Nonprofit. Tri (Aug-June). Assoc: A/OPR/OS CIS EARCOS WASC.

Offering a small-class setting in an English-language environment, the school serves expatriate and local children who are interested in an international program. Although the greatest numbers of pupils come from the US, Laos, Germany, Korea and Australia, no one nationality dominates the student body. VIS comprises three sections: preschool, elementary (grades K-5) and middle school (grades 6-9).

The developmentally oriented preschool prepares children for an elementary program in which they develop intellect, creativity, independence and responsibility, and gain an appreciation of the local culture. During these years, the curriculum features two weekly art, music, French and physical education classes, all of which specialists teach. For middle schoolers, writing skills development is an important aspect of the English program, while science classes focus on hands-on activities and use of the scientific method. French instruction at the middle school level increases to three periods weekly. In addition to field trips to local markets, museums, temples, businesses, organizations and events, students in grades 4-9 embark on longer (overnight or weeklong) excursions to environmentally or historically significant sites outside of the city.

Among daily after-school activities are field games, sports, reading clubs, crafts, Lao dance, tae kwon do, woodworking and music.

MALAYSIA

Sq. Miles: 127,316 (Slightly larger than New Mexico). **Country Pop:** 23,300,000 (2000). **Capital:** Kuala Lumpur. **Terrain:** Coastal plains and interior, jungle-covered mountains. **Ethnic Group(s):** Malay Chinese Indigenous Indian. **Religion(s):** Islam Buddhist Christian Hindu Confucian Taoist. **Other Language(s):** Malay Cantonese Hokkien Mandarin English Tamil Indigenous. **Government:** Constitutional Monarchy. **Independence:** 1957 (from United Kingdom). **Per Capita Income:** $4352 (2003). **GDP:** $229.3 billion (2003). Agriculture 7%. Industry 34%. Services 59%. **Currency:** Malaysian Ringgit (RM).

KINABALU INTERNATIONAL SCHOOL
Day — Coed Gr PS-10

88822 Kota Kinabalu, Sabah, Malaysia. PO Box 12080. Tel: 60-88-224526. Fax: 60-88-244203. EST+13.

www.kismy.org   E-mail: kismy@po.jaring.my

Martin Spice, Prin.

Col Prep. Curr—UK. Exams—IGCSE. Feat—Fr Bahasa_Malaysia Comp_Sci Studio_Art Music Bus. Supp—ESL.

Enr 135.

Est 1973. Tri (Sept-Aug).

GARDEN INTERNATIONAL SCHOOL
Day — Coed Ages 3-18

50480 Kuala Lumpur, Malaysia. 16 Jalan Kiara 3, Off Jalan Bukit Kiara. Tel: 60-3-6209-6888. Fax: 60-3-6201-2468. EST+13.

www.gardenschool.edu.my   E-mail: admissions@gardenschool.edu.my

Raymond P. Davis, Prin. MA. Karen Lim, Adm.

Col Prep. Gen Acad. Curr—UK. Exams—IGCSE AS-level A-level. Feat—Chin Fr Span Malay Comp_Sci Studio_Art Music. Supp—Dev_Read ESL LD Rem_Math Rem_Read Tut.

Activities—Acad Arts Govt/Pol Media Rec.

Enr 1790. B 890. G 900. Elem 1250. Sec 540. US 30. Host 635. Other 1125. Accepted: 98%. Avg class size: 24.
Fac 190. M 47. F 143. US 1. Host 90. Other 99. Adv Deg: 13%.
Tui '05-'06: Day RM18,660-33,990 (+RM1000). **Aid:** 10 pupils ($65,000).
Bldgs 4. Class rms 83. Libs 3. Sci labs 9. Lang labs 1. Comp labs 7. Art studios 7. Music studios 17. Dance studios 4. Drama studios 4. Gyms 1. Fields 1. Courts 6. Pools 1.
Est 1951. Inc. Tri (Sept-July). Assoc: ECIS.

GIS bases its curriculum on England's national curriculum, although modifications have been made to meet Malaysian requirements. The English system enables pupils to continue their education in other English-speaking countries without incurring an educational disadvantage. The kindergarten/early years department provides a curriculum that includes music, games, and arts and crafts.

Upon reaching the primary department, students receive instruction in basic reading, writing and arithmetic skills. The lower secondary school curriculum follows the general direction of the British curriculum at ages 11-14. This helps prepare students for the IGCSE examination. The Sixth Form places particular emphasis on college preparation.

Besides academic development, the school also stresses the importance of cocurricular activities as part of a balanced education. An array of clubs and societies is available.

INTERNATIONAL SCHOOL OF KUALA LUMPUR

Day — Coed Gr PS-12

50784 Kuala Lumpur, Malaysia. PO Box 12645. Tel: 60-3-4259-5600. Fax: 60-3-4257-9044. EST+13.
www.iskl.edu.my   E-mail: iskl@iskl.edu.my
Paul Chmelik, Head. BA, MEd, MA. **Stephanie Loo, Adm.**
  Col Prep. IB Diploma. Curr—Intl US. **Exams**—CEEB. **AP**—Eng Fr Span Calc Comp_Sci Bio Chem Physics US_Hist. **Feat**—Chin Malay SE_Asian_Hist Anthro Econ Psych Architect Film Photog Theater Music. **Supp**—ESL.
  Sports—Badminton Basket X country Rugby Soccer Softball Swim Tennis Track Volley. **Activities**—Acad Arts Govt/Pol Media Rec Service.
  Enr 1240. Elem 751. Sec 489. US 211. Host 120. Other 909. Accepted: 99%. Yield: 93%.
  Fac 142. M 45/1. F 89/7. US 65. Host 14. Other 63. Adv Deg: 61%.
  Grad '05—115. Avg SAT: M/V—1179. Avg ACT: 27.
  Tui '05-'06: Day RM24,014-45,194 (+RM1530-13,593). **Aid:** 2 pupils (RM200,000).
  Summer: Acad Rec. ESL. 3 wks.
  Est 1965. Nonprofit. Sem (Aug-June). Assoc: A/OPR/OS EARCOS WASC.

Reflecting the international atmosphere of Malaysia, ISKL has an enrollment representative of more than 50 nations. Courses in French, Spanish, Malay, Mandarin and Southeast Asian history enrich the standard American curriculum, which also features individualized instruction and the extensive use of audio-visual materials. Students prepare for the US College Boards, with graduates advancing to competitive colleges and universities in the US and throughout the world.

Advanced Placement and International Baccalaureate courses are offered in the secondary program.

Pupils in need of additional academic support receive assistance through the school's learning resources center.

MONT'KIARA INTERNATIONAL SCHOOL
Day — Coed Gr PS-12

50480 Kuala Lumpur, Malaysia. 22 Jalan Mont'Kiara. Tel: 603-2093-8604. Fax: 603-2093-6045. EST+13.
www.mkis.edu.my   E-mail: info@mkis.edu.my
Walter C. Morris, Head. Bridget Hall, Adm.

> **Col Prep. IB Diploma. Curr**—Intl US. **Exams**—CEEB. **Feat**—Chin Fr Span Visual_Arts Music Dance. **Supp**—ESL.
> **Sports**—Basket Golf Rugby Soccer Softball Swim Tennis Track Volley. **Activities**—Acad Arts Govt/Pol Rec Service.
> **Enr 700.**
> **Tui '05-'06: Day RM26,000-51,000** (+RM7000-8500).
> Class rms 32. Lib 16,000 vols. Comp labs 4. Art studios 4. Music studios 2. Dance studios 1. Gyms 1. Fields 2. Pools 1. Weight rms 1.
> **Est 1994.** Sem (Aug-June). Assoc: EARCOS WASC.

MKIS offers an American-style curriculum to the expatriate community of Kuala Lumpur. The elementary school curriculum includes information technology, art, music and Malaysian studies, and regular student-led conferences provide opportunities to showcase student work. All high school students pursue a traditional American diploma, although some prepare for the International Baccalaureate Diploma as well.

Students in grades 6-12 embark on three- to five-day trips to explore Malaysian culture and perform community service.

DALAT INTERNATIONAL SCHOOL
Bdg — Coed Gr 1-12; Day — Coed PS-12

11200 Penang, Malaysia. Tanjung Bunga. Tel: 60-4-899-2105. Fax: 60-4-890-2141. EST+13.
www.dalat.org   E-mail: office@dalat.org
Karl Steinkamp, Dir. Shelly Tuck, Adm.

> **Col Prep. Curr**—US. **Exams**—ACT AP CEEB. **AP**—Eng Calc Environ_Sci Psych. **Feat**—Chin Fr Span Astron Comp_Sci. **Supp**—ESL Tut.
> **Sports**—Badminton Basket Soccer Track Volley. **Activities**—Acad Arts Cultural/ Relig Govt/Pol Rec.
> **Enr 311.** Elem 177. Sec 134. US 108. Host 21. Other 182.
> **Fac 44.** M 16/2. F 21/5. US 28. Host 2. Other 14. Adv Deg: 40%.
> **Grad '05—22. Col—19. US Col—11.** (Tufts, Westmont, U of MI, U of IL-Urbana, Brigham Young, LeTourneau). Avg SAT: M/V—1156.
> **Tui '05-'06: Bdg RM41,250-63,000** (+RM2250-5550). **Day RM12,000-36,200** (+RM2250-5550).
> Dorms 5. Libs 1. Sci labs 2. Comp labs 3. Auds 1. Gyms 1. Fields 2. Courts 2.

Pools 1.
Est 1928. Nonprofit. Nondenom Christian. Sem (Aug-June). Assoc: EARCOS WASC.

Dalat serves the business expatriate and missionary communities in Southeast Asia. Its American-style college preparatory curriculum encompasses a wide choice of electives. With the exception of foreign languages, all courses are conducted in English; ESL support is available as needed.

The school is located on the beachfront of the island of Penang, the third-largest city in Malaysia and one of the earliest historical sites of European colonialism. This metropolis is the home of Malays, Chinese, Indians, Eurasians, Europeans and Americans. The Dalat School's international student body reflects this diverse community, and pupils are encouraged to explore foreign cultures. Many graduates matriculate at colleges in the US.

THE INTERNATIONAL SCHOOL OF PENANG
UPLANDS

Bdg — Coed Gr 3-12; Day — Coed PS-12

10250 Penang, Malaysia. Jalan Kelawei. Tel: 604-227-1764. Fax: 604-227-8972. EST+13.
www.uplands.org   E-mail: info@uplands.org
Ian Kerr, Prin. MBE.
   Col Prep. IB Diploma. Curr—Intl UK. **Exams**—IGCSE. **Feat**—Chin Fr Ger Japan Comp_Sci Econ Sociol Malaysian_Stud Studio_Art Bus. **Supp**—ESL.
   Tri (Aug-June). Assoc: EARCOS.

ST. CHRISTOPHER'S
INTERNATIONAL PRIMARY SCHOOL

Day — Coed Gr PS-5

10350 Penang, Malaysia. 10 Nunn Rd. Tel: 60-4-228-3589. Fax: 60-4-226-4340. EST+13.
www.scips.org.my   E-mail: scips@po.jaring.my
John Gwyn Jones, Prin.
   Gen Acad. Curr—UK. **Feat**—Ger Bahasa_Indonesia Computers Visual_Arts Music. **Supp**—ESL.
   Enr 500.
   Tui '05-'06: Day RM6900-15,000 (+RM1500-3500).
   Est 1965. Nonprofit. Tri (Sept-July).

THE ALICE SMITH SCHOOL

Day — Coed Gr PS-12

43000 Seri Kembangan, Selangor, Malaysia. 3 Jalan Equine, Taman Equine. Tel: 60-3-9543-3688. Fax: 60-3-9543-3788. EST+13.
www.alice-smith.edu.my   E-mail: klass@alice-smith.edu.my

Nik Bishop, Co-Prin. Steve Caulfield, Co-Prin.
    Col Prep. Curr—UK. Exams—GCSE IGCSE AS-level A-level. Feat—Fr Ger Comp_Sci Econ Studio_Art Drama Music Bus.
    Tui '05-'06: Day RM13,500-37,500 (+RM17,020-20,020).
    Est 1946. Tri (Sept-June).

MARSHALL ISLANDS

Sq. Miles: 70 (About the size of Washington, DC). **Country Pop:** 59,071 (2005). **Capital:** Majuro, pop. 25,000 (2005). **Terrain:** Low-lying coral atolls and islands. **Ethnic Group(s):** Marshallese American Filipino Chinese New_Zealander Korean. **Religion(s):** Protestant. **Other Language(s):** Marshallese English Japanese. **Government:** Parliamentary Democracy. **Independence:** 1986 (from United States). **GDP:** $135.3 million (1997). Agriculture 14%. Industry 16%. Services 70%. **Currency:** US Dollar ($).

KWAJALEIN SCHOOL SYSTEM
Day — Coed Gr PS-12

Kwajalein, Marshall Islands. Tel: 805-355-3761. Fax: 805-355-3584. EST+17.
Contact: PO Box 51, APO, AP 96555.
www.kwajalein-school.com   E-mail: frazierd@kwajalein-school.com
Dan Frazier, Supt.
    Col Prep. Curr—US. Exams—CEEB TOEFL. AP—Eng Calc Stats Comp_Sci Bio. Feat—Fr Span Studio_Art Music. Supp—Dev_Read ESL LD.
    Enr 400. Elem 275. Sec 125. US 345. Host 55. Avg class size: 11.
    Fac 42. US 42.
    Grad '05—25. Col—25. US Col—25. (U of HI-Manoa, Brown, MIT, U of TX-Austin, U of CA-Berkeley).
    Tui '02-'03: Day $9000-10,000.
    Summer: Rev. 6 wks.
    Bldgs 8. Class rms 34. Libs 2. Comp labs 3. Fields 1. Courts 1.
    Est 1963. Nonprofit. Sem (Aug-June).

Based on Kwajalein, the largest and most populous Marshall Island, this US Army-administered school offers an American curriculum that includes Advanced Placement courses. Most of its students are dependents of Americans employed on the Kwajalein missile range.

MONGOLIA

Sq. Miles: 604,103 (Slightly larger than Alaska). **Country Pop:** 2,791,272 (2005). **Capital:** Ulaanbaatar, pop. 760,077 (2000). **Terrain:** Almost all of land area is pasture or desert wasteland (of varying usefulness). **Ethnic Group(s):** Mongol Turkic Tungusic Chinese Russian. **Religion(s):** Buddhist_Lamaist Shamanist Muslim. **Official Language(s):** Khalkha_Mongol. **Other Language(s):** Kazakh Russian Chinese English. **Government:** Parliamentary. **Independence:** 1921 (from China). **GDP:** $4.9 billion (2003). Agriculture 21%. Industry 21%. Services 58%. **Currency:** Mongolian Tugrik (Tug).

INTERNATIONAL SCHOOL OF ULAANBAATAR
Day — Coed Gr PS-12

Ulaanbaatar, Mongolia. PO Box 49/564. Tel: 976-11-452-839. Fax: 976-11-450-340. EST+13.
www.isumongolia.org   E-mail: int.school.ub@gmail.com
Harvey Cohen, Int Dir. BSc, MA.
   Col Prep. IB PYP. IB MYP. IB Diploma. Curr—Intl. Exams—CEEB TOEFL IGCSE.
      Feat—Russ Korean Mongolian Comp_Sci Studio_Art Music Bus. Supp—LD.
   Est 1992. Nonprofit. Assoc: A/OPR/OS CIS EARCOS NEASC.

MYANMAR

Sq. Miles: 261,970 (Slightly smaller than Texas). **Country Pop:** 42,909,464 (2005). **Capital:** Rangoon, pop. 5,500,000. **Terrain:** Central lowlands ringed by steep, rugged highlands. **Ethnic Group(s):** Burman Shan Karen Rakhine Chinese Mon Indian. **Religion(s):** Buddhist Muslim Baptist Roman_Catholic. **Official Language(s):** Burmese. **Government:** Military Junta. **Independence:** 1948 (from United Kingdom). **Per Capita Income:** $225 (2004). **GDP:** $13.6 billion (2004). Agriculture 57%. Industry 9%. Services 34%. **Currency:** Myanmar Kyat (K).

INTERNATIONAL SCHOOL YANGON
Day — Coed Gr PS-12

Yangon, Myanmar. 20 Shwe Taungyar Rd, Bahann Township. Tel: 95-1-512793. Fax: 95-1-525020. EST+11.5.
www.isy.net.mm   E-mail: director@isy.net.mm
Thomas Tunny, Dir.
   Col Prep. Curr—US. Exams—AP CEEB. AP—Eng Calc Comp_Sci Bio Chem
      Physics Econ Psych. Feat—Fr Span Environ_Sci Web_Design Asian_Stud
      Studio_Art Drama. Supp—ESL.
   Tui '05-'06: Day $7600-9390 (+$1000-5000).
   Est 1955. Nonprofit. Sem (Aug-May). Assoc: A/OPR/OS EARCOS.

NEPAL

Sq. Miles: 56,136 (About the size of Tennessee). **Country Pop:** 27,676,547 (2005). **Capital:** Kathmandu, pop. 1,500,000. **Terrain:** Flat and fertile in the southern Terai region; terraced cultivation and swiftly flowing mountain rivers in the central hills; and the high Himalayas in the north. **Ethnic Group(s):** Brahman Chetri Newar Gurung Magar Tamang Rai Limbu Sherpa Tharu. **Religion(s):** Hindu Buddhist Muslim. **Official Language(s):** Nepali. **Government:** Parliamentary Democracy and Constitutional Monarchy. **Per Capita Income:** $279 (2003). **GDP:** $6.7 billion (2003). Agriculture 40%. Industry 20%. Services 40%. **Currency:** Nepali Rupee (NRs).

THE BRITISH SCHOOL
KATHMANDU

Day — Coed Gr K-12

Kathmandu, Nepal. PO Box 566. Tel: 977-1-5521794. Fax: 977-1-5522012. EST+10.75.

www.tbs.edu.np   E-mail: tbs@tbs.edu.np

Sandj L. Wilderspin, Prin.

    Gen Acad. Curr—UK. Exams—IGCSE. Feat—Nepali Econ Geog Psych Studio_ Art Music Bus.

    Enr 280. Avg class size: 22.

    Fac 25. Host 20.

    Tui '05-'06: Day £2310-2550 (+£1000-2000).

    Libs 1.

    Est 1966. Nonprofit. (July-June).

This school provides a British primary education for children of the international English-speaking population living in Kathmandu. Children attend principally from Britain, Australia, Canada, India, Europe and the US, with the student body comprising boys and girls from approximately 30 countries.

BUDHANILKANTHA SCHOOL

Bdg — Coed Gr 4-12

Kathmandu, Nepal. PO Box 1018. Tel: 977-1-4371637. Fax: 977-1-4371640. EST+10.75.

www.bnks.edu.np   E-mail: school@mail.com.np

N. P. Sharma, Prin. MEd.

    Col Prep. Curr—Nat UK. Exams—CEEB TOEFL A-level. Feat—Chin Comp_Sci. Supp—Dev_Read Makeup Rem_Math Rev Tut.

    Enr 928. B 616. G 312. Accepted: 100%. Avg class size: 30.

    Fac 75. M 59/2. F 14.

    Grad '05—84. US Col—35.

    Bldgs 20. Dorms 11. Class rms 40. Libs 2. Sci labs 6. Comp labs 1. Auds 1. Art studios 1. Music studios 1. Dance studios 1. Gyms 1. Fields 6. Courts 3. Pools 1. **Est 1972.** Nonprofit. Tri.

Founded as a national school, BNKS changed its program several times prior to converting to an English-medium school in 1983. Today, it concurrently runs both a UK-style curriculum and a national one. Interested students may work toward the A-level examinations.

KATHMANDU INTERNATIONAL STUDY CENTRE
Day — Coed Gr 6-12

Kathmandu, Nepal. Naya Baneshwor, Buddha Nagar, PO Box 126. Tel: 977-1-482604. Fax: 977-1-4780994. EST+10.75.
www.kisc.edu.np   E-mail: admin@kisc.edu.np
Judith Ellis, Prin. BSc, MBA.
  Col Prep. Gen Acad. Curr—UK. **Exams**—IGCSE AS-level A-level. **Feat**—Fr Ger Span Nepali Relig Studio_Art Drama Music Bus. **Supp**—ESL.
  Activities—Arts Rec.
  Enr 75. Elem 40. Sec 35. US 18. Host 9. Other 48. Accepted: 95%. Yield: 100%. Avg class size: 12.
  Fac 26. M 6/3. F 9/8. Adv Deg: 11%.
  Grad '05—10.
  Tui '05-'06: Day $4576.
  Bldgs 6. Class rms 20. Lib 6500 vols. Sci labs 1. Lang labs 4. Comp labs 1. Auds 1. Art studios 1. Music studios 1. Gyms 1. Fields 1. Courts 1.
  Est 1987. Nonprofit. Nondenom Christian. Quar (Aug-June).

KISC was founded in 1987 to serve expatriate mission families, and about 65 percent of students today are children of missionaries. Centrally located in Kathmandu, the school provides a Christian-based education within a culturally diverse environment. Preparation for the IGCSE and AS- and A-level exams is offered in conjunction with a standard US college preparatory curriculum.

Although it does not offer traditional boarding, KISC secures hostels for its students as the need arises.

LINCOLN SCHOOL
Day — Coed Gr PS-12

Kathmandu, Nepal. PO Box 2673, Rabi Bhawan. Tel: 977-1-4270482. Fax: 977-1-4272685. EST+10.75.
www.lsnepal.com   E-mail: info@lsnepal.com.np
Allan Bredy, Dir.
  Col Prep. Gen Acad. Curr—US. **Exams**—AP CEEB TOEFL. **AP**—Eng Fr Span Calc Stats Comp_Sci Bio Chem Physics Eur_Hist US_Hist Econ Studio_Art. **Supp**—ESL.
  Enr 260.
  Fac 30.
  Tui '05-'06: Day $9995-12,380 (+$2750).
  Est 1954. Nonprofit. Sem (Aug-June). Assoc: A/OPR/OS NEASC.

PAKISTAN

Sq. Miles: 310,527 (About twice the size of California). **Country Pop:** 162,419,946 (2005). **Capital:** Islamabad, pop. 3,700,000 (2005). **Largest City:** Karachi, pop. 11,624,219 (2005). **Terrain:** Flat Indus plain in east; mountains in north and northwest; Balochistan plateau in west. **Ethnic Group(s):** Punjabi Sindhi Pushtun Baloch Muhajir Saraiki Hazara. **Religion(s):** Muslim Christian Hindu. **Official Language(s):** Urdu. **Other Language(s):** English Punjabi Sindhi Pushtu Baloch. **Government:** Parliamentary Democracy. **Independence:** 1947 (from United Kingdom). **GDP:** $59 billion (1999). Agriculture 23%. Industry 24%. Services 53%. **Currency:** Pakistani Rupee (PRs).

INTERNATIONAL SCHOOL OF ISLAMABAD
Day — Coed Gr K-12

Islamabad 44000, Pakistan. PO Box 1124. Tel: 92-51-4434-950. Fax: 92-51-4440-193. EST+10.
www.isoi.edu.pk   E-mail: school@isoi.edu.pk
Rose Puffer, Supt.
 Col Prep. Curr—Intl US. Exams—CEEB. Feat—Fr Span Econ Photog Studio_Art Drama. Supp—Dev_Read ESL LD Rem_Math Rem_Read.
 Sports—Basket F_Hockey Soccer Swim Volley. Activities—Arts.
 Enr 287. B 177. G 110. Elem 187. Sec 100. US 40. Host 73. Other 174.
 Fac 44. M 10. F 34. US 24. Host 7. Other 13. Adv Deg: 59%.
 Tui '05-'06: Day $13,155-13,720.
 Bldgs 1. Lib 20,000 vols. Labs 2. Gym/auds 1. Fields 2. Tennis courts 2.
 Est 1964. Sem (Aug-June). Assoc: A/OPR/OS MSA.

Located on a 20-acre campus between Islamabad and Rawalpindi, this school provides an English-speaking education for an international enrollment composed mostly of Americans and Pakistanis. The American-style curriculum is geared toward US college admission.

KARACHI AMERICAN SCHOOL
Day — Coed Gr PS-12

Karachi 75350, Pakistan. Amir Khusro Rd, KDA Scheme 1. Tel: 92-21-453-9096. Fax: 92-21-454-7305. EST+10.
Contact: Dept of State Karachi, Washington, DC 20521.
www.kas.edu.pk   E-mail: admissions@kas.edu.pk
Peter Pelosi, Supt. PhD. Marilyn Nessel, Adm.
 Col Prep. Curr—US. Exams—ACT CEEB TOEFL. AP—Eng Fr Span Calc Chem Physics Eur_Hist US_Hist Studio_Art. Feat—British_Lit Creative_Writing Urdu Comp_Sci Econ Psych Drama Music Journ. Supp—ESL.
 Sports—Basket Soccer Swim Tennis Track Volley. Activities—Acad Arts Govt/Pol Media Rec Service.

Enr 333. B 190. G 143. Elem 207. Sec 126. US 62. Host 179. Other 92. Accepted: 50%. Avg class size: 25.

Fac 42. M 9/1. F 29/3. US 19. Host 17. Other 6. Adv Deg: 54%.

Grad '05—24. Col—24. US Col—14. (NYU 3, Boston U 2, Georgetown 1, Carnegie Mellon 1, U of MI 1, Franklin & Marshall 1). Avg SAT: M/V—1184.

Tui '05-'06: Day $7220-11,095 (+$3500). **Aid:** 2 pupils ($11,095).

Plant val $50,000,000. Bldgs 3. Class rms 40. 2 Libs 33,000 vols. Sci labs 3. Comp labs 2. Auds 1. Art studios 1. Music studios 1. Gyms 1. Fields 2. Courts 2. Pools 1.

Est 1952. Nonprofit. Sem (Aug-May). Assoc: A/OPR/OS MSA.

Located on a 10-acre campus, KAS follows an American-style curriculum. ESL is conducted throughout. While pupils of all nationalities may enroll, the school seeks to accommodate primarily those transient students from the expatriate business and diplomatic communities who stand to benefit from a US-style program.

In addition to athletics, boys and girls may take part in field trips, music organizations, cultural programs and interest clubs.

MURREE CHRISTIAN SCHOOL

Bdg and Day — Coed Gr 4-12

Murree 47180, Punjab, Pakistan. PO Jhika Gali. Tel: 92-51-3410321. Fax: 92-51-3411668. EST+10.

www.mcs.org.pk   E-mail: mcs@mcs.org.pk

Andrew Gordon, Dir. BEd.

Col Prep. Gen Acad. Curr—US. **Exams**—AP CEEB. **AP**—Eng Comp_Sci Bio Chem Physics Studio_Art. **Feat**—Fr Ger Span Urdu Relig Photog Music. **Supp**—LD Tut.

Sports—Basket F_Hockey Soccer Volley. **Activities**—Acad Arts Govt/Pol Media.

Enr 71. B 38/4. G 25/4. Elem 32. Sec 39. US 26. Host 5. Other 40. Accepted: 100%. Avg class size: 8.

Fac 14. M 3/3. F 8. US 5. Host 1. Other 8. Adv Deg: 14%.

Grad '05—8. Avg SAT: M/V—1203, Essay—575.

Tui '05-'06: Bdg PRs517,400 (+PRs5000). **Day PRs275,000.**

Bldgs 5. Dorms 3. Dorm rms 36. Class rms 20. Sci labs 2. Comp labs 2. Art studios 1. Gyms 1. Fields 2. Courts 2.

Est 1956. Inc. Nondenom Christian. Sem (Aug-June).

This interdenominational Christian school follows an American curriculum and offers preparation for the US College Boards and Advanced Placement examinations. The enrollment consists primarily of missionary children (who qualify for a discounted tuition fee) from roughly a dozen countries. An annual fine arts festival showcases students' art displays, variety shows and theater productions

MCS is located 7000 feet above sea level in the foothills of the Himalayan Mountains. With its physical attractiveness and amenable climate, Murree is a popular vacation destination.

PAPUA NEW GUINEA

Sq. Miles: 174,850 (About the size of California). **Country Pop:** 5,545,268 (2005). **Capital:** Port Moresby, pop. 320,000. **Terrain:** Mostly mountains with coastal lowlands and rolling foothills. **Ethnic Group(s):** Melanesian Papuan Negrito Micronesian Polynesian. **Religion(s):** Roman_Catholic Lutheran Presbyterian Anglican Seventh-Day_ Adventist Indigenous_Beliefs. **Official Language(s):** English. **Other Language(s):** Tok_Pisin Motu. **Government:** Constitutional Monarchy with Parliamentary Democracy. **Independence:** 1975. **Per Capita Income:** $744. **GDP:** $5 billion (1999). Agriculture 34%. Industry 35%. Services 31%. **Currency:** Papua New Guinean Kina (PK).

HIGHLAND LUTHERAN INTERNATIONAL SCHOOL
Day — Coed Gr PS-12

Wabag, Enga Province, Enga Province Papua New Guinea. PO Box 363. Tel: 675-547-1235. Fax: 675-547-1235. EST+15.
www.hlischool-png.org   E-mail: bkilback@nucleus.com
Brent Kilback, Head.
   Gen Acad. Curr—Nat. Feat—Relig.
   Enr 150.
   Fac 16.
   Est 1953. Lutheran-Missouri Synod.

PHILIPPINES

Sq. Miles: 117,187 (Slightly larger than Arizona). **Country Pop:** 87,857,473 (2005). **Capital:** Manila, pop. 9,930,000 (2000). **Terrain:** Islands, mostly mountainous, with narrow coastal lowlands. **Ethnic Group(s):** Malay Chinese. **Religion(s):** Roman_Catholic Protestant Muslim Buddhist. **Official Language(s):** Filipino. **Other Language(s):** English. **Government:** Republic. **Independence:** 1946 (from Spain). **Per Capita Income:** $976 (2004). **GDP:** $84.2 billion (2004). Agriculture 15%. Industry 32%. Services 53%. **Currency:** Philippine Peso (PP).

BRENT INTERNATIONAL SCHOOL BAGUIO
Bdg — Coed Gr 4-12; Day — Coed PS-12

2600 Baguio City, Philippines. Brent Rd, PO Box 35. Tel: 63-74-442-4050. Fax: 63-74-442-3638. EST+13.
www.brentschoolbaguio.com   E-mail: brent@brentschoolbaguio.com
Dick B. Robbins, Head. Lourdes Balanza, Adm.

Col Prep. IB Diploma. Curr—Intl UK US. **Exams**—CEEB ACT. **Feat**—Chin Fr Span Filipino Korean Comp_Sci Relig Studio_Art Music. **Supp**—ESL Tut.

Enr 232. B 28/109. G 14/81. Elem 154. Sec 78. US 40. Host 79. Other 113. Accepted: 90%. Avg class size: 16.

Fac 30. M 9/2. F 17/2. Adv Deg: 40%.

Grad '05—12. Col—12. US Col—3. Avg SAT: M/V—987. Avg ACT: 24.

Tui '05-'06: Bdg $14,250. Day $7500. Aid: 5 pupils ($40,749).

Endow $4,970,000. Bldgs 19. Dorms 2. Dorm rms 38. Class rms 32. Lib 22,000 vols. Sci labs 4. Lang labs 3. Comp labs 2. Theaters 1. Art studios 1. Music studios 1. Gyms 1. Fields 1. Tennis courts 2.

Est 1909. Nonprofit. Episcopal. Quar (Aug-June). Assoc: EARCOS.

Known originally as the Baguio School and renamed in 1922 in honor of its founder, Rt. Rev. Charles Henry Brent, first bishop of the Episcopal Church in the Philippines, the school accepts students of all religions and nationalities. Combining Christian ideals and high standards of scholarship, BISB offers an enriched international curriculum that prepares students for entrance to universities around the world. Although most pupils enroll from the US and the Philippines, the student body also includes boys and girls from over a dozen other countries.

Located on a 13-acre campus some 5000 feet above sea level, the school enjoys a temperate climate year-round. Outdoor sports include basketball, soccer, track and field, volleyball, rugby and badminton.

CEBU INTERNATIONAL SCHOOL

Day — Coed Gr PS-12

6000 Cebu City, Philippines. PO Box 735, Pit-os. Tel: 63-32-417-6390. Fax: 63-32-417-6394. EST+13.

www.cis.edu.ph   E-mail: markb@cis.edu.ph

Mark Bretherton, Supt. BS, MA.

Col Prep. Gen Acad. IB Diploma. Curr—Intl US. **Exams**—ACT CEEB TOEFL. **Feat**—Ger Span Filipino Comp_Sci Bible Studio_Art Drama Music Journ. **Supp**—ESL.

Sports—Basket Soccer Swim Volley. **Activities**—Acad Govt/Pol Rec.

Enr 371. Elem 258. Sec 113. US 74. Host 74. Other 223. Accepted: 98%. Yield: 100%. Avg class size: 16.

Fac 47. M 8/2. F 35/2. Host 39. Other 8. Adv Deg: 19%.

Grad '05—17.

Tui '05-'06: Day $920-7640.

Plant val $2,000,000. Bldgs 6. Class rms 39. 2 Libs 22,573 vols. Sci labs 3. Comp labs 2. Art studios 2. Music studios 1. Dance studios 1. Gyms 1. Fields 1. Pools 2.

Est 1924. Nonprofit. Quar (Aug-June). Assoc: EARCOS WASC.

CIS was established as a small elementary school named the American School of Cebu. It assumed its current name in 1973 and eventually added a secondary division; the first senior class graduated in 1987. The self-contained elementary school (nursery through grade 5) focuses on the traditional disciplines. German, Spanish and Filipino are the foreign language options, and ESL is available at all levels. The college preparatory middle and upper school program, which leads to

the IB Diploma, includes yearlong courses and electives in such areas as information technology, journalism and home economics.

FAITH ACADEMY

Day — Coed Gr PS-12

**0706 Makati City, Philippines. PO Box 2016 MCPO. Tel: 632-658-0048. Fax: 632-
658-0026. EST+13.**
www.faith.edu.ph   E-mail: vanguard@faith.edu.ph
Martha Macomber, Supt.
  Col Prep. Gen Acad. Curr—UK US. Exams—IGCSE.
  Enr 600.
  Tui '05-'06: Day **$4244** (+$4420).
  Est 1957. Nonprofit. Sem (Aug-May). Assoc: EARCOS WASC.

BRENT INTERNATIONAL SCHOOL MANILA

Day — Coed Gr PS-12

**1603 Pasig City, Philippines. University of Life Complex, PO Box 12201, Meralco
Ave. Tel: 63-2-631-1265. Fax: 63-2-633-8420. EST+13.**
www.brentmanila.edu.ph   E-mail: bism@brentmanila.edu.ph
Dick B. Robbins, Head.
  Col Prep. IB Diploma. Curr—Intl. **Supp**—ESL.
  Enr 1052.
  Est 1984. Nonprofit. Sem (Aug-May). Assoc: EARCOS.

THE BRITISH SCHOOL MANILA

Day — Coed Gr PS-12

**Taguig, Metro Manila, Philippines. 36th St, University Park, Bonifacio Global City.
Tel: 63-2-840-1561. Fax: 63-2-840-1520. EST+13.**
www.britishschoolmanila.org   E-mail: admissions@britishschoolmanila.org
Chris Mantz, Head. BA, MA.
  Col Prep. IB Diploma. Curr—Intl UK. **Exams**—CEE GCSE IGCSE. **Feat**—Fr Span
  Comp_Sci Psych Relig Studio_Art Drama Music Bus.
  Activities—Arts Rec.
  Enr 580. Elem 360. Sec 220. US 56. Host 129. Other 395. Avg class size: 17.
  Fac 48. M 22. F 25/1. Adv Deg: 14%.
  Grad '05—10.
  Tui '05-'06: Day £7400-8900.
  Sci labs 3. Comp labs 4. Auds 1. Music studios 1. Fields 1. Pools 1.
  Est 1976. Nonprofit. Tri (Sept-July).

Students from the United Kingdom make up approximately half of the enrollment at this school, which follows a modified version on the English National Curriculum with some modifications. As they progress, boys and girls prepare for the
National Curriculum Tests and the GCSE exams. Secondary school students pursue

the International Baccalaureate Diploma. All instructors arrive at the school with British or Commonwealth training.

INTERNATIONAL SCHOOL MANILA
Day — Coed Gr PS-12

1634 Taguig, Metro Manila, Philippines. University Pky, Fort Bonifacio. Tel: 63-2-840-8400. Fax: 63-2-840-8405. EST+13.
www.ismanila.com   E-mail: admission@ismanila.com
David Toze, Supt. MEd. **Gary Jerome, Adm.**

   Col Prep. IB Diploma. Curr—Intl US. **Exams**—ACT CEEB TOEFL. **Feat**—Chin Ger Japan Filipino Korean Econ Pol_Sci Psych Asian_Stud Drama Music. **Supp**—ESL LD Tut.

   Enr 1524. Elem 956. Sec 568. US 332. Host 279. Other 913. Accepted: 38%. Avg class size: 20.

   Fac 154. M 50/5. F 87/12. US 38. Host 55. Other 61. Adv Deg: 36%.

   Grad '05—147. US Col—84. (Bentley, Fordham, NYU, U of San Diego, Stanford). Avg SAT: M/V—1119.

   Tui '05-'06: Day $9980-13,510 (+$510-1790).

   Summer: Acad Enrich. 2 wks.

   Bldgs 1. Class rms 127. 3 Libs 82,330 vols. Sci labs 14. Comp labs 7. Auds 2. Theaters 2. Art studios 16. Music studios 16. Dance studios 6. Gyms 3. Fields 3. Tennis courts 6. Pools 3. Tracks 1. Weight rms 1.

   Est 1920. Quar (Aug-June). Assoc: A/OPR/OS EARCOS WASC.

The highly international student body at ISM follows a broad, US-style college preparatory curriculum that includes Advanced Placement courses, the two-year International Baccalaureate Diploma program, various electives, independent study opportunities, and extensive computer and fine arts programs.

Athletic competition, both interscholastic and intramural, as well as a full range of activities, rounds out the program. Limited scholarship aid is available only to Filipino pupils. Each year, ISM sends its graduates to colleges throughout the world, although most students matriculate at US institutions.

SINGAPORE

Sq. Miles: 263 (Slightly more than three and a half times the size of Washington, DC). **Country Pop:** 4,425,720 (2005). **Capital:** Singapore, pop. 4,154,500 (2002). **Terrain:** Lowland. **Ethnic Group(s):** Chinese Malay Indian. **Religion(s):** Buddhist Taoist Muslim Christian Hindu. **Other Language(s):** English Mandarin Chinese Malay Tamil. **Government:** Parliamentary Republic. **Independence:** 1965. **GDP:** $110 billion (2004). Agriculture 1%. Manufacturing 32%. Services 67%. **Currency:** Singaporean Dollar (S$).

AUSTRALIAN INTERNATIONAL SCHOOL
SINGAPORE

Day — Coed Gr PS-12

Singapore 596468, Singapore. 201 Ulu Pandan Rd. Tel: 65-6463-9595. Fax: 65-6463-9555. EST+13.
www.ais.com.sg   E-mail: enrolments@ais.com.sg
Peter Bond, Prin.
> Gen Acad. Curr—Australia. Feat—Chin Fr Comp_Sci Econ Geog Visual_Arts Music Bus. Supp—ESL.
> Enr 1200.
> Tui '05-'06: Day S$16,360-21,942 (+S$2100).
> Est 1993. Quar (Jan-Dec).

CANADIAN INTERNATIONAL SCHOOL

Day — Coed Gr PS-12

Singapore 289759, Singapore. 71 Bukit Tinggi Rd. Tel: 65-6875-1519. Fax: 65-6875-1516. EST+13.
www.cis.edu.sg   E-mail: admissions@cis.edu.sg
Gary Pettigrew, Head Prin.
> Col Prep. IB PYP. IB MYP. IB Diploma. Curr—Intl Can. Feat—Chin Fr Environ_Sci Econ Studio_Art Drama Music Bus. Supp—ESL.
> Enr 1200.
> Fac 120.
> Est 1989. Sem (Aug-June).

CHATSWORTH INTERNATIONAL SCHOOL

Day — Coed Gr PS-12

Singapore 229313, Singapore. 37 Emerald Hill Rd. Tel: 65-6737-5955. Fax: 65-6737-5655. EST+13.
www.chatsworth-international.com
E-mail: information@chatsworth-international.com
Jennifer Gay, Prin. BA.
> Col Prep. Curr—UK US. Exams—IGCSE A-level. Feat—Humanities Chin Fr Comp_Sci Studio_Art Music. Supp—ESL.
> Enr 630.
> Fac 55.
> Est 1994. Quar (Aug-June). Assoc: WASC.

DOVER COURT PREPARATORY SCHOOL

Day — Coed Gr PS-9

Singapore 139644, Singapore. Dover Rd. Tel: 65-6775-7664. Fax: 65-6777-4165. EST+13.
www.dovercourt.edu.sg   E-mail: admin@dovercourt.edu.sg

Maureen Roach, Dir.
   Gen Acad. Curr—UK. **Supp**—ESL.
   Enr 650.
   Tui '05-'06: Day $3500-5600.
   Est 1971. Tri (Aug-July).

ETON HOUSE INTERNATIONAL SCHOOL
Day — Coed Gr PS-6

Singapore 439501, Singapore. 51 Broadrick Rd. Tel: 65-6346-6922. Fax: 65-6346-6522. EST+13.
www.etonhouse.com.sg   E-mail: enquiry@etonhouse.com.sg
John Cooley, Prin. BA, BEd. **Caroline Barrett, Adm.**
   Pre-Prep. IB PYP. Curr—Intl UK. **Bilingual**—Chin. **Feat**—Japan Hindi Malay Studio_Art Music. **Supp**—ESL LD Rem_Math Rem_Read.
   Sports—X-country Gymnastics Soccer. **Activities**—Arts.
   Enr 440. B 230. G 210. Elem 440. US 26. Host 80. Other 334. Accepted: 95%. Yield: 95%. Avg class size: 22.
   Fac 53. M 6. F 47. Host 15. Other 38. Adv Deg: 3%.
   Grad '05—12. Prep—12.
   Tui '05-'06: Day S$12,000-13,400 (+S$1500).
   Summer: Rec. Tui Day S$250/wk. 8 wks.
   Bldgs 2. Class rms 25. Lib 7000 vols. Lang labs 4. Comp labs 1. Auds 1. Art studios 1. Music studios 1. Fields 2. Courts 1.
   Est 1995. Inc. Sem (Aug-June).

Eton House provides a bilingual, multicultural education within the framework of the British National Curriculum. Beginning in preschool (at age 3), EHIS emphasizes English and Mandarin Chinese language skills. Children learn to read and write in both languages in kindergarten, at which time the school introduces Japanese, Hindi and Malay language courses. Older boys and girls develop research, public speaking and computer skills.

An extensive after-school care and activities schedule includes sports, arts and crafts, and language study.

INTERNATIONAL COMMUNITY SCHOOL
Day — Coed Gr PS-12

Singapore 099450, Singapore. 514 Kampong Bahru Rd. Tel: 65-6324-4287. Fax: 65-6324-4050. EST+13.
www.ics.edu.sg   E-mail: info@ics.edu.sg
Joe Beeson, Prin.
   Col Prep. Curr—US. **Exams**—ACT CEEB TOEFL. **Feat**—British_Lit Chin Span Anat Comp_Sci Econ Govt Bible Fine_Arts Speech. **Supp**—ESL Tut.
   Enr 200. Accepted: 95%. Avg class size: 18.
   Fac 30.
   Grad '05—9. Col—8. US Col—5. (John Brown, Pensacola Christian, VA Milit, Union U). Avg SAT: M/V—1225. Avg ACT: 28.
   Tui '06-'07: Day S$13,122-18,615 (+S$1150).

Plant val S$1,900,000. Bldgs 3. Class rms 18. Lib 10,000 vols. Sci labs 1. Comp labs 1. Auds 1. Art studios 1. Courts 1.
Est 1993. Nonprofit. Nondenom Christian. Quar (Aug-June). Assoc: WASC.

Founded by a group of parents to meet the needs of corporate and missionary expatriate families, ICS lies in the south-central part of the city near Sentosa Island. The school offers a US-based curriculum to students from more than a dozen countries.

At the elementary (grades pre-K-6) and middle school (grades 7 and 8) levels, teachers employ a hands-on approach and integrate Bible instruction. The high school program features course work in such areas as British literature, consumer math and Mandarin, as well as various electives. Students may prepare for both the SAT and the ACT.

ISS INTERNATIONAL SCHOOL SINGAPORE
Day — Coed Gr PS-12

Singapore 109355, Singapore. 21 Preston Rd. Tel: 65-6475-4188. Fax: 65-6273-7065. EST+13.
www.iss.edu.sg   E-mail: admissions@iss.edu.sg
Tony Race, Head. BA, MA. **Angelia Toh, Adm.**

> **Col Prep. IB PYP. IB MYP. IB Diploma. Curr**—Intl. **Exams**—CEEB IGCSE. **Feat**—Chin Fr Japan Span Comp_Sci Asian_Stud Studio_Art Drama Music. **Supp**—Dev_Read ESL LD Rem_Math.
> **Sports**—Badminton Basket Bowl Rugby Soccer Squash Swim Track Volley. **Activities**—Acad Rec Service.
> **Enr 502.** B 274. G 228. Elem 327. Sec 175. US 26. Host 18. Other 458. Accepted: 95%. Avg class size: 16.
> **Fac 57.** M 15/2. F 33/7. US 10. Host 3. Other 44. Adv Deg: 10%.
> **Tui '05-'06: Day S$10,080-20,580.**
> **Summer:** Acad Enrich Rec. Tui Day S$400/2-wk ses. 4 wks.
> Bldgs 10. Class rms 30. 2 Libs 20,000 vols. Sci labs 2.
> **Est 1981.** Nonprofit. Sem (Aug-June).

ISS conducts the full International Baccalaureate curriculum: IB PYP, IB MYP and IB Diploma. Members of the international student body may alternatively pursue the American high school diploma or the IGCSE certificate. Pupils in the American high school diploma track who also sit for individual IB Diploma certificates may graduate with an advanced diploma.

An intensive English as a Second Language program, usually completed within one year, prepares non-English speakers for mainstream class work.

OVERSEAS FAMILY SCHOOL
Day — Coed Gr K-JC

Singapore 238515, Singapore. 25F Paterson Rd. Tel: 65-6738-0211. Fax: 65-6733-8825. EST+13.
www.ofs.edu.sg   E-mail: soma_mathews@ofs.edu.sg
Irene Chee, Exec Dir. Bhim M. Mozoomdar, Head.

Col Prep. IB PYP. IB MYP. IB Diploma. Curr—Intl UK US. **Exams**—CEEB IGCSE.
   Feat—Chin Fr Ger Japan Span Comp_Sci Econ Studio_Art Drama Bus.
   Supp—Dev_Read EFL ESL Rem_Math Rem_Read Rev Tut.
Sports—Basket Rugby Soccer Softball Volley. **Activities**—Arts.
Enr 2363. B 1179. G 1184. Elem 1857. Sec 506. US 212. Host 64. Other 2087.
   Accepted: 100%.
Fac 220. M 76/2. F 120/22. US 24. Host 17. Other 179. Adv Deg: 14%.
Grad '05—94.
Tui '05-'06: Day S$16,000-22,000.
Summer: Acad Enrich. Tui Day S$800-1600. 4 wks.
Bldgs 4. Class rms 105. Libs 2. Sci labs 1. Comp labs 3. Art studios 1. Music studios
   5. Pools 1.
Est 1991. Sem (Aug-June). Assoc: WASC.

Enrolling pupils from more than 50 countries, OFS provides an English-language education that prepares students to return to their national systems or to enter college in the US, Europe, Japan or Australia, among other countries. Students lacking fluency in English participate (for an additional fee) in the school's ESL program, and all children in grades 1-8 study a second language: either French, Japanese, Mandarin, Spanish or German. The curriculum maintains an international focus throughout, and all high schoolers take the IGCSE or IB exams prior to graduation.

OFS also operates a two-year college program featuring courses similar in content and difficulty to those offered during the first two years at California State University-Dominguez Hills.

SINGAPORE AMERICAN SCHOOL
Day — Coed Gr PS-12

Singapore 738547, Singapore. 40 Woodlands St 41. Tel: 65-6363-3403. Fax: 65-6363-3408. EST+13.
www.sas.edu.sg   E-mail: sasinfo@sas.edu.sg
Robert Gross, Supt.
   Col Prep. Gen Acad. Curr—US. **Exams**—CEEB. **Supp**—ESL.
   Enr 2900.
   Fac 300.
   Tui '05-'06: Day S$18,950-23,100 (+S$6500).
   Est 1956. Nonprofit. Sem (Aug-June). Assoc: A/OPR/OS EARCOS WASC.

TANGLIN TRUST SCHOOL
Day — Coed Ages 3-18

Singapore 139299, Singapore. Portsdown Rd. Tel: 65-67780771. Fax: 65-67775862. EST+11.
www.tts.edu.sg   E-mail: devmt@tts.edu.sg
Ronald Stones, Head. BSc, MBA, MBE.
   Col Prep. Gen Acad. Curr—UK. **Exams**—GCSE AS-level A-level. **Feat**—Chin Fr
      Ger Lat Span Comp_Sci Econ Psych Govt & Pol Studio_Art Drama Music Bus.
   Activities—Acad Arts Media Rec.

Enr 1950. Avg class size: 24.
Fac 170.
Tui '05-'06: Day S$15,600-22,275 (+S$4450).
Bldgs 4. Libs 3. Sci labs 2. Comp labs 3. Auds 3. Art studios 3. Music studios 3. Dance studios 3. Gyms 1. Fields 3. Pools 2.
Est 1925. Nonprofit. Tri (Sept-July).

This British-style school provides a broad-based curriculum that begins with a nursery program and extends through Sixth Form A levels. In addition to the core curriculum, Tanglin places emphasis upon the areas of music, art, information technology and physical education. Although the school accepts English-speaking pupils of all nationalities, most children enroll from the United Kingdom.

UNITED WORLD COLLEGE OF SOUTH EAST ASIA
Bdg — Coed Gr 6-12; Day — Coed PS-12

Singapore 139654, Singapore. 1207 Dover Rd. Tel: 65-6775-5344. Fax: 65-6778-5846. EST+13.
www.uwcsea.edu.sg   E-mail: info@uwcsea.edu.sg
Julian Whiteley, Head. BSc, MBA. **David Shephard, Adm.**
Col Prep. IB Diploma. **Curr**—Intl. **Exams**—GCSE. **AP**—Span. **Feat**—Chin Fr Ger Japan Hindi Korean Environ_Sci Comp_Sci Econ Pol_Sci Studio_Art Drama Music Bus. **Supp**—ESL.
Sports—Badminton Basket F_Hockey Golf Gymnastics Soccer Swim Tennis Track. **Activities**—Arts Rec Service.
Enr 2855. Elem 1521. Sec 1334. US 222. Host 184. Other 2449. Avg class size: 20.
Grad '05—263. Col—256. US Col—66.
Tui '05-'06: Bdg S$40,225 (+S$2100). **Day S$17,010-20,175** (+S$2100).
Est 1975. Tri (Aug-June).

UWCSEA is one of 10 related UWC international schools dedicated to promoting international understanding through education. The organization has campuses in Britain, Canada, Hong Kong, India, Italy, Norway, Singapore, Swaziland, the US and Venezuela, and each school is a community representing more than 70 countries. The program covers all elementary and secondary grades, and students follow the International Baccalaureate Diploma curriculum in grades 11 and 12.

Community service, outdoor programs and events pertaining to global issues supplement the school's academic offerings.

SOUTH KOREA

Sq. Miles: 38,000 (About the size of Indiana). **Country Pop:** 48,422,644 (2005). **Capital:** Seoul, pop. 10,300,000 (2004). **Terrain:** Partially forested mountain ranges separated by deep, narrow valleys; cultivated plains along the coasts, particularly in the west and south. **Ethnic Group(s):** Korean Chinese. **Religion(s):** Christian Buddhist Shamanist Confucian. **Official Language(s):** Korean. **Government:** Republic. **Independence:** 1945 (from Japan). **GDP:** $680.1 billion (2004). Agriculture 3%. Industry 41%. Services 56%. **Currency:** South Korean Won (W).

INTERNATIONAL SCHOOL OF BUSAN
Day — Coed Gr PS-8

Busan, South Korea. 1492-12 Jung-2-Dong, Haeundae-gu. Tel: 82-51-742-3332. Fax: 82-51-742-3375. EST+14.
www.ispusan.co.kr   E-mail: ispusan@ispusan.co.kr
Stephen Palmer, Prin. BSc.
   Gen Acad. Curr—Intl. **Feat**—Span Korean Comp_Sci Studio_Art Music. **Supp**—ESL.
   Enr 94. B 45. G 49. Elem 94. US 21. Host 12. Other 61.
   Fac 13. M 2/1. F 7/3.
   Tui '05-'06: Day W5,560,000-14,780,000 (+W1,050,000-1,110,000).
   Bldgs 1. Class rms 14. Lib 10,000 vols. Sci labs 1. Comp labs 1. Auds 1. Art studios 1. Music studios 1. Courts 1.
   Est 1983. Nonprofit. Tri (Aug-June). Assoc: ECIS.

Serving expatriate and qualified Korean national children, this elementary school combines methodologies used throughout the world, particularly those found in English-speaking nations such as England, the US, Australia, Canada and New Zealand. ISB offers a curriculum that enables children to move on to other international schools or return to the home country with a minimum of difficulty. The school, which limits class size to 15 pupils, maintains a strong computer program and places an emphasis on arts appreciation.

Scheduled to meet each Monday, Wednesday and Thursday, afternoon activities include sports, art, tae kwon do and dance.

INTERNATIONAL CHRISTIAN SCHOOL PYONGTAEK
Day — Coed Gr K-12

Pyongtaek 450-600, South Korea. PO Box 24. Tel: 82-31-651-1376. Fax: 82-31-653-1375. EST+14.
www.ics-stn.org   E-mail: johnpeterson@nics.org
John L. Peterson, Dir.
   Col Prep. Curr—US. **Feat**—Relig. **Supp**—ESL.
   Tui '05-'06: Day W6,345,000-6,975,000 (+W550,000).
   Est 1983. Nondenom Christian. Sem (Sept-June). Assoc: EARCOS WASC.

INTERNATIONAL CHRISTIAN SCHOOL OF SEOUL
Day — Coed Gr K-12

Seoul 140-022, South Korea. 1-206 Yongsan-dong 2 ga, Yongsan-gu. Tel: 82-2-773-1993. Fax: 82-2-773-2976. EST+14.

www.icseoul.org   E-mail: admissions@icseoul.org
Jeff Pinnow, Dir.
   Col Prep. Curr—US. **Exams**—CEEB. **AP**—Stats. **Feat**—Span Comp_Sci Bible
      Studio_Art. **Supp**—ESL.
   Enr 520.
   Tui '05-'06: Day W9,500,000-10,800,000 (+W700,000-2,400,000).
   Est 1990. Quar (Aug-May). Assoc: EARCOS WASC.

SEOUL FOREIGN SCHOOL

Day — Coed Gr PS-12

Seoul 120-113, South Korea. 55 Yunhi-Dong, Suhdaemoon-ku. Tel: 82-2-335-3100.
   Fax: 82-2-335-1857. EST+14.
www.sfs.or.kr   E-mail: sfsoffice@sfs.or.kr
Harlan E. Lyso, Head. PhD. Esther Kim Myong, Adm.
   Col Prep. IB Diploma. Curr—Intl UK US. **Exams**—ACT AP CEEB. **AP**—Calc
      US_Hist. **Feat**—Fr Span Korean Comp_Sci Econ Psych Relig Studio_Art
      Drama Music. **Supp**—ESL Rem_Read Tut.
   Sports—Basket X-country Soccer Swim Tennis Volley. **Activities**—Arts Govt/Pol
      Media.
   Enr 1344. B 656. G 688. Elem 988. Sec 356. US 790. Other 554. Accepted: 58%.
      Yield: 985%. Avg class size: 19.
   Fac 123. M 41. F 68/14. US 71. Host 5. Other 47. Adv Deg: 56%.
   Grad '05—85. US Col—62. (NYU 6, Parsons Sch of Design 3, U of MI 3, Boston
      Col 2, Wm & Mary 2, U of PA 2). Avg SAT: M/V—1240, Essay—600.
   Tui '05-'06: Day $8460-20,370. Aid: 47 pupils ($530,000).
   Bldgs 6. Class rms 96. 3 Libs 54,000 vols. Sci labs 4. Comp labs 5. Auds 2. Art
      studios 1. Music studios 3. Dance studios 1. Perf arts ctrs 1. Gyms 2. Fields 1.
      Courts 4. Tennis courts 4. Pools 1.
   Est 1912. Nonprofit. Nondenom Christian. Sem (Aug-June). Assoc: EARCOS
      WASC.

The oldest English-language school in Korea, SFS serves a predominantly
American enrollment, although many other nations are represented. At the elementary level, children may follow either a US- or a UK-style program. The full American curriculum comprises SAT test preparation, an array of elective offerings and
some Advanced Placement courses. The school also provides course work leading
to the International Baccalaureate Diploma.

In addition to its academic programs, the school plans excursions to sites of
historical, cultural, economic and manufacturing interest throughout the country.
Korea Emphasis Week allows pupils to acquaint themselves with local customs,
culture and history.

SEOUL INTERNATIONAL SCHOOL

Day — Coed Gr PS-12

Seoul 138-600, South Korea. Songpa PO Box 47. Tel: 82-2-2233-4551. Fax: 82-31-
   759-5133. EST+14.
www.sis-lhs.gyeonggi.kr   E-mail: kimka@siskorea.or.kr

Kim Hyung-Shik, Head. EdD.
  Col Prep. Curr—Intl. **Exams**—AP CEEB. **AP**—Eng Calc Bio Chem Environ_Sci Physics Eur_Hist US_Hist Psych Studio_Art. **Feat**—British_Lit Chin Span Comp_Sci E_Asian_Stud Ceramics Drama Music. **Supp**—ESL.
  Fac 83.
  Tui '05-'06: Day $12,700-15,700.
  Est 1973. Inc. Sem (Aug-June). Assoc: EARCOS WASC.

TAEJON CHRISTIAN INTERNATIONAL SCHOOL
Bdg — Coed Gr 6-12; Day — Coed K-12

Taejon 306-010, South Korea. 210-1 O-Jung Dong, PO Box 310, Daeduck Ku. Tel: 82-42-633-3663. Fax: 82-42-631-5732. EST+14.
www.tcis.or.kr E-mail: tcisinfo@tcis.or.kr
Thomas J. Penland, Head. BS, MEd, EdD.
  Col Prep. IB Diploma. Curr—Intl US. **Exams**—AP CEEB. **AP**—Eng Calc Stats Comp_Sci Bio Chem Studio_Art. **Feat**—Drama Music. **Supp**—ESL.
  Enr 600.
  Fac 50.
  Tui '05-'06: Bdg W6826-8613. Day W4,444-6,231.
  Est 1958. Nonprofit. Quar (Aug-June). Assoc: EARCOS WASC.

INDIANHEAD INTERNATIONAL SCHOOL
Bdg — Coed Gr 7-12; Day — Coed PS-12

Uijeongbu City, Gyeonggi-Do 480-701, South Korea. 233-3 Howon-Dong. Tel: 82-31-870-3475. Fax: 82-31-826-3476. EST+14.
www.iis.or.kr E-mail: es@iis.or.kr
Jeong Jin Park, Pres. Edmund Fitzgerald, Prin.
  Col Prep. Curr—US. **Exams**—AP CEEB TOEFL. **AP**—Span Calc Chem Physics Studio_Art. **Feat**—Comp_Sci Econ Sociol Music. **Supp**—Dev_Read ESL.
  Sports—Basket Soccer Volley. **Activities**—Acad Arts Service.
  Enr 161. Elem 94. Sec 67. US 113. Host 18. Other 30. Avg class size: 11.
  Fac 28. M 11/1. F 15/1. US 6. Host 5. Other 17.
  Grad '05—11. Col—11. US Col—10. (U of MI, U of IL-Urbana, Pepperdine, RI Sch of Design, Parsons Sch of Design). Avg SAT: M/V—1109.
  Tui '05-'06: Day W13,590,000-14,900,000.
  Summer: Enrich. Tui Day $2000. 4 wks.
  Bldgs 3. Class rms 23. Libs 1. Sci labs 3. Lang labs 4. Comp labs 3. Auds 1. Art studios 2. Music studios 8. Dance studios 1. Gyms 1. Fields 1. Courts 1.
  Est 1979. Nonprofit. Quar (Aug-June). Assoc: EARCOS WASC.

Founded as an elementary school to meet the needs of the local expatriate community, Indianhead relocated to a 20-acre campus in 1996 to accommodate expansion of its academic program and its physical plant.

The school's early childhood center provides a developmentally appropriate curriculum for children ages 3-6. Elementary-level instruction emphasizes basic academic skills while providing a foundation in phonics, math and critical-thinking skills. Computer science, art and music classes supplement traditional elementary subjects. In the middle school, pupils continue to develop fundamental learning skills and also gain familiarity with more abstract concepts. High school course work meets the needs of both college-bound students and those wishing to pursue nonacademic careers.

INTERNATIONAL CHRISTIAN SCHOOL
Day — Coed Gr PS-12

Uijongbu 480-600, South Korea. PO Box 23. Tel: 82-31-855-1277. Fax: 82-31-872-1458. EST+14.

Contact: PSC 311, Box 44, APO, AP 96258.

www.ics-ujb.org   E-mail: ics_ujb@hotmail.com

Rex Freel, Dir. MEd. **Bible Jang, Adm.**

    Gen Acad. Curr—US. **Feat**—Fr Span Korean Comp_Sci Music. **Supp**—ESL.

    Enr 268. Elem 187. Sec 81.

    Fac 21. US 20. Other 1.

    Tui '06-'07: Day W6,437,200-7,375,500 (+$500).

    Summer: Acad Rem. 3 wks.

    Bldgs 2. Class rms 15. Libs 1. Sci labs 1. Comp labs 1.

    Est 1983. Nonprofit. Nondenom Christian. Sem (Aug-June). Assoc: EARCOS WASC.

Founded as a ministry of the Liberty Mission of Korea, ICS-UJB conducts a basic US-style curriculum with a spiritual emphasis. In addition to the Uijongbu location, the school maintains campuses in Seoul and Pyong-Taek. Computer literacy and programming courses, as well as basic, intermediate and intensive English as a Second Language instruction, are noteworthy aspects of the curriculum. (ESL courses result in an additional fee.)

Students may take part in the following sports: cross-country, basketball, volleyball, soccer and cheerleading.

SRI LANKA

Sq. Miles: 25,332 (About the size of West Virginia). **Country Pop:** 20,064,776 (2005). **Capital:** Colombo, pop. 1,300,000 (2005). **Terrain:** Coastal plains in the northern third of country; hills and mountains in south. **Ethnic Group(s):** Sinhalese Tamil Muslim. **Religion(s):** Buddhist Hindu Muslim Christian. **Official Language(s):** Sinhala Tamil. **Other Language(s):** English. **Government:** Republic. **Independence:** 1948 (from United Kingdom). **GDP:** $18.4 billion (2003). Agriculture 20%. Industry 26%. Services 54%. **Currency:** Sri Lankan Rupee (SLRs).

THE OVERSEAS SCHOOL OF COLOMBO
Day — Coed Gr PS-12

Battaramulla, Sri Lanka. Pellawatte, PO Box 9. Tel: 94-11-2784920. Fax: 94-11-2784999. EST+11.
www.osc.lk   E-mail: admin@osc.lk
Laurie McLellan, Head. BA, DipEd, MA. Lilamanie de Zoysa, Adm.

   Col Prep. IB PYP. IB MYP. IB Diploma. Curr—Intl. Exams—IGCSE. Feat—Fr Span Drama Music. Supp—ESL LD.
   Sports—Basket Soccer Swim Track. Activities—Arts Govt/Pol Service.
   Enr 401. B 197. G 204. Elem 288. Sec 113. US 38. Host 52. Other 311. Avg class size: 24.
   Fac 57. M 19/1. F 35/2. US 8. Host 18. Other 31. Adv Deg: 31%.
   Grad '05—31. US Col—3. (Reed, U of FL, Marymount Col-NY).
   Tui '05-'06: Day $5635-14,099 (+$2875).
   Bldgs 6. Class rms 50. 2 Libs 20,000 vols. Sci labs 6. Comp labs 3. Auds 1. Art studios 2. Arts ctrs 1. Gyms 1. Fields 2. Pools 1.
   Est 1957. Nonprofit. Sem (Aug-June). Assoc: A/OPR/OS CIS MSA.

Conducting an international program designed to prepare students for either a return to the home country's school system or university matriculation, OSC enrolls pupils from approximately 30 nations. In grades K-8, children follow a curriculum based on the International Baccalaureate Primary Years and Middle Years programs. The IGCSE and the IB Diploma course of studies form the core of the program in grades 9-12, with the first two years devoted to the IGCSE and the final two years focused on IB preparation.

Students with language or learning difficulties may obtain assistance through the school's special-education department.

COLOMBO INTERNATIONAL SCHOOL
Day — Coed Gr PS-13

Colombo 7, Sri Lanka. 28 Gregory's Rd. Tel: 94-11-2697587. Fax: 94-11-2699592. EST+11.
www.cis.lk   E-mail: principal@cis.lk
David C. Sanders, Prin. BSc, MEd. Cheryl Thomasz, Adm.

   Col Prep. Gen Acad. Curr—UK. Exams—CEEB TOEFL O-level AS-level A-level. Feat—Fr Ger Sinhala Tamil Econ Studio_Art Accounting Bus. Supp—ESL Rem_Math Rem_Read.
   Sports—Badminton Basket F_Hockey Gymnastics Rugby Soccer Tennis. Activities—Acad Arts Service.
   Enr 1400. B 750. G 650. Elem 950. Sec 450. US 5. Host 1100. Other 295. Accepted: 70%. Yield: 90%. Avg class size: 24.
   Fac 160. M 30. F 125/5. Host 130. Other 30. Adv Deg: 12%.
   Grad '05—120. Col—110. US Col—10. (U of PA 2, GA Inst of Tech 1, Harvard 1, U of MD-Col Park 1, U of AZ 1, MI St 1). Avg SAT: M/V—1250, Essay—600.
   Tui '05-'06: Day $2500. Aid: 15 pupils ($25,000).
   Plant val $4,000,000. Class rms 60. 3 Libs 30,000 vols. Sci labs 7. Comp labs 3. Auds 1. Art studios 3. Gyms 1. Fields 1. Courts 2. Pools 2.
   Est 1982. Inc. Tri (Aug-July).

Offering an elementary and secondary English-language program, CIS follows the British academic system. Older students typically prepare for the GCE and GCSE examinations; the school can, however, also provide preparation for the SAT, thereby allowing graduates to enter universities throughout the world. The infant program (ages 3-6) consists of a play group and a kindergarten and offers instruction in music, art and drama. The junior section follows, providing a standard curriculum supplemented by computer, French, Sinhala and Tamil classes.

Students in the senior section take a varied three-year curriculum before selecting eight to 11 subjects for study at the GCSE level. Pupils may not proceed to the Sixth Form A-level courses until they have passed the GCE O-, AS- or A-level exams. Extracurricular pursuits consist of cultural activities, athletics, and community service opportunities at hospitals, orphanages and other sites.

ELIZABETH MOIR SCHOOL
Day — Coed Gr PS-12

Colombo 5, Sri Lanka. 4/20 Thalakotuwa Gardens. Tel: 94-11-2512275. Fax: 94-11-2512109. EST+11.
www.eureka.lk/moir   E-mail: moir@eureka.lk
Elizabeth Moir, Head. MA, DipEd.
  Col Prep. Curr—UK. **Exams**—O-level AS-level A-level. **Feat**—Fr Sinhala Tamil Comp_Sci Econ.
  Tri (Aug-July).

TAIWAN

Sq. Miles: 14,000 (About the size of West Virginia). **Country Pop:** 22,894,384 (2005). **Capital:** Taipei, pop. 2,600,000 (2004). **Terrain:** Largely mountainous. **Ethnic Group(s):** Taiwanese Chinese Aborigine. **Religion(s):** Buddhist Confucian Taoist Christian. **Official Language(s):** Mandarin. **Other Language(s):** Taiwanese Hakka. **Government:** Democracy. **GDP:** $355 billion (2004). Agriculture 2%. Industry 25%. Services 73%. **Currency:** Taiwanese New Dollar (NT$).

NATIONAL EXPERIMENTAL HIGH SCHOOL
BILINGUAL DEPARTMENT
Day — Coed Gr 1-12

Hsinchu 300, Taiwan. Jieshou Rd. Tel: 886-3-5777011. Fax: 886-3-5785565. EST+13.
http://bilingual.nehs.hc.edu.tw   E-mail: bilingual@mail.nehs.hc.edu.tw
Rong-feng Wu, Prin. Christine Huang, Dir. Christine Yin, Adm.
  Col Prep. Curr—US. **Bilingual**—Chin. **Exams**—ACT AP CEEB SSAT. **AP**—Eng Calc Bio Chem Environ_Sci Physics Eur_Hist US_Hist Econ Psych. **Feat**—Chin Fr Japan Govt Studio_Art Drama Music Bus Journ. **Supp**—Rem_Read.

Enr 537. Avg class size: 20.
Fac 56. US 17. Host 36. Other 3. Adv Deg: 58%.
Grad '05—46. Col—45. US Col—12. (Stanford, U of CA-Berkeley, Purdue, North-western, U of CA-Irvine, U of MI). , Essay—622
Bldgs 2. Class rms 21. Lib 55,000 vols. Sci labs 4. Comp labs 1. Auds 1. Art studios 2. Music studios 2. Dance studios 1. Gyms 1. Fields 1. Courts 12. Pools 2.
Est 1983. Sem (Aug-June).

The Bilingual Department, which operates alongside a traditional Taiwanese program that follows the national curriculum and prepares boys and girls for domestic colleges, provides American-based programs for English-speaking children. NEHS' student body in this section consists largely of ethnic Chinese children who were raised overseas and can speak both English and Chinese, although English is generally the first language. The curriculum's design enables departing students to either pursue Taiwanese education or continue Western-style education (and eventually attend college) overseas, usually in the US.

Students in the bilingual program take compulsory Chinese language (grades 1-12) and Chinese social studies (grades 1-8) courses in Mandarin. The college preparatory curriculum also includes requirements in such areas as math, science, US history and economics. Pupils in this section may receive preparation for the US College Boards, in addition to the ACT and AP exams. Various electives, honors and AP courses, and extracurricular activities are available at the high school level.

AMERICAN SCHOOL IN TAICHUNG

Bdg — Coed Gr 9-12; Day — Coed PS-12

Taichung 40661, Taiwan. 21-1 Chu Yuan Ln, Pei-Tun. Tel: 886-4-2239-7532. Fax: 886-4-2239-7520. EST+13.
www.ast.tc.edu.tw   E-mail: director@ast.tc.edu.tw
Irwin Stein, Dir. BA, MA.
   Col Prep. Curr—US. **Exams**—ACT CEEB. **Feat**—British_Lit Chin Span Stats Environ_Sci Comp_Sci Intl_Relations Studio_Art Drama Music. **Supp**—ESL.
   Enr 185. US 21. Host 19. Other 145. Avg class size: 17.
   Fac 29. M 15. F 13/1. Host 2. Other 27.
   Summer: Acad Enrich. Tui Day $1000. 4 wks.
   Bldgs 10. Dorms 2. Dorm rms 12. Class rms 24. Libs 1. Sci labs 2. Comp labs 2. Theaters 1. Art studios 1. Music studios 2. Fields 1. Courts 1.
   Est 1989. Quar (Aug-June). Assoc: EARCOS WASC.

Founded with a student body of six and originally housed in a remodeled shoe factory, LAS has grown substantially over the years. A largely expatriate enrollment follows a US-style program at all grade levels. Advanced Placement courses are part of the curriculum when student interest exists, and graduates commonly matriculate at American colleges.

MORRISON CHRISTIAN ACADEMY

Bdg — Coed Gr 9-12; Day — Coed K-12

Taichung 406, Taiwan. 136-1 Shui Nan Rd. Tel: 886-4-2292-3927. Fax: 886-4-2292-1174. EST+13.

www.mca.org.tw   E-mail: morrison@mca.org.tw

Tim McGill, Supt. MA. **Eloise Harder, Jill de Boer & Sue Chang, Adms.**

  Col Prep. Curr—US. **Exams**—AP CEEB. **AP**—Eng Calc Bio Chem US_Hist. **Feat**—Chin Span Comp_Sci Econ Psych Sociol Bible Ceramics Studio_Art Orchestra. **Supp**—ESL LD.

  Sports—Basket Soccer Track Volley Wrestling. **Activities**—Acad Arts Cultural/ Relig.

  Enr 916. B 42/437. G 36/401. Avg class size: 23.

  Fac 116. M 42/4. F 51/19. US 78. Host 12. Other 26. Adv Deg: 37%.

  Grad '05—55. Col—45. US Col—37. (USC 3, U of WA 3, Santa Monica 2, U of IL-Urbana 2, U of MI 2, Wheaton-MA 2). Avg SAT: M/V—1180, Essay—539.

  Tui '05-'06: Bdg $18,830. Day $8240-9850.

  Bldgs 12. Dorms 5. Dorm rms 40. Class rms 60. 5 Libs 60,000 vols. Sci labs 6. Comp labs 5. Auds 1. Gyms 4. Fields 4. Courts 5. Pools 1.

  Est 1952. Nonprofit. Nondenom Christian. Sem (Aug-June). Assoc: EARCOS WASC.

MCA offers an American-based program on three separate campuses. The curriculum is religiously oriented, with Bible courses required for every student at all grade levels. Advanced Placement courses are available in several disciplines at the high school level, and pupils may take up to three years of Chinese. The majority of students are American, with about 40 percent coming from missionary homes.

Aside from the Taichung campus, which serves pupils in grades K-12, the academy operates programs in Taipei (grades K-9) and Kaohsiung (grades K-8).

DOMINICAN INTERNATIONAL SCHOOL

Day — Coed Gr K-12

Taipei 104, Taiwan. 76 Tah Chih St. Tel: 886-2-2533-8451. Fax: 886-2-2533-0914. EST+13.

www.dishs.tp.edu.tw   E-mail: dspt@sirius.com

Sr. Zenaida T. Ancheta, OP, Dir.

  Col Prep. Gen Acad. Curr—US. **Exams**—CEEB. **Feat**—Chin Fr Span Relig. **Supp**—ESL.

  Sports—Volley. **Activities**—Service.

  Enr 386. B 203. G 183. Elem 257. Sec 129. US 46. Other 340. Accepted: 90%. Yield: 83%. Avg class size: 25.

  Fac 38. M 14. F 19/5. Adv Deg: 31%.

  Grad '05—90. US Col—15. (Purdue 6, U of WI-Madison 2, U of WA 1, SUNY-Stony Brook 1, U of CA-Riverside 1, U of OR 1). Avg SAT: M/V—1170, Essay—510.

  Tui '05-'06: Day NT$247,302-297,236.

  Bldgs 5. Class rms 40. Libs 2. Chapels 1. Sci labs 1. Lang labs 4. Comp labs 4. Auds 1. Theaters 1. Art studios 1. Music studios 3. Dance studios 1. Gyms 1. Fields 1. Courts 2.

  Est 1957. Nonprofit. Roman Catholic. Quar (Aug-May). Assoc: EARCOS.

Operated by the Dominican Sisters, DIS provides an American-style curriculum for an enrollment that is roughly half American. Religious education and community service are integral to the curriculum.

TAIPEI AMERICAN SCHOOL

Day — Coed Gr K-12

Taipei 111, Taiwan. 800 Chung Shan N Rd, Section 6, Shihliin District. Tel: 886-2-2873-9900. Fax: 886-2-2873-1641. EST+13.
www.tas.edu.tw   E-mail: admissions@tas.edu.tw
Charles C. Hanna, Supt.

Col Prep. IB Diploma. Curr—Intl US. Exams—AP CEEB. AP—Eng Fr Span Calc Comp_Sci Bio Chem Environ_Sci Physics US_Hist Econ Art_Hist Studio_Art. Feat—Chin Japan Psych Asian_Stud Theater_Arts. Supp—ESL.

Enr 2200. B 1157. G 1043.

Fac 210. M 100. F 110.

Tui '05-'06: Day NT$351,100-389,700 (+NT$160,000-167,000).

Est 1949. Nonprofit. Quar (Aug-June). Assoc: A/OPR/OS EARCOS WASC.

TAIPEI EUROPEAN SCHOOL

Day — Coed Gr PS-12

Taipei 111, Taiwan. 31 Chien Yeh Rd, Yang Ming Shan. Tel: 886-2-2862-2920. Fax: 886-2-2862-1458. EST+13.
www.taipeieuropeanschool.com   E-mail: registrar@tes.tp.edu.tw
John Nixon, CEO. William Butcher, Adm.

Col Prep. Gen Acad. IB Diploma. Curr—Intl Nat UK. Exams—IGCSE. Feat—Chin Fr Ger Comp_Sci Studio_Art Drama. Supp—ESL.

Sports—Basket Soccer Softball Volley.

Enr 920. B 477. G 443. Elem 767. Sec 153. US 210. Other 710. Accepted: 85%. Yield: 85%. Avg class size: 18.

Fac 160. M 67. F 93. Adv Deg: 30%.

Grad '05—18. US Col—2. (U of AZ, U of WA).

Tui '05-'06: Day $12,700.

Bldgs 3. Class rms 68. Libs 3. Sci labs 4. Lang labs 6. Comp labs 5. Auds 2. Theaters 1. Art studios 3. Gyms 2. Fields 3. Courts 2.

Est 1990. Sem (Aug-June).

Sharing its secondary and high school campus with two affiliated international schools, Deutsche Schule Taipei and Ecole Francais de Taipei, TES British School Section provides a UK-style program for pupils from approximately 30 nations. Although programming is based upon the British curriculum, the program has been modified to suit the varied student community. Chinese language and culture courses begin at age 4, while French language classes commence at age 8. Boys and girls typically study between five and eight subjects as they prepare for the IGCSE examinations. During the final two years of high school, students pursue the IB Diploma.

The infant and junior school occupies separate quarters at 731 Wen Lin Rd., Shihlin Taipei.

THAILAND

Sq. Miles: 198,114 (Slightly smaller than Texas). **Country Pop:** 65,444,371 (2005). **Capital:** Bangkok, pop. 9,668,854 (2005). **Terrain:** Densely populated central plain; northeastern plateau; mountain range in the west. **Ethnic Group(s):** Thai. **Religion(s):** Buddhist Muslim Christian Hindu Brahmin. **Official Language(s):** Thai. **Other Language(s):** English. **Government:** Constitutional Monarchy. **Per Capita Income:** $2578 (2004). **GDP:** $163 billion (2004). Agriculture 9%. Industry 44%. Services 47%. **Currency:** Thai Baht (Bt).

BANGKOK PATANA SCHOOL
Day — Coed Gr PS-12

Bangkok 10260, Thailand. 2/38 Soi La Salle, Sukhumvit 105. Tel: 66-2-398-0200. Fax: 66-2-399-3179. EST+12.

www.patana.ac.th   E-mail: reception@patana.ac.th

Andy Homden, Head. MA, MEd. **Robert Thornhill, Adm.**

    Col Prep. IB Diploma. Curr—Intl UK. **Exams**—GCSE IGCSE. **Feat**—Chin Fr Ger Japan Span Thai Comp_Sci Econ Thai_Stud Drama Music Bus. **Supp**—Dev_ Read ESL LD Rem_Math Rem_Read.

    Sports—Badminton Basket Rugby Soccer Swim Tennis Volley. **Activities**—Acad Arts Govt/Pol.

    Enr 2145. B 1041. G 1104. Elem 1665. Sec 480. US 187. Host 436. Other 1522. Avg class size: 22.

    Fac 220. M 96/1. F 121/2. US 6. Host 22. Other 192. Adv Deg: 17%.

    Grad '05—76. Col—68. US Col—18. (USC 2, U of GA 1, Carnegie Mellon 1, OH St 1, U of New Haven 1).

    Tui '05-'06: Day Bt317,040-590,670. Aid: 74 pupils (Bt9,998,650).

    Bldgs 25. Class rms 134. 2 Libs 50,000 vols. Sci labs 10. Comp labs 3. Auds 3. Art studios 5. Dance studios 2. Drama studios 2. Gyms 1. Fields 5. Tennis courts 11. Pools 3.

    Est 1957. Nonprofit. Tri (Sept-July). Assoc: CIS NEASC.

Founded to provide a British-style elementary education for the children of expatriates living in Bangkok, the school added a high school division in 1992. While the UK national curriculum forms the basis for the syllabi, adaptations are made to accommodate the international student body and to reflect the local culture. Secondary school students take a full range of IGCSE examination subjects that prepare them for the IB Diploma courses. Students who are nonnative English speakers take intensive ESL courses to achieve fluency.   **See Also Page 549**

CONCORDIAN INTERNATIONAL SCHOOL
Day — Coed Gr PS-8

Bangkok 10540, Thailand. 100-100/1 Moo 4 km, 14 Bangna-Trad Hwy, Bangch-along, Bangplee, Samutprakarn. Tel: 66-2-336-1155. Fax: 66-2-336-1134.

EST+12.
www.concordian.ac.th   E-mail: enquiries@concordian.ac.th
Edwin Coyle, Dir. Supanee Sungkasuwan, Adm.

Gen Acad. IB MYP. Curr—Intl. Bilingual—Mandarin Thai. Feat—Music. Supp— ESL.

Enr 120. B 55. G 65. Elem 120. Host 110. Other 10. Accepted: 96%. Avg class size: 16.

Fac 19. M 3. F 13/3. US 2. Host 4. Other 13. Adv Deg: 73%.

Tui '05-'06: Day Bt265,200-379,500.

Summer: Enrich. Tui Day Bt10,000/wk. 4 wks.

Bldgs 3. Class rms 13. Lib 3000 vols. Art studios 1. Music studios 1. Gyms 1. Fields 1. Courts 1. Pools 2.

Est 2001. Tri (Aug-June). Assoc: CIS NEASC.

CIS conducts an elementary curriculum in three languages: English, Mandarin and Thai. In nursery through grade 1, children spend 40 percent of their time studying in English, 40 percent in Mandarin and 20 percent in Thai. Pupils develop comprehension skills, then work on expanding vocabulary in each of the languages. Arithmetic skills are also integral to the program. Classes such as music and physical education are taught by specialists; any one of the three languages may serve as the medium of instruction in these courses. The IB Primary Years Program functions as the curricular framework.

Piano, ballet, golf, swimming, cooking, sewing, arts and crafts, tennis, tae kwon do, painting, drama and soccer are among CIS' extracurricular activities.

HARROW INTERNATIONAL SCHOOL

Day — Coed Gr PS-12

Bangkok 10120, Thailand. 289 New Sathorn Rd Soi 24, Chongnonsee, Yannawa. Tel: 662-672-0123. Fax: 662-672-0127. EST+12.
www.harrowschool.ac.th   E-mail: info@harrowschool.ac.th
Mark Hensman, Head.

Col Prep. Gen Acad. Curr—UK. Exams—CEEB GCSE IGCSE A-level. Feat— Chin Fr Ger Japan Comp_Sci Studio_Art Drama Music Bus. Supp—Dev_Read EFL LD Rev Tut.

Enr 730. Avg class size: 20.

Fac 95. M 37/3. F 49/6. Adv Deg: 10%.

Grad '05—30. Col—30.

Tui '02-'03: Bdg Bt600,000 (+Bt30,000). Day Bt350,000 (+Bt30,000). Aid: 10 pupils (Bt5,000,000).

Summer: Acad Enrich Rev Rec. Tui Day Bt48,000. 4 wks.

Bldgs 7. Dorm rms 15. Class rms 60. Lib 10,000 vols. Sci labs 3. Lang labs 3. Comp labs 3. Auds 1. Theaters 1. Art studios 2. Music studios 5. Gyms 3. Fields 1. Pools 2.

Est 1998. Inc. Tri (Sept-June).

HIS follows the UK national curriculum and thus leads boys and girls to the IGCSE, AS-level and A-level examinations. In addition to classes in the core disciplines of English, math and science, students engage in course work in Thai language and culture, information technology, the arts, business and physical education. Full departmentalization begins at age 9.

Comprehensive activity programs are available throughout. Junior school offerings include sketching, dance and aerobics, drama workshop, art club, ballet and jazz, swimming, choir, school newspaper and dramatic productions. Senior school pupils choose from soccer, jazz and contemporary dance, jazz band, Japanese, free-form painting and drawing, watersports, Web page design, badminton, rugby, digital photography, orchestra and school productions.

INTERNATIONAL COMMUNITY SCHOOL

Day — Coed Gr PS-12

Bangkok 10120, Thailand. 72 Soi Prong Jai, Sribhumpen Rd, Thungmahamek, Sathorn. Tel: 66-2-679-7175. Fax: 66-2-287-4530. EST+12.
www.icsbangkok.com   E-mail: info@icsbangkok.com
Tom VanHeukelem, Head. EdD. Susan Ostrowski, Adm.

    Col Prep. Curr—US. **Exams**—AP CEEB TOEFL. **AP**—Eng Span Calc Bio Physics. **Feat**—Chin Thai Environ_Sci Comp_Sci Studio_Art Music. **Supp**—ESL Tut.

    Sports—Badminton Basket Soccer Volley.

    Enr 661. Elem 470. Sec 191. US 95. Host 337. Other 229. Accepted: 78%. Avg class size: 25.

    Fac 65. M 24/2. F 38/1. US 44. Host 10. Other 11. Adv Deg: 49%.

    Grad '05—33. Col—33. **US Col**—7. (UCLA 2, Purdue 1, U of UT 1, Lafayette 1, Boston Col 1, Chapman 1). Avg SAT: M/V—1071.

    Tui '05-'06: Day Bt227,200-269,000 (+Bt200,000). **Aid:** 108 pupils (Bt4,500,000).

    Summer: Acad. 5 wks.

    Plant val Bt30,000,000. Bldgs 7. Class rms 35. 3 Libs 14,000 vols. Sci labs 2. Lang labs 3. Comp labs 4. Auds 1. Theaters 1. Art studios 1. Music studios 3. Dance studios 1. Gyms 2. Fields 2. Courts 1. Pools 1.

    Est 1993. Nonprofit. Nondenom Christian. Quar (Aug-June). Assoc: WASC.

Providing a US-style program that readies graduates for American and other English-speaking colleges, ICS conducts a Christian program for students from more than 30 countries. Roughly half of the pupils are Thai nationals. Emphasizing critical thinking, the school combines electives and activities with the core subjects of math, science, foreign language and history.

Hands-on computer classes enable pupils to work with applications and on subject-specific software. Beginning in prekindergarten, all boys and girls participate in art classes that provide exposure to such media as drawing, painting, sculpture, printmaking and crafts. Music instruction commences with instrumental lessons during the elementary years, then progresses to band and choir in the middle and high schools. Traditional dance, field trips to cultural sites, and Thai craft making and cooking help students learn more about Thailand.

ICS' original campus, at Prong Jai, now serves children in grades K-5. A second location, located at 1125 The Parkland Rd., Khwaeng Bangna, Bangkok 10260, accommodates students in grades pre-K-12.

KIS INTERNATIONAL SCHOOL
Day — Coed Gr PS-9

Bangkok 10320, Thailand. 999/124 Kesinee Ville, Pracha U-tit Rd, Huay-Kwang. Tel: 66-2-274-3444. Fax: 66-2-274-3452. EST+17.
www.kis.ac.th   E-mail: info@kis.ac.th
Sally Holloway, Head. MA. June Ven Den Bos, Prin. Sakonwan Kangsaviboon, Adm.

> Gen Acad. IB PYP. IB MYP. Curr—Intl. Feat—Humanities Span Thai Comp_Sci Studio_Art Drama Music Dance. Supp—ESL.
> Sports—Basket Soccer Track. Activities—Arts Rec.
> Enr 301. B 168. G 133. Accepted: 80%. Avg class size: 23.
> Fac 35. M 12. F 23. US 6. Host 9. Other 20. Adv Deg: 28%.
> Tui '05-'06: Day Bt175,500-343,500 (+Bt18,000).
> Summer: Rec. 3 wks.
> Bldgs 4. Class rms 31. Libs 2. Sci labs 3. Lang labs 4. Comp labs 4. Auds 1. Art studios 1. Music studios 2. Dance studios 1. Gyms 2. Fields 3. Courts 8. Pools 1.
> Est 1998. Inc. Tri (Aug-June). Assoc: ECIS.

Founded to meet the educational needs of Bangkok's large international community and those local families interested in an international curriculum, KIS follows the programming of the International Baccalaureate Organization. Children in grades PS-5 take part in the inquiry-based Primary Years Program, while students in grades 6-9 engage in the Middle Years Program. In addition to the IB programs, KIS offers a prekindergarten program for children ages 2½-3 that focuses on developmentally appropriate learning.

Field trips are integral to the PYP and MYP programs, beginning with day trips in kindergarten. Boys and girls in grade 3 and up embark on residential trips to such places as Rayong, Kanchanaburi, Chiang Mai and Khao Yai. Through an association with 14 other international schools, KIS offers a full program of cultural activities and competitive athletics.

NEW INTERNATIONAL SCHOOL OF THAILAND
Day — Coed Gr PS-12

Bangkok 10110, Thailand. 36 Sukhumvit Soi 15. Tel: 66-2651-2065. Fax: 66-2253-3800. EST+12.
www.nist.ac.th   E-mail: nist@nist.ac.th
Simon Leslie, Head.

> Col Prep. IB PYP. IB MYP. IB Diploma. Curr—Intl UK. Exams—CEEB. Feat—Comp_Sci Econ Psych Thai_Stud Studio_Art Drama Music. Supp—ESL.
> Enr 1346.
> Tui '05-'06: Day Bt252,860-517,330 (+Bt279,000-484,000).
> Est 1992. Nonprofit. Sem (Aug-June). Assoc: CIS EARCOS NEASC.

RUAMRUDEE INTERNATIONAL SCHOOL
Day — Coed Gr K-12

Bangkok 10510, Thailand. 42 Moo 4, Ramkhamhaeng 184, Minburi. Tel: 66-2-518-0320. Fax: 66-2-518-0334. EST+12.
www.rism.ac.th   E-mail: info@rism.ac.th
Rev. Apisit Kritsaralam, Head.

> Col Prep. IB Diploma. Curr—Intl US. Exams—AP CEEB TOEFL. AP—Eng Calc Stats Bio Chem Econ Psych. Feat—Chin Fr Japan Span Thai Anat Environ_Sci Zoology Pol_Sci Asian_Stud Ethics Relig Photog Studio_Art Drama Dance Bus Journ. Supp—ESL LD.
>
> Enr 1649. Elem 943. Sec 706. Avg class size: 25.
>
> Fac 230.
>
> Grad '05—175. Col—175. US Col—48. Avg SAT: M/V—1050.
>
> Tui '05-'06: Day Bt299,000-342,000 (+Bt350,000).
>
> Summer: Acad Enrich Rev Rem Rec. 4 wks.
>
> Est 1957. Nonprofit. Roman Catholic. Sem (Aug-June). Assoc: EARCOS WASC.

Founded by the Redemptorist Fathers of Thailand and the Sisters of Holy Infant Jesus, RIS first operated as a four-room elementary school for expatriate children of Catholic parishioners. The present-day program, which extends through grade 12, consists of a modified US curriculum that is tailored to the needs of the international student. Although English is the language of instruction, pupils may study French, Spanish, Mandarin, Japanese and Thai as foreign languages. Older students choose from Advanced Placement courses in many disciplines, and the two-year International Baccalaureate is a curricular option in grades 11 and 12.

RIS offers the following among its extracurricular options: astronomy, drama, forensics and golf.

ST. JOHN'S INTERNATIONAL SCHOOL
Day — Coed Gr PS-12

Bangkok 10900, Thailand. Viphavadi Rd Soi 22, Ladprao. Tel: 66-2-513-8575. Fax: 66-2-513-5273. EST+12.
www.stjohn.ac.th/International   E-mail: sjiadmin@stjohn.ac.th
Martin Scott, Head.

> Col Prep. Curr—UK. Exams—GCSE IGCSE A-level. Feat—Chin Fr Thai Comp_ Sci Studio_Art Drama Music. Supp—Dev_Read EFL ESL LD Rem_Math Rem_Read Tut.
>
> Enr 393. Accepted: 98%. Avg class size: 15.
>
> Fac 52. M 26. F 26. Adv Deg: 82%.
>
> Grad '05—27.
>
> Tui '05-'06: Day Bt262,950-333,000.
>
> Bldgs 3. Class rms 45. Libs 2. Sci labs 3. Lang labs 5. Comp labs 3. Theaters 1. Art studios 2. Music studios 2. Dance studios 2. Gyms 1. Fields 1. Courts 1. Pools 1.
>
> Est 1992. Inc. Roman Catholic. Tri (Aug-July).

A largely British staff conducts a full elementary and secondary program that follows that employed in the United Kingdom. The play-based early years focus on language and literacy, math skills, and knowledge and understanding of the world, as well as personal development. St. John's supplements its primary school courses with Thai language and culture classes. Students at the secondary level work toward the IGCSE and GCSE examinations. An increasing number of electives are available during these years.

Tae kwon do, art, Latin club, dance, ceramics, soccer, cooking, juggling, netball and tennis are some of the school's extracurricular options.

ST. STEPHEN'S INTERNATIONAL SCHOOL
BANGKOK

Day — Coed Gr PS-5

Bangkok 10900, Thailand. 107 Viphavadi Rangsit Rd, Lad Yao, Chatuchak. Tel: 66-2-513-0270. Fax: 66-2-930-3307. EST+12.
www.sis.edu   E-mail: info@sis.edu
Richard A. Ralphs, Dir. BEd. John Zermani, Prin. BA.
  Gen Acad. Curr—UK. Feat—Chin Thai.
  Enr 402. B 225. G 177. Elem 402. Accepted: 90%.
  Fac 50. M 14. F 36. US 4. Host 22. Other 24. Adv Deg: 12%.
  Tui '02-'03: Day $3857-5667 (+$600). Aid: 11 pupils ($44,500).
  Summer: Acad Rec. Tui Day $395-465/3-wk ses. 4 wks.
  Bldgs 2. Class rms 18. Libs 1. Comp labs 1. Fields 1. Pools 1.
  Est 1998. Inc. Tri (Sept-July). Assoc: CIS NEASC.

While the SIS' program borrows significantly from the English national curriculum, it also incorporates other international approaches to best serve the varied student body. Thai courses are available at all levels, and the school also conducts Mandarin classes throughout.

Pupils choose from a full complement of activities each term, among them interest clubs music, the arts, swimming, soccer, basketball and cricket. A coordinator oversees the extracurricular program.

AMERICAN PACIFIC INTERNATIONAL SCHOOL

Bdg — Coed Gr 6-12; Day — Coed 1-12

Chiang Mai 50230, Thailand. 158/1 Moo 3 Hangdong-Samoeng Rd, Banpong, Hangdong. Tel: 66-53-365-303. Fax: 66-53-365-304. EST+12.
www.apis.ac.th   E-mail: admissions@apis.ac.th
  Col Prep. Curr—US. Exams—AP TOEFL. AP—Calc Stats Bio Chem Physics. Feat—Creative_Writing Chin Japan Thai Comp_Sci SE_Asian_Hist Studio_Art Drama Dance. Supp—ESL.
  Fac 24.
  Est 1997. Sem (Aug-June). Assoc: EARCOS WASC.

CHIANG MAI INTERNATIONAL SCHOOL
Day — Coed Gr K-12

Chiang Mai 50000, Thailand. 13 Chetupon Rd. Tel: 66-53-242027. Fax: 66-53-242455. EST+12.
www.cmis.ac.th   E-mail: info@cmis.ac.th
Supaporn Yanasarn, Dir.

Col Prep. Gen Acad. Curr—US. Exams—AP CEEB. AP—Eng Fr Calc Bio Physics World_Hist Econ. Feat—Japan Span Thai Oceanog Comp_Sci Psych Studio_ Art Drama Music. Supp—ESL.

Enr 400.

Est 1954. Nondenom Christian. Sem (Aug-June). Assoc: A/OPR/OS EARCOS WASC.

NAKORN PAYAP INTERNATIONAL SCHOOL
Day — Coed Gr PS-12

Chiang Mai 50000, Thailand. 240 Moo 6, San Phi Sua, Muang. Tel: 66-053-110-6803. Fax: 66-053-110-687. EST+12.
www.nis.ac.th   E-mail: info@nis.ac.th
John Allen, Jr., Prin.

Col Prep. Gen Acad. Curr—US. Exams—CEEB. Feat—Comp_Sci Econ Psych Philos. Supp—ESL.

Fac 29.

Tui '05-'06: Day Bt96,000-300,000.

Est 1993. Sem (Aug-June). Assoc: WASC.

PREM TINSULANONDA INTERNATIONAL SCHOOL
Bdg — Coed Gr 4-12; Day — Coed K-12

Chiang Mai 50180, Thailand. PO Box 1, Mae Rim. Tel: 66-53-301500. Fax: 66-53-301507. EST+12.
www.premcenter.in.th   E-mail: enquiry@premcenter.in.th
David Baird, Head. BEd, MEd. Davidene Hannah, Adm.

Col Prep. Gen Acad. IB PYP. IB MYP. IB Diploma. Curr—Intl. Feat—Chin Fr Span Thai Comp_Sci Econ Thai_Stud Studio_Art Music. Supp—ESL.

Activities—Arts Service.

Enr 414. B 47/175. G 44/148. US 28. Host 117. Other 269. Accepted: 95%. Avg class size: 12.

Fac 56. M 22/2. F 27/5. US 6. Host 4. Other 46. Adv Deg: 23%.

Grad '05—24. Col—18. US Col—1. (Bucknell).

Tui '05-'06: Bdg Bt243,080. Day Bt173,600-335,720.

Bldgs 3. Dorm rms 120. Class rms 37. Libs 1. Sci labs 2. Comp labs 1. Auds 1. Gyms 1. Pools 1.

Est 2001. Nonprofit. Quar (Aug-June).

At all grade levels, the school follows the curriculum developed by the International Baccalaureate Organization. Students progress from the IB Primary Years

Program to the IB Middle Years Program, then conclude their studies in pursuit of the IB Diploma.

Operating daily each term, Prem Center's after-school activities program comprises approximately four dozen options. Students may take part in these activities (which include the arts, athletics and service) beginning in grade 1.

INTERNATIONAL SCHOOL EASTERN SEABOARD
Day — Coed Gr PS-12

Chonburi 20150, Thailand. PO Box 6, Banglamung. Tel: 66-38-345-556. Fax: 66-38-345-156. EST+12.
www.ise.ac.th   E-mail: ise@ise.ac.th
Ronald Schultz, Supt. PhD. **Joan Fedoruk, Adm.**

> **Col Prep. IB Diploma. Curr**—Intl US. **Exams**—CEEB. **Feat**—Fr Japan Span Thai Comp_Sci Studio_Art Drama Music. **Supp**—EFL ESL Tut.
> **Sports**—Basket Golf Softball Swim Volley.
> **Enr 375.** Elem 300. Sec 75. US 45. Host 65. Other 265. Accepted: 90%. Avg class size: 16.
> **Fac 42.** M 17/2. F 22/1. US 28. Host 2. Other 12. Adv Deg: 71%.
> **Grad '05—14. Col—14. US Col—13.** (U of WI-Madison 6, U of TX-Austin 2, Webster 2, U of IL-Urbana 1, Cornell 1, Occidental 1). Avg SAT: M/V—1250.
> **Tui '05-'06: Day $5066-10,000** (+$2500).
> **Summer:** Acad Enrich Rec. 4-6 wks.
> Plant val $4,000,000. Bldgs 3. Class rms 45. 2 Libs 10,000 vols. Sci labs 2. Lang labs 3. Comp labs 3. Auds 1. Art studios 2. Music studios 3. Dance studios 1. Gyms 2. Fields 1. Courts 1. Pools 1.
> **Est 1994.** Sem (Aug-June). Assoc: EARCOS WASC.

Offering a US-style education for students at all grade levels, ISE supplements core courses in English, science, math, social studies, and health and physical education with classes in foreign language, computer, music and art. The elementary school years emphasize thinking, listening, writing, reasoning and problem-solving skills, while the middle school program provides more opportunities for hands-on involvement and further develops pupils' thinking skills. Students who successfully complete the high school program earn the American high school diploma, the IB Diploma or both.

After-school extracurriculars enable students to participate in enrichment activities in supplemental foreign languages, various arts and crafts, and Thai studies.

THE REGENT'S SCHOOL
Bdg — Coed Gr 3-12; Day — Coed PS-12

Chonbury 20150, Thailand. PO Box 33, Naklua, Banglamung. Tel: 66-38-734-777. Fax: 66-38-734-778. EST+12.
www.regents.ac.th   E-mail: enquiry@regents.ac.th
Michael Walton, Prin. BA, MA. **Andrew Watt, Adm.**

> **Col Prep. IB Diploma. Curr**—Intl UK. **Exams**—IGCSE A-level. **Feat**—Chin Fr Ger Japan Thai Comp_Sci Econ Studio_Art Drama Music Bus Design. **Supp**—ESL Rem_Math Rem_Read Tut.

Sports—Soccer Swim Tennis. **Activities**—Arts Service.

Enr 780. Elem 400. Sec 380. US 50. Host 180. Other 550. Accepted: 60%. Avg class size: 20.

Fac 91. M 60. F 31. US 2. Host 6. Other 83. Adv Deg: 28%.

Grad '05—35. Col—33. US Col—6. (Stanford, U of MI, GA Inst of Tech, U of WI-Madison).

Tui '05-'06: Bdg $16,000. Day $9000. Aid: 60 pupils ($800,000).

Summer: Acad Enrich Rev Rem Rec. Tui Bdg $1200. Tui Day $900. 3 wks.

Plant val $30,000,000. Bldgs 10. Dorms 4. Dorm rms 50. Class rms 90. 2 Libs 12,000 vols. Sci labs 3. Lang labs 4. Comp labs 4. Auds 3. Theaters 1. Art studios 3. Music studios 10. Dance studios 2. Gyms 1. Fields 1. Courts 4. Pools 1.

Est 1995. Inc. Tri (Aug-June).

In the lower grades at Regent's, teachers use play to stimulate learning; a more formal approach to literacy and numeracy follows as children progress. Conducted in a small-class setting, the primary program (grades 2-5) includes instruction in music, information technology and physical education. The school provides frequent opportunities to learn about Thai culture and festivals, as well as the Thai language. In grades 6-8, pupils study core subjects, then have increased course options from grade 9. Boys and girls dedicate themselves to preparing for the IGCSE and A-level examinations in grades 9-12.

Regent's offers an array of extracurricular opportunities. Primary school children engage in an after-school program that operates two days per week. Older students participate in a varied program that features performing arts, land and water sports, and community service options.

A second campus, also enrolling boys and girls in grades PS-12, operates at 592 Pracha-Uthit Rd., Huai Kwang, Bangkok 10310 (66-2-690-3777).

ST. STEPHEN'S INTERNATIONAL SCHOOL
KHAO YAI

Bdg and Day — Coed Gr 3-12

Nakhorn Ratchasima 30130, Thailand. 49/1-3 Moo 4, Thanarat Rd, Nongnam-daeng, Pak Chong. Tel: 66-44-328-336. Fax: 66-44-365-019. EST+12.

www.sis.edu   E-mail: marketing@sis.edu

Panida Patrapisespong, Mgr. BA. **Visit Charoensiriwatana, Head.** PhD.

Col Prep. Curr—UK. **Exams**—IGCSE AS-level A-level. **Feat**—Chin Thai Comp_ Sci Studio_Art Drama Music. **Supp**—ESL Tut.

Sports—Badminton Basket Golf Soccer Swim Tennis Volley.

Enr 108. Elem 65. Sec 43. US 1. Host 95. Other 12. Avg class size: 11.

Fac 20. M 13. F 7. US 3. Host 3. Other 14. Adv Deg: 35%.

Tui '05-'06: Bdg Bt490,000 (+Bt81,000). **Day Bt310,000** (+Bt81,000).

Summer: Music. Tui Bdg Bt13,000. Golf. Tui Bdg Bt14,500. 1 wk.

Bldgs 5. Dorms 2. Class rms 51. Lib 50,000 vols. Sci labs 3. Lang labs 2. Auds 1. Theaters 2. Art studios 2. Music studios 2. Dance studios 1. Gyms 1. Fields 1. Courts 1. Pools 1.

Est 1995. Tri (Sept-June). Assoc: WASC.

Emphasizing a hands-on approach to learning, SIS-Khao Yai follows the British national curriculum at all grade levels. The elementary year program (grades 1-4) features instruction in the Thai and Mandarin languages, as well as in computers and drama, while the middle year curriculum (grades 5-8) devotes time to the development of sound study skills. Pupils in grades 9 and 10 prepare for the IGCSE examinations, then may take courses at AS or A level during their final two years.

Boys and girls choose from a wide selection of activities. Choices include mountain biking, riding, cooking, martial arts, Thai dance and music, and interscholastic and intramural sports.

INTERNATIONAL SCHOOL BANGKOK
Day — Coed Gr K-12

Nonthaburi 11120, Thailand. 39/7 Soi Nichada Thani, Samakee Rd, Pakkret. Tel: 66-2-963-5800. Fax: 66-2-583-5432. EST+12.
www.isb.ac.th   E-mail: register@isb.ac.th
Bill Gerritz, Head.
> **Col Prep. IB Diploma. Curr**—Intl US. **AP**—Eng Fr Span Calc Comp_Sci Bio Chem Physics Econ Studio_Art. **Feat**—Chin Japan Thai Anat Environ_Sci Psych Drama Music. **Supp**—ESL.
> **Enr 1878.** B 955. G 923.
> **Fac 114.**
> **Tui '05-'06: Day Bt499,400-581,600** (+Bt20,000).
> **Est 1951.** Nonprofit. Sem (Aug-June). Assoc: A/OPR/OS EARCOS WASC.

BRITISH CURRICULUM INTERNATIONAL SCHOOL
Bdg — Coed Gr 2-12; Day — Coed PS-12

Phuket 83200, Thailand. 59 Moo 2, Thepkrasattri Rd, Tambon Koh Kaew, Amphur Muang. Tel: 66-76-238-711. Fax: 66-76-238-750. EST+12.
www.bcis.ac.th   E-mail: info@bcis.ac.th
George A. Hickman, Head. BA, MEd, PhD. **Sutarsinee Suanplee, Adm.**
> **Col Prep. Gen Acad. IB Diploma. Curr**—Intl UK. **Exams**—GCSE IGCSE. **Feat**—Chin Fr Ger Japan Thai Comp_Sci Thai_Stud Studio_Art Drama Music. **Supp**—EFL ESL.
> **Sports**—Badminton Basket F_Hockey Gymnastics Rugby Soccer Softball Swim Tennis Volley. **Activities**—Arts Govt/Pol Media Rec Service.
> **Enr 800.** B 80/320. G 75/325. Elem 630. Sec 170. US 32. Host 295. Other 473. Accepted: 60%. Avg class size: 22.
> **Fac 100.** M 53/1. F 44/2. US 4. Host 11. Other 85. Adv Deg: 22%.
> **Grad '05—31.**
> **Tui '05-'06: Bdg $12,000-15,000. Day $7000-10,000.**
> **Summer:** ESL. Sports. Tui Bdg $1200-1500. 3-4 wks.
> Bldgs 13. Dorms 8. Class rms 70. 2 Libs 25,000 vols. Sci labs 7. Comp labs 4. Photog labs 1. Auds 1. Art studios 2. Music studios 2. Dance studios 1. Gyms 2. Fields 6. Courts 6. Pools 2.
> **Est 1996.** Inc. Tri (Aug-June).

BCIS' academic program combines elements from British and other international curricula. The primary program stresses language skills and course work in such core subjects as mathematics, science, history and geography. In the secondary school, the formal curriculum prepares the students for the IGCSE and the International Baccalaureate Diploma.

An array of sports, games, extracurricular activities and field trips during and after the school day completes the program.

QSI INTERNATIONAL SCHOOL OF PHUKET
Day — Coed Gr PS-12

Phuket 83000, Thailand. Box 432. Tel: 66-76-354-077. Fax: 66-76-354-076. EST+11. www.qsi.org/pkt_home   E-mail: pkt@qsi.org
Alan Siporin, Dir. MEd.
   Col Prep. Gen Acad. Curr—US. **Exams**—CEEB. **Feat**—Thai Econ Studio_Art Music. **Supp**—ESL Rev.
   Enr 97. B 57. G 40. Elem 77. Sec 20. US 16. Host 14. Other 67. Accepted: 90%. Yield: 100%. Avg class size: 11.
   Fac 18. M 6. F 12. US 10. Host 5. Other 3. Adv Deg: 38%.
   Tui '05-'06: Day $3700-8600. Aid: 19 pupils ($35,800).
   Summer: ESL. 4 wks.
   Plant val $504,000. Bldgs 3. Class rms 16. Lib 10,000 vols. Sci labs 1. Comp labs 1. Art studios 1. Fields 2. Courts 1.
   Est 2000. Nonprofit. Spons: Quality Schools International. Tri (Aug-June). Assoc: MSA.

The US-style curriculum at this school offers personalized instruction to Thai citizens, as well as to pupils from the US and other foreign countries. The medium of instruction is English, with intensive ESL classes provided to pupils with a limited knowledge of the language. The school offers Thai both for native speakers and as a foreign language.

Elementary-age children partake of various activities two afternoons each week.

ST. ANDREWS INTERNATIONAL SCHOOL RAYONG
Day — Coed Gr PS-10

Rayong 21130, Thailand. 1 Moo 7, Banchang-Makham Koo Rd, Banchang. Tel: 66-38-893716. Fax: 66-38-893720. EST+12.
www.st-andrews.ac.th/rayong   E-mail: rayong@st-andrews.ac.th
Andrew Harrison, Head. BEd.
   Gen Acad. Curr—Intl UK. **Exams**—IGCSE. **Feat**—Humanities Fr Ger Thai Comp_Sci Geog Studio_Art Music. **Supp**—Dev_Read ESL LD Rem_Math Rem_Read.
   Sports—Basket Gymnastics Soccer Swim. **Activities**—Arts Govt/Pol Rec.
   Enr 235. B 112. G 123. US 3. Host 59. Other 173. Accepted: 100%. Yield: 98%. Avg class size: 15.
   Fac 24. M 8/2. F 14. US 2. Host 2. Other 20.
   Grad '05—8.
   Tui '06-'07: Day Bt255,000-300,000 (+Bt45,000). **Aid:** 2 pupils (Bt1,200,000).
   Summer: Sports. Tui Day Bt12,000-15,000. 2 wks.
   Bldgs 4. Class rms 23. Lib 4000 vols. Sci labs 1. Lang labs 1. Comp labs 1. Art stu-

dios 1. Music studios 1. Fields 1. Courts 2. Pools 1. Riding rings 1. Stables 1.
Est 1996. Tri (Sept-July).

This British-style elementary school maintains a hands-on nursery school that accepts children as young as age 2. The program for boys and girls ages 3-5 focuses on language development, communication with both adults and children, artistic expression, and facility with letters and numbers. For children ages 5-7, the curriculum continues to stress clear communication, while also addressing listening skills, phonetic awareness and knowledge, and introductory subject matter pertaining to history, geography and science.

During the middle school years (ages 7-11), a structured, sequential program features course work in the standard subjects, as well as in art, music, and Thai language and culture. The lower high school (ages 11-16), again based on the British national curriculum, has the flexibility to accommodate pupils of various ability levels. Noteworthy courses at this level include humanities, information technology, and design and technology.

VIETNAM

Sq. Miles: 127,243 (Equivalent in size to Ohio, Kentucky and Tennessee combined). **Country Pop:** 83,535,576 (2005). **Capital:** Hanoi, pop. 2,842,000 (2002). **Largest City:** Ho Chi Minh City, pop. 5,378,000 (2002). **Terrain:** Varies from mountainous to coastal delta. **Ethnic Group(s):** Vietnamese Chinese Hmong Thai Khmer Cham. **Religion(s):** Buddhist Indigenous_Beliefs Roman_Catholic Protestant Muslim. **Official Language(s):** Vietnamese. **Other Language(s):** English French Chinese Khmer. **Government:** Communist. **Independence:** 1945 (from France). **Per Capita Income:** $553 (2004). **GDP:** $45.4 billion (2004). Agriculture 22%. Industry 40%. Services 38%. **Currency:** Vietnamese Dong (D).

HANOI INTERNATIONAL SCHOOL
Day — Coed Gr K-12

Hanoi, Vietnam. 48 Lieu Giai St, Ba Dinh. Tel: 84-4-832-7379. Fax: 84-4-832-7535. EST+12.
www.hisvietnam.com   E-mail: mainoffice@hisvietnam.com
Terry Hamilton, Prin.
  Col Prep. IB Diploma. **Curr**—Intl. **Exams**—IGCSE. **Feat**—Fr Japan Korean Vietnamese Comp_Sci Econ Studio_Art Music Bus. **Supp**—ESL.
  Enr 240.
  Tui '05-'06: Day $7000-9600 (+$1000).
  Est 1996. Quar (Aug-June).

UNITED NATIONS INTERNATIONAL SCHOOL OF HANOI
Day — Coed Gr PS-12

Hanoi, Vietnam. GPO Box 313. Tel: 84-4-8461284. Fax: 84-4-8463635. EST+12.
Contact: Box 1608 GRNL, New York, NY 10163.
www.unishanoi.org   E-mail: info@unishanoi.org
Alun Cooper, Head.

> Gen Acad. IB PYP. IB MYP. IB Diploma. Curr—Intl. Feat—Humanities Fr Span
> Korean Swedish Vietnamese Environ_Sci Comp_Sci Econ Psych Drama Music.
> Supp—ESL.
>
> Enr 700. Elem 546. Sec 154.
>
> Fac 92.
>
> Tui '06-'07: Day $8536-12,411 (+$3000).
>
> Est 1988. Nonprofit. Quar (Aug-June). Assoc: A/OPR/OS CIS EARCOS NEASC.

INTERNATIONAL SCHOOL
HO CHI MINH CITY
Day — Coed Gr PS-12

Ho Chi Minh City, Vietnam. 649A Vo Truong Toan St, An Phu, District 2. Tel: 84-8-8989100. Fax: 84-8-8989382. EST+12.
www.ishcmc.com   E-mail: enroll-ishcmc@hcm.vnn.vn
Sean O'Maonaigh, Head. BA, MEd. Christine Byrne, Adm.

> Col Prep. IB Diploma. Curr—Intl. Exams—IGCSE. Feat—Fr Korean Vietnamese
> Comp_Sci Studio_Art Music. Supp—ESL.
>
> Enr 589. Accepted: 99%. Avg class size: 20.
>
> Fac 67. M 27. F 40. US 8. Host 2. Other 57. Adv Deg: 32%.
>
> Grad '05—30.
>
> Tui '05-'06: Day $9950-13,850.
>
> 2 Libs 32,000 vols. Sci labs 4. Comp labs 3. Auds 1. Art studios 3. Music studios 2.
> Drama studios 1. Gyms 3. Fields 1. Courts 3. Pools 1.
>
> Est 1993. Nonprofit. Quar (Aug-June). Assoc: EARCOS ECIS.

Enrolling both expatriate pupils and older Vietnamese students (grades 10-12), the school maintains an international focus at all grade levels. Boys and girls prepare for the IGCSE examinations in grades 9 and 10, then pursue the IB Diploma the following two years; ISHCMC also conducts a four-year program that leads to the school's own diploma.

Specialists teach art, music, Vietnamese studies and physical education. English as a Second Language programming is available throughout. Pupils from Korea, Vietnam, the US, Japan, Australia, the United Kingdom and Malaysia constitute much of the enrollment, while most teachers are British, Australian or American.

Children in grades PS-1 attend school at a campus in the middle of Ho Chi Minh City, while those in grades 2-12 study at a location in an outer suburb of the city.

SAIGON SOUTH INTERNATIONAL SCHOOL
Day — Coed Gr PS-12

Ho Chi Minh City, Vietnam. Saigon S Pky, Tan Phong Ward, District 7. Tel: 84-8-413-0901. Fax: 84-8-413-0902. EST+12.
www.ssischool.org   E-mail: ssischool@hcm.vnn.vn
Gerry H. Keener, Head. BA, MDiv, STM. **Brie Goolbis, Adm.**

    Col Prep. Gen Acad. Curr—US. **Exams**—CEEB TOEFL. **AP**—Eng Calc Chem. **Feat**—Span Vietnamese Anthro Asian_Stud Ceramics Drama. **Supp**—ESL.

    Sports—Basket X-country Soccer Softball Swim Volley. **Activities**—Acad Arts Rec.

    Enr 382. Elem 295. Sec 87. US 55. Host 75. Other 252. Avg class size: 16.

    Fac 37. M 10. F 25/2. US 25. Host 2. Other 10. Adv Deg: 54%.

    Grad '05—6.

    Tui '05-'06: Day $5800-11,200 (+$1000).

    Bldgs 2. Class rms 30. Libs 1. Sci labs 2. Comp labs 2. Dance studios 1. Gyms 1. Fields 2. Pools 1.

    Est 1997. Quar (Aug-June). Assoc: EARCOS WASC.

SSIS offers a US-style elementary and secondary curriculum to a culturally diverse student body. A comprehensive ESL program forms an integral part of the program.

AUSTRALIA &
NEW ZEALAND

INDEX TO AUSTRALIA & NEW ZEALAND

AUSTRALIA & NEW ZEALAND

AUSTRALIA

Sq. Miles: 3,000,000 (About the size of the Continental United States). **Country Pop:** 20,090,437 (2005). **Capital:** Canberra, pop. 323,000 (2003). **Largest City:** Sydney, pop. 4,200,000 (2003). **Terrain:** Varied, but generally low lying. **Ethnic Group(s):** European Asian Aboriginal. **Religion(s):** Anglican Roman_Catholic Christian. **Official Language(s):** English. **Government:** Democracy. **Independence:** 1901 (from United Kingdom). **GDP:** $587.3 billion (2004). Agriculture 4%. Industry 28%. Services 68%. **Currency:** Australian Dollar (A$).

AUSTRALIAN CAPITAL TERRITORY

NARRABUNDAH COLLEGE
Day — Coed Gr 11-12

Kingston, Australian Capital Territory 2604, Australia. Jerrabomberra Ave. Tel: 61-2-6205-6999. Fax: 61-2-6205-6969. EST+16.5. www.narrabundahc.act.edu.au E-mail: the.principal@narrabundahc.act.edu.au Steve Kyburz, Prin. DipEd.

Col Prep. IB Diploma. Fr Bac. Curr—Intl. **Supp Lang**—Fr. **Feat**—Chin Fr Ger Ital Japan Span Bahasa_Indonesia Korean Comp_Sci Econ Psych Studio_Art Theater_Arts Music. **Supp**—ESL Rem_Math Tut.

Sports—Basket Golf Soccer.

Enr 920. B 370. G 550. Sec 920. Accepted: 90%. Avg class size: 20.

Fac 72. M 30. F 42.

Tui '06-'07: Day A$12,000-14,000 (+A$300).

Tri (Jan-Dec).

The international students' program, first started at Narrabundah in the early 1990s, has grown through the years and now attracts boys and girls predominantly from Asia, Europe and South America. The IB program serves pupils who may wish to pursue their education outside Australia. The college also offers a selection of courses designed to prepare students for tertiary institutions in Australia.

Nine languages, taught at all levels, allow native speakers to maintain fluency in their home languages through advanced course work. Tutorials and special English courses organized to help non-English speakers are also available.

NEW SOUTH WALES

NEW ENGLAND GIRLS' SCHOOL
Bdg — Girls Gr 5-12; Day — Girls K-12

Armidale, New South Wales 2350, Australia. Uralla Rd. Tel: 61-2-6774-8700.
Fax: 61-2-6772-7057. EST+15.
www.negs.nsw.edu.au   E-mail: info@negs.nsw.edu.au
Rebecca Ling, Prin.
   Col Prep. Gen Acad. IB Diploma. Curr—Intl Nat.
   Tui '05-'06: Bdg A$22,232-33,794. Day A$8014-18,775.
   Est 1895. Nonprofit. Anglican. Quar (Jan-Dec).

AMERICAN INTERNATIONAL SCHOOL
Day — Coed Gr PS-12

Oatlands, New South Wales 2117, Australia. Locked Bag 204. Tel: 61-2-9890-3488.
Fax: 61-2-9890-3499. EST+15.
www.amschool.com.au   E-mail: enquiry@ais.thin-ed.net
Lyn Cheetham, Supt.
   Col Prep. IB Diploma. Curr—Intl US.
   Enr 150. B 80. G 70.
   Fac 19.
   Tui '05-'06: Day A$11,018-20,602 (+A$1000-2000).
   Est 1999. Sem (Aug-June).

SOUTH AUSTRALIA

GLENUNGA INTERNATIONAL HIGH SCHOOL
Day — Coed Gr 8-12

Glenunga, South Australia 5064, Australia. 99 L'Estrange St. Tel: 61-8-8379-5629.
Fax: 61-8-8338-2518. EST+14.5.
www.gihs.sa.edu.au   E-mail: glenunga@gihs.sa.edu.au
Robert A. Knight, Prin. BA, DipEd.
   Col Prep. Gen Acad. IB MYP. IB Diploma. Curr—Intl Nat. Feat—Chin Fr Ger
      Japan Comp_Sci Econ Studio_Art Drama Music. Supp—Dev_Read ESL LD.
   Sports—Badminton Basket Fencing Rugby Soccer Swim Volley W_Polo. Activi-
      ties—Acad Arts Cultural/Relig Govt/Pol Rec Service.
   Enr 1250. Accepted: 100%. Avg class size: 26.
   Fac 95. M 45. F 50. Host 95.
   Grad '05—230.
   Tui '06-'07: Day A$550-1250. Aid: 200 pupils (A$40,000).
   Plant val A$20,000,000. Bldgs 3. Class rms 70. Lib 20,000 vols. Sci labs 7. Lang
      labs 7. Auds 1. Theaters 1. Art studios 5. Music studios 2. Dance studios 1.
      Gyms 1. Fields 2. Courts 10.

Est 1898. Nonprofit. Quar (Jan-Dec).

Glenunga's broad curriculum, which basically follows the national model, provides opportunities for specialization. The middle school features a specially modified version of the IB Middle Years Program that serves as a bridge between primary school and high school and allows pupils to advance to either a national or international program in succeeding years. In grades 11 and 12, students pursue either the International Baccalaureate Diploma or the South Australian certificate. This dual programming provides older boys and girls with a more extensive course selection, as they can enroll in certain classes in the other section.

Cocurricular activities such as public-speaking competitions, student council, interscholastic athletics and camps complement academics.

MERCEDES COLLEGE

Day — Coed Gr K-12

Springfield, South Australia 5062, Australia. 540 Fullarton Rd. Tel: 61-8-8372-3200. Fax: 61-8-8379-9540. EST+14.5.
www.mercedes.adl.catholic.edu.au   E-mail: info@mercedes.adl.catholic.edu.au
Peter Daw, Prin.
  Col Prep. Gen Acad. IB PYP. IB MYP. IB Diploma. Curr—Intl Nat. **Feat**—Comp_ Sci Studio_Art Drama Music Bus.
  Enr 1124. B 687. G 437.
  Tui '05-'06: Day A$4146-14,330.
  Est 1954. Inc. Roman Catholic. Quar (Jan-Dec).

ST. ANDREW'S SCHOOL

Day — Coed Gr PS-6

Walkerville, South Australia 5081, Australia. 22 Smith St, PO Box 87. Tel: 61-8-8168-5555. Fax: 61-8-8344-8670. EST+14.5.
www.standrews.sa.edu.au   E-mail: principal@standrews.sa.edu.au
David G. Woolnough, Prin. BEd. Susan Wilkins, Adm.
  Pre-Prep. IB PYP. IB MYP. Curr—Intl. **Feat**—Chin Ital Computers Relig Performing_Arts Visual_Arts.
  Sports—Basket Gymnastics Soccer Softball Tennis. **Activities**—Acad Arts Rec.
  Enr 630.
  Est 1850. Nonprofit. Anglican. Quar (Feb-Dec).

This Christian primary school follows both the International Baccalaureate Primary Years Program and the IB Middle Years Program. The liberal arts program accommodates boys and girls with varying learning styles. The IB frameworks at St. Andrew's comprise transdisciplinary, inquiry-based units of study in the PYP (reception through grade 4) and multidisciplinary units of study in the MYP (grades 5 and 6). High levels of specialization and an array of cocurricular electives add depth to the core curriculum.

Students may participate in interscholastic athletics and a varied selection of musical options. In addition, children attend nearby orchestral, dance and dramatic performances, as well as local art exhibitions.

VICTORIA

ST. LEONARD'S COLLEGE
Day — Coed Gr PS-12

Brighton East, Victoria 3187, Australia. 163 South Rd. Tel: 61-3-9592-2266. Fax: 61-3-9592-3439. EST+15.
www.stleonards.vic.edu.au   E-mail: enrolment@stleonards.vic.edu.au
Roger Hayward, Prin. BSc, PhD.

> **Col Prep. IB PYP. IB Diploma. Curr**—Intl Nat US. **Feat**—Fr Ger Japan Bahasa_ Indonesia Comp_Sci Econ Pol_Sci Australian_Stud Relig Drama Music Dance.
> **Sports**—Basket F_Hockey Soccer Softball Tennis Volley. **Activities**—Acad Arts.
> **Enr 1700.** B 850. G 850. Elem 950. Sec 750. US 15. Host 1605. Other 80.
> **Fac 340.** Host 340.
> **Grad '05—160.**
> **Tui '05-'06: Day A$7830-15,433** (+A$389-1562).
> **Est 1911.** Quar (Feb-Dec).

For the benefit of its substantial international enrollment, St. Leonard's offers both International Baccalaureate and Victoria Certificate of Education tracks. In addition to its main Brighton campus, the school maintains two other locations: the Patterson River campus serves children from early childhood through grade 10, while Camp Ibis, situated on the Banksia Peninsula in Gippsland, allows for outdoor education in the Australian bush. Each location has water sports facilities. All pupils take Christian religion courses.

GEELONG GRAMMAR SCHOOL
Bdg — Coed Gr 5-12; Day — Coed PS-12

Corio, Victoria 3214, Australia. 50 Biddlecombe Ave. Tel: 61-3-5273-9200. Fax: 61-3-5274-1695. EST+15.
www.ggscorio.vic.edu.au   E-mail: ggscorio@ggscorio.vic.edu.au
Stephen Meek, Prin.

> **Col Prep. IB Diploma. Curr**—Intl Nat. **Feat**—Chin Fr Ger Japan Span Comp_Sci Relig Studio_Art Drama Music. **Supp**—Dev_Read ESL LD Rem_Math Tut.
> **Enr 1500.** Elem 720. Sec 780. US 13. Host 1240. Other 247.
> **Fac 180.**
> **Tui '05-'06: Bdg A$28,960-39,960. Day A$7240-17,780.**
> Bldgs 150. Dorms 26. Dorm rms 800. Class rms 60. Libs 5. Sci labs 5. Gyms 2. Fields 5. Courts 34. Pools 2. Riding rings 1. Stables 24.
> **Est 1855.** Nonprofit. Anglican. Quar (Jan-Dec).

This large boarding and day school offers a full elementary and secondary program on four campuses in the Victoria area of Southeastern Australia. At all grade levels, GGS emphasizes the development of academic skills and sound work habits.

Specialist teachers provide instruction in art, music and physical education, and the school's well-developed foreign language department provides boys and girls with an unusually extensive choice of classes. The school primarily serves Australian students, but IB course work provides the school with an international dimension.

CAREY BAPTIST GRAMMAR SCHOOL
Day — Coed Gr PS-12

Kew, Victoria 3101, Australia. 349 Barkers Rd. Tel: 61-3-9816-1222. Fax: 61-3-9816-1263. EST+15.
www.carey.com.au   E-mail: registrar@carey.com.au
Phil De Young, Prin.

> Col Prep. IB Diploma. Curr—Intl Nat. Feat—Lib_Skills Chin Fr Ger Bahasa_Indonesia Environ_Sci Comp_Sci Econ Philos Relig Studio_Art Music Accounting Bus.
> Tui '06-'07: Day A$10,656-20,680 (+A$500-1000).
> Est 1923. Quar (Jan-Dec). Assoc: ECIS.

METHODIST LADIES' COLLEGE
Bdg and Day — Girls Gr PS-12

Kew, Victoria 3101, Australia. 207 Barkers Rd. Tel: 61-3-9274-6333. Fax: 61-3-9819-2345. EST+15.
www.mlc.vic.edu.au   E-mail: college@mlc.vic.edu.au
Rosa Storelli, Prin. BEd, MEd. Paul Nettelbeck, Adm.

> Col Prep. Gen Acad. IB Diploma. Curr—Intl. Feat—Fr Ger Japan Bahasa_Indonesia Comp_Sci Psych Relig Studio_Art Drama Music Home_Ec. Supp—Dev_Read ESL Rem_Math Rem_Read Tut.
> Activities—Arts Rec.
> Enr 2064. Elem 845. Sec 1219. Avg class size: 25.
> Fac 249.
> Tui '05-'06: Bdg A$34,155-35,115. Day A$15,475-16,435.
> Libs 1. Sci labs 1. Comp labs 1. Auds 1. Theaters 1. Art studios 1. Music studios 1. Gyms 1. Fields 1. Courts 2. Pools 1.
> Est 1882. Nonprofit. Quar (Jan-Dec).

MLC provides an Australian and international-style education for elementary and secondary students from North and South America, Asia, Europe and the Pacific Islands, as well as the home country. The school supplements core courses in English, science and math with foreign language and business management classes.

Junior school programs introduce students to library skills, art and computer usage. MLC's middle school program combines a wide range of academic, cocurricular and community activities. Senior school girls progress toward the IB Diploma and may also engage in vocational training programs.

WESLEY COLLEGE
Day — Coed Gr PS-12

**Melbourne, Victoria 3004, Australia. 577 St Kilda Rd. Tel: 61-3-9510-8694.
Fax: 61-3-9521-3164. EST+15.**
www.wesleycollege.net   E-mail: registrar@wesleycollege.net
Helen Drennen, Prin. Kathy Boburka, Adm.

   Col Prep. Gen Acad. IB PYP. IB MYP. IB Diploma. Curr—Intl Nat. **Feat**—Chin Fr
   Ger Japan Bahasa_Indonesia. **Supp**—ESL LD Rem_Math Rem_Read.

   Enr 3500. Accepted: 95%.

   Fac 358.

   Tui '05-'06: Day $9750-14,706.

   Lib 40,000 vols. Sci labs 2. Gyms 3. Fields 2. Tennis courts 12. Squash courts 2.
   Pools 2.

   Est 1865. Nonprofit. Sem (Feb-Dec).

This college preparatory school occupies three campuses. The Prahran campus,
situated three miles from the center of Melbourne, serves students in grades K-
12. Its urban setting is accessible to the city's galleries, courts and art center. The
program at Glen Waverly campus, located about nine miles from the center of the
city, offers a more suburban setting and accepts boys and girls in grades K-10. The
Elsternwick campus, where pupils in grades K-10 may enroll, lies about seven miles
from the city center. Students in grades 11 and 12 attend classes at the Prahran
campus.

On all three campuses, the school conducts a broad-based program. Children age
3 through grade 4 enroll in Wesley's early childhood program, where they learn in
a homeroom setting. Students in the junior school (grades 8-10) develop learning
skills while also becoming increasingly independent. The senior college program
(grades 11 and 12) allows interested pupils to pursue the IB Diploma.

In addition, Wesley maintains two campsites: Chum Creek is situated in the
Australian bush helps to develop pupils' hiking, camping, rock climbing, canoeing
and bushcraft skills; Camp Mallana provides canoeing and sailing opportunities
near the Gippsland Lakes; and a seaside farm in the state's far west enables boys
and girls to study coastal and rural life patterns. All students spend time at each of
these camps.   **See Also Page 555**

NEW ZEALAND

Sq. Miles: 103,483 (About the size of Colorado). **Country Pop:**
4,035,461 (2005). **Capital:** Wellington, pop. 367,600 (2003). **Largest
City:** Auckland, pop. 1,223,200 (2003). **Terrain:** Highly varied, from
snowcapped mountains to lowland plains. **Ethnic Group(s):** European
Maori Polynesian. **Religion(s):** Anglican Roman_Catholic Presbyterian.
Other Language(s): English Maori. **Government:** Parliamentary. **Independence:** 1907 (from United Kingdom). **Per Capita Income:** $23,900
(2004). **GDP:** $99.69 billion (2005). Agriculture 5%. Industry 27%. Ser-
vices 68%. **Currency:** New Zealand Dollar (NZ$).

AUCKLAND INTERNATIONAL COLLEGE

Bdg and Day — Coed Gr 10-12

Auckland, New Zealand. 85 Airedale St, PO Box 3966. Tel: 64-9-309-4480. Fax: 64-9-309-4484. EST+17.

www.aic.ac.nz   E-mail: info@aic.ac.nz

Craig Monaghan, Prin. BSc, MEd.

Col Prep. IB Diploma. Curr—Intl. Exams—ACT CEEB TOEFL. Feat—Chin Fr Ger Japan Comp_Sci Econ Visual_Arts.

Tri (July-June).

KRISTIN SCHOOL

Day — Coed Gr PS-12

Auckland 1331, New Zealand. PO Box 300-087, Albany. Tel: 64-9-415-9566. Fax: 64-9-415-8495. EST+17.

www.kristin.school.nz   E-mail: kristin@kristin.school.nz

Marge Scott, Exec Prin.

Col Prep. IB PYP. IB Diploma. Curr—Intl Nat. Feat—Chin Fr Japan Korean Comp_Sci Psych Relig Performing_Arts Photog Studio_Art Music Dance Outdoor_Ed. Supp—EFL.

Enr 1400.

Tui '06-'07: Day NZ$10,100-12,790 (+NZ$4600).

Est 1973. Quar (Jan-Dec).

CANADA

INDEX TO CANADA

CANADA

Sq. Miles: 3,800,000 (Slightly larger than the US). **Country Pop:** 32,805,041 (2005). **Capital:** Ottawa, pop. 1,000,000. **Largest City:** Toronto, pop. 4,500,000. **Terrain:** Mostly plains with mountains in the west and lowlands in the southeast. **Ethnic Group(s):** British French European Asian Arab African Amerindian. **Religion(s):** Roman Catholic Protestant Christian Muslim. **Other Language(s):** English French. **Government:** Parliamentary Democracy. **Independence:** 1867 (from United Kingdom). **Per Capita Income:** $31,029 (2004). **GDP:** $991 billion (2004). Agriculture 2%. Industry 27%. Services 71%. **Currency:** Canadian Dollar (Can$).

ALBERTA

STRATHCONA-TWEEDSMUIR SCHOOL
Day — Coed Gr 1-12

Okotoks, Alberta T1S 1A2, Canada. RR 2. Tel: 403-938-4431. Fax: 403-938-4492. EST-2. (Dial 1+ from US).
www.sts.ab.ca   E-mail: macount@sts.ab.ca
Catherine Raaflaub, Head. Tina Ierakidis, Adm.
   Col Prep. Gen Acad. IB PYP. IB Diploma. Curr—Intl Nat. **Feat**—Fr Lat Comp_Sci Film Studio_Art Drama Music Outdoor_Ed.
   Enr 685.
   Fac 70.
   Tui '05-'06: Day Can$10,890-13,480.
   Bldgs 4. Lib 30,000 vols. Sci labs 3. Comp labs 3. Theaters 1. Arts ctrs 1. Gyms 2. Fields 4.
   Est 1929. Nonprofit. Tri (Sept-June).

The result of a 1971 merger of Strathcona School for Boys and Tweedsmuir Girls' School, this nondenominational school offers a basic curriculum supplemented by electives. The study of French begins in grade 1, Latin in grade 9. International Baccalaureate courses and diplomas that vary according to each student's level of achievement are offered. The on-campus location of the Wilson Coulee Observatory, which is operated by the Royal Astronomical Society of Canada, provides students with an unusual opportunity to study astronomy under excellent conditions.

The school's outdoor education program involves students at all grade levels in expeditions that range from cross-country skiing and mountaineering to hiking and canoeing. Recreational clubs and physical education are important aspects of STS's program. Opportunities include white-water canoeing, tennis, rugby, ice skating, basketball, gymnastics, track and field, swimming, golf and volleyball.

BRITISH COLUMBIA

ST. GEORGE'S SCHOOL
Bdg — Boys Gr 6-12; Day — Boys 1-12

Vancouver, British Columbia V6S 1V1, Canada. 4175 W 29th Ave. Tel: 604-224-1304. Fax: 604-224-5820. EST-3. (Dial 1+ from US).
www.stgeorges.bc.ca   E-mail: info@stgeorges.bc.ca
Nigel R. L. Toy, Head. MA, DipEd. Bill McCracken, Adm.

    Col Prep. Curr—Nat. Exams—CEEB. AP—Eng Fr Ger Lat Calc Stats Comp_Sci Bio Chem Human_Geog Physics US_Hist Comp_Govt & Pol Econ Psych Art_Hist Music_Theory. Feat—Chin Japan Span Law Ceramics Film Studio_Art Journ Outdoor_Ed.

    Sports—Badminton Basket Crew X-country F_Hockey Golf Ice_Hockey Rugby Soccer Swim Tennis Track Volley W_Polo. Activities—Arts Rec Service.

    Enr 1130. B 126/1004. Accepted: 20%. Yield: 98%. Avg class size: 25.

    Fac 110. M 75. F 35. Adv Deg: 34%.

    Grad '05—143. Col—142. US Col—25. (Columbia 6, USC 4, Yale 3, U of PA 2, Duke 2, NYU 2). Avg SAT: M/V—1350.

    Tui '05-'06: Bdg Can$34,000 (+Can$1000). Day Can$12,600 (+Can$1000). Aid: 90 pupils (Can$450,000).

    Summer: Rec. Tui Bdg Can$3500/2-wk ses. Tui Day Can$500/2-wk ses. 8 wks.

    Endow Can$4,500,000. Plant val Can$14,800,000. Bldgs 3. Dorms 1. Dorm rms 30. Class rms 60. 2 Libs 30,000 vols. Sci labs 10. Comp labs 6. Theaters 1. Art studios 2. Music studios 2. Gyms 4. Fields 4. Courts 6. Pools 1.

    Est 1930. Nonprofit. Anglican. Tri (Sept-June).

Located in suburban Vancouver, St. George's follows the core curriculum outlined by the provincial ministry of education. In addition, the school features a comprehensive Advanced Placement program that is notable for its popularity, with approximately 90 percent of grade-eligible students taking one or more AP classes each year. Streamed courses in English, math and French promote accelerated completion of the core curriculum. While most graduates matriculate at Canadian universities, a substantial number attend competitive institutions in the US, and all pupils are encouraged to take the SAT exam.

    The school's location places it in proximity to the University of British Columbia, ocean beaches and the trails of Pacific Spirit Park. A strong sports program includes both interscholastic and recreational sports. In addition, boys choose from many fine and performing arts opportunities and productions.

YORK HOUSE SCHOOL
Day — Coed Gr K-12

Vancouver, British Columbia V6J 2V6, Canada. 4176 Alexandra St. Tel: 604-736-6551. Fax: 604-736-6530. EST-3. (Dial 1+ from US).

www.yorkhouse.ca   E-mail: development@yorkhouse.ca
G. Gail Ruddy, Head.
   Col Prep. Curr—Nat US. **Supp Lang**—Fr. **Exams**—AP. **AP**—Eng Fr Calc Bio
   Chem Eur_Hist Econ Studio_Art.
   Enr 600.
   Tui '05-'06: Day Can$12,075-13,000 (+$1200-2700).
   Est 1932. Nonprofit. Tri (Sept-June).

GLENLYON NORFOLK SCHOOL
Day — Coed Gr K-12

Victoria, British Columbia V8S 4A8, Canada. 801 Bank St. Tel: 250-370-6801.
   Fax: 250-370-6838. EST-3. (Dial 1+ from US).
www.glenlyonnorfolk.bc.ca   E-mail: gns@glenlyonnorfolk.bc.ca
Simon Bruce-Lockhart, Head.
   Col Prep. IB Diploma. Curr—Intl Nat.
   Tui '05-'06: Day Can$9060-28,843.
   Est 1913. Nonprofit. Tri (Sept-June).

LESTER B. PEARSON
UNITED WORLD COLLEGE OF THE PACIFIC
Bdg — Coed Gr 11-12

Victoria, British Columbia V9C 4H7, Canada. 650 Pearson College Dr. Tel: 250-
   391-2411. Fax: 250-391-2412. EST-3. (Dial 1+ from US).
www.pearsoncollege.ca   E-mail: admin@pearsoncollege.ca
David B. Hawley, Dir.
   Col Prep. IB Diploma. Curr—Intl. **Feat**—Fr Span Environ_Sci Econ Pol_Sci
   Peace_Stud Philos World_Relig Studio_Art Music. **Supp**—Tut.
   Enr 203. B 81. G 122.
   Fac 20. M 15/1. F 4.
   Tui '05-'06: Bdg $0.
   Est 1974. Sem (Sept-May).

LBPC is one of 10 related UWC international schools dedicated to promoting international understanding through education. The organization has campuses in Britain, Canada, Hong Kong, India, Italy, Norway, Singapore, Swaziland, the US and Venezuela, and each school is a community representing more than 70 countries. All students follow the International Baccalaureate curriculum in preparation for the IB exams.

Community service, outdoor programs and events pertaining to global issues supplement the academic offerings. All students admitted to the school attend on full scholarship.

MANITOBA

BALMORAL HALL SCHOOL

Bdg — Girls Gr 6-12; Day — Boys PS-K, Girls PS-12

Winnipeg, Manitoba R3C 3S1, Canada. 630 Westminster Ave. Tel: 204-784-1600. Fax: 204-774-5534. EST-1. (Dial 1+ from US).
www.balmoralhall.com　E-mail: info@balmoralhall.com
Claire Sumerlus, Head. BEd. Pamela McGhie, Adm.

Col Prep. Curr—Nat. AP—Eng Calc Bio Chem Physics. Feat—Fr Japan Span Studio_Art Theater Chorus Music Debate.

Enr 500. Avg class size: 20.

Fac 100.

Grad '05—31.

Tui '05-'06: Bdg Can$30,400-34,300. Day Can$11,550.

Bldgs 7. Dorms 1. Dorm rms 23. Class rms 32. Lib 12,000 vols. Sci labs 3. Comp labs 3. Theaters 1. Art studios 1. Gyms 2.

Est 1901. Nonprofit. Tri (Sept-June).

BH resulted from the 1950 merger of the Riverbend and Rupert's Land Schools. The boarding program serves both international students, who may take part in an integrated ESL program, and Canadian residents. Advanced Placement courses are part of the curriculum in the upper grades.

Extracurricular activities include sports, drama, public speaking and debate.

ST. JOHN'S-RAVENSCOURT SCHOOL

Bdg — Coed Gr 7-12; Day — Coed 1-12

Winnipeg, Manitoba R3T 3K5, Canada. 400 South Dr. Tel: 204-477-2400. Fax: 204-477-2446. EST-1. (Dial 1+ from US).
www.sjr.mb.ca　E-mail: info@sjr.mb.ca
David Howie, Head. PhD.

Col Prep. Curr—Nat US. Exams—CEEB. AP—Fr Calc Stats Bio Chem Physics Eur_Hist Econ. Feat—Span Law Canadian_Stud Studio_Art Music. Supp—ESL.

Fac 71.

Tui '05-'06: Bdg Can$22,850-30,550. Day Can$9700-12,090.

Est 1820. Nonprofit. (Sept-June).

NEW BRUNSWICK

ROTHESAY NETHERWOOD SCHOOL

Bdg and Day — Coed Gr 6-12

Rothesay, New Brunswick E2E 5H1, Canada. 40 College Hill Rd. Tel: 506-847-8224, 866-768-4372. Fax: 506-848-0851. EST+1. (Dial 1+ from US).
www.rns.cc　E-mail: admissions@rns.cc

Paul G. Kitchen, Head. BEd. **Peter Davidson & Elizabeth Kitchen, Adms.**
  Col Prep. Curr—Nat. **Exams**—ACT AP CEEB TOEFL. **AP**—Eng Fr Calc Comp_
    Sci Bio Chem Human_Geog Physics Eur_Hist Econ Music_Theory. **Feat**—Span
    Studio_Art Drama Music Outdoor_Ed. **Supp**—ESL.
  Sports—Badminton Basket Crew X-country F_Hockey Golf Ice_Hockey Rugby
    Soccer Squash Tennis Track Volley. **Activities**—Acad Arts Media Rec.
  Enr 230. B 68/53. G 43/66. Elem 56. Sec 174. US 5. Host 186. Other 39. Accepted:
    85%. Yield: 90%. Avg class size: 15.
  Fac 40. M 19. F 17/4. Host 38. Other 2. Adv Deg: 25%.
  Grad '05—49. Col—49. US Col—2. (U of WA, NYU).
  Tui '05-'06: Bdg Can$27,000 (+Can$3000). **Day Can$15,000** (+Can$2000). **Aid:**
    70 pupils (Can$380,000).
  Endow Can$3,500,000. Plant val Can$28,000,000. Bldgs 24. Dorms 4. Dorm rms
    60. Class rms 23. Libs 1. Chapels 1. Sci labs 4. Theaters 1. Art studios 1. Music
    studios 1. Dance studios 1. Gyms 1. Fields 5. Courts 8. Tennis courts 2. Squash
    courts 2. Rinks 1.
  Est 1877. Nonprofit. Anglican. Tri (Sept-June).

Rothesay Netherwood's program features Advanced Placement preparation, an advisor system, extensive arts offerings and a community service program. A technology program provides a laptop to each student in a campus-wide wireless network. A partnership with Outward Bound provides boys and girls with experiential learning opportunities.

All students participate in athletics and extracurricular activities.

ONTARIO

ST. ANDREW'S COLLEGE
Bdg and Day — Boys Gr 6-12

Aurora, Ontario L4G 3H7, Canada. 15800 Yonge St. Tel: 905-727-3178, 877-378-1899. Fax: 905-727-9032. EST. (Dial 1+ from US).
www.sac.on.ca   E-mail: admission@sac.on.ca
Ted Staunton, Head. BA, BEd, MEd. **Michael Roy, Adm.**
  Col Prep. Curr—Nat. **Exams**—AP CEEB. **AP**—Eng Calc Stats Chem Econ. **Feat**—
    Fr Span Comp_Sci Studio_Art Drama Music. **Supp**—ESL LD Rev Tut.
  Sports—Badminton Basket Baseball X-country Football Ice_Hockey Lacrosse
    Rugby Ski Soccer Swim Tennis Track Volley. **Activities**—Acad Arts Media Rec
    Service.
  Enr 530. B 265/265. US 6. Host 390. Other 134. Accepted: 67%. Yield: 50%. Avg
    class size: 17.
  Fac 62. M 47. F 15. Host 61. Other 1. Adv Deg: 29%.
  Grad '05—94. Col—94. US Col—12. (U of PA, Carnegie Mellon, Cornell, North-
    western, Hamilton, U of TX-Austin). Avg SAT: M/V—1165, Essay—500.
  Tui '05-'06: Bdg Can$36,680 (+Can$5500). **Day Can$22,775** (+Can$6500). **Aid:**
    72 pupils (Can$850,000).
  Summer: Acad. 3 wks.
  Endow Can$20,000,000. Plant val Can$56,000,000. Bldgs 18. Dorms 4. Dorm rms
    120. Class rms 40. Lib 18,000 vols. Sci labs 7. Auds 1. Theaters 2. Art studios 2.

Music studios 2. Gyms 2. Fields 9. Courts 12. Pools 1.
Est 1899. Nonprofit. Tri (Sept-June).

Located on a 110-acre campus 40 miles from Toronto, this boys' school prepares its students for competitive undergraduate programs in Canada, the United States and abroad. The middle school program (grades 6-8) emphasizes structure, creativity and physical activity. In addition to the standard middle school curriculum, boys have the opportunity to earn high school credit for ninth-grade math and comprehensive arts. Daily meetings with an advisor assist pupils with study techniques, exam preparation and time management.

At the upper school level (grades 9-12), boys work toward the Ontario (Canada) Secondary School Diploma. During these years, SAC also offers a selection of Advanced Placement courses for qualified students. High schoolers meet weekly with an advisor to discuss academic and nonacademic matters. At all grade levels, each student participates in the laptop program, as St. Andrew's is completely wireless.

To reinforce classroom learning and instill sound study habits for boarders, the school requires 90 minutes of supervised nightly study time for middle schoolers and two hours for upper schoolers; day pupils frequently spend time on campus into the evening as well. Guest speakers and field trips enhance classroom learning.

ALBERT COLLEGE

Bdg — Coed Gr 7-13; Day — Coed 1-13

Belleville, Ontario K8P 1A6, Canada. 160 Dundas St W. Tel: 613-968-5726. Fax: 613-968-9651. EST. (Dial 1+ from US).
www.albertc.on.ca   E-mail: info@albertc.on.ca
Keith Stansfield, Head. Heather Kidd, Adm.
  Col Prep. Curr—Nat. **Exams**—CEEB TOEFL. **Feat**—Fr Comp_Sci Econ Geog Psych Visual_Arts Drama Music Outdoor_Ed. **Supp**—ESL Tut.
  Enr 229. B 71/58. G 51/49. Elem 93. Sec 136. US 7. Host 156. Other 66. Avg class size: 15.
  Fac 35. M 17. F 18. Host 35. Adv Deg: 11%.
  Grad '05—59. Col—57. US Col—1. (U of MI).
  Tui '05-'06: Bdg Can$32,400-37,100. Day Can$9400-17,900. Aid: 45 pupils (Can$360,000).
  Endow Can$1,400,000. Bldgs 6. Dorms 4. Dorm rms 94. Class rms 25. Lib 11,000 vols. Gyms 1. Fields 2. Pools 1.
  Est 1857. Nonprofit. Sem (Sept-June).

The oldest boarding school of its kind in Canada, this culturally diverse school enrolls students from approximately two dozen countries. In addition to meeting provincial educational requirements, Albert offers Advanced Placement courses for qualified pupils. Frequent field trips reinforce class work at all grade levels. A well-developed equestrian program is available, and boys and girls have many waterfront and boating opportunities on the Bay of Quinte. The Outward Bound program provides wilderness adventure and leadership opportunities for students.

ASHBURY COLLEGE

Bdg — Coed Gr 9-12; Day Boys 4-12, Girls 9-12

Ottawa, Ontario K1M 0T3, Canada. 362 Mariposa Ave. Tel: 613-749-5954. Fax: 613-749-9724. EST. (Dial 1+ from US).
www.ashbury.on.ca   E-mail: admissions@ashbury.on.ca
Tam Matthews, Head. BS, MEd. Lisa Lewicki, Adm.
  Col Prep. IB Diploma. Curr—Intl. Bilingual—Fr. Exams—CEEB SSAT. Feat—Span Comp_Sci Can_Hist Econ Geog Sociol Philos Studio_Art. Supp—ESL Tut.
  Sports—Badminton Crew X-country F_Hockey Football Ice_Hockey Ski Soccer Squash Swim Tennis Track Volley. Activities—Acad Govt/Pol Media Service.
  Enr 645. B 42/402. G 41/160. Elem 160. Sec 485. US 18. Host 542. Other 85. Accepted: 60%. Avg class size: 16.
  Fac 75. M 40. F 35. Adv Deg: 28%.
  Tui '05-'06: Bdg Can$33,700 (+Can$2000). Day Can$16,120 (+Can$1500). Aid: 129 pupils (Can$350,000).
  Summer: Acad. Tui Day Can$500. 5 wks.
  Lib 8000 vols. Sci labs 6. Lang labs 1. Comp labs 3. Theaters 1. Art studios 1. Music studios 1. Gyms 2. Fields 2. Courts 2.
  Est 1891. Nonprofit. Anglican. Tri (Sept-June).

Offering a full college preparatory program, Ashbury prepares boys and girls for university entrance and the International Baccalaureate Diploma. Interested students may pursue a bilingual (English and French) diploma. Among extracurricular options are an outdoor education program that features skiing, canoeing, hiking, cycling and orienteering.

ELMWOOD SCHOOL

Day — Coed Gr PS-13

Ottawa, Ontario K1M 0V9, Canada. 261 Buena Vista Rd. Tel: 613-749-6761. Fax: 613-741-8210. EST. (Dial 1+ from US).
www.elmwood.on.ca   E-mail: admissions@elmwood.on.ca
Helen Hirsch Spence, Head.
  Col Prep. IB PYP. IB MYP. IB Diploma. Curr—Intl Nat. Supp Lang—Fr. Exams—CEEB. Feat—Fr Ger Lat Span Comp_Sci Econ Philos Studio_Art Drama Theater_Arts Music. Supp—ESL Tut.
  Enr 500. B 30. G 470. Elem 270. Sec 230. US 18. Host 453. Other 29.
  Fac 82. M 8/1. F 69/4.
  Grad '05—45. Col—45.
  Tui '05-'06: Day Can$14,600-16,700.
  Endow Can$360,000. Plant val Can$11,000,000. Bldgs 3. Libs 2. Sci labs 4. Comp labs 3. Theater/auds 1. Art studios 1. Music studios 1. Gyms 1.
  Est 1915. Nonprofit. Tri (Sept-June).

Elmwood offers a enriched course of study at all grade levels that progressively readies students for college. While boys are accepted only into the early grades, girls may attend through grade 13. For girls seeking additional challenge in the upper grades, the school supplements the Ontario curriculum with the two-year International Baccalaureate Diploma program. A notable feature of the foreign language department is the French curriculum: Students may learn French as a second language, as Elmwood offers three levels of instruction in each grade; those who follow a prescribed sequence of courses that lead to fluency in French may earn a bilingual certificate.

The school maintains a highly international environment. Boys and girls enroll from countries around the world, and Elmwood conducts exchange programs with schools in such countries as Switzerland, France, Spain, Germany and Italy.

BISHOP STRACHAN SCHOOL
Bdg — Girls Gr 7-12; Day — Girls PS-12

Toronto, Ontario M4V 1X2, Canada. 298 Lonsdale Rd. Tel: 416-483-4325. Fax: 416-481-5632. EST. (Dial 1+ from US).
www.bss.on.ca   E-mail: admissions@bss.on.ca
Kim Gordon, Head. Catherine Hant, Adm.
> **Col Prep. Curr**—Nat. **Exams**—AP. **AP**—Eng Fr Lat Span Calc Stats Comp_Sci Bio Chem Human_Geog Eur_Hist US_Hist Comp_Govt & Pol. **Feat**—Chin Studio_Art Drama.
> **Activities**—Acad Arts Cultural/Relig Govt/Pol Media Rec Service.
> **Enr 625.** G 90/535.
> **Fac 83.**
> **Grad '05—120.**
> **Tui '06-'07: Bdg Can$39,600** (+Can$1000-1500). **Day Can$21,200** (+Can$1000-1500).
> **Summer:** Acad. 5 wks.
> Bldgs 1. Dorm rms 58. Class rms 50. Libs 2. Gyms 2. Fields 1. Courts 2. Pools 1.
> **Est 1867.** Nonprofit. Anglican. Sem (Sept-June).

BSS, which is located near downtown Toronto, offers a standard Canadian curriculum in a residential and day setting. French is taught at all grade levels, and Mandarin and Italian are also among Bishop Strachan's foreign languages. Girls choose from a wide selection of Advanced Placement courses. A laptop program facilitates the integration of technology into the curriculum.

BRANKSOME HALL
Bdg — Girls Gr 8-12; Day — Girls PS-12

Toronto, Ontario M4W 1N4, Canada. 10 Elm Ave. Tel: 416-920-9741. Fax: 416-920-5390. EST. (Dial 1+ from US).
www.branksome.on.ca   E-mail: admissions@branksome.on.ca
Karen Murton, Prin. BA, BEd, MEd. **Ruth Ann Penny, Adm.**
> **Col Prep. IB Diploma. Curr**—Intl Nat. **Supp Lang**—Fr. **Exams**—SSAT. **Feat**—Comp_Sci Econ Drama Music Accounting. **Supp**—ESL.
> **Enr 885.** G 65/820. Avg class size: 19.
> **Fac 100.** Adv Deg: 52%.
> **Grad '05—104. Col—104. US Col—6.** (Harvard, Columbia, Brown, NYU, Princeton, Yale).
> **Tui '06-'07: Bdg Can$39,000** (+Can$5000). **Day Can$20,700** (+Can$5000). **Aid:** 5 pupils (Can$30,000).

Endow Can$9,000,000. Bldgs 12. Dorms 2. Dorm rms 35. Class rms 50. Libs 2. Sci
  labs 4. Comp labs 5. Theaters 1. Art studios 2. Music studios 2. Gyms 2. Fields
  2. Courts 6. Pools 1.
Est 1903. Nonprofit. Tri (Sept-June).

Girls at Branksome choose between the national curriculum and International
Baccalaureate programming. The coordinated junior school program (grades PS-
6) provides a solid grounding in the basics, with core courses in English, French,
math, science and social studies. All students take part in hands-on computer classes
and environmental studies course work. In grade 6, an extended French program
enables girls to study social studies in French.

The middle division's academic program (grades 7 and 8) focuses mainly on
core subjects, while also preparing students for advanced classes. In the senior
division (grades 9-12), electives such as computer studies, accounting, economics,
Latin, Spanish, art, music and drama complement course work in required subjects.
Pupils may also take Advanced Placement classes in the higher grades.

Assemblies, field trips, drama, musical ensembles, debate, public speaking,
community service, and various clubs and athletic activities complete Branksome's
program.

CAMBRIDGE INTERNATIONAL COLLEGE OF CANADA
Bdg and Day — Coed Gr 11-12

**Toronto, Ontario M8Z 4E1, Canada. 35 Ourland Ave. Tel: 416-252-9195, 877-422-
2422. Fax: 416-252-4266. EST.** (Dial 1+ from US).
www.cambridgeinternational.com E-mail: cambridge@globalserve.net
Irwin Diamond, Prin. BA, BEd.
  Col Prep. Gen Acad. Curr—Intl Nat. **Exams**—TOEFL O-level A-level. **Feat**—
    Comp_Sci Econ Pol_Sci Studio_Art Accounting Bus. **Supp**—Dev_Read ESL
    Makeup Rem_Math Rem_Read Rev Tut.
  Sports—Basket Soccer. **Activities**—Acad Govt/Pol Rec.
  Enr 97. B 26/31. G 22/18. Sec 97. Host 5. Other 92. Accepted: 85%. Yield: 95%.
    Avg class size: 9.
  Fac 12. M 8. F 4. Adv Deg: 33%.
  Grad '05—56. Col—45.
  Tui '05-'06: Bdg $9800 (+$2100). **Day $6820. Aid:** 12 pupils.
  Summer: Acad Enrich Rev Rem Rec. Tui Day $645/4-wk ses. 10 wks.
  Plant val $3,000,000. Bldgs 1. Dorms 1. Class rms 10. Lib 7600 vols. Sci labs 1.
    Comp labs 1. Auds 1. Art studios 1. Gyms 1. Fields 2. Courts 3. Pools 1.
  Est 1980. Nonprofit. Tri (Sept-July).

Cambridge International's curriculum prepares students, many of whom enroll
from Asia, the Middle East and the Caribbean, for entrance into universities in the
US, Canada, the UK and other countries. The basic program of arts and sciences is
broadened in grades 11 and 12 by environmental and family studies, and in grade 12
by courses in accounting, economic reasoning, people and politics, world religions
and American history. The school's year-round trimester system allows pupils to
complete one academic year in two terms. International pupils may receive intensive English as a Second Language on a daily basis.

Cultural field trips to museums, plays, sporting events, Parliament, Niagara Falls and other local sites complement academics.

CRESCENT SCHOOL
Day — Boys Gr 3-12

Toronto, Ontario M2L 1A2, Canada. 2365 Bayview Ave. Tel: 416-449-2556. Fax: 416-449-7950. EST. (Dial 1+ from US).
www.crescentschool.org   E-mail: info@crescentschool.org
Geoff Roberts, Head. BA, BEd, MEd. **David Budden, Adm.**

> **Col Prep. Curr**—Nat. **Exams**—AP CEEB. **AP**—Eng Fr Calc Stats Comp_Sci Bio Chem Human_Geog Physics World_Hist Econ. **Feat**—Span Anthro Law Pol_Sci Sociol Philos World_Relig Studio_Art Drama Music Accounting.
>
> **Sports**—Badminton Basket X-country Golf Ice_Hockey Rugby Ski Soccer Softball Squash Tennis Track Volley. **Activities**—Acad Arts Rec Service.
>
> **Enr 664.** B 664. Elem 307. Sec 357. Host 664. Accepted: 62%. Yield: 64%. Avg class size: 19.
>
> **Fac 68.** M 45. F 18/5. Host 68. Adv Deg: 17%.
>
> **Grad '05—87. US Col—10.** (Cornell, Princeton, Colgate, Hamilton, U of Chicago, Carnegie Mellon).
>
> **Tui '05-'06: Day Can$19,950** (+Can$3500). **Aid:** 20 pupils (Can$237,000).
>
> **Summer:** Acad Rec. Tui Day Can$1350. 5 wks.
>
> Endow Can$2,700,000. Plant val Can$35,000,000. Bldgs 3. Class rms 45. Libs 1. Sci labs 5. Lang labs 1. Comp labs 4. Theaters 1. Art studios 2. Music studios 2. Gyms 3. Fields 2. Courts 3.
>
> **Est 1913.** Nonprofit. Tri (Sept-June).

Comprising lower, middle and upper schools, Crescent emphasizes sound academic skills development and, in the higher grades, college preparation. Programming meets Ontario curricular requirements; in addition, older students choose from Advanced Placement courses in most major disciplines. The arts form an integral aspect of the curriculum, and boys also have many opportunities to take part in artistic endeavors outside the classroom.

Both intramural and interscholastic athletics are available each term, as are various interest clubs. Students may also participate in Outward Bound and community service.

ST. CLEMENT'S SCHOOL
Day — Girls Gr 1-12

Toronto, Ontario M4R 1G8, Canada. 21 St Clement's Ave. Tel: 416-483-4835. Fax: 416-483-8242. EST. (Dial 1+ from US).
www.scs.on.ca   E-mail: admissions@scs.on.ca
Patricia D. Parisi, Prin. BA, BEd, MSSc, EdS. **Martha Perry, Adm.**

> **Col Prep. Curr**—Nat. **Bilingual**—Fr. **Exams**—AP CEEB SSAT. **AP**—Eng Fr Lat Comp_Sci Bio Chem Environ_Sci Human_Geog Physics Eur_Hist US_Hist Econ Art_Hist Studio_Art Music_Theory.
>
> **Enr 425.** G 425.
>
> **Fac 51.** M 9. F 42. Adv Deg: 33%.

Grad '05—57. Col—57. US Col—2. (Brown, Smith).
Tui '05-'06: Day Can$17,450.
Summer: Acad. Tui Day Can$1275. 4 wks.
Bldgs 1. Class rms 26. Libs 1. Sci labs 3. Lang labs 1. Comp labs 2. Auds 1. Art
   studios 1. Music studios 1. Gyms 1. Fields 1.
Est 1901. Nonprofit.

St. Clement's, located in the center of the city, offers a bilingual, Canadian-style
curriculum. Academic instruction in French is provided for all grades, while pupils
in grades 11 and 12 choose from Advanced Placement courses in the major disciplines. Students may take AP courses between school years by enrolling in a special
summer program for an additional fee. Test preparation for both the SAT and the
SSAT examinations is part of the curriculum.

TORONTO FRENCH SCHOOL
Day — Coed Gr PS-12

**Toronto, Ontario M4N 1T7, Canada. 306 Lawrence Ave E. Tel: 416-484-6533.
   Fax: 416-488-3090. EST.** (Dial 1+ from US).
www.tfs.on.ca   E-mail: admissions@tfs.on.ca
Jean Brugniau, Head. Consuelo Ramos, Adm.
   Col Prep. IB Diploma. Curr—Intl. **Bilingual**—Fr. **Feat**—Fr Greek Lat Span Comp_
      Sci Econ Studio_Art Theater_Arts Music.
   Sports—Badminton Basket Baseball X-country Gymnastics Soccer Tennis Track
      Volley. **Activities**—Acad Arts Govt/Pol Media Service.
   Enr 1260.
   Fac 150.
   Grad '05—63.
   Tui '05-'06: Day Can$9035-19,620.
   Est 1962. Nonprofit. Tri (Sept-June).

TFS was founded in response to the need to educate children primarily from
English-speaking families in both constitutionally recognized cultures. In the lower
grades, French is the primary language of instruction: French is spoken exclusively
in the preschool, while 75 percent of the course work in grades 2-7 is in the language. Intensive language programs in grades PS-7 assist children who have had
little or no prior exposure to French. In the upper grades, language of instruction
varies according to individual course selection. Classes in French are conducted by
native French speakers, while classes in English are taught by teachers whose native
language is English.
   Branches of the school operate in Toronto and Mississauga.

THE YORK SCHOOL
Day — Coed Gr PS-13

**Toronto, Ontario M4T 1X2, Canada. 1320 Yonge St. Tel: 416-926-1325. Fax: 416-
   926-9592. EST.** (Dial 1+ from US).
www.yorkschool.com   E-mail: admin@tys.on.ca
Barbara Goodwin Zeibots, Head. Marilyn Andrews, Adm.

Col Prep. IB PYP. IB MYP. IB Diploma. Curr—Intl. **Feat**—Fr Span Studio_Art
Music.
Enr 600. Elem 370. Sec 230. Avg class size: 19.
Fac 75.
Grad '05—14. Col—14.
Tui '05-'06: Day Can$18,675 (+Can$2500).
Summer: Rec. 2-4 wks.
Bldgs 1. Libs 2. Comp labs 2. Auds 1. Theaters 1. Gyms 1.
Est 1965. Nonprofit. Tri (Sept-June).

York places particular emphasis on literacy, arithmetic computation, critical
thinking, research, problem solving and communication. Integration of computer
technology enhances the curriculum. Strong programs in art, music and physical
education complement course work in the standard subjects. Graduates of the international program receive the widely accepted IB Diploma.

QUEBEC

BISHOP'S COLLEGE SCHOOL
Bdg and Day — Coed Gr 7-12

Lennoxville, Quebec J1M 1Z8, Canada. 80 Moulton Hill Rd. Tel: 819-566-0227.
Fax: 819-822-8917. EST. (Dial 1+ from US).
www.bishopscollegeschool.com
E-mail: admissions@bishopscollegeschool.com
Lewis Evans, Head. Theodora Brinckman, Adm.

Col Prep. Curr—Nat. **Bilingual**—Fr. **Exams**—ACT AP CEEB. **AP**—Eng Calc
Comp_Sci Eur_Hist. **Feat**—Creative_Writing Robotics Sociol Philos Studio_Art
Drama Music Accounting. **Supp**—ESL Tut.
Sports—Basket X-country Football Golf Gymnastics Ice_Hockey Rugby Ski
Soccer Softball Swim Tennis Track. **Activities**—Arts Govt/Pol Rec.
Enr 257. B 120/31. G 77/29. Elem 68. Sec 189. Accepted: 66%. Avg class size: 11.
Fac 39. M 19/1. F 18/1. Adv Deg: 25%.
Tui '06-'07: Bdg Can$33,800 (+Can$2000). **Day Can$16,200** (+Can$2000).
Summer: Rec. Fr. ESL. Tui Bdg Can$2850. Tui Day Can$1750. 4 wks.
Endow Can$9,000,000. Bldgs 20. Dorms 8. Dorm rms 114. Lib 22,000 vols. Comp
labs 2. Theaters 1. Art studios 1. Music studios 1. Gyms 2. Fields 7. Courts 2.
Riding rings 1. Weight rms 2.
Est 1836. Inc. Tri (Sept-June).

Located on a 350-acre campus one and a half hours from Montreal and 40 minutes from the Vermont border, BCS maintains a college preparatory curriculum that
includes bilingual options, Advanced Placement courses, enrichment programs and
a range of extracurricular activities. Among other aspects of school life are study
abroad opportunities, outdoor education, arts activities and a mandatory sports
program.

SEDBERGH SCHOOL

Bdg and Day — Coed Gr 7-12

Montebello, Quebec J0V 1L0, Canada. 810 cote Azelie. Tel: 819-423-5523, 877-423-5523. Fax: 819-423-5769. EST. (Dial 1+ from US).
www.sedbergh.com   E-mail: admissions@sedbergh.com
Jeremy I. D. McLean, Head. Joanna A. A. Hoad, Adm.
  Col Prep. Curr—Nat. Exams—CEEB TOEFL. Feat—Fr Environ_Sci Marine_Biol/ Sci Econ Visual_Arts Outdoor_Ed Wilderness_Ed. Supp—ESL Tut.
  Sports—Rugby Ski Soccer. Activities—Govt/Pol Media Rec Service.
  Enr 95. B 55/3. G 35/2. Elem 28. Sec 67. US 5. Host 60. Other 30. Accepted: 65%. Yield: 60%. Avg class size: 12.
  Fac 23. M 9. F 14. Host 21. Other 2. Adv Deg: 21%.
  Grad '05—35. Col—34. US Col—2.
  Tui '05-'06: Bdg Can$41,275 (+Can$2000-5000). Day Can$17,000 (+Can$2000-5000). Aid: 28 pupils (Can$145,000).
  Bldgs 2. Dorms 2. Dorm rms 27. Class rms 12. Lib 16,000 vols. Sci labs 2. Comp labs 1. Art studios 1. Gyms 1. Fields 4. Courts 2.
  Est 1939. Nonprofit. (Sept-June).

Located on 1200 acres in the Laurentian Mountains of southern Quebec, Sedbergh offers an integrated experiential curriculum that allows students to learn across disciplines. Outdoor education and environmental awareness are important aspects of the curriculum. Students prepare for the US College Boards and the Quebec Matriculation examinations. While English is the language of instruction, students study French each year.

The school's mandatory sports program includes such offerings as downhill and cross-country skiing, kayaking, mountain biking, soccer and rugby.

MISS EDGAR'S AND MISS CRAMP'S SCHOOL

Day — Girls Gr K-11

Montreal, Quebec H3Y 3H6, Canada. 525 Mt Pleasant Ave. Tel: 514-935-6357. Fax: 514-935-1099. EST. (Dial 1+ from US).
www.ecs.qc.ca   E-mail: dmac@ecs.qc.ca
Susyn E. Borer, Head. BEd.
  Col Prep. Curr—Nat. Bilingual—Fr. Feat—Comp_Sci Econ Women's_Stud Can_Stud Studio_Art Drama Music.
  Sports—Badminton Basket X-country Golf Soccer Swim Tennis Track Volley. Activities—Acad Arts Media Service.
  Enr 323. G 323. Elem 205. Sec 118. Yield: 50%. Avg class size: 19.
  Fac 39. M 5. F 29/5. Host 39. Adv Deg: 35%.
  Grad '05—28.
  Tui '05-'06: Day Can$11,400-12,975 (+Can$1000). Aid: 30 pupils (Can$87,910).
  Bldgs 2. Class rms 25. Lib 5000 vols. Comp labs 2. Theaters 1. Art studios 1. Music studios 1. Gyms 1. Fields 1.
  Est 1909. Nonprofit. Quar (Sept-June).

ECS provides a varied college preparatory curriculum that emphasizes critical-thinking skills. The study of French begins at the junior school level (grades K-5) with a French immersion program that enables children to study half the day in English and half in French. Mother-tongue instruction in French is available in grades 6-11. The senior school (grades 9-11) features a laptop program as part of its integrated technology curriculum.

Girls take part in a cocurricular program that comprises community service, athletics, interest clubs and opportunities in the arts.

PRIORY SCHOOL
Day — Coed Gr K-6

Montreal, Quebec H3Y 1R9, Canada. 3120 The Boulevard. Tel: 514-935-5966. Fax: 514-935-1428. EST. (Dial 1+ from US).
www.priory.qc.ca   E-mail: info@priory.qc.ca
John Marinelli, Prin. BEd, DipEd, MSc. **Debra Merritt, Adm.**

  Pre-Prep. Curr—Nat. **Feat**—Fr Computers Relig Studio_Art Music.
  Sports—Basket Soccer Track. **Activities**—Acad Rec.
  Enr 170. Elem 170. Accepted: 55%. Yield: 85%. Avg class size: 24.
  Fac 14. M 1. F 11/2. Host 14. Adv Deg: 14%.
  Grad '05—24. Prep—24.
  Tui '05-'06: Day Can$8040 (+Can$2120). **Aid:** 6 pupils (Can$22,000).
  Endow Can$1,000,000. Plant val Can$4,000,000. Bldgs 3. Class rms 12. Lib 2000 vols. Comp labs 1. Art studios 1. Music studios 1. Gyms 1. Rinks 1.
  Est 1947. Nonprofit. Roman Catholic. Quar (Aug-June).

Although the school's primary language of instruction is English, French language and culture are featured in the curriculum at all grade levels. Computer literacy and religion courses are part of the program. Hands-on instruction in chess begins in the early grades, and the school hosts an annual tournament. Priory is located in a residential area near downtown.

STANSTEAD COLLEGE
Bdg and Day — Coed Gr 7-12

Stanstead, Quebec J0B 3E0, Canada. 450 Dufferin St. Tel: 819-876-2223. Fax: 819-876-5891. EST. (Dial 1+ from US).
www.stansteadcollege.com   E-mail: admissions@stansteadcollege.com
Michael T. Wolfe, Head. MA, MMgt. **Joanne Carruthers, Adm.**

  Col Prep. Curr—Nat. **Bilingual**—Fr. **Exams**—AP CEEB. **AP**—Fr Calc Bio Chem Environ_Sci Physics Comp_Govt & Pol Econ Studio_Art. **Supp**—ESL Tut.
  Sports—Basket X-country Football Ice_Hockey Rugby Ski Soccer Squash Swim Tennis. **Activities**—Acad Arts Govt/Pol Media Rec Service.
  Enr 205. US 38. Host 81. Other 86. Avg class size: 12.
  Fac 32. Adv Deg: 12%.
  Tui '05-'06: Bdg Can$34,660 (+Can$2000). **Day Can$15,590.**
  Summer: Acad Rec. ESL. 4 wks.
  Bldgs 9. Dorms 4. Lib 20,000 vols. Auds 1. Art studios 2. Music studios 1. Gyms 1. Fields 6. Courts 2. Pools 1.
  Est 1872. Nonprofit. Tri (Sept-June). Assoc: NEASC.

Situated on a 620-acre site in Quebec's Eastern Townships, Stanstead enrolls students from throughout Canada, the US and several other nations. The school's rigorous college preparatory curriculum reflects the bilingual nature of Quebec, as there are formal programs in both French and English.

Younger pupils develop learning strategies and study skills as they follow a varied program that emphasizes the core subjects of English, French and math. In the later grades, students pursue a two-year advanced curriculum leading to Quebec's diploma. Grade 12 at Stanstead focuses on preparing boys and girls for matriculation at schools outside of the province. Computer instruction is integral to class work at all grade levels.

SELWYN HOUSE SCHOOL

Day — Coed Gr K-11

Westmount, Quebec H3Y 2H8, Canada. 95 Chemin Cote St-Antoine Rd. Tel: 514-931-9481. Fax: 514-931-6118. EST. (Dial 1+ from US).
www.selwyn.ca   E-mail: admission@selwyn.ca
William Mitchell, Head. BA, BEd, MEd.
   Col Prep. Curr—Nat. **Bilingual**—Fr.
   Enr 565. Elem 391. Sec 174.
   Fac 67. Adv Deg: 35%.
   Tui '05-'06: Day Can$12,590-16,675.
   Est 1908. Nonprofit. Sem (Sept-June).

SASKATCHEWAN

LUTHER COLLEGE HIGH SCHOOL

Bdg and Day — Coed Gr 9-12

Regina, Saskatchewan S4T 5A5, Canada. 1500 Royal St. Tel: 306-791-9150. Fax: 306-359-6962. EST-1. (Dial 1+ from US).
www.luthercollege.edu   E-mail: lutherhs@luthercollege.edu
Berbel Knoll, Prin. BEd. **Sue Stinson, Adm.**
   Col Prep. IB Diploma. Curr—Intl Nat. **Exams**—CEEB TOEFL. **Feat**—Fr Ger Lat Comp_Sci Can_Stud Ethics Studio_Art Drama Accounting. **Supp**—ESL.
   Sports—Badminton Basket Baseball Cheer X-country Football Golf Ice_Hockey Soccer Softball Track Volley. **Activities**—Acad Cultural/Relig Govt/Pol Media Rec Service.
   Enr 450. B 50/175. G 50/175. Sec 450. US 1. Host 359. Other 90. Avg class size: 25.
   Fac 34. M 18/3. F 9/4. Host 33. Other 1. Adv Deg: 11%.
   Grad '05—102.
   Tui '05-'06: Bdg Can$14,690-14,890. Day Can$7940-8140.
   Bldgs 3. Dorms 2. Dorm rms 100. Class rms 15. Lib 12,000 vols. Chapels 1. Sci labs 3. Comp labs 1. Auds 1. Art studios 1. Music studios 1. Gyms 1. Fields 2.
   Est 1913. Nonprofit. Lutheran. Sem (Sept-June).

Offering college preparation in a Christian context, LCHS conducts a rigorous liberal arts program for students from more than a dozen countries. Foreign language offerings are noteworthy: Luther College is the only high school in the province to offer Latin, and one of the few to offer German. In addition to fulfilling curricular requirements set by the Government of Saskatchewan, boys and girls take a course in Christian Ethics each year; religion is an important aspect of school life.

Students wishing to pursue higher education outside of Canada may enroll in the two-year International Baccalaureate Diploma Program. A well-developed music program comprises several singing groups; instrumental ensembles; and junior, intermediate and senior handbell choirs.

CARIBBEAN ISLANDS

INDEX TO COUNTRIES IN THE
CARIBBEAN ISLANDS

CARIBBEAN ISLANDS

ARUBA

Sq. Miles: 75 (Slightly larger than Washington, DC). **Country Pop:** 71,566 (2005). **Capital:** Oranjestad, pop. 60,000 (2003). **Terrain:** Flat with a few hills; scant vegetation. **Ethnic Group(s):** Caribbean Amerindian. **Religion(s):** Roman_Catholic Protestant Hindu Muslim Methodist Anglican Methodist Evangelist Jehovah's_Witness Jewish. **Official Language(s):** Dutch. **Other Language(s):** Papiamento English Spanish. **Government:** Parliamentary Democracy. **Governed By:** The Netherlands. **GDP:** $2.15 billion (2002). **Currency:** Aruban Guilder (Af.).

INTERNATIONAL SCHOOL OF ARUBA
Day — Coed Gr PS-12

Wayaca Aruba. Tel: 297-845365. Fax: 297-847-341. EST+1.
www.isaruba.com   E-mail: intschool@setarnet.aw
Robert Werner, Head. BS, MEd. Carol Waymire, Adm.
  Col Prep. Curr—US. Exams—CEEB. AP—Eng. Feat—Dutch Fr Span Comp_Sci Econ Psych Studio_Art Drama Music Bus. Supp—ESL Rem_Read Tut.
  Enr 135. Avg class size: 15.
  Fac 26. M 8. F 13/5. US 14. Host 4. Other 8. Adv Deg: 65%.
  Grad '05—19. Col—17. US Col—17. (U of FL, Boston U, U of PA, Emory, Hardin-Simmons).
  Tui '02-'03: Day Af.15,120-18,920. Aid: 2 pupils ($14,500).
  Summer: Enrich Rec. Tui Day $280/wk. 4 wks.
  Bldgs 1. Class rms 28. Lib 10,000 vols. Sci labs 2. Lang labs 1. Comp labs 1. Art studios 1. Fields 1. Courts 3.
  Est 1986. Nonprofit. Sem (Aug-June). Assoc: A/OPR/OS SACS.

ISA, which was founded by local parents, provides English-language education to island children. The curriculum incorporates a selection of liberal arts courses and aims to prepare students for the transition to US schools and universities. After-school activities complement academic work.

BAHAMAS

Sq. Miles: 5382 (Slightly larger than Connecticut and Rhode Island combined). **Country Pop:** 301,790 (2005). **Capital:** Nassau, pop. 179,300 (2002). **Terrain:** Low and flat. **Ethnic Group(s):** African European

Asian Hispanic. **Religion(s):** Baptist Roman_Catholic Anglican Evangelical Methodist Rastafarian. **Official Language(s):** English. **Other Language(s):** Creole. **Government:** Constitutional Parliamentary Democracy. **Independence:** 1973 (from United Kingdom). **GDP:** $5.7 billion (2003). Financial Services 15%. Manufacturing 8%. Tourism 40%. **Currency:** Bahamian Dollar (B$).

LUCAYA INTERNATIONAL SCHOOL
Day — Coed Gr PS-12

Freeport, Bahamas. PO Box 44066. Tel: 242-373-4004. Fax: 242-373-6510. EST. (Dial 1+ from US).
www.lucaya-is.org   E-mail: lis@coralwave.com
Anthony Baron, Dir. BA, MA.
  Col Prep. IB PYP. IB Diploma. Curr—Intl.

LYFORD CAY INTERNATIONAL SCHOOL
Day — Coed Gr PS-12

Nassau, Bahamas. Lyford Cay Dr, PO Box N-7776. Tel: 242-362-4774. Fax: 242-362-5198. EST. (Dial 1+ from US).
www.lyfordcayschool.net   E-mail: info@lyfordcayschool.net
Paul Lieblich, Prin. Rose-Marie Taylor, Adm.
  Col Prep. Gen Acad. IB MYP. IB Diploma. Curr—Intl Nat. **Feat**—Humanities Fr Ger Span Comp_Sci Geog Studio_Art Drama Music. **Supp**—EFL LD Tut.
  Sports—Basket Golf Soccer Softball Tennis Volley. **Activities**—Acad Arts.
  Enr 305. B 158. G 147. Elem 265. Sec 40. US 50. Host 130. Other 125. Avg class size: 16.
  Fac 40. M 7/1. F 27/5. US 7. Host 11. Other 22. Adv Deg: 17%.
  Tui '05-'06: Day B$8200-11,950 (+B$3000). **Aid:** 21 pupils (B$70,000).
  Summer: Rec. Tui Day $250/wk. 5 wks.
  Endow B$300,000. Plant val B$4,881,000. Bldgs 6. Class rms 24. Lib 1000 vols. Sci labs 1. Comp labs 1. Art studios 1. Music studios 1. Fields 2. Pools 1.
  Est 1960. Nonprofit. Sem (Sept-June). Assoc: CIS NEASC.

Located within walking distance of the island's beaches, LCIS encourages students to use their tropical surroundings for exploration and recreation. Middle school students follow the International Baccalaureate Middle Years Program and also take the Bahamas Junior Certificate Examinations, while pupils in grades 11 and 12 work toward the International Baccalaureate Diploma. The program of studies emphasizes Bahamian culture and features local field trips.

ST ANDREW'S SCHOOL
THE INTERNATIONAL SCHOOL OF THE BAHAMAS

Day — Coed Gr PS-12

Nassau, Bahamas. PO Box EE 17340. Tel: 242-324-2621. Fax: 242-324-0816. EST. (Dial 1+ from US).

www.st-andrews.com   E-mail: sandrews@st-andrews.com

Robert Wade, Prin. Sally Varani-Jones, Adm.

Col Prep. Curr—Intl Nat UK. **Feat**—Fr Span Comp_Sci Econ Drama Theater_Arts Music. **Supp**—LD.

Enr 710.

Fac 60.

Tui '05-'06: Day B$6040-10,940 (+B$500).

Summer: Acad Rec. 4 wks.

Bldgs 5. Lib 12,000 vols.

Est 1948. Nonprofit. Tri (Sept-June). Assoc: CIS NEASC.

The elementary program at St Andrew's features the International Baccalaureate Primary Years Program, while students at the secondary level prepare for the Bahamas General Certificate of Secondary Education, which is a modified version of the British GCSE. Diagnosis, assessment and support are available through a special program for pupils with learning differences.

Among the school's extracurricular options are interest clubs, dance, drama, scuba, academic clubs, Model UN, student council, music, choir, student council, yearbook, and various intramural and interscholastic sports.

TAMBEARLY SCHOOL

Day — Coed Gr PS-9

Nassau, Bahamas. PO Box N-4284. Tel: 242-327-5965. Fax: 242-327-5963. EST. (Dial 1+ from US).

www.tambearly.com   E-mail: tambearly@coralwave.com

Alice Langford, Prin. BA, BS.

Pre-Prep. Curr—US. **Exams**—SSAT. **Feat**—Fr Lat Span Computers Geog Studio_Art Drama. **Supp**—ESL.

Sports—Basket F_Hockey Soccer Tennis. **Activities**—Arts Rec.

Enr 145. US 15. Host 73. Other 57. Accepted: 60%. Yield: 56%. Avg class size: 16.

Fac 15. M 3. F 9/3. Adv Deg: 20%.

Tui '05-'06: Day B$1875-2700. Aid: 10 pupils (B$20,000).

Summer: Span. 6 wks.

Bldgs 4. Class rms 14. Lib 1000 vols. Sci labs 1. Lang labs 3. Comp labs 16. Auds 1. Gyms 1. Fields 1. Courts 1. Pools 1.

Est 1985. Nonprofit. Tri (Sept-June).

Located in Sandyport, on the western side of the island of New Providence, Tambearly prepares students of average and above-average intelligence for further study in the US, the UK or Canada, or at local high schools. The traditional curriculum incorporates elements and materials from other countries, particularly Britain and Canada.

BERMUDA

Sq. Miles: 23 (About three-tenths the size of Washington, DC). **Country Pop:** 65,365 (2005). **Capital:** Hamilton, pop. 3461 (2001). **Terrain:** Hilly islands. **Ethnic Group(s):** Black White. **Religion(s):** Anglican Roman_Catholic African_Methodist_Episcopal Seventh-Day_Adventist Methodist. **Official Language(s):** English. **Government:** Parliamentary. **Governed By:** United Kingdom. **GDP:** $3.97 billion (2003). Agriculture 1%. Industry 10%. Services 89%. **Currency:** Bermudian Dollar (Bd$).

MOUNT ST. AGNES ACADEMY
Day — Coed Gr K-12

Hamilton, Bermuda. PO Box HM 1004. Tel: 441-292-4134. Fax: 441-295-7265. EST+1. (Dial 1+ from US).
www.msa.bm   E-mail: msaoffice@msa.bm
Jim Silcott, Prin.

> **Col Prep. Curr**—US. **Exams**—CEEB. **Feat**—Fr Span Stats Comp_Sci Relig Music Accounting. **Supp**—Rem_Math Rem_Read Tut.
> **Enr 600.** B 280. G 320. US 18. Host 570. Other 12.
> **Fac 34.** M 5. F 29. US 8. Host 13. Other 13. Adv Deg: 35%.
> **Grad '05**—42. **Col**—42. **US Col**—2. (Notre Dame).
> **Tui '05-'06: Day $9930-10,530** (+$750). **Aid:** 20 pupils ($20,000).
> Libs 1. Sci labs 1. Comp labs 1. Auds 1. Art studios 1. Gyms 1.
> **Est 1890.** Roman Catholic. Quar (Sept-June).

Composed of an elementary school (grades K-8) and a high school (grades 9-12), this Catholic institution conducts a program based on the US system. Advanced Placement courses are available in several subjects in the higher grades, and students prepare for the SAT exam. All MSA pupils fulfill a four-year graduation requirement in religion.

Boys and girls may join volleyball, basketball, cricket, track and field, and soccer squads. In addition, the school offers a quiz team, debate, glee club, yearbook, student council, an environmental club, yearbook and performing arts options.

SALTUS GRAMMAR SCHOOL
Day — Coed Gr K-12

Hamilton HM JX, Bermuda. PO Box HM 2224. Tel: 441-292-6177. Fax: 441-295-4977. EST+1. (Dial 1+ from US).
www.saltus.bm   E-mail: headmaster@saltus.bm
Nigel J. Kermode, Head.

> **Col Prep. Curr**—UK. **Exams**—GCSE IGCSE. **Feat**—Fr Span Computers Studio_Art Music.
> **Enr 1066.**
> **Fac 82.**
> **Tui '05-'06: Day $12,670.**
> **Est 1888.** Nonprofit. Tri (Sept-June).

BERMUDA HIGH SCHOOL FOR GIRLS
Day — Girls Gr K-PG

Pembroke HM 08, Bermuda. 27 Richmond Rd. Tel: 441-295-6153. Fax: 441-278-3017. EST+1. (Dial 1+ from US).
www.bhs.bm   E-mail: head.school@bhs.bm
Roy Napier, Head. BSc, MEd. **Lorna Andersen, Adm.**
 Col Prep. IB Diploma. Curr—Intl UK. **Exams**—CEEB GCSE IGCSE. **Feat**—Fr Lat Span Econ Studio_Art Drama Music Bus. **Supp**—Rem_Read Tut.
 Activities—Acad Media.
 Enr 680. G 680. US 30. Host 600. Other 50. Avg class size: 12.
 Fac 69. M 10. F 55/4. US 1. Host 40. Other 28. Adv Deg: 24%.
 Grad '05—23. **Col**—23. **US Col**—12. (Parsons Sch of Design, Boston Col, U of Tampa, Hampton).
 Tui '05-'06: Day $12,560-13,560 (+$500). **Aid:** 206 pupils ($300,000).
 Endow $5,000,000. Plant val $13,000,000. Bldgs 5. Libs 2. Sci labs 3. Comp labs 1. Auds 1. Art studios 1. Music studios 1. Dance studios 1. Gyms 1. Fields 1.
 Est 1894. Nonprofit. (Sept-June).

Located in the island's capital of Hamilton, BHS prepares girls for entry into American and British schools and colleges. In the lower and primary schools, emphasis is on basic skills. The senior school curriculum, which includes courses in the arts, commerce and business, leads to the GCSE, IGCSE and SAT examinations, as well as the IB Diploma.

BRITISH VIRGIN ISLANDS

Sq. Miles: 58 (About nine-tenths the size of Washington, DC). **Country Pop:** 22,643 (2005). **Capital:** Road Town, pop. 8800 (2002). **Terrain:** Coral islands relatively flat; volcanic islands steep, hilly. **Ethnic Group(s):** Black White Indian Asian. **Religion(s):** Methodist Anglican Seventh-Day_Adventist Baptist Jehovah's_Witness Roman_Catholic. **Official Language(s):** English. **Governed By:** United Kingdom. **GDP:** $311 million (2000). Agriculture 2%. Industry 6%. Services 92%. **Currency:** US Dollar ($).

CEDAR SCHOOL
Day — Coed Gr PS-12

Cruz Bay, VI 00831. PO Box 8309, PMB 5000. Tel: 284-494-5262. Fax: 284-495-9695. EST+1. (Dial 1+ from US).
www.cedarschoolbvi.com   E-mail: cedaroffice@surfbvi.com
Janet Tennikait, Head.
 Col Prep. IB MYP. Curr—Intl US. **Exams**—CEEB. **Feat**—Span Comp_Sci Econ Govt Psych Sociol Studio_Art Music.
 Fac 31.
 Tui '05-'06: Day $5350-8450 (+$600).
 Est 1990. Tri (Sept-June).

CUBA

Sq. Miles: 44,200 (About the size of Pennsylvania). **Country Pop:** 11,346,670 (2005). **Capital:** Havana, pop. 2,000,000. **Terrain:** Flat or gently rolling plains, hills; mountains in the southeast. **Ethnic Group(s):** Mulatto White Black Chinese. **Religion(s):** Roman_Catholic Protestant Jehovah's_Witness Jewish Santeria. **Official Language(s):** Spanish. **Government:** Communist. **Independence:** 1902. **GDP:** $33.92 billion (2004). Agriculture 7%. Industry 28%. Services 65%. **Currency:** Cuban Peso (Cu$).

INTERNATIONAL SCHOOL OF HAVANA

Day — Coed Gr PS-12

CP 10400 Havana, Cuba. 315 Calle 18, Miramar. Tel: 53-7-204-2540. Fax: 53-7-204-2723. EST.
www.ishav.org   E-mail: office@ish.co.cu
Ian Morris, Prin. Julien Cruz, Adm.

> Col Prep. IB Diploma. **Curr**—Intl UK US. **Exams**—CEEB TOEFL IGCSE. **Feat**—Span Comp_Sci Studio_Art Drama Music. **Supp**—EFL ESL LD.
>
> **Sports**—Basket F_Hockey Soccer Squash Swim Tennis Volley. **Activities**—Acad Arts Rec.
>
> **Enr 190.** B 107. G 83. Elem 161. Sec 29. US 19. Other 171. Avg class size: 10.
>
> **Fac 42.** M 10. F 31/1. Host 32. Other 10. Adv Deg: 4%.
>
> **Grad '05—20. Col—5. US Col—1.**
>
> **Tui '05-'06: Day Cu$7070-7980** (+$4000).
>
> **Summer:** Rec. Tui Day Cu$60/wk. 4 wks.
>
> Bldgs 4. Class rms 30. Libs 2. Sci labs 1. Lang labs 1. Comp labs 3. Art studios 1. Music studios 1. Courts 3.
>
> **Est 1965.** Sem (Aug-June). Assoc: CIS NEASC.

The school was founded to provide an English-language education for children of the expatriate business and diplomatic communities in Havana. Preparation for the IGCSE examinations begins in grade 6, and students' progress is moderated through checkpoint tests. After the IGCSE, students in grades 11 and 12 pursue an internationally focused program leading to the ISH diploma.

DOMINICAN REPUBLIC

Sq. Miles: 18,704 (About the size of Vermont and New Hampshire combined). **Country Pop:** 8,950,034 (2005). **Capital:** Santo Domingo, pop. 2,400,000. **Terrain:** Mountainous. **Ethnic Group(s):** European African. **Religion(s):** Roman_Catholic. **Official Language(s):** Spanish. **Government:** Representative Democracy. **Independence:** 1844. **Per Capita Income:** $1896 (2003). **GDP:** $16.12 billion (2003). Agriculture 12%. Industry 31%. Services 47%. **Currency:** Dominican Peso (RD$).

AMERICAN SCHOOL OF SANTO DOMINGO
Day — Coed Gr PS-12

Santo Domingo, Dominican Republic. PO Box 20212. Tel: 809-565-7946. Fax: 809-549-5841. EST+1. (Dial 1+ from US).
Contact: EPS P-2240, PO Box 02-5261, Miami, FL 33102.
www.assd.edu.do   E-mail: info@assd.edu.do
Janet Reyes, Dir.

    Col Prep. Curr—US. **Exams**—AP CEEB. **AP**—Span Comp_Sci US_Hist World_Hist. **Feat**—Fr Lat-Amer_Hist Econ Govt Psych Dominican_Stud Studio_Art Music. **Supp**—ESL.

    Tui '05-'06: Day $2620-5775 (+$280-850).

    Est 1981. Quar (Aug-June). Assoc: ACCAS.

CAROL MORGAN SCHOOL
Day — Coed Gr PS-12

Santo Domingo, Dominican Republic. Apartado 1169. Tel: 809-947-1000. Fax: 809-533-9222. EST 1. (Dial 1 + from US).
Contact: BM 1-09221, 6911 NW 87th Ave, Ste A, Miami, FL 33178.
www.cms.edu.do   E-mail: headmaster@cms.edu.do
Jack Delman, Head. Ruth Sanchez, Adm.

    Col Prep. Curr—US. **Exams**—AP CEEB. **AP**—Eng Span Calc Stats Bio Chem Physics Eur_Hist US_Hist Comp_Govt & Pol Psych US_Govt & Pol Studio_Art. **Feat**—Lat-Amer_Lit Ceramics Sculpt. **Supp**—ESL LD.

    Sports—Basket Soccer Softball Volley. **Activities**—Arts Rec.

    Enr 1127. Elem 802. Sec 325. US 395. Host 575. Other 157. Accepted: 60%. Avg class size: 20.

    Fac 122. US 63. Host 36. Other 23. Adv Deg: 82%.

    Avg SAT: M/V—1031.

    Tui '06-'07: Day $3723-8990 (+$2000-2571).

    Summer: Acad Enrich Rem Rec. 4 wks.

    Bldgs 10. Class rms 101. Libs 2. Sci labs 8. Comp labs 6. Theaters 1. Art studios 4. Music studios 3. Gyms 1. Fields 4. Courts 2. Weight rms 1.

    Est 1933. Nonprofit. Quar (Aug-June). Assoc: ACCAS A/OPR/OS SACS.

Carol Morgan conducts a North American-style college preparatory curriculum. All instruction is in English; Spanish is available as a foreign language elective. Students from the Dominican Republic and the US constitute most of the enrollment. Prior to admission, pupils must complete entry examinations and must display English proficiency.

HAITI

Sq. Miles: 10,714 (About the size of Maryland). **Country Pop:** 8,121,622 (2005). **Capital:** Port-au-Prince, pop. 2,000,000. **Terrain:** Rugged mountains with small coastal plains and river valleys, and a large east-central elevated plateau. **Ethnic Group(s):** African European. **Religion(s):**

Roman_Catholic Protestant Voodoo. **Official Language(s):** French Creole. **Government:** Republic. **Independence:** 1804 (from France). **Per Capita Income:** $422 (2002). **GDP:** $3.5 billion (2002). Agriculture 30%. Industry 20%. Services 50%. **Currency:** Haitian Gourde (G).

CARIBBEAN-AMERICAN SCHOOL
Day — Coed Gr PS-12

Petion Ville, Haiti. 56 rue Lambert. Tel: 509-558-50-77. EST.
Contact: PO Box 407139, Fort Lauderdale, FL 33340.
Ernestine Rochelle Robinson, Prin.
  Col Prep. Curr—US. Exams—ACT CEEB TOEFL. Feat—Fr Span Comp_Sci
    Psych. Supp—Dev_Read ESL Makeup Rem_Math Rem_Read Rev Tut.
  Enr 137. Avg class size: 10.
  Fac 5. M 1. F 4. US 2. Host 2. Other 1.
  Tui '06-'07: Day $1000 (+$100).
  Summer: Acad Enrich Rev Rem. Tui Day $300/wk. 10 wks.
  Bldgs 2. Class rms 13. Lib 10,000 vols. Sci labs 1. Lang labs 1. Art studios 1.
  Est 1979. Nonprofit. Quar (Sept-May).

The school offers a US curriculum that prepares students for the SAT exams. Environmental studies courses take place at the nearby coastline.

UNION SCHOOL
Day — Coed Gr PS-12

Port-au-Prince, Haiti. PO Box 1175. Tel: 509-260-0637. Fax: 509-257-3131. EST.
Contact: PO Box 407139, Fort Lauderdale, FL 33340.
www.unionschoolhaiti.net   E-mail: unionschool@direcway.com
Marie Jean-Baptiste, Dir.
  Col Prep. Curr—US. Supp Lang—Fr. Feat—Fr Span Comp_Sci Geog Haitian_
    Stud Studio_Art Music.
  Enr 385.
  Fac 38.
  Est 1919. Nonprofit. Sem (Aug-June). Assoc: ACCAS A/OPR/OS SACS.

JAMAICA

Sq. Miles: 4244 (Slightly smaller than Connecticut). **Country Pop:** 2,731,832 (2005). **Capital:** Kingston, pop. 628,000. **Terrain:** Mountainous, coastal plains. **Ethnic Group(s):** African East_Indian Chinese. **Religion(s):** Anglican Baptist Protestant Roman_Catholic Rastafarian Jewish. **Other Language(s):** English Patois. **Government:** Constitutional Parliamentary Democracy. **Independence:** 1962. **Per Capita Income:** $2771 (2001). **GDP:** $7.34 billion (2002). Agriculture 6%. Industry 33%. Services 61%. **Currency:** Jamaican Dollar (J$).

AMERICAN INTERNATIONAL SCHOOL OF KINGSTON
Day — Coed Gr PS-12

Kingston 8, Jamaica. 1A Olivier Rd. Tel: 876-755-2634. Fax: 876-925-4749. EST.
(Dial 1+ from US).
www.aisk.com
Bruce Goforth, Dir.
   Col Prep. Curr—US. **Exams**—ACT AP CEEB. **AP**—Eng Fr Span Bio US_Hist.
      Feat—Comp_Sci Studio_Art Music.
   Enr 199. Elem 165. Sec 34.
   Fac 27.
   Tui '05-'06: Day $2998-5995.
   Est 1994. Tri (Sept-June). Assoc: A/OPR/OS SACS.

NETHERLANDS ANTILLES

Sq. Miles: 371 (More than five times the size of Washington, DC).
Country Pop: 219,958 (2005). **Capital:** Willemstad, pop. 54,800 (2002).
Terrain: Generally hilly, volcanic interiors. **Ethnic Group(s):** Black
Carib_Amerindian White East_Asian. **Religion(s):** Roman_Catholic
Protestant Jewish Seventh-Day_Adventist. **Official Language(s):**
Dutch. **Other Language(s):** Papiamento English Spanish. **Government:** Parliamentary. **Governed By:** The Netherlands. **GDP:** $2.8 billion (2003). Agriculture 1%. Industry 15%. Services 84%. **Currency:**
Netherlands Antillean Guilder (Ant.f.).

INTERNATIONAL SCHOOL OF CURACAO
Day — Coed Gr K-12

Curacao, Netherlands Antilles. PO Box 3090, Koninginnelaan, Emmastad.
   Tel: 599-9-737-3633. Fax: 599-9-737-3142. EST+1.
www.isc.an   E-mail: iscmec@attglobal.net
Margie Elhage, Dir.
   Col Prep. IB Diploma. Curr—Intl US. **Exams**—AP CEEB. **AP**—Span. **Feat**—Lib_
      Skills Dutch Comp_Sci Fine_Arts Performing_Arts Bus. **Supp**—ESL.
   Fac 46.
   Tui '05-'06: Day Ant.f.4300-15,750 (+Ant.f.4000).
   Nonprofit. Quar (Aug-June). Assoc: AASSA A/OPR/OS SACS.

INTERNATIONAL SCHOOL OF ST. MAARTEN
Day — Coed Gr 4-12

St Maarten, Netherlands Antilles. 4 Oyster Pond Rd, PO Box 381. Tel: 599-543-
   7965. Fax: 599-543-7965. EST+1.
www.intlschoolstmaarten.org   E-mail: info@intlschoolstmaarten.org

Catherine Kretzschmar, Dir. BA, MA.
  Col Prep. Curr—US. **Exams**—AP CEEB.
  Fac 5. M 1. F 4. US 2. Other 3. Adv Deg: 40%.
  Tui '05-'06: Day $6560.
  Est 1995. Quar (Aug-June).

PUERTO RICO

Sq. Miles: 3515 (Slightly less than three times the size of Rhode Island).
Country Pop: 3,916,632 (2005). **Capital:** San Juan, pop. 421,958 (2000).
Terrain: Mostly mountains, with coastal plain belt in north; mountains
precipitous to sea on west coast; sandy beaches along most coastal
areas. **Ethnic Group(s):** White Black Amerindian Asian. **Religion(s):**
Roman_Catholic Protestant. **Other Language(s):** Spanish English.
Government: Commonwealth. **Governed By:** United States. **GDP:** $69
billion (2004). Agriculture 1%. Industry 45%. Services 54%. **Currency:**
US Dollar ($).

BALDWIN SCHOOL

Day — Coed Gr PS-12

Bayamon, PR 00960. PO Box 1827. Tel: 787-720-2421. Fax: 787-790-0619. EST+1.
  (Dial 1+ from US).
www.baldwin-school.org   E-mail: admission@baldwin-school.org
Gunther Brandt, Head.
  Col Prep. Curr—US. **Exams**—AP CEEB. **AP**—Fr Span Calc Comp_Sci Chem
    Eur_Hist. **Feat**—Port Econ Psych Studio_Art Drama Music Public_Speak.
    Supp—ESL.
  Tui '05-'06: Day $8020-9500 (+$2175-3575).
  Est 1968. Nonprofit. Sem (Aug-May).

THE TASIS SCHOOL IN DORADO

Day — Coed Gr PS-8

Dorado, PR 00646. 11 Carretera 693. Tel: 787-796-0440. Fax: 787-796-0240. EST+1.
  (Dial 1+ from US).
www.tasisdorado.com   E-mail: td@tasisdorado.com
Louis R. Christiansen, Dir. BA, EdM. **Maritere G. Matosantos, Prin.** BA, MAEd.
  Gen Acad. Curr—US. **Feat**—Span Computers Studio_Art Music.
  Tui '06-'07: Day $6400-8100 (+$625-1025).
  Est 2002. (Aug-May).

CARIBBEAN SCHOOL
Day — Coed Gr PS-12

Ponce, PR 00730. Urb La Rambla, 1689 Calle Navarra. Tel: 787-843-2048. Fax: 787-843-5626. EST+1. (Dial 1+ from US).
www.caribbeanschool.org   E-mail: webmaster@caribbeanschool.org
Lynn Roberts, Head.

Col Prep. Curr—US. Exams—ACT CEEB. AP—Eng Span Calc Bio Chem Physics US_Hist. Feat—Fr Comp_Sci Psych Studio_Art Music Public_Speak. Supp—Dev_Read.

Enr 610. B 312. G 298. Elem 446. Sec 164. US 51. Host 549. Other 10. Accepted: 90%. Avg class size: 25.

Fac 46.

Grad '05—26. Col—26. US Col—14. (Miami U-OH, PA St, Loyola U-LA, Yale, Brown, UNC-Chapel Hill).

Tui '05-'06: Day $3330-4515 (+$750-1500). Aid: 19 pupils ($52,885).

Summer: Enrich Rem Rec. Tui Day $250. 4 wks.

Bldgs 3. Libs 2. Sci labs 4. Comp labs 2. Art studios 1. Music studios 1. Gyms 1. Fields 2. Courts 2.

Est 1954. Nonprofit. Sem (Aug-May).

The school prepares students for college entrance in the Continental US, as well as Spanish-speaking academic institutions in Puerto Rico. Although most students are native-born, Spanish-speaking children, all instruction is in English. The school emphasizes Spanish culture and language.

The athletic program consists of volleyball, basketball, track, softball and cross-country. Other activities include art, computer club, newspaper, yearbook, public speaking and student government.

ACADEMIA DEL PERPETUO SOCORRO
Day — Coed Gr K-12

San Juan, PR 00907. 704 Jose Marti St. Tel: 787-721-4540. Fax: 787-723-4550. EST+1. (Dial 1+ from US).
www.perpetuo.org   E-mail: perpetuo@perpetuo.org
Rev. Armand0 Alvarez, Dir.

Col Prep. Gen Acad. Curr—US. Supp Lang—Span. Exams—CEEB TOEFL. AP—Eng Fr Span Calc Eur_Hist. Feat—Humanities Ital Port Comp_Sci Psych Ethics Relig Studio_Art Drama Music.

Enr 1360.

Fac 60.

Est 1921. Nonprofit. Roman Catholic. Sem (Aug-May).

CARIBBEAN PREPARATORY SCHOOL
Day — Coed Gr PS-12

San Juan, PR 00936. PO Box 70177. Tel: 787-765-4411. Fax: 787-764-3809. EST+1. (Dial 1+ from US).
www.cpspr.org   E-mail: jaranguren@cpspr.org

F. Richard Marracino, Head. BA, MPA. **Jo-Ann Aranguren, Adm.**

    Col Prep. Curr—US. **Feat**—Poetry Comp_Sci Puerto_Rican_Hist Ethics Studio_ Art Music. **Supp**—ESL LD.

    Enr 741. Elem 609. Sec 132. Other 12. Avg class size: 25.

    Fac 72. M 11. F 61. US 72. Adv Deg: 25%.

    Grad '05—42. Col—42. US Col—25. (Harvard, Tufts, Boston Col, Boston U, PA St). Avg SAT: M/V—900.

    Tui '02-'03: Day $2810-6730 (+$1960). **Aid:** 34 pupils ($50,000).

    Summer: Enrich Rem Rec. Tui Day $225-350/crse. 4 wks.

    Endow $5,500,000. Bldgs 5. Class rms 72. 2 Libs 40,000 vols. Sci labs 5. Comp labs 4. Auds 1. Art studios 3. Music studios 2. Dance studios 1. Gyms 1. Fields 2.

    Est 1952. Nonprofit. Sem (Aug-May).

Located on two campuses, CPS offers an English-language curriculum that prepares students for college entrance in Puerto Rico and in the Continental US. Lower school (grades pre-K-4) and middle school (grades 5-8) classes, which are held at the Parkville campus in Guaynabo (ten miles south of San Juan), emphasize hands-on activities in the traditional subjects. Conducted on the Commonwealth campus in Hato Rey, the high school (grades 9-12) features a wide selection of honors and Advanced Placement courses, as well as opportunities in the arts, with school publications and in athletics. ESL instruction is available for an additional fee, as is a support program that serves pupils in grades 1-12 who have mild learning differences or attention deficit disorder.

Rounding out CPS' program are field trips, after-school activities and community service opportunities.

ROBINSON SCHOOL

Day — Coed Gr PS-12

San Juan, PR 00907. 5 Nairn St. Tel: 787-728-6767. Fax: 787-727-7736. EST+1. (Dial 1+ from US).

www.robinsonschool.org   E-mail: exdir@robinsonschool.org

Robert E. Graves, Head.

    Col Prep. Curr—US. **Exams**—CEEB. **Feat**—Comp_Sci Relig Studio_Art Drama Music.

    Tui '05-'06: Day $5000-7560 (+1175-2675).

    Est 1902. Nonprofit. Quar (Aug-May).

SAINT JOHN'S SCHOOL

Day — Coed Gr PS-12

San Juan, PR 00907. 1454-66 Ashford Ave. Tel: 787-728-5343. Fax: 787-268-1454. EST+1. (Dial 1+ from US).

www.sjspr.org

Barry Farnham, Head.

    Col Prep. Curr—US.

    Enr 750.

    Fac 75.

    Tui '06-'07: Day $7705-11,005 (+$750).

Est 1915. Nonprofit. Sem (Aug-June).

TRINIDAD AND TOBAGO

Sq. Miles: 1980 (About one and a half times the size of Rhode Island). **Country Pop:** 1,088,644 (2005). **Capital:** Port of Spain, pop. 310,000. **Terrain:** Plains and low mountains. **Ethnic Group(s):** East_Indian African European Chinese. **Religion(s):** Roman_Catholic Hindu Anglican Pentecostal Baptist Methodist Muslim. **Official Language(s):** English. **Government:** Parliamentary Democracy. **Independence:** 1962 (from United Kingdom). **Per Capita Income:** $8923 (2004). **GDP:** $11.6 billion (2004). Agriculture 3%. Industry 47%. Services 50%. **Currency:** Trinidadian Dollar (TT$).

INTERNATIONAL SCHOOL OF PORT OF SPAIN
Day — Coed Gr PS-12

Westmoorings, Trinidad and Tobago. 1 International Dr. Tel: 868-633-4777. Fax: 868-632-4595. EST+1. (Dial 1+ from US).
Contact: POS 1369, 1601 NW 97th Ave, PO Box 025307, Miami, FL 33102.
www.isps.edu.tt   E-mail: blatham@Isps.edu.tt
Barney Latham, Dir. MA. **Jackie Fung Kee Fung, Adm.**

    Col Prep. Curr—US. **Exams**—ACT CEEB. **AP**—Eng Studio_Art. **Feat**—Fr Span Environ_Sci Comp_Sci. **Supp**—ESL.

    Sports—Basket Soccer Volley. **Activities**—Acad Arts Govt/Pol Media Rec Service.

    Enr 379. B 201. G 178. Elem 260. Sec 119. US 101. Host 119. Other 159. Avg class size: 15.

    Fac 56. M 11/1. F 42/2. US 7. Host 47. Other 2. Adv Deg: 71%.

    Grad '05—20. Col—15. US Col—5. (U of Miami 2, U of Denver 1, Appalachian St 1, Embry-Riddle 1). Avg SAT: M/V—1103.

    Tui '06-'07: Day $8650-13,000 (+$4000).

    Bldgs 1. Class rms 38. Lib 11,809 vols. Sci labs 3. Comp labs 2. Auds 1. Art studios 2. Music studios 1. Gyms 1. Fields 2.

    Est 1994. Nonprofit. Sem (Aug-June). Assoc: AASSA A/OPR/OS SACS.

ISPS bases its English-medium program on the US model. The elementary school curriculum takes a holistic, child-centered approach while promoting critical and creative thinking, providing cooperative learning opportunities and making accommodations for individual learning styles. Course work integrates art, music, foreign language, computer technology and physical education classes. At the middle school level, pupils follow an alternating schedule in which core classes meet every other day for 80 minutes. The college preparatory high school program features AP classes and such electives as art, drama and yearbook, as well as an alternating schedule that includes 85-minute classes. Graduates earn a US high school diploma.

Students engage in educational and experiential trips as part of the curriculum. Community service is actively encouraged. Sporting events, cultural programs, student government and regularly scheduled drama productions balance academics.

TURKS AND CAICOS ISLANDS

Sq. Miles: 166 (About two and a half times the size of Washington, DC). **Country Pop:** 20,556 (2005). **Capital:** Cockburn Town, pop. 4900 (2002). **Terrain:** Low, flat limestone; extensive marshes and mangrove swamps. **Ethnic Group(s):** African European. **Religion(s):** Baptist Methodist Anglican. **Official Language(s):** English. **Governed By:** United Kingdom. **GDP:** $216 million (2002). **Currency:** US Dollar ($).

THE ASHCROFT SCHOOL
Day — Coed Gr PS-8

Providenciales, Turks and Caicos Islands. PO Box 278, Leeward. Tel: 649-946-5523. Fax: 649-941-4614. EST. (Dial 1+ from US).
www.leewardtci.com/AshcroftSchool.htm   E-mail: taschool@tciway.tc
Gabriella Sullivan, Prin. BA, BEd, MEd.
    Gen Acad. Curr—Intl. **Feat**—Fr Span Comp_Sci Studio_Art Music. **Supp**—Tut.
    Enr 120. B 50. G 70. Elem 120. US 20. Host 30. Other 70. Avg class size: 16.
    Fac 15. M 1/1. F 11/2. Host 3. Other 12. Adv Deg: 33%.
    Grad '05—10.
    Tui '02-'03: Day $3300-6300 (+$750). **Aid:** 8 pupils ($16,000).
    Bldgs 4. Sci labs 1. Comp labs 1. Fields 1.
    Est 1986. Nonprofit. Tri (Sept-June).

Ashcroft provides an international-style elementary program for children from such areas as the Bahamas, Canada, the Dominican Republic, the US, Ireland, the UK, and the Turks and Caicos Islands. Course work in information technology, art and music complements classes in the standard subjects.

Extracurricular activities play an important role in school life. After-school clubs meet two days per week, with children divided into two groups: grades 1-3 and grades 4-8. Typical offerings include arts and crafts, computers, cooking, drama, magazine, and card and board games. In addition, students may take part in intramural sports beginning in grade 3, and interscholastic teams in the upper grades.

US VIRGIN ISLANDS

Sq. Miles: 136 (About twice the size of Washington, DC). **Country Pop:** 108,708 (2005). **Capital:** Charlotte Amalie, pop. 18,914 (1998). **Terrain:** Mostly hilly to rugged and mountainous with little level land. **Ethnic Group(s):** West_Indian Puerto_Rican. **Religion(s):** Baptist

Roman_Catholic Episcopal. **Official Language(s):** English. **Other Language(s):** Spanish Creole French. **Governed By:** United States. **GDP:** $2.5 billion (2002). Agriculture 1%. Industry 19%. Services 10%. Tourism 70%. **Currency:** US Dollar ($).

THE GOOD HOPE SCHOOL
Day — Coed Gr PS-12

Frederiksted, VI 00840. 170 Estate Whim. Tel: 340-772-0022. Fax: 340-772-0951. EST. (Dial 1+ from US).
www.ghsvi.org   E-mail: postmaster.ghs@gmail.com
Michael Mongeau, Head. BA, MA. **Patricia Swan, Adm.**

  Col Prep. Curr—US. **Exams**—ACT AP CEEB. **AP**—Eng Fr Span Calc Bio Chem Physics Eur_Hist US_Hist Studio_Art Music_Theory. **Feat**—British_Lit Creative_Writing 20th-Century_Amer_Lit Environ_Sci Marine_Biol/Sci Comp_Sci Caribbean_Hist Acting. **Supp**—Dev_Read ESL LD Rem_Math Rem_Read Tut.
  Sports—Basket Golf Soccer Softball Tennis Volley. **Activities**—Acad Arts Govt/Pol Rec.
  Enr 300. B 150. G 150. Elem 220. Sec 80. Accepted: 85%. Avg class size: 15.
  Fac 36. M 8. F 28. Adv Deg: 25%.
  Grad '05—28. **Col**—27. **US Col**—27. (Princeton 2, Stanford 1, US Naval Acad 1, Dickinson 1, Bennington 1).
  Tui '05–'06: Day $6900-9900 (+$400). **Aid:** 75 pupils ($185,000).
  Bldgs 12. Lib 15,000 vols. Sci labs 2. Comp labs 3. Theaters 1. Art studios 2. Music studios 2. Gyms 1. Fields 3. Pools 1.
  Est 1965. Nonprofit. Quar (Aug-June).

Located on 32 acres on the southwestern coast of St. Croix, the school offers an academic program that prepares students for postsecondary education. The lower school program provides instruction in self-contained classrooms, with specialists teaching art, music, physical education and computer. Middle school students gain exposure to various teaching techniques and learn from teams of teachers. Upper school pupils prepare for the US College Boards and the AP exams.

Serving pupils of all ages, Good Hope's resource center provides remedial services, diagnostic testing, and enrichment classes in reading and math for accelerated students.

ST. CROIX COUNTRY DAY SCHOOL
Day — Coed Gr PS-12

Kingshill, VI 00850. Rte 1, Box 6199. Tel: 340-778-1974. Fax: 340-779-3331. EST+1. (Dial 1+ from US).
www.stxcountryday.com   E-mail: sccds@stxcountryday.com
William D. Sinfield, Head. BA, BEd, MA.

  Col Prep. Curr—US. **Exams**—ACT AP CEEB. **AP**—Eng Fr Span Calc Comp_Sci Environ_Sci US_Hist Music_Theory. **Feat**—Creative_Writing Marine_Biol/Sci Caribbean_Hist Art_Hist. **Supp**—Rem_Math Rem_Read Tut.
  Sports—Basket Baseball Football Golf Sail Soccer Softball Swim Tennis Volley. **Activities**—Acad.

Enr 470. B 310. G 160. Accepted: 60%. Avg class size: 15.
Fac 50. M 12. F 38. US 50. Adv Deg: 50%.
Avg SAT: M/V—1070. Avg ACT: 22.
Tui '05-'06: Day $6500-9600. Aid: 120 pupils ($310,000).
Summer: Rec. Tui Day $165/wk. 7 wks.
Endow $800,000. Plant val $8,000,000. Lib 21,000 vols. Sci labs 3. Comp labs 6.
   Auds 1. Art studios 2. Music studios 2. Gyms 1. Fields 2. Pools 1.
Est 1964. Nonprofit. Quar (Aug-June).

The school's curriculum ultimately prepares students for the College Boards. The program places particular importance on technology: Networked computers are in every classroom, and pupils have Internet access. Enrichment is available through art, music, Spanish, computer, physical education, after-school activities, and intramural and interscholastic sports. Drama students deliver two productions annually, and Country Day maintains an art gallery.

ANTILLES SCHOOL
Day — Coed Gr PS-12

St Thomas, VI 00802. Frenchman's Bay 16-1. Tel: 340-776-1600. Fax: 340-776-1019.
   EST+1. (Dial 1+ from US).
www.antilles.vi   E-mail: admin@antilles.vi
Theodore F. Morse, Head. BA, MA. **Barbara Birt, Adm.**
   Col Prep. Curr—US. **Exams**—AP CEEB. **AP**—Eng Fr Span Calc Bio Chem
      US_Hist Econ Psych. **Feat**—Humanities Fine_Arts. **Supp**—Tut.
   Sports—Basket Baseball X-country Football Sail Soccer Softball Swim Volley.
      Activities—Acad Arts Govt/Pol.
   Enr 520. B 263. G 257. Elem 357. Sec 163. US 231. Host 274. Other 15. Avg class
      size: 20.
   Fac 48. M 13/2. F 26/7. US 43. Other 5. Adv Deg: 33%.
   Grad '05—42. Col—42. US Col—9. (Johnson & Wales 3, Boston U 2, Eckerd 2, U
      of Tampa 2). Avg SAT: M/V—1135.
   Tui '05-'06: Day $10,850-13,000. Aid: 312 pupils ($750,000).
   Bldgs 8. 2 Libs 14,000 vols. Sci labs 3. Comp labs 2. Auds 1. Art studios 2. Music
      studios 1. Dance studios 1. Gyms 1. Fields 1. Courts 2.
   Est 1950. Nonprofit. Quar (Aug-June).

A college preparatory country day school, Antilles occupies a 27-acre campus in Frenchman's Bay Estates. Antilles places equal emphasis on cognitive, social and physical development through its rigorous academic program. An intersession of minicourses planned jointly by faculty, students and the administration includes special classes, field trips and projects; over the years, offerings have included archaeological digs and environmental studies.

EUROPE

INDEX TO COUNTRIES IN EUROPE

EUROPE

ALBANIA

Sq. Miles: 28,748 (Slightly larger than Maryland). **Country Pop:** 3,563,112 (2005). **Capital:** Tirana, pop. 700,000. **Terrain:** Generally mountainous, but flat along the country's coastline with the Adriatic Sea. **Ethnic Group(s):** Albanian Greek Vlach Roma Serbian Montenegrin Macedonian Egyptian Bulgarian. **Religion(s):** Muslim Albanian_Orthodox Roman_Catholic Greek_Orthodox. **Official Language(s):** Albanian. **Government:** Parliamentary Democracy. **Independence:** 1912 (from Ottoman Empire). **GDP:** $10.5 billion (2000). Agriculture 24%. Industry 20%. Services 56%. **Currency:** Albanian Lek (AL).

TIRANA INTERNATIONAL SCHOOL
Day — Coed Ages 3-13

Tirana, Albania. Kutia Postare 1527. **Tel: 355-42-27734. Fax: 355-42-27734.** EST+6.
www.qsi.org/ALB_HOME E-mail: qsialb@albaniaonline.net
Scott D'Alterio, Dir.
  Gen Acad. Curr—US.
  Enr 75.
  Fac 16.
  Tui '05-'06: Day $4900-12,000 (+$1700).
  Est 1991. Nonprofit. Spons: Quality Schools International. Tri (Sept-June). Assoc: A/OPR/OS MSA.

AUSTRIA

Sq. Miles: 32,377 (Slightly smaller than Maine). **Country Pop:** 8,184,691 (2005). **Capital:** Vienna, pop. 1,600,000 (2003). **Terrain:** Alpine, northern highlands that form part of the Bohemian Massif, lowlands to the east. **Ethnic Group(s):** German Croat Slovene Hungarian Czech Slovak Roma. **Religion(s):** Roman_Catholic Lutheran Muslim. **Official Language(s):** German. **Government:** Parliamentary Democracy. **Per Capita Income:** $35,820 (2004). **GDP:** $290 billion (2004).

Agriculture 2%. Industry 30%. Services 68%. **Currency:** European Union Euro (€).

AMERICAN INTERNATIONAL SCHOOL SALZBURG
Bdg and Day — Coed Gr 7-12

A-5020 Salzburg, Austria. Moosstrasse 106. Tel: 43-662-824617. Fax: 43-662-824555. EST+6.
www.ais-salzburg.at   E-mail: office@ais-salzburg.at
Paul McLean, Head. BA. **Charise Neugebauer, Adm.**

> **Col Prep. Curr**—US. **Exams**—AP CEEB TOEFL. **AP**—Eng Fr Ger Span Calc Bio Chem Environ_Sci Human_Geog Eur_Hist US_Hist. **Feat**—Comp_Sci Photog Studio_Art Drama Music Dance. **Supp**—ESL Tut.
>
> **Enr 76.** Elem 9. Sec 67. Accepted: 80%. Avg class size: 7.
>
> **Fac 12.**
>
> **Grad '05—24. Col—17. US Col—7.** (AZ St, Wm & Mary, USC, San Jose St, U of Richmond). Avg SAT: M/V—1022.
>
> **Tui '05-'06: Bdg €20,000-24,000** (+€3500). **Day €12,000-13,750** (+€3500). **Aid:** 1 pupil (€16,500).
>
> **Summer:** Acad. Tui Bdg €5000. 7 wks.
>
> Libs 1. Comp labs 1. Art studios 1. Music studios 1.
>
> **Est 1976.** Nonprofit. Tri (Sept-May).

AIS offers American and ESL curricula as preparation for colleges in North America and throughout the world. Classes are small, permitting individualized attention and Advanced Placement courses are available in most subjects. Cultural and historical excursions to Vienna; Paris, France; Venice and Rome, Italy; Budapest, Hungary; and Prague, Czech Republic represent an extension of classroom work. Each year, pupils choose up to two elective offerings in such areas as computer, a second foreign language, drama, photography, and art and design.

The school occupies an 18th-century, palais-style building with modernized facilities. Students attend dramatic and musical productions in the city. The nearby mountains and countryside are opportune for skiing, ice skating, sailing and riding.

THE AMERICAN INTERNATIONAL SCHOOL
Day — Coed Gr PS-12

1190 Vienna, Austria. Salmannsdorfer Strasse 47. Tel: 43-1-40132. Fax: 43-1-401325. EST+6.
www.ais.at   E-mail: info@ais.at
Kevin Haverty, Dir. Margit Mahrenhorst, Adm.

> **Col Prep. IB Diploma. Curr**—Intl US. **Feat**—Fr Ger Span Econ Theater_Arts.
>
> **Enr 730.**
>
> **Fac 97.**
>
> **Tui '02-'03: Day €8340-14,900** (+$3600).
>
> Bldgs 1. Class rms 70. Lib 9000 vols. Gyms 3. Fields 1. Tracks 1.
>
> **Est 1959.** Nonprofit. Quar (Aug-June). Assoc: A/OPR/OS MSA.

Located on a 15-acre campus in northwest Vienna, this international school was founded by the American and Canadian embassies. Although Americans account for a substantial portion of the enrollment, students from more than 50 countries attend the school. The basic program is modeled after the American system, but preparation for the International Baccalaureate diploma is available to students in the secondary program. The language of instruction is English, with pupils taking German at all grade levels.

AIS conducts full sports and extracurricular programs.

DANUBE INTERNATIONAL SCHOOL
Day — Coed Gr K-12

1020 Vienna, Austria. Josef Gall-gasse 2. Tel: 43-1-720-3110. Fax: 43-1-720-3110-40. EST+6.
www.danubeschool.at   E-mail: info@danubeschool.at
Andrew R. Scott, Dir.
   Col Prep. IB MYP. IB Diploma. Curr—Intl. **Feat**—Comp_Sci Studio_Art Music.
   Tui '05-'06: Day €6995-14,575.
   Est 1990. Tri (Aug-June).

VIENNA CHRISTIAN SCHOOL
Day — Coed Gr K-12

1220 Vienna, Austria. Wagramer Strasse 175, Panethgasse 6A. Tel: 43-1-25122-501. Fax: 43-1-25122-517. EST+6.
www.viennachristianschool.org   E-mail: office@vcs-austria.org
Ken Norman, Dir.
   Col Prep. Curr—US. **Exams**—ACT AP CEEB. **AP**—Eng Ger Calc Comp_Sci US_Hist. **Feat**—Span Anat & Physiol Web_Design Econ Psych Bible Studio_Art Chorus. **Supp**—ESL.
   Tui '05-'06: Day €7790-8990.
   Est 1985. Nonprofit. Nondenom Christian. Quar (Aug-June).

VIENNA INTERNATIONAL SCHOOL
Day — Coed Gr PS-12

1220 Vienna, Austria. Strasse der Menschenrechte 1. Tel: 43-1-203-5595. Fax: 43-1-203-0366. EST+6.
www.vis.ac.at   E-mail: info@vis.ac.at
Michael Chapman, Dir. Tina Lackner, Adm.
   Col Prep. Gen Acad. IB Diploma. Curr—Intl. **Feat**—Fr Ger Span Comp_Sci. **Supp**—ESL.
   Enr 1386. Avg class size: 25.
   Fac 154.
   Tui '05-'06: Day €9632-13,500.
   Bldgs 1. Class rms 95. Sci labs 1. Comp labs 1. Theaters 1. Gyms 1.
   Est 1978. Nonprofit. Tri (Aug-June). Assoc: ECIS.

VIS serves families of the United Nations, Vienna's diplomatic corps and the international business community; some local students also enroll. The comprehensive curriculum, which progresses from preschool through high school, emphasizes the development of fundamental learning skills, creativity, tolerance and responsibility. The secondary program of study prepares the student for either a general diploma or the International Baccalaureate.

Extracurricular activities include team sports and interest clubs.

BELARUS

Sq. Miles: 80,100 (Slightly smaller than Kansas). **Country Pop:** 10,300,483 (2005). **Capital:** Minsk, pop. 1,719,000. **Terrain:** Landlocked, low-lying with thick forests, flat marshes and fields. **Ethnic Group(s):** Belarusian Russian Polish Ukrainian. **Religion(s):** Eastern_ Orthodox Roman_Catholic Greek_Catholic Protestant Jewish Muslim. **Official Language(s):** Belarusian Russian. **Government:** Republic. **Independence:** 1991 (from Soviet Union). **Per Capita Income:** $1965 (2003). **GDP:** $17.5 billion (2003). Agriculture 11%. Industry 36%. Services 53%. **Currency:** Belarusian Ruble (BR).

QSI INTERNATIONAL SCHOOL
MINSK

Day — Coed Ages 5-15

Minsk 220002, Belarus. Kropotkeena 74. Tel: 375-172-343035. Fax: 375-172-343035. EST+7.
www.qsi.org/blr_home   E-mail: minsk@qsi.org
Stan Ore, Dir. MS, EdS.
  Gen Acad. Curr—US. Feat—Russ Computers Econ. Supp—ESL.
  Sports—Basket Volley.
  Enr 20. B 9. G 11. US 5. Other 15. Accepted: 95%. Yield: 95%. Avg class size: 3.
  Fac 11. M 2/2. F 4/3. US 2. Host 9. Adv Deg: 27%.
  Est 1993. Nonprofit. Spons: Quality Schools International. Sem (Sept-June). Assoc: A/OPR/OS MSA.

QSI-Minsk offers an English-language education to international students and Belarusian student who intend to pursue higher studies in another country. Intensive English classes are available based on student placement testing, and Russian is taught as a foreign language. The school is located in a wing of a Belarusian public school, near the city center of Minsk.

BELGIUM

Sq. Miles: 12,566 (About the size of Maryland). **Country Pop:** 10,364,388 (2005). **Capital:** Brussels, pop. 992,041. **Terrain:** Flat coastal plains in northwest, central rolling hills, rugged mountains of Ardennes Forest in southeast. **Ethnic Group(s):** Fleming Walloon. **Religion(s):** Roman_Catholic Protestant Jewish Muslim Anglican Greek_Orthodox Russian_Orthodox. **Other Language(s):** Dutch French German. **Government:** Parliamentary Democracy. **Independence:** 1830 (from The Netherlands). **Per Capita Income:** $34,518 (2004). **GDP:** $355.5 billion (2004). Agriculture 1%. Industry 26%. Services 73%. **Currency:** European Union Euro (€).

BRITISH INTERNATIONAL SCHOOL OF BRUSSELS

Day — Coed Gr PS-5

1030 Brussels, Belgium. 163 Ave Emile Max. Tel: 32-2-736-8981. Fax: 32-2-736-8981. EST+6.
www.bisb.org   E-mail: schooloffice@bisb.org
Stephen Prescott, Head.
   Gen Acad. Curr—UK. **Feat**—Computers Comp_Rellg Studio_Art Music.
   Tui '05-'06: Day €9220-11,950 (+€500).
   Tri (Sept-July).

THE BRITISH JUNIOR ACADEMY OF BRUSSELS

Day — Coed Gr PS-5

1040 Brussels, Belgium. 83 Blvd Saint Michel. Tel: 32-2-732-5376. Fax: 32-2-732-5376. EST+6.
www.bjab.org   E-mail: bjabrussels@yahoo.com
Diane Perry, Head.
   Gen Acad. Curr—UK. **Feat**—Fr Studio_Art Music.
   Enr 120. Avg class size: 15.
   Fac 12. F 8/4.
   Tui '05-'06: Day €9475-11,850.
   Est 1992. Tri (Sept-June).

BJAB, located in an Edwardian residence near the center of the city, offers a program based on the British curriculum. The school serves children of the expatriate, commercial and diplomatic communities. In addition to core subject work in English, math and the sciences, students participate in a history and geography syllabus that reflects Brussels' international environment. French (taught by native speakers), art, and design and technology are other curricular elements.

Reviewed on a regular basis and adjusted to meet student interests, extracurriculars include such options as computers, drama, karate, ceramics, ballet, soccer, cricket, dancing, gymnastics and choir.

BRUSSELS ENGLISH PRIMARY SCHOOL
Day — Coed Ages 2½-11

1050 Brussels, Belgium. 23 Ave Franklin Roosevelt. Tel: 32-2-648-4311. Fax: 32-2-687-2968. EST+6.
www.beps.com   E-mail: brussels@beps.com
Charles A. Gellar, Dir.
   Gen Acad. Curr—Intl.
   Enr 240.
   Tui '02-'03: Day €10,690-14,850.
   Est 1972. Inc. Sem (Sept-June).

EUROPEAN SCHOOL OF BRUSSELS
UCCLE
Day — Coed Gr PS-12

1180 Brussels, Belgium. Ave du Vert Chasseur 46. Tel: 32-2-373-86-11. Fax: 32-2-375-47-16. EST+6.
www.eeb1.com   E-mail: kari.kivinen@eursc.org
Kari Kivinen, Dir.
   Col Prep. Curr—Intl. Feat—Greek Lat Comp_Sci Econ Relig Studio_Art Music.
   Est 1958.

INTERNATIONAL SCHOOL OF BRUSSELS
Day — Coed Gr PS-PG

1170 Brussels, Belgium. Kattenberg 19. Tel: 32-2-661-4211. Fax: 32-2-661-4200. EST+6.
www.isb.be   E-mail: admissions@isb.be
Kevin Bartlet, Dir. BA, MA. David Willows, Adm.
   Col Prep. IB Diploma. Curr—Intl. Exams—AP. AP—Eng Fr Calc Stats Bio Eur_Hist US_Hist. Feat—Ger Japan Lat Span Comp_Sci Geog Music. Supp—ESL.
   Sports—Basket Baseball X-country F_Hockey Golf Rugby Soccer Softball Swim Tennis Track Volley. Activities—Acad Arts Govt/Pol Media Rec Service.
   Enr 1397. Elem 917. Sec 480. US 414. Host 82. Other 901. Accepted: 99%. Avg class size: 20.
   Fac 165. M 43/6. F 82/34. US 56. Host 27. Other 82. Adv Deg: 57%.
   Tui '05-'06: Day €6350-24,350 (+€2050). Aid: 145 pupils (€1,680,000).
   Summer: Acad Enrich Rec. 3 wks.
   Bldgs 10. Class rms 105. 2 Libs 65,000 vols. Theaters 1. Art studios 1. Gyms 2. Fields 3. Courts 2.
   Est 1951. Nonprofit. Quar (Aug-June). Assoc: A/OPR/OS CIS MSA.

The oldest English-speaking international school in Brussels, ISB occupies a 40-acre campus with separate facilities for the early childhood center and the elementary, middle and high schools. Americans constitute approximately one-third of the enrollment, with the remainder enrolling from several dozen other nations. The school's curriculum provides the IB Diploma option at the high school level, while Advanced Placement courses are also available in the upper grades.

ISB maintains extensive programs both in the arts and in sports. Students are encouraged to take advantage of the school's location by becoming involved in community projects and activities. In addition, the school schedules extended field trips in Europe for enrichment purposes.

ANTWERP INTERNATIONAL SCHOOL
Day — Coed Gr PS-12

2180 Ekeren, Belgium. Veltwijcklaan 180. Tel: 32-3-543-93-00. Fax: 32-3-541-82-01. EST+6.
www.ais-antwerp.be   E-mail: ais@ais-antwerp.be
Steven Murray, Head.
> **Col Prep. IB Diploma. Curr**—Intl. **Exams**—CEEB TOEFL IGCSE. **Feat**—Dutch Fr Ger Span Comp_Sci Econ Geog.
> **Enr 572.** Elem 372. Sec 200. Accepted: 100%.
> **Fac 73.** M 23/1. F 30/19. US 19. Host 13. Other 41. Adv Deg: 32%.
> **Tui '05-'06: Day €15,100-19,970.**
> Bldgs 6. Class rms 45. Lib 10,000 vols. Labs 4. Auds 1. Gyms 1.
> **Est 1967.** Nonprofit. Sem (Aug-June). Assoc: A/OPR/OS CIS NEASC.

Founded to meet the educational needs of the local international community, AIS draws almost half of its enrollment from the United States. Many other countries, however, are represented in the student body; most pupils have lived in one or more other countries before arriving in Antwerp. The school teaches French and Dutch on a daily basis, and German is available at the secondary level. The curriculum places particular emphasis on languages and the social sciences.

WORLD INTERNATIONAL SCHOOL
Day — Coed Gr PS-10

1640 Rhode St Genese, Belgium. Chaussee de Waterloo 280. Tel: 32-2-358-56-06. Fax: 32-2-358-31-32. EST+6.
www.wis.be   E-mail: info@wis.be
Chris Mordue, Head.
> **Pre-Prep. IB MYP. Curr**—Intl. **Feat**—Humanities Fr Comp_Sci Studio_Art Drama Music.
> **Tui '05-'06: Day €17,200** (+€500).
> **Est 2000.**

BRITISH PRIMARY SCHOOL
Day — Coed Gr PS-5

3080 Tervuren, Belgium. Stationsstraat 3, Vossem. Tel: 32-2-767-30-98. Fax: 32-2-767-03-51. EST+6.
www.britishprimary.com   E-mail: info@britishprimary.com
Grainne O'Reilly, Head.
> **Gen Acad. Curr**—UK. **Feat**—Lib_Skills Fr Computers Music. **Supp**—ESL LD.
> **Enr 250.**

Tui '05-'06: Day €12,000-13,000.
Est 1975. Tri (Sept-July).

BRITISH SCHOOL OF BRUSSELS
Day — Coed Gr PS-12

3080 Tervuren, Belgium. Leuvensesteenweg 19. Tel: 32-2-766-04-30. Fax: 32-2-767-80-70. EST+6.
www.britishschool.be   E-mail: admissions@britishschool.be
Roland Chant, Prin.
> **Col Prep. IB Diploma. Curr**—Intl. **Feat**—Dutch Fr Ger Russ Span Comp_Sci Econ Sociol Studio_Art. **Supp**—ESL.
> **Tui '05-'06: Day €8350-22,900.**
> **Est 1970.** Tri (Sept-July).

INTERNATIONAL MONTESSORI SCHOOL
Day — Coed Gr PS-10

3080 Tervuren, Belgium. Rotselaerlaan 1. Tel: 32-2-767-63-60. Fax: 32-2-767-63-60. EST+6.
www.international-montessori.org   E-mail: montessori-tervuren@online.be
Annie R. Hoekstra-de Roos, Admin. MEd, MBA. **Rinze Hoekstra, Prin.**
> **Gen Acad. IB MYP. Curr**—Intl. **Bilingual**—Fr. **Feat**—Dutch Ger Comp_Sci Music. **Supp**—ESL Tut.
> **Enr 230.** B 120. G 110. Elem 220. Sec 10. US 30. Host 30. Other 170. Avg class size: 24.
> **Fac 32.** M 2/2. F 24/4. US 2. Host 15. Other 15. Adv Deg: 18%.
> **Grad '05—5.**
> **Tui '05-'06: Day €10,903-16,695** (+€300).
> **Summer:** Rec. Tui Day €240/wk. 2 wks.
> Bldgs 6. Class rms 14. Music studios 1.
> **Est 1993.** Inc. Sem (Sept-June).

This traditional Montessori school staffs each classroom with both an English-speaking teacher and a French-speaking teacher or assistant, thereby creating a completely bilingual environment. Students learn vocabulary in both languages through general conversation and interaction, songs, poems, books, stories and class presentations.

Children may enter the toddler program at 14 months, the Children's House at age 2½ and the primary class at age 5½. As the child progresses through the program, he or she gains familiarity with the basic concepts of language, mathematics and culture that are appropriate to the child's developmental level. Individualized learning, the development of decision-making skills and the pursuit of student interests are particular points of emphasis.

ST. JOHN'S INTERNATIONAL SCHOOL
Day — Coed Gr PS-13

1410 Waterloo, Belgium. 146 Dreve Richelle. Tel: 32-2-352-0610. Fax: 32-2-352-0630. EST+6.
www.stjohns.be   E-mail: admissions@stjohns.be
Joseph Doenges, Dir. DEd.

> **Col Prep. IB Diploma. Curr**—Intl UK US. **Exams**—AP CEEB TOEFL. **AP**—Eng Fr Ger Span Calc Chem Physics US_Hist Econ Music_Theory. **Feat**—Dutch Swedish Stats Comp_Sci Relig Visual_Arts.
> **Enr 930.** Elem 639. Sec 291.
> **Fac 120.**
> **Grad '05—67.**
> **Tui '05-'06: Day €18,500-23,800** (+€3250).
> **Summer:** Enrich Rem Rec. 2-8 wks.
> Bldgs 7. Class rms 54. Lib 22,000 vols. Arts ctrs 1. Gyms 2. Fields 1. Courts 3.
> **Est 1964.** Nonprofit. Ecumenical. Tri (Sept-June). Assoc: CIS MSA.

Situated in a residential area a short distance from the historic battlefields of Waterloo, St. John's offers a US/UK course of study that prepares students for the SAT and IGCSE examinations and the International Baccalaureate Diploma. General instruction is in English, with French taught daily from nursery through grade 13, and German and Spanish optional from grade 8. The elementary school emphasizes basic skills in language arts and math and offers a wide range of other subjects, including religion, health, information technology, music and art. Preparation for high school studies through a strong curriculum is provided within the middle school program, while the high school program readies students for both US college entrance and for British and European universities. Advanced Placement and honors courses are available in several disciplines.

A strong intramural and interscholastic program encourages participation in a wide range of sports, and fine arts offerings are available. During midwinter vacation, St. John's organizes separate ski trips for middle and senior high school students. Field trip destinations include various locations in Belgium, as well as sites of interest in neighboring countries.

BOSNIA AND HERZEGOVINA

Sq. Miles: 19,781 (Slightly smaller than West Virginia). **Country Pop:** 4,025,476 (2005). **Capital:** Sarajevo, pop. 387,876. **Terrain:** Mountains in the central and southern regions, plains along the Sava River in the north. **Ethnic Group(s):** Bosniak Serb Croat. **Religion(s):** Muslim Orthodox Catholic Protestant. **Other Language(s):** Bosnian Serbian Croatian. **Government:** Parliamentary Democracy. **Independence:** 1992 (from Yugoslavia). **Per Capita Income:** $6500 (2004). **GDP:** $26.21 billion (2004). Agriculture 14%. Industry 31%. Services 55%. **Currency:** Bosnian Mark (KM).

QSI INTERNATIONAL SCHOOL OF SARAJEVO

Day — Coed Gr PS-12

71320 Sarajevo, Bosnia and Herzegovina. Donji Hotorj 8, Vogosca. Tel: 387-33-434-756. Fax: 387-33-434-756. EST+6.
www.qsi.org/BHZ_HOME   E-mail: sarajevo@qsi.org
Jeffery Jenkins, Dir.

Pre-Prep. Curr—US. **Feat**—Fr Ger Bosnian Comp_Sci Studio_Art Music. **Supp**—ESL.

Enr 82. Accepted: 100%. Avg class size: 10.

Fac 29. Adv Deg: 6%.

Grad '05—5. Prep—5. US Prep—2. (UN Intl).

Tui '05-'06: Day $4600-12,000 (+$1600). **Aid:** 7 pupils ($77,000).

Plant val $500,000. Bldgs 1. Class rms 7. Lib 3500 vols. Sci labs 1. Comp labs 1.

Est 1997. Nonprofit. Spons: Quality Schools International. Tri (Sept-June). Assoc: A/OPR/OS MSA.

This school addresses the educational needs of expatriate children living in Sarajevo who are interested in a US-style program. Instruction in the basic skills is of primary importance. In addition to course work in the standard subjects, QSIS maintains a fully networked computer lab and conducts Bosnian, French and German language classes. Afternoon activities are available, and field trips enrich class work each term. Students typically spend two or three years at the school.

BULGARIA

Sq. Miles: 42,855 (Slightly larger than Tennessee). **Country Pop:** 7,450,349 (2005). **Capital:** Sofia, pop. 1,200,000. **Terrain:** The terrain is varied, containing large mountainous areas, fertile valleys, plains and a coastline along the Black Sea. **Ethnic Group(s):** Bulgarian Turkish Roma. **Religion(s):** Bulgarian_Orthodox Muslim Roman_Catholic Protestant. **Official Language(s):** Bulgarian. **Government:** Parliamentary Democracy. **Independence:** 1908 (from Ottoman Empire). **Per Capita Income:** $8200 (2004). **GDP:** $61.63 billion (2004). Agriculture 12%. Industry 30%. Services 58%. **Currency:** Bulgarian Lev (Lv).

THE AMERICAN COLLEGE OF SOFIA

Day — Coed Gr 8-12

Sofia 1000, Bulgaria. PO Box 873. Tel: 359-2-975-3695. Fax: 359-2-974-3129. EST+8.
www.acs.bg   E-mail: acs@acs.bg
Louis J. Perske, Pres. BA, MPA.

Col Prep. IB Diploma. Curr—Intl Nat US. **Exams**—AP CEEB TOEFL. **Feat**—Fr Ger Russ Span Bulgarian Comp_Sci Psych Philos Studio_Art. **Supp**—Tut.

Sports—Badminton Basket Soccer Tennis Volley. **Activities**—Acad Arts Cultural/Relig Govt/Pol Media Rec.

Enr 635. B 300. G 335. Elem 142. Sec 493. US 4. Host 596. Other 35. Accepted: 10%. Yield: 90%. Avg class size: 18.

Fac 72. M 26. F 46. US 12. Host 52. Other 8. Adv Deg: 68%.

Grad '05—97. Col—97. US Col—36. (Adelphi 4, St John's U-NY 3, Brown 2, Dartmouth 2, Tufts 2, Vassar 2). Avg SAT: M/V—1412, Essay—704.

Tui '05-'06: Day €12,000 (+€1000). **Aid:** 412 pupils (€1,220,000).

Summer: Acad Enrich Rec. Tui Day €500. 4 wks.

Bldgs 8. Class rms 64. Lib 15,000 vols. Sci labs 3. Comp labs 3. Auds 2. Theaters 1. Art studios 1. Music studios 3. Dance studios 1. Gyms 1. Fields 2. Courts 4.

Est 1860. Nonprofit. Sem (Sept-June).

The oldest American educational institution outside of the US, ACS was shut down by the Bulgarian government in 1942 and reopened 50 years later. Although the student body is predominantly Bulgarian, more than a dozen other countries are represented at the school.

In addition to the four high school grades, the school conducts a prep year (grade 8) that provides students who need it intensive English language training. While incorporating US curricular elements, the school follows guidelines set by the Bulgarian Ministry of Education. In grades 9 and 10, ACS teaches all courses in English except for foreign language (including Bulgarian). Geography and philosophy are also taught in Bulgarian in grades 11 and 12.

Significant financial assistance is available to Bulgarian citizens; however, virtually all international pupils must pay full tuition.

ANGLO-AMERICAN SCHOOL OF SOFIA

Day — Coed Gr PS-9

Sofia 1407, Bulgaria. c/o US Embassy, 16 Kozyak St. Tel: 359-2-974-4575. Fax: 359-2-974-4483. EST+7.

Contact: Dept of State, 5740 Sofia Pl, Washington, DC 20521.

http://sofia.ecis.org E-mail: aasregist@infotel.bg

Eric Larson, Dir. MA.

Gen Acad. Curr—Intl. **Feat**—Fr Bulgarian Comp_Sci Studio_Art Drama Music. **Supp**—ESL.

Activities—Acad Arts Rec Service.

Enr 190. B 96. G 94. US 47. Host 19. Other 124. Avg class size: 17.

Fac 27. M 5. F 15/7. US 5. Host 7. Other 15. Adv Deg: 25%.

Tui '05-'06: Day $3700-11,560 (+$1900-3815).

Bldgs 1. Class rms 10. Lib 9000 vols. Sci labs 1. Lang labs 3. Comp labs 1. Art studios 1. Music studios 1. Gyms 1. Courts 1.

Est 1967. Nonprofit. Quar (Aug-June). Assoc: A/OPR/OS CIS NEASC.

Established to provide appropriate educational facilities for the children of US and UK embassy personnel, the school now also serves boys and girls whose parents are working in Sofia with other embassies or with multinational companies. The academic program is American oriented and also incorporates British curricular elements. ESL courses assist students lacking English fluency, and French and Bulgarian are taught as foreign languages. Computer instruction is an important aspect of the curriculum at all grade levels.

CROATIA

Sq. Miles: 21,829 (Slightly smaller than West Virginia). **Country Pop:** 4,495,904 (2005). **Capital:** Zagreb, pop. 779,145 (2002). **Terrain:** Diverse, containing rocky coastlines, densely wooded mountains, plains, lakes and rolling hills. **Ethnic Group(s):** Croat Serb Bosnian Hungarian Slovenian Czech Roma. **Religion(s):** Roman_Catholic Orthodox Muslim. **Official Language(s):** Croatian. **Government:** Parliamentary Democracy. **Independence:** 1991 (from Yugoslavia). **Per Capita Income:** $11,600 (2005). **GDP:** $53.29 billion (2005). Agriculture 3%. Industry 33%. Services 64%. **Currency:** Croatian Kuna (HRK).

AMERICAN INTERNATIONAL SCHOOL OF ZAGREB
Day — Coed Gr PS-12

Zagreb 10000, Croatia. Vocarska 106. Tel: 385-1-46-80-133. Fax: 385-1-46-80-171. EST+6.
Contact: Dept of State, 5080 Zagreb Pl, Washington, DC 20521.
www.aisz.hr   E-mail: aisz@aisz.hr
James Swetz, Dir. MA.

Gen Acad. IB Diploma. Curr—Intl US. **Exams**—CEEB. **Feat**—Fr Ger Comp_Sci Studio_Art Music. **Supp**—ESL.
Activities—Arts Rec.
Enr 165. Elem 130. Sec 35. US 52. Host 27. Other 86. Accepted: 99%. Yield: 100%. Avg class size: 15.
Fac 31. M 5/2. F 19/5. US 10. Host 12. Other 9. Adv Deg: 54%.
Grad '05—6. Col—4.
Tui '05-'06: Day $15,540-16,765 (+$500). **Aid:** 13 pupils.
Summer: Acad Rec. Tui Day $80/wk. 4 wks.
Bldgs 2. Class rms 20. Lib 5000 vols. Sci labs 1. Comp labs 2. Auds 1. Art studios 1. Music studios 1. Gyms 1. Courts 1.
Est 1966. Nonprofit. Quar (Aug-June). Assoc: A/OPR/OS MSA.

AISZ serves the children of the American and international community who are temporarily residing in the Zagreb area. Pupils applying for admission to grade 5 and above should have some degree of English proficiency; a strong ESL program is available. The curriculum is that of an American school. French and German are available as foreign languages at all grade levels, and as native languages in certain grades.

After-school activities include sports, computers, board games, math enrichment, cooking, jazz dance, art, homework club, chorus and Croatian language.

CZECH REPUBLIC

Sq. Miles: 30,450 (About the size of Virginia). **Country Pop:** 10,230,000 (0). **Capital:** Prague, pop. 1,160,000. **Terrain:** Low mountains to the north and south, hills in the west. **Ethnic Group(s):** Czech Moravian Slovak Roma Silesian Polish German Ukrainian Vietnamese. **Religion(s):** Roman_Catholic Protestant. **Official Language(s):** Czech. **Government:** Parliamentary Republic. **Independence:** 1993. **Per Capita Income:** $10,479 (2004). **GDP:** $107.05 billion (2004). Agriculture 4%. Industry 39%. Services 57%. **Currency:** Czech Koruna (Kc).

THE BRITISH INTERNATIONAL SCHOOL OF PRAGUE

Day — Coed Gr PS-12

142 00 Prague 4, Czech Republic. K Lesu 558/2. Tel: 420-226-096200. Fax: 420-226-096201. EST+6.
www.bisp.cz   E-mail: mainoffice@bisp.cz
Jeremy G. R. Long, Dir.
    Col Prep. IB Diploma. Curr—Intl UK. Exams—IGCSE. Feat—Fr Ger Russ Czech Environ_Sci Econ Bus. Supp—EFL ESL.
    Activities—Arts.
    Enr 600. Avg class size: 15.
    Fac 75.
    Grad '05—10. Col—10.
    Tui '05-'06: Day €10,600-14,900.
    Bldgs 3. Class rms 40. Libs 4. Sci labs 3. Lang labs 2. Comp labs 4.
    Est 1992. Nonprofit. Tri (Sept-June).

Founded to fill a perceived need for a British-style educational establishment in the city, the school now serves children age 1½ and up through its infant, junior and senior divisions. In addition to the Kamyk site, the school maintains two other campuses in Prague. As BISP seeks to maintain continuity with schools in the UK, students follow the standard IGCSE program, and preparation for the IB is also provided. Although all nonlanguage faculty and much of the student body are British, the school enrolls pupils from dozens of other nations as well. A varied language program comprises 12 years of French, German and Czech instruction, as well as six years of Russian.

THE ENGLISH COLLEGE IN PRAGUE

Day — Coed Gr 8-12

190 00 Prague 9, Czech Republic. Sokolovska 320, Vysocany. Tel: 420-2-838-93113. Fax: 420-2-838-90118. EST+6.
www.englishcollege.cz   E-mail: office@englishcollege.cz
Peter de Voil, Head.
    Col Prep. IB Diploma. Curr—Intl UK. Exams—IGCSE. Feat—Fr Ger Span Czech Econ Psych Philos Visual_Arts Music.
    Enr 320.
    Tui '05-'06: Day £6540.
    Est 1994. Tri (Sept-June).

THE ENGLISH INTERNATIONAL SCHOOL
PRAGUE

Day — Coed Gr PS-8

142 00 Prague 4, Czech Republic. Na Okruhu 395. Tel: 420-2-61-91-23-68. Fax: 420-2-61-91-00-74. EST+6.
www.eisp.cz   E-mail: school@eisp.cz
Sylvia May, Head.
   Gen Acad. Curr—Intl UK. Feat—Ger Czech Studio_Art Music. Supp—EFL LD Rem_Read.
   Enr 174. Accepted: 100%. Avg class size: 16.
   Fac 30. M 4/1. F 21/4. US 7. Adv Deg: 3%.
   Grad '05—3.
   Tui '02-'03: Day Kc231,000-362,500.
   Summer: Acad Enrich Rec. Tui Day Kc5600/wk. 3 wks.
   Libs 1.
   Est 1995. Tri (Sept-July).

Housed on two sites on the southern outskirts of the city, EISP bases its program on that offered in England and Wales; however, the curriculum has been broadened and enriched to make it more suitable for an international student body. Children receive preparation for entrance examinations to senior schools in Prague, the UK and elsewhere. Most children learn some Czech; German is available as a second foreign language. Music, art and drama figure significantly in the school day, and many children study a musical instrument in school.

A limited number of boys and girls may enroll despite a lack of English fluency; they immediately enroll in EISP's English as a Foreign Language program. English serves as the medium of instruction at all grade levels, however.

Sister schools operate in the United Kingdom and Central Europe.

INTERNATIONAL SCHOOL OF PRAGUE

Day — Coed Gr PS-12

164 00 Prague 6, Czech Republic. Nebusicka 700. Tel: 420-2-2038-4111. Fax: 420-2-2038-4555. EST+6.
www.isp.cz   E-mail: ispmail@isp.cz
Robert Landau, Dir. Bohumila Limova, Adm.
   Col Prep. IB Diploma. Curr—Intl. Exams—CEEB. Feat—Creative_Writing Fr Ger Span Econ Psych Studio_Art Music. Supp—ESL Tut.
   Sports—Basket X-country Soccer Softball Swim Tennis Volley. Activities—Acad Arts Govt/Pol Media.
   Enr 750. US 150. Host 75. Other 525. Accepted: 99%. Avg class size: 20.
   Fac 94. M 33. F 58/3. US 58. Other 36. Adv Deg: 48%.
   Grad '05—50. US Col—26.
   Tui '05-'06: Day $17,075-20,075.
   Bldgs 1. Class rms 86. Labs 6. Theaters 1.
   Est 1948. Nonprofit. Sem (Sept-June). Assoc: A/OPR/OS ECIS.

Providing elementary and secondary education for children of the international community of Prague, this school offers a standard American curriculum that also prepares interested students for the International Baccalaureate. A wide range of nationalities is represented in the student body, including children from the US and approximately 30 other countries.

Located in the village of Nebusice, on the outskirts of Prague's residential area, the school organizes excursions to local sites of interest.

RIVERSIDE SCHOOL

Day — Coed Gr PS-12

160 00 Prague 6, Czech Republic. Roztocka 9, Sedlec. Tel: 420-224-315-336. Fax: 420-224-325-765. EST+6.
www.riversideschool.cz   E-mail: administration@riversideschool.cz
Peter Daish, Dir.
   Col Prep. Curr—Intl UK. **Exams**—IGCSE. **Feat**—Fr Span Czech Comp_Sci Relig Studio_Art Drama Music Journ. **Supp**—ESL.
   Tui '05-'06: Day £4089-6597.
   Est 1994. Nondenom Christian. Tri (Sept-June).

DENMARK

Sq. Miles: 16,640 (Slightly smaller than Vermont and New Hampshire combined). **Country Pop:** 5,432,335 (2005). **Capital:** Copenhagen, pop. 500,000. **Terrain:** Low and flat or slightly rolling. **Ethnic Group(s):** Scandinavian German Inuit Faroese. **Religion(s):** Evangelical_Lutheran Catholic Jewish. **Official Language(s):** Danish. **Other Language(s):** German Faroese Greenlandic English. **Government:** Constitutional Monarchy. **Per Capita Income:** $37,883 (2003). **GDP:** $212 billion (2003). Agriculture 2%. Industry 24%. Services 74%. **Currency:** Danish Krone (Dkr).

BJORN'S INTERNATIONAL SCHOOL

Day — Coed Gr 1-9

2100 Copenhagen, Denmark. Gartnerivej 5. Tel: 45-39-29-29-37. Fax: 45-39-18-38-42. EST+6.
www.b-i-s.dk   E-mail: kontoret.101152@b-i-s.dk
Pia Drabowicz, Prin.
   Gen Acad. Curr—Intl. **Exams**—IGCSE. **Feat**—Danish.
   Enr 150.
   Tui '06-'07: Day Dkr14,300 (+Dkr1100).
   Est 1967. Sem (Aug-June).

BERNADOTTE SCHOOL

Day — Coed Gr PS-10

2900 Hellerup, Denmark. Hellerupvej 11. Tel: 45-39-62-28-37. Fax: 45-39-62-27-37. EST+6.

www.bernadotteskolen.dk E-mail: tlh@bernadotteskolen.dk

 Pre-Prep. Curr—Nat. Feat—Fr Ger Danish Comp_Sci Drama Music.

 Tui '04-'05: Day Dkr14,220 (+Dkr2500).

 Est 1949.

COPENHAGEN INTERNATIONAL SCHOOL

Day — Coed Gr PS-12

2900 Hellerup, Denmark. Hellerupvej 22-26. Tel: 45-39-46-33-00. Fax: 45-39-61-22-30. EST+6.

www.cis-edu.dk E-mail: cis@cisdk.dk

Claes-Goran Widlund, Dir.

 Col Prep. IB PYP. IB MYP. IB Diploma. Curr—Intl. Exams—CEEB IGCSE. Feat—Fr Ger Danish Comp_Sci Anthro Theater_Arts. Supp—ESL.

 Enr 560.

 Fac 67.

 Tui '05-'06: Day Dkr88,000-99,000 (+Dkr12,000).

 Est 1963. Nonprofit. Quar (Aug-June). Assoc: A/OPR/OS CIS NEASC.

RYGAARDS SCHOOL
INTERNATIONAL DEPARTMENT

Day — Coed Ages 4-16

2900 Hellerup, Denmark. Bernstorffsvej 54. Tel: 45-39-62-10-53. Fax: 45-39-62-10-81. EST+6.

www.rygaardsskole.dk E-mail: admin@rygaards.com

Charles Dalton, Head.

 Gen Acad. Curr—UK. Exams—GCSE O-level. Feat—Fr Ger Danish Relig Studio_Art Bus.

 Enr 340.

 Tui '05-'06: Day Dkr19,085.

 Est 1909. Nonprofit. Roman Catholic. Sem (Aug-June).

HORSHOLM INTERNATIONAL SCHOOL

Day — Coed Gr PS-10

2970 Horsholm, Denmark. Cirkelhuset, Christianshusvej 16. Tel: 45-45-57-26-16. Fax: 45-45-57-26-69. EST+6.

www.his.dk E-mail: his@ngg.dk

Jan Thrane, Prin.

 Pre-Prep. IB PYP. IB MYP. Curr—Intl. Feat—Fr Ger Span Danish Comp_Sci Studio_Art.

Enr 180.
Fac 30.
Tui '05-'06: Day Dkr19,140.
Est 1996. Tri (Sept-June).

ENGLAND

Sq. Miles: 50,356 (Slightly larger than New York). **Country Pop:** 49,138,831 (2001). **Capital:** London, pop. 7,200,000 (2005). **Terrain:** Mostly rugged hills and low mountains. **Government:** Constitutional Monarchy. **Currency:** British Pound (£).

ACS COBHAM INTERNATIONAL SCHOOL
Bdg — Coed Gr 7-12; Day — Coed PS-12

Cobham, Surrey KT11 1BL, England. Heywood, Portsmouth Rd. Tel: 44-1932-867251. Fax: 44-1932-869789. EST+5.
www.acs-england.co.uk E-mail: cobhamadmissions@acs-england.co.uk
Thomas Lehman, Head. BA, MA. **Elizabeth Allis, Adm.**
>**Col Prep. IB Diploma. Curr**—Intl US. **Exams**—AP. **AP**—Eng Fr Ger Span Calc Stats Bio Chem Human_Geog Physics Eur_Hist US_Hist Econ Psych Studio_Art. **Feat**—Ceramics Photog Theater_Arts Journ. **Supp**—EFL ESL.
>**Sports**—Basket Baseball Cheer X-country Golf Rugby Soccer Softball Swim Tennis Track Volley. **Activities**—Acad Arts Govt/Pol Media Rec Service.
>**Enr 1309.** B 59/679. G 43/528. Elem 856. Sec 453. US 667. Host 127. Other 515. Avg class size: 20.
>**Fac 149.** M 44. F 92/13. US 69. Host 45. Other 35. Adv Deg: 38%.
>**Grad '05**—108. **Col**—97. **US Col**—48. (Boston U, U of VA, James Madison, Harvard, U of CA-Berkeley, Cornell).
>**Tui '05-'06: Bdg £25,100-26,200. Day £4900-15,650.**
>Bldgs 14. Dorms 3. Dorm rms 60. Class rms 110. 3 Libs 26,000 vols. Auds 1. Fields 2. Tennis courts 2. Pools 1. Tracks 1.
>**Est 1967.** Inc. Sem (Aug-June). Assoc: NEASC.

The oldest of three American Community Schools, ACS Cobham conducts a full preschool through high school program for its highly international student body. Originally designed to meet the educational needs of American families based in London, the school now provides both American and international pupils with two curricular options: one leading to the traditional US high school diploma, the other culminating with the International Baccalaureate diploma. Advanced Placement selections in all disciplines are an important aspect of the American program.

Accredited on both sides of the Atlantic, ACS maintains a flexible program that eases the student's transition back to schools in the US and other countries while also providing preparation for colleges around the world. Field trips to sites of interest in and around London are also part of the school program.

Two other London-area branches of the American Community Schools are in operation. ACS Hillingdon (108 Vine Ln., Hillingdon, Uxbridge, Middlesex

UB10 0BE) also conducts a full preschool through grade 12 program that includes Advanced Placement course work, while ACS Egham (London Rd., Egham, Surrey TW20 0HS) offers both the IB Primary Years Program (for children ages 3-11) and the IB Middle Years Program (ages 11-16). All three campuses follow the same educational approach.

ROSSALL SCHOOL
Bdg — Coed Ages 11-18; Day Coed 2-18

Fleetwood, Lancashire FY7 8JW, England. Tel: 44-1253-774201. Fax: 44-1253-772052. EST+5.
www.rossall.co.uk   E-mail: info@rossall.co.uk
Tim Wilbur, Prin.

> Col Prep. IB Diploma. Curr—Intl UK. Exams—GCSE A-level. Feat—Fr Ger Span Econ Psych Visual_Arts Music. Supp—ESL.
> Enr 1019.
> Tui '05-'06: Bdg €4735-7570 (+€100). Day €1855-3713 (+€100).
> Est 1844. Tri.

MARYMOUNT INTERNATIONAL SCHOOL
Bdg and Day — Girls Gr 6-12

Kingston upon Thames, Surrey KT2 7PE, England. George Rd. Tel: 44-208-949-0571. Fax: 44-208-336-2485. EST+5.
www.marymountlondon.com   E-mail: info@marymountlondon.com
Sr. Kathleen Fagan, RSHM, Head. BEd, MS. Chris Hiscock, Adm.

> Col Prep. IB Diploma. Curr—Intl. Exams—ACT CEEB TOEFL. Feat—Arabic Chin Fr Ger Ital Japan Span Econ Psych Philos Relig Studio_Art Music. Supp—Dev_ Read ESL Rem_Math Rem_Read Tut.
> Sports—Badminton Basket X-country Soccer Softball Tennis Volley. Activities— Arts Govt/Pol Rec.
> Enr 230. G 90/140. US 19. Host 50. Other 161. Accepted: 80%. Yield: 98%. Avg class size: 11.
> Fac 32. M 14/1. F 14/3. US 5. Host 17. Other 10. Adv Deg: 31%.
> Grad '05—47.
> Tui '05-'06: Bdg £22,000 (+£300). Day £13,000 (+£300).
> Bldgs 8. Dorms 4. Dorm rms 54. Class rms 29. Lib 7000 vols. Comp labs 3. Art studios 1. Music studios 1. Gyms 1. Athletic ctrs 1. Fields 1.
> Est 1955. Roman Catholic. Sem (Sept-June). Assoc: ECIS.

One of the many Marymount schools located throughout the world that takes direction from the Religious of the Sacred Heart of Mary, this school enrolls students of many different nationalities. The college preparatory program leads to an American high school diploma and the International Baccalaureate. Graduates pursue university degrees throughout the world.

AMERICAN SCHOOL IN LONDON

Day — Coed Gr PS-12

London NW8 0NP, England. 1 Waverly Pl. Tel: 44-20-7449-1200. Fax: 44-20-7449-1350. EST+5.
www.asl.org   E-mail: admissions@asl.org
William C. Mules, Head. AB, MEd, EdD. Jody Coats, Adm.

    Col Prep. Curr—US. **Exams**—ACT CEEB SSAT. **AP**—Fr Ger Span Calc Stats Comp_Sci Bio Chem Physics Eur_Hist US_Hist Econ Art_Hist Studio_Art Music_Theory. **Feat**—Web_Design Psych African_Stud World_Relig.
    Sports—Basket Baseball Cheer Crew X-country F_Hockey Golf Rugby Soccer Softball Swim Tennis Track Volley Wrestling. **Activities**—Acad Arts Govt/Pol Service.
    Enr 1313. B 676. G 637.
    Fac 163. M 58. F 105.
    Grad '05—87.
    Tui '05-'06: Day £15,150-18,570.
    Summer: Rec. 1-8 wks.
    Bldgs 1. Class rms 80. 2 Libs 50,000 vols. Sci labs 9. Comp labs 7. Theaters 2. Art studios 5. Music studios 5. Gyms 2. Fields 1.
    Est 1951. Nonprofit. Sem (Aug-June). Assoc: A/OPR/OS CIS MAIS MSA.

ASL, the oldest American-curriculum school in the UK, was established to provide a US-style academic program for children of American business and government personnel on assignment in London. Enrichment courses from the modern language, computer and fine arts departments complement the core curriculum of English, math, science and history. Advanced Placement courses in all major disciplines are offered, as are a variety of electives. Fine arts trips and the international school athletic program foster strong cultural ties with Continental Europe. While the enrollment is approximately 70 percent American, the school accepts pupils of all nationalities, including non-English speakers under age 12, who meet entry requirements. Graduates attend competitive colleges in the US, the UK and elsewhere in the world.

ASL's location on a three-acre site in central London allows students to take advantage of the city's theaters, art galleries and museums as part of curriculum-related field trips. The school operates a bus service covering most of north and central London.

SOUTHBANK INTERNATIONAL SCHOOL

Day — Coed Gr PS-12

London W11 3BU, England. 36-38 Kensington Park Rd, Nottinghill. Tel: 44-20-72433803. Fax: 44-20-77273290. EST+5.
www.southbank.org   E-mail: admissions@southbank.org
Nigel Hughes, Head. BSc, MEd. Margaret Anne Khoury, Adm.

    Col Prep. IB PYP. IB MYP. IB Diploma. Curr—Intl. **Feat**—Arabic Chin Fr Ger Greek Hebrew Ital Japan Lat Russ Span Farsi Finnish Norwegian Swedish Comp_Sci Studio_Art Drama Music. **Supp**—EFL ESL LD Tut.
    Sports—Basket Golf Soccer Volley. **Activities**—Arts Govt/Pol.
    Enr 670. B 338. G 332. Elem 499. Sec 171. US 208. Host 86. Other 376. Avg class

size: 16.
Fac 115. M 24/4. F 70/17. Adv Deg: 80%.
Grad '05—31. Col—29. US Col—3.
Tui '05-'06: Day £9000-17,700.
Summer: Acad Rec. EFL. 6 wks.
Bldgs 4. Sci labs 4. Comp labs 4. Auds 1. Theaters 2. Art studios 3. Music studios 3.
Est 1979. Nonprofit. Tri (Sept-June).

Founded by a group of British and American educators, Southbank has evolved over the years into an institution with three London locations: Southbank Kensington (in Notting Hill on Kensington Park Road) serves pupils ages 3-11, Southbank Hampstead (16 Netherhall Gardens, NW3 5TH) enrolls boys and girls ages 3-14, and Southbank Westminster (63-65 Portland Pl., W1B 1QR) accepts students ages 11-19.

The school conducts an individualized college preparatory curriculum for pupils from approximately 50 nations. Although English is the language of instruction, the school accommodates those boys and girls who arrive with little of no facility with the language. Numerous languages are part of the curriculum for older students both as foreign languages and as mother-tongue literature courses. Southbank follows all three International Baccalaureate programs.

The school's city campuses enable pupils to take advantage of many learning opportunities outside of the classroom, among them visits to exhibitions, museums and galleries. Most graduates—regardless of their nationality—matriculate at British universities.

WOODSIDE PARK INTERNATIONAL SCHOOL

Day — Coed Gr K-12

London N12 8SH, England. Friern Barnet Rd. Tel: 44-208-445-9670. Fax: 44-208-368-3220. EST+5.
www.wpis.org   E-mail: director@wpis.org
David Rose, Head.
   Col Prep. Gen Acad. IB PYP. IB MYP. IB Diploma. Curr—Intl Nat. **Exams—**GCSE. **Feat—**Fr Ger Ital Span Econ Relig Studio_Art Music. **Supp—**Dev_Read EFL ESL LD Makeup Rem_Math Rem_Read Rev Tut.
   Enr 560. B 370. G 190. US 25. Host 320. Other 215. Avg class size: 16.
   Fac 60. M 20/2. F 18/20. US 3. Host 45. Other 12. Adv Deg: 8%.
   Grad '05—15.
   Tui '02-'03: Day £4512-9900. **Aid:** 50 pupils (£250,000).
   Sci labs 3. Lang labs 2. Comp labs 3. Theaters 1. Art studios 2. Music studios 2. Gyms 3. Fields 1. Courts 2.
   Est 2000. Inc. Tri (Sept-July).

This school offers both international and national curricula. The junior department focuses on the pupils' development, with the curriculum designed to provide a sound training in basic literacy and arithmetic skills, while stimulating interest and participation in other activities such as games, music and the arts. In the senior department, each pupil takes nine or 10 courses at GCSE level, chosen from a varied curriculum. In the Sixth Form, students prepare for the International Baccalaureate Diploma.

The visual and performing arts are integral to school life at WPIS. Boys and girls study painting, sculpture, graphic arts, ceramics, collage and mosaics as part of the art curriculum, and all school divisions take part in dramatic productions. A choir and an orchestra provide performance opportunities for those interested in music, and students are also able to attend nearby concerts. Instrumental music instruction in piano, cello, guitar, violin, keyboard, flute and clarinet is available for an additional fee.

MALVERN COLLEGE
Bdg — Coed Ages 8-18; Day — Coed 3-18

Malvern, Worcestershire WR14 3DF, England. College Rd. Tel: 44-1684-581-500. Fax: 44-1684-581-617. EST+5.
www.malcol.org   E-mail: registry@malcol.org
Hugh C. Carson, Head.
> Col Prep. IB Diploma. Curr—Intl Nat. Exams—GCSE A-level. Feat—Fr Ger Greek Ital Lat Russ Span Cantonese Comp_Sci Econ Pol_Sci Relig Studio_Art Drama Music Bus.
> Tui '05-'06: Bdg £3805-7330. Day £1430-4740.
> Est 1865. Nonprofit. Tri (Sept-July).

ST. CLARE'S
OXFORD
Bdg — Coed Ages 16-19

Oxford OX2 7AL, England. 139 Banbury Rd. Tel: 44-1865-552031. Fax: 44-1865-513359. EST+5.
www.stclares.ac.uk   E-mail: admissions@stclares.ac.uk
Paula Holloway, Prin.
> Col Prep. IB Diploma. Curr—Intl. Feat—Comp_Sci Econ Pol_Sci Psych Sociol Philos Relig Art_Hist Studio_Art Communications.
> Fac 45.
> Est 1953. Nonprofit. Tri (Aug-June).

TASIS
THE AMERICAN SCHOOL IN ENGLAND
Bdg — Coed Gr 9-12; Day — Coed PS-12

Thorpe, Surrey TW20 8TE, England. Coldharbour Ln. Tel: 44-1932-565252. Fax: 44-1932-564644. EST+6.
Contact: 1640 Wisconsin Ave NW, Washington, DC 20007. Tel: 202-965-5800. Fax: 202-965-5816.
www.tasis.com   E-mail: ukadmissions@tasis.com
James A. Doran, Head. PhD. Bronwyn Thorburn-Riseley, Adm.
> Col Prep. IB Diploma. Curr—Intl US. Exams—ACT AP CEEB TOEFL. AP—Eng

Fr Span Calc Stats Comp_Sci Bio Chem Environ_Sci Physics Eur_Hist US_Hist Comp_Govt & Pol Econ Art_Hist Music_Theory. **Feat**—Humanities Ger Lat Studio_Art Drama Music. **Supp**—Dev_Read ESL LD Rem_Math Rem_Read Tut.

Sports—Basket Baseball Cheer X-country Golf Rugby Soccer Softball Tennis Volley. **Activities**—Arts Govt/Pol Media.

Enr 725. Accepted: 75%. Avg class size: 12.

Fac 105. M 34/4. F 57/10. Adv Deg: 29%.

Grad '05—80. US Col—41. (Boston U, Northeastern U, Geo Wash, U of TX-Austin). Avg SAT: M/V—1210.

Tui '06-'07: Bdg £24,550. Day £5300-15,950. Aid: 50 pupils (£250,000).

Summer: Ages 12-18. Acad Enrich Rev Rec. ESL. Sports. Tui Bdg $5600. 7 wks.

Sci labs 5. Comp labs 3. Theaters 1. Art studios 1. Music studios 1. Dance studios 1. Gyms 1. Fields 1. Courts 1.

Est 1976. Nonprofit. Sem (Sept-June). Assoc: CIS NEASC.

Located on a 35-acre campus, TASIS conducts a rigorous college preparatory curriculum that incorporates the International Baccalaureate Diploma Program and Advanced Placement courses in the major disciplines, in addition to an array of electives. TASIS combines academics with extensive facilities for art, drama, music, computers and sports.

During the school's October break, all students participate in a weeklong travel program that allows them to embark on trips to destinations ranging from historically interesting sites throughout Europe (including former Eastern Bloc countries) to more distant locations such as Northern Africa. For the February break, this travel program is optional and incurs an additional fee. Other travel abroad opportunities are also available during the winter and spring breaks.

See Also Pages 552-4

ESTONIA

Sq. Miles: 18,086 (About the size of New Hampshire and Vermont). **Country Pop:** 1,332,893 (2005). **Capital:** Tallinn, pop. 397,150. **Terrain:** Flat, elevation is slightly higher in the east and southeast. Steep limestone banks and 1,520 islands mark the coastline. **Ethnic Group(s):** Estonian Russian Ukrainian Belarusian Finnish. **Religion(s):** Lutheran Estonian_Apostolic_Orthodox Estonian_Orthodox Baptist. **Official Language(s):** Estonian. **Other Language(s):** Russian. **Government:** Parliamentary Democracy. **Independence:** 1991 (from Soviet Union). **GDP:** $19.2 billion (2004). Agriculture 4%. Manufacturing 29%. Services 67%. **Currency:** Estonian Kroon (KR).

INTERNATIONAL SCHOOL OF ESTONIA
Day — Coed Gr PS-12

10132 Tallinn, Estonia. Juhkentali 18. Tel: 372-660-6072. Fax: 372-660-6128. EST+7.
www.ise.edu.ee   E-mail: office@ise.edu.ee
Sharon A. Sperry, Dir. BSEd, MA.

    Col Prep. IB PYP. IB MYP. IB Diploma. Curr—Intl. **Exams**—CEEB TOEFL. **Feat**—Fr Ger Estonian Comp_Sci Studio_Art Music. **Supp**—ESL LD.
    Activities—Arts Rec.
    Enr 109. B 50. G 59. Elem 91. Sec 18. US 30. Host 14. Other 65. Accepted: 100%. Avg class size: 8.
    Fac 24. M 8/1. F 13/2. US 5. Host 10. Other 9. Adv Deg: 29%.
    Grad '05—5. Col—5.
    Tui '05-'06: Day €2746-13,310 (+€560). **Aid:** 9 pupils (€70,140).
    Bldgs 1. Class rms 19. Lib 10,000 vols. Sci labs 1. Comp labs 1. Gyms 1.
    Est 1995. Nonprofit. Quar (Aug-June). Assoc: A/OPR/OS.

ISE provides a comprehensive elementary and secondary program, beginning at age 3, for pupils interested in maintaining continuity with their home country's educational system, as well as those wishing to take part in a curriculum that features English as the language of instruction. Beginning in the primary years, the school follows the International Baccalaureate curriculum. An international faculty instructs pupils drawn primarily from Western European, Scandinavian and North American families who are in the country due to business or diplomatic assignments.

ISE encourages participation in after-school activities as an extension to the academic day.

FINLAND

Sq. Miles: 130,160 (About the size of New England, New Jersey and New York combined). **Country Pop:** 5,200,000. **Capital:** Helsinki, pop. 560,500. **Terrain:** Low but hilly, more than 70% forested, with more than 60,000 lakes. **Ethnic Group(s):** Finn Swede Lapp Sami Roma Tatar. **Religion(s):** Lutheran Orthodox_Christian. **Official Language(s):** Finnish Swedish. **Other Language(s):** Lapp Russian. **Government:** Constitutional Republic. **Independence:** 1917 (from Russia). **Per Capita Income:** $29,000 (2004). **GDP:** $171.6 billion (2004). Agriculture 3%. Industry 30%. Services 67%. **Currency:** European Union Euro (€).

THE ENGLISH SCHOOL
Day — Coed Gr PS-12

00270 Helsinki, Finland. Mantytie 14. Tel: 358-9-477-1123. Fax: 358-9-477-1980. EST+7.
www.eschool.edu.hel.fi   E-mail: english.school@edu.hel.fi

Juhani Kulmala, Prin.
> **Col Prep. Gen Acad. Curr**—Nat. **Bilingual**—Finnish. **Exams**—AP CEEB. **AP**—Eng Fr Ger Calc Physics. **Feat**—Ital Span Swedish Visual_Arts Music. **Supp**—LD Rev Tut.
> **Enr 492.** B 214. G 278. Elem 364. Sec 128.
> **Fac 67.**
> Avg SAT: M/V—1100.
> **Tui '05-'06: Day €508-2508.**
> **Est 1945.** Nonprofit. Nondenom Christian. Sem (Aug-May).

This bilingual school follows a course of study based on the Finnish school plan. Instruction is given in both English and Finnish, and pupils may choose to study French, German or Swedish as well. This international setting is reinforced by a faculty that includes individuals from Finland, Canada, Senegal, the UK and the US.

HELSINGIN SUOMALAINEN YHTEISKOULU
INTERNATIONAL BACCALAUREATE SECTION
Day — Coed Gr 10-12

00320 Helsinki, Finland. Isonnevantie 8. Tel: 358-9-4774180. Fax: 358-9-47741810. EST+7.
www.syk.edu.hel.fi   E-mail: minna.ankkuri@edu.hel.fi
Anja-Liisa Alanko, Head. MA.
> **Col Prep. IB Diploma. Curr**—Intl. **Bilingual**—Finnish. **Feat**—Fr Ger Span Swedish Econ.
> **Activities**—Arts Rec.
> **Enr 75.** B 30. G 45. Sec 75. US 1. Host 69. Other 5. Accepted: 33%. Avg class size: 25.
> **Fac 13.** M 4/1. F 8. US 2. Host 10. Other 1. Adv Deg: 84%.
> **Grad '05**—25. **Col**—25.
> **Tui '05-'06: Day €0** (+€600-1080).
> Bldgs 2. Class rms 51. Lib 15,000 vols. Sci labs 3. Lang labs 1. Comp labs 2. Auds 1. Art studios 1. Music studios 2. Gyms 1. Courts 1. Pools 1.
> **Est 1990.** Nonprofit. Sem (Aug-June).

The IB section at this school offers the two-year IB curriculum, as well as a preparatory year. During this preparatory year, pupils follow the Finnish national curriculum while also receiving intensive English language instruction; students in the IB program have English as their language of instruction. The IB curriculum comprises course work in six areas: English; Finnish and a second foreign language; history and economics; the experimental sciences; math; and electives.

Students pay no tuition charges (except for the English A1 course), although they incur textbook and IB examination fees.

INTERNATIONAL SCHOOL OF HELSINKI
Day — Coed Gr K-12

00180 Helsinki, Finland. Selkamerenkatu 11. Tel: 358-9-686-6160. Fax: 358-9-685-6699. EST+7.

www.ish.edu.hel.fi   E-mail: mainoffice@ish.edu.hel.fi
Bob Woods, Head. Katja Lehtonen, Adm.

   Col Prep. IB PYP. IB MYP. IB Diploma. Curr—Intl. **Exams**—CEEB. **Feat**—Fr Finnish Swedish Comp_Sci Studio_Art Music. **Supp**—ESL LD.
   Enr 331. Elem 208. Sec 123. US 38. Host 124. Other 169. Avg class size: 15.
   Fac 46. M 15/2. F 28/1. US 9. Host 12. Other 25. Adv Deg: 54%.
   Grad '05—25. US Col—3. (Bucknell, Smith, Bryant).
   Tui '05-'06: Day €10,344-13,517 (+€1000).
   Bldgs 2. Lib 1200 vols. Sci labs 3. Comp labs 4. Auds 1. Theaters 1. Art studios 1. Music studios 1. Gyms 1. Fields 1.
   Est 1963. Nonprofit. (Aug-June). Assoc: A/OPR/OS CIS NEASC.

ISH primarily enrolls expatriate children whose stay in Finland is limited. The basic elementary program offers math, music, social studies, and arts and crafts. At all grade levels, coursework follows the International Baccalaureate curriculum, with pupils working toward the IB Diploma. Students learn in small groups or individually, with the school maintaining a low student-teacher ratio.

After-school activities include pottery, ballet, drama, puppetry, gymnastics, swimming and ice skating.

FRANCE

Sq. Miles: 220,668 (About four-fifths the size of Texas). **Country Pop:** 60,656,178 (2005). **Capital:** Paris, pop. 2,125,246 (1999). **Terrain:** Varied. **Ethnic Group(s):** Celtic Latin Teutonic Slavic North African Indochinese Basque. **Religion(s):** Roman_Catholic. **Official Language(s):** French. **Government:** Republic. **GDP:** $2.02 trillion (2004). Agriculture 3%. Industry 21%. Services 76%. **Currency:** European Union Euro (€).

GREENFIELD BILINGUAL SCHOOL
(ECOLE BILINGUE GREENFIELD)

Day — Coed Gr PS-5

69660 Collonges-au-Mont-d'Or, Lyon, France. 14 rue de la Mairie. Tel: 33-4-72-27-87-80. EST+6.
www.greenfield.fr   E-mail: info@greenfield.fr
Marie-Fabienne Clement, Head.

   Gen Acad. Curr—Nat. **Bilingual**—Fr. **Feat**—Lib_Skills Comp_Sci Studio_Art.
   Enr 160. B 80. G 80. Elem 160. US 4. Host 138. Other 18. Avg class size: 20.
   Fac 10. US 1. Host 5. Other 4.
   Grad '05—5.
   Tui '02-'03: Day €2650.
   Bldgs 2. Class rms 9. Libs 1. Comp labs 7. Fields 1.
   Est 1988. Inc. Tri (Sept-June).

Enrolling children as young as age 2, Greenfield conducts bilingual nursery and primary school programs on separate campuses. While following the national curriculum, students spend half of each school day studying in English, and half in French. French and math classes are taught in French, while history, geography, science, civic education and art use English as the language of instruction. Instructors utilize songs, games, dancing and manual work to help students become fluent in both languages. British and American teachers conduct all English classes.

INTERNATIONAL SCHOOL OF TOULOUSE
Day — Coed Gr PS-12

31770 Colomiers, France. 2 allee de l'Herbaudiere, Rte de Pibrac. Tel: 33-5-62-74-26-74. Fax: 33-5-62-74-26-75. EST+6.
www.intst.net   E-mail: ist@intst.net
Leslie G. Albiston, Prin. BA. **Tess Perrussel, Adm.**
    Col Prep. IB Diploma. Curr—Intl UK. **Exams**—IGCSE. **Feat**—Fr Span Comp_Sci Studio_Art Music. **Supp**—EFL ESL Rem_Math Rem_Read.
    Activities—Arts.
    Enr 307. B 153. G 154. Avg class size: 22.
    Fac 50. M 19/4. F 19/8.
    Tui '05-'06: Day €7880-14,040 (+€1100).
    Summer: Rec. 3 wks.
    Libs 1. Sci labs 2. Art studios 1. Music studios 5. Gyms 2. Fields 1.
    Est 1999. Tri (Sept-July).

With its program based upon the UK national curriculum, IST prepares students for the IGCSE and the International Baccalaureate. Instruction places particular emphasis on the creative and sophisticated use of communications technology across the curriculum. Although English is the language of instruction, faculty give a high priority to developing pupils' competence in French to promote academic achievement and increased participation in the global community.

Programming provides continuity for children who have attended international schools in the past, as well as for those whose parents are employed with one of the area's multinational corporations. Beginning in grade 2, IST loans laptop computers to all students for classroom use. Also noteworthy is the school's well-regarded music program, which features the use of software that allows students to create and record music simultaneously.

BRITISH SCHOOL OF PARIS
Day — Coed Gr K-12

78290 Croissy-sur-Seine, France. 38 Quai de l'Ecluse. Tel: 33-1-34-80-45-90. Fax: 33-1-39-76-12-69. EST+6.
www.ecis.org/bsp   E-mail: bspregistrar@wanadoo.fr
Richard J. Woodall, Head. MA. **V. Joynes, Adm.**
    Col Prep. Curr—UK. **Exams**—GCSE AS-level A-level. **Feat**—Fr Ger Span Art_Hist Bus. **Supp**—EFL LD Rem_Math Rem_Read Tut.
    Sports—Basket X-country F_Hockey Rugby Soccer Track. **Activities**—Arts Govt/Pol.

Enr 830. B 420. G 410. Elem 597. Sec 233. US 15. Host 22. Other 793. Accepted: 90%. Yield: 97%. Avg class size: 18.

Fac 90. M 28/1. F 54/7. US 2. Host 4. Other 84. Adv Deg: 32%.

Grad '05—52. Col—52. US Col—2.

Tui '05-'06: Day €13,293-18,040 (+€900). **Aid:** 32 pupils (€38,700).

Bldgs 11. Class rms 58. 2 Libs 15,000 vols. Sci labs 5. Comp labs 2. Art studios 2. Music studlos 2. Dance studios 1. Gyms 1. Fields 3. Courts 16. Pools 1.

Est 1954. Nonprofit. Tri (Sept-June).

Situated on the banks of the Seine, about 10 miles outside of Paris, this school serves boys and girls from more than 50 countries. Emphasizing French in all grades, the program follows a British syllabus and prepares students for the GCSE, AS- and A-level examinations, for which the school is the French center. Two Advanced level passes on these tests afford sophomore standing at most American colleges. French-speaking students are provided with special English classes.

A small number of students reside with school-selected French or English host families.

COLLEGE INTERNATIONAL DE FONTAINEBLEAU
ANGLOPHONE SECTION

Day — Coed Gr 1-12

77300 Fontainebleau, France. 48 rue Guerin. Tel: 33-1-64-22-11-77. Fax: 33-1-64-23-43-17. EST+6.

www.anglosection.com   E-mail: admin@anglosection.com

Glenys Kennedy, Head.

Col Prep. Curr—UK. Bilingual—Fr. Exams—GCSE O-level A-level.

Activities—Arts Govt/Pol Rec.

Enr 400. B 200. G 200. Elem 300. Sec 100. US 100. Host 192. Other 102. Accepted: 90%. Avg class size: 18.

Fac 12. M 4/1. F 5/2. US 2. Other 10.

Tui '05-'06: Day €2000-4000 (+€400).

Est 1979. Nonprofit. Quar (Sept-June).

Consisting of primary, middle and high school divisions, the Anglophone Section conducts a fully bilingual program at all grade levels. Fluency in English is a prerequisite for admission to the section, but boys and girls may enroll until grade 10 with little or no knowledge of French. For the benefit of such students, Fontainebleau conducts special language courses designed to facilitate the rapid acquisition of necessary linguistic skills. Older pupils may prepare for the GCSE, A- and O-level examinations.

A small town in the heart of a large forest south of Paris, Fountainebleau offers many social, cultural and sporting options. The amenities of Paris are easily accessible by train.

ECOLE ACTIVE BILINGUE JEANNINE MANUEL
ECOLE INTERNATIONALE DE LILLE MÉTROPOLE
Bdg and Day — Coed Gr 6-12

59700 Marcq-en-Baroeul, France. 418 bis rue Albert Bailly. Tel: 33-3-20-65-90-50. Fax: 33-3-20-98-06-41. EST+6.
www.eabjmlille.com   E-mail: s.deblandere@eabjm.com
Francis Gianni, Head.

> **Col Prep. IB Diploma. Fr Bac. Curr**—Intl Nat. **Bilingual**—Fr. **Exams**—CEEB TOEFL IGCSE. **Feat**—Chin Ger Ital Span Comp_Sci Econ Studio_Art.
> **Enr 546.** B 53/225. G 45/223. US 3. Host 463. Other 80. Avg class size: 25.
> **Fac 48.** M 12/1. F 23/12.
> **Tui '05-'06: Bdg €11,210** (+€187-196). **Day €2340** (+€187-196).
> Bldgs 2. Dorms 2. Dorm rms 70. Class rms 27. Lib 5000 vols. Comp labs 1. Art studios 1.
> **Est 1992.** Tri (Sept-June).

Affiliated with the Paris-based institutions bearing the Ecole Active Bilingue name, this bilingual school maintains two divisions: one for grades 6-9, the other for grades 10-12. In the younger section, the curriculum includes English-language instruction in history, geography, the experimental sciences, art and physical education within the context of the French national program. The school places students in ability-appropriate English classes, and boys and girls receive French as a foreign language instruction as needed.

In the upper division, pupils prepare for the French and International baccalaureates; those wishing to pursue a college education in the US are readied for the SAT, and IGCSE preparation is also available. Boarders reside in housemaster-supervised dorms.

MOUGINS SCHOOL
Day — Coed Gr PS-12

06251 Mougins, France. 615 Ave Dr Maurice Donat, Font de l'Orme, BP 401. Tel: 33-493-90-15-47. Fax: 33-493-75-31-40. EST+6.
www.mougins-school.com   E-mail: information@mougins-school.com
Brian G. Hickmore, Head.

> **Col Prep. Curr**—UK. **Exams**—IGCSE AS-level A-level. **Feat**—Fr Ger Span Comp_Sci Geog Studio_Art Music Bus.
> **Tui '05-'06: Day €8100-11,250** (+€600).
> **Est 1982.** Nonprofit. Tri (Sept-June).

MARYMOUNT SCHOOL
Day — Coed Gr PS-8

92200 Neuilly sur Seine, France. 72 Blvd de la Saussaye. Tel: 33-1-46-24-10-51. Fax: 33-1-46-24-93-26. EST+6.
www.marymount.fr   E-mail: info@marymount.fr
Sr. Anne Marie Hill, Head. Teresa Geronazzo, Adm.

> **Col Prep. Curr**—US. **Feat**—Chin Lat Span Relig Studio_Art Music. **Supp**—ESL.

Sports—Basket Soccer. **Activities**—Arts Rec.
Enr 400. Elem 400. Avg class size: 18.
Fac 55. M 9/4. F 33/9. US 10. Host 10. Other 35. Adv Deg: 27%.
Tui '05-'06: Day €13,200-17,300 (+€4500).
Est 1923. Nonprofit. Roman Catholic. Tri (Sept-June). Assoc: CIS MAIS MSA.

This Catholic school accepts children of all faiths. An American elementary curriculum serves English-speaking children from many different countries, including the US, France, Ireland, Canada, Australia and Great Britain; others enroll from Africa, the Middle East, South America and Asia. Marymount's learning center addresses the needs of children requiring assistance with class work. The academic program is enriched by a full range of extracurricular activities.

Neuilly sur Seine is near the Bois de Boulogne, immediately to the west of Paris. The school is situated on a 1½-acre campus. Other Marymount schools are located in London, England, and Rome, Italy.

THE INTERNATIONAL SCHOOL OF NICE

Day — Coed Gr K-12

06200 Nice, France. 15 ave Claude Debussy. Tel: 33-4-93-21-04-00. Fax: 33-4-93-21-84-90. EST+6.
www.isn-nice.com   E-mail: edwige.roussel@cote-azur.cci.fr
Dorothy Foster, Dir. BA, MSc.

    Col Prep. IB Diploma. Curr—Intl. **Exams**—AP CEEB TOEFL CEE IGCSE AS-level. **Feat**—Dutch Fr Ger Ital Span Danish Comp_Sci Studio_Art Music. **Supp**—ESL LD.
    Sports—Hand Soccer. **Activities**—Arts Govt/Pol Rec.
    Enr 303. B 161. G 142. Elem 203. Sec 100. US 19. Host 30. Other 254. Accepted: 95%. Avg class size: 20.
    Fac 36. M 10/2. F 20/4. US 6. Host 8. Other 22.
    Grad '05—23. Col—23. US Col—6.
    Tui '05-'06: Day €8307-12,107.
    Class rms 25. Libs 2. Sci labs 2. Lang labs 2. Comp labs 1. Theaters 1. Art studios 2. Music studios 1. Gyms 1. Fields 1. Courts 1.
    Est 1977. Nonprofit. Tri (Sept-June). Assoc: CIS MSA.

Serving the international community of the Cannes-Nice-Monte Carlo region, this school conducts a full English-language curriculum. The course of instruction follows models utilized by major international schools around the world. The lower school (grades K-5) emphasizes language and math skills and features programs in science, social studies, music, arts and crafts, drama and physical education. Children attend mandatory French classes each day. The self-contained middle school (grades 6-8) continues to stress skill development in all academic areas. The school gears its high school curriculum primarily toward the IGCSE and the IB, but students may also prepare for the TOEFL, as well as for certain American exams. Most graduates continue their studies at British universities.

In addition to sports and other extracurriculars, the school organizes excursions to cultural events in southern France. A limited number of students may board with local French families.

ECOLE ACTIVE BILINGUE
ENGLISH-SPEAKING BRANCH

Day — Coed Gr 9-12

75008 Paris, France. 117 Blvd Malesherbes. Tel: 33-1-45-63-01-00. Fax: 33-1-45-63-62-23. EST+6.
www.eab.fr   E-mail: cdelesal@eab.fr
Georges Pannier, Head.

> Col Prep. IB Diploma. Fr Bac. Curr—Intl Nat UK US. Exams—CEEB TOEFL IGCSE O-level A-level. Feat—Fr Ger Ital Japan Span Korean Civics Econ Bus. Supp—EFL.
> Tui '05-'06: Day €8000-12,000 (+€500).
> Est 1954. Sem (Sept-June).

ECOLE ACTIVE BILINGUE JEANNINE MANUEL

Day — Coed Gr PS-12

75015 Paris, France. 70 rue du Theatre. Tel: 33-1-44-37-00-80. Fax: 33-1-45-79-06-66. EST+6.
www.eabjm.com   E-mail: info@eabjm.com
Elizabeth Zeboulon, Head.

> Col Prep. IB Diploma. Fr Bac. Curr—Intl Nat. Bilingual—Fr. Exams—TOEFL. Feat—Ger Hebrew Japan Span Comp_Sci Studio_Art.
> Enr 2900.
> Fac 230.
> Grad '05—244.
> Tui '05-'06: Day €3225-5025.
> Summer: Rec. 2 wks.
> Bldgs 7. 4 Libs 5000 vols. Sci labs 7. Comp labs 1. Auds 1. Gyms 1. Fields 1. Pools 2.
> Est 1954. Tri (Sept-June).

This school offers a bilingual elementary and secondary program that prepares boys and girls for the US College Boards, the French Baccalaureate and the International Baccalaureate. Pupils from more than 60 countries receive instruction in French and English from kindergarten; they may elect another language in grade 6. Non-French speakers enroll in adaptation classes at all levels. Japanese, Italian, Spanish and German constitute the foreign language program.

The school's three locations are within walking distance of the Eiffel Tower. The main building, completed in 1979, houses science labs, an audio-visual center, and other academic and recreational facilities.

INTERNATIONAL SCHOOL OF PARIS

Day — Coed Gr PS-12

75016 Paris, France. 6 rue Beethoven. Tel: 33-1-42-24-09-54. Fax: 33-1-45-27-15-93. EST+6.
www.isparis.edu   E-mail: info@isparis.edu
Gareth Jones, Head. MS.

Col Prep. **IB PYP. IB MYP. IB Diploma. Curr**—Intl. **Exams**—IGCSE. **Feat**—Humanities Fr Ger Japan Span Korean Comp_Sci Studio_Art Music. **Supp**—ESL.
Enr 500. Elem 300. Sec 200.
Fac 88.
Tui '05-'06: Day €13,038-18,444 (+€4500).
Est 1964. Nonprofit. Tri (Sept-June). Assoc: CIS NEASC.

THE LENNEN BILINGUAL SCHOOL
Day — Coed Gr PS-5

75007 Paris, France. 65 Quai d'Orsay. Tel: 33-1-47-05-66-55. Fax: 33-1-47-05-17-18. EST+6.
www.lennenbilingual.com   E-mail: school@lennenbilingual.com
Michelle Lennen, Head. BA, MA.
Gen Acad. Curr—Nat US. **Bilingual**—Fr. **Feat**—Computers Music.
Enr 120.
Tui '03-'04: Day €7600-8800.
Summer: Rec. 8 wks.
Class rms 6. Gyms 1. Fields 1.
Est 1960. Nonprofit. Sem (Sept-June).

Founded to fill Paris's need for bilingual (English and French) education at the preschool level, this school now provides a flexible, individualized program that runs from preschool through primary school. Each classroom features two instructors: one whose native language is English and another whose mother tongue is French. Half of the course work is taught in English, half in French. The school enriches its curriculum with field trips to local museums, farms and zoos.

Lennen has three locations in the city: a preschool on Quai d'Orsay, a second preschool at 145 rue Saint Dominique (33-1-53-59-90-73) and a division serving grades K-5 at 168 rue de Grenelle (33-1-44-42-99-00).

UNITED NATIONS NURSERY SCHOOL
Day — Coed Ages 2-5

75016 Paris, France. 40 rue Pierre Guerin. Tel: 33-1-45-27-20-24. Fax: 33-1-42-88-71-46. EST+6.
www.unns.net   E-mail: unns@noos.fr
Christine Pierson, Dir.
Gen Acad. Curr—Nat US. **Bilingual**—Fr.
Enr 59. B 28. G 31. Elem 59. Avg class size: 15.
Fac 6. F 4/2.
Tui '05-'06: Day €5700.
Summer: Enrich Rec. Tui Day €144-220/wk. 4 wks.
Est 1951. Nonprofit. Tri (Sept-June).

This international, cooperative, bilingual preschool, founded by several UNESCO staff members, is under the aegis of the French Ministry of Health and its office for Protection Maternelle et Infantile. Bilingual (English and French) teachers conduct a program based on active methods of instruction, and bilingualism is encouraged.

Children gain an appreciation of different cultures through introductions to foreign languages, customs and foods. Crafts, music, movement and outings are among the activities offered. Although the school is located in an urban setting, pupils have access to a garden with animals and play equipment.

SCHOOL YEAR ABROAD

Bdg — Coed Gr 11-12

35700 Rennes, France. 5 allee Sainte Marie. Tel: 33-299-382-333. Fax: 33-299-636-894. EST+6.

Contact: 439 S Union St, Lawrence, MA 01843. Tel: 978-725-6828. Fax: 978-725-6833.

www.sya.org   E-mail: mail@sya.org

Woodruff W. Halsey II, Exec Dir. AB, MA. Whitney Hermann, Adm.

  Col Prep. Curr—US. Bilingual—Fr. Exams—CEEB. AP—Fr Calc. Feat—Fr_Hist Art_Hist.

  Activities—Arts.

  Enr 60. Accepted: 66%. Yield: 85%. Avg class size: 15.

  Fac 14. M 4/4. F 4/2. US 3. Host 11. Adv Deg: 85%.

  Avg SAT: M/V—1315, Essay—668.

  Tui '05-'06: Bdg $36,000 (+$2000). Aid: 25 pupils ($639,942).

  Est 1967. Nonprofit. Quar (Sept-June).

School Year Abroad was established by Phillips Academy and is now a consortium of 26 independent schools. SYA France provides a fully accredited year of study for high school students in Rennes. The program is open to qualified juniors and seniors who have completed at least two years of French language study. With the exception of English and math courses, the medium of instruction is French.

Students live with native families and travel during vacation periods. American instructors teach math and English courses in English from American texts. Program participants learn about the culture and customs of the native country. Students prepare for the US College Boards and for certain Advanced Placement exams.

Similar programs operate in China, Italy and Spain (see separate listings).

AMERICAN SCHOOL OF PARIS

Day — Coed Gr PS-12

92216 Saint Cloud, France. 41 rue Pasteur, BP 82. Tel: 33-1-41-12-82-82. Fax: 33-1-46-02-23-90. EST+6.

www.asparis.org   E-mail: admissions@asparis.fr

Pilar Cabeza de Vaca, Head. John Guse, Adm.

  Col Prep. IB Diploma. Curr—Intl US. Exams—AP CEEB. AP—Eng Fr Span Calc Comp_Sci Bio Chem Physics US_Hist Econ. Feat—Web_Design Psych Filmmaking Photog Sculpt Studio_Art Theater_Arts Band Chorus. Supp—ESL LD.

  Sports—Basket Baseball Cheer X-country Golf Soccer Softball Swim Tennis Track Volley. Activities—Acad Arts Govt/Pol Media Service.

  Enr 751. Elem 412. Sec 336. PG 3. US 338. Host 48. Other 365. Avg class

size: 18.
Fac 103.
Grad '05—87. US Col—21. (Boston U 5, Geo Wash 4, NYU 4, Johns Hopkins 3, Stanford 3, Duke 2).
Tui '05-'06: Day €12,940-19,320 (+€7030).
Summer: Acad Rec. Tui Day €296-1268. 1-4 wks.
Sci labs 5. Music studios 1.
Est 1946. Nonprofit. (Aug-June). Assoc: A/OPR/OS CIS MAIS MSA.

Located on a 12-acre campus adjacent to the Parc de Saint Cloud, ASP provides an American-style curriculum for students from some 50 countries. The school teaches English and French as both first and second languages, and ESL instruction is available in grades 1-7.

The lower school (grades pre-K-5) includes an integrated language arts program and specialist teachers in several disciplines; in addition, a teacher serves pupils with special needs. Middle schoolers (grades 6-8) follow an interdisciplinary program that features team teaching in the core subjects. A selection of cocurricular courses enriches the curriculum. Students in the upper school participate in the International Baccalaureate and AP programs before ultimately earning the American high school diploma. Graduates go on to universities throughout the world, especially institutions in the US, Canada, the UK and France.

ASP emphasizes students' acquisition of French language skills while making extensive use of Paris and its environs as curricular resources. Pupils embark on field trips at all grade levels, and on extended study trips in grades 2-8. A varied program of fine and performing arts offerings, sports and other extracurricular activities supplements coursework.

LYCEE INTERNATIONAL
AMERICAN SECTION
Day — Coed Gr PS-12

78175 Saint-Germain-en-Laye, France. rue du Fer a Cheval, BP 5230. Tel: 33-1-34-51-74-85. Fax: 33-1-30-87-00-49. EST+6.
www.lycee-intl-american.org   E-mail: admissions.american@wanadoo.fr
Ted Faunce, Dir. BA, PhD. **Mary Friel, Adm.**
   Col Prep. Fr Bac. Curr—US. **Bilingual**—Fr. **Exams**—AP CEEB SSAT. **AP**—Eng. **Feat**—Ger Ital Lat Span Pol_Sci. **Supp**—Tut.
   Sports—Soccer. **Activities**—Arts Govt/Pol Media Service.
   Enr 680. B 340. G 340. Elem 440. Sec 240. US 300. Host 300. Other 80. Accepted: 33%. Yield: 80%. Avg class size: 18.
   Fac 20. M 5. F 11/4. US 19. Other 1. Adv Deg: 70%.
   Grad '05—56. Col—56. US Col—14. (Harvard 2, NYU 2, Brown 1, Northwestern 1, Tufts 1, Vassar 1). Avg SAT: M/V—1273, Essay—672.
   Tui '05-'06: Day €5000. Aid: 15 pupils ($22,000).
   Bldgs 7. Gyms 1.
   Est 1954. Nonprofit. Tri (Sept-June).

Located in a western suburb of Paris, the Lycee International features a strong academic curriculum that centers on the French national program, but accommodates additional course work for 11 national sections. Although it is a French public school, its faculty and student body comprise many nationalities, and are divided into sections according to country. Within each section, the school offers preparation for the different national university entrance exams, including the US College Boards and the international option of the French Baccalaureate.

In the American section, pupils study English and social studies in English, science, math and all other subjects in French. Students whose language ability does not allow them to follow the French curriculum enter adaptation classes.

The Lycee International has a strong theatrical arts department and offers an array of other extracurricular activities. The school encourages students to take advantage of the many cultural opportunities in nearby Paris, and boys and girls have frequent excursion opportunities.

SECTIONS INTERNATIONALES DE SEVRES
COLLEGE D'ETAT DE SEVRES
Day — Coed Gr K-12

92310 Sevres, France. 7 Rue Lecocq. Tel: 33-1-72-77-70-40. Fax: 33-1-45-34-06-15. EST+6.
www.sis-sevres.net   E-mail: sis@sis-sevres.net
Anne Potonnier, Dir.

Col Prep. IB Diploma. Fr Bac. Curr—Intl Nat. Bilingual—Fr. Exams—CEEB IGCSE. Feat—Greek Ital Japan Lat. Supp—Tut.
Activities—Arts Govt/Pol Media.
Enr 1063. Elem 420. Sec 643. Avg class size: 18.
Fac 50.
Tui '05-'06: Day €630-2200.
Est 1960. Nonprofit. Tri (Sept-June).

The International Sections supplement the school's traditional French program with instruction in either English or German. The English program syllabuses at the college (ages 11-15) and lycee (ages 16-18) levels stress reading skills and integrate the latest educational initiatives from Britain and the US. Native English-speaking instructors teach language, literature, international history and geography, while course work in all other subjects follows the normal French program, carried out by teachers from the French state educational system.

Notable aspects of the curriculum include three distinct levels of English instruction, intensive French instruction for pupils lacking fluency in the language, and mixed-language-ability history and geography classes. Most graduates of the English program proceed to American or British universities.

INTERNATIONAL SCHOOL OF SOPHIA ANTIPOLIS
(CENTRE INTERNATIONAL DE VALBONNE)
Bdg — Coed Gr 6-12; Day — Coed 1-12

06902 Sophia Antipolis, France. BP 097, 190 rue Frederic Mistral. Tel: 33-4-92-38-17-20. Fax: 33-4-92-38-17-21. EST+6.
www.issa.net   E-mail: secretary@issa.net
Andrew Derry, Head.

Col Prep. IB Diploma. Fr Bac. Curr—Intl Nat. **Bilingual**—Fr. **Feat**—Environ_Sci Comp_Sci Econ Studio_Art Drama Music.
Enr 840.
Fac 36.
Tui '05-'06: Bdg €22,000. Day €11,500 (+€229-762).
Est 1979. Nonprofit. Tri (Sept-June).

STRASBOURG INTERNATIONAL SCHOOL
Day — Coed Gr PS-10

67100 Strasbourg, France. 1 rue de Metzeral. Tel: 33-3-88-31-50-77. Fax: 33-3-88-84-98-71. EST+6.
www.strasbourgis.org   E-mail: admin@strasbourgis.org
Geoff Tomlinson, Dir.
  Gen Acad. Curr—UK US. **Feat**—Fr Studio_Art Music.
  Enr 35. US 13. Host 2. Other 20. Accepted: 100%. Avg class size: 8.
  Fac 7. M 1. F 5/1. Host 1. Other 6. Adv Deg: 14%.
  Grad '05—5.
  Tui '05-'06: Day €10,000 (+€1000). **Aid:** 2 pupils (€5000).
  Bldgs 1. Libs 1. Gyms 1. Fields 1.
  Est 1995. Nonprofit. Tri (Sept-July).

SIS provides a strictly English-medium curriculum that draws predominantly on the American and British educational systems. Individualization and small-group instruction are integral elements of the program. The school divides its pupils into six classes.

GEORGIA

Sq. Miles: 27,027 (Slightly larger than South Carolina). **Country Pop:** 4,677,401 (2005). **Capital:** Tbilisi, pop. 1,100,000 (2002). **Terrain:** Mostly rugged and mountainous. **Ethnic Group(s):** Georgian Azeri Armenian Russian. **Religion(s):** Georgian_Orthodox Muslim Russian_Orthodox Armenian_Apostolic. **Official Language(s):** Georgian. **Other Language(s):** Abkhaz. **Government:** Republic. **Independence:** 1991 (from Soviet Union). **Per Capita Income:** $744 (1997). **GDP:** $3.6 billion (1997). Agriculture 20%. Industry 23%. Services 57%. **Currency:** Georgian Lari (GEL).

QSI INTERNATIONAL SCHOOL OF TBILISI
Coed — Day Ages 3-13

Tbilisi, Georgia. 10 Topuria St, Saburtalo District. Tel: 995-32-982909. Fax: 995-32-322607. EST+9.
www.qsi.org/grg_home   E-mail: tbilisi@qsi.org
Robert Hinman, Dir.

Gen Acad. Curr—US. **Feat**—Fr Russ Georgian Comp_Sci Econ Studio_Art Music.
Enr 72.
Tui '05-'06: Day $5000-13,000.
Nonprofit. Spons: Quality Schools International. 5 terms. Assoc: A/OPR/OS MSA.

GERMANY

Sq. Miles: 137,821 (About the size of Montana). **Country Pop:** 82,431,390 (2005). **Capital:** Berlin, pop. 3,400,000. **Terrain:** Low plain in the north; high plains, hills, and basins in the center and east; mountainous alpine region in the south. **Ethnic Group(s):** German Danish Slavic. **Religion(s):** Protestant Roman_Catholic Muslim. **Official Language(s):** German. **Government:** Federal Republic. **Per Capita Income:** $22,900 (2001). **GDP:** $1.8 trillion (2001). Agriculture 1%. Industry 29%. Services 70%. **Currency:** European Union Euro (€).

BERLIN INTERNATIONAL SCHOOL
Day — Coed Gr PS-13

14195 Berlin, Germany. Lentzealle 8-14. Tel: 49-30-820077-90. Fax: 49-30-820077-99. EST+7.
www.berlin-international-school.de
E-mail: office@berlin-international-school.de
Peggy Bleyberg-Shor, Dir. MA.
    Col Prep. IB PYP. IB Diploma. Curr—Intl Nat. **Supp Lang**—Ger. **Exams**—TOEFL IGCSE. **Feat**—Fr Span Comp_Sci Econ Pol_Sci Studio_Art Music. **Supp**—EFL ESL Tut.
    Sports—Basket X-country Soccer. **Activities**—Arts Govt/Pol Media.
    Enr 788. US 41. Host 350. Other 397. Accepted: 60%. Yield: 92%. Avg class size: 22.
    Fac 92. M 39/1. F 48/4. US 18. Host 20. Other 54. Adv Deg: 26%.
    Grad '05—25. Col—22. US Col—5. (U of FL 3, Georgetown 1, Luther 1).
    Tui '05-'06: Day €7500-9000 (+€1000). **Aid:** 157 pupils.
    Bldgs 3. Class rms 71. 2 Libs 6000 vols. Sci labs 3. Comp labs 2. Art studios 4. Music studios 3. Dance studios 1. Gyms 1. Fields 1.
    Est 1998. Nonprofit. Sem (Aug-June).

Serving both local families and English-speaking ones from more than 60 nations, BIS offers English-medium instruction for international families (with German taught as a foreign language).

Children in the primary program follow the comprehensive, inquiry-based IB Primary Years Program. During the middle school years (grades 6-10), the curriculum includes compulsory course work in English, German, math, the natural sciences, history, geography, art, music and athletics. Computer science begins in grade 2, and a third language becomes available in grade 6. In the senior school (grades 11-13), international pupils usually follow the English-language IB Diploma Program, while German-speaking boys and girls prepare for the German Abitur.

INDEPENDENT BONN INTERNATIONAL SCHOOL
Day — Coed Ages 3-11

53117 Bonn, Germany. Tulpenbaumweg 42. Tel: 49-228-32-31-66. Fax: 49-228-32-39-58. EST+6.
www.ibis-school.com   E-mail: ibis@ibis-school.com
Irene Bolik, Head.
>   **Gen Acad. Curr**—Intl UK. **Feat**—Ger Computers Geog Studio_Art Music. **Supp**—ESL.
>   **Enr 190.**
>   **Fac 32.**
>   **Tul '05-'06: Day €6180-9600** (+€500-1500).
>   **Est 1963.** Nonprofit. Tri (Aug-July).

INTERNATIONAL SCHOOL OF BREMEN
Day — Coed Gr PS-12

28213 Bremen, Germany. Thomas-Mann-Strasse 8. Tel: 49-421-337-9272. Fax: 49-421-337-9273. EST+6.
www.isbremen.de   E-mail: office@isbremen.de
Malcolm Davis, Dir.
>   **Col Prep. Gen Acad. IB Diploma. Curr**—Intl UK US. **Exams**—AP IGCSE AS-level A-level. **Curr**—Ger Span Comp_Sci Econ Studio_Art Music. **Supp**—ESL.
>   **Sports**—F_Hockey. **Activities**—Rec.
>   **Enr 120.** B 70. G 50. Elem 100. Sec 20. US 5. Host 40. Other 75. Accepted: 98%. Avg class size: 14.
>   **Fac 26.** M 4/7. F 12/3. Adv Deg: 26%.
>   **Tul '05-'06: Day €7000-9900. Aid:** 6 pupils (€2000).
>   Plant val €5,000,000. Bldgs 2. Libs 1. Sci labs 1. Comp labs 1. Auds 1. Music studios 1. Gyms 1. Courts 1.
>   **Est 1998.** Inc. Quar (Aug-June). Assoc: MSA.

Located in the Schwachhausen area of Bremen near the center of the city, ISB offers an international program to students of more than a dozen nationalities. Originally an elementary school, the school gradually added the secondary grades, culminating in fall 2006 with the opening of grade 12.

The program incorporates curricular elements from the US and the UK: Boys and girls may prepare for the AP, the AS-level and the A-level examinations. Secondary students may ready themselves for the IGCSE and may then pursue the IB Diploma. English is the language of instruction, and German is available on both native and second-language levels.

ST. GEORGE'S SCHOOL
Day — Coed Gr PS-12

50937 Cologne, Germany. Anton-Antweiler-Strasse 4. Tel: 49-221-297899-0. Fax: 49-221-297899-14. EST+6.
www.stgeorgesschool.de   E-mail: info@stgeorgesschoolcologne.de
Marietta Horton, Prin. F. J. Nyman, Dir. BEd. N. Mayer, Adm.

> **Col Prep. Gen Acad. Curr**—UK. **Exams**—GCSE A-level. **Feat**—Fr Ger Comp_Sci Studio_Art Drama Music Bus. **Supp**—Dev_Read EFL ESL Rem_Math Rem_Read Tut.
> **Activities**—Arts Media Rec.
> **Enr 550.** B 290. G 260.
> **Fac 56.** M 32. F 24.
> **Tui '06-'07: Day $7650-9150** (+$700).
> Bldgs 3. Libs 3. Sci labs 1. Auds 1. Art studios 1. Music studios 1. Gyms 1. Courts 2.
> **Est 1985.** Nonprofit. Tri (Sept-July).

Instruction at St. George's is in English, with students following the English national curriculum in preparation for the GCSE and A and AS-level examinations. German language classes begin in preschool, while advanced-level courses commence during the high school years. From middle school on, the curriculum integrates information technology into all subjects. The school places importance on subjects that are unrelated to standardized exams, and a range of post-GCSE courses are available.

DRESDEN INTERNATIONAL SCHOOL
Day — Coed Gr PS-12

01309 Dresden, Germany. Goetheallee 18. Tel: 49-351-340-0428. Fax: 49-351-340-0430. EST+6.
www.dresden-is.de   E-mail: dis@dresden-is.de
Geoff Clark, Dir.

> **Col Prep. Gen Acad. IB PYP. IB MYP. IB Diploma. Curr**—Intl. **Feat**—Fr Ger Japan Econ Studio_Art Theater_Arts Music. **Supp**—ESL LD.
> **Activities**—Acad Arts Media Rec.
> **Enr 492.** B 261. G 231. US 57. Host 257. Other 178. Avg class size: 15.
> **Fac 62.** US 14. Host 18. Other 30.
> **Grad '05—16.**
> **Tui '05-'06: Day €5400-9500.**
> Bldgs 4. Libs 2. Sci labs 1. Comp labs 2. Art studios 1. Music studios 2.
> **Est 1996.** Nonprofit. Tri (Aug-June).

DIS, located near the Elbe River and the center of Dresden, offers an international curriculum to the growing area expatriate community. The main language of instruction is English. Taught by a largely bilingual staff, course work in grades PS-5 follows the International Baccalaureate Primary Years Program, which revolves around six organizing themes. Children then progress to the IB Middle Years Program, where instructors place particular emphasis on language skills. DIS' curriculum culminates in the two-year IB Diploma Program.

After-school activities and care programs, as well as study trips, complement academics. A summer language camp is also available.

INTERNATIONAL SCHOOL OF DUSSELDORF
Day — Coed Gr PS-13

40489 Dusseldorf, Germany. Niederrheinstrasse 336. Tel: 49-211-94066. Fax: 49-211-4080774. EST+6.
www.isdedu.info   E-mail: info@isdedu.de
Neil A. McWilliam, Dir.
   Col Prep. IB PYP. IB MYP. IB Diploma. Curr—Intl. **Exams**—CEEB TOEFL. **Feat**—Fr Ger Japan Span Comp_Sci Econ Psych Visual_Arts Music Bus. **Supp**—ESL.
   Enr 920.
   Fac 110.
   Tui '05-'06: Day €6570-14,700 (+€3990).
   Est 1968. Nonprofit. Sem (Aug-June). Assoc: A/OPR/OS CIS NEASC.

INTERNATIONALE SCHULE FRANKFURT-RHEIN-MAIN
Day — Coed Gr PS-13

65931 Frankfurt, Germany. Verwaltungs-GmbH, Strasse zur Internationalen Schule 33. Tel: 49-69-954-3190. Fax: 49-69-954-31920. EST+6.
www.isf-net.de   E-mail: info@isf-net.de
Angus Slesser, Dir.
   Col Prep. Curr—UK US. **Exams**—IGCSE AS-level A-level. **Feat**—Fr Ger Comp_Sci Econ Geog Studio_Art Music.
   Enr 900.
   Fac 81.
   Tui '05-'06: Day €11,460-14,520.
   Est 1995. Tri (Sept-June).

BAVARIAN INTERNATIONAL SCHOOL
Day — Coed Gr PS-12

85778 Haimhausen, Germany. Schloss Haimhausen, Hauptstrasse 1. Tel: 49-8133-917-121. Fax: 49-8133-917-135. EST+6.
www.bis-school.com   E-mail: admissions@bis-school.com
Matthew Mills, Dir. MEd. **Erika Swedberg, Adm.**
   Col Prep. Gen Acad. IB PYP. IB Diploma. Curr—Intl. **Exams**—IGCSE. **Feat**—Fr Ger Japan Span Comp_Sci Geog Visual_Arts Music Bus. **Supp**—ESL LD.
   Activities—Acad Govt/Pol Media Rec.
   Enr 654. B 346. G 308. Elem 486. Sec 168. US 160. Host 180. Other 314. Accepted: 90%. Yield: 90%. Avg class size: 19.
   Fac 63. M 16. F 44/3. US 12. Host 7. Other 44. Adv Deg: 31%.
   Grad '05—22. Col—20. US Col—2. (UCLA, Northwestern). Avg SAT: M/V—1270.
   Tui '06-'07: Day €9600-12,450 (+€8000).

Bldgs 1. Class rms 33. Libs 1. Sci labs 3. Comp labs 1. Auds 1. Theaters 1. Art studios 1. Music studios 3. Dance studios 1. Gyms 1.
Est 1991. Nonprofit. Tri (Aug-June). Assoc: CIS NEASC.

Serving the international community of Greater Munich and the surrounding areas, BIS conducts a primary and secondary day program that meets the needs of English-speaking pupils from around the world. Daily German classes are part of the curriculum, thus promoting increased fluency in the national language.

The International Baccalaureate Primary Years Program, enrolling children from age 4 through grade 5, emphasizes inquiry-based learning and the development of sound academic skills. Specialist teachers conduct English, German, music and physical education classes. A well-developed instrumental music program, art, environmental studies, study trips and extracurricular activities enrich the core curriculum in grades 6-8. The program in grades 9-12 begins with preparation for the IGCSE examination and culminates in the two-year International Baccalaureate Diploma program.

INTERNATIONAL SCHOOL HAMBURG

Day — Coed Gr PS-12

22605 Hamburg, Germany. Holmbrook 20. Tel: 49-40-883-0010. Fax: 49-40-881-1405. EST+6.
www.international-school-hamburg.de
E-mail: info@international-school-hamburg.de
Peter Gittins, Head. Catherine Bissonnet, Adm.

> **Col Prep. IB Diploma. Curr**—Intl. **Exams**—ACT TOEFL. **Feat**—Fr Ger Comp_Sci Geog Visual_Arts Drama Music. **Supp**—Dev_Read EFL ESL Rem_Math Rem_Read Tut.
> **Enr 640.** Elem 493. Sec 147. US 80. Host 220. Other 340. Accepted: 80%. Avg class size: 20.
> **Fac 92.**
> **Grad '05—40. Col—32. US Col—6.** (Cornell, Duke, Middlebury, USC, Emory, Wm & Mary).
> **Tui '05-'06: Day €7980-15,300** (+€5250).
> Bldgs 3. Lib 20,000 vols. Gyms 1.
> **Est 1957.** Nonprofit. Sem (Sept-June). Assoc: A/OPR/OS CIS NEASC.

Drawing its enrollment from more than 40 different countries, ISH conducts an international curriculum. Many students enroll from either Germany, the US, the UK or Japan. Foreign language instruction begins in grade 1 with German and continues with French in grade 7. Elective courses include computer, photography, drama and Model UN. The school prepares boys and girls for the US College Boards and the International Baccalaureate.

INTERNATIONAL SCHOOL HANNOVER REGION

Day — Coed Gr PS-12

30169 Hannover, Germany. Bruchmeisterallee 6. Tel: 49-511-270-41650. Fax: 49-511-270-41651. EST+6.

www.is-hr.de   E-mail: intschh@aol.com
Patricia Baier, Dir.
> **Col Prep. IB PYP. IB MYP. IB Diploma. Curr**—Intl. **Exams**—CEEB. **Feat**—Fr Ger
> Comp_Sci Econ Studio_Art Music. **Supp**—ESL LD.
>
> **Enr 300.** B 160. G 140. Elem 240. Sec 60. US 20. Host 100. Other 180. Avg class
> size: 18.
>
> **Fac 57.**
>
> **Grad '05—10.**
>
> **Tui '05-'06: Day €7190-10,380** (+€2500). **Aid:** 16 pupils (€40,000).
>
> Bldgs 1. Class rms 25. Sci labs 2. Comp labs 1. Auds 1. Art studios 1. Music studios
> 1. Gyms 1.
>
> **Est 1996.** Nonprofit. Tri (Aug-June).

This English-medium school first accepts children into its international pre-school at age 3. The development that occurs during the preschool years prepares youngsters for the primary section (grades K-5), in which pupils follow the IB Primary Years Program. In grades 6-10, boys and girls progress through the IB Middle Years Program. Grades 11 and 12 are devoted to pursuit of the IB Diploma.

Course work in music, art, information technology, personal and social education, and physical education complements core classes. Students study German as either a second language or a first language, depending upon proficiency.

HEIDELBERG INTERNATIONAL SCHOOL

Day — Coed Gr PS-9

69123 Heidelberg, Germany. Wieblinger Weg 9. Tel: 49-6221-75-90-60-0. Fax: 49-6221-75-90-60-99. EST+6.
www.hischool.de   E-mail: info@hischool.de
Kathleen Macdonald, Dir. Lori Novak, Adm.
> **Gen Acad. Curr**—Intl. **Feat**—Lib_Skills Ger Span Comp_Sci Studio_Art Music.
> **Activities**—Service.
>
> **Enr 110.** B 60. G 50. US 43. Host 31. Other 36. Avg class size: 14.
>
> **Fac 16.** M 2. F 11/3. US 4. Host 2. Other 10.
>
> **Tui '05-'06: Day €8800-11,800** (+€5500).
>
> **Est 2000.** Sem (Aug-June).

Employing English as the language of instruction and offering German at all levels, HIS conducts an international-style curriculum. Course work emphasizes learning and organizational skills, as well as collaborative learning. Subject areas include language arts, math, science and technology, humanities, social studies, physical education, computers, music, library skills and the creative arts.

FRANCONIAN INTERNATIONAL SCHOOL

Day — Coed Gr K-9

91074 Herzogenaurach, Germany. Christoph-Dassler Strasse 1. Tel: 49-9132-797910. Fax: 49-9132-797912. EST+6.
http://fis.ecis.org   E-mail: info@the-fis.de
Fred Runkel, Dir.
> **Gen Acad. Curr**—Intl. **Feat**—Ger Span Comp_Sci Geog Studio_Art Music.

Supp—ESL.
Enr 216.
Fac 29.
Tui '05-'06: Day €9080-11,120 (+€55-2310).
Est 1998. Nonprofit. Quar (Aug-June). Assoc: CIS NEASC.

BLACK FOREST ACADEMY

Bdg — Coed Gr 7-12; Day — Coed 1-12

79396 Kandern, Germany. Postfach 1109. Tel: 49-7626-91610. Fax: 49-7626-8821.
EST+6.
www.bfacademy.com   E-mail: admissions@bfacademy.com
Timothy P. Shuman, Dir. BRE, BS, MEd.

Col Prep. **Curr**—US. **Exams**—ACT AP CEEB TOEFL. **AP**—Eng Fr Ger Calc Bio
Chem Eur_Hist US_Hist Music_Theory. **Feat**—Creative_Writing Span Stats
Environ_Sci Programming Econ Geog Korean_Stud Bible Fine_Arts Graphic_
Arts Music Journ Indus_Arts. **Supp**—ESL LD.

Sports—Basket X-country Soccer Track Volley. **Activities**—Arts Govt/Pol Media.

Enr 359. B 95/90. G 89/85. Elem 123. Sec 236. US 251. Host 11. Other 97. Avg
class size: 14.

Fac 65. M 20/9. F 24/12. US 58. Other 7. Adv Deg: 47%.

Grad '05—74. Avg SAT: M/V—1107.

Tui '05-'06: Bdg €11,020-27,142 (+€2500). **Day** €11,020-13,923 (+€2700).

Bldgs 3. Dorms 8. Class rms 27. 2 Libs 12,000 vols. Sci labs 3. Comp labs 2. Auds
2. Art studios 2. Music studios 4. Gyms 2. Courts 2.

Est 1956. Nonprofit. Nondenom Christian. Quar (Aug-June). Assoc: CIS MSA.

BFA provides a Christian elementary and secondary education primarily for children of missionaries in Europe and North Africa. Approximately 10 percent of the students are children of North American expatriates employed at area businesses. The student population is representative of roughly 50 countries.

BFA is staffed by mission societies, and Biblical principles are integrated into the college preparatory curriculum. Preparation for the Advanced Placement exams is available. Approximately three-quarters of the school's graduates matriculate at North American colleges each year.

BERLIN BRANDENBURG INTERNATIONAL SCHOOL

Day — Coed Gr PS-12

14532 Kleinmachnow, Germany. Am Hochwald 30, Haus 2. Tel: 49-33203-80-36-0.
Fax: 49-33203-80-36-21. EST+6.
www.bbis.de   E-mail: office@bbis.de
Thomas Schaedler, Dir. BA, MBA.

Col Prep. IB PYP. IB MYP. IB Diploma. **Curr**—Intl. **Exams**—IGCSE. **Feat**—Fr Ger
Comp_Sci Econ Studio_Art Theater_Arts Music. **Supp**—ESL.

Sports—Badminton Basket X-country Soccer Track. **Activities**—Acad Arts Govt/
Pol Media.

Enr 425. B 220. G 205. Elem 294. Sec 131. US 54. Host 156. Other 215. Accepted:
95%. Avg class size: 18.

Fac 55. M 17. F 30/8. US 18. Host 11. Other 26. Adv Deg: 63%.
Grad '05—30. Avg SAT: M/V—1160.
Tui '05-'06: Day €7600-12,100. Aid: 40 pupils (€320,000).
Bldgs 2. Class rms 35. Lib 10,000 vols. Sci labs 3. Comp labs 1. Theaters 1. Art studios 1. Music studios 2.
Est 1991. Nonprofit. Sem (Sept-June). Assoc: A/OPR/OS CIS MSA.

Founded as Berlin-Potsdam International School, BBIS assumed its current name in spring 2002. The program, which serves students from approximately 25 nations, employs English as the classroom language and has an international character.

From the early years, children work within the International Baccalaureate curriculum: the Primary Years Program in preschool through grade 6, the Middle Years Program in grades 7-10 and the Diploma Program in grades 11 and 12. Pupils with limited English skills receive necessary support, while all boys and girls study the country's home language. In addition to the core subjects, instructors at the primary level teach foreign language, computer, art, music and physical education. Full departmentalization is in effect by grade 7, the start of secondary school. Grades 7 and 8 serve as transitional years between elementary and secondary education, while grades 9 and 10 involve preparation for the IGCSE. Students conclude their secondary years in pursuit of the IB Diploma, in which they take six academic courses and devote at least 150 hours to community service.

Particularly noteworthy among BBIS' activities is a strong sailing program. After learning about sailing theory and rope work in the winter, interested boys and girls may take sailing classes in the summer.

LEIPZIG INTERNATIONAL SCHOOL
Day — Coed Gr PS-12

04229 Leipzig, Germany. Konneritzstrasse 47. Tel: 49-341-421-0674. Fax: 49-341-421-2154. EST+6.
www.intschool-leipzig.com E-mail: admin@intschool-leipzig.com
Michael J. Webster, Head. BSc.
Col Prep. Gen Acad. IB Diploma. Curr—Intl. **Exams**—IGCSE. **Feat**—Fr Ger Comp_Sci Studio_Art Music. **Supp**—ESL.
Enr 353. Accepted: 80%. Avg class size: 15.
Fac 28. Adv Deg: 21%.
Grad '05—5.
Tui '05-'06: Day $5000-8000. Aid: 50 pupils ($200,000).
Summer: Bdg & Day. Acad Rec. Tui Bdg $600. Tui Day $300. 2 wks.
Libs 1. Sci labs 2. Comp labs 1. Theater/auds 1. Art studios 1. Music studios 1. Gyms 2. Fields 1.
Est 1992. Nonprofit. Sem (Aug-June). Assoc: A/OPR/OS.

This elementary and secondary school enrolls pupils from approximately two dozen nations. As English is the medium of instruction, LIS offers an intensive ESL program for those lacking fluency in the language. German is also available as both a second language and a first language. During the high school years, students work toward the IGCSE examinations, then prepare for the International Baccalaureate Diploma.

Popular activities at LIS include chess club, Web club, publications, modern dance, music, community service and sports.

FRANKFURT INTERNATIONAL SCHOOL
Day — Coed Gr PS-12

61440 Oberursel, Germany. An der Waldlust 15. Tel: 49-6171-2020. Fax: 49-6171-202384. EST+6.
www.fis.edu   E-mail: petra_rischke@fis.edu
Mark E. Ulfers, Head. Jutta Alice Kuehne, Adm.
    Col Prep. IB Diploma. Curr—Intl. **Exams**—CEEB IGCSE. **Feat**—Fr Span Comp_ Sci Studio_Art Drama Music. **Supp**—ESL.
    Sports—Basket Baseball X-country Soccer Softball Tennis Track Volley.
    Enr 1750. Elem 1322. Sec 428. US 504. Host 405. Other 841. Accepted: 95%. Yield: 99%. Avg class size: 20.
    Fac 293.
    Tui '05-'06: Day €13,290-16,120 (+€2080).
    Plant val €27,000,000. Bldgs 3. Class rms 150. Libs 4. Sci labs 10. Lang labs 1. Comp labs 5. Auds 3. Gyms 4. Fields 2.
    Est 1961. Nonprofit. Tri (Aug-June). Assoc: A/OPR/OS CIS NEASC.

Frankfurt International School was founded to provide a college preparatory education for children of the international community residing in the metropolitan area of Frankfurt/Main. The curriculum follows international school models, and the primary language of instruction is English. German is obligatory for most students from grade 1, and children in grades 4-6 take part in a bilingual program. The school enrolls many Americans, as well as high numbers of British and German students.

Elementary school programs are presented with an emphasis on small-group instruction. The middle school continues to build on the foundation laid in the elementary school. The school prepares students for the International Baccalaureate program.

Active intramural and interscholastic sports are offered at all grade levels. Throughout the school year, educational field trips supplement classroom work. The campus, located about 10 miles from central Frankfurt, is surrounded by a natural forest near the Taunus Mountains. The school is easily accessible by public transportation.

ERASMUS INTERNATIONAL SCHOOL
Bdg — Coed Gr 11-12; Day — Coed PS-12

14480 Potsdam, Germany. Flotowstrasse 10. Tel: 49-331-748-1690. Fax: 49-331-740-4361. EST+6.
www.eis-b.de   E-mail: info@eis-b.de
Stephen Wilkerson, Dir.
    Col Prep. Gen Acad. Curr—Intl Nat US. **Exams**—IGCSE. **Feat**—Fr Greek Russ

Polish Film Studio_Art Music Bus. **Supp**—EFL ESL Rem_Math Rem_Read Tut.

Enr 80. Accepted: 95%. Avg class size: 12.

Fac 22. Adv Deg: 36%.

Grad '05—53.

Tui '02-'03: Bdg €17,500-19,500. Day €9500-11,500. Aid: 50 pupils (€400,000).

Summer: Enrich Rev Rem. Ger. EFL. Tui Bdg €3250. 8 wks.

Endow €150,000. Bldgs 2. Dorms 1. Dorm rms 45. Class rms 25. Sci labs 1. Comp labs 2. Art studios 1. Music studios 1. Gyms 1. Fields 2.

Est 2000. Nonprofit. Tri (Aug-July).

This English-medium school basically follows the IB curriculum, beginning with the Primary Years Program and extending through the Middle Years and Diploma programs. In grades 11 and 12, however, students have two alternatives: They may pursue the German Abitur or follow a US-style curriculum that includes Advanced Placement course work. Erasmus IS provides children with an introduction to computers in grade 1, and the curriculum features integrated information and communication technology from grade 5. The foreign language program is particularly varied, with typical offerings including Russian, Polish and Greek.

SCHULE SCHLOSS SALEM

Bdg and Day — Coed Gr 5-13

88682 Salem, Germany. Schlossbezirk. Tel: 49-7553-919-0. Fax: 49-7553-919-380. EST+6.

www.salemcollege.de   E-mail: info@salem-net.de

Ingrid Sund, Prin. Margaret Tzanakakis, Adm.

Col Prep. IB Diploma. Curr—Intl Nat. **Bilingual**—Ger. **Feat**—Fr Lat Span Comp_ Sci Econ Psych Relig Studio_Art.

Sports—Basket F_Hockey Rugby.

Enr 700. B 334/37. G 306/23. Avg class size: 17.

Fac 121. M 47/11. F 20/43.

Grad '05—154.

Tui '05-'06: Bdg €26,760-28,800. Day €11,520-12,360.

Summer: Acad Rec. Lang. Tui Bdg €1850. 2½ wks.

Libs 4. Sci labs 6. Comp labs 10. Auds 3. Theaters 3. Gyms 3. Fields 3. Pools 1.

Est 1920. Nonprofit. Tri (Sept-July).

Predominantly a boarding school, Salem offers a secondary program that culminates in either the International Baccalaureate (conducted in English) or the German Abitur (taught in German). The three school divisions occupy separate campuses: the lower school at Burg Hohenfels, the middle school in Schloss Salem and the upper school at Salem International College. Most faculty teach at two of these schools.

Special features of the curriculum in the lower grades include Greek language courses among the foreign language options, and a choice of Protestant or Catholic religious instruction or interdenominational ethics lessons. During the later years, those boys and girls who pursue the IB take three or four of their six courses each term at the higher level, and the remainder at standard level.

Community service—most of which takes place off campus—is an integral aspect of school life. All students in grades 10-13 spend at least one afternoon weekly engaging in service. The arts are also important at Salem: Pictorial art displays, musical performances and theatrical productions, for example, take place regularly. Various compulsory and voluntary sports, as well as interest clubs, complete the program.

MUNICH INTERNATIONAL SCHOOL
Day — Coed Gr PS-12

82319 Starnberg, Germany. Schloss Buchhof. Tel: 49-8151-366-120. Fax: 49-8151-366-129. EST+6.
www.mis-munich.de   E-mail: admissions@mis-munich.de
Mary Seppala, Head. Ola Schmidt, Adm.

Col Prep. IB PYP. IB MYP. IB Diploma. Curr—Intl. **Exams**—ACT CEEB SSAT IGCSE. **Feat**—Fr Ger Japan Span Comp_Sci Econ Studio_Art Drama Music Bus. **Supp**—ESL.

Sports—Basket X-country Golf Ski Soccer Softball Swim Tennis Track Volley. **Activities**—Acad Arts Media Rec.

Enr 1281. B 632. G 649. Elem 296. Sec 446. PG 539. Avg class size: 20.

Fac 137. M 36/3. F 88/10. US 32. Host 21. Other 83.

Grad '05—91. Col—22. US Col—10. (Boston U 5, Columbia 1, Princeton 1, Rice 1, VA Polytech 1, Swarthmore 1). Avg SAT: M/V—1193.

Tui '05-'06: Day €11,370-13,960 (+€1300-4600).

Bldgs 6. Libs 2. Sci labs 6. Lang labs 2. Comp labs 3. Auds 2. Theaters 1. Art studios 3. Music studios 3. Gyms 3. Fields 5. Courts 3.

Est 1966. Nonprofit. Sem (Aug-June). Assoc: A/OPR/OS CIS NEASC.

Located on a 26-acre site near Lake Starnberg, MIS attracts students from more than 50 countries. The college preparatory curriculum prepares students for the US College Boards, the International Baccalaureate Diploma and the IGCSE exams. Daily instruction is offered in German, and there is special tutoring in English as a Second Language.

MIS is within an hour's drive of the Bavarian Alps, thereby enabling the students to benefit from the area's ski resources. Pupils also travel to other countries within Europe for athletic and musical competitions.

INTERNATIONAL SCHOOL OF STUTTGART
Day — Coed Gr PS-12

70597 Stuttgart, Germany. Sigmaringerstrasse 257. Tel: 49-711-769-6000. Fax: 49-711-769-60010. EST+6.
www.international-school-stuttgart.de   E-mail: iss@issev.de
David Gatley, Dir. Wendy Kielman, Adm.

Col Prep. IB Diploma. Curr—Intl. **Exams**—CEEB IGCSE. **Feat**—Fr Comp_Sci Studio_Art Music Design. **Supp**—ESL.

Enr 455. Elem 350. Sec 105. US 157. Host 98. Other 200. Avg class size: 22.

Fac 97. US 10. Host 24. Other 63.

Tui '05-'06: Day €7800-11,850 (+€260-3000).

Bldgs 2. Class rms 46. Libs 2. Sci labs 3. Comp labs 2. Auds 1. Art studios 2. Music

studios 2. Gyms 1. Fields 1.
Est 1985. Nonprofit. Sem (Sept-July). Assoc: CIS NEASC.

ISS provides an English-language education for a multicultural student body that enrolls from approximately 30 nations. Elementary-level children take part in the International Baccalaureate Primary Years Program. Specialists teach music, computers and physical education, and a small portion of the curriculum is taught in German. The middle school serves as a transitional period between elementary school and high school. Middle schoolers experience increased independence; participate in strong music, art and computer programs; and engage in school and community service. During the high school years, pupils follow an internationally recognized curriculum that provides preparation for the SAT, AP and IGCSE examinations. The two-year IB program is available in grades 11 and 12.

At all grade levels, programming emphasizes the culture, language and traditions of Germany. Frequent field trips into the local community help students learn about their host country.

THURINGIA INTERNATIONAL SCHOOL
WEIMAR
Day — Coed Gr K-7

99423 Weimar, Germany. Gutenbergstrasse 32. Tel: 49-3643-776904. Fax: 49-3643-776905. EST+6.
www.this-weimar.de   E-mail: this-weimar@t-online.de
Kerstin Machts, Head.
  Gen Acad. Curr—Intl. **Feat**—Fr Ger. **Supp**—ESL Tut.
  Enr 66. Elem 66. US 2. Host 59. Other 5. Accepted: 100%. Avg class size: 9.
  Fac 11. M 1. F 6/4. US 3. Host 2. Other 6.
  Tui '02-'03: Day €3645-4050.
  Bldgs 1. Class rms 8. Libs 1.
  Est 2000. Nonprofit. Sem (Aug-June).

Conducted by a multinational teaching staff, THIS provides an international education that incorporates elements from the American, British and German systems. While English is the language of instruction, pupils take daily German as a second language classes. In addition to international students residing in the Thuringen area due to business or government relocation, the school serves children from German families who are anticipating a move to an English-speaking country.

GREECE

Sq. Miles: 51,146 (Roughly the size of Alabama). **Country Pop:** 10,668,354 (2005). **Capital:** Athens, pop. 3,566,060. **Terrain:** Mountainous interior with coastal plains **Religion(s):** Greek_Orthodox Muslim. **Official Language(s):** Greek. **Other Language(s):** English. **Government:** Parliamentary Republic. **Independence:** 1830 (from Ottoman

Empire). **GDP:** $204 billion (2004). Agriculture 6%. Manufacturing 22%. Services 72%. **Currency:** European Union Euro (€).

AMERICAN COMMUNITY SCHOOLS OF ATHENS
Day — Coed Gr PS-12

152 34 Halandri, Athens, Greece. 129 Aghias Paraskevis St. Tel: 30-210-639-3200. Fax: 30-210-639-0051. EST+7.
www.acs.gr   E-mail: acs@acs.gr
Stefanos Gialamas, Dir.

> **Col Prep. IB MYP. IB Diploma. Curr**—Intl US. **Exams**—CEEB TOEFL. **Feat**—Arabic Greek Comp_Sci Econ Psych Sociol Photog Studio_Art Music. **Supp**—ESL.
> **Fac 84.**
> **Tui '05-'06: Day €5600-9650.**
> **Est 1945.** Nonprofit. Sem (Sept-June). Assoc: A/OPR/OS MSA.

INTERNATIONAL SCHOOL OF ATHENS
Day — Coed Gr PS-12

145 10 Kifissia, Greece. Xenias & Artemidos Sts, PO Box 51051. Tel: 30-210-6233888. Fax: 30-210-6233160. EST+7.
www.isa.edu.gr   E-mail: info@isa.edu.gr
C. N. Dardoufas, Dir. Betty Haniotakis, Adm.

> **Col Prep. IB PYP. IB MYP. IB Diploma. Curr**—Intl US. **Exams**—AP CEEB. **AP**—Eng Human_Geog World_Hist Art_Hist Studio_Art. **Feat**—Humanities Arabic Fr Greek Span Computers Econ Psych Drama Journ. **Supp**—Dev_Read ESL LD Rem_Math Rem_Read.
> **Sports**—Basket Soccer Volley. **Activities**—Arts.
> **Enr 196.** B 121. G 75. Elem 125. Sec 71. US 25. Host 59. Other 112. Accepted: 90%. Yield: 95%. Avg class size: 14.
> **Fac 61.** M 11/3. F 39/8. US 19. Host 12. Other 30. Adv Deg: 42%.
> **Grad '05—37. Col—36. US Col—1.** Avg SAT: M/V—1050.
> **Tui '05-'06: Day €5000-8700.**
> **Summer:** Ages 14-18. Enrich. ESL. Tui Day €730. 5 wks.
> Bldgs 2. 2 Libs 15,000 vols. Sci labs 5. Comp labs 2. Art studios 3. Music studios 1. Fields 1. Courts 4.
> **Est 1979.** Inc. (Sept-June). Assoc: MSA.

ISA's curriculum addresses the needs of its highly international student body. A college preparatory program that features Advanced Placement work serves American students and those planning to attend college in the US. For English-speaking European students, a course of study leading to the IB Diploma is available. Instruction in computers, sociology, art history, music, drama, studio art and journalism supplements work in the standard subject areas.

The school expects all boys and girls to participate in athletic activities such as basketball, soccer, tennis, swimming and volleyball. Pupils embark on excursions to sites of historical and cultural interest in the surrounding city, countryside and islands, as well as to other European destinations and the Middle East.

ISA maintains two Athens-area campuses within a short drive of each other. Serving the primary, middle and high schools, the main campus is located in Kifissia, a northern suburb of Athens. The kindergarten (ages 2-5) occupies nearby quarters in a traditional villa.

CAMPION SCHOOL

Day — Coed Gr PS-12

15302 Pallini, Greece. PO Box 67484. Tel: 30-1-607-1700. Fax: 30-1-607-1750. EST+7.
www.campion.edu.gr   E-mail: info@campion.edu.gr
Stephen Atherton, Head.
   Col Prep. IB Diploma. Curr—Intl UK. **Exams**—GCSE. **Feat**—Greek Studio_Art Drama Music. **Supp**—ESL.
   Fac 68.
   Tui '05-'06: Day €5480-10,200 (+€860).
   Est 1970. Nonprofit. Tri (Sept-June). Assoc: ECIS.

PINEWOOD INTERNATIONAL SCHOOL
OF THESSALONIKI

Bdg — Coed Gr 9-12; Day — Coed PS-12

555 10 Pilea, Thessaloniki, Greece. PO Box 21001. Tel: 30-2310-301221. Fax: 30-2310-323196. EST+7.
www.pinewood.gr   E-mail: info@pinewood.gr
Frederick L. Thompson, Dir. PhD.
   Col Prep. IB MYP. IB Diploma. Curr—Intl US. **Exams**—CEEB TOEFL. **Feat**—Comp_Sci Econ Studio_Art Bus. **Supp**—ESL.
   Activities—Acad Govt/Pol Service.
   Tui '05-'06: Day €4330-7730.
   Est 1950. Nonprofit. Sem (Aug-June). Assoc: A/OPR/OS MSA.

Pinewood is located in Thessaloniki, the second largest city in Greece. Housed on the Anatolia College campus (where boarders reside), it was first established as an elementary school by a group of British and American parents.

Students work in traditional, self-contained classrooms with specialists in physical education, foreign languages and ESL. Electives at the secondary level include computer, creative writing and consumer math. Students are prepared for the US College Boards, and information and counseling sessions serve both those interested in matriculating at American colleges and those planning to attend universities in the United Kingdom.

ANATOLIA COLLEGE

Bdg and Day — Coed Gr 7-12

555 10 Pylea, Thessaloniki, Greece. PO Box 21021. Tel: 30-2-310-398-201. Fax: 30-2-310-327-500. EST+7.
www.anatolia.edu.gr   E-mail: jpg@ac.anatolia.edu.gr
Richard Jackson, Pres.

>Col Prep. IB Diploma. Curr—Intl Nat. Supp Lang—Greek. Feat—Comp_Sci Econ Studio_Art Music.
>
>Enr 1299.
>
>Fac 122.
>
>Est 1886. Nonprofit. Tri (Sept-June).

ST. LAWRENCE COLLEGE

Day — Coed Gr PS-12

16602 Varkiza, Greece. PO Box 74221. Tel: 30-210-8917000. Fax: 30-210-8917010. EST+7.
www.st-lawrence.gr   E-mail: info@st-lawrence.gr
George N. Kladidis, Head. BA. Emily Naoum, Adm.

>Col Prep. Gen Acad. Curr—UK. Exams—IGCSE AS-level A-level. Feat—Arabic Fr Greek Russ Comp_Sci Sociol Art_Hist Studio_Art Drama Music Bus Health. Supp—Dev_Read EFL ESL LD Rem_Math Rem_Read Tut.
>
>Sports—Basket Rugby Soccer Tennis Volley. Activities—Acad Arts Govt/Pol Media Rec Service.
>
>Enr 800. B 380. G 420. Elem 466. Sec 334. US 102. Host 155. Other 543. Accepted: 90%. Avg class size: 15.
>
>Fac 79. M 12/2. F 64/1. Adv Deg: 18%.
>
>Grad '05—65. Col—60.
>
>Tui '05-'06: Day €5405-8825 (+€2500).
>
>Summer: Ages 3-14. Acad Enrich Rem Rec. Tui Day €1500. 4 wks.
>
>Bldgs 8. Class rms 66. 2 Libs 10,000 vols. Sci labs 6. Comp labs 2. Theaters 1. Art studios 3. Music studios 1. Dance studios 1. Gyms 1. Fields 1. Courts 2. Pools 1. Stables 1. Tracks 1.
>
>Est 1980. Inc. Tri (Sept-June).

St. Lawrence's curriculum, which operates along British public and preparatory school lines, readies students for the IGCSE and A-level examinations. Modern Greek classes are compulsory through grade 10. The school maintains two resource rooms to address special learning needs.

All students are encouraged to learn about the native culture and language through participation in clubs, activities and excursions.

HUNGARY

Sq. Miles: 35,910 (About the size of Indiana). **Country Pop:** 10,006,835 (2005). **Capital:** Budapest, pop. 2,000,000. **Terrain:** Mostly flat, with low mountains in the north and northeast and north of Lake Balaton.

Ethnic Group(s): Magyar Romany German Serb Slovak Romanian. **Religion(s):** Roman_Catholic Calvinist Lutheran Jewish. **Official Language(s):** Magyar. **Government:** Republic. **GDP:** $101.5 billion (2004). Agriculture 3%. Industry 32%. Services 65%. **Currency:** Hungarian Forint (Ft).

AMERICAN INTERNATIONAL SCHOOL OF BUDAPEST
Day — Coed Gr PS-12

Budapest 1525, Hungary. PO Box 53. Tel: 36-26-556-000. Fax: 36-26-556-003. EST+6.

www.aisb.hu   E-mail: admissions@nk.aisb.hu

Raymond Holliday, Dir. Gabriella Thomas, Adm.

  Col Prep. IB Diploma. Curr—Intl. Exams—CEEB TOEFL. Feat—Fr Ger Span Comp_Sci Photog Studio_Art Drama. Supp—ESL LD.

  Sports—Basket Soccer Softball Swim Tennis Track Volley. Activities—Acad Arts Govt/Pol Service.

  Enr 678. B 390. G 288. Elem 481. Sec 197. US 112. Host 94. Other 472. Accepted: 95%. Yield: 98%. Avg class size: 16.

  Fac 105. M 36/5. F 50/14. US 62. Host 5. Other 38. Adv Deg: 71%.

  Grad '05—43. Avg SAT: M/V—1165.

  Tui '05-'06: Day $14,560-17,350.

  Summer: Rec. 1-7 wks.

  Bldgs 2. Class rms 85. 2 Libs 40,300 vols. Sci labs 6. Comp labs 5. Theaters 4. Art studios 3. Music studios 4. Dance studios 1. Gyms 3. Fields 2. Courts 6. Pools 2. Weight rms 1.

  Est 1973. Nonprofit. (Aug-June). Assoc: A/OPR/OS CIS MSA.

A typical American curriculum is offered at this school for American dependent children and children of other English-speaking foreign residents in Budapest. Foreign language instruction commences in grade 4, and a Hungarian culture program is offered. High school students pursue the International Baccalaureate Diploma, and graduates enroll at universities in North America and Europe. The school's elementary and secondary divisions occupy separate campuses.

INTERNATIONAL SCHOOL OF BUDAPEST
Day — Coed Gr PS-8

Budapest 1121, Hungary. Konkoly Thege utca 21B. Tel: 36-1-395-6543. Fax: 36-1-395-5376. EST+6.

www.isb.hu   E-mail: isb@elender.hu

Mark Davies, Head.

  Gen Acad. Curr—Intl US. Supp—ESL.

  Enr 52. B 25. G 27.

  Fac 10.

  Tui '05-'06: Day €6600-9200.

  Est 1992. (Aug-June). Assoc: CIS MSA.

INTERNATIONAL CHRISTIAN SCHOOL OF BUDAPEST
Day — Coed Gr 1-12

Diosd 2049, Hungary. Ifjusag utca 11. Tel: 36-23-381-986. Fax: 36-23-381-552. EST+6.
www.icsbudapest.org   E-mail: registrar@icsbudapest.org
David M. Welsh, Dir. BA, MEd.

  Col Prep. Curr—US. Exams—ACT AP CEEB TOEFL. AP—Calc Physics. Feat—British_Lit Creative_Writing Ger Span Hungarian Anat & Physiol Econ Bible Studio_Art Drama Music_Theory Journ. Supp—ESL LD Rem_Math Tut.

  Sports—Basket Soccer Track Volley. Activities—Arts Govt/Pol Service.

  Enr 204. B 86. G 118. Elem 105. Sec 99. US 117. Host 30. Other 57. Accepted: 99%. Yield: 99%. Avg class size: 18.

  Fac 32. M 5/6. F 13/8. US 29. Host 3. Adv Deg: 9%.

  Grad '05—20. Col—15. US Col—12. (Campbell 4, Cedarville 2, Calvin 1, U of KY 1, Belhaven 1, Greenville Col 1).

  Tui '05-'06: Day $10,490-10,850. Aid: 6 pupils ($3000).

  Bldgs 1. Class rms 14. Libs 1. Sci labs 2. Comp labs 1. Art studios 1.

  Est 1994. Nonprofit. Evangelical. Quar (Aug-June). Assoc: MSA.

While providing an English-medium education that prepares students for entrance into North American colleges, ICSB places significant emphasis on its Christian worldview: Boys and girls take Bible each year and attend weekly chapel services, and all courses are taught from a Christian perspective. In addition, community outreach activities and spiritual events are integral to the program. Non-native English speakers may enroll in ESL classes, and the school also provides special services for pupils with learning disabilities or particular physical needs. Although the student body is predominantly American, boys and girls come from roughly a dozen countries.

ICSB's location just outside of downtown Budapest enables faculty and students to make use of the city's resources.

ICELAND

Sq. Miles: 39,600 (About the size of Virginia). Country Pop: 296,737 (2005). Capital: Reykjavik, pop. 113,730. Terrain: Rugged. Ethnic Group(s): Norwegian Celtic. Religion(s): Evangelical. Official Language(s): Icelandic. Government: Parliamentary. Independence: 1918 (from Denmark). GDP: $12.54 billion (2004). Agriculture 11%. Industry 10%. Services 79%. Currency: Icelandic Krona (IKr).

REYKJAVIK INTERNATIONAL SCHOOL
Day — Coed Gr K-6

Reykjavik, Iceland. Tel: 354-694-3341. Fax: 354-545-2701. EST+5.
Contact: c/o US Embassy, PSC 1003, Box 40, FPO, AE 09728. Tel: 354-562-9100.
www.vikurskoli.is/RIS/   E-mail: ris@vikurskoli.is

Berta Faber, Head.
 Gen Acad. Curr—US. **Feat**—Computers Fine_Arts Music.
 Enr 11. Elem 11. Accepted: 98%. Avg class size: 5.
 Fac 3.
 Tui '05-'06: Day $6000-10,000 (+$25).
 Est 1959. Nonprofit. Sem (Aug-June). **Assoc:** A/OPR/OS.

Serving the children of US Embassy personnel and other international residents in the port city of Reykjavik, this small elementary school follows a highly individualized US-style curriculum. Children have biweekly swimming lessons and access to a small library. AES schedules frequent field trips to community areas of interest. Pupils may receive Icelandic language lessons after school three times per week.

IRELAND

Sq. Miles: 27,136 (Slightly larger than West Virginia). **Country Pop:** 4,015,676 (2005). **Capital:** Dublin, pop. 495,101. **Terrain:** Arable, meadows and pastures, rough grazing in use, inland water. **Ethnic Group(s):** Irish English. **Religion(s):** Roman_Catholic. **Official Language(s):** English. **Other Language(s):** Gaelic. **Government:** Parliamentary Republic. **Independence:** 1921 (from United Kingdom). **Per Capita Income:** $21,600 (2001). **GDP:** $86.3 billion (2001). Agriculture 5% Industry 46%. Services 49%. **Currency:** European Union Euro (€).

ST. ANDREW'S COLLEGE
Day — Coed Gr PS-12

Blackrock, County Dublin, Ireland. Booterstown Ave. Tel: 353-1-288-2785. Fax: 353-1-283-1627. EST+5.
www.st-andrews.ie   E-mail: information@st-andrews.ie
Arthur Godsill, Head. MA, MEd. **Ronnie Hay, Adm.**
 Col Prep. Gen Acad. IB Diploma. Curr—Intl US. **Exams**—CEEB. **Feat**—Fr Ger Span Comp_Sci Studio_Art Music. **Supp**—EFL ESL LD Rem_Math Rem_Read Tut.
 Sports—Badminton Basket F_Hockey Rugby. **Activities**—Acad Arts Govt/Pol Media Rec Service.
 Enr 1184. US 45. Host 914. Other 225. Avg class size: 18.
 Fac 127. M 40/2. F 80/5. US 4. Host 109. Other 14. Adv Deg: 14%.
 Grad '05—163. Col—145. US Col—5. (Stanford, U of PA, U of Portland, Santa Clara, Friends World).
 Tui '05-'06: Day $5162-6543. Aid: 375 pupils ($307,515).
 Endow $12,874,000. Plant val $6,220,000. Bldgs 4. Class rms 85. Libs 2. Sci labs 4. Comp labs 1. Auds 1. Gyms 1. Athletic ctrs 1. Fields 4. Courts 3.
 Est 1894. Nonprofit. Presbyterian. Tri (Sept-June). Assoc: A/OPR/OS CIS NEASC.

St. Andrew's provides a liberal education that ultimately prepares students for the IB Diploma and the Irish Intermediate and Leaving Certificate examinations.

The preparatory department (grades PS-6) offers specialist art, music, drama and computer instructors. Native speakers teach European languages. The two courses of study (the IB and the national programs) run parallel to each other during the final two secondary years.

Although a day school, St. Andrew's boards some students with local families.

ITALY

Sq. Miles: 116,303 (About the size of Georgia and Florida combined). **Country Pop:** 58,103,033 (2005). **Capital:** Rome, pop. 2,800,000. **Terrain:** Mostly rugged and mountainous. **Ethnic Group(s):** Italian German French. **Religion(s):** Roman_Catholic. **Official Language(s):** Italian. **Government:** Republic. **Per Capita Income:** $21,500 (2002). **GDP:** $1.2 trillion (2002). Agriculture 2%. Industry 29%. Services 69%. **Currency:** European Union Euro (€).

INTERNATIONAL SCHOOL OF NAPLES
Day — Coed Gr PS-12

80125 Bagnoli, Naples, Italy. Viale della Liberazione 1. Tel: 39-081-721-20-37. Fax: 39-081-570-02-48. EST+6.
www.intschoolnaples.it   E-mail: info@intschoolnaples.it
Josephine Sessa, Prin. BA, MA.

Col Prep. Curr—US. **Exams**—CEEB. **Feat**—Ital Environ_Sci Comp_Sci Sociol Art_Hist Studio_Art Music. **Supp**—ESL Tut.

Activities—Arts Media.

Enr 237. B 121. G 116. Elem 161. Sec 76. US 20. Host 81. Other 136. Accepted: 100%. Avg class size: 20.

Fac 26. M 4. F 18/4. US 7. Host 10. Other 9. Adv Deg: 23%.

Grad '05—17. Col—15. US Col—2. (U of Chicago). Avg SAT: M/V—1370, Essay—650.

Tui '05-'06: Day €2340-5760 (+€1000).

Bldgs 3. Class rms 17. Lib 8000 vols. Sci labs 1. Comp labs 1. Gyms 1. Fields 1. Courts 4. Pools 1.

Est 1979. Nonprofit. Quar (Sept-June).

Located on the outskirts of Naples, ISN draws more than half its enrollment from the NATO community. The school follows a traditional American college preparatory curriculum. Specialized classes offering preparation for Italy's state exams are also available. Staff specialists teach music, art, computer science, physical education and ESL courses.

Field trips to places of curricular and cultural interest enrich the program.

UNITED WORLD COLLEGE OF THE ADRIATIC

Bdg — Coed Gr 11-12

34103 Duino, Italy. Via Trieste 29. Tel: 39-040-373-9221. Fax: 39-040-373-9225. EST+6.

www.uwcad.it   E-mail: uwcad@uwcad.it

M. Marc Abrioux, Head. MA, PhD.

Col Prep. IB Diploma. Curr—Intl. Feat—Ital Russ Slovene Environ_Sci Econ Philos Studio_Art Music. Supp—Tut.

Sports—F_Hockey. Activities—Acad Arts Media Rec.

Enr 196. US 6. Host 30. Other 160. Avg class size: 14.

Fac 23. M 13. F 10. US 1. Host 5. Other 17. Adv Deg: 78%.

Tui '06-'07: Bdg $0.

Est 1983. Nonprofit.

UWCAC is one of 10 related UWC international schools dedicated to promoting international understanding through education. The organization has campuses in Britain, Canada, Hong Kong, India, Italy, Norway, Singapore, Swaziland, the US and Venezuela, and each school is a community representing more than 70 countries. Each student accepted into the program attends for two years on a full scholarship. Pupils follow the International Baccalaureate curriculum in preparation for the IB exams.

Community service, outdoor programs and events pertaining to global issues supplement the academic offerings.

THE INTERNATIONAL SCHOOL OF FLORENCE

Day — Coed Gr PS-12

50125 Florence, Italy. Villa Torri di Gattaia, viuzzo di Gattaia 9. Tel: 39-055-2001515. Fax: 39-055-2008400. EST+6.

www.isfitaly.org

Laura Mongiat, Head. BA, BEd. Heidi Flores & Ellin Ragusa, Adms.

Col Prep. IB PYP. IB MYP. IB Diploma. Curr—Intl Nat US. Supp Lang—Ital. Exams—CEEB TOEFL. Feat—Fr Ital Comp_Sci Studio_Art Drama Music. Supp—EFL LD.

Sports—Soccer Tennis Track Volley. Activities—Arts Govt/Pol Media Service.

Enr 368. Elem 259. Sec 109. US 135. Host 147. Other 86. Accepted: 90%. Yield: 80%. Avg class size: 15.

Fac 52. M 11. F 39/2. US 29. Host 8. Other 15. Adv Deg: 23%.

Grad '05—24. Col—22. US Col—10. (U of CO-Boulder, PA St, U of Richmond, U of MI, Tufts, Wash & Lee). Avg SAT: M/V—1178.

Tui '05-'06: Day €6300-11,700 (+€2750).

Bldgs 2. 2 Libs 15,000 vols. Sci labs 3. Comp labs 2. Art studios 2. Music studios 2. Fields 2. Courts 1.

Est 1952. Nonprofit. Quar (Sept-June). Assoc: A/OPR/OS CIS MAIS MSA.

Founded in Rome as St. Michael's Country Day School, this school offers elementary and secondary education to children of local and expatriate families. American and IB curricula are available, with all three International Baccalaureate programs in place. In addition, ISF conducts junior and middle school programs for native and nonnative Italian speakers.

For English-speaking students, Italian language is taught at all grade levels, beginning in grade 1; French is introduced in grade 6. Supplementary courses include music, art and computers, as well as sports activities and journalism. The junior school occupies a separate campus in Bagno a Ripoli.

AMERICAN INTERNATIONAL SCHOOL IN GENOA
Day — Coed Gr PS-12

16148 Genoa, Italy. Via Quarto 13C. Tel: 39-010-386528. Fax: 39-010-398700. EST+6.
www.aisge.it   E-mail: info@aisge.it
John Paduano, Dir. EdD.
> **Gen Acad. IB Diploma. Curr**—Intl Nat US. **Exams**—CEEB. **Feat**—Fr Ital Studio_ Art Music. **Supp**—EFL ESL LD.
> **Enr 241.** Accepted: 100%. Avg class size: 13.
> **Fac 23.**
> **Grad '05—15.**
> **Tui '05-'06: Day €5360-10,390** (+€516). **Aid:** 3 pupils (€5000).
> **Summer:** Enrich. Tui Day €700. 4 wks.
> Bldgs 4. Class rms 15. 2 Libs 5500 vols. Sci labs 1. Comp labs 1. Art studios 1. Gyms 1. Fields 1.
> **Est 1966.** Nonprofit. Sem (Sept-June). Assoc: CIS MAIS NEASC.

Formerly the Overseas School of Liguria, AISG enrolls pupils from more than a dozen countries. Located in a villa near the sea, 20 minutes from the center of Genoa, the school is accessible to public transportation. English is the medium of instruction in all academic subjects, and classes are small, with an average student-teacher ratio of 10:1. Departmentalization begins in grade 6. The study of Italian is compulsory for all students, and French is also available from grade 6.

CASTELLI INTERNATIONAL SCHOOL
Day — Coed Gr 1-8

00046 Grottaferrata, Rome, Italy. Via degli Scozzesi 13. Tel: 39-06-94315779. Fax: 39-06-94315779. EST+6.
www.castelli-international.it   E-mail: maryac@castelli-international.it
Marianne Palladino, Dir. BA, MA, PhD.
> **Gen Acad. Curr**—Intl. **Bilingual**—Ital. **Feat**—Lib_Skills Fr Comp_Sci Geog Studio_Art Drama Music. **Supp**—Dev_Read EFL ESL Rem_Math Rev Tut.
> **Activities**—Arts Rec Service.
> **Enr 110.** B 50. G 60. Elem 20. Sec 40. PG 50. Accepted: 80%. Avg class size: 16.
> **Fac 18.** M 1/5. F 8/4. US 4. Host 2. Other 12. Adv Deg: 16%.
> **Tui '05-'06: Day €6100-7500** (+€1000).
> Bldgs 2. Class rms 9. Lib 5000 vols. Sci labs 1. Lang labs 1. Comp labs 1. Art studios 1. Music studios 1. Dance studios 1. Fields 1. Tennis courts 1.
> **Est 1977.** Nonprofit. Tri (Sept-June).

CIS is a bilingual (Italian and English) elementary and middle school that prepares students for secondary schools in Europe and around the world. The multifaceted program addresses individual learning needs within a small-class environment.

An annual ski trip supplements a sports program consisting of soccer, volleyball, tennis and table tennis.

AMERICAN SCHOOL OF MILAN
Day — Coed Gr PS-12

20090 Milan, Italy. Noverasco di Opera. Tel: 39-02-530-0001. Fax: 39-02-5760-6274. EST+6.

www.asmilan.org   E-mail: director@asmilan.org

Alan Austen, Dir.

Col Prep. IB MYP. IB Diploma. Curr—Intl US. Exams—CEEB. Feat—Fr Ital Span Comp_Sci Econ Psych Ital_Stud Philos Studio_Art Music.

Enr 496.

Fac 56.

Tui '05-'06: Day €7460-13,170 (+€2000).

Est 1962. Nonprofit. Sem (Sept-June). Assoc: A/OPR/OS MAIS MSA.

INTERNATIONAL SCHOOL OF MILAN
Day — Coed Gr PS-12

20153 Milan, Italy. Via Caccialepori 22. Tel: 39-02-48708076. Fax: 39-02-48703644. EST+6.

www.ism-ac.it   E-mail: admin@ism-ac.it

Terence F. Haywood, Head. MA.

Col Prep. IB PYP. IB MYP. IB Diploma. Curr—Intl UK. Exams—GCSE IGCSE. Feat—Fr Ger Ital Ecol Econ Visual_Arts Theater_Arts Bus.

Enr 1160.

Est 1958. Tri (Sept-June).

ST. LOUIS SCHOOL
Day — Coed Gr PS-8

20139 Milan, Italy. Via Caviglia 1. Tel: 39-02-55231235. Fax: 39-02-56610885. EST+6.

www.stlouisschool.it   E-mail: info@stlouisschool.com

Pre-Prep. Curr—UK. Supp Lang—Ital. Feat—Fr Ital Lat Computers Studio_Art Music.

SIR JAMES HENDERSON
BRITISH SCHOOL OF MILAN
Day — Coed Ages 3-18

20134 Milan, Italy. Via Pisano Dossi 16. Tel: 39-02-210-941. Fax: 39-02-2109-4224. EST+6.

www.sjhschool.com   E-mail: info@sjhschool.com

Trevor Church, Prin. MA.

Col Prep. Curr—Nat UK. Exams—GCSE IGCSE A-level. Feat—Creative_Writing

Fr Ger Ital Span Comp_Sci Ital_Stud Studio_Art Music Bus. **Supp**—ESL.
Enr 622. B 319. G 303. Elem 388. Sec 234.
Fac 66. M 11/3. F 38/14.
Tui '01-'02: Day €4054-8553 (+€2531).
Est 1969. Nonprofit. Tri (Sept-June).

INTERNATIONAL SCHOOL OF MODENA

Day — Coed Gr K-9

**41042 Modena, Italy. Via Silvio Pellico 9, Fiorano Modenese. Tel: 39-0536-832904.
Fax: 39-0536-911189. EST+6.**
www.ismmodena.org   E-mail: office@ismmodena.org
Soheila Mathison, Prin.

Pre-Prep. Gen Acad. IB PYP. IB MYP. **Curr**—Intl UK. **Exams**—GCSE IGCSE.
Feat—Ger Ital Computers Studio_Art Music. **Supp**—EFL ESL.
Activities—Arts Govt/Pol Rec.
Enr 83. Elem 73. Sec 10. US 7. Host 7. Other 69. Accepted: 100%. Yield: 90%. Avg
class size: 13.
Fac 16. M 6/1. F 9. Host 4. Other 12. Adv Deg: 18%.
Tui '05-'06: Day €9600 (+€3050).
Class rms 10. Libs 1. Sci labs 1. Lang labs 1. Comp labs 1. Art studios 1. Music
studios 1. Gyms 1.
Est 1998. Tri (Sept-June).

After initially following the British national curriculum, ISM adopted the IB
Primary Years and Middle Years programs. Boys and girls follow a traditional curriculum that includes computers, geography, history, art and design technology,
music, foreign languages, drama and physical education. The school draws its
students from roughly 15 nations.

INTERNATIONAL SCHOOL OF TURIN

Day — Coed Gr PS-12

**10024 Moncalieri, Turin, Italy. Vicolo Tiziano 10. Tel: 39-11-645-967. Fax: 39-11-
643-298. EST+6.**
www.acat-ist.it   E-mail: info@acat-ist.it
Jonathan Cramb, Head.

Col Prep. IB Diploma. **Curr**—Intl Nat US. **Bilingual**—Ital. **Exams**—CEEB. **Feat**—
Econ Visual_Arts Music Bus. **Supp**—ESL.
Tui '05-'06: Day €5390-10,200 (+€500-1000).
Est 1963. Nonprofit. Sem (Aug-June). Assoc: CIS NEASC.

PLAY ENGLISH
THE BILINGUAL SCHOOL OF MONZA

Day — Coed Gr PS-6

**20052 Monza, Milan, Italy. Via Confalonieri 18. Tel: 39-039-231-2282. Fax: 39-039-
232-0591. EST+6.**

www.playenglish.it   E-mail: playengl@tin.it
Eugenia Papadaki, Head. BA, MA.

    Pre-Prep. Gen Acad. Curr—Intl. **Bilingual**—Ital. **Feat**—Fr Comp_Sci Studio_Art Drama Music.

    Enr 116. Accepted: 95%. Avg class size: 18.

    Fac 20. Adv Deg: 10%.

    Tui '05-'06: Day €3080-7170.

    Summer: Rec. Tui Day €700. 6 wks.

    Class rms 11. Lib 7000 vols. Comp labs 1. Art studios 1. Music studios 1. Gyms 2. Fields 1. Courts 1.

    Est 1995. Inc. Tri (Sept-July).

Enrolling children from age 1, this primary school utilizes a play-centered approach to learning. Both Italian pupils and children of the international community engage in a bilingual program that allows them to gain fluency in two languages. The curriculum follows the guidelines set forth by the Italian and British ministries of education. Upon departure from the school, students are able to transition easily into either an English- or an Italian-language school.

    In the early years, most subjects employ English as the language of instruction; as the student progresses, however, more and more course work is taught in Italian. Mixed-ability teaching accommodates children of varying aptitudes and allows students in need to receive extra attention. Use of the computer, drama activities and music serve as important language-learning tools. The curriculum comprises four main areas: language and literacy; mathematics, science and information technology; history, geography and social sciences; and the expressive arts.

    Music, choir, sports, art, ceramics, drama and interest clubs are among the Bilingual School's extracurriculars.

THE ENGLISH INTERNATIONAL SCHOOL OF PADUA

Day — Coed Gr PS-12

35128 Padova, Italy. Via Forcellini 168. Tel: 39-049-802-2503. Fax: 39-049-802-0660. EST+6.
www.eisp01.com   E-mail: eisp@eisp01.com
Lucio Rossi, Dir. PhD.

    Col Prep. IB Diploma. Curr—Intl. **Exams**—GCSE. **Feat**—Fr Ger Ital Lat Span Comp_Sci Philos Studio_Art. **Supp**—Dev_Read EFL ESL LD Makeup Rem_Math Rem_Read Rev Tut.

    Enr 644. Elem 572. Sec 72. US 42. Host 553. Other 49. Accepted: 97%. Avg class size: 20.

    Fac 59. M 10/4. F 41/4. US 9. Host 9. Other 31.

    Grad '05—66.

    Tui '05-'06: Day €5000-10,000 (+€100-500).

    Endow €9,000,000. Plant val €5,000,000. Bldgs 3. Class rms 34. 3 Libs 7000 vols. Sci labs 1. Comp labs 2. Music studios 1. Gyms 1. Fields 1.

    Est 1987. Sem (Sept-June).

Founded in response to meet the international community in Padova's desire for appropriate schooling, the school provides a full elementary and secondary program that employs English as the language of instruction. Although a large percentage of students are Italian, increasing numbers of boys and girls (many of whom are native English speakers) now enroll from other countries.

A dual approach results in EISP's melding of the curricula of Italy and England. The resulting program addresses skill development in the areas of communication, comprehension, vocabulary and writing. Instruction in the elementary grades, which takes a cross-curricular approach at times, includes specialist teachers in certain areas. More structure is evident at the middle school level, and programming seeks to improve pupils' academic skills, familiarity with concepts, overall knowledge and study habits. During the first year of middle school, pupils are introduced to a third language, either German, Spanish or French. Pursuit of the International Baccalaureate Diploma is possible during the final two years of high school.

AMERICAN OVERSEAS SCHOOL OF ROME

Bdg — Coed Gr 9-12; Day — Coed PS-PG

00189 Rome, Italy. Via Cassia 811. Tel: 39-06-334-381. Fax: 39-06-332-62608. EST+6.

Contact: PSC 59, Box 68, APO, AE 09624.

www.aosr.org   E-mail: information@aosr.org

Larry Dougherty, Head. BA, MAT, EdD. Donald Levine, Adm.

Col Prep. IB Diploma. Curr—Intl US. Exams—ACT AP CEEB TOEFL. AP—Eng Fr Span Calc Bio Chem Physics Eur_Hist US_Hist Psych Art_Hist. Feat—Ital Comp_Sci Archaeol. Supp—Dev_Read EFL ESL LD Rem_Read Tut.

Sports—Basket X-country Soccer Tennis Volley Wrestling. Activities—Arts Govt/ Pol Media Rec.

Enr 620. B 8/302. G 8/302. Elem 412. Sec 207. PG 1. US 176. Host 196. Other 248. Accepted: 90%. Avg class size: 17.

Fac 73. M 14/4. F 46/9. US 46. Host 10. Other 17. Adv Deg: 50%.

Grad '05—52. Col—45. US Col—21. (Brown, Emerson, US Air Force Acad, U of PA, U of TX-Austin, Wash U).

Tui '05-'06: Bdg €36,000 (+€2500). Day €7900-16,700 (+€1800). Aid: 61 pupils (€230,000).

Summer: Rec. 2-4 wks.

Bldgs 4. 2 Libs 20,000 vols. Sci labs 4. Comp labs 3. Theaters 1. Art studios 2. Music studios 2. Gyms 1. Fields 1. Tennis courts 2.

Est 1947. Nonprofit. Sem (Sept-June). Assoc: A/OPR/OS MAIS MSA.

The school offers an American-based curriculum to the English-speaking and international communities of Rome. A comprehensive program of academics features the International Baccalaureate Diploma Program, as well as Advanced Placement courses in all major disciplines. AOSR's boarding program enables high school pupils to reside at the nearby Hotel Villa St. Dominique.

See Also Page 548

GREENWOOD GARDEN SCHOOL

Day — Coed PS-K

00189 Rome, Italy. Via Vito Sinisi 5. Tel: 39-06-3326-6703. Fax: 39-06-3326-6703. EST+6.

E-mail: greenwoodgarden@libero.it

Donna Selbert, Dir. BA, MEd.

 Gen Acad. Curr—US.

 Enr 40. Elem 40. Avg class size: 11.

 Fac 5. F 4/1. US 3. Host 1. Other 1. Adv Deg: 20%.

 Tui '06-'07: Day €5200-5850.

 Summer: Rec. 4 wks.

 Bldgs 1. Class rms 4. Libs 1.

 Est 1974. Tri (Sept-June).

This American-style nursery school and kindergarten is located near the Via Cassia. Individual attention aids children in their transition from home to school. The early childhood center provides a play-oriented experience in which children learn by engaging in hands-on activities.

A play group involving various physical play activities is available for two-year-olds. In nursery school, three- and four-year-olds enter a more structured environment with greater group participation. Coloring, cutting, prewriting exercises, matching and sorting, and alphabet and counting activities commence. Kindergarten prepares five-year-olds for their entrance into first grade. Basic readiness activities are developed to include alphabet and phonic recognition, reading, mathematics and number activities, science, and visual and perceptual concepts. Attention focuses on the building of verbal and communicational skills.

All children participate in arts and crafts projects. Daily outdoor activities allow the children to use the garden and to engage in gymnastics and movement exercises.

MARYMOUNT INTERNATIONAL SCHOOL

Day — Coed Gr PS-12

00191 Rome, Italy. Via di Villa Lauchli 180. Tel: 39-06-362-9101. Fax: 39-06-3630-1738. EST+6.

www.marymountrome.com   E-mail: marymount@marymountrome.org

Yvonne Hennigan, Head. Debbie Woods, Adm.

 Col Prep. IB Diploma. Curr—Intl US. **Exams**—ACT CEEB. **Feat**—Fr Ital Span Comp_Sci Relig Studio_Art Drama Music. **Supp**—ESL LD.

 Enr 835. B 394. G 441. Elem 609. Sec 226. US 250. Host 385. Other 200. Avg class size: 15.

 Fac 90.

 Grad '05—45. **Col**—43.

 Tui '06-'07: Day €8100-15,600.

 Bldgs 4. Sci labs 4. Comp labs 2. Auds 1. Theaters 1. Art studios 2. Music studios 2. Fields 1. Courts 1. Pools 1.

 Est 1946. Nonprofit. Roman Catholic. Sem (Sept-June). Assoc: CIS MAIS NEASC.

Founded by the Religious of the Sacred Heart of Mary and part of the worldwide network of Marymount schools, the school provides a US-style curriculum that also includes International Baccalaureate programming. During the elementary years, classroom instructors teach the core subjects of language arts, math, science, social studies and religion, while specialists provide lessons in art, music, Italian language and physical education. ESL classes serve children lacking proficiency in English, and a learning specialist assists those with specific learning needs. In addition to the IB Diploma option, students at the secondary level may take Advanced Placement courses in grades 11 and 12. Electives supplement course requirements in grades 10-12. Field trips, which make use of the school's accessibility to the center of Rome, provide enrichment at all grade levels.

At the elementary level, children pursue interests in art, music, drama, soccer and basketball through the extracurricular program. During the middle school years, pupils may take part in such activities as drama, after-school sports and socials. High schoolers choose from student council, yearbook, chess club, choir, sports and cheerleading. Artistically inclined students may enter their work in local art competitions, while interested boys and girls are able to participate in Model UN.

THE NEW SCHOOL
Day — Coed Gr PS-12

00135 Rome, Italy. Via della Camilluccia 669. Tel: 39-06-329-4269. Fax: 39-06-329-7546. EST+6.
www.newschoolrome.com   E-mail: info@newschoolrome.com
Armando MacRory, Head.
> **Col Prep. Curr**—UK. **Exams**—GCSE AS-level A-level. **Feat**—Fr Ital Span Econ Studio_Art Drama Music Bus.
> **Tui '05-'06: Day €8600-12,300.**
> **Est 1972.** Nonprofit. Tri (Sept-June).

ROME INTERNATIONAL SCHOOL
Day — Coed Gr PS-9

00197 Rome, Italy. Viale Romania 32. Tel: 39-06-844-82650. Fax: 39-06-844-82653. EST+6.
www.romeinternationalschool.it   E-mail: office@romeinternationalschool.it
Patricia M. Smith, Head.
> **Gen Acad. Curr**—UK. **Supp Lang**—Ital. **Feat**—Ital Comp_Sci Studio_Art Music. **Supp**—ESL.
> **Enr 374.**
> **Fac 31.**
> **Est 1988.** Sem (Sept-June).

ST. FRANCIS INTERNATIONAL SCHOOL
Day — Coed Ages 3-14

00168 Rome, Italy. Via S Borgia 85. Tel: 39-06-35-5110-23. Fax: 39-06-35-5110-23. EST+6.
www.stfrancis-school.it   E-mail: info@stfrancis-school.it
Diane Proietti, Prin. BA.
    Pre-Prep. Curr—US. **Feat**—Ital Drama Music. **Supp**—EFL.
    Enr 104.
    Fac 14.
    Tui '06-'07: Day €4700-6100 (+€300).
    Est 1984. Tri (Sept-June).

ST. GEORGE'S BRITISH INTERNATIONAL SCHOOL
Day — Coed Gr PS-12

00123 Rome, Italy. Via Cassia, La Sorta. Tel: 39-06-308-6001. Fax: 39-06-308-92490. EST+6.
www.stgeorge.school.it   E-mail: secretary@stgeorge.school.it
Nicholas P. Johnson, Prin. BA, MA, MEd.
    Col Prep. IB Diploma. Curr—Intl UK. **Exams**—GCSE IGCSE. **Feat**—Fr Ger Ital Span Comp_Sci World_Relig Drama Music.
    Sports—Basket F_Hockey Soccer Swim Tennis Track Volley.
    Enr 644.
    Fac 90. M 40/2. F 46/2. Adv Deg: 26%.
    Grad '05—58.
    Tui '05-'06: Day €7950-15,250 (+€5000).
    Est 1958. Nonprofit. Tri (Sept-June).

This British-oriented school, which occupies a 27-acre campus, is divided into upper and lower schools. Students follow a college preparatory syllabus directed toward the GCSE and IB exams. Religion class is required for all students under age 14. Graduates typically matriculate at universities in Europe, Australia, Canada and the US.

ST. STEPHEN'S SCHOOL
Bdg and Day — Coed Gr 9-PG

00153 Rome, Italy. Via Aventina 3. Tel: 39-06-575-0605. Fax: 39-06-574-1941. EST+6.
www.ststephens-rome.com   E-mail: ststephens@ststephens-rome.com
Philip H. Allen, Head. BA, MA.
    Col Prep. IB Diploma. Curr—Intl US. **Exams**—AP CEEB. **AP**—Eng Fr Lat Eur_ Hist US_Hist Art_Hist. **Feat**—Econ Geog Islamic_Stud Drawing Sculpt Drama Music Dance. **Supp**—ESL Tut.
    Sports—Basket Soccer Volley. **Activities**—Acad Arts Govt/Pol Media Rec Service.
    Enr 211. B 15/79. G 16/101. Sec 208. PG 3. US 77. Host 45. Other 89. Accepted: 60%. Avg class size: 13.

Fac 39. M 9/5. F 16/9. US 25. Host 5. Other 9. Adv Deg: 41%.
Grad '05—51. Col—47. US Col—16. (U of Chicago 2, Columbia 2, Haverford 2, NYU 1, Boston U 1, Tufts 1).
Tui '05-'06: Bdg €26,500 (+€470). **Day €15,700** (+€1350). **Aid:** 60 pupils (€210,000).
Endow $1,800,000. Bldgs 1. Dorms 1. Dorm rms 36. Class rms 10. Lib 14,000 vols. Sci labs 3. Comp labs 2. Auds 1. Art studios 2. Music studios 1. Dance studios 1. Perf arts ctrs 1. Gyms 1. Courts 2.
Est 1964. Nonprofit. Sem (Sept-June). Assoc: A/OPR/OS CIS NEASC.

Situated in central Rome, the school is a few minutes' walk from the Colosseum and the Roman Forum. Students are prepared for an American secondary school diploma and have the opportunity for Advanced Placement work and pursuit of the International Baccalaureate. The fine arts, history, classical studies, literature and languages play a strong part in the curriculum, as do math, science and computer. An extensive field trip program enriches class work.

Graduates enter competitive American colleges, in addition to universities in Australia, Canada, Italy, Japan, England and other countries.   **See Also Page 551**

SOUTHLANDS ENGLISH SCHOOL
Day — Coed Gr PS-8

00124 Rome, Italy. Casal Palocco, Via Teleclide 20. Tel: 39-06-50-53-93-2. Fax: 39-06-50-91-71-92. EST+6.
www.southlands.it   E-mail: sesir@southlands.it
Vivien Franceschini, Prin.
  Gen Acad. Curr—UK. **Exams**—GCSE. **Feat**—Fr Ital Comp_Sci Geog Studio_Art Drama Music.
  Enr 390.
  Tui '06-'07: Day €5400-11,138 (+€260).
  Tri (Sept-June).

ENGLISH INTERNATIONAL SCHOOL
Day — Coed Gr K-8

36027 Rosa, Italy. Via Segafredo 50. Tel: 39-0424-582191. Fax: 39-0424-582385. EST+6.
www.eischool.it   E-mail: info@eischool.it
Francesca Eger, Prin.
  Pre-Prep. Curr—Intl. **Bilingual**—Ital. **Feat**—Fr Ger Span Comp_Sci Studio_Art Drama Music. **Supp**—ESL LD Rem_Read Rev Tut.
  Sports—Volley. **Activities**—Arts.
  Enr 260. Elem 260. Accepted: 99%. Yield: 100%.
  Fac 20. M 2/3. F 12/3. Host 9. Other 11. Adv Deg: 100%.
  Tui '05-'06: Day €5000.
  Summer: Rec. Tui Day €320/2-wk ses. 4 wks.
  Bldgs 1. Class rms 15. Lib 4000 vols. Sci labs 1. Comp labs 1. Auds 1. Art studios 1. Gyms 2. Fields 1. Courts 1. Pools 1.
  Est 1992. Inc. Sem (Sept-June).

Founded as an elementary school by a group of parents interested in providing for their children an international curriculum taught in English, EIS opened a middle school division in fall 2000. While most courses are taught in English, Italian is the language of instruction in the following classes: math, history, geography, music and Italian language; students not fluent in Italian receive tutoring in these subjects in English. In addition, the school provides Italian tutoring for those in need. Programming is based on the British national curriculum and meets the requirements of the Italian ministerial curriculum as well.

Lunchtime athletic clubs enable children to work with a trainer in such sports as soccer, athletics, volleyball and basketball. Theatrical performances and art workshops are among EIS' other activities.

INTERNATIONAL SCHOOL OF TRIESTE
Day — Coed Gr PS-9

34016 Trieste, Italy. Via Conconello 16, Opicina. Tel: 39-040-211452. Fax: 39-040-213122. EST+6.
www.istrieste.org   E-mail: info@istrieste.org
James Pastore, Dir. MEd.
  Gen Acad. Curr—Intl US. **Feat**—Lib_Skills Fr Ger Ital Lat Span Computers Studio_Art Music. **Supp**—ESL LD.
  Sports—Soccer. **Activities**—Arts.
  Enr 263. US 3. Host 221. Other 39. Accepted: 95%. Avg class size: 22.
  Fac 35. M 5/2. F 23/5. US 6. Host 16. Other 13. Adv Deg: 14%.
  Tui '05-'06: Day €5040-6700 (+€1400).
  Bldgs 1. Class rms 17. Lib 3500 vols. Sci labs 1. Comp labs 1. Art studios 1. Gyms 1. Fields 1. Courts 1.
  Est 1964. Nonprofit. Quar (Sept-June). Assoc: MAIS MSA.

Originally founded to accommodate children of scientists from the International Centre for Theoretical Physics of Trieste, the school patterns its program on the standard American curriculum. Art, music, physical education and Italian are required of all students. English as a Second Language is taught in nursery and kindergarten.

Chief seaport of the Austrian Empire until World War I, when it passed to Italy, and claimed by Yugoslavia after World War II, Trieste is situated on the gulf of the same name in a setting of great scenic beauty.

VICENZA INTERNATIONAL SCHOOL
Day — Coed Gr 9-12

36100 Vicenza, Italy. Contra San Marcello 9. Tel: 39-0444-525080. Fax: 39-0444-525083. EST+6.
E-mail: info@internationalyceum.it
Mary Bussino Cappellari, Head.
  Col Prep. IB Diploma. Curr—Intl. **Feat**—Ital Span Comp_Sci Econ Psych Philos Studio_Art Theater_Arts Music Bus. **Supp**—Makeup Tut.
  Avg class size: 10.

Fac 12. M /2. F /10. Host 7. Other 5. Adv Deg: 100%.
Tui '05-'06: Day €6550.
Class rms 5. Libs 1. Chapels 1. Sci labs 1. Comp labs 2. Auds 1.
Est 1989. Inc. Sem (Sept-June).

As is the case with all schools participating in the International Baccalaureate Diploma Program, VIS requires its students to select one class from each of the six IB subject areas. IB instruction is in English; those pupils whose mother tongue differs from the language of instruction earn a bilingual diploma. Although they are not part of the regular foreign language curriculum, French, German and Swedish may be offered upon request.

Situated in northern Italy, Vincenza is an architecturally renowned city that lies between Verona and Padua. Venice is less than an hour away.

SCHOOL YEAR ABROAD

Bdg — Coed Gr 11-12

01100 Viterbo, Italy. Via Cavour 77. Tel: 39-0761-326-856. Fax: 39-0761-304-529. EST+6.
Contact: 439 S Union St, Lawrence, MA 01843. Tel: 978-725-6828. Fax: 978-725-6833.
www.sya.org   E-mail: mail@sya.org
Woodruff W. Halsey II, Exec Dir. AB, MA. **Whitney Hermann, Adm.**
  Col Prep. Curr—US. **Exams**—CEEB. **AP**—Lat Calc. **Feat**—Greek Ital Art_Hist.
  Sports—Rugby Soccer Tennis Volley. **Activities**—Arts.
  Enr 60. Accepted: 66%. Yield: 85%. Avg class size: 15.
  Fac 8. M 4. F 4. US 4. Host 4. Adv Deg: 87%.
  Avg SAT: M/V—1315, Essay—668.
  Tui '05-'06: Bdg $36,000 (+$2000). **Aid:** 25 pupils ($639,942).
  Est 2001. Nonprofit. Quar (Sept-June).

School Year Abroad was established by Phillips Academy and is now a consortium of 26 independent schools. SYA provides a fully accredited year of study for high school students in Viterbo. The program is open to qualified juniors and seniors who have completed at least two years of Latin language study. With the exception of the Italian course, the medium of instruction is English.

Students live with native families and travel during vacation periods. Program participants learn about the culture and customs of the native country. Students prepare for the US College Boards and for certain Advanced Placement exams.

Similar programs operate in China, France and Spain (see separate listings).

LATVIA

Sq. Miles: 25,640 (About the size of West Virginia). **Country Pop:** 2,290,237 (2005). **Capital:** Riga, pop. 739,232 (2002). **Terrain:** Fertile low-lying plains predominate in central Latvia, highlands in Vidzeme and Latgale to the east, and hilly moraine in the western Kurzeme region. **Ethnic Group(s):** Latvian Russian Belarusian Ukrainian Polish. **Religion(s):** Lutheran Orthodox Roman_Catholic. **Official Language(s):** Latvian. **Other Language(s):** Russian. **Government:** Parliamentary Democracy. **Independence:** 1991 (from Soviet Union). **Per Capita Income:** $3359 (2002). **GDP:** $8.41 billion (2002). Agriculture 5%. Financial Services 5%. Manufacturing 15%. Services 60%. Transport & Communications 15%. **Currency:** Latvian Lat (Ls).

INTERNATIONAL SCHOOL OF LATVIA
Day — Coed Gr PS-12

Jurmala LV 2010, Latvia. Viestura iela 6A. Tel: 371-7755018. Fax: 371-7755009. EST+7.
www.isl.edu.lv   E-mail: isloffice@isl.edu.lv
Michael P. Mack, Dir. PhD.
   Col Prep. IB PYP. IB MYP. IB Diploma. **Curr**—Intl. **Exams**—CEEB. **Feat**—Fr Ger Comp_Sci Latvian_Stud Studio_Art Visual_Arts Drama Music. **Supp**—ESL.
   Activities—Acad Govt/Pol Rec.
   Enr 172. B 93. G 79. Elem 127. Sec 45. US 27. Host 56. Other 89. Accepted: 95%. Avg class size: 12.
   Fac 31. M 11. F 16/4. US 18. Host 7. Other 6. Adv Deg: 48%.
   Grad '05—7. Col—4.
   Tui '05-'06: Day €5200-11,900 (+€2250). **Aid:** 17 pupils (€65,000).
   Bldgs 1. Class rms 25. Lib 14,000 vols. Sci labs 1. Comp labs 2. Auds 1. Theaters 1. Art studios 1. Music studios 1. Gyms 1. Fields 1. Pools 1.
   Est 1994. (Aug-June). Assoc: A/OPR/OS CIS NEASC.

With a curriculum that combines North American and European elements, ISL offers the full International Baccalaureate Program. The Primary Years Program (grades PS-5) and Middle Years Program (grades 6-10) lead up to the IB Diploma Program. Children in grades PS-5 remain in self-contained classes, while older students follow a departmentalized program. Instructors incorporate individualization as they see fit to meet the needs of the international student body.

ISL is located in the coastal town of Jurmala, not far from Riga.

LITHUANIA

Sq. Miles: 26,080 (About the size of West Virginia). **Country Pop:** 3,596,617 (2005). **Capital:** Vilnius, pop. 541,278. **Terrain:** Central lowland plains are separated by hilly uplands created by glacial drift. **Ethnic Group(s):** Lithuanian Polish Russian. **Religion(s):** Catholic Orthodox Protestant. **Official Language(s):** Lithuanian. **Other Language(s):** Russian Polish. **Government:** Parliamentary Democracy. **Independence:** 1990 (from Soviet Union). **Per Capita Income:** $6474 (2004).

GDP: $22.3 billion (2004). Agriculture 6%. Manufacturing 32%. Services 62%. **Currency:** Lithuanian Litai (LTL).

AMERICAN INTERNATIONAL SCHOOL OF VILNIUS
Day — Coed Gr PS-10

Vilnius 03106, Lithuania. c/o American Embassy, 6 Akmenu St. Tel: 370-5-212-10-31. Fax: 370-5-264-72-02. EST+7.
Contact: c/o American Embassy, PSC 78, Box V, APO, AE 09723.
www.aisv.lt   E-mail: office@aisvilnius.lt
Jeffrey Z. Haun, Dir.
  Pre-Prep. Curr—US. Feat—Fr Ger Lithuanian Computers Studio_Art Music. Supp—ESL.
  Enr 84.
  Tui '05-'06: Day €4100-19,500 (+€100-500).
  Est 1993. Nonprofit. Quar (Sept-June). Assoc: A/OPR/OS.

LUXEMBOURG

Sq. Miles: 1034 (About the size of Rhode Island). **Country Pop:** 468,571 (2005). **Capital:** Luxembourg, pop. 77,300 (2004). **Terrain:** Continuation of Belgian Ardennes in the north, heavily forested and slightly mountainous; extension of French Lorraine plateau in the south, with open, rolling countryside. **Ethnic Group(s):** Celtic French German. **Religion(s):** Roman_Catholic. **Official Language(s):** Luxembourgish French German. **Other Language(s):** English. **Government:** Constitutional Monarchy. **Independence:** 1839 (from The Netherlands). **Per Capita Income:** $58,900 (2004). **GDP:** $29.02 billion (2004). Agriculture 1%. Industry 16%. Services 83%. **Currency:** European Union Euro (€).

INTERNATIONAL SCHOOL OF LUXEMBOURG
Day — Coed Gr PS-12

1430 Luxembourg, Luxembourg. 36 Blvd Pierre Dupong. Tel: 352-260440. Fax: 352-26-044704. EST+6.
www.islux.lu   E-mail: information@islux.lu
Clayton W. Lewis, Dir.
  Col Prep. Gen Acad. IB Diploma. Curr—Intl. Exams—ACT CEEB TOEFL. Feat—Fr Ger Comp_Sci Geog Studio_Art Drama Music. Supp—ESL.
  Enr 598. B 279. G 319. Elem 441. Sec 157. US 113. Host 32. Other 453. Avg class size: 15.
  Fac 75. M 22/1. F 40/12. US 38. Host 3. Other 34. Adv Deg: 56%.
  Grad '05—28. Col—19. US Col—6.

Tui '05-'06: Day €10,250-14,070 (+€1000).
Summer: Enrich Rec. Tui Day €90/wk. 2 wks.
Bldgs 1. Libs 2. Sci labs 4. Comp labs 4. Auds 1. Art studios 2. Music studios 3. Gyms 1. Fields 1. Pools 1.
Est 1963. Nonprofit. Tri (Sept-June). Assoc: CIS MSA.

ISL serves children of the international community living in Luxembourg. Many students come from the US, with others from Norway, Sweden and the UK. The school's flexible college preparatory curriculum draws upon different national traditions and includes the International Baccalaureate Diploma program in grades 11 and 12.

Basketball, soccer, swimming, track, volleyball, yearbook, student council, choir and band are among the available activities.

ST. GEORGE'S INTERNATIONAL SCHOOL
Day — Coed Gr PS-8

2127 Weimershof, Luxembourg. Rue des Marguerites. Tel: 352-42-32-24. Fax: 352-42-32-34. EST+6.
www.st-georges.lu   E-mail: info@st-georges.lu
Heather Duxbury, Head.
Pre-Prep. **Curr**—UK. **Feat**—Fr Comp_Sci Studio_Art Music. **Supp**—ESL LD.
Tui '05-'06: Day €4919-9152 (+€400).
Est 1990. Tri (Sept-July).

MACEDONIA

Sq. Miles: 9781 (Slightly larger than Vermont). **Country Pop:** 2,045,262 (2005). **Capital:** Skopje, pop. 600,000 (2001). **Terrain:** Mountainous territory covered with deep basins and valleys; three large lakes, each divided by a frontier line; country bisected by the Vardar River. **Ethnic Group(s):** Macedonian Albanian Turkish Roma Serb. **Religion(s):** Eastern_Orthodox Muslim Catholic. **Other Language(s):** Macedonian Albanian Turkish Serbo-Croatian. **Government:** Democracy. **Independence:** 1991 (from Yugoslavia). **GDP:** $5.07 billion (2000). Agriculture 12%. Industry 32%. Services 56%. **Currency:** Macedonian Denar (MKD).

AMERICAN SCHOOL MACEDONIA
Day — Coed Gr PS-12

Skopje Macedonia. Ul Nikola Parapunov BB, Makoteks Kompleks, Karpos IV. Tel: 389-2-3063-265. Fax: 389-2-3091-332. EST+6.
Contact: 4430 Fountain Ave, Ste A, Los Angeles, CA 90029. Tel: 323-662-9787. Fax: 323-662-1569.

www.asm.edu.mk   E-mail: contact@asm.edu.mk
Mike Bujko, Supt. MA.

> **Col Prep. Curr**—US. **Exams**—ACT AP CEEB SSAT TOEFL. **Feat**—Fr Span Comp_Sci Studio_Art Drama. **Supp**—EFL ESL Tut.
>
> **Enr 63.** B 33. G 30. Elem 45. Sec 18. US 6. Other 57. Accepted: 90%. Yield: 100%. Avg class size: 6.
>
> **Fac 10.** M 3/2. F 3/2. US 3. Host 7. Adv Deg: 30%.
>
> **Grad '05—5. Col—4. US Col—4.** (Stanford 2, UCLA 1, Harvard 1).
>
> **Tui '05-'06: Day €3500.**
>
> Plant val $300,000. Bldgs 1. Lib 1200 vols. Comp labs 1. Gyms 1. Fields 1. Courts 1. Pools 1.
>
> **Est 1994.** Nonprofit. Sem (Sept-June).

Located in Macedonia's capital city, ASM conducts a traditional US-style program in a small-class setting. The student body at the elementary level consists of children from all over the world; in the higher grades, a higher number of Macedonian pupils enroll. Teachers come largely from the US, Canada or Macedonia. Typical of an American school, ASM prepares students for various US examinations, including the College Boards and the ACT.

QSI INTERNATIONAL SCHOOL OF SKOPJE

Day — Coed Gr PS-8

1000 Skopje, Macedonia. Inlindenska BB, Reon 55. Tel: 389-2-3067-678. Fax: 389-2-3062-250. EST+6.
www.qsi.org/mcn   E-mail: skopje@qsi.org
Eric Nelis, Dir.

> **Gen Acad. Curr**—US. **Feat**—Fr Ger Span Macedonian Comp_Sci Studio_Art Music. **Supp**—ESL.
>
> **Tui '05-'06: Day $5600-13,000** (+$100-1700).
>
> **Est 1996.** Nonprofit. Spons: Quality Schools International. Tri (Sept-June). Assoc: A/OPR/OS MSA.

MALTA

Sq. Miles: 122 (About one-tenth the size of Rhode Island.). **Country Pop:** 398,534 (2005). **Capital:** Valletta, pop. 7000 (2002). **Largest City:** Birkirkara, pop. 21,600 (2002). **Terrain:** Low hills. **Ethnic Group(s):** Arab Sicilian Norman Spanish Italian English. **Religion(s):** Roman_ Catholic. **Other Language(s):** Maltese English. **Government:** Republic. **Independence:** 1964 (from United Kingdom). **Per Capita Income:** $12,173 (2003). **GDP:** $4.85 billion (2003). Agriculture 2%. Industry 23%. Services 75%. **Currency:** Maltese Lira (Lm).

VERDALA INTERNATIONAL SCHOOL
Bdg — Coed Gr 7-12; Day — Coed PS-12

St Andrews STJ 14, Malta. Fort Pembroke. Tel: 356-21-375133. Fax: 356-21-372387. EST+6.
www.verdala.org   E-mail: vis@verdala.org
Adam Pleasance, Head. BA, MA.

Col Prep. IB Diploma. Curr—Intl UK US. Exams—IGCSE O-level. Feat—Fr Ital Span Comp_Sci Psych Visual_Arts Theater_Arts Bus.

Enr 230.

Fac 38.

Tui '05-'06: Bdg Lm4750-5200 (+Lm100-400). Day Lm2050-2500 (+Lm100-400).

Est 1976. Nonprofit. Sem (Sept-June). Assoc: A/OPR/OS MSA.

ST. EDWARD'S COLLEGE
MALTA
Day — Boys Gr K-10

Vittoriosa CSP 09, Malta. Triq San Dwardu, Birgu. Tel: 356-21827077. Fax: 356-21891557. EST+6.
www.stedwards.edu.mt   E-mail: hm@stedwards.edu.mt
Anthony Saliba, Head. BS, MEd.

Col Prep. Curr—Nat UK. Exams—IGCSE. Feat—Fr Ital Maltese Environ_Sci Comp Sci Econ Relig Studio_Art Drama Bus. Supp—LD

Sports—Basket X-country Gymnastics Hand Soccer Volley. Activities—Arts Govt/Pol Media Rec Service.

Enr 600. Accepted: 92%. Avg class size: 21.

Fac 71. M 32/3. F 34/2. Host 69. Other 2. Adv Deg: 5%.

Tui '05-'06: Day Lm786-1299 (+Lm70).

Libs 2. Sci labs 3. Comp labs 4. Theaters 1. Art studios 4. Music studios 1. Gyms 1. Basketball courts 2. Tennis courts 2.

Est 1929. Roman Catholic. Tri (Sept-June).

Conducted in the manner of an English public school, St. Edward's ultimately prepares its students for the IGCSE examinations. Course offerings broaden as boys progress through the junior school, the middle school and the senior school. Preparation for Malta's SEC examinations is also part of the senior school program. A learning disabilities specialist identifies, assesses and manages a range of learning disorders that includes dyslexia, dyspraxia, attentional disorders, Asperger's syndrome and specific language impairment.

Located in the virtual center of the Mediterranean, Malta has a sunny, warm climate. Vittoriosa is a fortified city whose buildings often date back to the 16th century.

MOLDOVA

Sq. Miles: 13,000 (Slightly larger than Maryland). Country Pop: 4,455,421 (2005). Capital: Chisinau, pop. 655,000. Terrain: Rolling steppe, gradual slope south to Black Sea. **Ethnic Group(s):** Moldovan Romanian Ukrainian Russian Gagauz Jewish Bulgarian. **Religion(s):** Orthodox_Christian Jewish Baptist. **Official Language(s):** Romanian. **Other Language(s):** Russian Ukrainian Gagauz. **Government:** Republic. **Independence:** 1991 (from Soviet Union). **Per Capita Income:** $760 (2004). **GDP:** $2.6 billion (2004). Agriculture 20%. Industry 24%. Services 56%. **Currency:** Moldovan Leu (MDL).

QSI INTERNATIONAL SCHOOL OF CHISINAU
Day — Coed Gr PS-7

Chisinau, Moldova. 18 Anton Crihan St. Tel: 373-2-2240-822. Fax: 373-2-2240-822. EST+7.
www.qsi.org/mdv   E-mail: chisinau@qsi.org
Mary Kay Smith, Dir.
    Gen **Acad. Curr**—US. **Feat**—Russ Romanian Computers Studio_Art Drama Music.
    Tui '05-'06: Day $5000-16,000 (+$100-1700).
    Nonprofit. Spons: Quality Schools International. Assoc: A/OPR/OS MSA.

MONACO

Sq. Miles: 1 (About the size of New York City's Central Park). **Country Pop:** 32,409 (2005). **Capital:** Monaco, pop. 32,409 (2005). **Terrain:** Hilly. **Ethnic Group(s):** French Italian Monegasque British Swiss German Belgian American. **Religion(s):** Roman_Catholic. **Official Language(s):** French. **Other Language(s):** English Italian Monegasque. **Government:** Constitutional Monarchy. **GDP:** $870 million (2000). Agriculture 17%. **Currency:** European Union Euro (€).

THE INTERNATIONAL SCHOOL OF MONACO
Day — Coed Gr PS-12

Monte Carlo 98000, Monaco. 12 Quai Antoine Premier. Tel: 377-93-25-68-20. Fax: 377-93-25-68-30. EST+6.
www.ismonaco.org   E-mail: ecoleism@cote-dazur.com
Mary Maccaud, Dir.
    Col Prep. IB PYP. IB MYP. IB Diploma. **Curr**—Intl. **Bilingual**—Fr. **Exams**—IGCSE. **Feat**—Span Comp_Sci Studio_Art Drama Music. **Supp**—ESL.
    Enr 320.
    Tui '06-'07: Day €13,700-16,500 (+€5000).
    Est 1994. Nonprofit. (Aug-June). Assoc: ECIS.

THE NETHERLANDS

Sq. Miles: 16,485 (Slightly less than twice the size of New Jersey).
Country Pop: 16,407,491 (2005). **Capital:** Amsterdam, pop. 739,104.
Terrain: Coastal lowland. **Ethnic Group(s):** Dutch Moroccans Turks
Surinamese. **Religion(s):** Roman_Catholic Protestant Muslim. **Offi-
cial Language(s):** Dutch. **Government:** Constitutional Monarchy. **Per
Capita Income:** $36,236 (2004). **GDP:** $591 billion (2004). Agriculture
2%. Industry 24%. Services 74%. **Currency:** European Union Euro (€).

INTERNATIONAL SCHOOL OF AMSTERDAM
Day — Coed Gr PS-12

**1180 AX Amstelveen, The Netherlands. PO Box 920. Tel: 31-20-347-1111. Fax: 31-
20-347-1222. EST+6.**
www.isa.nl   E-mail: admissions@isa.nl
Edward Greene, Dir. BA, MA, PhD. Julia True, Adm.
  Col Prep. IB PYP. IB MYP. IB Diploma. Curr—Intl. Exams—CEEB TOEFL.
    Feat—Dutch Fr Ger Japan Span Comp_Sci Econ Geog Studio_Art Theater
    Music. Supp—ESL LD.
  Sports—Basket Soccer Softball Swim Tennis Track Volley. Activities—Arts Rec.
  Enr 870. Elem 645. Sec 225. US 230. Host 80. Other 560. Avg class size: 20.
  Fac 131. M 36. F 66/29. US 27. Host 21. Other 83. Adv Deg: 35%.
  Grad '05—47. Col—47. US Col—6. (Stanford, Boston U, U of OR, U of WI-Madi-
    son, Suffolk, CO St).
  Tui '05-'06: Day €12,250-19,100.
  Bldgs 2. Class rms 70. 2 Libs 15,000 vols. Sci labs 5. Comp labs 4. Theaters 1. Art
    studios 4. Dance studios 1. Gyms 2. Courts 2.
  Est 1964. Nonprofit. Tri (Sept-June). Assoc: A/OPR/OS CIS NEASC.

Designed to meet the needs of the international community in Amsterdam, ISA
enrolls students from around the world. Most pupils come from the US, Japan, the
UK and The Netherlands. The school follows the entire IB progression, from the
Primary Years Program (ages 3-11), to the Middle Years Program (ages 11-16) to
the Diploma Program (ages 16-18).

A wide selection of activities, many of which incur a participation fee, includes
athletics, foreign language lessons and performing arts groups. Offerings in the
visual and performing arts are also plentiful. In addition, ISA schedules various
social events.

BRITISH SCHOOL OF AMSTERDAM
Day — Coed Ages 2-11

**1077 ME Amsterdam, The Netherlands. Anthonie van Dijckstraat 1. Tel: 31-20-679-
7840. Fax: 31-20-675-8396. EST+6.**
www.britams.nl   E-mail: info@britams.nl
M. W. G. Roberts, Prin. MA, MBA.

Pre-Prep. Curr—UK. **AP**—Comp_Sci. **Feat**—Dutch Fr Lat Span Geog Visual_Arts Music.
Tui '05-'06: Day €7980-12,060 (+€1500).
Est 1978. Nonprofit. Tri (Sept-July).

ARNHEM INTERNATIONAL SCHOOL

Day — Coed Gr PS-12

6835 HZ Arnhem, The Netherlands. Lorentz Lyceum, Groningensingel 1245. Tel: 31-26-320-0111. Fax: 31-26-320-0113. EST+6.
www.arnheminternationalschool.nl
E-mail: info@arnheminternationalschool.nl
M. van de Louw, Prin.

Col Prep. IB MYP. IB Diploma. Curr—Intl. **Exams**—CEEB IGCSE. **Feat**—Dutch Fr Ger Lat Span Comp_Sci Econ Studio_Art Drama Music.
Enr 225.
Tui '05-'06: Day €3150-4650.
(Aug-June).

AFNORTH INTERNATIONAL SCHOOL

Day — Coed Gr PS-12

6445 EE Brunssum, The Netherlands. Ferdinand Bolstraat 1. Tel: 31-45-527-8220. Fax: 31-45-527-8233. EST+6.
Contact: Unit 21606, APO, AE 09703.
www.afno-is.eu.dodea.edu   E-mail: ais.directorate@eu.dodea.edu
Benjamin M. Brigg, Dir. PhD.

Col Prep. Curr—Intl US Can. **Supp Lang**—Ger. **Exams**—AP. **AP**—Eng Fr Ger Span Calc Stats Bio Chem Physics Eur_Hist US_Hist World_Hist Comp_Govt & Pol Econ Psych US_Govt & Pol Art_Hist Studio_Art Music_Theory. **Feat**—Humanities Shakespeare Arabic ASL Dutch Greek Japan Port Russ Icelandic Korean Turkish Anat & Physiol Marine_Biol/Sci Comp_Sci Ceramics Sculpt Drama Journ. **Supp**—ESL.

Sports—Basket Baseball Cheer X-country Soccer Softball Swim Tennis Track Volley Wrestling. **Activities**—Acad Arts Govt/Pol Media.
Enr 1200.
Fac 102.
Tui '05-'06: Day €14,950-17,050.
Libs 1. Gyms 3. Fields 2. Courts 1. Pools 1.
Est 1967. Nonprofit. Quar (Aug-June).

Founded to serve children of Allied Forces North Regional Headquarters (AFNORTH) and other NATO personnel in the area, AIS is sponsored by four nations: the US, Canada, Germany and the United Kingdom. American, British, Canadian and international students engage in an English-speaking program, while pupils in the smaller German section have German as their language of instruction. The American curriculum features an array of foreign languages, as well as an extensive Advanced Placement program.

INTERNATIONAL SECONDARY SCHOOL
OF EINDHOVEN
Day — Coed Ages 11-18

5602 BH Eindhoven, The Netherlands. PO Box 1310. Tel: 31-40-242-6835. Fax: 31-40-256-6344. EST+6.
www.isse-school.nl   E-mail: isse@iae.nl
David Garner, Head. MA.
> **Col Prep. IB MYP. IB Diploma. Curr**—Intl. **Feat**—Dutch Fr Span Comp_Sci Studio_Art Music. **Supp**—ESL.
> **Enr 305.** US 40. Host 100. Other 165. Accepted: 90%. Avg class size: 16.
> **Fac 44.** M 16/2. F 20/6. US 8. Host 14. Other 22. Adv Deg: 27%.
> **Tui '05-'06: Day €4300-5438.**
> Libs 1. Sci labs 4. Lang labs 1. Comp labs 2. Art studios 2. Music studios 1. Gyms 1. Courts 2.
> **Est 1974.** Tri (Sept-July).

The English section at this school provides a bicultural education for members of the international community who have an English-speaking background. Much of the student body is from The Netherlands, while the remainder comes from the UK, the US and more than 20 other nations. Students take either a pre-university program or a general course in preparation for technical training. All students study Dutch to facilitate communication with pupils in the other sections.

REGIONAL INTERNATIONAL SCHOOL
Day — Coed Gr PS-6

5654 PA Eindhoven, The Netherlands. Humperdincklaan 4. Tel: 31-40-251-9437. Fax: 31-40-252-7675. EST+6.
www.riseindhoven.nl   E-mail: info@riseindhoven.nl
Henk A. Schol, Head.
> **Gen Acad. Curr**—Intl UK. **Supp Lang**—Dutch. **Feat**—Dutch Fr Computers Geog Studio_Art Drama Music. **Supp**—Dev_Read EFL ESL Rem_Math Rem_Read.
> **Enr 441.** B 238. G 203. Elem 441. US 12. Host 149. Other 280. Avg class size: 18.
> **Fac 55.** M 10/1. F 19/25. US 2.
> **Grad '05—29.**
> **Tui '05-'06: Day €3010.**
> Bldgs 1. Class rms 30. Libs 2. Lang labs 2. Comp labs 1. Gyms 2. Fields 1.
> **Est 1965.** Nonprofit. Tri (Aug-July).

RIS was established to serve the needs of the international community in the Eindhoven area. The curriculum, which utilizes English as the language of instruction, is compatible with educational systems used in Holland, England, the US, France, Belgium and Germany. Friday afternoon activities, ranging from soccer to cooking and from aerobics to ceramics, along with various school outings, enrich the academic program.

INTERNATIONAL SCHOOL OF THE HAGUE
Day — Coed Ages 11-18

2597 GV The Hague, The Netherlands. Theo Mann Bouwmeesterlaan 75. Tel: 31-70-328-14-50. Fax: 31-70-328-20-49. EST+6.
www.ishthehague.nl   E-mail: admissions@ishthehague.nl
Pat Sullivan, Head. MA.
  Col Prep. IB Diploma. Curr—Intl. **Exams**—IGCSE. **Feat**—Dutch Fr Ger Span Comp_Sci Econ Geog Bus.
  Enr 600.
  Tui '03-'04: Day €4538-5445.
  Est 1991. Nonprofit. Sem. Assoc: A/OPR/OS.

THE INTERNATIONAL SCHOOL HILVERSUM
ALBERDINGK THIJM
Day — Coed Gr 1-12

1213 AL Hilversum, The Netherlands. Emmastraat 56. Tel: 31-35-672-9931. Fax: 31-35-672-9939. EST+6.
www.klg.nl/ish   E-mail: ish@klg.nl
Jetty van Driel, Head. MA. **Glyn Jones, Adm.**
  Col Prep. IB PYP. IB MYP. IB Diploma. Curr—Intl. **Supp Lang**—Dutch. **Exams**—CEEB. **Supp**—ESL.
  Activities—Arts Rec.
  Enr 400. B 200. G 200. Accepted: 80%. Yield: 80%. Avg class size: 22.
  Fac 50. US 4. Host 22. Other 24.
  Grad '05—52.
  Tui '05-'06: Day €4275-5370.
  (Sept-June).

ISH offers the three International Baccalaureate programs: the Primary Years Program for students ages 3-11, the Middle Years Program for students ages 11-16, and the Diploma Program for ages 16-18. Although English is the language of instruction, many students enter the school before reaching fluency, and ESL instruction is offered. Grade 6 students take Dutch and French, and beginning in grade 7 students choose from French, Spanish and German language studies.

Depending on the language of study, students in grades 8 and 9 participate in exchanges with international schools in France, Spain or Germany.

VIOLENSCHOOL INTERNATIONAL DEPARTMENT
Day — Coed Gr PS-6

1213 BH Hilversum, The Netherlands. Rembrandtlaan 30. Tel: 31-35-621-6053. Fax: 31-35-624-6878. EST+6.
www.violenschoolintdept.nl   E-mail: info@violenschoolintdept.nl
Atse R. Spoor, Head.
  Pre-Prep. IB PYP. Curr—Intl. **Feat**—Dutch Visual_Arts Drama Music. **Supp**—ESL.
  Enr 280.

Fac 16.
Tui '05-'06: Day €2300.
Est 1986. (Sept-July).

INTERNATIONAL SCHOOL MAASTRICHT
Day — Coed Ages 11-19

6201 BD Maastricht, The Netherlands. PO Box 1187. Tel: 31-43-367-4666. Fax: 31-43-367-0809. EST+6.
www.ismaastricht.nl   E-mail: admin@ism.portamosana.nl
Julia Paul, Head. BA.
   Col Prep. IB Diploma. Curr—Intl UK. **Exams**—IGCSE. **Feat**—Humanities Dutch Fr Ger Span Comp_Sci. **Supp**—ESL.
   Enr 215.
   Tui '05-'06: Day €5000 (+€150).
   Est 1984. Nonprofit. Spons: Jeanne d'Arc College. Tri (Sept-July).

HET RIJNLANDS LYCEUM OEGSTGEEST
INTERNATIONAL SCHOOL
Day — Coed Gr 6-12

2341 BA Oegstgeest, The Netherlands. Apollolaan 1. Tel: 31-71-519-35-55. Fax: 31-71-519-35-50. EST+6.
www.isrlo.nl   E-mail: administration@rijnlands.ros.nl
M. F. Elkerbout, Head. P. Taylor, Adm.
   Col Prep. Gen Acad. IB Diploma. Curr—Intl. **Feat**—Dutch Fr Ger Span Studio_Art Drama Music. **Supp**—ESL Tut.
   Enr 250. Accepted: 70%.
   Fac 55. M 14/7. F 7/27. US 2. Host 30. Other 23. Adv Deg: 85%.
   Grad '05—35. **Col**—33. **US Col**—2. (Brown, Boston U).
   Tui '05-'06: Day €4600-5500. Aid: 3 pupils (€9000).
   Bldgs 2. Class rms 65. Libs 1. Sci labs 9. Lang labs 6. Comp labs 2. Auds 1. Art studios 3. Music studios 1. Dance studios 1. Gyms 3. Fields 1.
   Est 1956. Nonprofit. Sem (Aug-July).

The international program, which serves pupils from more than 40 countries, progresses from the interdisciplinary International Baccalaureate Program to the IB Diploma Program. In addition to academic skills development, the curriculum addresses social and cultural issues relevant to the varied student body. Although boys and girls may not board on campus, Het Rijnlands provides assistance upon request for those students seeking accommodations.

Among the school's extracurricular options are sports, yearbook, orchestra, student council, drama, magazine and choir.

INTERNATIONAL SCHOOL EERDE

Bdg — Coed Gr 2-12; Day — Coed PS-12

7731 PJ Ommen, The Netherlands. Kasteellaan 1. Tel: 31-529-451452. Fax: 31-529-456377. EST+6.

www.eerde.nl   E-mail: info@eerde.nl

H. G. Voogd, Prin.

Col Prep. IB Diploma. Curr—Intl. Exams—IGCSE. Feat—Dutch Fr Ger Ital Russ Span Finnish Swedish Comp_Sci Econ. Supp—LD Rem_Math Rem_Read.

Sports—Swim Tennis. Activities—Acad Arts Media Rec.

Enr 130. Avg class size: 10.

Tui '05-'06: Bdg €37,785 (+€6500). Day €10,300-15,155 (+€5500).

Dorms 2. Sci labs 1. Comp labs 1. Art studios 1. Gyms 1. Fields 1. Courts 1. Pools 1.

Est 1933. Nonprofit. (Sept-July). Assoc: ECIS.

Located on an estate of 2000 acres, this school combines principles utilized in England and the US during the primary grades (K-5), then prepares students for the IGCSE and the IB in the secondary years. An individualized program is designed for each student after thorough assessment. Apart from formal lessons, there are scheduled periods of study when teachers are available for consultation and guidance.

The school's main building, surrounded by forest, moat and lawns, is a chateau in the manner of Louis XIV, dating from 1715 and located on a site occupied by successive castles going back for centuries. Enrollment is largely made up of Dutch and British students, with approximately six additional nationalities represented. Admission is granted only after a personal interview with the school head.

AMERICAN INTERNATIONAL SCHOOL OF ROTTERDAM

Day — Coed Gr PS-12

3055 WJ Rotterdam, The Netherlands. Verhulstlaan 21. Tel: 31-10-422-5351. Fax: 31-10-422-4075. EST+6.

www.aisr.nl   E-mail: information@aisr.nl

Brian Atkins, Dir.

Col Prep. IB Diploma. Curr—Intl. Exams—CEEB. Feat—Dutch Fr Ger Span.

Enr 226. B 112. G 114. Elem 180. Sec 46.

Fac 42.

Tui '05-'06: Day €10,400-14,500 (+€1700).

Est 1959. Nonprofit. Sem (Aug-June). Assoc: A/OPR/OS CIS NEASC.

ROTTERDAM INTERNATIONAL SECONDARY SCHOOL
WOLFERT VAN BORSELEN

Day — Coed Gr 7-12

3039 KK Rotterdam, The Netherlands. Bentincklaan 280. Tel: 31-10-890-7745. Fax: 31-10-890-7755. EST+6.

www.wolfert.nl/riss   E-mail: info.riss@wolfert.nl

Aidan Campbell, Head. Alexa Nijpels Bell, Adm.

Col Prep. IB Diploma. Curr—Intl UK. Exams—IGCSE. Feat—Dutch Fr Ger Studio_Art. Supp—ESL Rem_Math Rem_Read Tut.
Activities—Rec.
Enr 165. US 8. Host 21. Other 136. Accepted: 90%. Yield: 100%. Avg class size: 15.
Fac 31. M 7. F 8/16. US 1. Host 2. Other 28. Adv Deg: 12%.
Grad '05—18.
Tui '05-'06: Day €6800.
Est 1987. Tri.

Founded to educate the international community of Rotterdam, RISS emphasizes internationalism at all levels. In the Foundation Course (ages 11-14) students learn Dutch and may also study either French or German. Preparation for the IGCSE and IB Diploma is available for older students, with many earning a bilingual diploma. Students from other countries are encouraged to integrate native language and culture into their studies.

THE BRITISH SCHOOL IN THE NETHERLANDS
Day — Coed Gr PS-13

2252 BG Voorschoten, The Netherlands. Jan van Hooflaan 3. Tel: 31-71-560-2222. Fax: 31-71-560-2200. EST+6.
www.britishschool.nl   E-mail: info@britishschool.nl
Trevor Rowell, Prin. Rinske Drayer, Adm.
Col Prep. Curr—UK. Exams—ACI GCSE AS-level A-level. Feat—Dutch Fr Ger Span Environ_Sci Comp_Sci Econ Geog Govt Psych Studio_Art Drama Music. Supp—ESL.
Sports—Basket F_Hockey Golf Gymnastics Rugby Soccer Swim Tennis. Activities—Acad Arts Govt/Pol Rec.
Enr 1600. B 800. G 800. Elem 1200. Sec 400. Avg class size: 22.
Fac 153.
Grad '05—68. Col—62. US Col—3. (Vassar, PA St, U of IL-Urbana).
Tui '05-'06: Day €10,620-14,250 (+€450).
Est 1935. Tri (Sept-July).

The British School occupies five separate sites: three in The Hague, a senior school (serving ages 11-18) in Voorschoten and a small junior school (ages 5-11) in Assen. While the senior school provides a British education that follows the National Curriculum, the program also has an international dimension. Much of the student body, which represents roughly 60 nations, spends three or four years at the school prior to relocation, but about 30 percent of the pupils remain until graduation.

Music and drama are important elements of the curriculum, and course work places special emphasis on public speaking and oratory. Boys and girls may prepare for GCSE and AS- and A-level examinations in a wide range of subjects. Students make extensive cultural use of The Hague, and the school also schedules frequent cultural, language and athletic excursions to other countries.

AMERICAN SCHOOL OF THE HAGUE
Day — Coed Gr PS-12

2241 BX Wassenaar, The Netherlands. Rijksstraatweg 200. Tel: 31-70-512-1060. Fax: 31-70-511-2400. EST+6.
www.ash.nl   E-mail: admission@ash.nl
Richard Spradling, Supt.

    Col Prep. IB Diploma. Curr—Intl US. **Exams**—AP. **AP**—Eng Fr Ger Span Calc Bio Chem Human_Geog Physics US_Hist Econ Studio_Art Music_Theory. **Supp**—ESL.
    Enr 1050. Elem 695. Sec 355.
    Fac 141.
    Tui '05-'06: Day €12,300-14,900 (+€1500).
    Est 1953. Nonprofit. Sem (Aug-June). Assoc: CIS MSA.

NORWAY

Sq. Miles: 150,000 (Slightly larger than New Mexico). **Country Pop:** 4,593,041 (2005). **Capital:** Oslo, pop. 521,886 (2004). **Terrain:** Rugged with high plateaus, steep fjords, mountains, and fertile valleys. **Ethnic Group(s):** Norwegian Sami. **Religion(s):** Lutheran Pentecostal_Christian Roman_Catholic Muslim. **Official Language(s):** Bokmaal_Norwegian Nynorsk_Norwegian. **Other Language(s):** English. **Government:** Hereditary Constitutional Monarchy. **Independence:** 1905 (from Sweden). **GDP:** $183 billion (2004). Agriculture 2%. Industry 36%. Services 62%. **Currency:** Norwegian Krone (NKr).

OSLO INTERNATIONAL SCHOOL
Day — Coed Gr K-12

1318 Bekkestua, Norway. PO Box 53. Tel: 47-67-81-82-90. Fax: 47-67-81-82-91. EST+6.
www.oslointernationalschool.no   E-mail: ois.main@aktivepost.no
Barbara Carlsen, Dir.

    Col Prep. IB Diploma. Curr—Intl UK. **Exams**—GCSE IGCSE. **Feat**—Fr Ger Span Comp_Sci Studio_Art Drama Music. **Supp**—ESL.
    Sports—Basket Soccer. **Activities**—Arts Rec.
    Enr 500.
    Fac 71. M 10/3. F 36/22. US 11. Host 5. Other 55.
    Tui '05-'06: Day NKr30,000-130,000 (+NKr8525).
    Est 1963. Nonprofit. Tri (Aug-June). Assoc: A/OPR/OS CIS NEASC.

OIS provides an English-language education for the international community of Oslo. The primary school, which also provides English lessons to students who are nonnative speakers, emphasizes independent learning and multiculturalism. Secondary school students prepare for the IGCSE examinations and pursue the

International Baccalaureate Diploma. Graduates attend universities in Norway, Europe and North America.

THE INTERNATIONAL SCHOOL OF BERGEN

Day — Coed Gr PS-10

5081 Bergen, Norway. Vilhelm Bjerknesvei 15. Tel: 47-55-30-63-30. Fax: 47-55-30-63-31. EST+6.
www.isb.gs.hl.no   E-mail: info@isb.gs.hl.no
June Murison, Dir. BSc.
> **Gen Acad. IB MYP. Curr**—Intl. **Feat**—Fr Norwegian Comp_Sci Studio_Art Music. **Supp**—ESL LD.
> **Enr 210.** B 105. G 105. Elem 180. Sec 30. US 15. Host 90. Other 105. Accepted: 90%. Yield: 95%. Avg class size: 16.
> **Fac 27.** M 4. F 13/10. US 5. Host 3. Other 19. Adv Deg: 11%.
> **Grad '05—15.**
> **Tui '05-'06: Day NKr30,000-126,000.**
> Class rms 10. Lib 5000 vols. Sci labs 1. Comp labs 1. Art studios 1. Music studios 1. Gyms 2. Pools 1. Rinks 1.
> **Est 1975.** Nonprofit. Tri (Aug-June). Assoc: CIS NEASC.

ISB was founded to meet the educational needs of children of expatriate oil company personnel and to attract more international corporations to the Bergen area. The school has since become known outside of the corporate community, and an increasing number of students now enroll from the local area. Near the mountains, the school rests at the foot of a lake. Pupils follow the IB Middle Years Program, which is rarely conducted in Norway. The international curriculum also includes ESL and a program for children with learning disabilities.

Each year, boys and girls embark on numerous excursions into the countryside.

RED CROSS NORDIC UNITED WORLD COLLEGE

Bdg — Coed Gr 11-12

6968 Flekke, Fjaler, Norway. Tel: 47-57-73-70-00. Fax: 47-57-73-70-01. EST+6.
www.rcnuwc.uwc.org   E-mail: info@rcnuwc.uwc.org
> **Col Prep. IB Diploma. Curr**—Intl. **Feat**—Span Norwegian Environ_Sci Econ Pol_Sci Peace_Stud World_Relig Studio_Art Music.
> **Enr 200.**
> Dorms 5. Lib 5300 vols. Comp labs 1. Dark rms 1. Theaters 1.
> **Est 1995.**

RCNUWC is one of 10 related UWC international schools dedicated to promoting international understanding through education. The organization has campuses in Britain, Canada, Hong Kong, India, Italy, Norway, Singapore, Swaziland, the US and Venezuela, and each school is a community representing more than 70 countries. All students follow the International Baccalaureate curriculum in preparation for the IB exams.

Community service, outdoor programs and events pertaining to global issues supplement the academic offerings.

INTERNATIONAL SCHOOL OF STAVANGER
Day — Coed Gr PS-12

4043 Hafrsfjord, Norway. Treskeveien 3. Tel: 47-51-55-43-00. Fax: 47-51-55-43-01. EST+6.
www.isstavanger.no　E-mail: lduevel@isstavanger.no
Linda M. Duevel, Dir. PhD.

> **Col Prep. IB Diploma. Curr**—Intl. **Exams**—CEEB IGCSE. **Feat**—Fr Span Norwegian Comp_Sci Econ Geog Psych.
> **Enr 462.** Elem 325. Sec 137.
> **Fac 66.** M 20. F 46. Adv Deg: 72%.
> **Grad '05—34.**
> **Tui '05-'06: Day $23,076.**
> Bldgs 1. 2 Libs 13,700 vols. Art studios 1. Music studios 1. Theater/auds 1. Gyms 3. Fields 2. Courts 2.
> **Est 1966.** Nonprofit. Sem (Aug-June). Assoc: A/OPR/OS CIS NEASC.

Established by representatives of major oil companies operating in the North Sea, ISS draws the majority of its students from families associated with the oil industry and a local NATO base, but enrollment is open to all English-speaking pupils. The curriculum is internationally based, and elementary students work in traditional self-contained classrooms. The secondary school's college preparatory curriculum, which features advanced courses and independent study, offers both the IGCSE and the International Baccalaureate Diploma program. Stavenger administers a number of testing programs, in addition to school examinations. Graduates matriculate at competitive universities throughout the world.

Stavanger's 15-acre site is a short distance from the city center. Extracurricular activities include varsity team sports, intramural sports for elementary and secondary students, and a wide range of clubs. Company-sponsored pupils receive a tuition discount.

SKAGERAK INTERNATIONAL SCHOOL
Day — Coed Gr PS-12

3222 Sandefjord, Norway. Framnesveien 7. Tel: 47-33-42-38-00. Fax: 47-33-46-93-63. EST+6.
www.skagerak.org　E-mail: office@skagerak.org
Lars Martin Ask, Prin. BA.

> **Col Prep. IB Diploma. Curr**—Intl. **Feat**—Fr Ger Norwegian Econ Psych Theater_Arts.
> **Tui '06-'07: Day NKr28,000-34,000** (+NKr9000-10,000).
> **Est 1991.** Sem (Aug-June).

THE BRITISH INTERNATIONAL SCHOOL
OF STAVANGER
Day — Coed Gr PS-7

4032 Stavanger, Norway. Gauselbakken 107. Tel: 47-51950250. Fax: 47-51950251. EST+6.

www.biss.no   E-mail: office@biss.no
Zelma Roisli, Prin.
  Gen Acad. Curr—UK. Exams—CEE. Feat—Fr Norwegian Music.
  Enr 150.
  Tui '05-'06: Day NKr11,700-50,000 (+NKr100).
  Est 1977. Nonprofit. (Aug-June).

BIRRALEE INTERNATIONAL SCHOOL TRONDHEIM
Day — Coed Ages 4-13

7013 Trondheim, Norway. Bispegata 9C. Tel: 47-73-870260. Fax: 47-73-870265. EST+6.
www.birralee.no   E-mail: principal@birralee.no
Trude Farstad, Prin.
  Gen Acad. Curr—Intl Nat UK. Feat—Norwegian Computers Relig Studio_Art
    Drama Music. Supp—ESL.
  Activities—Arts Govt/Pol Rec.
  Enr 175. B 83. G 92. Accepted: 95%. Avg class size: 16.
  Fac 15. M /1. F 11/3. US 1. Host 3. Other 11.
  Tui '05-'06: Day NKr15,000-20,200.
  Bldgs 3. Class rms 15. Libs 2. Comp labs 1. Art studios 1. Music studios 1. Dance
    studios 1. Gyms 1.
  Est 1973. Nonprofit. Sem (Aug-June).

Serving both local families and those from overseas who are spending one to five years in the area, Birralee provides an English-speaking education for elementary-age children. During the junior years (ages 7-11), reading is a particular point of emphasis. Instructors often teach geography, history, art, drama, technology, home economics and music through cross-curricular topics. Children study Scandinavian geography and history to gain a better awareness of their environment. Pupils in the senior department (ages 11-13) take part in a program that stresses creative, practical and logical thinking. Projects and group work enrich the curriculum at this level.

The school is situated in the center of Trondheim, one of Norway's largest cities. Close to the city's older section, with its cathedral and museums, Birralee's location allows students to easily visit cultural and historical sites of interest. The expansive ski terrain surrounding the city provides opportunities for cross-country and downhill skiing and ski jumping. Pupils are encouraged to take part in both winter and summer sports.

POLAND

Sq. Miles: 120,725 (About the size of New Mexico). **Country Pop:** 38,635,144 (2005). **Capital:** Warsaw, pop. 1,690,821 (2004). **Terrain:** Flat plain, except mountains along southern border. **Ethnic Group(s):** Polish German Ukrainian Belorussian Lithuanian. **Religion(s):** Roman_Catholic Eastern_Orthodox Uniat Protestant Jewish. **Official**

Language(s): Polish. **Government:** Republic. **Independence:** 1918.
GDP: $244 billion (2004). Agriculture 3%. Industry 31%. Services 66%.
Currency: Polish Zloty (zl).

AMERICAN SCHOOL OF WARSAW
Day — Coed Gr PS-12

05-520 Konstancin-Jeziorna, Poland. Bielawa, ul Warszawska 202. Tel: 48-22-702-8500. Fax: 48-22-702-8599. EST+6.
www.asw.waw.pl   E-mail: admissions@asw.waw.pl
Charles Barder, Dir.

 Col Prep. IB Diploma. Curr—Intl US. Exams—ACT CEEB SSAT. Feat—Dutch Fr Ger Span Polish Swedish Comp_Sci Econ Govt Psych Photog Studio_Art Theater_Arts Music. Supp—Dev_Read ESL Makeup Rem_Math Rem_Read.
 Enr 824. Elem 598. Sec 226. Avg class size: 20.
 Fac 100.
 Grad '05—44. Col—42.
 Tui '05-'06: Day $9312-17,052.
 Bldgs 7. Class rms 56. Lib 7500 vols. Comp labs 2. Gyms 1. Fields 2.
 Est 1953. Nonprofit. Sem (Aug-June). Assoc: A/OPR/OS CIS NEASC.

This school offers a complete educational program to the children of the international diplomatic and business community of Warsaw. Situated in the district of Konstancin, the school is a short drive south of the center of the city. The elementary curriculum emphasizes individualized and small-group instruction in order to maximize development of basic communication, computational and thinking skills. The high school curriculum features an IB program and preparation for the SAT and AP exams. In addition to the basics, art, music and physical education are offered at all levels.

Student activities include intramural and interscholastic sports, music, drama and interest clubs.

BRITISH INTERNATIONAL SCHOOL OF CRACOW
Day — Coed Ages 3-19

31-108 Krakow, Poland. ul Smolensk 25. Tel: 48-12-292-64-80. Fax: 48-12-292-64-81. EST+6.
www.bisc.krakow.pl   E-mail: office@bisc.krakow.pl
Andy Harris, Head.

 Col Prep. IB Diploma. Curr—Intl UK. Exams—GCSE IGCSE AS-level A-level. Feat—Fr Ger Japan Polish Comp_Sci Studio_Art Drama Music. Supp—ESL LD.
 Activities—Acad Arts Media Rec.
 Enr 144. B 64. G 80. US 5. Host 20. Other 119. Accepted: 100%. Yield: 100%. Avg class size: 9.
 Fac 37. M 5/4. F 14/14. US 2. Host 17. Other 18. Adv Deg: 48%.
 Grad '05—3. Col—3.
 Tui '05-'06: Day €9900 (+€500).
 Est 1995. Tri (Sept-June).

Located in the center of the city, BISC follows the English National Curriculum. Preschool classes focus on creative play, while also addressing children's basic reading and writing skills. In the primary school, course work emphasizes the core subjects of English and math, with classes grouped according to ability. Secondary schoolers prepare first for the IGCSE, then either the IB Diploma or the AS- and A-level examinations.

Musical and dramatic productions take place throughout the year, and local field trips provide enrichment at all grade levels.

THE INTERNATIONAL SCHOOL OF KRAKOW
Day — Coed Gr PS-12

30-074 Krakow, Poland. ul Kazimierza Wielkiego 33. Tel: 48-12-632-25-42. Fax: 48-12-632-25-42. EST+6.
www.iskonline.org   E-mail: admin@iskonline.org
Erica T. Mazzeo, Dir. MEd.
  Gen Acad. Curr—Intl Nat US. **Exams**—AP CEEB TOEFL GCSE IGCSE A-level. **Feat**—Dutch Fr Ger Polish Comp_Sci Studio_Art Music. **Supp**—Dev_Read EFL ESL Rem_Math Rem_Read Rev Tut.
  Activities—Acad Arts Rec.
  Enr 72. Elem 55. Sec 17. US 26. Host 4. Other 42. Accepted: 100%. Avg class size: 10.
  Fac 20. M 2/5. F 8/5. Adv Deg: 50%.
  Tui '06-'07: Day €10,000 (+€900). **Aid:** 5 pupils ($50,000).
  Bldgs 1. Class rms 8. Lib 8000 vols. Sci labs 1. Lang labs 2. Comp labs 1. Art studios 1. Music studios 1. Gyms 1. Fields 1. Pools 1. Rinks 1.
  Est 1994. Nonprofit. Sem (Sept-June). Assoc: A/OPR/OS.

Focusing on core academic skills, ISK conducts an English-medium educational program for the international community of the Krakow area that facilitates the transition to a home country school or another international school. The US and international curricula incorporate ESL, TOEFL and SAT preparation, as well as language courses in French, German, Dutch and Polish.

The school's high school program resulted from a partnership with a well-regarded Polish school. Because of this relationship, a combined class of ISK students and Polish public school pupils receive a traditional, English-medium secondary education. The school maintains small-group settings for both academic courses and activities.

BRITISH SCHOOL WARSAW
Day — Coed Gr PS-12

02-943 Warsaw, Poland. Ul Limanowskiego 15. Tel: 48-22-842-32-81. Fax: 48-22-842-32-65. EST+6.
www.thebritishschool.pl   E-mail: british@thebritishschool.pl
Tom McGrath, Head.
  Col Prep. IB Diploma. Curr—Intl UK. **Exams**—GCSE IGCSE. **Feat**—Fr Polish

Comp_Sci Relig Studio_Art Music. **Supp**—ESL.
Enr 500.
Tui '05-'06: Day £3750-8825.
Est 1992. Tri (Sept-July).

PORTUGAL

Sq. Miles: 35,672 (Slightly smaller than Indiana). **Country Pop:** 10,566,212 (2005). **Capital:** Lisbon, pop. 1,900,000. **Terrain:** Mountainous in the north; rolling plains in the central south. **Religion(s):** Roman_Catholic. **Official Language(s):** Portuguese. **Government:** Republic. **GDP:** $188.7 billion (2004). Agriculture 6%. Industry 30%. Services 64%. **Currency:** European Union Euro (€).

ESCOLA INTERNACIONAL SAO LOURENCO
Day — Coed Gr PS-12

8135 Almancil, Algarve, Portugal. Cx 445N, Sitio da Rabona. Tel: 351-289-398-328. Fax: 351-289-398-298. EST+5.
www.eisl-pt.org   E-mail: eisl@mail.telepac.pt
Robert Taylor, Dir. BEd. **Brigitta Fluckiger, Adm.**

    Col Prep. Curr—UK. **Exams**—GCSE IGCSE A-level. **Feat**—Fr Port Comp_Sci Studio_Art Music Bus. **Supp**—Dev_Read ESL LD Rem_Math Rem_Read Tut.
    Sports—Basket X-country Soccer. **Activities**—Acad Arts Rec.
    Enr 266. B 140. G 126. Elem 204. Sec 62. US 3. Host 26. Other 237. Accepted: 95%. Yield: 98%. Avg class size: 20.
    Fac 35. M 5/2. F 23/5. US 1. Host 3. Other 31.
    Grad '05—8. **Col**—8.
    Tui '05-'06: Day €5205-9090 (+€275-400).
    Class rms 14. Sci labs 2. Comp labs 1. Gyms 1. Fields 1. Pools 1.
    Est 1991. Nonprofit. Tri (Sept-June).

This nonselective school follows a modified version of the English National Curriculum. Instruction in most subjects is in English, although Portuguese is introduced in the foundation stage and is integrated into each class' curriculum. Older students prepare for the IGCSE and A- and AS-level examinations. Drama and music are part of the curriculum through grade 8, while physical education is compulsory through grade 10. Frequent educational and recreational trips enrich classroom work.

Local community service, which is an area of emphasis, includes environmental projects, cultural events, sports competitions and fundraising work.

INTERNATIONAL PREPARATORY SCHOOL
Day — Coed Gr PS-6

2775-557 Carcavelos, Portugal. Rua do Boror 12. Tel: 351-21457-0149. Fax: 351-21457-3501. EST+5.
www.ipsschool.org
    Gen Acad. Curr—UK. **Feat**—Dutch Fr Port Studio_Art Drama Music. **Supp**—ESL. **Enr 160.**
    Est 1982. Sem (Sept-June).

ST. JULIAN'S SCHOOL
Day — Coed Gr PS-12

2776-601 Carcavelos, Portugal. Quinta Nova. Tel: 351-21-458-5300. Fax: 351-21-458-5313. EST+5.
www.stjulians.com   **E-mail:** mail@stjulians.com
David Smith, Head. BS, DipEd.
    Col Prep. IB Diploma. Curr—Intl Nat UK. **Exams**—GCSE IGCSE. **Feat**—Comp_Sci Econ Philos Studio_Art Music Bus.
    Enr 900.
    Est 1932. Nonprofit. Tri (Sept-June). Assoc: CIS NEASC.

ST. DOMINIC'S INTERNATIONAL SCHOOL
Day — Coed Gr PS-12

2789-506 Sao Domingos de Rana, Portugal. Rua Maria Brown. Tel: 351-21-444-04-34. Fax: 351-21-444-30-72. EST+5.
www.dominics-int.org   **E-mail:** adm@dominic.mailpac.pt
Maria do Rosario Empis, Prin.
    Col Prep. IB PYP. IB MYP. IB Diploma. Curr—Intl. **Exams**—CEEB IGCSE. **Feat**—Dutch Fr Ger Port Span Swedish Comp_Sci Ethics Relig Studio_Art Drama Music. **Supp**—ESL LD Makeup Rem_Math Rem_Read Tut.
    Enr 650. B 325. G 325. Accepted: 80%. Avg class size: 22.
    Fac 72. M 23. F 49. Adv Deg: 27%.
    Grad '05—50. Col—49. US Col—1.
    Tui '02-'03: Day €4981-12,656 (+€2000). **Aid:** 15 pupils (€30,000).
    Plant val €5,000,000. Bldgs 2. Class rms 40. Lib 7000 vols. Sci labs 5. Comp labs 2. Auds 1. Gyms 2. Fields 1. Courts 4.
    Est 1964. Nonprofit. Tri (Sept-June). Assoc: CIS NEASC.

St. Dominic's was established as the international branch of the Colegio do Bom Sucesso, which was founded more than a century ago in Belem by the Irish Dominican Sisters. The school provides English-medium instruction for children of the international community at all grade levels. The curriculum is geared towards ultimately preparing students for the IB examinations. Primary years (grades PS-6) course work includes Portuguese, Swedish, information technology and religion, in addition to the standard subjects. In grades 7-10, such classes as German, media studies, ethics and international studies join the curriculum. St. Dominic's final two years focus primarily on readying pupils for either vocational tests or the IB Diploma.

Cocurricular activities, held at lunchtime and after school, comprise art, drama, music, computer, sports, languages, ballet and judo.

CARLUCCI AMERICAN INTERNATIONAL SCHOOL OF LISBON

Day — Coed Gr PS-12

2710-301 Sintra, Portugal. Rua Antonio dos Reis 95, Linho. Tel: 351-21-923-9800. Fax: 351-21-923-9899. EST+5.

www.caislisbon.com   E-mail: tesc0893@mail.telepac.pt

Blannie M. Curtis, Dir. MEd. **Cindy Ferrell, Adm.**

  Col Prep. IB Diploma. Curr—Intl US. **Exams**—CEEB SSAT TOEFL GCSE. **Feat**— Fr Port Comp_Sci Studio_Art Music. **Supp**—Dev_Read EFL ESL LD Makeup Rem_Math Rem_Read Rev Tut.

  Enr 435. Elem 321. Sec 114. US 77. Host 191. Other 167. Avg class size: 18.

  Fac 56. M 14. F 41/1. US 36. Host 9. Other 11. Adv Deg: 58%.

  Grad '05—39. **Col**—39. **US Col**—6. (Wm & Mary, Mary Wash, CA St U, PA St, U of FL).

  Tui '02-'03: Day €6572-13,920 (+€1300-1484). **Aid:** 26 pupils (€120,623).

  Summer: Acad Enrich Rev Rem Rec. Tui Day €295-825. 1-3 wks. Soccer. Tui Day €295-570. 1-2 wks.

  Bldgs 3. 2 Libs 20,000 vols. Sci labs 3. Comp labs 1. Art studios 2. Music studios 2. Fields 1. Courts 1.

  Est 1956. Nonprofit. Quar (Sept-June). Assoc: A/OPR/OS CIS MAIS NEASC.

Maintaining an early childhood through grade 12 curriculum comparable to that present at US college preparatory schools, CAISL offers Advanced Placement courses in several subjects while preparing students for the SAT. Portuguese is taught as a foreign language, as English is the language of instruction. Graduates typically matriculate at colleges in the US, the UK and Portugal.

ROMANIA

Sq. Miles: 91,699 (Slightly smaller than New York and Pennsylvania combined). **Country Pop:** 22,329,977 (2005). **Capital:** Bucharest, pop. 2,020,000. **Terrain:** Consists mainly of rolling, fertile plains; hilly in the eastern regions of the middle Danube basin; and major mountain ranges running north and west in the center of the country, which collectively are known as the Carpathians. **Ethnic Group(s):** Romanian Hungarian German Ukrainian Serb Croat Russian Turk Roma. **Religion(s):** Orthodox Roman_Catholic Reformed_Protestant Baptist Pentecostal Greek_Catholic Muslim Jewish. **Official Language(s):** Romanian. **Other Language(s):** Hungarian German. **Government:** Republic. **Independence:** 1877 (from Ottoman Empire). **GDP:** $73.2 billion (2004).

Agriculture 11%. Industry 28%. Services 61%. **Currency:** Romanian Leu (plural, Lei) (RL).

FUNDATIA INTERNATIONAL BRITISH SCHOOL OF BUCHAREST

Day — Coed Gr K-12

Bucharest, Romania. 21 Agricultori St. Tel: 40-1-252-3704. Fax: 40-1-253-1697. EST+7.
www.ibsb.ro   E-mail: office@ibsb.ro
Julian M. Hingley, Prin. BA, MA.

Col Prep. Gen Acad. Curr—UK. Exams—IGCSE AS-level A-level. Feat—Fr Ger Ital Span Romanian Comp_Sci Law Pol_Sci Psych Bus. Supp—Dev_Read EFL ESL Makeup Rem_Math Rem_Read Rev Tut.

Sports—Basket Soccer Swim. Activities—Acad Arts Rec.

Enr 138. B 68. G 70. US 7. Host 45. Other 86. Accepted: 90%. Yield: 75%. Avg class size: 10.

Fac 30. M 11. F 17/2. US 2. Host 9. Other 19. Adv Deg: 66%.

Tui '05-'06: Day €10,000. Aid: 6 pupils (€60,000).

Summer: Acad Enrich Rev Rec. 2-6 wks.

Plant val €4,000,000.

Est 2000. Tri (Sept-June).

FIBSB, which follows the UK National Curriculum, prepares boys and girls for the University of Cambridge International Examinations. In the primary years, progress is monitored by standard attainment tests, required at the end of each key stage. Older students prepare for the IGCSE and A- and AS-level examinations, and optional Saturday-morning revision sessions focus on specific subjects. Romanian language and culture courses serve both native speakers and those new to the language.

The school schedules regular choir and chamber music concerts. Theatrical productions attract pupils interested in art, music and drama.

INTERNATIONAL SCHOOL OF BUCHAREST

Day — Coed Gr PS-12

Bucharest, Romania. 428 Mihai Bravu St, Dristor, Sector 3. Tel: 40-21-327-54-33. Fax: 40-21-327-50-58. EST+7.
www.isb.ro   E-mail: info@isb.ro
Selami Ahmet Salgur, Prin.

Col Prep. Curr—UK. Exams—IGCSE A-level. Feat—Ger Span Romanian Comp_Sci Relig Studio_Art Music. Supp—EFL ESL Makeup.

Enr 354. B 194. G 160. US 6. Host 94. Other 254. Accepted: 98%. Avg class size: 14.

Fac 47. M 14/8. F 18/7. US 4. Host 22. Other 21. Adv Deg: 100%.

Tui '05-'06: Day $3000-6950 (+$300).

Libs 1. Theaters 1. Gyms 1. Pools 1. Rinks 1. Riding rings 1.

Est 1996. Inc. Sem (Sept-June).

With a program adapted from that followed in England, ISB primarily serves staff children of embassies and international corporations. English is the language of instruction, although pupils lacking proficiency in the language may enroll in preschool, kindergarten or grade 1. Students follow the IGCSE curriculum in grades 9 and 10, then pursue A-level course work in grades 11 and 12.

AMERICAN INTERNATIONAL SCHOOL OF BUCHAREST
Day — Coed Gr PS-12

Judetul Ilfov, Romania. Sos Pipera-Tunari 196, Comuna Voluntari-Pipera. Tel: 40-21-204-4300. Fax: 40-21-204-4306. EST+7.
www.aisb.ro   E-mail: admiss@aisb.ro
Arnold Beiber, Dir. BS, MA, MEd, EdD. **Lynn Wells, Adm.**

> **Col Prep. IB PYP. IB MYP. IB Diploma. Curr**—Intl US. **Exams**—CEEB. **Feat**—Fr Span Romanian Comp_Sci Web_Design Econ Studio_Art Theater_Arts Music. **Supp**—ESL Tut.
>
> **Sports**—Basket Soccer Softball Swim Tennis Volley. **Activities**—Acad Arts Govt/Pol.
>
> **Enr 560.** B 280. G 280. Elem 405. Sec 155. US 98. Host 132. Other 330. Accepted: 99%. Yield: 95%. Avg class size: 17.
>
> **Fac 70.** M 21. F 49. US 20. Host 15. Other 35. Adv Deg: 60%.
>
> **Grad '05—30. Col—28. US Col—9.** (U of PA, Vassar, Cornell, Alvernia, Voorhees, U of NM). Avg SAT: M/V—1200.
>
> **Tui '05-'06: Day $10,075-19,430** (+$1000). **Aid:** 10 pupils ($160,000).
>
> **Summer:** Acad Enrich. ESL. 8 wks.
>
> Plant val $22,000,000. Bldgs 4. Lib 12,000 vols. Sci labs 4. Comp labs 3. Auds 1. Theaters 1. Art studios 2. Music studios 4. Dance studios 1. Gyms 2. Fields 2. Courts 4.
>
> **Est 1962.** Nonprofit. (Aug-June). Assoc: A/OPR/OS ECIS.

AISB serves the English-speaking community of Bucharest, as well as other foreign pupils as space permits. Students come from the US, Romania, Israel, Canada, the United Kingdom and Spain, along with roughly 40 other nations. The academic program combines American and international curricular elements. AISB caters to the needs of the international student body: In addition to the IB Diploma program (available in grades 11 and 12), the school offers both the IB Primary Years and the IB Middle Years programs.

Outdoor education in grades 6-12 includes an annual expedition to the nearby Carpathian Mountains. Community service is an integral part of the AISB curriculum, as students in grades 9-12 perform 25 hours of compulsory service each year.

RUSSIA

Sq. Miles: 6,500,000 (About one and four-fifths the size of the US). **Country Pop:** 143,420,309 (2005). **Capital:** Moscow, pop. 8,300,000. **Terrain:** Broad plain with low hills west of Urals; vast coniferous forest and tundra in Siberia; uplands and mountains along southern borders.

Ethnic Group(s): Russian Tatar Ukrainian. **Religion(s):** Russian_ Orthodox Muslim Jewish Roman_Catholic Protestant Buddhist. **Official Language(s):** Russian. **Government:** Federation. **Independence:** 1991 (from Soviet Union). **Per Capita Income:** $4000 (2004). **GDP:** $613 billion (2004). Agriculture 5%. Industry 34%. Services 61%. **Currency:** Russian Ruble (RR).

ANGLO-AMERICAN SCHOOL OF MOSCOW

Day — Coed Gr PS-12

Moscow, Russia. Tel: 7-495-231-4488. Fax: 7-495-231-4476. EST+8.
Contact: c/o US Embassy, Box M, 00140 Helsinki, Finland.
www.aas.ru   E-mail: admissions@aas.ru
Drew Alexander, Dir.

    Col Prep. IB PYP. IB Diploma. Curr—Intl. **Exams**—CEEB. **Feat**—Fr Russ Environ_Sci Comp_Sci Psych Studio_Art Drama Music. **Supp**—ESL.

    Enr 1200. B 592. G 608. Elem 914. Sec 286.

    Fac 175. M 44. F 87/44.

    Tui '05-'06: Day $11,300-17,500 (+$6000).

    Est 1949. Quar (Aug-June). Assoc: A/OPR/OS CIS NEASC.

MOSCOW ECONOMIC SCHOOL

Day — Coed Gr K-12

123022 Moscow, Russia. 29 Zamorenova St. Tel: 7-495-255-0070. Fax: 7-495-253-4323. EST+8.
www.mes.ru   E-mail: mes@mes.ru
Yuri Shamilov, Pres. Larisa Orischenko, Adm.

    Col Prep. IB PYP. IB MYP. IB Diploma. Curr—Intl. **Bilingual**—Russ. **Feat**—Fr Ger Span Econ Studio_Art Music.

    Sports—Basket Soccer Swim Tennis. **Activities**—Arts Media Service.

    Enr 715. Avg class size: 12.

    Fac 210. M 27/5. F 158/20. Host 206. Other 4.

    Est 1993. Nonprofit. Quar (Sept-June). Assoc: ECIS.

This bilingual school expects students to read and understand Russian and English by grade 4. Instruction in a second foreign language, either French, Spanish, or German, begins in the second year. Primary school programming combines the International Baccalaureate Primary Years Program with elements of the Russian curriculum. The IB Middle Years Program follows, with additional instruction provided in technology and the fine and performing arts. Pupils may graduate with either the IB Diploma or the traditional Russian diploma.

    MES strongly encourages all senior school boys and girls to participate in extracurricular activities and community service.

SLAVIC ANGLO-AMERICAN SCHOOL MARINA
Day — Coed Gr 1-11

119261 Moscow, Russia. 6 Panferov St, Block 2. Tel: 7-095-134-1547. Fax: 7-095-134-5035. EST+8.
www.saasmar.ru   E-mail: saasmar@mail.ru
Tatiana A. Yurovskaia, Prin.

> **Col Prep. Gen Acad. Curr**—Nat US. **Bilingual**—Russ. **Exams**—CEEB TOEFL GCSE IGCSE. **Feat**—Fr Ger. **Supp**—EFL ESL.
> **Enr 250.** B 118. G 132. Elem 180. Sec 70. US 5. Host 238. Other 7. Accepted: 80%. Yield: 95%. Avg class size: 16.
> **Fac 47.** M 6. F 32/9. US 3. Host 44. Adv Deg: 14%.
> **Grad '05**—15. **Col**—15. **US Col**—3. (Davidson, U of PA, Boston U).
> **Tui '05-'06: Day $5000.**
> Bldgs 2. Class rms 28. 3 Libs 27,000 vols. Sci labs 2. Lang labs 12. Comp labs 3. Auds 1. Theaters 1. Art studios 2. Music studios 3. Dance studios 3. Gyms 2.
> **Est 1990.** Quar (Sept-June).

SAAS Marina prepares students for higher education through American, British and Russian models. Instruction is in Russian and English, and students may elect to study French and German as foreign languages beginning in grade 4. The program includes student and staff exchanges with schools in the US, Great Britain, South Africa, Holland, Belgium, Germany and other countries.

QSI INTERNATIONAL SCHOOL OF VLADIVOSTOK
Day — Coed Gr K-7

690033 Vladivostok, Russia. 3B Gamarnika St. Tel: 7-4232-336-609. EST+15.
http://vlv.qsi.org   E-mail: vladivostok@qsi.org
Harold Strom, Dir.

> **Gen Acad. Curr**—US. **Feat**—Russ Computers Econ Studio_Art Music.
> **Enr 20.**
> **Tui '05-'06: Day $16,000** (+$1600).
> **Est 1996.** Nonprofit. Spons: Quality Schools International. Assoc: A/OPR/OS MSA.

SCOTLAND

Sq. Miles: 30,167 (About the size of Virginia). **Country Pop:** 5,062,011 (2001). **Capital:** Edinburgh, pop. 401,910 (2001). **Largest City:** Glasgow, pop. 662,954 (2001). **Terrain:** Mostly rugged hills and low mountains. **Government:** Constitutional Monarchy. **Currency:** British Pound (£).

FETTES COLLEGE

Bdg and Day — Coed Ages 7-18

Edinburgh EH4 1QX, Scotland. Carrington Rd. Tel: 44-131-332-2281. Fax: 44-131-332-3081. EST+5.
www.fettes.com   E-mail: enquiries@fettes.com
Michael C. B. Spens, Head.

    Col Prep. IB Diploma. Curr—Intl UK. **Exams**—GCSE AS-level A-level. **Feat**—Fr Ger Greek Lat Span Comp_Sci Pol_Sci Relig Art_Hist Studio_Art Drama Music. **Supp**—EFL.

    Sports—Badminton Basket X-country Equestrian Fencing F_Hockey Golf Gymnastics Lacrosse Rugby Soccer Squash Swim Tennis Volley. **Activities**—Acad Arts Rec.

    Enr 600.
    Fac 101.
    Tui '04-'05: Bdg £14,628-20,199. Day £9345-13,887.
    Bldgs 20. Dorms 8. 2 Libs 16,000 vols. Chapels 1. Drama studios 1. Gyms 1. Fields 2. Courts 4. Pools 1.
    Est 1870. Nonprofit. Tri (Sept-June).

Located on 85 acres near the center of Edinburgh, Fettes offers an individualized curriculum designed to prepare students for university entrance.

Boys and girls in the preparatory school (ages 7-13) follow a curriculum based upon the Scottish course of studies for ages 5-14. Specialists teach English, math, history, geography, religious studies, and personal and social education to children ages 7-9. Gradually, students spend less time with their homeroom teacher; by the last year of preparatory school, specialists lead all classes. During the middle school years (ages 14-16), boys and girls take five core subjects at GCSE level, in addition to five elective choices. In the Sixth Form (ages 16-18), pupils pursue either the A levels or the International Baccalaureate Diploma.

Divided into the medieval Old Town and the Georgian New Town, Edinburgh displays a variety of architectural styles. For three weeks each summer, the city hosts an internationally recognized arts festival.

INTERNATIONAL SCHOOL OF ABERDEEN

Day — Coed Gr PS-12

Milltimber, Aberdeen AB13 0AB, Scotland. 296 N Deeside Rd. Tel: 44-1224-732267. Fax: 44-1224-735648. EST+5.
www.isa.aberdeen.sch.uk   E-mail: admin@isa.aberdeen.sch.uk
Daniel Hovde, Dir. PhD.

    Col Prep. IB Diploma. Curr—Intl US. **Exams**—CEEB. **Feat**—Fr Span Comp_Sci Econ Psych Studio_Art Music. **Supp**—Dev_Read EFL ESL LD Rem_Math Rem_Read.

    Enr 340. Accepted: 99%. Avg class size: 15.
    Fac 47. M 9. F 38. US 17. Host 24. Other 6. Adv Deg: 42%.
    Grad '05—20. Col—6. US Col—7. (HI Pacific, Boston U, James Madison, TX A&M, Brown). Avg SAT: M/V—1100.
    Tui '02-'03: Day £9530-10,245 (+£400).
    Plant val £5,000,000. Bldgs 1. Class rms 50. Lib 15,000 vols. Sci labs 3. Lang labs

2. Comp labs 2. Art studios 2. Music studios 1. Gyms 1. Fields 1.
Est 1972. Nonprofit. Sem (Aug-June). Assoc: CIS MSA.

Founded as the American School in Aberdeen to provide a US-style education for children of oil industry workers from North America, ISA has served primarily families involved with the oil industry and the American military. Although approximately three-quarters of the enrollment continue to come from the US and Canada, a growing number of countries are represented in the student body; in response to this changing population, the school assumed its current name and initiated an IB program in 1994.

Located about 100 miles northeast of Edinburgh, Aberdeen is a port city on the North Sea, lying between the mouths of the Dee and the Don rivers.

SERBIA AND MONTENEGRO

Sq. Miles: 39,518 (Slightly smaller than Kentucky). **Country Pop:** 10,829,175 (2005). **Capital:** Belgrade. **Terrain:** Varied; in the north, rich fertile plains; in the east, limestone ranges and basins; in the southeast, mountains and hills; in the southwest, high shoreline with no islands off the coast. **Ethnic Group(s):** Serbian Albanian Montenegrin Hungarian. **Religion(s):** Orthodox Muslim Roman_Catholic Protestant. **Other Language(s):** Serbo-Croatian Albanian. **Government:** Republic. **Independence:** 1993. **Per Capita Income:** $2620 (2004). **GDP:** $24 billion (2004). Agriculture 17%. Industry 25%. Services 58%. **Currency:** Yugoslav Dinar (Din).

ANGLO-AMERICAN SCHOOL BELGRADE
Day — Coed Gr 6-12

11000 Belgrade, Serbia and Montenegro. Miloja Djaka 10. Tel: 381-11-669-996. Fax: 381-11-2660-763. EST+6.
www.aplus.edu.yu   E-mail: aplus@eunet.yu
Tijana Mandic, Prin. PhD.
    Col Prep. Curr—Intl UK US. **Exams**—ACT CEEB TOEFL IGCSE AS-level A-level.
      Feat—Fr Ger Ital Japan Span Studio_Art. **Supp**—EFL ESL LD Rem_Math Tut.
    Sports—Basket Soccer Swim. **Activities**—Acad Arts Govt/Pol Media Service.
    Enr 20. B 12. G 8. US 2. Host 9. Other 9. Accepted: 90%. Avg class size: 6.
    Fac 20. M 1/7. F 5/7. Adv Deg: 60%.
    Grad '05—6. Col—6. US Col—3.
    Tui '05-'06: Day €6600-11,000 (+€750). **Aid:** 4 pupils (€16,000).
    Lib 2320 vols. Sci labs 1. Lang labs 1. Comp labs 2.
    Est 2001. Nonprofit. Quar (Sept-June).

Founded by a group of teachers and others interested in establishing an English-medium program at the secondary level, AASB conducts two distinct curricula: an American-style program and a British-style one. Students in the American section fulfill core course requirements in language arts, social studies, math, science, multicultural studies, financial skills and career planning, then devote remaining classroom time to electives. Pupils enrolled in the British section prepare for the British O-level examinations in grades 9 and 10, then ready themselves for the A levels during their final two years.

THE BRITISH INTERNATIONAL SCHOOL OF BELGRADE
Day — Coed Gr PS-12

11000 Belgrade, Serbia and Montenegro. Brace Jerkovic, Padina, Kruzni Put 4.
Tel: 381-11-34-67-000. Fax: 381-11-34-67-182. EST+6.
www.ihsb.co.yu   E-mail: ihsb@eunet.yu
Aleksandra Keserovic, Dir. MA.
   Col Prep. Curr—UK US. **Exams**—CEEB TOEFL IGCSE A-level. **Feat**—Fr Ger
      Span Comp_Sci Geog Studio_Art Drama Music Bus. **Supp**—ESL.
   Enr 96. B 47. G 49.
   Fac 32. Adv Deg: 21%.
   Tui '05-'06: Day €6500-10,000.
   Est 1997. Tri (Sept-June).

INTERNATIONAL SCHOOL OF BELGRADE
Day — Coed Gr PS-12

11040 Belgrade, Serbia and Montenegro. Temisvarska 19. Tel: 381-11-2651-832.
Fax: 381-11-2652-619. EST+6.
Contact: Dept of State, 5070 Belgrade Pl, Washington, DC 20521.
www.isb.co.yu   E-mail: isb@isb.co.yu
Gerald F. Craig, Dir.
   Gen Acad. IB PYP. IB MYP. IB Diploma. Curr—Intl US. **Feat**—Fr Serbian. **Supp**—
      ESL Rem_Math Rem_Read.
   Enr 223. B 130. G 93. Accepted: 100%. Avg class size: 13.
   Fac 30. M 4/1. F 21/4.
   Grad '05—12.
   Tui '05-'06: Day $3500-11,730.
   Bldgs 5. Class rms 15. Lib 8700 vols. Sci labs 1. Comp labs 1. Gyms 1. Pools 1.
   Est 1948. Nonprofit. Quar (Sept-June). Assoc: A/OPR/OS.

Following a modified American curriculum to meet the needs of students from many nations, this school serves the diplomatic and business community of Belgrade. All instruction is in English, and about 20 percent of the pupils take English as a Second Language. French is taught in grades 2-8. The school facilities consist of a rented villa and adjacent buildings in a residential section of the city.

SLOVAKIA

Sq. Miles: 18,933 (About the size of West Virginia). **Country Pop:** 5,431,363 (2005). **Capital:** Bratislava, pop. 452,053. **Terrain:** High mountains in the north, low mountains in the center, hills to the west, Danube river basin in the south. **Ethnic Group(s):** Slovak Hungarian Roma Czech Ruthenian Ukrainian. **Religion(s):** Roman_Catholic Protestant Greek_Catholic Orthodox. **Official Language(s):** Slovak. **Other Language(s):** Hungarian Ruthenian Romany Ukrainian. **Government:** Parliamentary Republic. **Independence:** 1993. **Per Capita Income:** $7600 (2004). **GDP:** $41.1 billion (2004). Agriculture 3%. Industry 30%. Services 67%. **Currency:** Slovak Koruna (SLK).

THE BRITISH INTERNATIONAL SCHOOL BRATISLAVA
Day — Coed Gr PS-12

841 02 Bratislava, Slovakia. Dolinskeho 1. Tel: 421-2-6436-6992. Fax: 421-2-6436-4784. EST+6.
www.bis.sk   E-mail: info@bisb.sk
Peter Radoja, Head. BSc, MEd, MBA.
  Gen Acad. Curr—Intl UK. Exams—IGCSE AS-level A-level. Feat—Ger Slovak Comp_Sci Studio_Art Music. Supp—Dev_Read EFL ESL Rem_Math Rem_Read Tut.
  Enr 180. B 85. G 95. Elem 140. Sec 40. US 15. Host 35. Other 130. Accepted: 95%. Avg class size: 15.
  Fac 28. M 6/1. F 18/3. US 1. Host 12. Other 15. Adv Deg: 17%.
  Tui '02-'03: Day $4595-7365.
  Bldgs 1. Lib 2500 vols. Sci labs 1. Comp labs 1. Art studios 1. Music studios 1. Gyms 2.
  Est 1997. Tri (Sept-July).

BIS meets the educational needs of both international students and local children interested in English-medium instruction. Students enroll from approximately 20 nations in the Americas, Europe, Asia, Australia and Africa. The preschool program seeks the development of basic learning skills, while the primary (grades K-2) and elementary (grades 3-4) levels employ self-contained classrooms and small class size. Middle schoolers (grades 5-9) take courses in five departments: language arts, mathematics, science, social studies and foreign languages. Older pupils work toward the IGCSE examinations. Nonnative English speakers receive ESL instruction.

QSI INTERNATIONAL SCHOOL OF BRATISLAVA
Day — Coed Gr PS-12

842 20 Bratislava 4, Slovakia. Karloveska 64. Tel: 421-2-654-228-44. Fax: 421-2-654-116-46. EST+6.
www.qsi.org/svk   E-mail: bratislava@qsi.org
Merry Wade, Dir. BS, MA, EdS, PhD.
  Col Prep. IB Diploma. Curr—Intl US. Exams—AP CEEB. AP—Fr Bio. Feat—British_Lit Dutch Ger Slovak Comp_Sci Econ Studio_Art Music Dance.

Enr 155.
Tui '05-'06: Day $5300-10,400 (+$5700).
Est 1994. Nonprofit. Spons: Quality Schools International. Tri (Sept-June). Assoc: A/OPR/OS MSA.

QSI INTERNATIONAL SCHOOL OF KOSICE
Day — Coed Gr K-8

040 01 Kosice, Slovakia. Nam Ladislava Novomeskeho 2. Tel: 42-55-6250040. Fax: 42-55-6250040. EST+6.
www.qsi.org/ksc   E-mail: kosice@qsi.org
Ray Varey, Dir.
  Gen Acad. Curr—Intl. **Supp**—ESL.
  Enr 31. B 15. G 16.
  Fac 14.
  Tui '05-'06: Day $8400-11,000 (+$1700).
  Est 2001. Nonprofit. Spons: Quality Schools International. Assoc: MSA.

SLOVENIA

Sq. Miles: 7906 (Slightly smaller than New Jersey). **Country Pop:** 2,011,070 (2005). **Capital:** Ljubljana, pop. 265,881 (2002). **Terrain:** Mountains rising in the north, wide plateaus in the southeast, Karst limestone region of caves in the south-southwest, hills in the east. **Ethnic Group(s):** Slovene Croat Serb Bosnian Hungarian Montenegrin Macedonian Albanian Italian Roma. **Religion(s):** Roman_Catholic Atheist Orthodox_Christian Muslim Jewish. **Official Language(s):** Slovene. **Other Language(s):** Hungarian Italian German English. **Government:** Parliamentary Democracy. **Independence:** 1991 (from Yugoslavia). **Per Capita Income:** $16,112 (2004). **GDP:** $32.2 billion (2004). Agriculture 4%. Industry 37%. Services 60%. **Currency:** Slovene Tolar (SIT).

GIMNAZIJA BEZIGRAD
IB PROGRAM

Day — Coed Gr 3-12

1000 Ljubljana, Slovenia. Periceva 4. Tel: 386-1-300-0400. Fax: 386-1-300-0440. EST+6.
www.gimb.org   E-mail: barbara@gimb.org
Barbara Gostisa, Head.
  Col Prep. IB MYP. IB Diploma. Curr—Intl. **Feat**—Fr Ger Anthro Psych Philos. **Supp**—ESL.
  Sports—Basket Soccer Volley. **Activities**—Acad Arts.
  Enr 22.

Fac 155. M 87/4. F 60/4. US 1. Host 151. Other 3. Adv Deg: 9%.
Tui '05-'06: Day $5521.
Class rms 45. Sci labs 1. Comp labs 1. Gyms 1.
Est 1990. Nonprofit. Sem (Sept-June).

Three years after this long-established school introduced its International Baccalaureate Program in 1990, Gimnazija Bezigrad formed an international department to address the needs of foreign students enrolled in the IB Middle Years and IB Diploma programs. Diploma recipients matriculate at competitive European and American universities.

The school is a short walk north from the center of Ljubljana.

QSI INTERNATIONAL SCHOOL OF LJUBLJANA
Day — Coed Gr PS-12

1000 Ljubljana, Slovenia. Puharjeva ulica 10. Tel: 386-1-439-6300. Fax: 386-1-439-6305. EST+6.
http://sln.qsi.org   E-mail: ljubljana@qsi.org
Glenn Mosher, Dir.

Gen Acad. Curr—US. **Feat**—Slovene Comp_Sci Econ Studio_Art Music. **Supp**—ESL Tut.
Bldgs 1. Class rms 6. 2 Libs 700 vols. Comp labs 1. Music studios 1.
Est 1995. Nonprofit. Spons: Quality Schools International. 5 terms (Aug-June). Assoc: A/OPR/OS MSA.

Enrolling children as young as age 3, the school conducts an English-medium program that follows the US elementary model. The curriculum is geared toward minimizing adjustment problems for students upon their return to the home country. Course work in computer literacy, art, music and physical education complements classes in the traditional disciplines. In addition, Slovene culture is an integral part of each pupil's education, and boys and girls have Slovene as a foreign language option. Field trips enrich classroom work at all grade levels.

SPAIN

Sq. Miles: 194,884 (About the size of Arizona and Utah combined). **Country Pop:** 40,341,462 (2005). **Capital:** Madrid, pop. 5,500,000. **Terrain:** High plateaus and mountains. **Ethnic Group(s):** Basque Catalan Galician. **Religion(s):** Roman_Catholic. **Official Language(s):** Spanish. **Other Language(s):** Catalan-Valenciana Galician Basque. **Government:** Constitutional Monarchy. **Per Capita Income:** $22,421 (2004). **GDP:** $995.1 billion (2004). Agriculture 3%. Industry 29%. Services 68%. **Currency:** European Union Euro (€).

INTERNATIONAL COLLEGE SPAIN
Day — Coed Gr PS-12

28100 Alcobendas, Madrid, Spain. Calle Vereda Norte 3, La Moraleja. Tel: 34-91-650-2398. Fax: 34-91-650-1035. EST+6.
www.icsmadrid.com   E-mail: info@icsmadrid.com
Terry Hedger, Dir. Eunice Amondaray, Adm.

Col Prep. IB PYP. IB MYP. IB Diploma. Curr—Intl Nat. Exams—CEEB. Feat—Fr Span Comp_Sci Geog Drama Music. Supp—EFL ESL Tut.

Sports—Basket Soccer Volley. Activities—Arts.

Enr 602. Elem 441. Sec 161. US 82. Host 204. Other 316. Accepted: 90%. Yield: 87%. Avg class size: 20.

Fac 76. M 19. F 54/3. Adv Deg: 28%.

Grad '05—47. US Col—5. (Stanford, Tufts, Trinity Col-CT, Boston Col, U of PA).

Tui '05-'06: Day €6030-12,360.

Summer: Rec. Tui Day €600. 4 wks.

Bldgs 2. Libs 2. Sci labs 4. Comp labs 3. Auds 1. Art studios 2. Gyms 1. Fields 1. Courts 3.

Est 1980. Inc. Tri (Sept-June). Assoc: CIS MAIS NEASC.

ICS consists of three sections: the IB Primary Years Program (grades PS-5), the IB Middle Years Program (grades 6-10) and the IB Diploma Program (grades 11 and 12). Small classes in the primary school allow pupils to progress at an appropriate pace in English and math. Music, art and other activities supplement the traditional subjects, and Spanish is compulsory from grade 1. Secondary schoolers follow a broad curriculum that emphasizes math, science and languages while preparing students for the IB Diploma.

SIERRA BERNIA SCHOOL
Day — Coed Ages 3-18

03580 Alfaz del Pi, Alicante, Spain. La Caneta, San Rafael. Tel: 34-96-687-5149. Fax: 34-96-687-3633. EST+6.
www.nabss.org/sierra.htm   E-mail: duncan@ctv.es
Duncan M. Allan, Head. BA.

Col Prep. Curr—Nat UK. Exams—GCSE IGCSE A-level. Feat—Fr Span Comp_Sci.

Activities—Arts Rec.

Enr 200. Host 50. Other 150. Avg class size: 13.

Fac 13. M 6. F 7.

Tui '05-'06: Day €3000-6000 (+€900).

Bldgs 3. Class rms 16. Libs 1. Sci labs 1. Comp labs 1. Art studios 1. Pools 1.

Est 1973. Nonprofit. Tri (Sept-June).

Situated in a residential area near the village of Alfaz del Pi, Sierra Bernia follows the traditional British program of studies. Students, who enroll predominantly from European countries, prepare for the GCSE or IGCSE and the A-level examinations. Spanish language classes are taught at all levels, as are the required elements of the Spanish national curriculum. Graduates attend universities in the US and throughout Europe.

BENJAMIN FRANKLIN INTERNATIONAL SCHOOL
Day — Coed Gr PS-12

08017 Barcelona, Spain. Martorell i Pena 9. Tel: 34-93-434-2380. Fax: 34-93-417-3633. EST+6.
www.bfis.org   E-mail: bfranklin@bfisnet.org
Shirley Davis, Dir. MEd.

> Col Prep. Curr—US. Exams—AP CEEB SSAT TOEFL. AP—Eng Fr Span Calc Bio Chem Physics Eur_Hist Comp_Govt & Pol Studio_Art. Feat—Catalan Stats Marine_Biol/Sci Comp_Sci Music. Supp—ESL.
>
> Activities—Acad Arts Govt/Pol Media Rec.
>
> Enr 378. B 182. G 196. Elem 266. Sec 112. US 114. Host 118. Other 146. Accepted: 99%. Yield: 99%. Avg class size: 16.
>
> Fac 53. M 15. F 32/6. US 32. Host 16. Other 5. Adv Deg: 54%.
>
> Grad '05—30. Col—30. US Col—3. (UCLA, U of CA-Santa Barbara, VA Commonwealth).
>
> Tui '05-'06: Day €4550-8670 (+€1700).
>
> Summer: Acad Rec. Span. ESL. Tui Day €485. 4 wks.
>
> Bldgs 5. Class rms 27. Lib 12,000 vols. Sci labs 2. Comp labs 1. Art studios 1. Music studios 1. Courts 3.
>
> Est 1986. Nonprofit. Tri (Sept-June). Assoc: A/OPR/OS MAIS MSA.

BFIS conducts a comprehensive American-style curriculum that provides preparation for Advanced Placement exams and the SAT. In addition to the standard subjects, high schoolers take compulsory computer technology, music and art classes; pupils also choose from an array of electives. Advanced Placement offerings in a range of subjects ready students for the Advanced Placement International Diploma. ESL and Spanish as a Second Language are available, and the school also conducts a program that offers support to students with learning difficulties; those with talents in certain areas that require extra enrichment and challenge; and boys and girls in need of additional assistance with their English language skills.

Excursions designed to explore the history, culture and architecture of Barcelona and the Catalonian region supplement class work. Extracurricular offerings include musical and dramatic productions, recreational sports and academic competitions.

KENSINGTON SCHOOL
Day — Coed Ages 4-18

08034 Barcelona, Spain. Carrer dels Cavallers 31-33, Pedralbes. Tel: 34-93-203-5457. Fax: 34-93-280-5067. EST+6.
www.kensingtonschoolbcn.com
E-mail: kensingtonschoolbcn@kensingtonschoolbcn.com
Robin Giles, Head.

> Col Prep. Curr—UK. Exams—GCSE O-level AS-level A-level. Feat—Fr Span Comp_Sci Studio_Art.
>
> Sports—Basket Soccer Volley. Activities—Arts.
>
> Enr 250.
>
> Theaters 1. Art studios 1. Music studios 1. Gyms 1.
>
> Est 1966. Tri.

Kensington was founded to provide a British-style education for Barcelona's international community. The school is not selective and accepts pupils of all backgrounds and ability levels. Students in the junior school (ages 7-10) follow the British curriculum. At more advanced levels, course work emphasizes preparation for the GCSE and GCE A-level examinations. Field trips, dramatic productions and athletics round out the program.

THE AMERICAN SCHOOL OF BILBAO
Day — Coed Gr PS-12

48640 Berango, Vizcaya, Spain. Soparda Bidea 10. Tel: 34-94-668-08-60. Fax: 34-94-668-04-52. EST+6.
www.sarenet.es/asb   E-mail: asb@asb.sarenet.es
Roger West, Dir.

  Col Prep. Gen Acad. Curr—Intl Nat US. **Exams**—ACT CEEB. **Feat**—Fr Span Basque Comp_Sci Studio_Art Music. **Supp**—ESL Rem_Math Tut.
  Enr 313. B 153. G 160. Elem 238. Sec 75. US 12. Host 266. Other 35. Accepted: 50%. Avg class size: 23.
  Fac 24. M 6/1. F 16/1. US 10. Host 8. Other 6. Adv Deg: 62%.
  Grad '05—18. Col—18.
  Tui '02-'03: Day $3440-5350 (+$1800).
  Summer: EFL. Tui Day $500/4-wk ses. 8 wks.
  Bldgs 6. Class rms 19. Lib 12,000 vols. Sci labs 1. Comp labs 1. Auds 1. Art studios 1. Music studios 1. Gyms 1. Courts 4.
  Est 1967. Nonprofit. Quar (Sept-June). Assoc: CIS MAIS NEASC.

Located on a six-acre campus in the rolling countryside of Berango, the school conducts an academic program similar to that found at any progressive US school. ASB administers the PSAT to 11th and 12th graders, and qualified students may prepare for the Advanced Placement examinations. In addition to required course work, all students (beginning in grade 1) take Spanish.

Athletic facilities facilitate participation in basketball, vollcyball, baseball and soccer. The school makes ample use of its coastal location, and school life reflects the influence of the area's Basque heritage.

THE ENGLISH CENTRE
(EL CENTRO INGLES)
Day — Coed Gr PS-12

11500 El Puerto de Santa Maria, Cadiz, Spain. Apartado Correos 85. Tel: 34-956-850560. Fax: 34-956-873804. EST+6.
www.elcentroingles.es   E-mail: info@elcentroingles.es
Linda M. Randell, Prin. D. Manuel Ramirez, Head.

  Col Prep. Curr—Nat UK. **Bilingual**—Span. **Feat**—Fr Ger Studio_Art Music. **Supp**—Dev_Read EFL ESL LD Rem_Math Rem_Read Tut.
  Sports—Basket Gymnastics Soccer Tennis. **Activities**—Arts.
  Enr 820. B 328. G 492. Elem 541. Sec 279. US 50. Host 717. Other 53. Accepted: 60%. Avg class size: 25.
  Fac 59. M 13/3. F 36/7. US 6. Host 42. Other 11. Adv Deg: 54%.
  Tui '05-'06: Day €1709-3854 (+€37-140).

Summer: Rec. 2-8 wks.
Bldgs 4. Class rms 32. Libs 1. Gyms 1. Courts 2. Stadiums 1. Pools 1.
Est 1969. Inc. Tri (Sept-June).

The English Centre conducts a bilingual program with an intensive ESL component for pupils lacking fluency in English. All members of the English-language teaching staff are either native speakers or are fluent in the language. Courses such as computer studies, art, music and physical education are taught in English. An international faculty stresses immersion in Spanish culture by adding local and national field trips to the curriculum.

AMERICAN SCHOOL OF BARCELONA
Day — Coed Gr PS-12

08950 Esplugues de Llobregat, Barcelona, Spain. Calle Jaume Balmes 7. Tel: 34-93-371-4016. Fax: 34-93-473-4787. EST+6.
www.a-s-b.com   E-mail: info@a-s-b.com
Lee Fertig, Dir.
   Col Prep. Curr—Nat US. **Supp Lang**—Span. **Exams**—CEEB. **Feat**—Catalan
      Psych Studio_Art Music. **Supp**—EFL ESL LD Rem_Read.
   Enr 500. B 250. G 250. Elem 340. Sec 160. US 50. Avg class size: 18.
   Fac 67. US 31. Host 22. Other 14.
   Grad '05—34.
   Tui '05-'06: Day €4750-7850 (+€1800).
   Bldgs 3. 2 Libs 15,000 vols. Fields 1. Courts 2.
   Est 1962. Nonprofit. Tri (Sept-June). Assoc: A/OPR/OS MAIS MSA.

ASB provides a US-style curriculum emphasizing a bicultural education, with Spanish taught as a second language. Students whose native language is not English must meet the school's language requirements prior to admission. In the high school years, boys and girls may pursue the US high school diploma or the Spanish baccalaureate, or they may take part in a joint program that enables them to earn both certificates.

Extracurricular activities include basketball, soccer, volleyball, swimming, chess, art and music.

XABIA INTERNATIONAL COLLEGE
Day — Coed Gr PS-12

03730 Javea, Alicante, Spain. Carretera Cabo de la Nao 21. Tel: 34-96-647-1785. Fax: 34-96-647-1785. EST+6.
www.xabia-international-college.com
E-mail: info@xabia-international-college.com
Michael Bayes, Dir. BA, MA.
   Col Prep. Curr—UK. **Exams**—GCSE IGCSE AS-level A-level. **Feat**—Fr Ger Span
      Comp_Sci Econ Psych Bus. **Supp**—ESL Rev Tut.
   Activities—Arts Rec.
   Enr 300. B 140. G 160. Elem 195. Sec 105. US 7. Host 60. Other 233. Accepted:
      85%. Yield: 97%. Avg class size: 12.

Fac 49. M 10/5. F 24/10. US 1. Host 7. Other 41. Adv Deg: 14%.
Grad '05—45. US Col—2.
Tui '05-'06: Day €4950-7700 (+€500).
Est 1995. Inc. Tri (Sept-June).

Xabia integrates Spanish language and culture courses into the English National Curriculum. Children achieve fluency in at least two languages by the end of their primary education. Secondary school students prepare for the IGCSE and the A- and AS-level examinations.

All pupils have access to music, sports, computers and language lessons. Graduates go on to universities predominantly in the United Kingdom, Germany, Switzerland and Spain.

RUNNYMEDE COLLEGE
Day — Coed Gr PS-12

28109 La Moraleja, Madrid, Spain. Calle Salvia 30. Tel: 34-916-508-302. Fax: 34-916-508-236. EST+6.
www.runnymede-college.com   E-mail: mail@runnymede-college.com
Frank M. Powell, Head. BSc.
  Col Prep. Curr—UK. **Exams—**CEEB GCSE IGCSE A-level. **Feat—**Fr Lat Span Comp_Sci Art_Hist Drawing Studio_Art Music. **Supp—**ESL Rem_Math Rem_Read.
  Enr 540. B 282. G 258. Elem 443. Sec 97. PG 0. US 43. Host 270. Other 227.
  Fac 45. M 10. F 33/2. Host 43. Other 2. Adv Deg: 11%.
  Grad '05—22. Col—21. US Col—4. (Boston U, Tufts).
  Bldgs 2. Class rms 35. 2 Libs 20,000 vols. Sci labs 2. Comp labs 1. Auds 1. Art studios 1. Music studios 1. Gyms 1. Fields 1. Courts 1.
  Est 1967. Tri (Sept-June).

Founded in Madrid to provide a British-style secondary education for area students of all nationalities, RC added a primary division in 1987 and moved to suburban La Moraleja in 1990. In the junior school, English, math and science form the core of the curriculum, with boys and girls also taking history and geography, design technology, art and music. Pupils take Spanish, which is taught as a foreign language, three days per week. During the senior school years, Runnymede places considerable emphasis on the IGCSE, GCSE and A-level examinations. Boys and girls typically take three courses at A level.

BRITISH SCHOOL OF GRAN CANARIA
Day — Coed Gr PS-12

35017 Las Palmas de Gran Canaria, Spain. Carretera a Marzagan s/n. Tel: 34-928-351-167. Fax: 34-928-351-065. EST+6.
www.bs-gc.com   E-mail: hardes@bs-gc.com
Steven R. Hardes, Head.
  Col Prep. Curr—Nat UK. **Exams—**IGCSE A-level.
  Enr 476. B 222. G 254.
  Fac 48.

Est 1966. Tri (Sept-July).

OAKLEY COLLEGE

Day — Coed Gr PS-12

35017 Las Palmas de Gran Canaria, Spain. Calle Zuloaga 17, Tafira Alta. Tel: 34-928354247. Fax: 34-928354267. EST+6.
www.oakleycollege.com   E-mail: oakley@teleline.es
Donat Morgan, Dir. BA, MBA.

   Col Prep. Curr—UK. **Exams**—GCSE IGCSE O-level AS-level A-level. **Feat**—Humanities Fr Ger Span Comp_Sci Span_Stud Music. **Supp**—ESL.

   Sports—Basket Soccer Volley. **Activities**—Arts Rec.

   Enr 350. B 175. G 175. Accepted: 90%. Avg class size: 22.

   Grad '05—12.

   Summer: Enrich Rec. 4 wks.

   Bldgs 3. Class rms 20. Lib 5000 vols. Sci labs 1. Lang labs 1. Comp labs 1. Art studios 1. Music studios 1. Dance studios 1. Gyms 1. Fields 1. Courts 2.

   Est 1989. Tri (Sept-June).

Located in the Canary Islands, Oakley follows the English National Curriculum while also emphasizing Spanish language and culture. Primary school students spend about 20 percent of their time studying Spanish and become bilingual by age 11. A second foreign language, either French or German, is added in secondary school, as is a Spanish-language social studies course. Students prepare for the IGCSE and A- and AS-level examinations.

Overnight camping trips begin at age 5, and older student embark on environmental study trips. Fundraising and volunteer work are elements of the community service program.

AMERICAN SCHOOL OF MADRID

Day — Coed Gr PS-12

28080 Madrid, Spain. Apartado 80. Tel: 34-91-740-1900. Fax: 34-91-357-2678. EST+6.
www.asmadrid.org   E-mail: info@asmadrid.org
William D. O'Hale, Head. Sholeh Arab, Adm.

   Col Prep. IB Diploma. Curr—Intl Nat US. **Exams**—CEEB. **Feat**—Fr Span Comp_Sci Photog Studio_Art Drama Music. **Supp**—ESL.

   Sports—Basket Baseball Soccer Softball Track Volley. **Activities**—Arts Govt/Pol Media Rec.

   Enr 730. B 359. G 371. Elem 520. Sec 210. US 223. Host 230. Other 277.

   Fac 91. US 66. Host 19. Other 6.

   Grad '05—56. Col—55. US Col—19. (Georgetown, Purdue, PA St, NYU, Boston U, St Louis U). Avg SAT: M/V—1093.

   Tui '05-'06: Day €5222-16,044 (+€6000).

   Summer: Acad Enrich Rec. Span. Soccer. 4 wks.

   Bldgs 2. Sci labs 4. Comp labs 3. Auds 1. Art studios 3. Music studios 2.

   Est 1961. Nonprofit. Sem (Sept-June). Assoc: A/OPR/OS MAIS MSA.

Located on a site overlooking the city, this school, originally founded to serve the American community in Madrid, now attracts an international student body. During the high school years, ASM offers a US-style curriculum, an International Baccalaureate diploma program and the official Spanish curriculum, thus allowing pupils to prepare for colleges around the world. Many students graduate with the ability to speak three languages—English, Spanish and French—fluently.

Nonnative English speakers in grades 1-8 who have above-average skills in their home languages may participate in Immersion English, a component of the ESL program that enables children to develop proficiency in an accelerated time frame and thus be prepared to continue their studies in the school's international high school program.

BRITISH COUNCIL SCHOOL
Day — Coed Gr PS-12

28223 Madrid, Spain. Prado de Somosaguas, Calle Solano 3, Pozuelo de Alarcon. Tel: 34-91-337-3612. Fax: 34-91-337-3634. EST+6.
www.britishcouncil.es   E-mail: school@britishcouncil.es
Gillian Flaxman, Head. BA. **Piedad Huelves, Adm.**
   Col Prep. Curr—Nat UK. **Bilingual**—Span. **Exams**—GCSE IGCSE AS-level.
      Feat—Fr Ger Studio_Art Theater Music. **Supp**—Dev_Read EFL ESL.
   Activities—Arts.
   Enr 1892. Host 1854. Other 38. Avg class size: 22.
   Fac 170. US 2. Host 35. Other 133. Adv Deg: 5%.
   Grad '05—110.
   Tui '05-'06: Day €5745-6480 (+€624).
   Est 1940. Nonprofit. Tri (Sept-June).

Students at the school follow an integrated, bilingual program that incorporates British methodology. In addition to the Spanish Selectividad, pupils prepare for the IGCSE exam and several British tests. Approximately 60 percent of course work is conducted in English, while the remainder is taught in Spanish.

EVANGELICAL CHRISTIAN ACADEMY
Day — Coed Gr 1-12

28816 Madrid, Spain. Calle La Manda 47, Camarma de Esteruelas. Tel: 34-91-886-5003. Fax: 34-91-886-6419. EST+6.
www.ecaspain.org   E-mail: info@ecaspain.org
Scot Musser, Head.
   Col Prep. Curr—US. **Exams**—AP CEEB. **AP**—Span Calc. **Feat**—Humanities Bible Studio_Art Music.
   Activities—Govt/Pol Media.
   Enr 90. Avg class size: 10.
   Fac 23. M 9. F 11/3.
   Grad '05—2. Col—2.
   Tui '05-'06: Day $4500.
   Bldgs 2. Class rms 11. Lib 12,000 vols. Sci labs 1. Comp labs 1. Music studios 1. Courts 1.

Est 1973. Nonprofit. Evangelical. Sem (Aug-June).

Conducting a US curriculum taught from a Christian perspective, ECA was founded to serve missionary families, but the school now accepts nonmissionary pupils on a space-available basis. Although English is the language of instruction, the academy provides Spanish at all levels, including Advanced Placement. Students with special learning needs receive remedial and enrichment support at the school's learning center.

Among cocurricular activities are outdoor education opportunities at all grade levels and instrumental music lessons.

HASTINGS SCHOOL

Day — Coed Gr PS-12

28036 Madrid, Spain. Calle Azulinas 8. Tel: 34-91-359-9913. Fax: 34-91-359-3521. EST+6.
www.hastingsschool.com   E-mail: info@hastingsschool.com
Michael B. Mellor, Head.

Col Prep. Curr—UK. **Exams**—IGCSE A-level. **Feat**—Span Geog Studio_Art Music Bus.
Enr 400.
Tui '05-'06: Day €3834-7488.
Est 1971.

INTERNATIONAL SCHOOL OF MADRID

Day — Coed Gr PS-12

28033 Madrid, Spain. Serrano Galvache 13. Tel: 34-91-302-30-80. Fax: 34-91-302-66-53. EST+6.
E-mail: ismadrid@terra.es
Anne Mazon, Prin. Beatriz Novella & Emma Segura, Adms.

Col Prep. Gen Acad. **Curr**—Nat UK. **Exams**—CEEB IGCSE AS-level A-level. **Feat**—Fr Span Comp_Sci Econ Relig Studio_Art. **Supp**—Dev_Read ESL Rem_Math Rem_Read Tut.
Sports—Basket Gymnastics Soccer Volley. **Activities**—Arts Govt/Pol Rec.
Enr 550. B 250. G 300. US 5. Host 495. Other 50. Accepted: 70%. Yield: 70%. Avg class size: 20.
Fac 45. M 16/2. F 21/6. US 1. Host 43. Other 1. Adv Deg: 17%.
Grad '05—15. Col—15. US Col—2.
Tui '05-'06: Day €3675-7800 (+€45-1530).
Summer: Acad Enrich Rec. 1½-4 wks.
Bldgs 2. Class rms 30. 2 Libs 8000 vols. Sci labs 3. Comp labs 1. Art studios 1. Music studios 2. Dance studios 1. Gyms 2. Courts 2.
Est 1971. Tri (Sept-June).

Designed to meet the needs of both Spanish and non-Spanish students living in Madrid, ISM's curriculum follows the English National Curriculum and, for Spanish pupils, satisfies the educational requirements of the Spanish Government. Boys and girls prepare for the IGCSE examinations primarily in grade 10 (although tests for certain courses are taken in grade 9), then advance to the AS and A levels in grades 11 and 12. SAT preparation is available for those students wishing it. The school conducts Christian religion classes once a week.

ALOHA COLLEGE

Day — Coed Gr PS-12

29660 Marbella, Malaga, Spain. Urb El Angel, Nueva Andalucia. Tel: 34-952-814133. Fax: 34-952-812729. EST+6.
www.aloha-college.com   E-mail: info@aloha-college.com
Robert Clarence, Head.
    Col Prep. IB Diploma. Curr—Intl Nat UK. **Supp Lang**—Span. **Exams**—IGCSE.
    Enr 700.
    Fac 80.
    Tui '05-'06: Day €5100-10,920 (+€180).
    Est 1982. Nonprofit. Sem (Sept-June).

ENGLISH INTERNATIONAL COLLEGE

Day — Coed Gr PS-12

29600 Marbella, Malaga, Spain. Urb Ricmar, Carretera de Cadiz, Malaga Km 189½. Tel: 34-952-83-1058. Fax: 34-952-83-8992. EST+6.
www.eic.edu   E-mail: academicadmin@eic.edu
Ron Griffin, Dir.
    Col Prep. Curr—UK. **Exams**—GCSE IGCSE A-level. **Feat**—Fr Ger Econ Geog
    Studio_Art Drama Music Bus.
    Enr 500.
    Est 1982. Tri (Sept-June).

THE ACADEMY INTERNATIONAL SCHOOL

Day — Coed Gr PS-12

07141 Marratxi, Mallorca, Spain. Cami de Son Ametler Vell 16, Apartado 120. Tel: 34-971-605-008. Fax: 34-971-226-158. EST+6.
www.theacademyschool.com   E-mail: Info@theacademyschool.com
Hazel Stephens, Head. MEd. **Cynthia Walker, Prin.**
    Col Prep. Gen Acad. Curr—Nat UK. **Bilingual**—Span. **Exams**—IGCSE.
    Feat—Ger Catalan Studio_Art Music. **Supp**—Dev_Read EFL LD Rem_Math
    Rem_Read Tut.
    Activities—Arts Rec.
    Enr 226. B 112. G 114. Elem 196. Sec 30. US 5. Host 150. Other 71. Avg class
    size: 20.
    Fac 25. M 4/1. F 18/2. Host 3. Other 22. Adv Deg: 8%.
    Grad '05—20.
    Tui '05-'06: Day €4038-6994. Aid: 5 pupils.
    Summer: Enrich Rev Rec. EFL. Tui Day €170/wk. 4 wks.
    Bldgs 4. Class rms 13. Lib 300 vols. Sci labs 1. Comp labs 1. Art studios 1. Dance
    studios 1. Gyms 1. Fields 1. Courts 1. Pools 1. Riding rings 1. Stables 4.

Est 1985. Tri (Sept-June).

Within a bilingual structure, the school combines solid academics with offerings in the arts and athletics. The academy follows the British National Curriculum
and the Spanish curriculum in language, media studies and Catalan, thus allowing
students to progress easily to either Spanish- or English-medium schools. Due in
large part to the relatively high percentage of German students, English as a Foreign
Language instruction is available during both the academic year and the month-long
summer session.

SUNLAND INTERNATIONAL SCHOOL
Day — Coed Gr PS-9

**29580 Nueva Aljaima, Malaga, Spain. Carretera Cartama Estacion-Pizarra. Tel: 34-
952-42-42-53. Fax: 34-952-42-44-10. EST+6.**
www.sunland-int.com   E-mail: admin@sunland-int.com
Mary Langford, Actg Head. BA, MEd.
> **Gen Acad. IB PYP. Curr**—Intl Nat UK. **Supp Lang**—Span. **Feat**—Span Computers
> Geog Studio_Art Music. **Supp**—EFL ESL LD Tut.
> **Sports**—Basket F_Hockey Soccer. **Activities**—Arts Rec.
> **Enr 212.** B 100. G 112. US 4. Host 77. Other 131. Accepted: 97%. Yield: 100%. Avg
> class size: 18.
> **Fac 20.** M 6. F 13/1. US 1. Host 4. Other 15. Adv Deg: 5%.
> **Grad '05—15.**
> **Tui '05-'06: Day €4350-6255** (+€50). **Aid:** 15 pupils (€20,531).
> **Summer:** Acad Rec. Tui Day €425. 4 wks.
> Plant val €4,500,000. Bldgs 3. Class rms 14. Libs 1. Sci labs 1. Comp labs 1. Art
> studios 1. Music studios 1. Fields 1. Courts 2. Pools 1.
> **Est 2001.** Inc. Tri (Sept-June).

This international school employs the British National Curriculum and conducts
daily Spanish language and social studies courses. The primary school follows the
International Baccalaureate Primary Years Program. The secondary curriculum
includes courses in citizenship, technology, and personal, social and health education.

Sunland's campus lies to the west and north of Malaga and features academic
buildings, athletic facilities and a small school farm.

BELLVER INTERNATIONAL COLLEGE
Day — Coed Gr PS-12

**07015 Palma de Mallorca, Spain. Josep Costa Ferrer 5, Marivent-Calamayor.
Tel: 34-971-401-679. Fax: 34-971-401-762. EST+6.**
www.bellvercollege.com   E-mail: info@bellvercollege.com
Larry Longhurst, Head.
> **Col Prep. Curr**—UK. **Exams**—GCSE IGCSE AS-level A-level. **Feat**—Fr Span
> Comp_Sci Studio_Art Bus.
> **Tui '05-'06: Day €4140-7170** (+€1200).
> **Est 1950.** Tri.

CAXTON COLLEGE

Bdg — Coed Gr 6-12; Day — Coed PS-12

46530 Pucol, Valencia, Spain. Carretera de Barcelona s/n. Tel: 34-96-142-4500. Fax: 34-96-142-0930. EST+6.

www.caxtoncollege.com   E-mail: caxton@caxtoncollege.com

Amparo Gil Marques, Prin.

    Col Prep. Gen Acad. Curr—UK. **Bilingual**—Span. **Exams**—IGCSE AS-level A-level. **Feat**—Chin Fr Ger Span Studio_Art Bus. **Supp**—EFL ESL Rem_Math Rem_Read Rev Tut.

    Activities—Arts Rec.

    Enr 1295. Elem 958. Sec 337. US 12. Host 1157. Other 126. Avg class size: 25.

    Fac 200. Host 75. Other 125.

    Grad '05—67. Col—31.

    Tui '05-'06: Bdg €14,000 (+€2000). **Day €5200.**

    Summer: Acad Rev Rec. Tui Bdg €1301/4-wk ses. Tui Day €440/4-wk ses. 8 wks.

    Bldgs 4. Class rms 71. Lib 16,000 vols. Sci labs 5. Comp labs 2. Theaters 1. Art studios 2. Music studios 2. Dance studios 2. Gyms 2. Fields 5. Courts 2. Basketball courts 1. Pools 1.

    Est 1987. Inc. Tri (Sept-June).

Pupils learn three languages at Caxton—English, Spanish and German—while they study all subjects that are part of the national curricula of England and Spain. Instruction is available in both English and Spanish for most courses. Students take A-level course work during the later years.

Various complementary activities are available during and after school. A special Saturday program for boys and girls lacking in English proficiency combines two hours of English instruction with athletic participation in such sports as paddle tennis, tennis, miniature golf, soccer, basketball and volleyball.

Boarders reside with local host families.

BALEARES INTERNATIONAL SCHOOL

Day — Coed Gr PS-13

07015 San Agustin, Palma de Mallorca, Spain. Calle Cabo Mateu Coch 17. Tel: 34-971-40-31-61. Fax: 34-971-70-03-19. EST+6.

www.balearesint.net   E-mail: bis@ocea.es

J. Barrie Wiggins, Dir. BS.

    Col Prep. Curr—UK US. **Exams**—CEEB SSAT TOEFL GCSE A-level. **Feat**—Fr Ger Span Geog.

    Enr 225.

    Fac 23.

    Tui '05-'06: Day €3042-7356.

    Est 1957. Quar (Sept-June).

KING'S COLLEGE

Bdg — Coed Ages 11-18; Day — Coed 3-18

28761 Soto de Vinuelas, Madrid, Spain. Paseo de los Andes 35. Tel: 34-918-034-800. Fax: 34-918-036-557. EST+6.

www.kingscollege.es   E-mail: info@kingscollege.es

David Johnson, Head. MSc.

> Col Prep. Curr—Nat UK. Exams—GCSE IGCSE A-level. Feat—Fr Span Comp_ Sci Econ Geog Studio_Art Music.
>
> Enr 1350.
>
> Fac 100.
>
> Est 1969. Tri (Sept-June).

SOTOGRANDE INTERNATIONAL SCHOOL

Bdg — Coed Ages 10-18; Day — Coed 3-18

11310 Sotogrande, Cadiz, Spain. Apartado 15. Tel: 34-956-79-59-02. Fax: 34-956-79-48-16. EST+6.

www.sis.ac   E-mail: info@sis.ac

Christopher Charleson, Head. BSc, DipEd.

> Col Prep. IB PYP. IB MYP. IB Diploma. Curr—Intl UK. Exams—GCSE IGCSE. Feat—Econ Geog Visual_Arts Drama Music Bus. Supp—EFL ESL.
>
> Enr 614.
>
> Fac 77.
>
> Tui '02-'03: Bdg €14,703-17,106 (+€280). Day €3939-7776 (+€280).
>
> Est 1978. Nonprofit. Tri (Sept-June).

AMERICAN SCHOOL OF LAS PALMAS

Day — Coed Gr PS-12

35017 Tafira Alta, Las Palmas de Gran Canaria, Spain. Apartado 15. Tel: 34-928-430023. Fax: 34-928-430017. EST+6.

www.aslp.org   E-mail: info@aslp.org

Joyce Lujan Martinez, Dir. BA, MS, PhD.

> Col Prep. Curr—Nat US. Supp Lang—Span. Exams—AP CEEB.
>
> Enr 410.
>
> Fac 50.
>
> Est 1967. Nonprofit. Quar (Sept-June). Assoc: MAIS NEASC.

SCHOOL YEAR ABROAD

Bdg — Coed Gr 11-12

50004 Zaragoza, Spain. Plaza de Aragon 12. Tel: 34-976-239-208. Fax: 34-976-235-220. EST+6.

Contact: 439 S Union St, Lawrence, MA 01843. Tel: 978-725-6828. Fax: 978-725-6833.

www.sya.org   E-mail: mail@sya.org

Woodruff W. Halsey II, Exec Dir. AB, MA. Whitney Hermann, Adm.

Col Prep. Curr—US. **Bilingual**—Span. **Exams**—CEEB. **AP**—Span Calc. **Feat**—
Environ_Sci Art_Hist Film Theater Journ.
Sports—Basket Baseball Soccer Volley. **Activities**—Arts Media Service.
Enr 60. Accepted: 66%. Yield: 85%. Avg class size: 15.
Fac 8. M 4. F 4. US 3. Host 5. Adv Deg: 100%.
Avg SAT: M/V—1315, Essay—668.
Tui '05-'06: Bdg $36,000 (+$2000). **Aid:** 25 pupils ($639,942).
Est 1964. Nonprofit. Quar (Sept-June).

School Year Abroad was established by Phillips Academy and is now a consortium of 26 independent schools. SYA provides a fully accredited year of study for high school students in Zaragoza. The program is open to qualified juniors and seniors who have completed at least two years of Spanish language study. With the exception of English and math courses, the medium of instruction is Spanish.

Students live with native families and travel during vacation periods. American instructors teach math and English courses in English from American texts. Program participants learn about the culture and customs of the native country. Students prepare for the US College Boards and for certain Advanced Placement exams.

Similar programs operate in China, France and Italy (see separate listings).

SWEDEN

Sq. Miles: 173,731 (About the size of California). **Country Pop:** 9,001,774 (2005). **Capital:** Stockholm, pop. 765,044 (2005). **Terrain:** Generally flat or rolling. **Ethnic Group(s):** Swede Finn Sami. **Religion(s):** Lutheran Catholic Orthodox Baptist Jewish Buddhist Muslim. **Official Language(s):** Swedish. **Other Language(s):** Finn Sami. **Government:** Constitutional Monarchy. **Per Capita Income:** $26,200 (2004). **GDP:** $255.4 billion (2004). Agriculture 2%. Industry 28%. Services 70%. **Currency:** Swedish Krona (Sk).

BRITISH INTERNATIONAL PRIMARY SCHOOL OF STOCKHOLM
Day — Coed Ages 3-11

182 68 Djursholm, Sweden. Ostra Valhallavagen 17. Tel: 46-8-755-2375. Fax: 46-8-755-2635. EST+6.
www.britishinternationalprimaryschool.se
E-mail: borgen@britishinternationalprimaryschool.se
Jane Crowley, Prin.
Gen Acad. Curr—UK. **Supp**—ESL.
Enr 140.
Fac 17.
Tui '05-'06: Day Sk83,200-124,100.
Est 1980. Tri (Aug-June).

GRENNASKOLAN RIKSINTERNAT
IB PROGRAMME

Bdg and Day — Coed Ages 13-20

563 22 Granna, Sweden. Box 95. Tel: 46-390-561-50. Fax: 46-390-561-51. EST+6.
www.grennaskolan.se   E-mail: info@grennaskolan.se
Marianne Pollard, Coord.

Col Prep. IB MYP. IB Diploma. Curr—Intl. Feat—Fr Ger Swedish Geog Psych
Visual_Arts Theater_Arts Music.
Tui '05-'06: Bdg Sk120,000-220,000 (+Sk4500).
Est 1994.

INTERNATIONAL SCHOOL OF HELSINGBORG

Day — Coed Gr K-12

254 51 Helsingborg, Sweden. Vastra Allen 7. Tel: 46-42-105-705. Fax: 46-42-134-190. EST+6.
www.is-hbg.se   E-mail: julie.little@helsingborg.se
Anders Nilsson, Prin.

Col Prep. IB PYP. IB MYP. IB Diploma. Curr—Intl Nat. Feat—Fr Swedish Comp_
Sci Econ Philos Studio_Art Drama Music. Supp—EFL ESL LD.
Activities—Media Service.
Enr 333. Elem 245. Sec 88. US 35. Host 160. Other 138. Avg class size: 20.
Fac 30. M 11/1. F 14/4. US 4. Host 6. Other 20. Adv Deg: 100%.
Grad '05—10.
Tui '06-'07: Day $0.
Bldgs 2. Class rms 30. Lib 5000 vols. Sci labs 3. Comp labs 1. Auds 1. Art studios 1.
Music studios 1. Gyms 1. Fields 1. Courts 2.
Est 1995. Nonprofit. Sem (Aug-June).

Founded in response to local demand for international schooling, ISH employs English as its language of instruction and follows IB guidelines. International pupils, whose families are typically on short-term assignment to one of the area's multinational companies, enroll from Europe, North and South America, Asia and the Middle East. Beginning in kindergarten and continuing through grade 5, the school conducts the Primary Years Program. Boys and girls then progress to the Middle Years Program and, finally, the Diploma Program. As ISH is a state school, course work also fulfills requirements of the Swedish National Curriculum.

Located at the neck of the main entrance to the Baltic Sea, Helsingborg is accessible to Copenhagen, Denmark; Gothenburg; and Malmo.

BLADIN'S INTERNATIONAL SCHOOL

Day — Coed Gr PS-10

200 74 Malmo, Sweden. Box 20093. Tel: 46-40-300885. Fax: 46-40-910885. EST+6.
www.bladins.se   E-mail: info@bladins.se
Sandra Nilsson, Coord.

Gen Acad. IB PYP. IB MYP. Curr—Intl. Feat—Humanities Fr Span Computers
Studio_Art Drama Music. Supp—ESL LD.

Activities—Service.
Enr 238. B 119. G 119. Elem 208. Sec 30. Avg class size: 22.
Fac 24. M 4/5. F 9/6. Adv Deg: 12%.
Tui '05-'06: Day Sk60,500-66,900.
Libs 1. Sci labs 2. Comp labs 1. Art studios 1. Music studios 1. Gyms 1.
Est 1987. Sem (Aug-June).

BIS follows the programming of the International Baccalaureate Organization. Course work emphasizes creative and critical thinking, in addition to independent learning skills. Instruction is in English, and pupils study Swedish and either French, German or Spanish as foreign languages. Physical education, technology, community service and cross-curricular projects are integral to the program.

SODERKULLA INTERNATIONAL SCHOOL
Day — Coed Gr PS-8

200 46 Malmo, Sweden. Soderkullagatan 14, Box 240 46. Tel: 46-40-34-68-41. Fax: 46-40-34-68-63. EST+6.
www.pedc.se/soder   E-mail: soderkulla@malmo.se
Lars Mansson, Prin.
> **Gen Acad. Curr**—Nat. **Bilingual**—Swedish. **Feat**—Fr Ger Span Geog Relig Studio_Art Music Speech.
> **Enr 125.** B 56. G 69.
> **Fac 12.** M 3. F 6/3.
> **Est 1996.** Sem (Aug-June).

INTERNATIONAL SCHOOL IN NACKA
Day — Coed Gr PS-10

133 04 Saltsjobaden, Sweden. Box 4003. Tel: 46-8-718-8300. Fax: 46-8-718-8302. EST+6.
www.isn.nacka.se   E-mail: international.school@nacka.se
Anita Malmjarn-Askelof, Prin.
> **Col Prep. IB PYP. IB MYP. IB Diploma. Curr**—Intl Nat. **Supp Lang**—Swedish. **Feat**—Fr Ger Span Comp_Sci Studio_Art Music. **Supp**—ESL.
> **Enr 350.** B 165. G 185.
> **Fac 46.**
> **Est 1995.** Sem (Aug-June).

SIGTUNASKOLAN HUMANISTISKA LAROVERKET
Bdg and Day — Coed Gr 9-12

193 28 Sigtuna, Sweden. PO Box 508. Tel: 46-8-592-571-00. Fax: 46-8-592-572-50. EST+6.
www.sshl.se   E-mail: info@sshl.se
Rune Svaninger, Head.
> **Col Prep. IB MYP. IB Diploma. Curr**—Intl Nat. **Supp Lang**—Swedish.
> **Enr 590.** B 180/125. G 150/135.

Fac 92. M 30/3. F 29/30.
Tui '05-'06: Bdg Sk132,000-261,100. Day Sk16,000-20,500.
Est 1926. Sem (Aug-June).

STOCKHOLM INTERNATIONAL SCHOOL
Day — Coed Gr PS-12

111 38 Stockholm, Sweden. Johannesgatan 18. Tel: 46-8-412-40-00. Fax: 46-8-412-40-01. EST+6.
www.intsch.se   E-mail: admin@intsch.se
John Foulkes-Jones, Prin. Erik Bennett, Adm.

Col Prep. IB PYP. IB MYP. IB Diploma. Curr—Intl. Feat—Fr Ger Swedish Comp_ Sci Psych Studio_Art Drama Music. Supp—ESL.
Enr 357. Avg class size: 18.
Fac 40.
Tui '05-'06: Day Sk72,000-140,000 (+Sk4000-24,000).
Class rms 26. Libs 2. Sci labs 2. Comp labs 1. Art studios 1. Gyms 1.
Est 1951. Nonprofit. Sem (Aug-June). Assoc: A/OPR/OS CIS MSA.

Enrolling students from more than 50 countries, the school follows the International Baccalaureate curriculum and utilizes English as its language of instruction. Boys and girls progress from the IB Primary Years Program to the Middle Years Program, then conclude their studies in pursuit of the IB Diploma. English as a Second Language are available. The main goal of the program is to facilitate either the student's transfer to another international school or a return to his or her home country's school system.

UPPSALA INTERNATIONAL SCHOOL
Day — Coed Gr PS-9

754 21 Uppsala, Sweden. Kvarngardesskolan Thunmansgatan 47. Tel: 46-18-727-5900. Fax: 46-18-727-5905. EST+6.
www.kvarngardesskolan.uppsala.se   E-mail: kvarngardesskolan@uppsala.se
Marianna Lovenstad, Prin. Jerry Morrissey, Adm.

Gen Acad. Curr—Nat. Bilingual—Swedish. Feat—Fr Ger Span Studio_Art Drama Music. Supp—EFL ESL.
Activities—Arts.
Enr 160. Avg class size: 22.
Fac 16. M 4/3. F 5/4.
Grad '05—14.
Tui '05-'06: Day $0.
Bldgs 7. Class rms 25. Gyms 2. Fields 2. Courts 1. Rinks 1.
Est 1993. Nonprofit. Sem (Aug-June).

As the international section of Kvarngardet School, UIS offers a bilingual curriculum to children of guest workers in Sweden, children who speak English as their first language, and foreign or Swedish children with a strong command of English. The school's Swedish curriculum emphasizes multiculturalism, and language instruction is available in French, German and Spanish.

SWITZERLAND

Sq. Miles: 15,941 (About the size of Vermont and New Hampshire combined). **Country Pop:** 7,489,370 (2005). **Capital:** Bern, pop. 123,000. **Largest City:** Zurich, pop. 341,000. **Terrain:** Largely mountainous, with hills and plateaus. **Religion(s):** Roman_Catholic Protestant Muslim. **Other Language(s):** German French Italian Romansch. **Government:** Federal State. **Per Capita Income:** $22,898 (2001). **GDP:** $358 billion (2004). Agriculture 2%. Industry 30%. Services 67%. **Currency:** Swiss Franc (SwF).

INTERNATIONAL SCHOOL OF ZUG
Day — Coed Gr PS-8

6340 Baar, Switzerland. Walterswil. Tel: 41-41-768-11-88. Fax: 41-41-768-11-89. EST+6.
www.isoz.ch E-mail: office@isoz.ch
Martin Latter, Dir. Elaine Tomlinson, Prin.
>Pre-Prep. Gen Acad. IB PYP. IB MYP. Curr—Intl. Feat—Dutch Fr Ger Dutch Computers Studio_Art Drama Music. Supp—Dev_Read ESL LD Rem_Math Rem_Read Tut.
>Activities—Rec.
>Enr 522. Elem 522. US 120. Host 104. Other 298. Avg class size: 16.
>Fac 90. M 14/10. F 38/28. US 12. Host 10. Other 68.
>Grad '05—16.
>Tui '06-'07: Day SwF12,000-24,000.
>Bldgs 5. Class rms 55. 2 Libs 20,000 vols. Sci labs 1. Lang labs 5. Comp labs 2. Auds 1. Theaters 1. Art studios 1. Music studios 2. Dance studios 1. Gyms 2. Fields 1.
>Est 1961. Tri (Aug-June).

Situated on the edge of Lake Zug, the school offers a curriculum similar to that found in an international American elementary school. While enrollment is not strictly American, most students speak English upon arrival; an ESL program serves children requiring extra help with the language. The teaching approach is individual, with groups kept as small as possible. Field trips to local places of interest enrich the program.

INTERNATIONAL SCHOOL RHEINTAL
Day — Coed Gr 1-11

9470 Buchs, Switzerland. Aeulistrasse 10. Tel: 41-81-750-63-00. Fax: 41-81-750-63-01. EST+6.
www.isr.ch E-mail: office@isr.ch
Meg Sutcliffe, Head. BSc, DipEd.
>Gen Acad. IB PYP. IB MYP. Curr—Intl. Feat—Fr Ger Comp_Sci Studio_Art Music. Supp—ESL.
>Enr 90. B 48. G 42. Elem 85. Sec 15. US 10. Host 30. Other 50. Accepted: 95%.

Avg class size: 12.
Fac 13. M 4. F 3/6. US 1. Host 1. Other 11. Adv Deg: 15%.
Tui '05-'06: Day SwF14,000-22,000 (+SwF1000). **Aid:** 4 pupils (SwF30,000).
Bldgs 3. Class rms 11. Lib 2000 vols. Sci labs 1. Comp labs 1. Art studios 1. Music studios 1.
Est 2002. Nonprofit. Sem (Aug-June).

Serving the needs of the international community in the Liechtenstein, St. Gallen and Vorarlberg region, ISR conducts an English-medium program that emphasizes critical thinking, problem solving, qualitative and quantitative thinking, computation, research and information analysis, and communicational skills. Boys and girls follow the International Baccalaureate PYP and MYP curricula, which consist of course work in language arts, math, social studies, science, design and technology, arts and crafts, music, German (from grade 1), technology, and physical education and swimming.

In addition to weekly music classes, students may receive instrumental music instruction. Local and extended field trips that vary in length from a day to a week enrich the academic program. Pupils have opportunities to share music and drama performances and artwork displays.

After-school activities vary throughout the year according to student interest and the availability of instructors. Among typical offerings are interest clubs, sports, arts and crafts, and foreign languages.

AIGLON COLLEGE

Bdg and Day — Coed Ages 9-18

1885 Chesieres-Villars, Switzerland. Tel: 41-24-496-6161. Fax: 41-24-496-6162. EST+6.
www.aiglon.ch   E-mail: info@aiglon.ch
Jonathan Long, Head. MA, MTh, PhD. **Mary Sidebottom, Adm.**

    Col Prep. Curr—UK. **Supp Lang**—Fr. **Exams**—CEEB TOEFL O-level AS-level A-level. **Feat**—Arabic Dutch Fr Ger Greek Ital Japan Port Russ Span Swedish Econ Psych Philos Relig Studio_Art Drama Music. **Supp**—Dev_Read ESL Rem_Math Rem_Read Tut.

    Sports—Basket Gymnastics Rugby Ski Soccer Swim Volley. **Activities**—Rec Service.

    Enr 350. B 150/30. G 145/25. US 30. Host 30. Other 290. Avg class size: 11.

    Fac 85. Adv Deg: 25%.

    Grad '05—50. **Col**—50. US Col—23.

    Tui '05-'06: Bdg SwF46,400-65,200 (+SwF3000). **Day SwF19,000-45,600** (+SwF1000).

    Summer: Bdg. Ages 10-16. Acad Enrich Rec. Tui Bdg SwF5500. 3 wks. Winter Sports. Tui Bdg SwF2150. 1-2 wks.

    Bldgs 18. Dorms 8. Libs 30,000. Gyms 1. Fields 2. Courts 5. Rinks 1.

    Est 1949. Nonprofit. Tri (Sept-July). Assoc: CIS NEASC.

Offering a UK-style curriculum, Aiglon College stands on a sheltered south slope of the Swiss Alps, at a height of 4250 feet overlooking the Rhone Valley to the Dents du Midi and the Massif du Mont-Blanc. With approximately one-quarter of its students being either British or American, Aiglon operates along the lines of an English public school. The curriculum meets the requirements of the British GCSE and GCE and the US College Boards. Graduates matriculate at a variety of competitive American and British colleges.

In addition to skiing, swimming and other sports, the physical education program features skiing, hiking and cycling expeditions, as well as instruction in the techniques of rock climbing, camping and rescue work. Aiglon encourages pupils to engage in handicrafts and hobbies, and they may pursue other interests through clubs and societies.

ST. GEORGE'S SCHOOL

Bdg — Girls Gr 6-12; Day — Boys PS-9, Girls PS-12

1815 Clarens, Montreux, Switzerland. CP 213. Tel: 41-21-964-34-11. Fax: 41-21-964-49-32. EST+6.
www.st-georges.ch   E-mail: office@st-georges.ch
Carolyn S. Steinson, Prin. Vicky Perbos-Parsons, Adm.
   Col Prep. Curr—UK. Exams—CEEB TOEFL IGCSE A-level. Feat—Fr Ger Ital Japan Russ Span Studio_Art Music. Supp—EFL ESL Rev Tut.
   Sports—Badminton Basket X-country Golf Soccer Swim Track Volley. Activities—Arts Rec.
   Enr 158. B 51. G 38/69. US 17. Host 18. Other 123. Avg class size: 14.
   Fac 31.
   Grad '05—20.
   Tui '05-'06: Bdg SwF62,400-65,000 (+SwF3000). Day SwF20,400-30,000. Aid: 8 pupils (SwF53,000).
   Summer: Acad Rec. Tui Bdg SwF4500. Tui Day SwF2600. 4 wks.
   Bldgs 3. Dorms 2. Class rms 25. Lib 15,000 vols. Labs 2. Art studios 2. Gyms 1. Tennis courts 5. Pools 1.
   Est 1927. Nonprofit. Tri (Sept-June).

Overlooking Lake Geneva and the Savoy Alps, St. George's offers a British-style curriculum geared towards the IGCSE and GCE exams and the American College Boards. The program prepares students for admission to both American colleges and universities elsewhere.

The study of modern language is strongly emphasized, and the school's summer program provides intensive French and English instruction. Enriching the academic program are music, art and drama classes.

INTERNATIONAL SCHOOL OF GENEVA (ECOLE INTERNATIONALE DE GENEVE)

Day — Coed Gr PS-13

1208 Geneva, Switzerland. 62 Rte de Chene. Tel: 41-22-787-24-00. Fax: 41-22-787-24-10. EST+6.
www.ecolint.ch   E-mail: administration@ecolint.ch
Nicholas Tate, Dir. PhD. John Douglas, Adm.
   Col Prep. IB PYP. IB MYP. IB Diploma. Swiss Mat. Curr—Intl. Bilingual—Fr. Exams—TOEFL IGCSE. Feat—Arabic Ger Ital Span Ecol Comp_Sci Econ Philos Studio_Art Drama Theater_Arts Music. Supp—ESL LD Rem_Math

Rem_Read.

Sports—Basket Rugby Soccer Track. **Activities**—Arts Media.

Enr 3749. B 1961. G 1788. Elem 2570. Sec 1179. US 591. Host 548. Other 2610. Avg class size: 20.

Fac 394. M 71/33. F 219/71. US 30. Host 85. Other 279.

Grad '05—300.

Tui '05-'06: Day SwF14,240-24,190.

Bldgs 32. Libs 6. Labs 16. Theaters 1. Art studios 7. Music studios 6.

Est 1924. Nonprofit. Tri (Sept-June). Assoc: CIS MSA.

Founded by staff of the League of Nations as the world's first international school, this institution also offered an International Baccalaureate diploma program before any other school. Today, the IB continues to form the basis of the senior secondary school's college preparatory program.

Pupils in the IB program may earn their diplomas in French, English or a combination of the two. The school prepares students for several exams and also grants the American high school diploma. Boys and girls of varying ability levels enroll, and a support program serves individuals with learning difficulties. French and English courses are compulsory at the secondary level, while German, Italian and Spanish classes are part of the language program.

The school occupies three campuses. La Grande Boissiere, located in Geneva, is the largest of the three. Another secondary school location, La Chataigneraie, is 15 miles away in Fourex. The newest campus, Des Nations, serves elementary and secondary students at two sites adjacent to the United Nations in Geneva.

GENEVA ENGLISH SCHOOL

Day — Coed Gr PS-6

1294 Genthod, Switzerland. 36 Rte de Malagny. Tel: 41-22-755-18-55. Fax: 41-22-779-14-29. EST+6.

www.geneva-english-school.ch   E-mail: gesadmin@iprolink.ch

Denis Unsworth, Head. BA, DipEd, MA.

Gen Acad. Curr—UK. **Feat**—Fr Computers Studio_Art Music.

Enr 170. B 85. G 85. Elem 170.

Fac 18.

Tui '05-'06: Day SwF17,150 (+SwF900).

Class rms 7. Libs 1. Gyms 1. Fields 1.

Est 1962. Tri (Sept-June).

The British-based curriculum offered at GES, which is located near the north shore of Lake Geneva, prepares students for secondary education in the US and Switzerland, as well as in Britain. Emphasis is on the development of basic skills, especially those concerning arithmetic and reading, begun in preparatory classes. All students take French. Music, including instruction in singing and several instruments, and arts and crafts—ranging from collage, mosaics and modeling to sewing, embroidery and knitting—enrich the program.

Sports are an important part of school life, with several periods of physical education each week complemented by the opportunity to participate in cross-country, gymnastics, basketball, soccer and rugby. Excursions to museums and local sites of interest, a winter ski camp for older students, annual drama productions in English and French, and other school activities complete school life.

GSTAAD INTERNATIONAL SCHOOL
Bdg — Coed Gr 8-12

3780 Gstaad, Switzerland. Ahorn. Tel: 41-33-7442373. Fax: 41-33-7443578. EST+6.
www.gstaadschool.ch   E-mail: gis@gstaad.ch
Alain Souperbiet, Dir.

    Col Prep. Curr—UK US. **Exams**—AP CEEB TOEFL IGCSE A-level. **Feat**—Comp_ Sci Econ Studio_Art Music. **Supp**—ESL LD.

    Tui '05-'06: Bdg SwF65,800.

    Est 1962. Inc. Tri (Sept-June).

THE BRITISH SCHOOL
BERN
Day — Coed Gr PS-6

3073 Gumligen, Switzerland. Hintere Dorfgasse 20. Tel: 41-31-952-75-55. Fax: 41-31-952-75-57. EST+6.
www.britishschool.ch   E-mail: britishschool@bluewin.ch
Enid Potts, Head. BEd.

    Gen Acad. Curr—Intl UK. **Feat**—Ger Computers Geog Studio_Art Drama Music. **Supp**—ESL Rem_Math Rem_Read.

    Activities—Arts Media Rec.

    Enr 68. B 36. G 32. Elem 68. US 8. Host 14. Other 46. Avg class size: 11.

    Fac 13. F 6/7. US 1. Host 1. Other 11. Adv Deg: 7%.

    Grad '05—5.

    Tui '05-'06: Day SwF16,000.

    Bldgs 1. Class rms 8. Lib 3000 vols.

    Est 1988. Nonprofit. Sem (Aug-June).

With a program based upon British and international systems, the school supplements its elementary curriculum with field trips to museums, theaters and zoos, as well as visits to such nearby cities as Lucerne, Basel and Zurich. All children have access to a computer in class, as well as to a central computer for more involved projects and research. Older pupils regularly attend art workshops conducted for English-speaking children.

Swimming, ice skating, skiing and general physical education form an important part of the school's program. Scouting, instrumental music instruction, drama productions, musical performances and a summer fair represent some of the British School's activities.

INTERNATIONAL SCHOOL OF BERNE

Day — Coed Gr PS-12

3073 Gumligen, Switzerland. Mattenstrasse 3. Tel: 41-31-951-23-58. Fax: 41-31-951-17-10. EST+6.

www.isberne.ch   E-mail: office@isberne.ch

Kevin Page, Dir. MEd, MBA.

> Col Prep. IB PYP. IB MYP. IB Diploma. Curr—Intl. Exams—CEEB IGCSE. Feat—Fr Ger Comp_Sci Econ Studio_Art Theater_Arts Music. Supp—Dev_Read ESL Rem_Math.
>
> Sports—Basket Soccer Volley. Activities—Rec.
>
> Enr 236. B 122. G 114. US 36. Host 24. Other 176. Avg class size: 16.
>
> Fac 40. M 12. F 22/6. US 8. Host 1. Other 31. Adv Deg: 25%.
>
> Grad '05—15. Col—15.
>
> Tui '05-'06: Day SwF19,300-24,940 (+SwF4000).
>
> Bldgs 4. 2 Libs 16,000 vols. Sci labs 3. Comp labs 2. Auds 1. Art studios 2. Music studios 1. Gyms 1. Fields 1.
>
> Est 1960. Nonprofit. Tri (Aug-June). Assoc: A/OPR/OS CIS NEASC.

Located in the residential community of Gumligen (20 minutes from Berne), ISB consists of an early learning center (ages 3 and 4), an elementary section (grades K-5) and a secondary section (grades 6-12). The English-medium curriculum includes the humanities, language arts, foreign language, math, science, the arts and physical education. The school follows all three programs of the International Baccalaureate Organization.

Within its academic framework, the school makes full use of its location in the center of Switzerland. Alpine summer and winter athletics include skiing, skating, hiking and mountain sports.

ECOLE D'HUMANITE

Bdg — Coed Gr 5-12; Day — Coed 1-12

6085 Hasliberg-Goldern, Switzerland. Tel: 41-33-972-92-92. Fax: 41-33-972-92-11. EST+6.

www.ecole.ch   E-mail: us.office@ecole.ch

Kenneth C. Hill, Dir. BA.

> Col Prep. Gen Acad. Swiss Mat. Curr—Nat UK US. Bilingual—Ger. Exams—CEEB TOEFL. Feat—Fr Psych Philos World_Relig Music Dance. Supp—ESL Makeup Tut.
>
> Sports—Basket Equestrian Gymnastics Sail Ski Soccer Volley. Activities—Acad Govt/Pol Rec Service.
>
> Enr 146. B 73/4. G 65/4. Elem 33. Sec 113. Avg class size: 5.
>
> Fac 50. M 25. F 25. US 11. Host 16. Other 23. Adv Deg: 18%.
>
> Grad '05—6. Avg SAT: M/V—1320, Essay—610.
>
> Tui '05-'06: Bdg SwF36,000 (+SwF1680). Day SwF18,000. Aid: 12 pupils (SwF180,000).
>
> Endow SwF1,000,000. Bldgs 13. Dorm rms 75. Class rms 33. Lib 20,000 vols. Fields 2. Courts 1.
>
> Est 1934. Nonprofit. Tri (Sept-June).

Children of many nationalities, races and religions study and grow up together in a spirit of cooperation and cultural interchange at this unusual school in the Bernese Oberlands. About half of the students are Swiss nationals, while the rest come from the US and various nations in Europe, South America, Asia and Africa.

The educational structures of the school were developed by its founder, Paul Geheeb, who previously directed a school in Germany from 1910 until 1934, when he fled increasing Nazi pressure. Under his course system, only three academic subjects are studied during periods of five or six weeks. Rather than being divided into conventional classes, children are grouped by ability in subjects. They may pursue independent study under a teacher's supervision.

All students are required to learn German, and most classes are taught in this language. US history, math, science, sociology and English courses are taught in English. The program prepares students for the US College Boards and the Swiss Maturite. While no longer part of the curriculum, GCE preparation is arranged for any students who desire it.

Emphasizing artistic and practical work, the school reserves afternoons for courses in the fine arts and crafts, as well as for athletics, among them hiking and skiing. Living in small, family-style groups of faculty and students, the children share in the communal self-governing of the school and the upkeep of house and grounds.

Near the Brunig Pass, an hour's drive from Lucerne and Interlaken, the village of Goldern is situated on the terrace of the Hasliberg at an altitude of 3500 feet.

THE BILINGUAL SCHOOL TERRA NOVA

Day — Coed Gr PS-6

8700 Kusnacht, Switzerland. Florastrasse 19. Tel: 41-44-910-4300. Fax: 41-44-910-4305. EST+6.
www.terra-nova.ch   E-mail: info@terra-nova.ch
Daniel Landos, Head.

> **Gen Acad. Curr**—Intl Nat. **Bilingual**—Ger. **Feat**—Fr Studio_Art Theater Music. **Supp**—Dev_Read ESL Rem_Math Rem_Read Tut.
> **Enr 116.** B 62. G 54. Elem 116. US 15. Host 50. Other 51. Avg class size: 14.
> **Fac 18.** M 2/4. F 3/9. US 2. Host 10. Other 6. Adv Deg: 11%.
> **Tui '05-'06: Day** SwF23,400 (+SwF1700).
> **Est 1996.** (Aug-July).

This bilingual school emphasizes global communication and cultural variety. German and English are given equal status, and at each grade level a German-language teacher and English-language teacher share instructional time. In the lower grades, children acquire an oral command of the second language before written instruction begins. Cultural activities include theater, music, and arts and crafts.

LAKESIDE BILINGUAL DAYSCHOOL ZURICH (ZWEISPRACHIGE TAGESSCHULE ZURICHSEE)

Day — Coed Gr PS-7

8700 Kusnacht, Switzerland. Seestrasse 21. Tel: 41-1-9142050. Fax: 41-1-9142059. EST+6.

www.lakesideschool.ch   E-mail: office@lakesideschool.ch
Stefan Urner, Head.
  Gen Acad. Curr—Intl Nat. Bilingual—Ger.
  Enr 135.
  Fac 16.
  Tui '05-'06: Day SwF21,360.
  Est 1996. Sem.

BRILLANTMONT INTERNATIONAL COLLEGE
Bdg and Day — Coed Ages 13-19

1005 Lausanne, Switzerland. 16 Ave Secretan. Tel: 41-21-310-0400. Fax: 41-21-320-8417. EST+6.
www.brillantmont.ch   E-mail: info@brillantmont.ch
Philippe Pasche, Dir. Geraldine Boland, Adm.
  Col Prep. Curr—UK US. Supp Lang—Fr. Exams—CEEB SSAT TOEFL IGCSE A-level. Feat—Chin Ital Russ Comp_Sci Photog Studio_Art Drama Music Dance Bus. Supp—EFL ESL.
  Enr 150. B 40/30. G 50/30. US 8. Host 8. Other 134.
  Fac 28. M 10/4. F 10/4. US 1. Host 4. Other 23.
  Grad '05—18.
  Tui '06-'07: Bdg SwF54,000-56,000 (+SwF6000). Day SwF23,000-25,000 (+SwF500).
  Summer: Bdg. Acad Rec. Tui Bdg SwF2660/2-wk ses. 6 wks.
  Bldgs 7. Dorms 4. Libs 1. Sci labs 3. Lang labs 2. Comp labs 1. Gyms 2. Tennis courts 2.
  Est 1882. Tri (Sept-June). Assoc: CIS NEASC.

Located on a four-acre site in the university town of Lausanne, Brillantmont comprises five sections: a British division that offers a varied curriculum leading to the IGCSE and A-level examinations; an American section that includes AP classes and preparation for the US College Boards; a Swiss division; a language school; and a business section. The British and American sections are university oriented, with a vast majority of graduates matriculating at four-year colleges in the US or Europe.

Lausanne is one mile north of Lake Geneva, facing the Alps. Many extracurricular and outdoor activities are available as a complement to academics.

ECOLE NOUVELLE DE LA SUISSE ROMANDE
Bdg — Coed Gr 7-12; Day — Coed PS-12

1012 Lausanne, Switzerland. Chemin de Rovereaz 20, CP 161. Tel: 41-21-654-65-00. Fax: 41-21-654-65-05. EST+6.
www.ensr.ch   E-mail: info@ensr.ch
Nicolas Catsicas, Head.
  Col Prep. IB Diploma. Swiss Mat. Curr—Intl Nat. Bilingual—Fr. Exams—CEEB. Feat—Ger Ital Russ Span Comp_Sci Anthro Econ Psych Philos Studio_Art Drama Music. Supp—EFL ESL Tut.
  Enr 476. Elem 350. Sec 126. US 10. Host 360. Other 106. Accepted: 100%. Avg class size: 19.

Fac 65. M 25/15. F 22/3. US 4. Host 51. Other 10. Adv Deg: 60%.
Grad '05—27. Col—22. US Col—3. Avg SAT: M/V—1000.
Tui '05-'06: Bdg SwF25,100-33,200. Day SwF7600-19,200.
Endow SwF200,000. Plant val SwF15,000,000. Bldgs 6. Dorms 1. Dorm rms 28.
  Class rms 40. Lib 5000 vols. Sci labs 2. Comp labs 26. Auds 1. Art studios 1.
  Gyms 1. Fields 3. Courts 1.
Est 1906. Nonprofit. Sem (Aug-June).

Located on a hill overlooking Lake Geneva in the French-speaking region of the country, ENSR offers a bilingual program that has featured a growing concentration in English over the years. Children as young as age 3 take part in a Montessori nursery school and kindergarten. In the primary school, the program includes daily English lessons and the introduction of German in grade 4. The middle school program (grades 5-8) includes a common core syllabus of basic subjects, the continued study of German, and the addition of other foreign languages in grades 7 and 8.

In the senior school, boys and girls may pursue either the Swiss national diploma or the IB Diploma. The International Baccalaureate program is unusual in that students take four subjects taught in English and four in French. Those wishing to attend US colleges may prepare for the SAT examination during the later years.

Boarders choose from five- and seven-day options.

INTERNATIONAL SCHOOL OF LAUSANNE

Day — Coed Gr PS-12

1052 Le Mont-sur-Lausanne, Switzerland. Chemin de la Grangette 2. Tel: 41-21-
  560-0202. Fax: 41-21-560-0203. EST+6.
www.isl.ch   E-mail: info@isl.ch
Simon G. Taylor, Dir.
  Col Prep. IB PYP. IB Diploma. Curr—Intl UK. **Exams**—IGCSE. **Feat**—Fr Ger
    Span Comp_Sci Econ Geog Studio_Art. **Supp**—ESL.
  Sports—Basket X-country Rugby Ski Soccer Softball Track. **Activities**—Arts Rec.
  Enr 557. B 248. G 309.
  Fac 78. M 19/4. F 36/19.
  Tui '05-'06: Day SwF19,200-26,100 (+SwF1950-3800).
  Est 1962. Nonprofit. Tri (Sept-June). Assoc: CIS NEASC.

Children from the United States attend ISL with children from Great Britain, Canada, Holland and Scandinavia. The curriculum is comparable to that of primary schools in Britain and the US, and it prepares children for secondary education. Instruction is provided in traditional subjects and computer studies, with French studied as a second language. Special courses and individual tutoring are arranged for children whose first language is not English.

Older students spend one day a week during the winter term receiving professional skiing instruction in the Alps.

LEYSIN AMERICAN SCHOOL
IN SWITZERLAND
Bdg — Coed Gr 9-PG

1854 Leysin, Switzerland. Tel: 41-24-493-3777. Fax: 41-24-494-1585. EST+6.
Contact: PO Box 7154, Portsmouth, NH 03802. Tel: 603-431-7654. Fax: 603-431-1280.
www.las.ch   E-mail: admissions@las.ch
Timothy Kelley, Head.

Col Prep. IB Diploma. Curr—Intl US. **Exams**—CEEB TOEFL. **Feat**—Ger Span Environ_Sci Comp_Sci Drama Band Chorus Music. **Supp**—ESL.
Enr 330. Accepted: 70%. Avg class size: 13.
Fac 78. M 24/2. F 28/24.
Grad '05—90. Col—90. US Col—65. (U of CA, U of TX, Boston Col, U of VA, Oberlin, U of MI). Avg SAT: M/V—1050.
Tui '05-'06: Bdg SwF50,000-53,500 (+SwF1500).
Summer: Acad Enrich Rev Rec. Theater. Leadership. ESL. Tui Bdg $2900/3-wk ses. 6 wks.
Plant val $21,000,000. Bldgs 10. Dorms 5. Dorm rms 150. Class rms 35. Lib 17,000 vols. Sci labs 5. Comp labs 2. Auds 1. Theaters 1. Art studios 4. Music studios 3. Dance studios 1. Gyms 1. Rinks 1. Riding rings 1. Stables 1.
Est 1960. Inc. Sem (Sept-June). Assoc: AISA CIS MSA.

Students at this American-administered school prepare for entrance into US colleges. The curriculum includes a full complement of Advanced Placement courses, an IB diploma program and a comprehensive ESL program. Pupils come primarily from the US, as do faculty members (except for European language teachers).

Physical education (including a variety of winter and summer sports), publications, clubs and hobby groups supplement the academic program, which is further enriched by field trips and weekend excursions. The school arranges special cultural tours for students unable to go home during the Easter holiday.

LAS is located at the edge of the health and ski resort of Leysin, at an altitude of 5000 feet, above the Rhone Valley and Lake Geneva. Geneva, European headquarters of the UN, is approximately 90 minutes away by car.

TASIS
THE AMERICAN SCHOOL IN SWITZERLAND
Bdg — Coed Gr 7-PG; Day — Coed K-PG

6926 Montagnola-Lugano, Switzerland. Tel: 41-91-960-5151. Fax: 41-91-993-2979. EST+6.
Contact: 1640 Wisconsin Ave NW, Washington, DC 20007. Tel: 202-965-5800. Fax: 202-965-5816.
www.tasis.com   E-mail: usadmissions@tasis.com
Jeffrey C. Bradley, Head. BA, MA. **William E. Eichner, Adm.**

Col Prep. IB Diploma. Curr—Intl US. **Exams**—ACT AP CEEB TOEFL. **AP**—Eng Fr Span Calc Bio Chem Human_Geog Physics Eur_Hist US_Hist Econ Art_Hist Studio_Art. **Feat**—Shakespeare Ger Ital Environ_Sci Architect Ceramics Photog Drama. **Supp**—ESL Tut.
Sports—Basket Rugby Soccer Swim Tennis Track Volley. **Activities**—Acad Arts

Govt/Pol Media Rec Service.

Enr 384. B 127/67. G 145/45. Elem 86. Sec 293. PG 5. US 108. Host 35. Other 241. Accepted: 56%. Yield: 80%. Avg class size: 12.

Fac 65. M 29/2. F 19/15. US 39. Host 5. Other 21. Adv Deg: 47%.

Grad '05—86. Col—86. US Col—35. (Geo Wash 7, Boston U 3, Bentley 3, U of VA 3, Tufts 2, Bard 2). Avg SAT: M/V—1180.

Tui '05-'06: Bdg $36,000. Day $27,000. Aid: 44 pupils.

Summer: Enrich Rec. Lang. Arts. ESL. Tui Bdg $4100-5000. Tui Day $1850-2400. 3-4 wks.

Plant val SwF28,000,000. Bldgs 17. Dorms 10. Dorm rms 125. Class rms 26. Lib 22,000 vols. Labs 6. Theaters 1. Art studios 1. Music studios 3. Dance studios 1. Gyms 1. Athletic ctrs 1. Fields 1. Courts 1. Basketball courts 2. Volleyball courts 2. Pools 1.

Est 1956. Nonprofit. Sem (Sept-June). Assoc: CIS NEASC.

The first American boarding school on the continent, founded by Mary Crist Fleming to provide preparation for US colleges in a European setting, TASIS now offers both an American-style curriculum and an International Baccalaureate option. The varied student body represents approximately 50 nations.

The core college preparatory program consists of course work in English, math, science, social studies, drama and languages; French, Spanish, Italian and German are the available languages. Various electives broaden the curriculum, and qualified pupils may take Advanced Placement classes or may pursue the IB course of studies. Those requiring assistance with English may receive English as a Second Language instruction.

After operating as a secondary school for five decades, TASIS opened an elementary school for children in grades K-6 in September 2005. Housed in a building overlooking the TASIS campus, it is the only English-language elementary school in Ticino Canton.

Course-related travel is an important element of the program at all grade levels. TASIS' travel program includes 10 days of educational travel throughout Europe, as well as a weeklong ski term when the school relocates to Crans-Montana.

The city of Lugano is a medical, financial and trading center, situated in southern Switzerland, in the lake region and close to the Italian border. The school is situated on a nine-acre campus five minutes from the city and a short walk below the village of Montagnola, located on a hill overlooking Lake Lugano.

See Also Pages 552-4

INSTITUT MONTE ROSA

Bdg and Day — Coed Gr 6-PG

1820 Montreux, Switzerland. 57 ave de Chillon. Tel: 41-21-965-45-45. Fax: 41-21-965-45-46. EST+6.

www.monterosa.ch   E-mail: info@monterosa.ch

Bernhard Gademann, Dir. BS, MS. **Elizabeth Barrett, Adm.**

    Col Prep. Curr—US. **Exams**—AP CEEB TOEFL. **AP**—Fr Span Calc Econ. **Feat**— Ger Ital Comp_Sci Studio_Art Music Bus Finance. **Supp**—EFL ESL Makeup Rem_Math Tut.

    Activities—Rec.

Enr 65. US 1. Host 2. Other 62. Accepted: 98%. Avg class size: 8.
Fac 12.
Grad '05—12. Col—11.
Tui '05-'06: Bdg SwF42,800-50,000 (+SwF8000). **Day SwF28,000-33,000** (+SwF3000).
Summer: Acad Enrich. Tui Bdg SwF1500/wk. Tui Day SwF1250/wk. 9 wks.
Bldgs 5. Dorms 3. Class rms 24. 2 Libs 3000 vols. Sci labs 1. Comp labs 1. Gyms 1. Fields 1. Tennis courts 1.
Est 1874. Nonprofit. Tri (Sept-June).

Offering an international college preparatory program, the school maintains an Anglo-American section that readies students for the US College Boards and awards a high school diploma upon the successful completion of grade 12. Specially designed courses prepare interested students for business college entry. The postgraduate year combines intensive language study with business, economics and computer studies. Pupils, who enroll from more than 20 countries, remain at the school for an average of two to three years.

Monte Rosa's comprehensive athletic program consists of both team and individual sports, including a full skiing program during the winter months. The school expects all students to participate in the sports program at least three times a week.

The village of Territet, where the school is located, is on the eastern shore of Lake Geneva, close to Montreux and about 17 miles from Lausanne.

NEUCHATEL JUNIOR COLLEGE

Bdg — Coed Gr 12

2002 Neuchatel, Switzerland. Cret-Taconnet 4. Tel: 41-32-725-2700. Fax: 41-32-724-4259. EST+6.
Contact: 44 Victoria St, Ste 1310, Toronto, Ontario M5C 1Y2 Canada. Tel: 416-368-8169, 800-263-2923. Fax: 416-368-0956.
www.njc.ch   E-mail: admissions@neuchatel.org
Norman Southward, Prin. BA, BEd, MEd. **Dayle Leishman, Adm.**
    Col Prep. Curr—Can. **Supp Lang**—Fr. **Exams**—AP CEEB. **AP**—Eng Fr Ger Calc Chem Human_Geog Physics Eur_Hist Comp_Govt & Pol Studio_Art. **Feat**—Econ Law Philos Bus.
    Sports—Rugby Ski Soccer Swim Volley. **Activities**—Acad Arts Govt/Pol Media Service.
    Enr 90. B 25. G 65. Sec 90. US 5. Other 85. Accepted: 95%. Yield: 98%. Avg class size: 12.
    Fac 10. M 5/1. F 3/1. Host 2. Other 8. Adv Deg: 50%.
    Grad '05—110. Col—110. US Col—4.
    Tui '06-'07: Bdg SwF36,200 (+SwF15,000). **Aid:** 6 pupils (SwF18,000). Endow Can$120,000.
    Est 1956. Nonprofit. Sem (Sept-June).

NJC offers a one-year pre-university program that combines a Canadian curriculum with Advanced Placement courses. The study of French is mandatory, and a review course assists students who are not yet proficient in the language. Students live with host families and are immersed in French language and Swiss culture.

Travel opportunities include recreational ski trips to the Swiss Alps and educational excursions to destinations across Europe. The guest speaker series regularly features international diplomats and business executives. A summer internship program places graduates in the Canadian Embassy in Bern and the United Nations High Commission for Refugees.

INTERNATIONAL SCHOOL BASEL
Day — Coed Gr PS-12

4153 Reinach, Switzerland. Fleischbachstrasse 2, Postfach 678. Tel: 41-61-715-33-33. Fax: 41-61-715-33-15. EST+6.
www.isbasel.ch   E-mail: info@isbasel.ch
Lesley Barron, Dir. Jenny Dunning, Adm.

> **Col Prep. IB PYP. IB MYP. IB Diploma. Curr**—Intl. **Exams**—CEEB. **Feat**—Fr Ger Econ Pol_Sci Psych Studio_Art Theater Music Bus. **Supp**—ESL Tut.
>
> **Sports**—Basket Soccer Softball Swim Track Volley. **Activities**—Acad Arts Govt/Pol.
>
> **Enr 940.** B 493. G 447. Elem 680. Sec 260. US 158. Host 96. Other 686. Avg class size: 17.
>
> **Fac 116.** US 24. Host 20. Other 72. Adv Deg: 25%.
>
> **Grad '05**—47. **Col**—32. **US Col**—6. (Harvard, Stanford, Columbia, Am U, Worcester Polytech, NC St).
>
> **Tui '05-'06: Day SwF11,250-29,500** (+SwF4500).
>
> Bldgs 2. Class rms 70. 2 Libs 20,000 vols. Sci labs 4. Comp labs 5. Auds 1. Theaters 1. Art studios 2. Music studios 2. Dance studios 1. Gyms 3. Fields 1. Courts 1.
>
> **Est 1979.** Nonprofit. Sem (Aug-June). Assoc: CIS NEASC.

Consisting of a junior school (pre-school to grade 5), a middle school (grades 6-10) and a high school (grades 11-12), this international school moved to its six-acre, suburban campus in 2003. The curriculum, which follows the International Baccalaureate Primary Years, Middle Years and Diploma programs, is designed to facilitate a smooth transition for the pupil to another international school or back to the student's native country.

Junior school programming provides boys and girls with a thorough grounding in English, math, science and social studies. German is introduced in grade 1, French in grade 5. The middle school program culminates in a personal project completed by all students in grade 10. Courses in grades 11 and 12 lead toward either the IB Diploma or a general high school diploma. Students can arrange preparation for the SAT and for certain Advanced Placement exams. Most graduates attend college in either Europe or the US.

INSTITUT LE ROSEY
Bdg — Coed Gr 1-12; Day — Coed 3-6

1180 Rolle, Switzerland. Chateau du Rosey. Tel: 41-21-822-55-00. Fax: 41-21-822-55-04. EST+7.
www.rosey.ch   E-mail: rosey@rosey.ch
Philippe Gudin, Dir. Jacques Bounin, Adm.

> **Col Prep. IB Diploma. Fr Bac. Curr**—Intl. **Bilingual**—Fr. **Exams**—CEEB TOEFL.
> **Feat**—Arabic Chin Fr Ger Ital Japan Russ Span Bulgarian Polish Portugese

Romanian Turkish Comp_Sci Econ Psych Philos Drawing Sculpt Studio_Art
Chorus Music. **Supp**—ESL Tut.

Sports—Basket Baseball Crew Golf Hand Ice_Hockey Rugby Ski Soccer Swim
Volley.

Enr 340. B 166/4. G 166/4. Elem 140. Sec 200. US 35. Host 35. Other 270.
Accepted: 75%. Avg class size: 8.

Fac 90. M 40/5. F 40/5. US 20. Host 30. Other 40.

Grad '05—80. Col—80. US Col—40. (Bentley, Cornell, Vanderbilt, Parsons Sch of
Design, Sch of the Art Inst of Chicago, Mt Holyoke).

Tui '05-'06: Bdg SwF74,000 (+SwF6000). **Day SwF30,000** (+SwF6000). **Aid:** 4
pupils.

Summer: Acad Rec. Sports. Tui Bdg SwF3000-7000. 2-4 wks.

Bldgs 17. 2 Libs 16,000 vols. Sci labs 8. Comp labs 1. Auds 2. Theaters 1. Art studios 4. Music studios 12. Dance studios 1. Gyms 2. Fields 3. Tennis courts 11.
Pools 2. Rinks 1. Riding rings 2. Stables 1.

Est 1880. Inc. Tri (Sept-July). Assoc: CIS NEASC.

International from its founding, the school enrolls boys and girls from approximately 60 countries. Among the alumni are counted kings, princes and illustrious
persons from the United States. Students must complete an entrance exam and
furnish a school transcript prior to admission.

All subjects are taught in both French and English, as the school expects pupils
to be fully bilingual. The program meets the requirements of the French Baccalaureate and the International Baccalaureate. American graduates typically enter
competitive colleges in the US.

Extracurricular activities include music, the fine arts, carpentry, daily assemblies, debates, lectures, and other cultural and social events. Placing great stress on
physical education, the school offers a full athletic schedule.

The 13th-century Chateau du Rosey, as well as four other buildings and extensive athletic facilities, occupies the 50-acre campus in Rolle, a small town on the
shores of Lake Geneva, midway between Lausanne and Geneva. For the winter
term, the school moves to its Gstaad campus in the Bernese Oberland.

JOHN F. KENNEDY INTERNATIONAL SCHOOL
Bdg and Day — Coed Gr K-8

3792 Saanen, Switzerland. Tel: 41-33-744-13-72. Fax: 41-33-744-89-82. EST+6.
www.jfk.ch   E-mail: lovell@jfk.ch
William M. Lovell, Dir. BA.

Pre-Prep. Gen Acad. Curr—Intl. **Feat**—Fr Studio_Art Drama Music. **Supp**—ESL
Rem_Math Rem_Read Tut.

Enr 60. B 15/15. G 16/14. Elem 60. Avg class size: 10.

Fac 11. M 2. F 7/2. Adv Deg: 18%.

Grad '05—10. US Prep—1. (Choate).

Tui '05-'06: Bdg SwF45,300 (+SwF8000). **Day SwF24,800** (+SwF4500).

Summer: Rec. ESL. Tui Bdg SwF4800. Tui Day SwF2700. 3½ wks.

Bldgs 5. Dorms 1. Dorm rms 8. Class rms 10. Lib 9000 vols. Comp labs 1. Art
studios 1.

Est 1949. Inc. Tri (Sept-June).

Situated about two miles from the resort of Gstaad, the school is housed in five typical Bernese chalets in the village of Saanen. Combining traditional and modern teaching methods, the curriculum prepares students for enrollment into Canadian, American and British secondary schools. The program features small classes, with individualized instruction and a family-like atmosphere in an international environment. Beginning at age 6, all boys and girls take French, and English as a Second Language is available to pupils lacking fluency in the language. The Alpine location offers many opportunities for sports and activities, including daily skiing during the winter.

A summer camp program combining language instruction with an introduction to many sports and outdoor living skills operates during July and August.

INSTITUT AUF DEM ROSENBERG
Bdg and Day — Coed Gr 1-13

9000 St Gallen, Switzerland. Hohenweg 60. Tel: 41-71-277-77-77. Fax: 41-71-277-98-27. EST+6.
www.instrosenberg.ch   E-mail: info@instrosenberg.ch
Otto Gademann, Dir.

Col Prep. Curr—Nat UK US. Exams—AP CEEB TOEFL IGCSE O-level A-level.
   AP—Fr Ger Span Calc Bio Chem Environ_Sci Physics Eur_Hist Comp_Govt
   & Pol Econ. Feat—Humanities Ital 20th-Cent_Hist Art_Hist Studio_Art.
   Supp—EFL.
Enr 170. B 89/3. G 76/2.
Fac 38. M 9/8. F 12/9.
Tui '05-'06: Bdg SwF51,000. Day SwF30,000.
Est 1889. Nonprofit. Tri (Sept-June).

COLLEGE DU LEMAN INTERNATIONAL SCHOOL
Bdg — Coed Gr 7-13; Day — Coed PS-13

1290 Versoix, Geneva, Switzerland. Rte de Sauverny 74. Tel: 41-22-775-55-55. Fax: 41-22-775-55-59. EST+6.
www.cdl.ch   E-mail: info@cdl.ch
Francis A. Clivaz, Dir.

Col Prep. IB Diploma. Fr Bac. Swiss Mat. Curr—Intl UK US. Bilingual—Fr.
   Exams—AP CEEB TOEFL IGCSE. AP—Eng Fr Ger Span Calc Bio Chem
   Physics Eur_Hist US_Hist Econ Psych Studio_Art. Feat—Chin Ital Russ
   Comp_Sci Sociol Philos Journ. Supp—EFL ESL Rem_Math Rem_Read Tut.
Sports—Badminton Basket X-country Golf Rugby Ski Soccer Swim Tennis Track
   Volley. Activities—Acad Arts Govt/Pol Media Rec.
Enr 1752. B 108/778. G 107/759. US 167. Host 250. Other 1335. Accepted: 80%.
   Yield: 80%. Avg class size: 18.
Fac 195. M 42/15. F 89/49. US 16. Host 45. Other 134. Adv Deg: 16%.
Grad '05—156. Col—94.
Tui '05-'06: Bdg SwF50,000-52,000. Day SwF16,500-21,800.
Summer: Acad Enrich Rev Rec. Tui Bdg SwF4800-5400/3-wk ses. Tui Day
   SwF3300-4200/3-wk ses. 6 wks.

Bldgs 17. Dorms 8. Class rms 52. 2 Libs 19,000 vols. Sci labs 4. Lang labs 1. Comp labs 3. Auds 1. Theaters 1. Art studios 3. Music studios 1. Gyms 3. Fields 2. Courts 3. Pools 1. Weight rms 1.
Est 1960. Nonprofit. Spons: Meritas. (Sept-June). Assoc: CIS NEASC.

Dual sectioning at this school provides English-language instruction preparing for the US College Boards, the British examinations and the International Baccalaureate Diploma, as well as French-language instruction leading to the French Baccalaureate and the Swiss Maturite. The English-speaking section, which affords opportunities for advanced work in several subject areas, particularly stresses the study of French. Many countries have representation in the student body, giving College du Leman a strongly international flavor.

COLLEGE ALPIN BEAU SOLEIL
INTERNATIONAL SECTION
Bdg — Coed Gr 6-12

1884 Villars-sur-Ollon, Switzerland. Tel: 41-24-496-2626. Fax: 41-24-496-2627. EST+6.
www.beausoleil.ch   E-mail: administration@beausoleil.ch
Jerome de Meyer, Dir.
> **Col Prep. IB Diploma. Fr Bac. Curr**—Intl UK US. **Bilingual**—Fr. **Exams**—CEEB TOEFL IGCSE A-level. **Feat**—Ger Ital Russ Span Environ_Sci Econ Philos Relig Studio_Art Music Bus.
> **Enr 163.**
> **Tui '05-'06: Day SwF63,000-69,000.**
> **Est 1910.** Tri. Assoc: CIS NEASC.

ZURICH INTERNATIONAL SCHOOL
Day — Coed Gr PS-12

8820 Wadenswil, Switzerland. Steinacherstrasse 140. Tel: 41-43-833-22-22. Fax: 41-43-833-22-23. EST+6.
www.zis.ch   E-mail: zis@zis.ch
Peter C. Mott, Head. BA, MA. **Dale Braunschweig, Adm.**
> **Col Prep. IB PYP. IB Diploma. Curr**—Intl US. **Exams**—AP CEEB TOEFL. **AP**—Eng Fr Ger Calc Stats Comp_Sci Bio Chem Physics Eur_Hist US_Hist Econ Art_Hist Studio_Art Music_Theory. **Feat**—Swedish Environ_Sci Philos Photog Acting Music. **Supp**—ESL LD Tut.
> **Sports**—Basket Soccer Softball Swim Tennis Track Volley. **Activities**—Acad Arts Govt/Pol Media Service.
> **Enr 928.** B 504. G 424. Elem 630. Sec 292. PG 6. US 226. Host 117. Other 585. Accepted: 99%. Yield: 99%. Avg class size: 18.
> **Fac 150.** M 36/18. F 64/32. US 45. Host 10. Other 95. Adv Deg: 66%.
> **Grad '05—60. Col—43.** Avg SAT: M/V—1242.
> **Tui '05-'06: Day SwF21,700-30,300.**
> Bldgs 4. Lib 10,000 vols. Sci labs 2. Comp labs 2. Fields 1.
> **Est 2001.** Nonprofit. Sem (Aug-June). Assoc: CIS NEASC.

Offering a college preparatory curriculum that combines elements from

American and international curricula, ZIS resulted from the merger of the American International School of Zurich (established in 1963) and the International Primary School of Zurich (founded in 1970). The school provides a full preschool (age 3) through high school program for students from approximately 35 nations. Advanced Placement courses, an independent study program, and numerous electives (particularly in the arts) supplement the standard program of study.

The active extracurricular and sports program is similar to that found in American secondary schools, and it includes athletic activities with students from Swiss schools, excursions to cultural events in Zurich, and vacation study trips to various parts of Europe. Zurich, the largest city in Switzerland, is an important financial center and the home of a university.

The school's upper school campus is in Kilchberg, a small community a few miles south of the city, on the western shore of the Lake of Zurich, while the lower school occupies quarters at Steinacherstrasse 140, Wadenswil 8820.

THE RIVERSIDE SCHOOL
Day — Coed Gr 7-12

6300 Zug, Switzerland. Artherstrasse 55. Tel: 41-41-7260450. Fax: 41-41-7260452. EST+6.
www.riverside.ch   E-mail: info@riverside.ch
Dominic Currer, Dir. BA, MSc.

> **Col Prep. IB MYP. Curr**—Intl. **Exams**—AP CEEB. **AP**—Eng Fr Ger Calc Comp_Sci Bio Chem Environ_Sci Human_Geog Physics Eur_Hist Econ Art_Hist Studio_Art. **Feat**—Performing_Arts Visual_Arts. **Supp**—EFL LD Tut.
>
> **Sports**—Basket X-country Ski Soccer Track. **Activities**—Arts Govt/Pol Media Rec Service.
>
> **Enr 115.** B 51. G 64. Elem 14. Sec 111. US 15. Host 18. Other 82. Accepted: 90%. Avg class size: 12.
>
> **Fac 20.** M 7. F 9/4. US 2. Host 1. Other 17. Adv Deg: 25%.
>
> **Grad '05—22. Col**—15. US Col—2. (Boston U, U of Denver). Avg SAT: M/V— 1190.
>
> **Tui '06-'07: Day SwF26,000-30,000** (+SwF1000-2000). **Aid:** 20 pupils (SwF300,000).
>
> Bldgs 1. Class rms 6. Lib 5000 vols. Sci labs 3. Comp labs 2. Art studios 1. Music studios 1. Dance studios 1. Courts 1.
>
> **Est 1990.** Nonprofit. Sem (Aug-June).

Drawing students from approximately two dozens countries, this middle school and high school bases academic promotion on achievement, not age. Most pupils take at least one AP class prior to graduation. Boys and girls must meet various minimum requirements by the end of grade 10 through four years of study and the completion of a personal project. By this point, Riverside demands proficiency in English, math, computer, design and technology, a foreign language, humanities, the fine and performing arts, and physical education. During the following two years, students follow an advanced curriculum consisting of five or more courses per year, including a senior-level English class.

Boys and girls who have been identified with learning or language difficulties may receive assistance through the school's learning support department, which provides individually formulated educational programs for these pupils.

INSTITUT MONTANA
Bdg and Day — Coed Gr 5-12

6300 Zugerberg, Switzerland. Tel: 41-41-711-17-22. Fax: 41-41-711-54-65. EST+6.
www.montana-zug.ch   E-mail: info@montana-zug.ch
Oliver Schmid, Dir.

    Col Prep. IB Diploma. Swiss Mat. Curr—Intl US. **Exams**—CEEB TOEFL. **Feat**— Dutch Fr Ital Span Comp_Sci Econ Studio_Art Music. **Supp**—EFL.
    Enr 145. B 55/25. G 42/23. Accepted: 90%. Avg class size: 10.
    Fac 24. M 6/3. F 9/6.
    Grad '05—32. US Col—26.
    Tui '05-'06: Bdg SwF46,300-48,300 (+SwF5000). **Day SwF25,300-27,300** (+SwF550). **Aid:** 1 pupil (SwF10,000).
    Summer: Bdg. Acad Rec. Tui Bdg SwF5500. 5 wks.
    Bldgs 5. Dorms 4. Dorm rms 85. Class rms 35. Libs 3. Gyms 1. Fields 3. Tennis courts 4.
    Est 1926. Nonprofit. Sem (Sept-June).

Located on a 75-acre campus just outside of Zug, the cantonal capital, this international institute has separate American, Dutch, German-Swiss and Italian divisions. Each section studies in its own language and prepares for the university requirements of the respective country. The student body represents more than 30 different nationalities. Pupils from countries other than the US apply to the American division if they are proficient in English.

The rigorous academic program includes the study of German, French or both every year, commencing in grade 5. Honors and Advanced Placement courses are part of the program. US graduates matriculate at a variety of competitive colleges.

The international atmosphere is enhanced through the integrated dormitories and school teams and organizations. The athletic program offers a wide range of team and individual sports, including obligatory skiing, while publications, choir, dramatics and hobby clubs are other activities. Travel workshops concentrating on specialized interests are organized to visit various countries during the Easter holidays. The school also arranges shorter trips throughout the school year.

THE INTER-COMMUNITY SCHOOL OF ZURICH
Day — Coed Gr PS-12

8126 Zumikon, Switzerland. Strubenacher 3. Tel: 41-1-919-8300. Fax: 41-1-919-8320. EST+6.
www.icsz.ch   E-mail: admin@icsz.ch
Michael Matthews, Head.

    Col Prep. IB PYP. IB MYP. IB Diploma. Curr—Intl. **Feat**—Humanities Fr Ger Comp_Sci Econ Studio_Art Drama Music Dance. **Supp**—ESL Tut.
    Enr 683. B 350. G 333. Avg class size: 22.
    Fac 110. M 28/4. F 50/28.
    Grad '05—40.

Tui '05-'06: Day SwF24,500-29,500 (+SwF4500-6900).
Bldgs 1. Class rms 40. Lib 12,000 vols. Gym/auds 1.
Est 1960. Nonprofit. Sem (Aug-June).

Offering an individualized program that integrates national and international teaching methods, ICS seeks to ease the transition to and from students' home systems. Roughly half of the pupils are either British or American. While the medium of instruction is English, all children except kindergartners study German, and French is compulsory from grade 7 on. Boys and girls prepare for the IB Diploma in grades 11 and 12.

The school is situated in a residential area on the outskirts of Zurich.

UKRAINE

Sq. Miles: 233,000 (Slightly smaller than Texas). **Country Pop:** 47,425,336 (2005). **Capital:** Kiev, pop. 2,800,000. **Terrain:** A vast plain bounded by the Carpathian mountains in the southwest and by the Black Sea and the Sea of Oziv in the South. **Ethnic Group(s):** Ukrainian Russian Belarusian Moldovan Hungarian Bulgarian Jewish Crimean. **Religion(s):** Ukrainian_Orthodox Greek_Catholic Jewish Roman_Catholic Muslim. **Official Language(s):** Ukrainian. **Other Language(s):** Russian. **Government:** Parliamentary. **Independence:** 1991 (from Soviet Union). **Per Capita Income:** $1324 (2004). **GDP:** $62.77 billion (2004). Agriculture 18%. Industry 45%. Services 37%. **Currency:** Ukrainian Hryvnia (UAH).

KIEV INTERNATIONAL SCHOOL
Day — Coed Gr PS-12

Kiev Ukraine. 3A Svyatoshynsky Provulok. Tel: 380-44-452-27-92. Fax: 380-44-452-29-98. EST+7.
www.qsi.org/ukr   E-mail: kiev@qsi.org
Michael Seefried, Dir. BS, MS.
   Col Prep. IB Diploma. Curr—Intl US. **Exams**—AP. **AP**—Eng Fr Studio_Art. **Feat**—Russ Comp_Sci.
   Enr 186.
   Est 1992. Nonprofit. Spons: Quality Schools International. Tri (Aug-June). Assoc: A/OPR/OS.

PECHERSK SCHOOL INTERNATIONAL
Day — Coed Gr PS-12

03039 Kiev, Ukraine. Victora Zabily 7A. Tel: 380-44-455-9585. Fax: 380-44-455-9580. EST+7.
www.psi.kiev.ua   E-mail: johny@psi.kiev.ua

Steven Alexander, Dir. BA, MEd.

    Col Prep. IB PYP. IB MYP. IB Diploma. Curr—Intl. **Exams**—CEEB TOEFL. **Feat**— Fr Ger Russ Comp_Sci Studio_Art Theater_Arts. **Supp**—ESL LD Rem_Math Rem_Read.

    Sports—Basket X-country Soccer Volley. **Activities**—Arts Govt/Pol Rec Service.

    Enr 320. Elem 250. Sec 70. US 35. Host 40. Other 245.

    Fac 47. M 15. F 32. US 12. Host 20. Other 15. Adv Deg: 48%.

    Grad '05—14. Col—14. US Col—5. (Pace, Johns Hopkins, FL Inst of Tech, Geo Mason, U of OR).

    Tui '05-'06: Day $11,500-12,500 (+$1000-3000). **Aid:** 8 pupils ($15,000).

    Bldgs 3. Class rms 26. 2 Libs 10,000 vols. Sci labs 3. Comp labs 2. Art studios 1. Music studios 1. Drama studios 1. Gyms 1. Fields 1. Courts 1.

    Est 1995. Nonprofit. Quar (Aug-June). Assoc: CIS NEASC.

Welcoming students from more than 30 nations, PSI offers the International Baccalaureate Primary Years, Middle Years and Diploma programs. Students who choose not to fulfill the IB Diploma requirements may pursue a standard Ukrainian diploma. Community service is required of all students in Kindergarten through grade 12.

Students and their parents may participate in college and career counseling sessions, and boys and girls prepare for the US College Boards.

WALES

Sq. Miles: 8023 (Slightly smaller than Massachusetts). **Country Pop:** 2,903,085 (2001). **Capital:** Cardiff, pop. 305,340 (2001). **Terrain:** Mostly rugged hills and low mountains. **Government:** Constitutional Monarchy. **Currency:** British Pound (£).

ATLANTIC COLLEGE
Bdg — Coed Gr 11-12

Vale of Glamorgan CF61 1WF, Wales. St Donat's Castle, Llantwit Major. Tel: 44-1-446-799000. Fax: 44-1-446-799013. EST+5.

www.atlanticcollege.org   E-mail: principal@uwcac.uwc.org

Malcolm McKenzie, Prin. BA, MA.

    Col Prep. IB Diploma. Curr—Intl. **Exams**—CEEB TOEFL. **Feat**—Arabic Fr Ger Japan Span Environ_Sci Econ Pol_Sci Peace_Stud World_Relig Studio_Art Music. **Supp**—Tut.

    Activities—Govt/Pol Service.

    Enr 330. B 150. G 180. Sec 330. US 18. Host 70. Other 242. Avg class size: 14.

    Fac 37. M 24. F 9/4. US 2. Host 26. Other 9. Adv Deg: 37%.

    Grad '05—161. Col—155. US Col—61. (Middlebury 9, Colby 7, U of PA 6, Macalester 5, Princeton 5, Wellesley 5).

    Tui '05-'06: Bdg £17,400.

    Endow £3,000,000. Plant val £5,000,000. Bldgs 30. Dorms 7. Dorm rms 84. Class rms 41. Lib 25,000 vols. Sci labs 10. Art studios 1. Music studios 6. Gyms 1. Fields 2. Courts 3. Pools 2.

Est 1962. Nonprofit. (Aug-May).

Atlantic College is one of 10 related UWC international schools dedicated to promoting international understanding through education. The organization has campuses in Britain, Canada, Hong Kong, India, Italy, Norway, Singapore, Swaziland, the US and Venezuela, and each school is a community representing more than 70 countries. All students follow the International Baccalaureate curriculum in preparation for the IB exams.

Community service, outdoor programs and events pertaining to global issues supplement the academic offerings.

MEXICO &
CENTRAL AMERICA

INDEX TO COUNTRIES IN
MEXICO & CENTRAL AMERICA

MEXICO & CENTRAL AMERICA

COSTA RICA

Sq. Miles: 19,652 (About twice the size of Vermont). **Country Pop:** 4,016,173 (2005). **Capital:** San Jose, pop. 2,100,000. **Terrain:** A rugged, central range separates the eastern and western coastal plains. **Ethnic Group(s):** European Mestizo African Chinese. **Religion(s):** Roman_Catholic Protestant. **Official Language(s):** Spanish. **Other Language(s):** Caribbean_Creole. **Government:** Democratic Republic. **Independence:** 1821 (from Spain). **Per Capita Income:** $4670 (2004). **GDP:** $18.4 billion (2004). Agriculture 9%. Industry 28%. Services 63%. **Currency:** Costa Rican Colon (CR¢).

COUNTRY DAY SCHOOL

Day — Coed Gr PS-12

1250 Escazu, Costa Rica. Apartado 1139. Tel: 506-289-0919. Fax: 506-228-2076. EST-1.
www.cds.ed.cr   E-mail: codash@racsa.co.cr
Robert Trent, Dir. BA, MA, MEd, MDiv.

> **Col Prep. Curr**—Nat US. **Exams**—ACT AP CEEB TOEFL. **AP**—Eng Span Calc Bio Chem Physics Eur_Hist US_Hist Comp_Govt & Pol. **Feat**—British_Lit Fr Costa_Rican_Stud Studio_Art Drama Music. **Supp**—ESL.
> **Sports**—Basket Soccer Volley. **Activities**—Acad Arts Media Rec.
> **Enr 840.** Elem 697. Sec 143. US 287. Host 216. Other 337. Avg class size: 18.
> **Fac 102.** M 18/3. F 69/12. US 49. Host 43. Other 10. Adv Deg: 55%.
> **Grad '05—33. US Col—6.** (Geo Wash, U of San Francisco, U of PA, Tufts, Purdue, Trinity U). Avg SAT: M/V—1154.
> **Tui '05-'06: Day $5476-8426.**
> Bldgs 3. Libs 2. Sci labs 5. Comp labs 3. Auds 1. Art studios 3. Music studios 1. Gyms 1. Fields 2. Courts 1. Pools 1.
> **Est 1963.** Inc. Quar (Aug-June). Assoc: AASCA MSA.

CDS follows a US curriculum that provides preparation for the US College Boards. Students are predominantly North American, with lesser numbers coming from Europe, Asia and Latin America. Spanish instruction begins in elementary school, when children are placed in a class appropriate to their proficiency. Students in grades 9 and 10 take a sequence of special courses including art and music appreciation, physical education, speech, and vocabulary development. High school students may pursue either a traditional US diploma or the Costa Rican Baccalaureate. Students who are strong in math may take part in an honors sequence.

The school's location in the Central Valley lies about four miles from the center of San Jose.

AMERICAN INTERNATIONAL SCHOOL
OF COSTA RICA
Day — Coed Gr PS-12

San Jose, Costa Rica. Apartado Postal 4941-1000. Tel: 506-293-2567. Fax: 506-293-0974. EST-1.
Contact: c/o US Embassy San Jose, Dept of State, Washington, DC 20521.
www.aiscr.com   E-mail: ais@aiscr.com
Larue Goldfinch, Dir. Eliana Carvalho, Prin. BA, MS.

Col Prep. Curr—Nat US. **Supp Lang**—Span. **Exams**—ACT CEEB TOEFL. **Feat**—Comp_Sci Studio_Art Music Journ. **Supp**—EFL ESL LD Tut.
Enr 210. Elem 130. Sec 80. Accepted: 80%. Avg class size: 16.
Fac 37. Adv Deg: 29%.
Grad '05—23. Col—20. US Col—15. Avg SAT: M/V—1050.
Tui '05-'06: Day $3675-6150 (+$550-2050). **Aid:** 4 pupils ($30,000).
Plant val $1,200,000. Bldgs 5. Lib 8000 vols. Comp labs 2. Art studios 1. Music studios 2. Gyms 2. Fields 1.
Est 1970. Nonprofit. Sem (Aug-June). Assoc: AASCA A/OPR/OS.

Located on a five-acre site, this school, which is open to students of all nationalities living in San Jose, features an American curriculum that includes Advanced Placement courses. Costa Rican history and geography are taught in the elementary grades. Specialized education is available for students with learning disabilities.

LINCOLN SCHOOL
Day — Coed Gr PS-12

1000 San Jose, Costa Rica. Apartado Postal 1919. Tel: 506-247-0800. Fax: 506-247-0900. EST-1.
Contact: PO Box 025216, Miami, FL 33102.
www.lincoln.ed.cr   E-mail: director@lincoln.ed.cr
Jack J. Bimrose, Dir. MEd. **Irene Tovar, Adm.**

Col Prep. IB Diploma. **Curr**—Intl US. **Bilingual**—Span. **Exams**—CEEB TOEFL. **Feat**—Fr Comp_Sci Anthro Econ Intl_Relations Costa_Rican_Stud Comp_Relig Theater_Arts Bus Design. **Supp**—ESL LD.
Sports—Badminton Basket Soccer. **Activities**—Acad Arts Govt/Pol Media Service.
Enr 1148. US 72. Host 1011. Other 65. Avg class size: 22.
Fac 128. M 25/2. F 91/10. US 24. Host 97. Other 7. Adv Deg: 42%.
Avg SAT: M/V—1151.
Tui '05-'06: Day $3436-4763 (+$1000).
Bldgs 15. Class rms 70. 2 Libs 24,000 vols. Sci labs 4. Theaters 1. Gyms 1. Fields 1.
Est 1945. Nonprofit. Sem (Aug-June). Assoc: AASCA A/OPR/OS SACS.

Located in a suburban area four miles from San Jose, the school's enrollment is composed mostly of Costa Ricans. The bilingual curriculum prepares students for either the US diploma, the International Baccalaureate or the Costa Rican Bachillerato. Lincoln conducts a program for pupils with learning disabilities.

Students participate in exchange programs with schools in France; Atlanta, GA; and New York City.

MARIAN BAKER SCHOOL
Day — Coed Gr PS-12

San Jose, Costa Rica. Apartado 4269-1000. Tel: 506-273-3426. Fax: 506-273-4609. EST-1.
Contact: PO Box 025216-751, Miami, FL 33102.
E-mail: mbschool@racsa.co.cr
Linda Niehaus, Dir.
> Col Prep. Curr—Nat US. Exams—CEEB. AP—Eng Span Calc Bio Chem Physics US_Hist Psych. Feat—Comp_Sci Lat-Am_Hist Costa_Rican_Stud Studio_Art Music. Supp—ESL.
> Enr 201. US 60. Host 68. Other 73.
> Fac 51.
> Tui '05-'06: Day $5150-7725 (+$670).
> Est 1985. Quar (Aug-June). Assoc: AASCA SACS.

EL SALVADOR

Sq. Miles: 8260 (About the size of Massachusetts). **Country Pop:** 6,704,932 (2005). **Capital:** San Salvador, pop. 1,700,000. **Terrain:** Mountains separate country into three distinct regions: southern coastal belt, central valleys and plateaus, and northern mountains. **Ethnic Group(s):** Mestizo. **Religion(s):** Roman_Catholic Protestant. **Official Language(s):** Spanish. **Government:** Republic. **Independence:** 1821 (from Spain). **Per Capita Income:** $2258 (2003). **GDP:** $13.1 billion (2003). Agriculture 1%. Industry 30%. Services 60%. **Currency:** Salvadoran Colon (ES¢).

COLEGIO INTERNACIONAL DE SAN SALVADOR
(THE INTERNATIONAL SCHOOL OF SAN SALVADOR)
Day — Coed Gr PS-12

San Salvador, El Salvador. Calle La Reforma 169, Colonia San Benito, Box 05-15. Tel: 503-2224-1330. Fax: 503-2265-7860. EST-1.
Contact: VIPSAL 1214, Box 025364, Miami, FL 33102.
www.intschoolsansal.com   E-mail: c_stemp@intschoolsansal.com
Chester Stemp, Head. BS, MS.
> Col Prep. Curr—Nat US. Supp Lang—Span. Exams—CEEB. AP—Calc Econ Psych. Feat—British_Lit Fr Sociol. Supp—ESL.
> Sports—Basket Cheer Volley. Activities—Acad Arts Govt/Pol Media.

Enr 310. B 146. G 164. Elem 220. Sec 90. US 70. Host 110. Other 130. Accepted: 60%. Yield: 90%. Avg class size: 22.

Fac 34. M 5/4. F 22/3. US 12. Host 19. Other 3. Adv Deg: 38%.

Grad '05—23. Col—23. US Col—6. (Purdue, Loyola U-LA, Converse, Mercer, Bridgewater Col, Grand Valley St). Avg SAT: M/V—1068.

Tui '05-'06: Day $3000-4400 (+$1300). **Aid:** 40 pupils ($70,000).

Summer: Acad Enrich Rev Rem. Tui Day $300. 6 wks.

Plant val $2,000,000. Bldgs 13. Class rms 19. Lib 5000 vols. Sci labs 1. Comp labs 1. Courts 2. Pools 1.

Est 1979. Inc. Quar (Aug-June). Assoc: AASCA.

CISS provides its international student body with a US-style curriculum that utilizes English as the primary language of instruction. Those fluent in Spanish may take Spanish and social studies in the language, but all other instruction is in English. High schoolers who wish to do so may earn the Salvadoran government diploma by successfully completing certain supplemental courses. Spanish as a Second Language instruction is part of the program

Extracurricular activities are similar to those found in US schools. Scholarship aid is not available to first-year pupils.

ESCUELA AMERICANA
(AMERICAN SCHOOL)
Day — Coed Gr PS-12

San Salvador, El Salvador. PO Box 01-35. Tel: 503-2528-8300. Fax: 503-2528-8319. EST-1.

www.amschool.edu.sv   E-mail: lopez.yolanda@amschool.edu.sv

Charles Skipper, Gen Dir.

Col Prep. Gen Acad. Curr—Nat US. **Exams**—CEEB.

Enr 1720. Elem 1275. Sec 445.

Est 1946. Nonprofit. Sem (Aug-June). Assoc: AASCA SACS.

ACADEMIA BRITANICA CUSCATLECA
Day — Coed Gr PS-12

Santa Tecla, El Salvador. Apartado Postal 121. Tel: 503-2241-44-00. Fax: 503-2228-29-56. EST-1.

www.abc.edu.sv   E-mail: headmaster@abc.edu.sv

J. George Hobson, Head.

Col Prep. IB Diploma. Curr—Intl UK. **Exams**—CEEB TOEFL IGCSE. **Feat**—Fr Span Comp_Sci Econ Psych Studio_Art Music Bus. **Supp**—ESL.

Enr 1299.

Fac 126.

Tui '05-'06: Day $3566-4368 (+$2020-2520).

Tri (Aug-June). Assoc: ECIS.

GUATEMALA

Sq. Miles: 42,000 (About the size of Tennessee). **Country Pop:** 14,655,189 (2005). **Capital:** Guatemala City, pop. 2,500,000. **Terrain:** Mountainous, with fertile coastal plain. **Ethnic Group(s):** Mestizo Indigenous. **Religion(s):** Roman_Catholic Protestant Traditional_Mayan. **Official Language(s):** Spanish. **Other Language(s):** Kiche Kaqchikel Q'eqchi Mam. **Government:** Constitutional Democratic Republic. **Independence:** 1821 (from Spain). **Per Capita Income:** $2200 (2004). **GDP:** $27.2 billion (2004). Agriculture 23%. Manufacturing 19%. Services 58%. **Currency:** Guatemalan Quetzal (Q).

AMERICAN SCHOOL OF GUATEMALA
Day — Coed Gr K-12

Guatemala City, Guatemala. 11 Calle 15-79, Zona 15, Vista Hermosa III. Tel: 502-23690791. Fax: 502-23698335. EST-1.
Contact: CAG/E-910, 9381 NW 13th St, Miami, FL 33172.
www.cag.edu.gt   E-mail: cagadm@cag.edu.gt
Ettie Zilber, Dir. EdD.
> Col Prep. Curr—Nat US. Bilingual—Span. Exams—AP CEEB. AP—Eng Span Calc Bio Chem Environ_Sci Physics Comp_Govt & Pol Econ. Feat—Stats Comp_Sci Philos Studio_Art Music.
> Enr 1429. Elem 687. Sec 318. PG 424.
> Fac 194.
> Est 1945. Nonprofit. Sem (Aug-June). Assoc: AASCA NEASC SACS.

COLEGIO INTERAMERICANO
Day — Coed Gr PS-12

01016 Guatemala City, Guatemala. Boulevard La Montana, Finca El Socorro Zona 16. Tel: 502-364-1803. Fax: 502-364-1779. EST-1.
Contact: Section 4134, PO Box 02-5339, Miami, FL 33102.
www.interamericano.edu.gt   E-mail: migularte@interamericano.edu.gt
Robert M. Farr, Dir.
> Col Prep. Gen Acad. Curr—Nat US. AP—Span Calc World_Hist Psych. Feat—Comp_Sci Studio_Art Music.
> Quar (Jan-Aug). Assoc: AASCA SACS.

COLEGIO MAYA
(THE AMERICAN INTERNATIONAL SCHOOL)
Day — Coed Gr PS-12

01073 Santa Catarina Pinula, Guatemala. Apartado Postal 2C. Tel: 502-2365-0037. Fax: 502-2365-0116. EST-1.

Contact: Section 0280, PO Box 02-5289, Miami, FL 33102.
www.cm.edu.gt   E-mail: info@cm.edu.gt
Sherry Miller, Dir. PhD.
   Col Prep. Curr—US. **Exams**—AP CEEB. **AP**—Eng Span Calc Bio Chem Envi-
      ron_Sci US_Hist World_Hist Psych. **Supp**—ESL LD.
   Sports—Basket Soccer. **Activities**—Arts Rec.
   Enr 325. US 116. Host 69. Other 140. Accepted: 80%. Yield: 80%. Avg class size:
      15.
   Fac 50. M 15/3. F 32. US 34. Host 10. Other 6. Adv Deg: 52%.
   Grad '05—29. US Col—6. (U of PA, U of VA, Notre Dame, Duke, Wheaton-MA,
      Miami U-OH). Avg SAT: M/V—1130, Essay—570. Avg ACT: 29.
   Tui '05-'06: Day $6435-9601 (+$6000-7000).
   Summer: Rec. Q500/wk. 4 wks.
   Bldgs 10. Class rms 34. 2 Libs 21,000 vols. Sci labs 2. Comp labs 3. Auds 1. Art
      studios 1. Music studios 1. Gyms 1. Fields 1. Courts 2.
   Est 1958. Nonprofit. Sem (Aug-June). Assoc: AASCA A/OPR/OS SACS.

Maya offers small-class instruction, and individual help is available to students
with specific remedial and learning problems. Spanish is required of students at all
levels. Most students are from either the US or Guatemala.

HONDURAS

Sq. Miles: 43,270 (About the size of Louisiana). **Country Pop:**
6,975,204 (2005). **Capital:** Tegucigalpa, pop. 1,150,000. **Terrain:**
Mountainous. **Ethnic Group(s):** Mestizo European Arab African Asian
Indigenous_Indians. **Religion(s):** Roman_Catholic Protestant. **Official Language(s):** Spanish. **Government:** Democratic Constitutional
Republic. **Independence:** 1821 (from Spain). **Per Capita Income:** $2600
(2003). **GDP:** $17.46 billion (2003). Agriculture 13%. Industry 31%. Ser-
vices 56%. **Currency:** Honduran Lempira (L).

MAZAPAN SCHOOL
Day — Coed Gr 1-12

La Ceiba, Honduras. PO Box 96. Tel: 504-443-2716. Fax: 504-443-3559. EST-1.
Contact: MIA 951, 1601 NW 97th Ave, PO Box 025365, Miami, FL 33102.
www.mazapanschool.org   E-mail: mazapan@la.dole.com
Martha Counsil, Supt. MEd. **Mirtha de Martinez, Dir.** BA. **Emma Nufio, Adm.**
   Col Prep. Curr—US. **Bilingual**—Span. **Exams**—ACT CEEB TOEFL. **Feat**—Fr.
   Enr 307. B 157. G 150. Elem 200. Sec 107. US 27. Host 275. Other 5. Avg class
      size: 25.
   Fac 26. M 7/1. F 16/2. US 11. Host 14. Other 1. Adv Deg: 34%.
   Grad '05—25. Col—22. US Col—4. (LA St-Baton Rouge, Loyola Marymount, Notre
      Dame, Harding). Avg SAT: M/V—1012. Avg ACT: 21.
   Tui '05-'06: Day $3679-4056 (+$1000-2000).
   Endow $1,000,000. Sci labs 1. Comp labs 1. Art studios 1. Music studios 1. Gyms

2. Fields 4. Courts 1.
Est 1928. Inc. Spons: Dole Fresh Fruit International. Sem (Aug-June). Assoc: AASCA SACS.

This company-sponsored school offers a college preparatory program preparing students for the US College Boards. Athletics include basketball, soccer, volleyball and softball.

ESCUELA INTERNACIONAL SAMPEDRANA
Day — Coed Gr PS-12

San Pedro Sula, Honduras. Colonia El Pedregal. Tel: 594-566-2722. Fax: 594-566-1458. EST-1.
www.seishn.org   E-mail: info@seishn.org
  Col Prep. **Curr**—Nat US. **Supp Lang**—Span. **Exams**—AP TOEFL. **AP**—Eng Span Calc Bio Chem Human_Geog Econ Psych Studio_Art. **Feat**—Honduran_Stud. **Supp**—ESL.
  Enr 1811.
  Fac 78.
  Est 1953. Nonprofit. Sem (Aug-June). Assoc: AASCA SACS.

AMERICAN SCHOOL OF TEGUCIGALPA
Day — Coed Gr PS-12

Tegucigalpa, Honduras. c/o US Embassy. Tel: 504-239-3333. Fax: 504-239-6162. EST-1.
www.amschool.org   E-mail: info@amschool.org
Liliana Jenkins, Supt.
  Col Prep. **IB MYP. IB Diploma. Curr**—Intl Nat US. **Supp Lang**—Span. **Feat**—Comp_Sci Honduran Stud Studio_Art Music.
  Enr 1120.
  Fac 103.
  Est 1946. Nonprofit. Sem (Aug-June). Assoc: AASCA A/OPR/OS SACS.

DISCOVERY SCHOOL
Day — Coed Gr PS-12

Tegucigalpa, Honduras. Colonia Lara, Calle Benito Juarez, Casa 3602. Tel: 504-236-7006. Fax: 504-221-4149. EST-1.
Contact: TGU 00015, PO 025387, Miami, FL 33102.
www.discoveryschool.edu.hn   E-mail: dsoffice@mundo123.hn
Glenn Jones, Dir. BA, MA.
  Col Prep. **Curr**—US. **Exams**—AP CEEB TOEFL. **AP**—Eng Calc. **Feat**—Lib_Skills Span Comp_Sci Studio_Art Music. **Supp**—ESL Tut.
  Activities—Arts Rec.
  Enr 194. B 102. G 92. Elem 153. Sec 41. US 50. Host 57. Other 87. Accepted: 50%. Yield: 90%. Avg class size: 10.
  Fac 26. M 6. F 20. US 14. Host 11. Other 1. Adv Deg: 30%.

Grad '05—1. Col—1.
Tui '05-'06: Day $3950-5450. Aid: 10 pupils ($12,500).
Plant val $1,750,000. Bldgs 9. Class rms 28. Libs 1. Sci labs 1. Comp labs 1. Art studios 1. Music studios 1. Fields 1. Courts 1.
Est 1995. Nonprofit. Quar (Aug-June). Assoc: A/OPR/OS SACS.

Founded as an elementary school by area parents and three teachers, Discovery now offers a US-oriented program that runs through grade 12. Comprising nursery (age 3), prekindergarten (age 4) and kindergarten (age 5), the early childhood program emphasizes direct sensory experiences and facilitates both the development of mental abilities such as verbal skills and the proper use of English.

During the elementary years (grades 1-5), children remain with the homeroom teacher for the core subjects, while specialists teach physical education, art, music, computer and library skills. Daily Spanish instruction is another aspect of the elementary curriculum. Basic skills are the focus at the secondary level (grades 6-12). Although fact acquisition is important, more stress is placed on research, synthesis, discussion and presentation.

Cocurricular offerings are integral to school life. Notable examples include holiday celebrations, a science fair and a music festival. Extracurricular athletics round out the program.

MEXICO

Sq. Miles: 761,600 (About three times the size of Texas). **Country Pop:** 106,202,903 (2005). **Capital:** Mexico City, pop. 13,000,000 (2000). **Terrain:** Coastal lowlands, central high plateaus, and mountains. **Ethnic Group(s):** Mestizo Indian Caucasian. **Religion(s):** Roman_Catholic Protestant. **Official Language(s):** Spanish. **Government:** Federal Republic. **Independence:** 1810 (from Spain). **Per Capita Income:** $6517 (2004). **GDP:** $677 billion (2004). Agriculture 4%. Financial Services 12%. Industry 24%. Services 30%. Transport & Communications 10%. Tourism 20%. **Currency:** Mexican Peso (Mex$).

THE AMERICAN SCHOOL FOUNDATION
OF GUADALAJARA
Day — Coed Gr PS-12

44630 Guadalajara, Jalisco, Mexico. Colomos 2100, Col Providencia, Apartado Postal 6-280. Tel: 52-333-648-0299. Fax: 52-333-817-3356. EST-1.
www.asfg.mx   E-mail: asfg@asfg.mx
Janet Heinze, Dir. BA, MA. **Julia Gil de Madrigal, Adm.**
  Col Prep. **Curr**—Nat US. **Supp Lang**—Span. **Exams**—ACT AP CEEB. **AP**—Eng Span Calc Stats Comp_Sci Bio Chem Physics US_Hist. **Feat**—Fr Mexican_Hist Econ Psych Drama Marketing. **Supp**—Dev_Read ESL LD Rem_Math Rem_Read Tut.
  Sports—Basket Soccer Swim Track Volley. **Activities**—Acad Govt/Pol Media Rec.

Enr 1421. Elem 1111. Sec 310. US 165. Host 1206. Other 50. Accepted: 95%. Yield: 100%. Avg class size: 24.
Fac 124. US 46. Host 63. Other 15. Adv Deg: 41%.
Grad '05—62. Col—54. US Col—12. (UCLA 2, U of MI 1, Stanford 1, Tulane 1, Savannah Col of Art & Design 1). Avg SAT: M/V—1080.
Tui '05-'06: Day Mex$48,600 (+Mex$21,000).
Summer: Acad Enrich Rev Rem. Tui Day $3300-3500. 4 wks.
Bldgs 7. Class rms 90. 2 Libs 30,000 vols. Sci labs 6. Comp labs 4. Auds 1. Art studios 3. Music studios 3. Gyms 1. Fields 2. Courts 3. Pools 1.
Est 1956. Nonprofit. Sem (Aug-June). Assoc: A/OPR/OS ASOMEX SACS.

This American-style program (which employs English as the primary language of instruction) comprises early childhood (nursery and kindergarten), elementary (pre-1-4), middle school (grades 5-8) and high school (grades 9-12) divisions. Honors and Advanced Placement courses are both part of the college preparatory high school curriculum. Most high schoolers enroll in ASFG's dual program, which allows students to receive both a US high school diploma and the Mexican Bachillerato upon graduation.

All pupils fulfill a mandatory community service requirement as a supplement to academic work. School graduates typically go on to universities in the US, Mexico and Canada.

AMERICAN SCHOOL FOUNDATION

Day — Coed Gr PS-12

01120 Mexico City, Mexico. Bondojito 215, Tacubaya. Tel: 52-55-5227-4900. Fax: 52-55-5273-4357. EST-1.
www.asf.edu.mx   E-mail: personnel@asf.edu.mx
Dario A. Cortes, Pres. Julie Hellmund, Adm.
Col Prep. IB Diploma. Curr—Intl Nat US. Bilingual—Span. Exams—ACT CEEB SSAT. Feat—Fr Ital Psych Photog Photojourn. Supp—ESL LD Tut.
Enr 2400. Accepted: 50%. Avg class size: 22.
Fac 235. Adv Deg: 34%.
Grad '05—152. Col—148. US Col—73. (U of Miami, Boston U, NYU, U of TX-Austin, Stanford, Tufts). Avg SAT: M/V—1094. Avg ACT: 23.
Tui '05-'06: Day Mex$73,000-106,000. Aid: 514 pupils ($99,600).
Summer: Acad Rem Rec. Tui Day $3000-5000. 2-6 wks.
Bldgs 12. Class rms 90. 4 Libs 33,000 vols. Sci labs 9. Comp labs 8. Art studios 4. Music studios 5. Gyms 3. Fields 3. Courts 4. Pools 1.
Est 1888. Nonprofit. Sem (Aug-June). Assoc: A/OPR/OS ASOMEX SACS.

Located on a 17-acre tract on the western edge of the city, the ASF provides a full early childhood through high school program for a student body composed largely of Mexicans and Americans. While English is the primary language of instruction, children follow a completely bilingual curriculum in grades 1-6. Skills classes serve pupils that require English language support. In addition, the school maintains a special-needs program for those in grades 1-12.

Student council; school publications; opportunities in drama, music and the arts; interest clubs; intramural and interscholastic sports; and Model UN are some of the extracurricular options.

GREENGATES SCHOOL
Day — Coed Gr K-12

11002 Mexico City, Mexico. Apartado Postal 10-1112. Tel: 52-55-53730088. Fax: 52-55-53730765. EST-1.
www.greengates.edu.mx   E-mail: sarav@greengates.edu.mx
Susan E. Mayer, Prin. BA.

> **Col Prep. IB PYP. IB Diploma. Curr**—Intl UK. **Exams**—ACT CEEB IGCSE. **Feat**—Fr Span Environ_Sci Comp_Sci Econ Psych Ceramics Studio_Art Drama Music. **Supp**—EFL ESL Tut.
>
> **Sports**—Basket Rugby Soccer Swim Volley. **Activities**—Arts Govt/Pol Rec Service.
>
> **Enr 1170.** B 640. G 530. Elem 860. Sec 310. US 146. Host 562. Other 462. Avg class size: 23.
>
> **Fac 126.** M 37. F 89. US 13. Host 38. Other 75. Adv Deg: 23%.
>
> **Grad '05—61. Col—60. US Col—24.** (Yale 2, Harvard 1, Princeton 1, MIT 1). Avg SAT: M/V—1228, Essay—565. Avg ACT: 26.
>
> **Tui '05-'06: Day $5820-13,850** (+$500). **Aid:** 234 pupils.
>
> **Summer:** Acad Enrich Rem. Tui Day $600-950. 5 wks.
>
> Bldgs 6. Lib 10,000 vols. Gyms 1. Fields 1. Courts 1. Pools 1.
>
> **Est 1951.** Tri (Aug-June).

The UK-based curriculum at Greengates prepares students for the IGCSE examinations and the IB Diploma and accommodates boys and girls from some 50 nations. Though English is the medium of instruction, all pupils must study Spanish at the appropriate level. ESL and EFL courses serve students whose native language is not English.

AMERICAN SCHOOL FOUNDATION OF MONTERREY
Day — Coed Gr PS-12

64000 Monterrey, Nuevo Leon, Mexico. Apartado Postal 1762. Tel: 52-81-8153-4400. Fax: 52-81-8378-2535. EST-1.
Contact: 1001 S 10th St, PMB 311, Ste G, McAllen, TX 78501.
www.asfm.edu.mx   E-mail: jeff.keller@asfm.edu.mx
D. Jeffrey Keller, Supt. EdD. **Teresa Canales, Adm.**

> **Col Prep. Curr**—Nat US. **Supp Lang**—Span. **Exams**—AP CEEB. **AP**—Eng Span Calc Comp_Sci Physics Econ Psych. **Feat**—Art_Hist Studio_Art Drama Music Accounting.
>
> **Enr 2000.** Elem 1550. Sec 450. Avg class size: 20.
>
> **Fac 199.** Adv Deg: 31%.
>
> **Grad '05—85. Col—85. US Col—25.** (U of TX-Austin, Yale, U of Chicago, NYU, Boston Col, Syracuse).
>
> **Tui '05-'06: Day Mex$64,650-89,850** (+Mex$18,415-23,915). **Aid:** 100 pupils.
>
> **Summer:** Rem. Tui Day Mex$4000. 4 wks.
>
> Bldgs 4. Class rms 150. 2 Libs 25,000 vols. Sci labs 10. Comp labs 8. Auds 2. Theaters 1. Art studios 4. Music studios 5. Gyms 4. Fields 5. Courts 8.
>
> **Est 1928.** Nonprofit. Sem (Aug-June). Assoc: A/OPR/OS ASOMEX SACS.

Offering a combined Mexican-US curriculum, ASFM prepares students for the

US College Boards or the Mexican Bachillerato. Advanced Placement courses in the major disciplines provide further challenge for older pupils.

Student council, drama, music and art are among the school's activities.

PAN AMERICAN SCHOOL
Day — Coed Gr PS-9

64000 Monterrey, Nuevo Leon, Mexico. Apartado Postal 474. Tel: 52-83-42-07-78. Fax: 52-83-40-27-49. EST-1.
www.pas.edu.mx   E-mail: admissions_spc@pas.edu.mx
L. H. Arpee, Dir. PhD.

> **Gen Acad. Curr**—Nat. **Bilingual**—Span. **Feat**—Comp_Sci Studio_Art Band Dance.
>
> **Enr 1386.** Elem 1269. Sec 117. US 26. Host 1351. Other 9. Avg class size: 23.
>
> **Fac 123.** M 21/10. F 80/12. US 30. Host 91. Other 2. Adv Deg: 2%.
>
> Bldgs 2. Class rms 63. 2 Libs 6000 vols. Sci labs 2. Lang labs 2. Comp labs 2. Art studios 2. Dance studios 2. Fields 1. Courts 3.
>
> **Est 1952.** Nonprofit. Quar (Aug-June).

Organized as an elementary and junior high school, the Pan American School also includes a one-year commercial course. While the official language of instruction is English, the curriculum is national; students who wish to earn the Mexican diploma must take specified courses that are taught in Spanish.

THE EDRON ACADEMY
(EL COLEGIO BRITANICO)
Day — Coed Gr PS-12

01740 Olivar de los Padres, Mexico. Calz al Desierto de los Leones 5578. Tel: 52-5-585-19-20. Fax: 52-5-585-28-30. EST-1.
www.edron.edu.mx   E-mail: information@edron.edu.mx
Michael Spooner, Head.

> **Col Prep. IB Diploma. Curr**—Intl UK. **Bilingual**—Span. **Exams**—IGCSE. **Feat**—Fr Econ Studio_Art Drama Theater_Arts Music. **Supp**—ESL.
>
> **Enr 850.**
>
> **Fac 90.**
>
> **Est 1963.** Nonprofit.

THE AMERICAN SCHOOL OF PACHUCA
Day — Coed Gr PS-9

42086 Pachuca, Hidalgo, Mexico. Valle de Anahuac s/n. Tel: 52-771-713-9608. Fax: 52-771-718-5077. EST-1.
www.americana.edu.mx   E-mail: mail@americana.edu.mx
Niceforo Ramirez Castillo, Gen Dir.

> **Pre-Prep. Curr**—Nat US. **Bilingual**—Span. **Feat**—Comp_Sci Studio_Art Music. **Supp**—EFL Tut.
>
> **Enr 968.** B 514. G 454. Elem 898. Sec 70. US 4. Host 960. Other 4. Accepted: 80%.

Avg class size: 23.
Fac 81. M 15/15. F 46/5. US 21. Host 53. Other 7. Adv Deg: 7%.
Grad '05—63.
Tui '01-'02: Day Mex$3347-4445 (+Mex$20,000). **Aid:** 48 pupils (Mex$475,000).
Bldgs 6. Class rms 42. Libs 1. Sci labs 1. Comp labs 2. Auds 1. Studios 1. Fields
1. Courts 1.
Est 1920. Nonprofit. Sem (Aug-July). Assoc: ASOMEX.

Founded as a company school by the Real del Monte Mining Company, this
school offers a bilingual program that follows both American and Mexican courses
of study. While a significant number of administrators and faculty members hail
from the US, most pupils come from upper-middle-class Mexican households.

The preschool, which serves children ages 3-5, features one native English-
speaking teacher and one Mexican instructor. During the primary grades, students
receive three hours of instruction daily in both Spanish and English. Junior high
pupils study the English language, math, physical science and social studies in
English, while taking all other courses in Spanish. Spanish-language instruction is
provided weekly in computer and the arts.

Located at an elevation of 8000 feet, the city of Pachuca lies north-northeast of
Mexico City. Noteworthy colonial cities and pre-Columbian archeological sites are
within a half-day's drive of the city.

AMERICAN SCHOOL OF PUERTO VALLARTA
Day — Coed Gr PS-12

**48300 Puerto Vallarta, Jalisco, Mexico. Apartado Postal 2-280, Marina Vallarta.
Tel: 52-322-221-1525. Fax: 52-322-221-2373. EST-1.**
www.aspv.edu.mx   E-mail: gsel@aspv.edu.mx
Gerald Selitzer, Dir. MA. **Elise Langley, Adm.**
 Col Prep. Gen Acad. Curr—Nat US. **Bilingual**—Span. **Exams**—AP CEEB.
 AP—Eng Span US_Hist. **Feat**—Comp_Sci Studio_Art Drama Music. **Supp**—
 Dev_Read ESL Rem_Math Rem_Read Tut.
 Sports—Basket Soccer. **Activities**—Acad Arts Govt/Pol.
 Enr 367. Elem 272. Sec 95. US 93. Host 244. Other 30. Avg class size: 25.
 Fac 42. M 13/4. F 22/3. US 19. Host 14. Other 9. Adv Deg: 33%.
 Grad '05—68. US Col—12. (Menlo 2, Wellesley 1, Hamilton 1, W WA 1, Suffolk 1).
 Avg ACT: 26.
 Tui '05-'06: Day Mex$51,862-74,948.
 Summer: Rec. Sports. 3 wks.
 Bldgs 4. Class rms 23. Libs 2. Sci labs 2. Comp labs 2. Theaters 1. Fields 2. Courts
 3.
 Est 1986. Nonprofit. Sem (Aug-June). Assoc: A/OPR/OS ASOMEX SACS.

ASPV offers a bilingual education. Its curriculum of arts and sciences emphasizes skill development in written and spoken English and Spanish and also
incorporates computer technology. Community activities and sports supplement
academic work.

JOHN F. KENNEDY SCHOOL
AMERICAN SCHOOL OF QUERETARO

Day — Coed Gr PS-12

76100 Queretaro, Queretaro, Mexico. Ave Sabinos 272, Jurica Campestre. Tel: 52-442-218-00-75. Fax: 52-442-218-17-84. EST-1.
www.jfk.edu.mx   E-mail: admissions@jfk.edu.mx
Mirtha Stappung Ruff, Dir. MEd, MA. **Milton Zuniga, Adm.**

Col Prep. IB Diploma. Curr—Intl Nat US. **Bilingual**—Span. **Exams**—CEEB TOEFL. **Feat**—Span Comp_Sci Econ Pol_Sci Studio_Art Music. **Supp**—Rem_ Math Tut.

Sports—Basket Soccer Track Volley. **Activities**—Arts Rec.

Enr 1336. B 694. G 642. Elem 1024. Sec 312. US 69. Host 1162. Other 105. Accepted: 85%. Avg class size: 25.

Fac 131. M 14/28. F 74/15. US 14. Host 107. Other 10. Adv Deg: 20%.

Grad '05—59. Col—54.

Tui '05-'06: Day $3371-5705 (+$2600). **Aid:** 284 pupils ($490,864).

Plant val $6,600,000. Bldgs 21. Class rms 65. Lib 17,500 vols. Sci labs 2. Comp labs 4. Auds 1. Art studios 3. Music studios 2. Gyms 1. Fields 2. Courts 2.

Est 1964. Nonprofit. (Aug-June). Assoc: ASOMEX SACS.

Founded by industrialists from Mexico and the US who were residing in the Queretaro area, JFK conducts bilingual elementary and secondary curricula. As most children enroll from Mexico, the school provides intensive English immersion during the three-year preschool program. In grades 1-12, students follow a dual curriculum. Classes are taught in Spanish for half of the school day, while course work during the remainder of the day features English as the language of instruction and adheres to the US system.

JFK provides special Spanish and English courses for pupils lacking fluency in either of the two languages. In addition to the standard subjects, the curriculum includes music, art, computation, technical drawing and physical education classes. Boys and girls study Mexican and American culture at all grade levels.

AMERICAN SCHOOL OF TAMPICO
(ESCUELA AMERICANA DE TAMPICO)

Day — Coed Gr PS-10

89320 Tampico, Tamaulipas, Mexico. Calle Hidalgo s/n, Col Tancol. Tel: 52-833-227-2081. Fax: 52-833-227-2080. EST-1.
www.ats.edu.mx   E-mail: webmaster@ats.edu.mx
Emma Gutierrez, Dir.

Pre-Prep. Curr—US. **Supp Lang**—Span.

Enr 956.

Est 1917. Nonprofit. Sem (Aug-June). Assoc: ASOMEX SACS.

AMERICAN SCHOOL OF TORREON
(COLEGIO AMERICANO DE TORREON)
Day — Coed Gr PS-12

27019 Torreon, Coahuila, Mexico. Paseo del Algodon y Blvd Carlos Lopez Sosa, Fracc Los Vinedos. Tel: 52-871-733-26-60. Fax: 52-871-733-26-68. EST-1.
Contact: 344 Rio Dulce, Ste 871-152, El Paso, Texas 79932.
www.cat.mx   E-mail: cat@cat.mx
Makhlouf Ouyed, Dir. Astrid Martinez, Adm.

> Col Prep. Curr—Nat US. Bilingual—Span. Exams—ACT AP CEEB. Feat—Fr Comp_Sci Studio_Art Band Music Orchestra. Supp—ESL Rem_Math Tut.
>
> Sports—Basket Baseball Football Soccer Volley. Activities—Acad Arts Govt/Pol Media.
>
> Enr 1191. Elem 873. Sec 318. Host 1161. Other 30. Avg class size: 20.
>
> Fac 87. M 17. F 70. US 12. Host 66. Other 9. Adv Deg: 43%.
>
> Grad '05—50. Avg SAT: M/V—1008, Essay—443.
>
> Tui '05-'06: Day $2700-5500 (+$470). Aid: 269 pupils.
>
> Bldgs 2. Class rms 71. Libs 2. Sci labs 2. Comp labs 3. Art studios 1. Music studios 2. Gyms 2. Fields 3. Pools 1.
>
> Est 1950. Nonprofit. Sem (Aug-June). Assoc: ASOMEX SACS.

Offering bilingual instruction in English and Spanish, this coeducational school provides a college preparatory program. While the school offers a US-style curriculum, it incorporates many aspects of Mexican culture and enables students to meet the requirements for both the Mexican Bachillerato and the US diploma. Students may prepare for the US College Boards, and most graduates go on to college in the US or Mexico.

NICARAGUA

Sq. Miles: 50,446 (Slightly larger than New York). Country Pop: 5,465,100 (2005). Capital: Managua, pop. 1,000,000. Terrain: Extensive Atlantic coastal plains rising to central interior mountains; narrow Pacific coastal plain interrupted by volcanoes. Ethnic Group(s): Mestizo Jamaican. Religion(s): Roman_Catholic Evangelical. Official Language(s): Spanish. Other Language(s): English. Government: Republic. Independence: 1821 (from Spain). GDP: $2.4 billion (2001). Agriculture 21%. Industry 21%. Services 58%. Currency: Nicaraguan Cordoba (C$).

AMERICAN-NICARAGUAN SCHOOL
Day — Coed Gr PS-12

Managua, Nicaragua. PO Box 2670. Tel: 505-278-0029. Fax: 505-267-3088. EST-1.
www.ans.edu.ni   E-mail: adminoff@ans.edu.ni
Elsa Lamb, Dir.

> Col Prep. Curr—Nat US. Exams—AP CEEB. AP—Eng Fr Span Calc Bio

Chem Human_Geog Physics Eur_Hist US_Hist Econ Psych US_Govt & Pol. **Feat**—Amer_Stud Lat-Amer_Stud Comp_Relig Studio_Art Drama Music. **Supp**—ESL.
Enr 1021. Elem 624. Sec 397.
Fac 102. US 48. Host 39. Other 15.
Tui '05-'06: Day $1800-4200 (+$2000-3500).
Est 1944. Nonprofit. Sem (Aug-July). Assoc: AASCA AASSA A/OPR/OS SACS.

PANAMA

Sq. Miles: 29,762 (Slightly smaller than South Carolina). **Country Pop:** 3,039,150 (2005). **Capital:** Panama City, pop. 827,828. **Terrain:** Mountainous. **Ethnic Group(s):** Mestizo West_Indian Caucasion Amerindian. **Religion(s):** Roman_Catholic Protestant. **Official Language(s):** Spanish. **Other Language(s):** English. **Government:** Constitutional Democracy. **Independence:** 1903 (from Colombia). **GDP:** $13.83 billion (2004). Agriculture 5%. Industry 8%. Services 77%. **Currency:** Panamanian Balboa (B).

BALBOA ACADEMY
Day — Coed Gr PS-12

Panama, Panama. World Trade Ctr, PO Box 0832-1482. Tel: 507-211-0035. Fax: 507-211-3319. EST.
Contact: Unit 0945, APO, AA 34002.
www.balboaacademyweb.org   E-mail: jquinn@balboa-academy.org
Jean Lamb, Dir. MA.
   Col Prep. Curr—Nat US. **Exams**—AP CEEB. **AP**—Eng Span Bio Environ_Sci Physics Eur_Hist US_Hist World_Hist US_Govt & Pol Studio_Art. **Feat**—Creative_Writing Fr Stats Botany Marine_Biol/Sci Zoology Comp_Sci Psych Philos Journ. **Supp**—ESL Rem_Math Rem_Read Tut.
   Sports—Basket Soccer Volley. **Activities**—Service.
   Enr 593. B 317. G 276. Elem 433. Sec 160. US 189. Host 208. Other 196. Accepted: 95%. Yield: 90%. Avg class size: 15.
   Fac 58. M 6. F 51/1. US 40. Host 13. Other 5. Adv Deg: 44%.
   Grad '05—51. US Col—15. (FL St 9, U of Tampa 2, U of Louisville 1, Duke 1, Ringling Sch of Art & Design 1, Savannah Col of Art & Design 1). Avg SAT: M/V—991.
   Tui '05-'06: Day $3200-5920 (+$6000).
   Bldgs 4. Sci labs 4. Comp labs 6. Art studios 3. Music studios 2. Gyms 2. Fields 2.
   Est 1999. Nonprofit. Sem (Aug-June). Assoc: AASCA SACS.

The academy conducts a college preparatory program similar to that of an American private school. English is the medium of instruction, with Spanish being offered as both a native and a foreign language. A well-developed Advanced Placement program features course work in all major disciplines. To satisfy both US and Panamanian requirements, the school integrates American and Panamanian history, geography and government into the social studies curriculum. All graduates qualify for a US diploma, and they may also earn a Panamanian one.

THE INTERNATIONAL SCHOOL OF PANAMA
Day — Coed Gr PS-12

Panama, Panama. PO Box 0819-02588. Tel: 507-266-7037. Fax: 507-266-7808. EST.

Contact: Apartado 6-7589, El Dorado, Panama City, Panama.

www.isp.edu.pa   E-mail: isp@isp.edu.pa

Alexander Bennett, Dir.

> **Col Prep. IB Diploma. Curr**—Intl Nat US. **Exams**—ACT CEEB SSAT. **Feat**—Fr Span Environ_Sci Comp_Sci Econ Psych Panamanian_Stud Philos Graphic_ Arts Studio_Art Drama Chorus. **Supp**—EFL ESL Tut.
>
> **Enr 480.** Accepted: 98%. Avg class size: 21.
>
> **Fac 73.** M 9. F 62/2. US 23. Host 40. Other 10. Adv Deg: 54%.
>
> **Grad '05—47. Col—42. US Col—12.** (Northeastern U, Loyola U-LA, SMU, Notre Dame, U of PA, UNC-Chapel Hill).
>
> **Tui '05-'06: Day $6408-8280** (+$1000-6000).
>
> **Summer:** Enrich. 4-6 wks.
>
> Bldgs 6. Class rms 36. 2 Libs 14,000 vols. Sci labs 2. Comp labs 2. Gyms 1. Fields 2. Courts 2.
>
> **Est 1982.** Nonprofit. Quar (Aug-June). Assoc: AASCA A/OPR/OS SACS.

ISP occupies an eight-acre campus in an eastern suburb of Panama City. With the exception of Spanish language and Panamanian history courses, all instruction is in English. The student body encompasses pupils from approximately 40 nations, and the curriculum meets US, Panamanian and international requirements. Students may pursue the International Baccalaureate Diploma in grades 11 and 12.

Available sports include basketball, soccer and volleyball.

MIDDLE EAST

INDEX TO COUNTRIES IN THE
MIDDLE EAST

MIDDLE EAST

ARMENIA

Sq. Miles: 11,500 (Slightly larger than Maryland). **Country Pop:** 2,982,904 (2005). **Capital:** Yerevan, pop. 1,248,700 (1999). **Terrain:** High plateau with mountains, little forestland. **Ethnic Group(s):** Armenian Yezidi Russian Greek. **Religion(s):** Armenian_Apostolic. **Official Language(s):** Armenian. **Other Language(s):** Russian. **Government:** Republic. **Independence:** 1991 (from Soviet Union). **Per Capita Income:** $880 (2003). **GDP:** $2.8 billion (2003). Agriculture 25%. Industry 35%. Services 40%. **Currency:** Armenian Dram (AMD).

QSI INTERNATIONAL SCHOOL OF YEREVAN
Day — Coed Ages 3-17

375010 Yerevan, Armenia. PO Box 82. Tel: 374-1-391030. Fax: 374-1-284913. EST+9.
www.qsi.org/ARM_HOME   E-mail: yerevan@qsi.org
Richard Ryden, Dir.
  Gen Acad. Curr—US. Feat—Fr Russ Armenian Studio_Art Music.
  Enr 84.
  Fac 14.
  Tui '05-'06: Day $9400-12,000 (+$1600).
  Est 1995. Nonprofit. Spons: Quality Schools International. Assoc: A/OPR/OS MSA.

AZERBAIJAN

Sq. Miles: 33,774 (Slightly smaller than Maine). **Country Pop:** 7,911,974 (2005). **Capital:** Baku, pop. 1,900,000 (2003). **Terrain:** Caucasus Mountains to the north, lowland in the central area through which the Kura River flows. **Ethnic Group(s):** Azeri Dagestani Russian Armenian. **Religion(s):** Muslim Russian_Orthodox Armenian_Orthodox. **Official Language(s):** Azerbaijani. **Other Language(s):** Russian Armenian. **Government:** Republic. **Independence:** 1991 (from Soviet Union). **GDP:** $10.2 billion (2004). Agriculture 14%. Industry 46%. Services 40%. **Currency:** Azerbaijani Manat (AZM).

BAKU INTERNATIONAL SCHOOL

Day — Coed Gr PS-12

Baku, Azerbaijan. 128 Azadlig Prospect. Tel: 994-12-656352. Fax: 994-12-410595.
EST+9.

www.qsi.org/AZB_HOME   E-mail: phildale@qsi.org

Scott Root, Dir.

Gen Acad. Curr—US. Feat—Fr Russ Azeri Comp_Sci Studio_Art.

Enr 102.

Fac 24.

Tui '05-'06: Day $8000-12,000 (+$1600).

Est 1994. Nonprofit. Spons: Quality Schools International. Assoc: A/OPR/OS
MSA.

THE INTERNATIONAL SCHOOL OF AZERBAIJAN

Day — Coed Gr PS-12

Baku, Azerbaijan. Stonepay, Royal Park, Yeni Yasamal. Tel: 994-12-4973208.
Fax: 994-12-4972194. EST+9.

Contact: 501 Westlake Park Blvd, PO Box 4381, Houston, TX 72210.

www.tisa.az   E-mail: admissions@tisa.az

Peter J. Harding, Dir. BEd. Gayle Berger, Adm.

Col Prep. IB PYP. IB MYP. IB Diploma. Curr—Intl. Exams—ACT CEEB TOEFL.
Feat—Fr Russ Span Comp_Sci Econ Psych Studio_Art. Supp—Dev_Read
ESL Rem_Math Rem_Read.

Sports—Basket Soccer. Activities—Acad Arts Rec Service.

Enr 429. B 213. G 216. Elem 355. Sec 74. US 129. Host 59. Other 241. Accepted:
98%. Yield: 95%. Avg class size: 18.

Fac 60. M 16. F 39/5. US 7. Host 9. Other 44.

Grad '05—15. Col—8. US Col—3. (Guilford, USC, U of UT). Avg SAT: M/V—1150.

Tui '05-'06: Day $15,500 (+$5000). Aid: 29 pupils.

Plant val $10,000,000. Bldgs 4. Class rms 34. Lib 12,000 vols. Sci labs 3. Lang
labs 6. Photog labs 2. Art studios 2. Music studios 1. Dance studios 1. Gyms
1. Fields 1.

Est 1996. Nonprofit. Tri (Aug-June). Assoc: ECIS.

TISA's program of study borrows elements from European, Australian, and
North American curricula. Elementary school students follow the IB Primary Years
Program. Foreign language options during these years are French, Spanish and Russian, and music, physical education and information technology are also part of the
curriculum. Students in grades 6-10 complete the IB Middle Years Program, with
a further emphasis on interdisciplinary projects and schoolwide activities. All high
schoolers work toward the traditional TISA diploma (which is equivalent to a US
high school diploma), and many students also prepare for the IB Diploma.

BAHRAIN

Sq. Miles: 268 (About four times the size of Washington DC). **Country Pop:** 688,345 (2005). **Capital:** Manama, pop. 148,000 (2002). **Terrain:** Low interior plateau and hill on main island. **Ethnic Group(s):** Bahraini Asian Arab Iranian. **Religion(s):** Muslim Roman_Catholic Jewish Hindu. **Official Language(s):** Arabic. **Other Language(s):** English Farsi Urdu. **Government:** Constitutional Monarchy. **Independence:** 1971 (from United Kingdom). **GDP:** $7.7 billion (2002). Agriculture 1%. Financial Services 16%. Industry 17%. Manufacturing 12%. Public Administration 20%. Transport & Communications 9%. **Currency:** Bahraini Dinar (BD).

BAHRAIN SCHOOL
Bdg — Coed Gr 9-12; Day — Coed K-12

Juffair, Bahrain. PO Box 934. Tel: 973-17-727828. Fax: 973-17-725714. EST+8.
Contact: PSC 451, Box 690, FPO, AE 09834.
www.bahr-ehs.eu.dodea.edu   E-mail: trevor.burt@eu.dodea.edu
Jennifer Beckwith, Prin. PhD.

> Col Prep. IB Diploma. Curr—Intl US. Exams—ACT AP CEEB TOEFL. AP—Eng Calc Chem Physics Econ. Feat—Arabic Fr Ger Span Comp_Sci Studio_Art. Supp—ESL LD Tut.
>
> Sports—Basket X-country Soccer Swim Tennis Track. Activities—Acad Arts Govt/Pol Media.
>
> Enr 400. B 35/175. G 30/160. US 150. Host 150. Other 100. Accepted: 80%. Yield: 99%. Avg class size: 15.
>
> Fac 60. M 15. F 40/5. US 51. Host 7. Other 2.
>
> Grad '05—67. Col—60.
>
> Tui '05-'06: Bdg $27,732. Day $18,156.
>
> Dorms 1. Libs 1. Sci labs 6. Auds 1. Art studios 3. Music studios 1. Gyms 2. Fields 2. Tennis courts 4. Pools 1. Tracks 1.
>
> Est 1968. Nonprofit. Quar (Aug-June).

Beginning as an elementary school for US Defense Department employees, Bahrain School has since undergone significant expansion. The school currently admits English-speaking children, including Bahraini nationals, through grade 12.

The academic program meets American curricular requirements, with preparation given for the International Baccalaureate Diploma. Extensive elective offerings complement core courses within each department. The school offers business education and design technology classes for the small percentage of students not planning to attend college.

CYPRUS

Sq. Miles: 3572 (About the size of Connecticut). **Country Pop:** 780,133 (2005). **Capital:** Nicosia, pop. 197,800 (2000). **Terrain:** Central plain with mountain ranges to the north and south. **Ethnic Group(s):** Greek Turkish Armenian. **Religion(s):** Greek_Orthodox Muslim Romanite Armenian_Orthodox. **Official Language(s):** Greek Turkish English. **Government:** Republic. **Independence:** 1960 (from United Kingdom). **GDP:** $15.4 billion (2004). Agriculture 5%. Industry 19%. Services 76%. **Currency:** Cyprian Pound (£C).

AMERICAN ACADEMY LARNACA
Day — Coed Gr 1-13

6301 Larnaca, Cyprus. Gregory Afxentiou Ave, PO Box 4112. Tel: 357-24-815400. Fax: 357-24-651046. EST+7.
www.academy.ac.cy   E-mail: info@academy.ac.cy
Tom Robertson, Dir.

> **Col Prep. Curr**—Nat UK. **Supp Lang**—Greek. **Exams**—TOEFL GCSE IGCSE O-level A-level. **Feat**—Humanities Fr Ger Greek Comp_Sci Econ Psych Relig Studio_Art Music.
> **Enr 1000.** Elem 430. Sec 570. US 5. Host 700. Other 295. Accepted: 35%.
> **Fac 62.** M 13/4. F 40/5. Adv Deg: 19%.
> **Grad '05—99. US Col—6.** (MIT, UCLA, IN U, Georgetown, U of TX-Austin, U of WI-Madison).
> **Tui '02-'03: Day $2370-3760** (+$100-350). **Aid:** 25 pupils ($17,000).
> **Summer:** Enrich Rem Rec. 6 wks.
> Bldgs 3. 2 Libs 8000 vols. Sci labs 6. Comp labs 2. Auds 1. Art studios 3. Dance studios 1. Gyms 1. Fields 1. Courts 2.
> **Est 1908.** Nonprofit. Nondenom Christian. Sem (Sept-June).

The academy (grades 7-13) and the junior school (grades 1-6) were established by the Reformed Presbyterian Church of North America as a Christian Mission school. In addition to a general education, pupils receive preparation for college entrance.

A full range of extracurricular activities includes drama, dance and music. The school's extensive facilities provide many athletic opportunities.

MEDITERRANEAN HIGH SCHOOL/
MEDITERRANEAN JUNIOR PRIVATE SCHOOL
Day — Coed Gr 1-12

6500 Larnaca, Cyprus. 10 Kilkis St, PO Box 42572. Tel: 357-24-664733. Fax: 357-24-664734. EST+7.
www.medhigh.com.cy   E-mail: info@medhigh.com.cy
Niki Georghiou, Prin.

> **Col Prep. Curr**—UK. **Exams**—CEEB TOEFL IGCSE O-level AS-level A-level.

Feat—Fr Greek Comp_Sci Relig Studio_Art Music. **Supp**—EFL ESL LD Rem_Math Tut.

Sports—Basket Volley. **Activities**—Acad Arts Media.

Enr 310. B 152. G 158. Elem 178. Sec 132. Host 169. Other 141. Accepted: 80%. Avg class size: 18.

Fac 45. M 13/2. F 29/1. US 2. Host 34. Other 9. Adv Deg: 15%.

Grad '05—49.

Tui '05-'06: Day £C1700-2750 (+£C150).

Summer: Rec. Tui Day £C120. 5 wks.

Bldgs 1. Class rms 18. Lib 1000 vols. Sci labs 1. Comp labs 1. Auds 1. Art studios 1. Music studios 1. Dance studios 1. Gyms 1. Fields 1. Courts 1. Pools 1.

Est 1995. Inc. Tri (Sept-June).

These schools provide English-language primary and secondary programs that incorporate elements of the British and American systems, with adaptations made to the local environment. At Med Junior, children receive a firm grounding in the fundamentals while gaining both an appreciation of the arts and an exposure to computer technology.

All Med High students complete course work in the following areas: English, math, modern Greek, computer, religious studies and physical education. In addition, each pupil takes various compulsory classes relevant to his or her area of concentration. Students may take up to four courses at A-level, and the program's final three years provide preparation for various external exams, including the SAT and the TOEFL.

AMERICAN ACADEMY LIMASSOL

Day — Coed Gr PS-12

Limassol, Cyprus. Despinas Pattichi St, PO Box 1867. Tel: 357-5-337054. Fax: 357-5-387488. EST+7.

www.american-academy-cyprus.com   E-mail: academy@cytanet.com.cy

Col Prep. Curr—UK. **Exams**—GCSE AS-level A-level. **Feat**—Arabic Fr Greek Russ Comp_Sci Econ Relig Studio_Art Drama Bus.

Tui '05-'06: Day £C856-2220 (+£C50).

Est 1971. Tri.

FOLEY'S GRAMMAR AND JUNIOR SCHOOL

Day — Coed Gr PS-12

3095 Limassol, Cyprus. 40 Homer St. Tel: 357-25-58-21-91. Fax: 357-25-58-41-19. EST+7.

www.foleysschool.com   E-mail: foley@spidernet.com.cy

Col Prep. Curr—UK. **Exams**—GCSE AS-level A-level. **Feat**—Fr Ger Greek Comp_Sci Studio_Art Drama Music.

Tui '05-'06: Day £2160-4380.

Tri (Sept-June).

LOGOS SCHOOL OF ENGLISH EDUCATION

Bdg — Coed Gr 6-13; Day — Coed K-13

3501 Limassol, Cyprus. 33-35 Yialousa St, PO Box 51075. Tel: 357-25-336061. Fax: 357-25-335578. EST+7.

www.logos.ac.cy   E-mail: pr@logos.ac.cy

Peter Ross, Prin. BSc.

> Col Prep. Curr—UK. Exams—TOEFL IGCSE A-level. Feat—Fr Ger Greek Comp_ Sci Relig Studio_Art. Supp—EFL ESL LD.
>
> Enr 280. B 10/138. G 3/129. Elem 200. Sec 80. US 20. Host 90. Other 170. Avg class size: 20.
>
> Fac 28. M 16/2. F 8/2. US 7. Host 10. Other 11. Adv Deg: 82%.
>
> Grad '05—16. US Col—5. Avg ACT: 21.
>
> Tui '02-'03: Bdg £C5200 (+£C1200). Day £C1725 (+£C300).
>
> Bldgs 4. Dorm rms 7. Class rms 20. Lib 4000 vols. Sci labs 2. Comp labs 1. Auds 1. Fields 1. Tennis courts 2. Pools 1.
>
> Est 1973. Nonprofit. Nondenom Christian. Tri (Sept-June).

Logos School provides a general English education within the context of the Christian faith, and all students attend morning Assembly. Students of many nationalities prepare for GCSE and A-level examinations and the high school diploma. Geography field trips, archaeological excavations and outings to local factories, as well as a variety of sports and clubs, are part of the program.

AMERICAN ACADEMY NICOSIA

Day — Coed Gr 1-13

1515 Nicosia, Cyprus. 3A Michael Parides St, PO Box 21967. Tel: 357-22-664-266. Fax: 357-22-669-290. EST+7.

www.aacademynicosia.ac.cy   E-mail: aacademy@spidernet.com.cy

Joe Worsham, Prin. BA, MA, EdD.

> Col Prep. Gen Acad. Curr—UK. Exams—IGCSE O-level AS-level A-level. Feat—Fr Greek Comp_Sci Econ Law Sociol Bible Accounting Bus Home_Ec. Supp—ESL Tut.
>
> Enr 305. B 160. G 145. US 5. Host 200. Other 100. Avg class size: 18.
>
> Fac 34. Adv Deg: 23%.
>
> Grad '05—25. Col—22. US Col—3.
>
> Tui '04-'05: Day £C1880-3000.
>
> Bldgs 3. Lib 20,000 vols. Sci labs 1. Comp labs 1. Auds 1. Art studios 1. Fields 1. Courts 2.
>
> Est 1922. Nonprofit. Sem (Sept-June).

While the school follows the British National Curriculum, it also meets the curricular standards of the US. All instruction is in English, with the exception of Greek and French language instruction; pupils of Greek descent take Greek, while others study French. The secondary program offers IGCSE, GCE O-level, and AS- and A-level examination preparation. A special program for older pupils prepares boys and girls for college study in the fields of law, international relations and politics, public service and international business.

Bible class is among American Academy's course requirements.

AMERICAN INTERNATIONAL SCHOOL IN CYPRUS

Day — Coed Gr PS-12

1686 Nicosia, Cyprus. 11 Kassos St, PO Box 23847. Tel: 357-22-316-345. Fax: 357-22-316-549. EST+7.
www.aisc.ac.cy   E-mail: aisc@aisc.ac.cy
Ron Joron, Dir.

> **Col Prep. IB Diploma. Curr**—Intl US. **Exams**—CEEB. **Feat**—Fr Greek Span Comp_Sci Psych Studio_Art Drama Music. **Supp**—ESL LD.
>
> **Sports**—Basket Soccer Swim Tennis Volley. **Activities**—Arts Govt/Pol Rec.
>
> **Enr 259.** Elem 159. Sec 100. US 72. Host 94. Other 93. Accepted: 95%. Yield: 95%. Avg class size: 15.
>
> **Fac 39.** M 6/2. F 26/5. US 18. Host 6. Other 15. Adv Deg: 48%.
>
> **Grad '05—20. Col—17. US Col—6.** (U of VA, Lawrence U, Savannah Col of Art & Design, U of S FL, Embry-Riddle, Boston Col). Avg SAT: M/V—1046, Essay—511.
>
> **Tui '05-'06: Day £C1680-5280** (+£C1350-3200).
>
> Bldgs 3. Class rms 27. Lib 11,000 vols. Sci labs 3. Comp labs 2. Auds 1. Art studios 1. Music studios 1. Gyms 1. Courts 1. Pools 1.
>
> **Est 1987.** Inc. Sem (Sept-June). Assoc: MAIS MSA.

The school offers a regular American elementary and secondary curriculum and the International Baccalaureate amid a rich cultural and historical setting. In addition to local families, AISC enrolls children whose parents work in the diplomatic corps, at international corporations or at the United Nations. The school's required preparatory courses are supplemented by many off-campus academic and extracurricular activities, and service learning is an important aspect of school life.

Comprehensive college planning and placement allows graduates to matriculate at many competitive US, British and international institutions.

THE GRAMMAR SCHOOL

Day — Coed Ages 12-19

1519 Nicosia, Cyprus. Anthoupolis Hwy, PO Box 22262. Tel: 357-22-695695. Fax: 357-22-623044. EST+7.
www.grammarschool.ac.cy   E-mail: info@grammarschool.ac.cy
Vassos Hajiyerou, Head. BA. **Marina Koni, Adm.**

> **Col Prep. Curr**—UK. **Exams**—CEEB TOEFL IGCSE O-level A-level. **Feat**—Fr Greek Comp_Sci Civics Econ Law World_Relig Accounting.
>
> **Sports**—Soccer Swim Track Volley. **Activities**—Acad Arts Service.
>
> **Enr 1080.** Accepted: 20%. Avg class size: 25.
>
> **Fac 82.** M 36. F 46.
>
> **Grad '05—145. Col—110. US Col—10.**
>
> Libs 1. Sci labs 4. Comp labs 3. Art studios 1. Music studios 1. Dance studios 1. Gyms 1. Fields 2. Pools 3.
>
> **Est 1963.** Nonprofit. Sem (Sept-June).

The school's curriculum consists of required courses in math, English, social studies, the sciences, information technology, art, religion and physical education. Field trips to the museums and historical landmarks of Cyprus are integral to the curriculum. Clubs and sports are among the student activities.

INTERNATIONAL SCHOOL OF PAPHOS
Bdg — Coed Gr 6-12; Day — Coed PS-12

Paphos, Cyprus. 22-26 Hellas Ave, PO Box 2018. Tel: 357-26-932236. Fax: 357-26-942541. EST+7.
www.spidernet.net/web/isop   E-mail: isop@spidernet.com.cy
L. Olympiou, Head. BA, PhD.
> Col Prep. Curr—UK. Exams—IGCSE AS-level A-level. Feat—Fr Ger Greek Stats Comp_Sci Econ Studio_Art Music. Supp—EFL ESL.
> Enr 300. Accepted: 70%. Avg class size: 24.
> Fac 38. M 5/1. F 18/14. Host 25. Other 13. Adv Deg: 10%.
> Grad '05—6. Col—4.
> Tui '05-'06: Day £C1571-2840 (+£C251).
> Fields 1.
> Est 1980. Nonprofit. Sem (Sept-June).

The academic program at ISOP utilizes a predominantly British approach as it prepares students for the GCE and GCSE examinations. Classes are small, and offerings in the arts complement courses in the core subjects.

Extracurricular activities include hikes through the forests and beaches of this Mediterranean island, cultural excursions, swimming and skiing.

IRAQ

Sq. Miles: 168,754 (About the size of California). **Country Pop:** 26,074,906 (2005). **Capital:** Baghdad, pop. 5,700,000 (2004). **Terrain:** Alluvial plains, mountains and desert. **Ethnic Group(s):** Arab Kurd Turcoman Chaldean Assyrian. **Religion(s):** Shiite_Muslim Sunni_Muslim Christian. **Other Language(s):** Arabic Kurdish Assyrian Armenian. **Government:** Transitional Democracy. **Independence:** 1932. **Per Capita Income:** $870 (2005). **GDP:** $24.3 billion (2005). Agriculture 7%. Industry 67%. Services 26%. **Currency:** Iraqi Dinar, New (ID).

BAGHDAD INTERNATIONAL SCHOOL
Day — Coed Gr PS-12

Baghdad, Iraq. PO Box 15117, Al Yarmouk. Tel: 964-1-5522410. Fax: 964-1-5522479. EST+8.
Contact: c/o UNDP Iraq, PO Box 1608, Grand Central Sta, New York, NY 10163.
E-mail: bised@uruklink.net
Nisreen Al-Awqati, Dir.
> Col Prep. Curr—UK. Exams—O-level A-level.
> Enr 47. B 21. G 26.
> Fac 56. Host 50. Other 6.
> Tui '02-'03: Day $1565-2145 (+$1300).
> Est 1984. Nonprofit. Sem (Sept-June).

ISRAEL

Sq. Miles: 7850 (About the size of New Jersey). **Country Pop:** 6,276,883 (2005). **Capital:** Jerusalem, pop. 657,543 (2000). **Largest City:** Tel Aviv, pop. 354,428 (2000). **Terrain:** Plains, mountains, desert and coast. **Ethnic Group(s):** Jewish. **Religion(s):** Jewish Muslim. **Official Language(s):** Hebrew Arabic. **Other Language(s):** English Russian. **Government:** Parliamentary Democracy. **Independence:** 1948. **GDP:** $117.4 billion (2002). Agriculture 3%. Industry 38%. Services 59%. **Currency:** Israeli Shekel (NIS).

ANGLICAN INTERNATIONAL SCHOOL JERUSALEM

Day — Coed Gr PS-12

Jerusalem 91001, Israel. 82 Rechov Haneviim, PO Box 191. Tel: 972-2-567-7200. Fax: 972-2-538-4874. EST+7.
www.aisj.co.il   E-mail: shermanj@aisj.co.il
Phil Billing, Dir. BEd, MEd.
  Col Prep. IB Diploma. Curr—Intl. **Exams**—CEEB IGCSE. **Feat**—Arabic Fr Hebrew Comp_Sci Middle_Eastern_Stud Jerusalem_Stud Relig Studio_Art Theater_Arts. **Supp**—EFL ESL Rem_Read Tut.
  Sports—Basket Soccer Swim Tennis. **Activities**—Arts Govt/Pol Media.
  Enr 203. Accepted: 90%. Avg class size: 15.
  Fac 22. M 8/2. F 6/6. US 5. Host 9. Other 8. Adv Deg: 45%.
  Grad '05—16. **Col**—16. **US Col**—11.
  Tui '05-'06: Day $7500-12,900 (+$1400). **Aid:** 30 pupils ($115,000).
  Bldgs 10. Class rms 24. Libs 2. Sci labs 2. Comp labs 3. Auds 1. Theaters 1. Art studios 2. Music studios 3. Gyms 1. Fields 1. Courts 2.
  Est 1948. Nonprofit. Anglican. Sem (Sept-June). Assoc: MSA.

The school bases its curriculum in grades PS-5 on the English national program, although modifications at all grade levels allow course work to meet American curricular requirements. Students in grades 6-10 follow the International Baccalaureate Middle Years Program, while boys and girls in grades 11 and 12 take part in the IB Diploma program and may receive preparation for the SAT examination. In the upper grades, pupils choose from an increasing number of electives, among them theater arts and computer science.

Field trips to Jerusalem's many religious, cultural and historical sites form the basis for the Jerusalem studies program.

WALWORTH BARBOUR AMERICAN INTERNATIONAL SCHOOL IN ISRAEL

Day — Coed Gr K-12

Kfar Shmaryahu 46910, Israel. PO Box 9005. Tel: 972-9-961-8100. Fax: 972-9-961-8111. EST+7.

www.wbais.org   E-mail: aisrael@wbais.org
Marsha L. Aaronson, Supt.
    Col Prep. Curr—US. Exams—AP CEEB. AP—Eng Fr Span Calc Comp_Sci Bio Physics Eur_Hist US_Hist Art_Hist Studio_Art. Feat—Hebrew Anat Environ_Sci Intl_Relations.
    Enr 450.
    Fac 72.
    Tui '05-'06: Day $14,500-16,550 (+$3550).
    Est 1958. Nonprofit. Sem (Sept-June). Assoc: A/OPR/OS MSA.

JORDAN

Sq. Miles: 34,573 (Slightly smaller than Indiana). Country Pop: 5,759,732 (2005). Capital: Amman, pop. 1,900,000. Terrain: Mostly desert plateau in east, highland area in west. Ethnic Group(s): Arab Circassian Armenian Kurd. Religion(s): Sunni_Muslim Christian. Official Language(s): Arabic. Other Language(s): English. Government: Constitutional Monarchy. Independence: 1946. Per Capita Income: $2164 (2004). GDP: $11.52 billion (2004). Agriculture 3%. Industry 30%. Services 67%. Currency: Jordanian Dinar (JD).

THE ABDUL HAMID SHARAF SCHOOL
Day — Coed Gr PS-12

Amman 11118, Jordan. PO Box 6008. Tel: 962-6-5924188. Fax: 962-6-5924623. EST+7.
www.ahss.edu.jo   E-mail: ahss@go.com.jo
Sue Dahdah, Dir. BSc, MA, EdD. Farid Dahdah, Admin Dir. BSc.
    Col Prep. Curr—Nat UK US. Bilingual—Arabic. Exams—CEEB IGCSE O-level A-level. Feat—Arabic Fr Comp_Sci. Supp—ESL LD.
    Sports—Basket Soccer Volley. Activities—Arts Rec.
    Enr 480. B 300. G 180. Elem 280. Sec 200. US 245. Host 170. Other 65. Accepted: 95%. Yield: 92%. Avg class size: 22.
    Fac 50. M 12/3. F 30/5. US 3. Host 45. Other 2. Adv Deg: 10%.
    Grad '05—67. Col—57. US Col—34. Avg SAT: M/V—1270, Essay—650.
    Tui '06-'07: Day $1000-4150 (+$450-560). Aid: 144 pupils ($135,000).
    Summer: Rec. 5 wks.
    Plant val $900,000. Bldgs 1. Class rms 28. Libs 2. Sci labs 3. Comp labs 1. Theaters 1. Art studios 1. Music studios 1. Fields 2.
    Est 1980. Inc. Sem (Aug-June).

Following a humanistic, child-centered approach to elementary and secondary education, AHSS conducts a bilingual program in which instructors teach the basic subjects in Arabic. Both Montessori and traditional kindergarten classes are available. French classes offer pupils a third language option beginning in grade 3, and the school provides computer training. Audio-visual materials and teaching aids supplement textbooks, especially in English, math, science and social studies courses. Boys and girls begin preparing for the US College Boards during junior year.

A special education center serves students with learning differences.

THE AHLIYYAH SCHOOL FOR GIRLS

Day — Girls Gr 1-12

Amman 11181, Jordan. PO Box 2035. Tel: 962-6-464-9861. Fax: 962-6-462-1549. EST+7.

www.asg.edu.jo   E-mail: asg@asg.edu.jo

Haifa Hajjar Najjar, Dir. BSc, MA. **Badiah Madbak, Adm.**

  Col Prep. Gen Acad. IB Diploma. Curr—Intl Nat UK. **Bilingual**—Arabic. **Exams**—GCSE IGCSE O-level A-level. **Feat**—Fr Comp_Sci Econ Relig Drama. **Supp**—LD.

  Sports—Basket Gymnastics Hand Track Volley. **Activities**—Acad Arts Govt/Pol Service.

  Enr 1000. G 1000. Elem 666. Sec 334. US 14. Host 952. Other 34. Accepted: 50%. Yield: 47%. Avg class size: 25.

  Fac 121. M 15/2. F 86/18. US 2. Host 116. Other 3. Adv Deg: 21%.

  Grad '05—74.

  Tui '05-'06: Day $2700-5000. Aid: 654 pupils ($118,000).

  Endow $700,000. Plant val $16,500,000. Bldgs 3. Class rms 44. Libs 2. Sci labs 3. Lang labs 2. Comp labs 4. Theaters 2. Art studios 4. Music studios 2. Dance studios 2. Courts 2.

  Est 1926. Nonprofit. Episcopal. Sem (Sept-June).

ASG's program enriches the national curriculum with suitable American and British syllabi in English language and literature, math, the sciences and social studies. The school employs both English and Arabic as languages of instruction, although non-Jordanian pupils preparing for the IGCSE or the IB Diploma receive instruction in English. Children begin to develop learning skills in grade 1, then build upon these abilities in grades 2-6. Students remain with a homeroom teacher in grades 1-3, with departmentalization beginning in grade 4.

Girls at the secondary level may pursue courses at the IGCSE O level in grades 9 and 10, then enroll in the IB Diploma Program. Alternatively, girls may follow the Jordanian curriculum in grades 9-12.

AMERICAN COMMUNITY SCHOOL

Day — Coed Gr PS-12

Amman 11831, Jordan. Box 310, Dahiat Al-Amir Rashid. Tel: 962-6-581-3944. Fax: 962-6-582-3357. EST+7.

www.acsamman.edu.jo   E-mail: school@acsamman.edu.jo

Brian Lahan, Supt.

  Col Prep. Curr—US. **Exams**—CEEB. **AP**—Eng Fr Span Calc Bio Chem US_Hist Econ Psych Studio_Art. **Supp**—ESL.

  Enr 500.

  Fac 40. US 21. Host 7. Other 12.

  Tui '05-'06: Day $5935-10,820 (+$300).

Est 1955. Nonprofit. Sem (Aug-June). Assoc: A/OPR/OS MSA.

INTERNATIONAL COMMUNITY SCHOOL
Day — Coed Gr PS-10

Amman 11181, Jordan. PO Box 2002. Tel: 962-6-552-10-70. Fax: 962-6-552-71-09. EST+7.
www.ics-amman.edu.jo   E-mail: office@ics-amman.index.com.jo
Phillip Brisley, Dir.
> **Pre-Prep. Curr**—UK. **Exams**—GCSE. **Feat**—Arabic Fr Comp_Sci Relig Studio_Art Music. **Supp**—ESL LD.
> **Tui '05-'06: Day JD4650-7370** (+JD1000).
> **Est 1954.** Tri (Sept-Aug).

INTERNATIONAL SCHOOL OF CHOUEIFAT AMMAN
Day — Coed Gr PS-12

Amman 11810, Jordan. PO Box 316. Tel: 962-6-4291133. Fax: 962-6-4291155. EST+7.
E-mail: iscamman@sabis.net
Victor Saad, Dir.
> **Col Prep. Curr**—UK US. **Exams**—CEEB GCSE IGCSE A-level.
> **Est 1997.**

MASHREK INTERNATIONAL SCHOOL
Day — Coed Gr K-12

Amman 11118, Jordan. PO Box 1412. Tel: 962-6-5412979. Fax: 962-6-5411143. EST+7.
www.mashrek.edu.jo   E-mail: mashrek@go.com.jo
Bassam Malhas, Dir. Hana Al Nasser Malhas, Prin.
> **Col Prep. IB Diploma. Curr**—Intl Nat. **Bilingual**—Arabic. **Exams**—IGCSE AS-level A-level. **Feat**—Fr Ger Comp_Sci Islamic_Hist Studio_Art Drama Music Public_Speak. **Supp**—Dev_Read ESL LD Rem_Math Rem_Read.
> **Sports**—Basket Gymnastics Soccer Swim Tennis Track Volley. **Activities**—Arts Govt/Pol Service.
> **Enr 700.** B 455. G 245. Elem 500. Sec 200. Accepted: 30%. Avg class size: 24.
> **Fac 120.** M 12/8. F 90/10. US 3. Host 110. Other 7. Adv Deg: 15%.
> **Grad '05—60. US Col—3.** (U of MA-Dartmouth, U of AZ, U of MA-Amherst).
> **Tui '06-'07: Day JD1250-4750** (+JD500).
> **Summer:** Rec. Tui Day JD120. 4 wks.
> Plant val JD4,000,000. Bldgs 3. Class rms 30. Sci labs 4. Lang labs 2. Comp labs 4. Auds 2. Art studios 2. Music studios 1. Dance studios 2. Gyms 1. Fields 1. Courts 4.
> **Est 1993.** Inc. Sem (Aug-June).

MIS offers a bilingual education emphasizing critical thinking skills. In addition to instruction in English and Arabic, elementary and middle school students may study French language. After grade 8, students enter either the English or the Arabic track. Those enrolled in the English track prepare for the IGCSE, A- and AS-level examinations, then enter the IB Diploma Program. The Arabic track leads to the Jordanian high school diploma. Physical education, performing arts and community service complement academics.

MODERN AMERICAN SCHOOL

Day — Coed Gr PS-12

Amman 11195, Jordan. PO Box 950553, Sweifieh. Tel: 962-6-5810027. Fax: 962-6-5816861. EST+7.
www.modernamericanschool.com   E-mail: admin@modernamericanschool.com
Omaya Zamel, Prin.
> **Col Prep. Curr**—UK US. **Exams**—CEEB TOEFL IGCSE A-level. **Feat**—Arabic Fr Comp_Sci Relig Islamic_Stud Studio_Art Music.
> **Enr 900.**
> **Fac 134.**
> **Tui '06-'07: Day JD1800-5350** (+JD550-1050).
> Sem (Aug-June).

MODERN MONTESSORI SCHOOL

Day — Coed Gr PS-12

Amman 11821, Jordan. PO Box 1941. Tel: 962-6-553-5190. Fax: 962-6-553-5831. EST+7.
www.montessori.edu.jo   E-mail: mms@montessori.edu.jo
Randa Hasan, Prin.
> **Col Prep. IB Diploma. Curr**—Intl. **Bilingual**—Arabic. **Feat**—Comp_Sci Studio_Art Theater_Arts Music.
> **Tui '06-'07: Day JD1350-4920** (+JD320-650).
> **Est 1985.**

AMMAN BACCALAUREATE SCHOOL

Day — Coed Gr PS-12

Sweileh 11910, Jordan. PO Box 441. Tel: 962-6-541-1572. Fax: 962-6-541-2603. EST+7.
www.abs.edu.jo   E-mail: proffice@abs.edu.jo
Samia Al Farra, Prin. MEd. Liza Khanfar, Adm.
> **Col Prep. IB MYP. IB Diploma. Curr**—Intl Nat UK. **Bilingual**—Arabic. **Exams**—ACT CEEB TOEFL. **Feat**—Fr Comp_Sci Econ Geog Relig Studio_Art Drama Music.
> **Sports**—Badminton Basket Gymnastics Hand Rugby Soccer Tennis Track Volley. **Activities**—Arts Rec Service.
> **Enr 976.** B 524. G 452. Accepted: 10%. Avg class size: 21.

Fac 149. M 37/3. F 101/8. US 10. Host 121. Other 18. Adv Deg: 20%.
Tui '05-'06: Day JD1900-6700. Aid: 25 pupils (JD25,000).
Summer: Acad Enrich Rec. 4 wks.
Bldgs 5. 3 Libs 35,000 vols. Sci labs 7. Comp labs 3. Auds 1. Theaters 1. Gyms 1.
    Fields 1. Courts 3. Tracks 1.
Est 1981. Nonprofit. Sem (Sept-June). Assoc: CIS NEASC.

Although the vast majority of its student body is Jordanian, ABS enrolls international pupils from more than 20 other nations. In addition to readying students for the national diploma, the curriculum provides preparation for the IB Diploma.

Grades K-8 conduct bilingual (Arabic and English) programs, after which students have the option of studying exclusively in English. A two-year kindergarten program and Junior School (grades 1-5) focus on the child's personal and social development. The school offers the Middle Years Program in grades 6-10 prior to the two-year IB Diploma curriculum. Among ABS' staff are a few instructors with special-needs expertise.

KUWAIT

Sq. Miles: 6880 (Slightly smaller than New Jersey). **Country Pop:** 2,335,648 (2005). **Capital:** Kuwait City, pop. 413,170 (2002). **Terrain:** Flat to slightly undulating desert plain. **Ethnic Group(s):** Kuwaiti Arab Asian. **Religion(s):** Sunni_Muslim Shiite_Muslim Hindu Christian Sikh. **Official Language(s):** Arabic. **Other Language(s):** English. **Government:** Nominal Constitutional Monarchy. **Independence:** 1961 (from United Kingdom). **GDP:** $48 billion (2004). Agriculture 1%. Industry 60%. Services 39%. **Currency:** Kuwaiti Dinar (KD).

DASMAN MODEL SCHOOL
Day — Coed Gr PS-12
Dasman 15455, Kuwait. PO Box 426. Tel: 965-243-0607. Fax: 965-243-0339. EST+8.
www.dasmanschool.com.kw   E-mail: dasmanms@qualitynet.net
C. Lance Curlin, Supt. Nadia Kawash, Adm.
    Col Prep. Curr—Nat US. **Bilingual**—Arabic. **Exams**—CEEB. **Feat**—Fr Span
    Comp_Sci Islamic_Stud Studio_Art Music. **Supp**—ESL Rem_Math Rem_Read
    Tut.
    Fac 133. M 26. F 107. Adv Deg: 9%.
    Summer: Rem Rec. Tui Day KD100/crse. 4 wks.
    Plant val $1,500,000. Bldgs 2. Class rms 53. Libs 1. Sci labs 1. Comp labs 2. Auds
        2. Art studios 2. Music studios 2. Dance studios 2. Gyms 2. Fields 1. Courts 1.
        Pools 1.
    Est 1996. Inc. Sem (Sept-June). Assoc: CIS NEASC.

This bilingual elementary school features Arabic studies courses at all grade levels. Learning through structured play is the main characteristic of the kindergarten program, where all work revolves around a central theme. This thematic approach continues during the lower elementary years. At this level, American or British homeroom teachers provide all instruction. Specialists teach all middle school courses, among them music, art, computers, swimming and physical education.

AMERICAN SCHOOL OF KUWAIT

Day — Coed Gr PS-12

Hawalli 32042, Kuwait. PO Box 6735. Tel: 965-266-4341. Fax: 965-265-0438. EST+8.

www.ask.edu.kw   E-mail: ask@ask.edu.kw

Andy Page-Smith, Supt. BEd, MEd, DEd. Rebecca Ness, Adm.

Col Prep. Curr—US. Exams—ACT AP CEEB. AP—Eng Fr Span Calc Stats Comp_Sci Bio Chem Physics US_Hist World_Hist Econ Studio_Art. Feat—Arabic Astron Oceanog Psych Sociol Relig Ceramics Drama Music. Supp—Dev_Read ESL Rem_Read.

Sports—Badminton Basket X-country Soccer Softball Swim Track Volley. Activities—Acad Arts Govt/Pol Media Rec.

Enr 1379. B 760. G 619. Elem 903. Sec 476. US 321. Host 635. Other 423. Accepted: 60%. Yield: 90%. Avg class size: 20.

Fac 132. M 45. F 87. US 69. Host 3. Other 60. Adv Deg: 48%.

Grad '05—131. Col—131. US Col—6. (U of Miami, Purdue, U of WI-Madison, Tufts, U of MI, Boston U). Avg SAT: M/V—987.

Tui '05-'06: Day $5308-11,322.

Summer: Acad Enrich Rev Rec. 4 wks.

Bldgs 2. Class rms 103. Libs 2. Sci labs 10. Comp labs 7. Auds 1. Art studios 4. Gyms 2. Fields 3. Pools 1.

Est 1964. Nonprofit. Sem (Sept-June). Assoc: A/OPR/OS MSA.

ASK attracts students of about 50 different nationalities. At the elementary level, the school features team teaching in an individualized instructional environment. At the high school level, all pupils in grade 9 take Arabic or Arabic as a Second Language; boys and girls in grades 10 and 11 need study Arabic only if they are citizens of Arab-speaking countries. High schoolers may prepare for the US College Boards, with the vast majority of graduates advancing to college.

NEW ENGLISH SCHOOL

Day — Coed Gr PS-12

Hawalli 32036, Kuwait. PO Box 6156. Tel: 965-531-8060. Fax: 965-531-9924. EST+8.

www.neskt.com   E-mail: admin@neskt.com

Ziad S. Rajab, Dir.

Col Prep. Curr—UK. Exams—GCSE IGCSE AS-level A-level. Feat—Arabic Fr Span Comp_Sci Econ Islamic_Stud Studio_Art Drama Music Accounting Bus. Supp—ESL.

Tui '05-'06: Day KD1100-2500.

Est 1969. Tri (Sept-June).

UNIVERSAL AMERICAN SCHOOL
Day — Coed Gr PS-12

Khaldiya 72451, Kuwait. PO Box 17035. Tel: 965-561-5857. Fax: 965-562-5343. EST+8.
www.uas.edu.kw   E-mail: uas@qualitynet.net
Daniel Sinnott, Supt.

> **Col Prep. Curr**—US. **Supp Lang**—Arabic. **Exams**—ACT CEEB TOEFL. **AP**—Eng Calc Bio Chem Environ_Sci Physics US_Hist Studio_Art. **Feat**—Fr Span. **Supp**—ESL.
> **Enr 1063.** B 672. G 391.
> **Tui '06-'07: Day KD1067-2644** (+KD50).
> **Est 1976.** Nonprofit. Quar (Aug-June). Assoc: NEASC.

THE AMERICAN CREATIVITY ACADEMY
Day — Coed Gr PS-12
(Coord — Day PS-12)

Kuwait 32018, Kuwait. PO Box 1740. Tel: 965-261-1711. Fax: 965-263-2478. EST+8.
www.aca.edu.kw   E-mail: aca_recruiting@yahoo.com
Gene Vincent, Supt.

> **Col Prep. Curr**—US. **Exams**—AP CEEB. **AP**—Eng Calc Bio Econ. **Feat**—Arabic World_Relig Studio_Art.
> **Enr 1813.** Elem 1603. Sec 210. US 24. Host 1758. Other 31.
> **Est 1997.** Quar (Sept-June). Assoc: CIS MSA.

THE ENGLISH SCHOOL FAHAHEEL
Day — Coed Gr PS-12

Kuwait 64003, Kuwait. PO Box 7209, Fahaheel. Tel: 965-371-1070. Fax: 965-371-5458. EST+8.
www.skee.com   E-mail: esf@skee.com
George Bowery, Prin.

> **Col Prep. Curr**—UK. **Exams**—IGCSE A-level. **Feat**—Arabic Fr Comp_Sci Islamic_Stud Music. **Supp**—Dev_Read EFL ESL Rem_Math Rem_Read Tut.
> **Sports**—Soccer Swim Volley. **Activities**—Acad Arts Rec.
> **Enr 800.** Avg class size: 23.
> **Tui '05-'06: Day KD1007-2087.**
> Bldgs 2. Class rms 60. Libs 3. Sci labs 4. Comp labs 6. Auds 1. Theaters 1. Art studios 2. Music studios 2. Gyms 2. Fields 2. Courts 2. Pools 1.
> **Est 1968.** Nonprofit. Tri (Sept-June).

Founded to provide an English education for expatriate children in Kuwait, ESF has occupied its current campus since 2005. The school follows the English National Curriculum, modified to include required courses in Arabic and Islamic studies. The primary school features a broad curriculum and additional instruction in computers, music and French. Secondary school students prepare for a wide range of IGCSE and A-level examinations.

A comprehensive after-school activities program is offered, and students volunteer with local humanitarian organizations.

KUWAIT ENGLISH SCHOOL

Day — Coed Gr PS-12

Kuwait 22057, Kuwait. PO Box 8640, Salmiya. Tel: 965-565-5216. Fax: 965-562-9356. EST+8.
www.kes.edu.kw   E-mail: keschool@kes.edu.kw
Rhoda Elizabeth Muhmood, Dir.
    Col Prep. Curr—UK. **Exams**—GCSE IGCSE AS-level A-level. **Feat**—Arabic Comp_Sci Islamic_Stud Studio_Art Drama Music. **Supp**—LD.
    Enr 2000.
    Tui '05-'06: Day KD1100-2755.
    Est 1979. Tri (Sept-June).

KUWAIT NATIONAL ENGLISH SCHOOL

Day — Coed Gr PS-12

Kuwait 32057, Kuwait. PO Box 44273, Hawally. Tel: 965-265-6904. Fax: 965-265-2459. EST+8.
www.knes.edu.kw   E-mail: knes@qualitynet.net
Chantal Al Gharabally, Dir.
    Col Prep. Curr—UK. **Exams**—TOEFL IGCSE AS-level A-level. **Feat**—Arabic Fr Comp_Sci Econ Islamic_Stud Studio_Art Music Accounting Bus. **Supp**—ESL.
    Nonprofit. Tri (Sept-June).

AL-BAYAN BILINGUAL SCHOOL

Day — Coed Gr PS-12

Safat 13105, Kuwait. PO Box 24472. Tel: 965-2632850. Fax: 965-2614845. EST+8.
www.bbs.edu.kw   E-mail: bbsjadm@bbs.edu.kw
Brian McCauley, Dir. PhD.
    Col Prep. Curr—Nat US. **Bilingual**—Arabic. **Exams**—AP CEEB TOEFL. **AP**—Eng Comp_Sci Bio Chem Physics Econ Psych Studio_Art. **Feat**—Fr Astron Environ_Sci Sociol Islamic_Stud Ceramics Drama Music_Theory Accounting Journ. **Supp**—Rev Tut.
    Enr 1700. B 900. G 800. Elem 1400. Sec 300. US 10. Host 1590. Other 100. Accepted: 85%. Avg class size: 24.
    Fac 170. M 70. F 100. US 65. Host 100. Other 5. Adv Deg: 18%.
    Grad '05—35. Col—35. US Col—25.
    Tui '05-'06: Day KD1405-2735.
    Endow $2,600,000. Plant val $15,000,000. Bldgs 4. Class rms 150. 4 Libs 40,000 vols. Sci labs 7. Comp labs 6. Auds 3. Art studios 2. Music studios 3. Gyms 2. Fields 1. Courts 6.
    Est 1977. Nonprofit. Sem (Sept-June). Assoc: CIS NEASC.

BBS' students at all grade levels take classes in both English and Arabic, thus enabling boys and girls to develop spoken and written mastery of the two languages. The preschool program, taught half in English and half in Arabic, stresses perceptual-motor, cognitive and language development. Core classes at the elementary level include language arts, math and science, with other courses including Islamic studies, art, music, computer, physical education and, in grade 4, social studies.

Departmentalization begins in the middle school (grades 5-8), at which time the school emphasizes sound study habits and independent learning skills. The college preparatory high school features a varied elective program and a selection of Advanced Placement courses.

THE BRITISH SCHOOL OF KUWAIT
Day — Coed Gr PS-12

Safat 13130, Kuwait. PO Box 26922. Tel: 965-562-1701. Fax: 965-562-4903. EST+8. www.bsk.edu.kw   E-mail: vam@bsk.edu.kw
Vera Al-Mutawa, Dir. Graham Hawkins, Prin.
>   **Col Prep. Curr**—UK. **Exams**—GCSE IGCSE A-level. **Feat**—Arabic Fr Comp_Sci Econ Relig Studio_Art Drama Music Bus. **Supp**—ESL LD.
>   **Enr 1450.**
>   **Est 1978.** 5 terms (Sept-June).

THE ENGLISH SCHOOL
Day — Coed Gr PS-8

Safat 13004, Kuwait. PO Box 379. Tel: 965-563-7205. Fax: 965-563-7147. EST+8. www.tes.edu.kw   E-mail: admin@tes.edu.kw
John Allcott, Head.
>   **Gen Acad. Curr**—UK. **Exams**—CEE. **Feat**—Arabic Fr Lat Studio_Art Drama Music.
>   **Sports**—Basket F_Hockey Soccer. **Activities**—Arts Rec.
>   **Tui '05-'06: Day KD1180-2175.**
>   **Est 1953.** Nonprofit. Tri (Sept-June).

Serving the English-speaking community in Kuwait, the school closely follows the British National Curriculum. Students choose from the traditional disciplines, as well as a foreign language program that includes Arabic. Excursions and field trips enrich classroom work. These trips increase in length for older pupils, to whom overseas treks are sometimes offered.

Many school graduates matriculate at independent schools in the United Kingdom.

LEBANON

Sq. Miles: 4015 (About half the size of New Jersey). **Country Pop:** 3,826,018 (2005). **Capital:** Beirut, pop. 1,500,000. **Terrain:** Narrow coastal plain backed by the Lebanon Mountains, the fertile Bekaa Valley and the Anti-Lebanon Mountains, which extend to the Syrian border. **Ethnic Group(s):** Arab Armenian. **Religion(s):** Christian Muslim Druze. **Official Language(s):** Arabic. **Other Language(s):** French English Armenian. **Government:** Parliamentary Republic. **Independence:** 1943. **GDP:** $18.8 billion (2004). Agriculture 12%. Industry 21%. Services 67%. **Currency:** Lebanese Pound (LL).

AMERICAN COMMUNITY SCHOOL AT BEIRUT
Day — Coed Gr PS-12

Beirut 11072260, Lebanon. PO Box 11-8129, Riad El Solh. Tel: 961-1-374-370. Fax: 961-1-366-050. EST+7.
Contact: 3 Dag Hammarskjold Plaza, 8th Fl, New York, NY 10017. Tel: 212-583-7634. Fax: 212-583-7635.
www.acs.edu.lb E-mail: acs@acs.edu.lb
George H. Damon, Jr., Head. EdD.
  Col Prep. IB Diploma. Curr—Intl Nat US. Supp Lang—Arabic. Exams—CEEB TOEFL. Supp—ESL.
  Enr 997.
  Fac 153. Adv Deg: 32%.
  Tui '05-'06: Day $6599-9884 (+$600-2600).
  Est 1905. Nonprofit. Tri (Sept-June). Assoc: A/OPR/OS MSA.

INTERNATIONAL COLLEGE
Day — Coed Gr PS-12

Beirut 1107 2020, Lebanon. PO Box 11-0236, Riad El-Solh. Tel: 961-1-371-294. Fax: 961-1-362-500. EST+7.
Contact: 215 Park Ave S, Ste 2016, New York, NY 10003. Tel: 212-529-3005. Fax: 212-529-8525.
www.ic.edu.lb E-mail: icny@aol.com
Arthur H. Charles, Jr., Pres. BS, MS, PhD.
  Col Prep. IB Diploma. Fr Bac. Curr—Intl Nat US. Supp Lang—Fr Arabic. Exams—CEEB. Feat—Arabic Fr Comp_Sci Econ Psych Philos Drawing Studio_Art Theater_Arts. Supp—ESL.
  Sports—Basket Soccer Swim Track Volley. Activities—Acad Arts Service.
  Enr 3407. US 523. Host 2060. Other 824. Avg class size: 24.
  Fac 312. M 53/14. F 232/13. US 8. Host 255. Other 49. Adv Deg: 28%.
  Grad '05—212. Col—212. US Col—20. (Georgetown, U of MI, Purdue).
  Tui '05-'06: Day $5024-5584. Aid: 424 pupils ($973,338).
  Endow $30,000,000.
  Est 1891. Nonprofit. Tri (Sept-June). Assoc: CIS NEASC.

IC utilizes English, French and Arabic as languages of instruction, depending upon which track the student chooses. Programming follows American, French and Lebanese curricular lines, preparing boys and girls in the various sections for the International, French and Lebanese baccalaureates, as well as the US College Boards. A three-year curriculum that begins in grade 10, the College Preparatory

Program offers a US-style program with course requirements in math, science, English, social studies, French and Arabic.

Founded in Izmir, Turkey, International College moved in 1936 to Lebanon, where it administered the preparatory section of the American University of Beirut. Affiliation with AUB ended in 1957, although the school continues to occupy part of the campus.

EASTWOOD COLLEGE
Day — Coed Gr PS-12

Mansourieh, Meten, Lebanon. PO Box 100. Tel: 961-4-409307. Fax: 961-4-400916. EST+7.
www.eastwoodcollege.com   E-mail: info@eastwoodcollege.com
Amine M. Khoury, Pres. BA, MA. **Rosemary Wallis, Adm.**

    Col Prep. Gen Acad. Curr—Nat US. **Supp Lang**—Fr Arabic. **Exams**—CEEB TOEFL. **Feat**—Arabic Dutch Fr Stats Comp_Sci Econ Psych Philos Studio_Art Drama Music Bus. **Supp**—Dev_Read EFL ESL LD Makeup Rem_Math Rem_Read Rev Tut.

    Enr 800. B 406. G 394. US 22. Host 350. Other 428. Accepted: 95%. Avg class size: 23.

    Fac 147. M 25. F 122. US 2. Host 125. Other 20. Adv Deg: 31%.

    Grad '05—36. US Col—9. (Notre Dame).

    Tui '05-'06: Day $2500-6000. Aid: 350 pupils ($250,000).

    Summer: Acad Enrich Rec. Tui Day $1200-1400. 6 wks.

    Plant val $1,500,000. Class rms 30. Lib 13,000 vols. Chapels 2. Sci labs 2. Comp labs 2. Art studios 2. Music studios 2.

    Est 1973. Evangelical. Tri (Sept-June).

Operating on campuses in Kafarshima and Mansourieh, this Evangelical Christian school enrolls students from various religious groups. Readiness programs and field trips are important elements of the preschool program, which serves children ages 3-5. The elementary program, which runs through grade 6, places considerable emphasis on English and Arabic language skills.

The curriculum emphasizes critical thinking, reasoning and problem solving, with drama, music, art, computer literacy and physical education. Pupils have two options at the secondary level: the official Lebanese curriculum and an international program that serves students from roughly two dozen countries and enables them to earn an American high school diploma.

SAGESSE HIGH SCHOOL
Bdg — Coed Gr 5-12; Day — Coed PS-12

Metn, Lebanon. Ain Saadeh. Tel: 961-1-872-145. Fax: 961-1-872-149. EST+7.
www.sagessehs.com   E-mail: sagesse@sagesse.com
Rev. Edgard Madi, President. PhD.

    Col Prep. IB Diploma. Curr—Intl Nat US. **Exams**—AP CEEB TOEFL. **Feat**—Ital Span Relig Studio_Art Music. **Supp**—ESL LD.

    Sports—Basket Soccer Swim Volley.

    Enr 1157. B 21/644. G 3/489. Elem 777. Sec 380. US 256. Host 635. Other 266.

Accepted: 95%. Yield: 85%. Avg class size: 20.
Fac 136. M 29/8. F 95/4. US 4. Host 125. Other 7.
Tui '05-'06: Bdg $14,000-15,000 (+$2000). **Day LL2,900,000-6,800,000** (+LL560,000-740,000).
Bldgs 2. Dorms 1. Dorm rms 40. Class rms 58. Lib 3000 vols. Sci labs 4. Comp labs 3. Theaters 2. Art studios 2. Music studios 2. Fields 1. Courts 6.
Est 1992. Roman Catholic. Sem (Sept-June).

Founded to meet the needs of English-speaking international students in Metropolitan Beirut, this Catholic school provides course work leading to the International Baccalaureate Diploma, the American high school diploma and the Lebanese Baccalaureate. Boys and girls in the American section may prepare for the College Board and Advanced Placement examinations, and nonnative English speakers ready themselves for the TOEFL. The broad-based curriculum facilitates entrance into colleges throughout the world. Pupils with dyslexia, attentional disorders and other learning differences may receive assistance through SHS' special-education unit.

A 30-minute drive from Beirut's airport, the mountainous campus setting in the village of Ain Saadeh overlooks the Mediterranean Sea.

OMAN

Sq. Miles: 82,031 (About the size of Kansas). **Country Pop:** 3,001,583 (2005). **Capital:** Muscat, pop. 880,200 (2005). **Terrain:** Mountains, plains and arid plateau. **Ethnic Group(s):** Arab Baluchi Zanzabari Indian Pakistani Bangladeshi. **Religion(s):** Ibadhi Sunni_Muslim Shiite_Muslim Hindu Christian. **Official Language(s):** Arabic. **Other Language(s):** English Baluchi Urdu Swahili Hindi. **Government:** Monarchy. **GDP:** $21.58 billion (2004). Agriculture 3%. Industry 40%. Services 57%. **Currency:** Omani Rial (RO).

THE AMERICAN INTERNATIONAL SCHOOL OF MUSCAT
Day — Coed Gr PS-12

Azaiba 130, Oman. PO Box 584. Tel: 968-2459-5180. Fax: 968-2450-3815. EST+9.
www.taism.com   E-mail: taism@omantel.net.om
Kevin Schafer, Dir. BA, MA.
  Col Prep. Curr—Intl US. **Exams**—AP CEEB. **AP**—Eng Fr Calc Bio Chem US_Govt & Pol. **Feat**—Creative_Writing Lib_Skills Arabic Span Comp_Sci Chorus Music Public_Speak. **Supp**—Dev_Read ESL LD Rem_Math Tut.
  Sports—Basket Soccer Swim Track Volley. **Activities**—Acad Arts Govt/Pol Media Rec.
  Enr 430. B 222. G 208. Elem 326. Sec 104. US 168. Host 11. Other 251. Accepted: 90%. Yield: 80%. Avg class size: 14.
  Fac 48. M 17/1. F 26/4. US 32. Other 16. Adv Deg: 52%.

Grad '05—18. Col—18. US Col—10. (Bard, Boston Col, Geo Wash, Emerson, Clark U, U of MD-Col Park). Avg SAT: M/V—1240.

Tui '05-'06: Day $5622-14,404 (+$3368-4184).

Plant val $7,800,000. Bldgs 1. Class rms 32. Lib 12,000 vols. Sci labs 3. Comp labs 2. Auds 1. Theaters 1. Art studios 3. Music studios 2. Gyms 1. Fields 1. Courts 1. Pools 1.

Est 1998. Nonprofit. Sem (Aug-June). Assoc: A/OPR/OS CIS NEASC.

TAISM enrolls expatriate children from dozens of nationalities into a US-style program that accounts for differing student abilities. Serving boys and girls from age 3 through grade 2, the early childhood program focuses on cognitive development, fundamental motor skills and language development. In grades 1 and 2, the school supplements classroom instruction in language arts, science, math, social studies and technology with specialist-taught classes in art, music, physical education, foreign language and library skills. During the elementary years (grades 3-5), the curriculum builds upon the foundation established in the earlier grades, with particular attention paid to analysis and critical thinking. Pupils gain responsibility at this time, as they receive homework assignments and complete extended projects.

The transitional middle school (grades 6-8) follows a developmentally appropriate, interdisciplinary program that is organized around broad themes. Emphasizing college preparation, the high school years include elective course work in art, music, physical education and technology. A well-developed Advanced Placement program allows students in grades 11 and 12 to pursue accelerated study in the major disciplines.

AMERICAN-BRITISH ACADEMY

Day — Coed Gr PS-12

Muscat 115, Oman. PO Box 372, Medinat Al Sultan Qaboos. Tel: 968-24603646. Fax: 968-24603544. EST+9.

www.abaoman.edu.om   E-mail: admin@abaoman.edu.om

Mona Nashman-Smith, Supt. BEd. Ann Smith, Adm.

Col Prep. Gen Acad. IB PYP. IB MYP. IB Diploma. Curr—Intl UK US. Exams—IGCSE. Feat—Arabic Fr Span Comp_Sci Econ Geog Drama Theater_Arts. Supp—ESL LD Rem_Math Rev Tut.

Sports—Basket Soccer Swim Volley. Activities—Acad Arts Govt/Pol Rec.

Enr 743. B 382. G 361. Elem 519. Sec 224. US 58. Host 18. Other 667. Accepted: 90%. Yield: 99%. Avg class size: 22.

Fac 75. M 30. F 43/2. US 11. Other 64. Adv Deg: 26%.

Grad '05—48. US Col—10.

Tui '05-'06: Day RO1800-4395 (+RO500-750).

Plant val RO3,000,000. Bldgs 8. Class rms 60. 2 Libs 20,000 vols. Sci labs 6. Lang labs 4. Comp labs 3

3. Theaters 1. Art studios 2. Music studios 3. Dance studios 2. Gyms 1. Fields 1. Courts 2. Pools 1.

Est 1987. Nonprofit. Tri (Aug-June). Assoc: CIS MSA.

This English-medium school's program follows the three programs of study of the International Baccalaureate Organization. In addition, many courses in grades 9 and 10 satisfy the requirements of the IGCSE. ABA places particular emphasis on the performing and visual arts as a complement to its IB course work.

See Also Page 547

THE BRITISH SCHOOL
MUSCAT

Day — Coed Gr PS-12

Ruwi 112, Oman. PO Box 1907. Tel: 968-24600842. Fax: 968-24601062. EST+9.
www.britishschool.edu.om   E-mail: admin@britishschool.edu.om
Steve Howland, Prin. BEd, MBA. Deirdre Selway, Adm.

> **Col Prep. Curr**—UK. **Exams**—GCSE A-level. **AP**—Comp_Sci. **Feat**—Dutch Fr Ger Geog Psych Studio_Art Bus. **Supp**—Dev_Read ESL LD Rem_Read Tut.
>
> **Sports**—Basket F_Hockey Gymnastics Soccer Swim Track. **Activities**—Acad Arts Govt/Pol Media.
>
> **Enr 800.** B 360. G 440. Elem 635. Sec 165. US 7. Host 2. Other 791. Accepted: 95%. Yield: 95%. Avg class size: 20.
>
> **Fac 67.** M 25. F 42. US 1. Other 66. Adv Deg: 26%.
>
> **Grad '05—15. Col—12. US Col—1.**
>
> **Tui '05-'06: Day** RO1740-4470 (+RO700).
>
> Bldgs 15. Class rms 62. 2 Libs 35,000 vols. Sci labs 5. Comp labs 4. Art studios 2. Music studios 2. Fields 1. Pools 1.
>
> **Est 1971.** Nonprofit. Tri (Sept-June).

Following the British National Curriculum, the school draws nearly half its students from the United Kingdom. Instruction in Key Stage 1 emphasizes the development of social and learning skills, and specialists introduce music, technology, drama and dance. French instruction begins in the first year of Key Stage 2. Senior school students prepare for the GCSE, AS- and A-level examinations through a curriculum augmented by educational trips to Vietnam and Switzerland.

MUSCAT PRIVATE SCHOOL

Day — Coed Gr PS-12

Ruwi, Oman. PO Box 1031, PC 112. Tel: 968-565550. Fax: 968-560957. EST+9.
www.mpsoman.org   E-mail: mpsmps@omantel.net.om
Nigel Melen, Prin.

> **Col Prep. Curr**—Nat UK. **Exams**—IGCSE A-level. **Feat**—Arabic Fr Comp_Sci Studio_Art Drama Music Accounting Bus. **Supp**—ESL.
>
> **Enr 700.**
>
> **Tui '05-'06: Day** RO1200-3500 (+RO100).
>
> **Est 1989.** Quar (Aug-June).

QATAR

Sq. Miles: 4427 (Slightly smaller than Rhode Island). **Country Pop:** 863,051 (2005). **Capital:** Doha, pop. 431,525 (2005). **Terrain:**

Mostly desert, flat, barren. **Ethnic Group(s):** Arab Pakistani Indian
Iranian. **Religion(s):** Muslim. **Official Language(s):** Arabic. **Other
Language(s):** English. **Government:** Constitutional Emirate. **Inde-
pendence:** 1971 (from United Kingdom). **Per Capita Income:** $32,996
(2004). **GDP:** $28.45 billion (2004). Agriculture 1%. Industry 50%.
Natural Resources 31%. Services 18%. **Currency:** Qatari Riyal (QR).

DOHA COLLEGE
Day — Coed Gr 6-12

Doha, Qatar. PO Box 7506. Tel: 974-4687379. Fax: 974-4685720. EST+8.
www.dohacollege.com   E-mail: enquiries@dohacollege.com
Jon Lawson, Prin. M. Al-Humaidi, Adm.

> **Col Prep. Curr**—UK. **Exams**—GCSE IGCSE A-level. **Feat**—Arabic Fr Ger Comp_
> Sci Studio_Art Drama Music. **Supp**—EFL ESL LD Tut.
> **Enr 740.** B 402. G 338. US 25. Host 50. Other 665. Accepted: 80%. Avg class size:
> 23.
> **Fac 63.** M 36. F 23/4. Other 63. Adv Deg: 9%.
> **Tui '05-'06: Day QR16,665-31,185** (+QR2000).
> Bldgs 1. Libs 1. Sci labs 1. Comp labs 1. Theaters 1. Gyms 1. Fields 1. Pools 1.
> **Est 1980.** Nonprofit. Tri (Sept-July).

Sponsored by the British Embassy, the school provides a complete UK-style
education for English-speaking students from the United Kingdom and more than
50 other countries. The program follows the national curriculum of England and
Wales through GCSE level. After age 16, pupils opt for either A-level study or
pursuit of the GNVQ business curriculum.

   The school encourages students to cultivate their interests in such areas as music,
drama and art. As part of the afternoon program, boys and girls can also participate
in basketball, cricket, netball, rounders, rugby, soccer, squash, swimming, bowling
and volleyball. Interscholastic athletic competition is available with local schools
and other similar international institutions in the Gulf region.

QATAR ACADEMY
Day — Coed Gr PS-12

Doha, Qatar. PO Box 1129. Tel: 974-4826666. Fax: 974-4802769. EST+8.
www.qf.edu.qa   E-mail: qataracademy@qf.org.qa
Hana Kanan, Dir. EdD.

> **Col Prep. IB PYP. IB MYP. IB Diploma. Curr**—Intl. **Feat**—Arabic Fr Comp_Sci
> Studio_Art Drama Music Bus. **Supp**—ESL.
> **Enr 630.**
> **Fac 85.**
> **Tui '05-'06: Day QR11,910-29,800.**
> **Est 1996.** Nonprofit. Tri (Sept-June). Assoc: CIS NEASC.

SAUDI ARABIA

Sq. Miles: 1,176,349 (About one-fourth the size of the continental United States). **Country Pop:** 26,417,599 (2005). **Capital:** Riyadh, pop. 3,700,000 (2003). **Terrain:** Primarily desert with rugged mountains in the southwest. **Ethnic Group(s):** Arab Afro-Asian. **Religion(s):** Muslim. **Official Language(s):** Arabic. **Government:** Monarchy. **Independence:** 1932. **GDP:** $242 billion (2002). Agriculture 3%. Industry 75%. Services 22%. **Currency:** Saudi Arabian Riyal (Srls).

DHAHRAN ACADEMY
Day — Coed Gr PS-12

Al-Khobar 31952, Saudi Arabia. PO Box 31677. Tel: 966-3-330-0555. Fax: 966-3-330-0555. EST+8.
www.isgdh.org   E-mail: dahs@isgdh.org
Norma Hudson, Supt.
  Col Prep. Curr—US. Exams—AP CEEB TOEFL.
  Enr 526. Elem 221. Sec 305.
  Fac 42.
  Tui '05-'06: Day Srls17,900-45,850.
  Est 1962. Nonprofit. Sem (Aug-June). Assoc: A/OPR/OS MSA.

SAUDI ARAMCO SCHOOLS
Day — Coed Gr K-9

Dhahran 31311, Saudi Arabia. Saudi Arabian Oil Co, Box 73. Tel: 966-3-877-1676. Fax: 966-3-872-0783. EST+8.
Contact: Aramco Services Co, 9009 W Loop S, Houston, TX 77096.
E-mail: brent.mutsch@aramco.com
Brent A. Mutsch, Supt.
  Pre-Prep. Curr—US. Exams—SSAT. Feat—Arabic Fr Span Studio_Art Music. Supp—Dev_Read ESL Makeup Rem_Math Rem_Read Rev Tut.
  Enr 1650. B 847. G 803. Elem 1480. Sec 170. US 1286. Host 35. Other 329. Avg class size: 15.
  Fac 190. M 55. F 93/42. US 176. Host 2. Other 12. Adv Deg: 43%.
  Grad '05—170. Prep—92. US Prep—51. (McCallie, Stony Brook, Williston Northampton, Baylor, Blair, Cate).
  Bldgs 6. 5 Libs 150,000 vols. Art studios 7. Music studios 8. Gyms 5. Fields 5. Courts 5. Pools 5.
  Est 1945. Nonprofit. Spons: Saudi Arabian Oil Company. Tri (Sept-July).

Established and sponsored by the Saudi Arabian Oil Company for children of its employees, the Saudi Aramco school system operates year-round on several campuses in Saudi Arabia. A US-style curriculum featuring individualized instruction serves a largely American enrollment.

AMERICAN INTERNATIONAL SCHOOL OF JEDDAH
Day — Coed Gr PS-12

Jeddah 21352, Saudi Arabia. PO Box 127328. Tel: 966-2-662-0051. Fax: 966-2-691-2402. EST+8.
www.aisjed.net   E-mail: aisj@aisjed.net
Paul Pescatore, Dir. Dima Kabani, Adm.

> **Col Prep. Curr**—US. **Exams**—ACT AP CEEB. **AP**—Eng Fr Calc Bio Chem World_ Hist Econ. **Feat**—Arabic Span Environ_Sci Comp_Sci Govt Intl_Relations Islamic_Stud Photog Studio_Art Drama Chorus. **Supp**—Dev_Read ESL Tut.
>
> **Sports**—Badminton Basket Soccer Softball Volley. **Activities**—Acad Arts Govt/Pol Media Rec Service.
>
> **Enr 647.** B 367. G 280. Elem 411. Sec 236. US 157. Host 78. Other 412. Accepted: 10%. Avg class size: 22.
>
> **Fac 84.** M 17. F 63/4. US 33. Host 3. Other 48. Adv Deg: 29%.
>
> **Grad '05—58. Col—58. US Col—11.** (Purdue 4, Duke 1, PA St 1, U of IL-Urbana 1, Oberlin 1, Geo Wash 1).
>
> **Tui '05-'06: Day Srls15,700-34,700.**
>
> Bldgs 11. Class rms 58. Lib 24,000 vols. Sci labs 1. Comp labs 6. Art studios 2. Music studios 3. Gyms 2. Fields 1. Weight rms 1.
>
> **Est 1952.** Nonprofit. Sem (Aug-June). Assoc: MSA.

Licensed by the Saudi Arabian Ministry of Education to operate as a school for expatriate children, AISJ conducts an American-style elementary and secondary curriculum featuring the traditional selection of core courses. Particularly able students choose from a selection of Advanced Placement courses. In addition to various extracurricular pursuits, pupils participate in local and international athletic competitions and fine arts festivals that often provide travel opportunities to other countries in the Middle East and Europe.

Located on the Red Sea, Jeddah is a modern city with a large seaport and an extensive business center. Site of a major international airport, it is also the departure point for pilgrimages to the Moslem holy cities of Mecca and Medina.

THE BRITISH INTERNATIONAL SCHOOL
(THE CONTINENTAL SCHOOL)
Day — Coed Gr PS-12

Jeddah 21442, Saudi Arabia. PO Box 6453. Tel: 966-2-699-0019. Fax: 966-2-699-1943. EST+8.
www.continentalschool.com   E-mail: conti@conti.sch.sa
Bruce Gamwell, Dir.

> **Col Prep. IB Diploma. Curr**—Intl UK. **Exams**—GCSE IGCSE. **Feat**—Arabic Fr Span Stats Comp_Sci Studio_Art Drama Music Bus Outdoor_Ed. **Supp**—EFL ESL.
>
> **Sports**—Soccer Swim Volley.
>
> **Enr 1431.** B 825. G 606. Elem 1022. Sec 409. US 115. Host 176. Other 1140. Accepted: 90%. Avg class size: 21.
>
> **Fac 135.** US 5. Host 6. Other 124.
>
> **Grad '05—47.**
>
> **Tui '05-'06: Day Srls27,900-51,900** (+Srls4500). **Aid:** Srls300,000.

Bldgs 10. Class rms 50. 3 Libs 15,000 vols. Sci labs 8. Comp labs 5. Theaters 1. Art studios 4. Music studios 4. Gyms 2. Courts 2. Pools 2.
Est 1977. Nonprofit. Tri (Sept-June). Assoc: CIS NEASC.

The school offers an English-language elementary and secondary education to students age 2 and up. Although approximately one-seventh of the student body is British, pupils of many other nations also take part in the UK-based curriculum. Some students continue at the Continental School through the IGCSEs and the IB Diploma, while others opt to take public examinations elsewhere. Graduates of the school advance to colleges worldwide, with destinations in the US and the UK being particularly popular.

JEDDAH PREP AND GRAMMAR SCHOOL
Day — Coed Gr PS-10

Jeddah 21442, Saudi Arabia. PO Box 6316. Tel: 966-2-654-2354. Fax: 966-2-238-0232. EST+8.
www.jpgs.org   E-mail: hmsec@jpgs.org
Paul Hay, Head.
    Gen Acad. Curr—UK. **Exams**—IGCSE A-level. **Feat**—Comp_Sci Econ Law Studio_Art Music Accounting Bus. **Supp**—ESL.
    Enr 600.
    Tui '05-'06: Day Srls23,250-36,150 (+Srls4300).
    Est 1967. Tri (Sept-July).

AMERICAN INTERNATIONAL SCHOOL-RIYADH
Day — Coed Gr PS-12

Riyadh 11421, Saudi Arabia. PO Box 990. Tel: 966-1-491-4270. Fax: 966-1-491-7101. EST+8.
www.aisr.org   E-mail: registration@ais-r.edu.sa
Matilda Fullerton, Supt.
    Col Prep. IB Diploma. Curr—Intl US. **Exams**—CEEB SSAT. **Feat**—Arabic Fr Span Comp_Sci Econ Visual_Arts Music. **Supp**—ESL.
    Enr 695.
    Tui '05-'06: Day Srls26,800-50,765 (+Srls6500).
    Est 1963. Nonprofit. Quar (Aug-June). Assoc: A/OPR/OS CIS NEASC.

THE BRITISH SCHOOL—RIYADH
(SAUDI ARABIAN INTERNATIONAL SCHOOL)
Day — Coed Gr PS-10

Riyadh 11612, Saudi Arabia. PO Box 85769. Tel: 966-1-248-2387. Fax: 966-1-248-0351. EST+8.
www.britishschoolriyadh.com   E-mail: principal@britishschoolriyadh.com
Dolores McNamara, Prin.
    Gen Acad. Curr—UK. **Exams**—GCSE IGCSE. **Feat**—Arabic Fr Span Comp_Sci Studio_Art Music.

Enr 1100.
Fac 85.
Tui '02-'03: Day Srls30,300-45,300 (+Srls4000).
Libs 1. Sci labs 1. Lang labs 1. Comp labs 1. Art studios 1. Music studios 1. Gyms 1. Fields 1. Courts 1.
Est 1979. Nonprofit. Tri (Sept-June).

This UK-style school educates English-speaking students from more than 40 nations. In the early years, the curriculum focuses on developing language skills, phonics and basic writing skills. Pupils next concentrate on the core subjects of math, science and history. Foreign language instruction begins at age 11 with a choice of French or Arabic. The following year, boys and girls continue with their chosen language, but they may also study Spanish. Preparation for the GCSE and IGCSE exams commences at age 13.

A comprehensive program of extracurricular activities features sports, crafts, music, drama and art.

SYRIA

Sq. Miles: 71,504 (About the size of North Dakota). **Country Pop:** 18,448,752 (2005). **Capital:** Damascus, pop. 5,000,000. **Terrain:** Narrow coastal plain with a double mountain belt in the west; large, semiarid and desert plateau to the east. **Ethnic Group(s):** Arab Kurd Armenian Circassian Turcoman. **Religion(s):** Sunni_Muslim Alawi Christian Druze. **Official Language(s):** Arabic. **Other Language(s):** English French Kurdish Armenian Aramaic Circassian. **Government:** Republic. **Independence:** 1946. **GDP:** $22.2 billion (2004). Agriculture 25%. Industry 31%. Services 44%. **Currency:** Syrian Pound (£S).

ICARDA INTERNATIONAL SCHOOL OF ALEPPO
Day — Coed Gr PS-12

Aleppo, Syria. PO Box 5466. Tel: 963-21-574-3104. Fax: 963-21-576-3936. EST+7. E-mail: iisa@net.sy
Robert Thompson, Head. BA, MA. **Maria Teresa Gaeta-Arejola, Adm.**
   Col Prep. IB PYP. IB Diploma. Curr—Intl UK US. **Exams**—CEEB TOEFL IGCSE. **Feat**—Arabic Fr Span Comp_Sci Econ Theater_Arts. **Supp**—Dev_Read ESL Rem_Math Rem_Read.
   Sports—Basket Soccer Volley. **Activities**—Govt/Pol.
   Enr 263. US 20. Host 106. Other 137. Accepted: 90%. Yield: 95%. Avg class size: 20.
   Fac 37. M 12. F 21/4. US 8. Host 12. Other 17. Adv Deg: 32%.
   Grad '05—15. Col—15. US Col—4. (Boston U, Brigham Young, Denison, Hamilton). Avg SAT: M/V—1105.
   Tui '05-'06: Day $2200-7548 (+$1500-2000).
   Class rms 25. Libs 1. Sci labs 3. Lang labs 3. Comp labs 2. Auds 1. Music studios 1.

Arts ctrs 1. Gyms 1. Fields 2. Courts 4.
Est 1977. Nonprofit. Sem (Aug-June). Assoc: MSA.

IISA's elementary and secondary curricula maintain standards similar to those found at other international schools and at national schools in the US and Europe. Elementary children follow the IB Primary Years Program, while high schoolers work toward a US-style high school diploma, with the option of also earning the IB Diploma. Boys and girls in grades 9 and 10 concentrate mainly on IGCSE courses. Graduates typically matriculate at universities in North America, the Middle East or Europe.

DAMASCUS COMMUNITY SCHOOL

Day — Coed Gr PS-12

Damascus, Syria. Al Mahdi Bin Baraka St, Abu Rumaneh. Tel: 963-11-333-7737. Fax: 963-11-332-1457. EST+7.
Contact: Dept of State, 6110 Damascus Pl, Washington, DC 20521.
www.dcssyria.org   E-mail: dcs@dcssyria.org
Mike Kent, Dir.
  Col Prep. Curr—US. **Exams**—CEEB. **AP**—Eng Fr Calc Bio Chem US_Hist Econ.
  Feat—Comp_Sci Psych Syrian_Stud Visual_Arts Music. **Supp**—ESL.
  Fac 47.
  Tui '05-'06: Day $4100-12,300.
  Est 1957. Nonprofit. Quar (Aug-June). Assoc: A/OPR/OS MSA.

TAJIKISTAN

Sq. Miles: 55,251 (Slightly smaller than Wisconsin). **Country Pop:** 7,163,506 (2005). **Capital:** Dushanbe, pop. 562,000 (2000). **Terrain:** Pamir and Alay mountains dominate landscape; western Ferghana valley in north, Kofarnihon and Vakhsh Valleys in southwest. **Ethnic Group(s):** Tajik Uzbek Russian. **Religion(s):** Sunni_Muslim Shiite_Muslim. **Official Language(s):** Tajik. **Other Language(s):** Russian. **Government:** Republic. **Independence:** 1991 (from Soviet Union). **GDP:** $2.3 billion (2005). Agriculture 24%. Industry 28%. Services 48%. **Currency:** Tajikistani Somoni (TJS).

DUSHANBE INTERNATIONAL SCHOOL

Day — Coed Gr K-11

Dushanbe, Tajikistan. Bofande 9. Tel: 992-372-214776. Fax: 992-372-510271. EST+10.
www.dushis.com   E-mail: dushis@dushis.com
Mehmet Basturk, Dir. BA. **Azamat Kholmatov, Adm.**
  Col Prep. Gen Acad. Curr—UK. **Exams**—CEEB TOEFL IGCSE. **Feat**—Fr Russ

Tajik Comp_Sci Relig Studio_Art Drama Music. **Supp**—Dev_Read EFL ESL Rev Tut.
Sports—Badminton Basket Rugby Soccer Volley.
Enr 228. B 148. G 80. Host 163. Other 65. Accepted: 60%. Yield: 56%. Avg class size: 20.
Fac 38. M 16/1. F 17/4. Host 22. Other 16. Adv Deg: 13%.
Grad '05—29. Col—15. US Col—3. (U of NE-Omaha, U of Houston, U of NE-Lincoln).
Tui '05-'06: Day $2000-9000 (+$200). **Aid:** 40 pupils ($60,000).
Summer: Acad Enrich Rev Rec. 2-8 wks.
Bldgs 2. Lib 20,000 vols. Sci labs 3. Lang labs 4. Comp labs 1. Art studios 1. Music studios 1. Fields 2.
Est 1997. Nonprofit. Sem (Sept-May).

Serving both native and expatriate students, DIS follows a modified version of the British National Curriculum that prepares boys and girls for the IGCSE exams and the Cambridge International Examinations. During the primary years, children learn mainly from classroom teachers, with specialists teaching certain subjects. Departmentalization is employed in the secondary program. Students interested in attending universities that require SAT results receive assistance with this exam, and nonnative English speakers gain preparation for the TOEFL.

TURKEY

Sq. Miles: 296,000 (Slightly larger than Texas). **Country Pop:** 69,660,559 (2005). **Capital:** Ankara, pop. 5,153,000 (2005). **Largest City:** Istanbul, pop. 11,322,000 (2005). **Terrain:** Narrow coastal plain surrounds Anatolia, an inland plateau becomes increasingly rugged as it progresses eastward. **Ethnic Group(s):** Turkish Kurdish. **Religion(s):** Muslim Christian Bahai Jewish. **Official Language(s):** Turkish. **Other Language(s):** Kurdish Zaza Arabic Armenian Greek. **Government:** Republic. **Independence:** 1923. **GDP:** $293.6 billion (2004). Agriculture 12%. Industry 30%. Services 58%. **Currency:** New Turkish Lira (TL).

ROBERT COLLEGE

Bdg and Day — Coed Gr 9-12

80820 Arnavutkoy, Istanbul, Turkey. Kurucesme Caddesi 87. Tel: 90-212-359-2222. Fax: 90-212-257-5443. EST+7.
Contact: 276 5th Ave, Ste 905, New York, NY 10001. Tel: 212-843-5550. Fax: 212-843-5556.
www.robcol.k12.tr   E-mail: robcol@robcol.k12.tr
John R. Chandler, Head. Peter Pelosi, Adm.

    Col Prep. Curr—Nat US. **Bilingual**—Turkish. **Exams**—CEEB. **Feat**—Turkish_Lit Fr Ger Comp_Sci Turkish_Stud Studio_Art.
    Enr 954. B 75/408. G 69/402. US 1. Host 953. Avg class size: 20.
    Fac 95. M 37/2. F 53/3. US 28. Host 42. Other 25.

Grad '05—134.
Bldgs 8. Dorms 2. Lib 30,000 vols. Theaters 1. Gyms 1. Fields 2. Courts 2.
Est 1863. Nonprofit. Sem (Sept-June).

The present-day Robert College is the result of the 1971 merger between Robert Academy for Boys, founded in 1863, and the American College for Girls, established in 1871. The university division of Robert College, the oldest American-sponsored college abroad, was given to the Turkish Government and is now the University of the Bosphorus.

While its enrollment comprises a high percentage of Turkish nationals, the school accepts a limited number of international day students. English is the language of instruction in math, science, English literature, arts and physical education classes, while the balance of the curriculum is conducted in Turkish.

ISTANBUL INTERNATIONAL COMMUNITY SCHOOL
Day — Coed Gr PS-12

**34866 Bebek, Istanbul, Turkey. Karaagac Koyu, Hadimkoy. Tel: 90-212-857-8264.
Fax: 90-212-857-8270. EST+7.**
www.iics.k12.tr   E-mail: parents@iics.k12.tr
Jeremy Lewis, Head. MEd. **Berrin Balik, Adm.**

   Col Prep. IB PYP. IB MYP. IB Diploma. Curr—Intl US. **Exams**—CEEB. **Feat**—Fr Span Turkish Comp_Sci Econ Philos Studio_Art Drama Music. **Supp**—EFL ESL.
   Sports—Basket X-country Soccer Softball Tennis Volley. **Activities**—Acad Arts Govt/Pol Rec.
   Enr 422. B 230. G 192. Elem 297. Sec 125. US 112. Other 310. Accepted: 97%. Yield: 75%. Avg class size: 15.
   Fac 53. M 17. F 34/2. US 16. Host 2. Other 35. Adv Deg: 50%.
   Grad '05—27. Col—27. **US Col**—3. (Skidmore, SUNY-Albany, NYU). Avg SAT: M/V—1093.
Tui '05-'06: Day $8800-19,500.
   Plant val $7,000,000. Bldgs 7. Class rms 54. 2 Libs 16,000 vols. Sci labs 4. Comp labs 4. Theaters 1. Art studios 3. Music studios 2. Gyms 2. Fields 1. Courts 5. Tracks 1.
   Est 1911. Nonprofit. (Aug-June). Assoc: A/OPR/OS CIS NEASC.

IICS serves provides a full elementary and secondary program for a student body that represents more than 40 other nations. Students follow the three curricula designed by the International Baccalaureate Organization: the Primary Years, Middle Years and Diploma programs. The school teaches French from grade 1, two years of Spanish during the secondary years and Turkish in grades 1-6.

Frequently scheduled field trips help pupils gain familiarity with Istanbul's many historic and cultural sites.

BILKENT UNIVERSITY PREPARATORY SCHOOL
BILKENT INTERNATIONAL SCHOOL

Day — Coed Gr PS-12

06800 Bilkent, Ankara, Turkey. East Campus. Tel: 90-312-266-4961. Fax: 90-312-266-4963. EST+7.
www.bupsbis.bilkent.edu.tr   E-mail: school@bups.bilkent.edu.tr
Gary Crippin, Dir. PhD.

> **Col Prep. IB Diploma. Curr**—Intl Nat UK US. **Supp Lang**—Turkish. **Exams**—CEEB IGCSE. **Feat**—Fr Ger Span Comp_Sci Econ Studio_Art Drama Music. **Supp**—ESL Tut.
> **Sports**—Basket Soccer Volley. **Activities**—Arts Govt/Pol Media.
> **Enr 560.** B 260. G 300. Elem 390. Sec 170. US 28. Host 514. Other 18. Accepted: 33%. Avg class size: 15.
> **Fac 89.** M 34. F 55. US 16. Host 32. Other 41. Adv Deg: 39%.
> **Grad '05—47. Col—47. US Col—21.** (Cornell, Stanford, Tufts, Purdue).
> **Tui '05-'06: Day $16,385.**
> Bldgs 8. Class rms 23. Lib 16,000 vols. Sci labs 6. Comp labs 2. Theaters 1. Art studios 4. Music studios 4. Dance studios 1. AV rms 2. Gyms 1. Fields 1. Courts 3.
> **Est 1993.** Nonprofit. Spons: Bilkent University. Sem (Sept-June). Assoc: CIS NEASC.

This elementary and secondary school is designed to prepare students for examinations inside and outside of Turkey. International pupils supplement traditional course work with such subjects as music, world history, world geography, computers and study skills. Coursework is conducted in both English and Turkish in grades 1-5. The curriculum in grades 9 and 10 prepares students for the IGCSE exam, while the last two years of high school are devoted to the International Baccalaureate. The IB program consists of a study of six courses over the two-year period.

Located on the east campus of Bilkent University (with which the school is affiliated), BUPS/BIS schedules educational field trips throughout the region. Interest clubs, musical groups and sporting pursuits cater to the interests of the student body.

THE BRITISH INTERNATIONAL SCHOOL
ISTANBUL

Day — Coed Gr PS-12

80600 Istanbul, Turkey. PDI-ER Uluslararasi Ozel Egitim, Hizmetleri Ticaret AS, Dilhayat Sok 18, Etiler. Tel: 90-212-2872264. Fax: 90-212-2577628. EST+7.
www.bis.k12.tr   E-mail: bisadmin@bis.k12.tr
Paul Johnstone, Prin. Tuba Guven, Adm.

> **Col Prep. IB Diploma. Curr**—Intl UK. **Exams**—IGCSE. **Feat**—Fr Ger Span Turkish Environ_Sci Comp_Sci Studio_Art Music Bus. **Supp**—Dev_Read ESL LD Rem_Math Rem_Read Tut.
> **Enr 350.** B 174. G 176. Avg class size: 10.
> **Fac 63.** M 18/1. F 43/1. US 1. Host 3. Other 59. Adv Deg: 19%.
> **Grad '05—8. Col—8.**
> **Tui '05-'06: Day $8995-19,995.**
> **Est 1999.** Inc. Tri (Sept-July).

BIS, which enrolls pupils from roughly 40 nations, conducts a British-style program that utilizes English as the language of instruction. BIS' preschool, which enrolls children beginning at age 2½, places emphasis upon communication, language and literacy; development of math skills; knowledge and understanding of the world; and creativity. Pupils continue to develop learning and study skills at the primary school level. During these years, the school also conducts a program for gifted students. Course work at the secondary level leads to the IGCSE examinations and the International Baccalaureate Diploma. Special programs in all school divisions serve nonnative speakers of English, as well as those with such learning differences as dyslexia.

A varied selection of extracurricular activities includes swimming, soccer, softball, volleyball, basketball and skiing, among other sports. Boys and girls may engage in concerts and theatrical productions as part of the school's performing arts program. BIS schedules annual educational trips to locations both in Turkey and abroad as a source of enrichment.

ENKA SCHOOLS

Day — Coed Gr PS-12

Istanbul, Turkey. Sadi Gulcelik Spor Sitesi, Istinye 34460. Tel: 90-212-276-05-45. Fax: 90-212-286-52-12. EST+7.
www.enkaschools.com   E-mail: mailbox@enkaschools.com
Col Prep. IB Diploma. Curr—Intl. Feat—Lib_Skills Fr Ger Turkish Comp_Sci Visual_Arts Music.
Enr 1000.
Est 1996. Sem (Sept-June).

EYUBOGLU SCHOOLS

Day — Coed Gr PS-12

34762 Istanbul, Turkey. Namik Kemal Mah, Dr Rustem Eyuboglu Sk, 8 Umraniye. Tel: 90-216-522-12-12. Fax: 90-216-522-12-14. EST+7.
www.eyuboglu.com   E-mail: eyuboglu@eyuboglu.k12.tr
Burcak Eyuboglu, Dir. MSc.
Col Prep. IB PYP. IB MYP. IB Diploma. Curr—Intl Nat. Bilingual—Turkish. Exams—CEEB TOEFL. Feat—Fr Ger Ital Span Astron Comp_Sci Turkish_Hist Civics Psych Milit_Sci Relig Studio_Art Music. Supp—LD Makeup Rem_Math Tut.
Sports—Arch Basket Fencing Gymnastics Swim Volley. Activities—Acad Arts Govt/Pol Media Rec.
Enr 2050. B 1070. G 980. Elem 1320. Sec 730. US 8. Host 2042. Accepted: 80%. Yield: 70%. Avg class size: 20.
Fac 362. M 80/2. F 280. US 5. Host 326. Other 31. Adv Deg: 14%.
Grad '05—120. Col—115. US Col—18.
Tui '05-'06: Day $8000 (+$2000). Aid: 180 pupils ($500,000).
Bldgs 13. Class rms 110. 2 Libs 50,000 vols. Sci labs 4. Comp labs 8. Auds 1. Theaters 3. Art studios 4. Music studios 4. Dance studios 1. Gyms 5. Fields 3. Courts 7. Pools 1.

Est 1985. Inc. Sem (Sept-June). Assoc: ECIS.

Offering bilingual instruction at all grade levels, Eyuboglu comprises two elementary sections and standard and science-oriented secondary divisions. Students may follow the entire International Baccalaureate curriculum: the Primary Years, Middle Years and Diploma programs. Boys and girls lacking proficiency in English may receive ESL instruction and may also prepare for the TOEFL examination. Beginning in grade 6, pupils choose from the following foreign languages: German, French and Italian.

IRMAK SCHOOL

Day — Coed Gr PS-12

34728 Istanbul, Turkey. Cemil Topuzlu Cad 112, Caddebostan. Tel: 90-216-411-3923. Fax: 90-216-411-3926. EST+7.
www.irmak.k12.tr   E-mail: info@irmak.k12.tr
Nilgun Akalin, Dir.

> **Col Prep. Gen Acad. IB Diploma. Curr**—Intl Nat. **Bilingual**—Turkish. **Exams**—CEEB TOEFL. **Feat**—Ger Comp_Sci Studio_Art Drama Music. **Supp**—ESL Tut.
>
> **Sports**—Badminton Basket Volley. **Activities**—Acad Arts Govt/Pol Rec Service.
>
> **Enr 585.** B 292. G 293. Elem 495. Sec 90. US 10. Host 556. Other 19. Accepted: 33%. Avg class size: 20.
>
> **Fac 89.** M 22. F 67. US 3. Host 84. Other 2. Adv Deg: 5%.
>
> **Grad '05**—28. **Col**—26.
>
> **Tui '05-'06:** Day $8500. **Aid:** 98 pupils ($620,000).
>
> Bldgs 3. Class rms 34. 2 Libs 47,000 vols. Sci labs 2. Comp labs 1. Auds 1. Art studios 2. Music studios 2. Dance studios 1. Gyms 1. Courts 4.
>
> **Est 1995.** Nonprofit. Sem (Sept-June).

Although Irmak primarily serves Turkish students, the school offers both the International Baccalaureate curriculum and the Turkish national program. Children begin building an academic foundation in the preschool, when they take part in such activities as computers, laboratory science, art, music, ballet and gymnastics. Refinement of learning skills continues during the elementary years. Math and science are taught in both English and Turkish in grade 6, the same year in which children may first take German as a foreign language. English is the medium of instruction in some high school classes, and Irmak provides preparations for the SAT examinations for interested pupils.

MEF INTERNATIONAL SCHOOL

Day — Coed Gr PS-12

34340 Istanbul, Turkey. Ulus Mahallesi, Dereboyu Caddesi, Ortakoy. Tel: 90-212-287-6900. Fax: 90-212-287-3870. EST+7.
www.international.mef.k12.tr   E-mail: mef@mef.k12.tr
Dilara Jane Sougstad, Prin.

> **Gen Acad. IB PYP. IB Diploma. Curr**—Intl. **Feat**—Fr Span Turkish Comp_Sci Photog Sculpt Drama Chorus Music. **Supp**—Dev_Read ESL LD Rem_Math

Rem_Read.

Enr 100. B 45. G 55. Elem 60. Sec 40. US 20. Host 10. Other 70. Accepted: 95%. Avg class size: 10.

Fac 22. M 10. F 12. US 2. Host 2. Other 18. Adv Deg: 50%.

Grad '05—8.

Tui '05-'06: Day $13,500-15,250 (+$50-100).

Bldgs 4. Class rms 12. 2 Libs 5000 vols. Sci labs 1. Comp labs 1. Auds 1. Theaters 1. Art studios 1. Music studios 1. Dance studios 1. Gyms 4. Fields 1. Courts 2. Pools 1.

Est 1999. Inc. Tri (Sept-June).

Located in central Istanbul, the school conducts this program for international pupils on the same campus as MEF National School. French and Turkish are available as foreign languages, as is a comprehensive ESL program. International in focus, MEF's curriculum is inquiry based and transdisciplinary. The school conducts two International Baccalaureate curricula: the Primary Years Program and the Middle Years Program.

Activities make use of MEF's extensive facilities; some of these extracurriculars take place during the school day. Options include various arts and crafts, athletics and interest clubs.

ISIKKENT SCHOOL

Day — Coed Gr PS-9

35070 Izmir, Turkey. 243 Sokak 35, Yesilova. Tel: 90-232-462-7100. Fax: 90-232-462-7102. EST+7.

www.isikkent.k12.tr   E-mail: isikkent@isikkent.k12.tr

Ralph Friedly, Head. EdD.

Gen Acad.Bilingual—Turkish. **Feat**—Fr Comp_Sci Studio_Art Music. **Supp**—EFL Tut.

Sports—Basket Swim Volley W_Polo. **Activities**—Arts Govt/Pol Rec Service.

Enr 323. B 182. G 141. Elem 300. Sec 23. US 1. Host 309. Other 13. Accepted: 99%. Avg class size: 20.

Fac 65. M 9/1. F 51/4. US 1. Host 57. Other 7. Adv Deg: 18%.

Grad '05—36.

Tui '05-'06: Day YTL10,377-14,300.

Plant val $11,000,000. Bldgs 5. Lib 8000 vols. Sci labs 3. Comp labs 2. Auds 1. Theaters 2. Art studios 3. Music studios 2. Dance studios 2. Gyms 4. Courts 3. Pools 1.

Est 1998. Nonprofit. Quar (Sept-June).

This bilingual school employs team teaching in grades K-4, as well as in some fifth-grade classes. An integrated arts program begins in grade 6, and pupils develop competency in technology as the years progress. Cultural field trips enrich classroom learning.

After-school music, sports and drama complement academics. Each student participates in at least four clubs during the course of the school year.

IZMIR OZEL TURK KOLEJI

Bdg — Coed Gr 6-12; Day — Coed PS-12

35280 Izmir, Turkey. Mithatpasa Cad 689, Kopru. Tel: 90-232-244-0500. Fax: 90-232-231-1007. EST+7.
www.ozelturkkoleji.com   E-mail: info@ozelturkkoleji.com
Oguz Tatis, Dir.

> **Gen Acad. Curr**—Nat. **Supp Lang**—Turkish. **Exams**—TOEFL. **Feat**—Fr Ger Turkish Comp_Sci Studio_Art Music.
> **Sports**—Basket Gymnastics Hand Sail Volley. **Activities**—Arts.
> **Enr 2750.** Avg class size: 24.
> **Fac 228.** M 59. F 169. Host 222. Other 6.
> **Tui '05-'06: Bdg $8245. Day $5850.**
> Bldgs 10. Dorms 2. Class rms 84. Sci labs 5. Lang labs 1. Comp labs 4. Auds 2. Theaters 1. Art studios 2. Music studios 2. Dance studios 1. Gyms 3. Fields 4. Courts 2.
> **Est 1950.** Sem.

Izmir Ozel Turk Koleji comprises a preschool, a primary school, and general and science high schools. Intensive preparation for interscholastic science competitions includes Saturday instruction. Among artistic and cultural activities are drama, literature, music and folk dance nights, in addition to panels and guest speakers during class time. The IT Academy program, offered in partnership with Microsoft Corporation, prepares students for careers in information technology. The school's forest campus provides opportunities for tree planting and ecological study.

TARSUS AMERICAN COLLEGE

Bdg — Boys Gr 9-12; Day — Coed 1-12

33400 Tarsus, Mersin, Turkey. PO Box 633400. Tel: 90-324-613-5402. Fax: 90-324-624-6347. EST+7.
www.tac.k12.tr   E-mail: school@tac.k12.tr
Daryl York, Dir. BA, MA, MSc.

> **Col Prep. Curr**—Nat US. **Bilingual**—Turkish. **Exams**—CEEB TOEFL. **Feat**—Fr Ger Comp_Sci Turkish_Stud Bus. **Supp**—LD Rem_Read.
> **Sports**—Badminton Basket Hand. **Activities**—Acad Arts Govt/Pol Rec Service.
> **Enr 522.** Elem 324. Sec 198. Host 521. Other 1. Avg class size: 18.
> **Fac 82.** US 9. Host 65. Other 8. Adv Deg: 18%.
> **Grad '05—139. Col—92. US Col—13.**
> **Tui '05-'06: Bdg $14,335. Day $9350. Aid:** 78 pupils ($373,662).
> **Summer:** Enrich. Tui Bdg $2750. 4 wks.
> Bldgs 8. Dorms 1. Class rms 62. 2 Libs 20,000 vols. Sci labs 4. Comp labs 2. Auds 1. Theaters 1. Art studios 3. Music studios 1. Gyms 1. Fields 1. Courts 2.
> **Est 1888.** Sem (Sept-June).

This bilingual school prepares students for entry into universities in Turkey and abroad. Intensive English language study begins in the earliest grades and is reinforced through the arts and extracurricular activities. In the primary school, Turkish is the language of instruction in social studies, math and science classes. Boys and girls have a second foreign language option (French or German) beginning in grade

7. High schoolers may pursue both the International Baccalaureate and the Turkish diplomas.

TURKMENISTAN

Sq. Miles: 88,100 (Slightly larger than California). **Country Pop:** 4,952,081 (2000). **Capital:** Ashgabat, pop. 605,000 (1999). **Terrain:** Mostly covered in subtropical, sandy Karakum Desert, with dunes rising to the Kopet Dag Mountains in the south along the border with Iran **Ethnic Group(s):** Turkmen Uzbek Russian. **Religion(s):** Muslim Eastern_Orthodox. **Other Language(s):** Turkmen Russian Uzbek. **Government:** Republic. **Independence:** 1991 (from Soviet Union). **GDP:** $28 billion (2004). Agriculture 27%. Industry 39%. Services 34%. **Currency:** Turkmen Manat (TMM).

ASHGABAT INTERNATIONAL SCHOOL
Day — Coed Gr PS-12

Ashgabat, Turkmenistan. Berzengi, Ataturk St. Tel: 993-12-489027. Fax: 993-12-489028. EST+10.
www.qsi.org/tkm   E-mail: paulbateman@qsi.org
Paul M. Bateman, Dir. BEd, MEd.
> **Gen Acad. Curr**—US. **Feat**—Fr Russ Turkmen Computers Econ Studio_Art Music. **Supp**—ESL Rem_Read Tut.
> **Enr 69.** Elem 60. Sec 9. US 11. Host 30. Other 28. Avg class size: 10.
> **Fac 23.** M 3/3. F 5/12. Adv Deg: 17%.
> **Tui '06-'07: Day $4400-12,200** (+$1600).
> Bldgs 1. Class rms 8. Lib 10,000 vols. Comp labs 1. Fields 1.
> **Est 1994.** Nonprofit. Spons: Quality Schools International. Tri (Aug-June). Assoc: A/OPR/OS MSA.

The only English-language school in Turkmenistan, AIS offers a US-style curriculum to boys and girls of all nationalities. Russian is taught from the earliest grades to fluency, and students may study French or Turkmen beginning in grade 5. Intensive ESL instruction serves nonnative speakers at all grade levels. High school students may either participate in the school's program or take correspondence courses through the University of Nebraska.

The campus is located in the foothills of the Kopet Dag Mountains.

UNITED ARAB EMIRATES

Sq. Miles: 30,000 (About the size of Maine). **Country Pop:** 2,563,212 (2005). **Capital:** Abu Dhabi, pop. 928,000 (2000). **Terrain:** Largely desert with some agricultural areas. **Ethnic Group(s):** Indian Pakistani

Bangladeshi Egyptian Jordanian Iranian Filipino. **Religion(s):** Muslim
Hindu Christian. **Official Language(s):** Arabic. **Other Language(s):**
English Hindi Urdu Persian. **Government:** Federation of Emirates.
Independence: 1971 (from United Kingdom). **GDP:** $102 billion (2004).
Agriculture 4%. Industry 26%. Natural Resources 32%. Services 38%.
Currency: United Arab Emirates Dirham (Dh).

AL NAHDA NATIONAL SCHOOLS
Day — Coed Gr PS-12
(Coord — Day PS-12)

Abu Dhabi, United Arab Emirates. PO Box 815. Tel: 971-2-445-4200. Fax: 971-2-445-1637. EST+9.
www.alnahdasch.com   E-mail: nahdab1@emirates.net.ae
Jihad Al Ghani, Prin.

> Col Prep. Gen Acad. Curr—UK US. Exams—CEEB TOEFL IGCSE A-level.
> Feat—Arabic Fr Urdu Comp_Sci Econ Islamic_Stud Accounting Bus. Supp—
> Dev_Read EFL LD Rem_Math.
> Enr 4000. B 1200. G 2800. Avg class size: 25.
> Fac 345. M 120. F 225. US 15. Host 3. Other 327. Adv Deg: 24%.
> Grad '05—300. Col—270. US Col—30.
> Tui '05-'06: Day Dh16,000 (+$300). Aid: 400 pupils ($200,000).
> Summer: Rem Rec. Tui Day $400.
> Bldgs 8. Class rms 160. 6 Libs 20,000 vols. Sci labs 10. Lang labs 1. Comp labs 14.
>   Auds 2. Theaters 2. Gyms 3. Fields 3. Pools 2.
> Est 1983. Inc. Sem (Sept-June). Assoc: CIS NEASC.

ANNS offers two academic programs. In the British program, English is the
medium of instruction for all subjects as students work toward the IGCSE and A-
level examinations. Arabic language programs are available for native speakers and
for those who regard Arabic as a second language. Students may take French or
Urdu as a third language.

Pupils in the other section, the American high school program, study all subjects in English, except for Arabic language and Islamic studies. Participants in
the American stream must achieve a minimum score on the TOEFL (if applicable)
and SAT exams prior to graduation. The school teaches English, math, science and
computers at the same level in both streams through grade 8. ANNS' student body
typically represents more than 30 nations.

AL-WOROOD SCHOOL
Day — Coed Gr PS-12

Abu Dhabi, United Arab Emirates. PO Box 46673. Tel: 971-2-4448855. Fax: 971-2-4449732. EST+9.
www.alworood.sch.ae   E-mail: alworood@emirates.net.ae
Abdullah Al-Nowais, Pres.

> Col Prep. Curr—UK. Exams—CEEB TOEFL IGCSE AS-level A-level. Feat—
> Arabic Fr Comp_Sci Studio_Art Music Accounting Bus.

Enr 2100.
Fac 114. M 34. F 80.
Tui '04-'05: Day Dh10,200-22,600 (+Dh1360-3480).
Est 1982. Sem (Sept-June). Assoc: MSA.

AMERICAN COMMUNITY SCHOOL OF ABU DHABI
Day — Coed Gr K-12

Abu Dhabi, United Arab Emirates. PO Box 42114. Tel: 971-2-681-5115. Fax: 971-2-681-6006. EST+9.
www.acs.sch.ae   E-mail: acs@acs.sch.ae
David Cramer, Supt. DEd.
  Col Prep. Curr—US. Exams—CEEB SSAT ACT. Feat—Arabic Span Studio_Art.
  Enr 634. Accepted: 80%. Avg class size: 16.
  Fac 75. US 62. Other 13. Adv Deg: 69%.
  Grad '05—38. Col—37. US Col—30.
  Tui '05-'06: Day Dh19,290-42,470 (+Dh1500). Aid: 9500 pupils.
  Plant val $15,000,000. Bldgs 3. Class rms 56. Lib 25,000 vols. Sci labs 4. Comp labs 4. Auds 1. Art studios 2. Music studios 2. Dance studios 1. Gyms 3. Fields 2. Pools 1.
  Est 1973. Nonprofit. Quar (Aug-June). Assoc: A/OPR/OS MSA.

ACS offers an American curriculum to the children of predominantly American families living in Abu Dhabi. Departmentalized instruction begins in grade 7, and all students take Arabic at either the beginning, intermediate or advanced level. In the upper grades, pupils choose from a selection of AP courses.

Sports, drama and chorus are among the school's extracurricular activities.

THE BRITISH SCHOOL-AL KHUBAIRAT
Day — Coed Gr PS-12

Abu Dhabi, United Arab Emirates. PO Box 4001. Tel: 971-2-4462280. Fax: 971-2-4461915. EST+9.
www.britishschool.sch.ae   E-mail: principal@britishschool.sch.ae
Paul Coackley, Prin.
  Gen Acad. Curr—UK. Exams—GCSE A-level. Feat—Arabic Fr Span Comp_Sci Econ Geog Studio_Art Drama Music Bus.
  Tui '05-'06: Day Dh19,845-34,650 (+Dh5565-6515).
  Est 1968. Tri (Sept-June).

INTERNATIONAL SCHOOL OF CHOUEIFAT
ABU DHABI
Day — Coed Gr K-PG

Abu Dhabi, United Arab Emirates. PO Box 7212. Tel: 971-2-4461444. Fax: 971-2-4461048. EST+9.
www.iscad-sabis.net   E-mail: iscad@sabis.net
John Ormerod, Dir. BA.

Col Prep. Curr—Intl UK US. **Exams**—AP CEEB TOEFL GCSE IGCSE O-level AS-level A-level. **AP**—Eng Fr Calc Comp_Sci Bio Chem Physics Econ. **Feat**—Arabic Ital. **Supp**—Dev_Read ESL Makeup Rem_Math Rem_Read Tut.

Sports—Basket F_Hockey Soccer Swim Volley. **Activities**—Arts.

Enr 3140. B 1775. G 1365. Elem 2458. Sec 668. PG 14. US 201. Host 438. Other 2501. Accepted: 90%. Yield: 90%. Avg class size: 28.

Fac 146. M 37. F 109. US 4. Other 142. Adv Deg: 34%.

Grad '05—150.

Tui '02-'03: Day Dh13,300-24,500.

Summer: Acad Enrich Rev Rem Rec. Tui Day $1200. 6 wks.

Bldgs 8. Libs 1. Sci labs 4. Auds 1. Art studios 1. Music studios 3. Dance studios 1. Gyms 1. Fields 1. Courts 2. Pools 2.

Est 1978. Tri (Sept-June).

Part of the international SABIS School Network, ISC-Abu Dhabi conducts a varied academic program that enables pupils to prepare for college in many different countries. Students may take course work leading up to the GCSE, IGCSE, GCE, SAT and Advanced Placement examinations; in addition, nonnative English speakers may ready themselves for the TOEFL. The final year, which is equivalent to freshman year at a US college, allows students to take further AP and A-level courses. Graduates matriculate at institutions in the UK, other European countries, the US, Canada, Australia, and the Middle and Far East.

The school's academic curriculum is supplemented by a full extracurricular program. Students are encouraged to take part in student life activities planned and run by student advisors and prefects. Social codes are strict, in accordance with the social and behavioral mores of the host country.

INTERNATIONAL SCHOOL OF CHOUEIFAT
AL AIN

Day — Coed Gr PS-13

Al Ain, United Arab Emirates. Box 15997. Tel: 971-3-7678444. Fax: 971-3-7678711. EST+9.

www.iscalain-sabis.net   E-mail: iscalain@sabis.net

Col Prep. Curr—UK US. **Exams**—CEEB TOEFL GCSE IGCSE O-level A-level.

Enr 652.

Tui '05-'06: Day DH14,400-26,400.

Est 1976. Tri (Sept-June).

AL MAWAKEB SCHOOL

Day — Coed Gr PS-12

Dubai, United Arab Emirates. PO Box 10799. Tel: 971-4-285-1415. Fax: 971-4-285-1988. EST+9.

www.almawakeb.sch.ae   E-mail: info@almawakeb.sch.ae

Nubugh Nasr, Dir. MA. **Alissar Soubra, Adm.**

Col Prep. Curr—Intl US. **Supp Lang**—Fr Arabic. **Exams**—CEEB TOEFL. **Feat**—Arabic Fr Comp_Sci Econ Islamic_Stud. **Supp**—ESL Makeup Rem_Math Rev

Tut.

Sports—Basket Soccer Track Volley. **Activities**—Acad Arts Govt/Pol Media.

Enr 2369. B 1258. G 1111. Elem 1748. Sec 621. US 126. Host 544. Other 1699. Accepted: 80%. Avg class size: 28.

Fac 150. M 31. F 119. US 14. Other 136. Adv Deg: 54%.

Grad '05—144.

Tui '05-'06: Day Dh10,280-23,670 (+Dh1000-12,000).

Summer: Acad Rem. 3 wks.

Bldgs 3. Class rms 53. Lib 9000 vols. Sci labs 1. Comp labs 1. Theaters 1. Art studios 1. Courts 2.

Est 1979. Inc. Quar (Sept-June).

This school offers a US-style college preparatory program with an enrollment representing more than 50 nationalities. Children begin studying English, French and Arabic in kindergarten, with English becoming the medium of instruction in grade 1. Pupils in grades 10-12 follow a required course of study that includes Islamic education for all Muslim boys and girls.

THE AMERICAN SCHOOL OF DUBAI

Day — Coed Gr PS-12

Dubai, United Arab Emirates. PO Box 71188. Tel: 971-4-344-0824. Fax: 971-4-344-1510. EST+9.

www.asdubai.org   E-mail: asdadmin@emirates.net.ae

Harold S. Fleetham, Supt.

Col Prep. Curr—US. **Feat**—Fr Span Studio_Art.

Enr 936. B 497. G 439. Elem 659. Sec 277.

Fac 77. M 29. F 48.

Tui '05-'06: Day $8752-12,692 (+$2542).

Bldgs 4. Class rms 67. Lib 40,000 vols. Comp labs 4. Music studios 1. Gyms 2. Fields 1. Tennis courts 2. Pools 1.

Est 1966. Nonprofit. Quar (Aug-June). Assoc: MSA.

Established by the Dubai Petroleum Company, ASD offers a traditional US curriculum. Middle Eastern culture classes are required for all students. Instruction is semidepartmentalized in grade 6, and completely departmentalized thereafter. The high school curriculum features Advanced Placement courses in grades 11 and 12.

ASD maintains strong vocal, instrumental music and drama programs. Students in grades 6-12 engage in various academic, service, athletic and social clubs and activities. Intramural sports are available at the middle school level, and at the varsity and junior varsity levels later in swimming, boys' wrestling, cross-country and tennis. In addition, competition in such areas as volleyball, soccer, basketball, softball, track and field, badminton, forensics, the performing arts and other activities is sponsored by an organization comprising schools in the Middle East. Boys and girls travel to other countries in the region to participate in certain sports or the fine arts festival.

ARAB UNITY SCHOOL

Day — Coed Gr PS-12

Dubai, United Arab Emirates. PO Box 10563, Rashidiya. Tel: 971-4-2886-226. Fax: 971-4-2886-321. EST+9.

www.arabunityschool.com   E-mail: auschool@emirates.net.ae

Zainab A. Taher, Prin. BA, BEd, MA.

> **Col Prep. Gen Acad. Curr**—Intl UK. **Exams**—IGCSE O-level A-level. **Feat**—Arabic Fr Hindi Urdu Bengali. **Supp**—Dev_Read ESL Rem_Math Rem_Read Rev Tut.
>
> **Enr 2815.** US 75. Host 50. Other 2690. Accepted: 15%. Avg class size: 30.
>
> **Fac 145.** M 15. F 130. Host 10. Other 135. Adv Deg: 44%.
>
> **Tui '05-'06: Day DH4545-8070** (+Dh250-350).
>
> Bldgs 5. Class rms 100. Libs 2. Sci labs 2. Lang labs 2. Comp labs 9. Auds 1. Gyms 1. Fields 3. Courts 3.
>
> **Est 1974.** Nonprofit. Sem (Sept-June).

The school prepares students for the IGCSE and O- and A-level examinations, and it administers the US College Boards as well. Although the curriculum follows the English system, it is international in scope, catering to a diverse expatriate community. Students of many nationalities enroll, with greatest representation coming from the Middle East, Africa and Asia.

DUBAI AMERICAN ACADEMY

Day — Coed Gr K-12

Dubai, United Arab Emirates. PO Box 32762. Tel: 97-14-347-9222. Fax: 97-14-347-6070. EST+9.

www.dubaiacademy.org   E-mail: dacademy@emirates.net.ae

Dan E. Young, Supt.

> **Col Prep. IB Diploma. Curr**—Intl US. **Feat**—Women's_Lit Arabic Fr Span Comp_Sci Psych Sociol Photog Theater_Arts. **Supp**—ESL.
>
> **Activities**—Rec.
>
> **Enr 1400.** US 602. Host 28. Other 770. Accepted: 75%. Yield: 97%. Avg class size: 20.
>
> **Fac 98.**
>
> **Grad '05—50.**
>
> **Tui '05-'06: Day Dh33,074-46,620** (+Dh350).
>
> Bldgs 2. Class rms 110. Libs 2. Sci labs 6. Comp labs 7. Auds 1. Theaters 1. Art studios 6. Music studios 6. Gyms 2. Pools 2.
>
> **Est 1998.** Quar (Aug-June). Assoc: NEASC.

Located on a 20-acre, suburban campus, DAA provides an American-style education for students from more than 60 countries. Elementary students receive instruction in health, physical education, computer technology, art, music and Arabic culture, and French is available in grades 4 and 5. High school students may pursue either an American high school diploma or the IB Diploma. English is the only language of instruction, and students must meet minimum language requirements; supplementary instruction in English is available to qualified students.

An extensive after-school activities program rounds out the program.

DUBAI COLLEGE
Day — Coed Gr 7-13

Dubai, United Arab Emirates. PO Box 837. Tel: 971-4-3999111. Fax: 971-4-3999175. EST+9.
www.dubaicollege.org   E-mail: admissions@dubaicollege.org
W. E. Parton, Head.
> **Col Prep. Curr**—UK. **Exams**—GCSE AS-level A-level. **Feat**—Arabic Fr Ger Comp_Sci Geog Studio_Art Drama Music.
> **Enr 742.** B 364. G 378.
> **Fac 65.**
> **Grad '05—80. Col—79. US Col—8.** (Boston U, Loyola U-LA, Columbia, UNC-Chapel Hill, U of MI, NYU).
> **Tui '05-'06: Day Dh44,880-50,820.**
> Bldgs 9. Lib 17,000 vols. Sci labs 1. Lang labs 1. Comp labs 1. Art studios 1. Music studios 1. Dance studios 1. Gyms 1. Fields 1. Courts 1. Pools 1.
> **Est 1978.** Nonprofit. Tri (Sept-June). Assoc: ECIS.

This school conducts a British-style curriculum for students from age 11 to university entrance. After first following a foundation program of 13 subjects, pupils progress to the two-year GCSE curriculum, then move on to the two-year GCE A-level program. Teachers possess British university credentials, and students enroll from more than 40 nations (although 70 percent are British). Graduates typically matriculate at universities in Britain, the US and Canada.

Extracurricular activities include interest clubs, publications, debate, dramatic productions, musical groups and outings. Students may also take part in such physical pursuits as basketball, tennis, swimming, soccer, cricket, netball, rugby, scuba diving, squash and table tennis.

EMIRATES INTERNATIONAL SCHOOL
Day — Coed Gr PS-12

Dubai, United Arab Emirates. PO Box 6446. Tel: 971-4-348-9804. Fax: 971-4-348-2813. EST+9.
www.eischool.com   E-mail: mail@eischool.com
> **Col Prep. IB Diploma. Curr**—Intl UK. **Exams**—IGCSE. **Feat**—Arabic Fr Ital Comp_Sci Econ Relig Studio_Art Drama Music Bus.
> **Enr 1813.**
> **Tui '06-'07: Day Dh21,000-44,500** (+Dh2500).
> **Est 1991.** Tri (Aug-June). Assoc: MSA.

JEBEL ALI PRIMARY SCHOOL
Day — Coed Gr PS-5

Dubai, United Arab Emirates. PO Box 17111, Jebel Ali Village. Tel: 971-4-884-6485. Fax: 971-4-884-5373. EST+9.
www.jebelalischool.com   E-mail: jaschool@emirates.net.ae
Maureen Chapman, Head. BEd.
> **Gen Acad. Curr**—UK. **Feat**—Arabic Fr Computers Geog Studio_Art Music.

Supp—Rem_Math Rem_Read.
Sports—Gymnastics Rugby Soccer Swim. **Activities**—Arts Media.
Enr 560. B 280. G 280. Elem 560. US 2. Host 1. Other 557. Accepted: 80%. Avg
class size: 24.
Fac 40. M 5. F 33/2. Other 40. Adv Deg: 12%.
Grad '05—56.
Tui '05-'06: Day Dh24,300.
Class rms 26. Libs 2. Sci labs 1. Comp labs 1. Art studios 1. Music studios 1. Gyms
1. Fields 1. Pools 1.
Est 1978. Nonprofit. Tri (Sept-June).

Jebel Ali's modified English National Curriculum is taught by a British faculty.
The foreign language curriculum features Arabic in grades K-5 and French in grades
2-5. A detailed social and health education program runs throughout the school. The
infant and junior divisions occupy separate campuses less than a mile apart.

SAFA SCHOOL

Day — Coed Gr PS-5

**Dubai, United Arab Emirates. PO Box 71091. Tel: 971-4-394-7879. Fax: 971-4-394-
7723. EST+8.**
www.safaschooldubai.com   E-mail: school@safaschooldubai.com
Jane M. Knight, Head.
Gen Acad. Curr—UK. **Feat**—Arabic Fr Computers Studio_Art Music.
Sports—Rugby Soccer Swim. **Activities**—Arts Rec.
Enr 200. Elem 200. Avg class size: 24.
Fac 13. M 2. F 11. Other 13.
Tui '05-'06: Day Dh15,000-24,000 (+Dh850).
Libs 1. Sci labs 1. Comp labs 1. Art studios 1. Music studios 1. Dance studios 1.
Gyms 1. Pools 1.
Est 1992. Tri (Sept-June).

The school offers a broad, child-centered course of studies based on England's
National Curriculum. The early program (ages 3-5) emphasizes multisensory, creative learning with special instruction in music, computers and physical education.
Key Stages 1 and 2 continue development in the core subjects, as well as French
and Arabic languages. The physical education program consists of sports, games,
gymnastics and dance.

INTERNATIONAL SCHOOL OF CHOUEIFAT
SHARJAH

Day — Coed Gr PS-13

**Sharjah, United Arab Emirates. PO Box 2077. Tel: 971-65-582211. Fax: 971-65-
582865. EST+9.**
www.iscshj-sabis.net   E-mail: iscshj@sabis.net
Jamal Hazbun, Dir.
Col Prep. Curr—UK US. **Exams**—CEEB TOEFL GCSE IGCSE O-level A-level.
Enr 1900.
Tui '05-'06: Day Dh12,300-24,000.

Est 1976. Tri (Sept-June).

UZBEKISTAN

Sq. Miles: 117,868 (Slightly larger than California). **Country Pop:** 26,851,195 (2005). **Capital:** Tashkent, pop. 2,500,000. **Terrain:** Flat-to-rolling sandy desert with dunes; broad, flat intensely irrigated river valleys along Amu Darya, Syr Darya; shrinking Aral Sea; semiarid grasslands in east. **Ethnic Group(s):** Uzbek Russian Tajik Kazakh Karakalpak Tatar. **Religion(s):** Sunni_Muslim Eastern_Orthodox. **Other Language(s):** Uzbek Russian Tajik. **Government:** Republic. **Independence:** 1991 (from Soviet Union). **GDP:** $52.21 billion (2005). Agriculture 38%. Industry 26%. Services 36%. **Currency:** Uzbekistani Som (UZS).

TASHKENT INTERNATIONAL SCHOOL
Day — Coed Gr K-12

Tashkent 700005, Uzbekistan. 3 Vasiliy Fetisov St. Tel: 998-71-191-9671. Fax: 998-71-120-6621. EST+10.
Contact: ADM/2 TIS, Dept of State, 7110 Tashkent Pl, Washington, DC 20521.
www.tashschool.org   E-mail: office@tashschool.org
Kevin Glass, Dir.
  Col Prep. IB Diploma. Curr—Intl US. Exams—AP CEEB. Feat—Russ Comp_Sci Studio_Art Drama Music. Supp—ESL.
  Enr 196.
  Fac 27.
  Tui '05-'06: Day $9925-14,400 (+$1250).
  Est 1994. Nonprofit. Sem (Aug-June). Assoc: A/OPR/OS CIS NEASC.

THE TASHKENT ULUGBEK INTERNATIONAL SCHOOL
Day — Coed Gr K-12

Tashkent 700070, Uzbekistan. 17 Usman Nasir St. Tel: 998-712-562-586. Fax: 998-71-152-14-20. EST+10.
www.tasulu.com   E-mail: ulugbek@tasulu.com
Alettin Duman, Prin.
  Col Prep. Curr—UK. Exams—O-level AS-level A-level. Feat—Russ Uzbek Comp_Sci Uzbek_Hist Geog Studio_Art Music.
  Enr 245.
  Fac 25.
  Est 1995. Nonprofit. Tri (Sept-June).

YEMEN

Sq. Miles: 203,796 (About the size of California and Pennsylvania combined). **Country Pop:** 20,727,063 (2005). **Capital:** Saana, pop. 1,747,627 (2004). **Terrain:** Mountainous interior bordered by desert with a flat and sandy coastal plain. **Ethnic Group(s):** Arab. **Religion(s):** Muslim Jewish Christian Hindu. **Official Language(s):** Arabic. **Government:** Republic. **Per Capita Income:** $647 (2004). **GDP:** $12.8 billion (2004). Agriculture 13%. Industry 48%. Services 39%. **Currency:** Yemeni Rial (YRls).

SANAA INTERNATIONAL SCHOOL
Day — Coed Gr PS-12

Sanaa, Yemen. Box 2002. Tel: 967-1-370191. Fax: 967-1-370193. EST+8.
www.qsi.org/yem   E-mail: jimgilson@qsi.org
Gordon Blackie, Dir. MA.
  Col Prep. Curr—US. **Feat**—Arabic Fr Comp_Sci Studio_Art Music. **Supp**—ESL.
  Enr 119. B 68. G 51. Elem 89. Sec 30. US 8. Host 54. Other 57. Accepted: 100%.
    Avg class size: 8.
  Fac 19. Adv Deg: 15%.
  Grad '05—7. Col—6. US Col—3. (Harvard, Fisher, Drexel).
  Tui '05-'06: Day $2500-12,000 (+$1600-4100). **Aid:** 11 pupils ($106,700).
  Bldgs 3. Class rms 19. Lib 10,000 vols. Sci labs 2. Comp labs 1. Auds 2. Art studios
    1. Music studios 1. Gyms 1. Fields 2. Courts 3.
  Est 1971. Nonprofit. Tri (Sept-June). Assoc: A/OPR/OS MSA.

Employing teaching methods and curriculum organization similar to those found in Europe and America, SIS enrolls students of many different nationalities. The four-year US-style high school curriculum includes the basic subjects and a limited selection of Advanced Placement courses. SIS' primary purpose is to enable each international pupil to continue his or her schooling in the home country with a minimum of adjustment problems. Students lacking fluency in English receive intensive ESL instruction.

Elementary children may engage in after-school activities two afternoons per week.

SOUTH AMERICA

INDEX TO COUNTRIES IN
SOUTH AMERICA

SOUTH AMERICA

ARGENTINA

Sq. Miles: 1,100,000 (About the size of the US east of the Mississippi River). **Country Pop:** 39,537,943 (2005). **Capital:** Buenos Aires, pop. 2,776,138 (2001). **Terrain:** Andes mountains and foothills in the west. Remainder of country is lowland; central region characterized by vast grassy plains. **Ethnic Group(s):** Spanish Italian Mestizo Amerindian. **Religion(s):** Roman_Catholic Protestant Jewish. **Official Language(s):** Spanish. **Government:** Republic. **Independence:** 1816 (from Spain). **GDP:** $152 billion (2004). Agriculture 10%. Industry 36%. Services 54%. **Currency:** Argentine Peso ($A).

BELGRANO DAY SCHOOL
Day — Coed Gr K-12

C1428DOA Buenos Aires, Argentina. Juramento 3035, Capital Federal. Tel: 54-11-4781-0011. Fax: 54-11-4786-4298. EST+2.
www.bdsnet.com.ar   E-mail: rrpp@bdsnet.com.ar
Matilde V. Green, Prin. Alicia Vallcaneras, Adm.
   Col Prep. Gen Acad. Curr—Intl Nat. **Bilingual**—Span. **Exams**—IGCSE AS-level A-level. **Feat**—Fr Econ Studio_Art. **Supp**—Rem_Math Rem_Read Rev Tut.
   Sports—F_Hockey Gymnastics Rugby Soccer Volley. **Activities**—Arts Rec.
   Enr 847. B 438. G 409. US 21. Host 782. Other 44. Accepted: 90%. Avg class size: 25.
   Fac 127. M 7/14. F 36/70. Host 125. Other 2. Adv Deg: 5%.
   Grad '05—56. Col—52. US Col—2.
   Tui '05-'06: Day $A3356-13,919 (+$A1650-1750).
   Bldgs 4. Class rms 70. 2 Libs 16,600 vols. Sci labs 2. Comp labs 3. Auds 1. Art studios 2. Music studios 3. Gyms 1. Fields 1. Courts 3.
   Est 1912. Roman Catholic. Sem (Mar-Dec).

Located in the city's Belgrano area, BDS is a bilingual school offering a curriculum that incorporates national and international elements. Beginning in kindergarten, the school places strong emphasis on bilingualism. During the primary years, which stress fundamental skills acquisition, the academic day is divided between English and Spanish. Middle schoolers (ages 12-15) further develop language fluency and also work on study, research and teamwork skills. The curriculum at this level incorporates field trips and special projects. Students at the senior school level may prepare for the IGCSE, AS- and A-level examinations, and BDS also offers the national Bilingual Baccalaureate.

Additional programs include art, drama, ballet, music production and competitive sports. Each school section produces an annual theater presentation. Over the years, senior athletic teams have participated in tournaments in Great Britain, New Zealand, Australia, South Africa and Chile.

BUENOS AIRES INTERNATIONAL CHRISTIAN ACADEMY

Day — Coed Gr PS-12

1642 Buenos Aires, Argentina. Chile 343, San Isidro. Tel: 54-11-4732-1941. Fax: 54-11-4732-3329. EST+2.
www.baica.com   E-mail: info@baica.com
Matt Greco, Dir.

> **Col Prep. Curr**—US. **Exams**—CEEB. **Feat**—Span Comp_Sci Bible. **Supp**—ESL Makeup Tut.
> **Enr 67.** B 34. G 33. Elem 43. Sec 24. US 40. Host 10. Other 17. Accepted: 98%. Avg class size: 5.
> **Fac 21.** M 2/2. F 16/1. US 15. Host 5. Other 1. Adv Deg: 14%.
> **Grad '05—8.**
> **Tui '02-'03: Day $3200-7400.**
> Bldgs 2. Class rms 15. Lib 3000 vols. Sci labs 1. Comp labs 1. Art studios 1. Music studios 1. Gyms 1. Fields 1. Courts 1.
> **Est 1998.** Nonprofit. Nondenom Christian. Sem (Aug-June).

Teaching its curriculum from a biblical perspective, BAICA offers an English-medium program that follows the Northern Hemisphere's school year. Classes remain unusually small, with the maximum number of students in a class being 12. A full-time staff consisting solely of instructors trained at US colleges conducts the US-style curriculum.

Among the school's activities are basketball, baseball and tennis.

NORTHLANDS SCHOOL

Day — Coed Gr PS-12

1636 Buenos Aires, Argentina. Roma 1248, Olivos. Tel: 54-11-4711-8400. Fax: 54-11-4711-8401. EST+2.
www.northlands.org.ar   E-mail: info@northlands.org.ar
Timothy H. Gibbs, Head. BA. **Gabriela Cosentino, Adm.**

> **Col Prep. IB Diploma. Curr**—Intl Nat. **Bilingual**—Span. **Exams**—IGCSE. **Feat**— Fr Comp_Sci Studio_Art Music.
> **Sports**—F_Hockey Rugby Soccer Softball Volley. **Activities**—Acad Arts Rec.
> **Enr 1531.** B 508. G 1023. Elem 1318. Sec 213. Avg class size: 25.
> **Fac 211.** M 12/10. F 54/135. Host 205. Other 6.
> **Grad '05—71.**
> **Tui '05-'06: Day $A6400-18,590.**
> Bldgs 9. Class rms 50. Libs 3. Sci labs 5. Comp labs 3. Auds 2. Theaters 1. Fields 2. Pools 1.
> **Est 1920.** Nonprofit. Tri (Feb-Dec).

With bilingual programming at all grade levels, the school combines international curricular features with Argentina's national program. Children progress from the International Baccalaureate Primary Years Program to the IB Middle Years Program to the IB Diploma. In addition, Northlands integrates preparation for the IGCSE examinations. The school operates two campuses: the main location in Olivos and a secondary site in Nordelta; both offer bilingual instruction at all grade levels.

ASOCIACION ESCUELAS LINCOLN
(LINCOLN AMERICAN INTERNATIONAL SCHOOL)
Day — Coed Gr PS-12

1637 La Lucila, Buenos Aires, Argentina. Andres Ferreyra 4073. Tel: 54-11-4794-9400. Fax: 54-11-4790-2117. EST+2.
www.lincoln.edu.ar   E-mail: admissions@lincoln.edu.ar
Philip T. Joslin, Supt.

   Col Prep. Gen Acad. IB Diploma. Curr—Intl US. Supp Lang—Span. Exams—ACT AP CEEB TOEFL. AP—Eng Fr Span Physics. Feat—Environ_Sci Comp_Sci Econ Intl_Relations Psych Antarctic_Stud Studio_Art Drama Music.
   Enr 705. US 204. Host 106. Other 395.
   Fac 95.
   Tui '05-'06: Day $9300-14,300 (+$1220-6000).
   Est 1936. Nonprofit. Quar (Aug-June). Assoc: AASSA A/OPR/OS SACS.

ST. ANDREW'S SCOTS SCHOOL
Day — Coed Gr PS-12

1636 Olivos, Argentina. R S Pena 654. Tel: 54-11-4799-5371. Fax: 54-11-4799-8318. EST+2.
www.sanandres.esc.edu.ar   E-mail: admissions@sanandres.esc.edu.ar
Gabriel Rshaid, Head. Ana Repila, Adm.

   Col Prep. IB Diploma. Curr—Intl Nat UK. Bilingual—Span. Exams—IGCSE. Feat—Fr Comp_Sci Studio_Art Music Bus.
   Sports—Basket F_Hockey Gymnastics Rugby. Activities—Arts Media Rec.
   Enr 1899. B 1010. G 889. Elem 1405. Sec 494. US 21. Host 1853. Other 25. Avg class size: 26.
   Fac 252. Host 244. Other 8.
   Grad '05—115.
   Bldgs 15. Class rms 80. 3 Libs 25,000 vols. Sci labs 11. Comp labs 3. Auds 3. Art studios 4. Music studios 2. Gyms 1. Fields 9. Pools 1.
   Est 1838. Nonprofit. Presbyterian. Tri (Feb-Dec).

This bilingual school offers a four-tiered system: three years of kindergarten (commencing at age 3), followed by six primary years and six secondary grades (consisting of three middle school and three senior school years). English is the medium of instruction during the kindergarten years, while children in grades 1-6 study in English during the morning hours and in Spanish in the afternoon. Pupils in grades 7-12 take part in a fully bilingual program in which English-medium course work leads to the IGCSE, and classes utilizing Spanish as the language of instruction follow the Argentine national curriculum. The vast majority of students prepare for the International Baccalaureate Diploma in grades 11 and 12.

St. Andrew's maintains two campuses: Olivos, a northern suburb of Buenos Aires, serves as the location of the administrative offices, one kindergarten, one primary school and the secondary school, while Punta Chica, a 20 minutes' drive further north, is the site of the other kindergarten and primary school.

ST. GEORGE'S COLLEGE
Bdg — Coed Gr 6-12; Day — Coed PS-12

1878 Quilmes, Buenos Aires, Argentina. Guido 800, Casilla Correo 2. Tel: 54-11-4257-3472. Fax: 54-11-4253-0030. EST+2.
www.stgeorge.com.ar   E-mail: info@stgeorge.com.ar
Nigel P. O. Green, Head. BS, DipEd.

> **Col Prep. IB Diploma. Curr**—Intl Nat. **Bilingual**—Span. **Exams**—IGCSE. **Feat**—Fr Comp_Sci Econ Relig Studio_Art Drama Music Bus.
> **Enr 650.** B 30/355. G 20/245. Avg class size: 20.
> **Fac 86.**
> **Grad '05**—53.
> **Tui '02-'03: Bdg $A22,800** (+$A1000). **Day $A5700-16,800** (+$A800).
> Bldgs 19. Dorms 2. Dorm rms 11. Lib 10,000 vols. Chapels 1. Sci labs 1. Comp labs 1. Fields 10. Courts 5. Pools 2.
> **Est 1898.** Nonprofit. Nondenom Christian. Sem (Feb-Dec).

Enrollment at this British-oriented school comes from Great Britain, South America and the United States. The curriculum prepares students for the IGCSE examinations, the International Baccalaureate, the US College Boards and the Argentine Bachillerato.

Among the sports and extracurricular activities available at St. George's are drama, choir, journalism, carpentry, squash, golf and graphic design.

BOLIVIA

Sq. Miles: 425,000 (About the size of Texas and California combined). **Country Pop:** 8,857,870 (2005). **Capital:** La Paz, pop. 800,385. **Terrain:** High plateau, temperate and semitropical valleys, and the tropical lowlands. **Ethnic Group(s):** Aymara Quechu Guarani European. **Religion(s):** Roman_Catholic. **Official Language(s):** Spanish. **Other Language(s):** Quechua Aymar Guarani. **Government:** Republic. **Independence:** 1825 (from Spain). **Per Capita Income:** $914 (2004). **GDP:** $8.1 billion (2004). Agriculture 13%. Industry 35%. Services 52%. **Currency:** Bolivian Boliviano (Bs).

AMERICAN INTERNATIONAL SCHOOL OF BOLIVIA

Day — Coed Gr PS-12

Cochabamba, Bolivia. PO Box 5309. Tel: 591-4-428-8577. Fax: 591-4-428-8576. EST+1.
www.aisb.edu.bo   E-mail: admin@mail.asb.edu.bo
Kathleen H. Asbun, Dir.

> **Col Prep. IB Diploma. Curr**—Intl Nat US. **Supp Lang**—Span. **Exams**—ACT CEEB TOEFL. **Feat**—Fr Ger Span Psych Philos Studio_Art Music.
>
> **Tui '05-'06: Day Bs1155-3355** (+Bs1160).
>
> **Est 1993.** (Aug-June). Assoc: AASSA A/OPR/OS SACS.

COCHABAMBA COOPERATIVE SCHOOL

Day — Coed Gr PS-12

Cochabamba, Bolivia. Casilla 1395. Tel: 591-4-4490-605. Fax: 591-4-4490-609. EST+1.
www.ccs.edu.bo   E-mail: contact@ccs.edu.bo
Christine Cunningham, Dir.

> **Col Prep. Curr**—Nat US. **Exams**—AP CEEB. **AP**—Span Bio Chem Physics Econ. **Feat**—Fr Fine_Arts Graphic_Arts. **Supp**—ESL.
>
> **Est 1954.** Sem (Aug-June). Assoc: AASSA SACS.

AMERICAN COOPERATIVE SCHOOL

Day — Coed Gr PS-12

La Paz, Bolivia. Calle 10 y Pasaje Kantutas, Calacoto. Tel: 591-2-279-2302. Fax: 591-2-279-7218. EST+1.
Contact: c/o US Embassy, La Paz, Bolivia.
www.acslp.org   E-mail: acs@acslp.org
David P. Cramer, Supt.

> **Col Prep. Curr**—US. **Exams**—ACT AP CEEB SSAT. **AP**—Eng Span Calc Bio Chem US_Hist World_Hist Psych. **Feat**—Lat-Amer_Lit Fr Comp_Sci Sociol Comp_Relig Philos Studio_Art Music. **Supp**—Dev_Read ESL LD Makeup Rem_Math Rem_Read Rev Tut.
>
> **Enr 479.** B 245. G 234. Elem 351. Sec 128. US 144. Host 214. Other 121. Accepted: 90%. Avg class size: 15.
>
> **Fac 51.** Adv Deg: 68%.
>
> **Grad '05—32. Col—32. US Col—28.** (Notre Dame, Boston U, Boston Col, U of SC, Johns Hopkins, U of AR-Fayetteville). Avg SAT: M/V—1098.
>
> **Tui '05-'06: Day $8900-9900** (+$2500-6000).
>
> **Summer:** Enrich Rev Rem Rec. Tui Day $250. 4 wks.
>
> Bldgs 8. Class rms 47. 2 Libs 17,000 vols. Sci labs 4. Comp labs 3. Auds 1. Theaters 1. Art studios 2. Music studios 2. Gyms 1. Fields 2. Courts 4. Pools 1. Weight rms 1.
>
> **Est 1955.** Nonprofit. Quar (Aug-May). Assoc: AASSA A/OPR/OS SACS.

Located in the suburb of Calacoto, ACS provides a college preparatory curriculum for students of roughly two dozen nationalities. The program mirrors that typically found in American schools. Children in grades PS-5 study in self-contained classrooms, while also receiving instruction from specialists in music, art, library, computers and physical education. Full departmentalization is in place during the middle school years (grades 6-8), and a well-developed Advanced Placement program complements required course work during the high school years (grades 9-12).

Varsity sports include soccer, volleyball, basketball and track. Band, drama, rock climbing, mountain biking and outdoor adventure constitute some of ACS' other activities.

SANTA CRUZ COOPERATIVE SCHOOL
Day — Coed Gr PS-12

Santa Cruz, Bolivia. Casilla 753. Tel: 591-3-3530808. Fax: 591-3-3526993. EST+1. www.sccs.edu.bo   E-mail: admissions@sccs.edu.bo
William McKelligott, Dir. BA, MA.
  Col Prep. Curr—US. **Supp Lang**—Span. **Exams**—ACT AP CEEB. **AP**—Eng Span Calc Chem Physics US_Hist World_Hist Comp_Govt & Pol Psych Studio_Art. **Feat**—Comp_Sci Music. **Supp**—LD.
  Sports—Basket Soccer Track Volley. **Activities**—Acad Govt/Pol.
  Enr 517. Elem 374. Sec 143. Avg class size: 18.
  Fac 46. US 24. Host 14. Other 8. Adv Deg: 60%.
  Avg SAT: M/V—1080.
  Tui '05-'06: Day $3937-4889 (+$300).
  Est 1959. Nonprofit. Sem (Aug-June). Assoc: AASSA A/OPR/OS SACS.

With approximately 15 percent of its enrollment coming from families of US citizens in Santa Cruz, this school offers a US-style curriculum. Spanish is taught at all grade levels. Elective courses include creative writing, art, drama, music and computers. Students may pursue either a traditional US diploma or the Bolivian diploma.

BRAZIL

Sq. Miles: 3,290,000 (Slightly smaller than the US). **Country Pop:** 186,112,794 (2005). **Capital:** Brasilia, pop. 2,200,000 (2004). **Largest City:** Sao Paulo, pop. 10,400,000 (2004). **Terrain:** Dense forests in northern regions including Amazon Basin; semiarid along norrtheast coast; mountains, hills, and rolling plains in the southwest, including Mato Grosso; and coastal lowland. **Ethnic Group(s):** Portuguese Italian German Spanish Japanese Arab African. **Religion(s):** Roman_Catholic. **Official Language(s):** Portuguese. **Government:** Federative Republic. **Independence:** 1822 (from Portugal). **GDP:** $604.9 billion (2004). Agriculture 10%. Industry 39%. Services 51%. **Currency:** Brazilian Real (R$).

AMAZON VALLEY ACADEMY

Day — Coed Gr PS-12

66613-970 Belem, Para, Brazil. Caixa Postal 5170, Agencia Cabanagem. Tel: 55-91-3245-2566. Fax: 55-91-3245-7202. EST+2.
www.avabrazil.org   E-mail: avab@amazon.com.br
E. Wade Underwood, Dir. DEd.

    Col Prep. Gen Acad. Curr—US. **Supp Lang**—Span. **Exams**—ACT CEEB. **Feat**—Fr Port Comp_Sci Bible. **Supp**—EFL ESL LD.

    Sports—Baseball Soccer. **Activities**—Media.

    Enr 69. B 36. G 33. Elem 49. Sec 20. US 36. Host 22. Other 11. Accepted: 100%. Avg class size: 8.

    Fac 18. M 2/4. F 9/3. US 12. Host 6. Adv Deg: 16%.

    Grad '05—4. **Col**—4. **US Col**—4. (Union U, Grace, Cedarville).

    Tui '06-'07: Day $3300-6600 (+$1300). **Aid:** 62 pupils ($146,480).

    Bldgs 5. Class rms 15. 2 Libs 8000 vols. Sci labs 1. Comp labs 1. Music studios 1. Gyms 1. Fields 2. Courts 1. Pools 1.

    Est 1957. Nonprofit. Nondenom Christian. Sem (Aug-June). Assoc: SACS.

Operating primarily for missionaries' children but admitting others as space permits, AVA provides a US-style elementary and secondary curriculum for both international and Brazilian students. College preparatory course work leads to the US and Brazilian high school diplomas. Boys and girls take a compulsory Bible study class each year.

THE AMERICAN SCHOOL OF BELO HORIZONTE
(ESCOLA AMERICANA DE BELO HORIZONTE)

Day — Coed Gr PS-12

30575-815 Belo Horizonte, Minas Gerais, Brazil. Av Deputado Cristovan Chiaradia 120, Bairro Buritis. Tel: 55-31-3378-6700. Fax: 55-31-3378-6878. EST+2.
www.eabh.com.br   E-mail: eabh@eabh.com.br
Molly Garner, Dir.

    Col Prep. Curr—US. **Exams**—CEEB. **Feat**—Port Span Comp_Sci Fine_Arts. **Supp**—ESL.

    Enr 140. Accepted: 95%. Avg class size: 12.

    Fac 22. Adv Deg: 36%.

    Grad '05—5. **Col**—5. **US Col**—5. (Georgetown, PA St, CO St, Am U, U of PA).

    Tui '05-'06: Day $13,908-16,404 (+$3500).

    Bldgs 2. Lib 12,000 vols. Sci labs 2. Comp labs 1. Gyms 1. Fields 2.

    Est 1956. Nonprofit. Sem (Aug-June). Assoc: AASSA A/OPR/OS SACS.

Enrolling students from such countries as the US, Brazil, China, India, Denmark and the Philippines, this school follows a US-based curriculum. Portuguese is taught at all grade levels as a foreign language, and a Portuguese as a Second Language program is also in place for non-Brazilians.

Extracurricular activities include yearbook, interest clubs, quiz bowl, student council, field trips, and such sports as basketball, volleyball and soccer.

AMERICAN SCHOOL OF BRASILIA
Day — Coed Gr PS-12

70200-650 Brasilia, Brazil. SGAS 605, Bloco E, Lotes 34-37. Tel: 55-61-442-9700. Fax: 55-61-244-4303. EST+2.
www.eabdf.br   E-mail: info@eabdf.br
John E. Gates, Head. BA, MEd.
> **Col Prep. Curr**—Nat US. **Exams**—CEEB. **AP**—Eng Fr Ger Span Calc Bio Chem Eur_Hist US_Hist World_Hist Econ Studio_Art. **Feat**—Comp_Sci Music.
> **Enr 450.** Elem 340. Sec 110.
> **Fac 47.**
> **Tui '05-'06:** Day $14,416-19,680.
> **Est 1961.** Sem (Aug-June). Assoc: AASSA A/OPR/OS SACS.

AMERICAN SCHOOL OF CAMPINAS
(ESCOLA AMERICANA DE CAMPINAS)
Day — Coed Gr PS-12

13090-860 Campinas, Sao Paulo, Brazil. Rua Cajamar 35, Jardim Alto da Barra. Tel: 55-19-2102-1000. Fax: 55-19-2102-1016. EST+2.
www.eac.com.br   E-mail: talktous@eac.com.br
Stephen Herrera, Supt.
> **Col Prep. Curr**—Nat US. **Supp Lang**—Port. **Exams**—ACT CEEB. **AP**—Eng Calc Bio Physics World_Hist Psych. **Feat**—Port Comp_Sci Studio_Art Music. **Supp**—ESL.
> **Enr 455.** Elem 365. Sec 90.
> **Fac 97.**
> **Est 1956.** Nonprofit. Quar (Aug-June). Assoc: AASSA SACS.

INTERNATIONAL SCHOOL OF CURITIBA
Day — Coed Gr PS-12

82410-530 Curitiba, Parana, Brazil. Ave Dr Eugenio Bertolli 3900. Tel: 55-41-3364-7400. Fax: 55-41-3364-9663. EST+2.
www.iscbrazil.com   E-mail: isc.communications@iscbrazil.com
Bill R. Pearson, Supt. Felicitas Kemmsies, Adm.
> **Col Prep. IB Diploma. Curr**—Intl US. **Exams**—CEEB. **Feat**—Lib_Skills Port Comp_Sci Brazilian_Hist Econ Studio_Art. **Supp**—ESL.
> **Sports**—Basket Soccer Volley. **Activities**—Acad Arts Govt/Pol Media Rec.
> **Enr 410.** US 53. Host 193. Other 164.
> **Fac 62.** US 18. Host 43. Other 1.
> **Grad '05**—15. **Col**—15. Avg SAT: M/V—1060.
> **Est 1959.** Nonprofit. Sem (Aug-June). Assoc: AASSA SACS.

Located in the hills of Jardim Schaffer, overlooking the city of Curitiba, ISC serves both the international and the Brazilian population in the area. The elementary school curriculum includes the study of Portuguese, and Portuguese as a second language for nonnative speakers. Middle school students remain with the same teacher for core subjects in grades 7 and 8, and instruction in computers and technology is integrated into the curriculum. ISC offers three diploma options: All pupils fulfill requirements for accredited US and Brazilian diplomas, and some elect to prepare for the International Baccalaureate Diploma as well.

PAN AMERICAN SCHOOL OF PORTO ALEGRE

Day — Coed Gr PS-12

91330-280 Porto Alegre, Rio Grande do Sul, Brazil. Rua Joao Paetzel 440. Tel: 55-51-3334-5866. Fax: 55-51-3334-5866. EST+2.
www.panamerican.com.br   E-mail: school@panamerican.com.br
Murray Vosper, Dir.

Col Prep. Gen Acad. Curr—Nat US. Supp Lang—Port. Exams—CEEB. Feat—Fr Port Comp_Sci Brazilian_Hist Studio_Art. Supp—Dev_Read EFL Rev Tut.
Enr 160. B 78. G 82. Elem 144. Sec 16. US 18. Host 99. Other 43. Accepted: 95%. Avg class size: 20.
Fac 21. M 6/3. F 10/2. US 2. Host 10. Other 9. Adv Deg: 38%.
Tui '05-'06: Day $14,784-15,840 (+$4616). Aid: 10 pupils ($100,000).
Summer: Acad Enrich Rec. Tui Day $300. 5 wks.
Plant val $1,500,000. Bldgs 2. Class rms 16. Lib 8000 vols. Sci labs 1. Comp labs 1. Auds 1. Gyms 1. Courts 1.
Est 1966. Nonprofit. Sem (Aug-June). Assoc: AASSA SACS.

The school provides a full US-style program, with Portuguese offered as a foreign language to the international student body. As Pan American wishes its students to be conversant in both languages, 20 percent of instruction is in Portuguese. Course work in art, computer and physical education supplements study of the standard subjects. The high school program combines correspondence courses with in-class instruction.

Frequently scheduled field trips provide academic enrichment, and after-school activities enable boys and girls to choose from various pursuits each weekday.

AMERICAN SCHOOL OF RECIFE

Day — Coed Gr PS-12

51030-060 Recife, Pernambuco, Brazil. Rua Sa e Souza 408. Tel: 55-81-3341-4716. Fax: 55-81-3341-0142. EST+2.
www.ear.com.br   E-mail: info@ear.com.br
Dennis Donatuti, Supt.

Col Prep. Curr—Nat US. Exams—ACT CEEB. Feat—Fr Port Span Genetics Photog Studio_Art Drama Music.
Enr 242. Elem 149. Sec 93.
Fac 36.
Tui '05-'06: Day $5808-6245 (+$1600).
Est 1956. Nonprofit. Quar (Aug-June). Assoc: AASSA A/OPR/OS SACS.

THE BRITISH SCHOOL OF RIO DE JANEIRO
Day — Coed Gr PS-11

22281-030 Rio de Janeiro, Brazil. Rua Real Grandeza 87, Botafogo. Tel: 55-21-2539-2717. Fax: 55-21-2266-5040. EST+1.
www.britishschool.g12.br   E-mail: edu@britishschool.g12.br
Paul R. Wiseman, Dir. BA, MA. **Denise Pinna, Adm.**

   Col Prep. Gen Acad. IB Diploma. Curr—Intl Nat UK. **Exams**—IGCSE. **Feat**—Fr Port Span Comp_Sci Drama Music Bus. **Supp**—Dev_Read ESL LD Rem_Math Rem_Read.
   Sports—Basket Soccer Volley. **Activities**—Govt/Pol Service.
   Enr 1353. B 670. G 683. Elem 1104. Sec 249. US 18. Host 1109. Other 226. Accepted: 70%. Yield: 90%. Avg class size: 21.
   Fac 194. M 24/10. F 106/54. US 2. Host 133. Other 59. Adv Deg: 10%.
   Grad '05—60. Col—60.
   Tui '05-'06: Day R$31,392-32,136. Aid: 55 pupils.
   Bldgs 13. Class rms 112. Libs 5. Sci labs 6. Comp labs 4. Auds 3. Art studios 6. Music studios 5. Dance studios 2. Gyms 2. Fields 2. Courts 4. Pools 1.
   Est 1924. Nonprofit. Quar (Feb-Dec). Assoc: ECIS.

While enrolling students primarily from Brazil, the school is essentially British in character and curriculum. During the primary years, pupils follow England's National Curriculum. Secondary programming leads to the IGCSE and then to the IB Diploma. As English is the medium of instruction, fluency in the language is emphasized through ESL and other support. Particularly in the early grades, a learning support unit assists pupils with specific learning difficulties, as well as those who are struggling with their English language skills. Practical experiences, evidenced through day trips and longer residential excursions, enrich classroom learning.

Community service, sports and the arts are especially popular elements of the extracurricular program.

ESCOLA AMERICANA DO RIO DE JANEIRO
Day — Coed Gr PS-12

22451-260 Rio de Janeiro, Brazil. Estrada da Gavea 132. Tel: 55-21-2512-9830. Fax: 55-21-2259-4722. EST+2.
www.earj.com.br   E-mail: admission@earj.com.br
Peter Cooper, Head. Caren Addis, Adm.

   Col Prep. IB Diploma. Curr—Intl Nat US. **Exams**—ACT CEEB SSAT. **Feat**—British_Lit Creative_Writing Fr Port Span Environ_Sci Marine_Biol/Sci Comp_Sci Econ Intl_Relations Psych Studio_Art. **Supp**—ESL LD Rev Tut.
   Sports—Basket Cheer Soccer Softball Volley. **Activities**—Acad Arts Govt/Pol Media Service.
   Enr 776. Elem 539. Sec 237. Accepted: 90%. Avg class size: 20.
   Fac 188. M 58. F 130. US 33. Host 149. Other 6. Adv Deg: 37%.
   Grad '05—60. Col—53. US Col—18. (U of VA). Avg SAT: M/V—1172, Essay—551.
   Tui '05-'06: Day R$22,440-50,376 (+$6500-7500). **Aid:** 70 pupils.
   Bldgs 8. Class rms 70. 2 Libs 45,000 vols. Sci labs 8. Comp labs 3. Theaters 1.

Gyms 2. Fields 2.
Est 1937. Nonprofit. Sem (Aug-June). Assoc: AASSA A/OPR/OS SACS.

EARJ offers distinct programs leading to the US high school diploma, the International Baccalaureate and the Brazilian diploma. While the curriculum is consistent with that offered at American public and independent schools, programming also incorporates Brazilian customs and culture. At the upper school level, the school provides advisory and tutorial sessions to address the developmental and social needs of the student body. Compulsory community service work and the completion of a senior project are important elements of the upper school program.

PAN AMERICAN SCHOOL OF BAHIA

Day — Coed Gr PS-12

41680-060 Salvador, Bahia, Brazil. Loteamento Patamares s/n. Tel: 55-71-367-9099. Fax: 55-71-367-9090. EST+2.
www.paspanthers.org.br   E-mail: info@escolapanamericana.com
Larry Smith, Supt.
  Col Prep. **Curr**—Nat US. **Supp Lang**—Port. **Exams**—ACT CEEB. **Feat**—Port Comp_Sci Studio_Art Music. **Supp**—ESL.
  Est 1960. Nonprofit. Sem (Aug-June). Assoc: AASSA SACS.

ASSOCIACAO ESCOLA GRADUADA DE SAO PAULO
(THE AMERICAN SCHOOL OF SAO PAOLO)

Day — Coed Gr PS-12

01059-970 Sao Paulo, Brazil. Caixa Postal 1976. Tel: 55-11-3747-4800. Fax: 55-11-3742-9358. EST+2.
www.graded.br   E-mail: hgoncalv@graded.br
David Randall, Supt. Heidi M. G. Goncalves, Adm.
  Col Prep. **IB Diploma. Curr**—Intl US. **Exams**—ACT CEEB. **Feat**—Fr Port Span Comp_Sci Econ Studio_Art Music. **Supp**—ESL.
  Enr 1119. B 547. G 572. Elem 799. Sec 320. US 301. Host 490. Other 328. Avg class size: 18.
  Fac 118. US 55. Host 51. Other 12. Adv Deg: 43%.
  Grad '05—79. US Col—6. (Harvard, Brown, Tufts, U of PA, Duke, Boston U).
  Tui '05-'06: Day R$36,408-48,612.
  Endow $240,000. Bldgs 15. Class rms 90. 2 Libs 45,000 vols. Sci labs 1. Lang labs 1. Comp labs 8. Auds 1. Gyms 1. Fields 1. Courts 2.
  Est 1920. Nonprofit. Sem (Aug-June). Assoc: AASSA A/OPR/OS SACS.

Enrolling students from Brazil, elsewhere in Latin America, the US, Europe and the Far East, this school offers an American curriculum. IB courses are available, as are electives in drama, choir, French, Portuguese, Spanish, computer and yearbook.

Extracurricular activities include dramatic and musical productions, academic competitions, athletics and community service.

CHAPEL SCHOOL
(ESCOLA MARIA IMACULADA)

Day — Coed Gr PS-12

04602-970 Sao Paulo, Brazil. Caixa Postal 21293. Tel: 55-11-5687-7455. Fax: 55-11-5521-7763. EST+2.
www.chapel.g12.br   E-mail: chapel@chapel.g12.br
John T. Ciallelo, Dir. MS. **Vera Prado, Adm.**

> **Col Prep. IB Diploma. Curr**—Intl. **Supp Lang**—Port. **Feat**—Fr Port Span Pol_Sci Sociol Brazilian_Stud Relig.
> **Enr 700.** US 111. Host 435. Other 154. Accepted: 50%. Avg class size: 25.
> **Fac 66.** M 18. F 36/12. US 22. Host 36. Other 8. Adv Deg: 45%.
> **Grad '05—44. Col—44. US Col—22.** (Boston U, Columbia, Brown, Stanford, Georgetown, PA St).
> **Tui '01-'02: Day R$14,400-27,600** (+R$6000).
> Bldgs 6. Class rms 55. Libs 2. Auds 1. Gyms 2. Fields 1. Courts 2.
> **Est 1947.** Nonprofit. Sem (Aug-June). Assoc: AASSA SACS.

Founded by the Oblate Fathers of Mary Immaculate to educate English-speaking Catholics in the area, Chapel provides a US-style education for elementary- and secondary-level pupils. All students take religion courses, and electives include Brazilian studies and Portuguese language classes. Pupils may prepare for the US College Boards, and interested boys and girls may work toward the International Baccalaureate Diploma.

Extracurricular activities include student government, drama, Model UN, quiz bowl, choral music, newspaper, yearbook, cheerleading and sports.

PAN AMERICAN CHRISTIAN ACADEMY

Day — Coed Gr K-12

04829-310 Sao Paulo, Brazil. Rua Cassio de Campos Nogueira 393. Tel: 55-11-5928-9655. Fax: 55-11-5928-9591. EST+2.
www.paca.com.br   E-mail: info@paca.com.br
Michael Epp, Supt.

> **Col Prep. Curr**—US. **Supp Lang**—Port. **Exams**—ACT AP CEEB. **AP**—Eng Bio Chem Physics US_Hist. **Feat**—Port Comp_Sci Bible Studio_Art Music. **Supp**—LD.
> **Sports**—Basket Soccer Softball Volley. **Activities**—Acad Arts Govt/Pol Media Service.
> **Enr 316.** Elem 200. Sec 116. US 94. Host 111. Other 111. Avg class size: 25.
> **Fac 33.** US 23. Host 10.
> **Grad '05—27. Col—27. US Col—20.** Avg SAT: M/V—1085.
> **Tui '05-'06: Day R$17,940-23,140** (+R$4260). **Aid:** 126 pupils.
> Bldgs 5. Class rms 19. 2 Libs 13,000 vols. Sci labs 2. Comp labs 2. Gyms 1. Fields 2. Courts 2. Pools 1.
> **Est 1959.** Nonprofit. Nondenom Christian. Quar (Aug-June). Assoc: AASSA SACS.

Founded by American missionaries to meet the educational needs of their families, PACA now serves both the business and Christian ministry communities from the US, Brazil and other nations. English is the medium of instruction in the main program, with students pursuing a US high school diploma. A Christian worldview is emphasized in all subject areas. Interested pupils have the option of earning the Brazilian diploma by concurrently completing course work in Portuguese.

The focus in kindergarten is on the development of reading, writing, oral language, math, music and art skills. An emphasis on the fundamentals continues during the elementary and middle school years, with special activities available in sports, music and drama. A learning lab serves boys and girls with learning disabilities. High schoolers choose from a selection of Advanced Placement courses.

ST. PAUL'S SCHOOL

Day — Coed Gr PS-12

01440-903 Sao Paulo, Brazil. Rua Juquia 166, Jardim Paulistano. Tel: 55-11-3085-3399. Fax: 55-11-3085-3708. EST+1.
www.stpauls.br   E-mail: spshead@stpauls.br
Rachid Benammar, Head. MA. **Sandra Abatepaulo, Adm.**

> **Col Prep. Gen Acad. IB Diploma. Curr**—Intl Nat UK. **Exams**—IGCSE. **Feat**—Fr Port Span Comp_Sci Econ Studio_Art Theater_Arts Music. **Supp**—Tut.
> **Sports**—Basket Hand Soccer Volley. **Activities**—Acad Arts Media Rec.
> **Enr 1001.** B 520. G 481. Elem 675. Sec 326. US 66. Host 741. Other 194. Avg class size: 20.
> **Fac 129.** M 31/1. F 96/1. US 3. Host 104. Other 22. Adv Deg: 55%.
> **Grad '05—35. Col—35. US Col—6.** (U of PA, Babson, Bentley, Sarah Lawrence, Barnard, Bard).
> **Tui '05-'06: Day $13,800** (+$150).
> Class rms 62. 2 Libs 27,300 vols. Chapels 1. Sci labs 8. Comp labs 3. Theaters 1. Art studios 2. Music studios 8. Dance studios 1. Drama studios 1. Gyms 2. Fields 1. Courts 2. Pools 2.
> **Est 1926.** Nonprofit. Sem (Aug-June).

Though the medium of instruction at St. Paul's is English, most pupils are not native speakers of the language. The structured pre-preparatory division (ages 3-5) provides an integrated curriculum that emphasizes fundamental reading, writing, science and math skills. The prep school (ages 6-11) stresses sound study habit development, as well as both independent and cooperative learning skills. Basically, the school's curriculum at the pre-preparatory and preparatory levels follows the British National Curriculum.

Students take IGCSE courses in forms four and five, then take part in the IB Diploma Program in the Sixth Form. Boys and girls select six subjects, three at A level and three at AS level. These six courses come from the following areas: math, languages, science, humanities and one other discipline.

CHILE

Sq. Miles: 302,778 (Nearly twice the size of California). **Country Pop:** 15,980,912 (2005). **Capital:** Santiago, pop. 6,000,000. **Terrain:** Desert in north; fertile central valley; volcanoes and lakes toward the south, giving way to rugged and complex coastline; Andes Mountains on the eastern border. **Ethnic Group(s):** Mestizo European Native-American. **Religion(s):** Roman_Catholic Protestant. **Official Language(s):** Spanish. **Government:** Republic. **Independence:** 1810 (from Spain). **GDP:** $94.1 billion (2004). Agriculture 6%. Commerce 8%. Financial Services 15%. Fisheries 12%. Industry 19%. Manufacturing 17%. Mining 13%. Natural Resources 3%. Transport & Communications 7%. **Currency:** Chilean Peso (Ch$).

ANTOFAGASTA INTERNATIONAL SCHOOL
Day — Coed Gr PS-12

Antofagasta, Chile. Ave Angamos 587. Tel: 56-55-256-613. Fax: 56-55-256-628. EST+1.
www.ais.cl   E-mail: ais@ais.cl
Carlos Ignacio Figueroa Ahumada, Prin.
  Gen Acad. Curr—Intl.
  Enr 50.
  Fac 11. M 5. F 6. US 1. Host 7. Other 3. Adv Deg: 36%.
  Est 1994. Nonprofit. Sem (Feb-Dec).

THE GRANGE SCHOOL
Day — Coed Gr PS-12

6870671 Santiago, Chile. Ave Principe de Gales 6154, La Reina. Tel: 56-2-586-0100. Fax: 56-2-277-0946. EST+1.
www.grange.cl   E-mail: rectoria@grange.cl
John A. Horsfall, Head. PhD. **Antonia Ferrer, Adm.**
  Col Prep. IB Diploma. Curr—Intl Nat. **Bilingual**—Span. **Exams**—IGCSE. **Feat**—Comp_Sci Econ Philos Relig Studio_Art Theater_Arts Music. **Supp**—Tut.
  Sports—F_Hockey Gymnastics Rugby Ski Soccer Tennis Volley. **Activities**—Acad Arts Rec Service.
  Enr 1740. B 902. G 838. Elem 1251. Sec 489. Host 1700. Other 40. Avg class size: 25.
  Fac 200. M 30/4. F 150/16. US 2. Host 168. Other 30. Adv Deg: 25%.
  Tui '05-'06: Day Ch$3,009,600-3,206,500.
  Bldgs 6. Class rms 92. Sci labs 4. Auds 2. Theaters 2. Art studios 2. Music studios 6. Gyms 3. Fields 6. Courts 3. Pools 1.
  Est 1928. Sem (Mar-Dec).

Combining instruction in English and Spanish and borrowing important curricular elements from the UK system, the Grange employs strictly bilingual teachers through grade 5. Two instructors per classroom in grades pre-K-1 conduct a program entirely in English that emphasizes the development of fundamental learning skills. During the primary and early middle school years, most work is done in English, whereas Spanish becomes the dominant language at the secondary level.

From prekindergarten through grade 4, children remain with their homeroom teacher for all classes except music, religion and physical education; more subject teaching begins in grade 5, and full departmentalization is in effect from grade 7 on. In grades 11 and 12, all pupils take Spanish, math, English, the history and geography of Chile, and physical education. In addition, boys and girls choose four subjects from this group: history, economics, social science, art, philosophy, physics, chemistry, biology, music, computer and theater studies. Some students follow the IB Diploma curriculum, while others take only certain IB subjects. Preparation for the IGCSE is part of the curriculum.

The school places strong emphasis on college preparation and also maintains a career education program.

INTERNATIONAL PREPARATORY SCHOOL
Day — Coed Gr PS-12

Santiago, Chile. Pastor Fernandez 16001, Lo Barnechea. Tel: 56-2-321-5800. Fax: 56-2-321-5821. EST+1.
www.tipschile.com   E-mail: info@tipschile.com
Lesley Easton Allen, Head. BS.
Col Prep. Gen Acad. Curr—UK. Exams—IGCSE AS-level A-level.
Enr 141.
Tui '05-'06: Day $6890-9040.
Est 1975. Sem (Mar-Dec).

INTERNATIONAL SCHOOL NIDO DE AGUILAS
Day — Coed Gr PS-12

Santiago, Chile. Casilla 27020, Correo 27. Tel: 56-2-339-8100. Fax: 56-2-216-7603. EST+1.
www.nido.cl   E-mail: ljaques@nido.cl
Donald Bergman, Head. BS, MS, PhD. Lilian Jaques, Adm.
Col Prep. IB Diploma. Curr—Intl US. Exams—ACT CEEB. Feat—Creative_Writing Fr Span Comp_Sci Econ Govt Philos Studio_Art. Supp—ESL.
Enr 1199. Elem 910. Sec 289. Accepted: 90%. Avg class size: 20.
Fac 121. Adv Deg: 28%.
Grad '05—67. US Col—6. (Cornell, Princeton, MIT, Stanford, Purdue, Duke).
Tui '05-'06: Day $11,000. Aid: 9 pupils ($7200).
Bldgs 14. 2 Libs 18,880 vols. Sci labs 4. Comp labs 3. Theaters 1. Gyms 1. Fields 2. Courts 4. Tracks 1.
Est 1934. Nonprofit. Quar (July-June). Assoc: AASSA A/OPR/OS SACS.

Located on a 130-acre site in the foothills of the Andes, this school offers a US-style curriculum to students in the international business community, as well as to qualified Chilean pupils who are interested in an English-medium program. As all instruction is in Spanish, Nido features an extensive ESL program. Boys and girls pursue either the US diploma, the International Baccalaureate Diploma or the Chilean diploma.

Among Nido's extracurricular activities are school newspaper and yearbook, dance, photography, band, chess club, computer club and ski club. In addition, students may participate in a sports program that includes soccer, tennis, basketball, track and horseback riding.

LINCOLN INTERNATIONAL ACADEMY
Day — Coed Gr PS-12

Santiago, Chile. Avenida Las Condes 13150. Tel: 56-2-496-7600. Fax: 56-2-496-7623. EST+1.
www.lintac.cl   E-mail: admisiones@lintac.cl
John Seaquist, Dir. Guacolda Espinace, Prin.

    Col Prep. Curr—Nat US. **Bilingual**—Span. **Exams**—CEEB. **Feat**—Fr Lat Comp_Sci Studio_Art Music.

    Enr 465. Elem 375. Sec 90. Accepted: 75%. Avg class size: 25.

    Fac 64. M 15/8. F 33/8.

    Grad '05—19. Col—19.

    Bldgs 9. Lib 6000 vols. Sci labs 2. Comp labs 2. Auds 1. Gyms 1. Fields 1.

    Est 1976. Inc. Sem (Mar-Dec). Ecumenical. Sem (Mar-Dec).

The bilingual, international curriculum at Lincoln prepares students for entrance to US and Chilean universities. Computer instruction commences in kindergarten and continues through grade 12. Pupils must pass an admission test prior to enrollment.

SANTIAGO COLLEGE
Day — Coed Gr PS-12

Santiago, Chile. Los Leones 584, Providencia. Tel: 56-2-751-3800. Fax: 56-2-751-3802. EST+1.
www.scollege.cl   E-mail: master@scollege.cl
Lorna Prado Scott, Dir.

    Col Prep. IB PYP. IB MYP. IB Diploma. Curr—Intl Nat US. **Bilingual**—Span. **Exams**—CEEB. **Feat**—Fr Comp_Sci Relig Studio_Art Music.

    Enr 1813.

    Fac 131. M 15/18. F 83/15.

    Tui '05-'06: Day $3460 (+$1970).

    Est 1880. Nonprofit. Sem (Mar-Dec). Assoc: CIS NEASC.

COLOMBIA

Sq. Miles: 440,000 (About the size of Texas, New Mexico and Arkansas combined). **Country Pop:** 42,954,279. **Capital:** Bogota, pop. 7,000,000 (2004). **Terrain:** Flat coastal areas, with extensive coastlines on the Pacific Ocean and Caribbean Sea three rugged parallel mountain chains, central highlands, and flat eastern grasslands. **Religion(s):** Roman_Catholic. **Official Language(s):** Spanish. **Government:** Republic. **Inde-**

pendence: 1810 (from Spain). **GDP:** $83.01 billion (2004). Agriculture 13%. Industry 34%. Services 53%. **Currency:** Colombian Peso (Col$).

COLEGIO KARL C. PARRISH

Day — Coed Gr PS-12

Barranquilla, Colombia. Km 2, Carretera Antigua a Puerto Colombia, Apartado Aereo 52962. Tel: 57-5-359-8929. Fax: 57-5-359-8828. EST.
www.kcparrish.edu.co   E-mail: mail@kcparrish.edu.co
Laura Horbal Potosky, Dir.

  Col Prep. Curr—Nat US. **Bilingual**—Span. **Exams**—SSAT TOEFL. **Feat**—Comp_ Sci Colombian_Hist Econ Ethics Philos Relig Photog Studio_Art Drama Music Dance. **Supp**—LD.
  Enr 730. Avg class size: 26.
  Fac 81. Adv Deg: 44%.
  Grad '05—45. Col—45.
  Tui '05-'06: Day $4000-4750 (+$4500).
  Lib 20,000 vols. Sci labs 1. Comp labs 1. Auds 1. Art studios 1. Music studios 1. Dance studios 1. Gyms 1. Fields 2. Courts 5. Pools 1.
  Est 1938. Nonprofit. Tri (Aug-June). Assoc: AASSA ACCAS A/OPR/OS SACS.

Offering a dual US-Colombian curriculum to students from those two nations and several other countries, the school prepares students for the US College Boards and the Colombian Bachillerato. Instruction in the US-based program is in English, while that in the Colombian program is approximately half English and half Spanish. Spanish study is required of all students. Many graduates matriculate at US colleges.

COLEGIO ANGLO-COLOMBIANO

Day — Coed Gr PS-12

2 Bogota, Colombia. Apartado Aereo 253393. Tel: 57-1-216-9200. Fax: 57-1-614-9673. EST.
www.anglocolombiano.edu.co   E-mail: adminanglocol@cable.net.co
James S. Walbran, Rector. BA, MA. **Dora Nelly Moreno, Adm.**

  Col Prep. IB PYP. IB MYP. IB Diploma. Curr—Intl Nat UK. **Bilingual**—Span. **Exams**—CEEB IGCSE. **Feat**—Fr Comp_Sci Drama. **Supp**—Dev_Read Makeup Rem_Math Rem_Read Tut.
  Enr 1681. B 840. G 841. Accepted: 33%. Avg class size: 22.
  Fac 140.
  Grad '05—105.
  Tui '02-'03: Day Col$4835-5762 (+Col$575-2120).
  Est 1956. Nonprofit. Quar (Aug-June). Assoc: ECIS.

Founded by a group of Colombian and British citizens, the Anglo maintains its links to Great Britain through representation on the school's board by members of the British Embassy and the British Council. The curriculum also remains connected to that found in the United Kingdom, as the IGCSE exams are part of the program, along with all three components of the International Baccalaureate sequence (the Primary Years, Middle Years and Diploma programs).

In prekindergarten, Spanish is the main language of instruction (with a daily English lesson incorporated). The process is reversed in kindergarten, with children studying in English and taking a daily Spanish lesson. This pattern continues in succeeding years through age 7. Specialists teach music, ESL, Spanish as a Second Language and physical education to these children. In the primary section (grades 2-5), the program features English as its primary language of instruction; sports and other extracurricular activities gain in prominence in this division.

The demanding secondary school program (grades 6-12) leads to the internationally recognized IB Diploma. Roughly three-quarters of secondary-level classes are taught in English in grades 6-10, while the language of instruction during the final two years depends upon the pupil's choice of subjects. The IB program at the Anglo fulfills all requirements of the Colombian Bachillerato. Graduates matriculate at colleges in Colombia, Europe and North America.

COLEGIO GRAN BRETANA
Day — Coed Gr PS-10

Bogota, Colombia. 215-20 Carrera 51. Tel: 57-1-676-0391. Fax: 57-1-676-0426. EST.
www.cgb.edu.co   E-mail: admissions@cgb.edu.co
Nicholas Reeves, Dir. Fiorella Rocha, Adm.

> Gen Acad. Curr—Nat UK. Supp Lang—Span. Exams—IGCSE. Feat—Fr Span Comp_Sci Econ Colombian_Stud Studio_Art Drama Music. Supp—ESL Tut.
> Sports—Baseball Rugby Soccer Swim Tennis Volley. Activities—Arts Media.
> Enr 223. B 116. G 107. Elem 204. Sec 19. US 38. Host 103. Other 82. Accepted: 75%. Avg class size: 13.
> Fac 31. M 8/3. F 17/3. Host 20. Other 11. Adv Deg: 25%.
> Grad '05—12.
> Tui '05-'06: Day $7400 (+$2000). Aid: 16 pupils.
> Libs 1. Sci labs 2. Comp labs 1. Theaters 1. Art studios 1. Music studios 1. Dance studios 1. Gyms 1. Fields 1. Courts 1.
> Est 1997. Quar (Aug-June). Assoc: CIS NEASC.

CGB was founded to provide an English-language education and diverse environment to Bogota's international community. The school follows the English National Curriculum, with adaptations made to meet requirements for the Colombian National Curriculum and the US high school diploma. Spanish language instruction begins in Key Stage 1, as boys and girls are placed in groups appropriate to their ability.

Students whose first language is neither English nor Spanish have opportunities to practice their home language. Secondary school students prepare for the IGCSE examinations.

COLEGIO NUEVA GRANADA
Day — Coed Gr PS-12

Bogota, Colombia. 70-20 Carrera 2E. Tel: 57-1-235-5350. Fax: 57-1-211-3720. EST.
Contact: 1025 NW 27th St, Ste 201, Miami, FL 33172. Tel: 305-463-7272.
www.cng.edu   E-mail: ccastro@cng.edu
Barry McCombs, Dir. PhD. **Katherine Ancizar, Adm.**

Col Prep. Curr—US. **Supp Lang**—Span. **Exams**—ACT AP CEEB TOEFL. **AP**— Eng Span Calc Bio Chem Environ_Sci Human_Geog Physics US_Hist Econ Studio_Art. **Feat**—Creative_Writing Chin Fr Port Comp_Sci Comp_Relig Ethics Drama Music Journ. **Supp**—ESL LD Makeup Rem_Math Rev Tut.

Sports—Basket Baseball Soccer Track Volley Weightlifting. **Activities**—Acad Arts Govt/Pol Rec.

Enr 1680. Elem 1259. Sec 421. US 374. Host 1089. Other 217. Accepted: 98%. Yield: 98%. Avg class size: 20.

Fac 160. M 41. F 119. US 55. Host 88. Other 17. Adv Deg: 35%.

Grad '05—92. Col—90. US Col—5. (Boston U, Columbia, Tufts, U of VA, Notre Dame). Avg SAT: M/V—1051.

Tui '05-'06: Day $5259 (+$680). **Aid:** 44 pupils ($69,775).

Bldgs 9. 2 Libs 40,000 vols. Comp labs 4. Theaters 1. Art studios 3. Music studios 3. Dance studios 1. Gyms 2. Fields 1. Courts 2.

Est 1938. Nonprofit. Sem (Aug-June). Assoc: AASSA ACCAS A/OPR/OS SACS.

CNG, which predominantly serves Colombian nationals and the dependents of the US expatriate community, provides a college preparatory curriculum similar to that found in the US. As English is the language of instruction in all classes except for Spanish and Colombian social studies, the school offers special assistance at the prekindergarten level for children that lack fluency in English. Interested pupils may enroll in a dual program allowing them to earn both a US high school diploma and the Colombian Bachillerato.

All students fulfill an after-school community service requirement. A leadership program trains selected students in communicational skills, group processes and human relations.

COLEGIO PANAMERICANO
Day — Coed Gr PS-12

Bucaramanga, Colombia. Apartado Aereo 522. Tel: 57-7-6386213. Fax: 57-7-6398970. EST.
www.panamericano.edu.co   E-mail: director@panamericano.edu.co
Jeffrey Michael Jurkovac, Dir. BS, EdS, MEd.

Col Prep. Gen Acad. Curr—Intl. **Bilingual**—Span. **Exams**—SSAT. **Feat**—Comp_ Sci Studio_Art Music. **Supp**—Tut.

Enr 550. B 280. G 270. Elem 486. Sec 64. US 10. Host 530. Other 10. Accepted: 50%. Avg class size: 25.

Fac 49. M 12/1. F 26/10. US 6. Host 43.

Grad '05—23. Col—23. US Col—2. (Boston U, Tulane).

Tui '02-'03: Day $1250. Aid: 1 pupil ($1250).

Bldgs 2. Class rms 31. Lib 10,500 vols. Sci labs 1. Comp labs 2. Auds 1. Art studios 2. Music studios 1. Courts 2. Pools 1.

Est 1963. Nonprofit. Tri (Jan-Nov). Assoc: ACCAS SACS.

Primarily enrolling Colombian students, Panamericano follows a bilingual curriculum that leads to both the US high school diploma and the Colombian Bachillerato. The academic program, similar to that found in US public schools, is supplemented by such recreational activities as basketball, volleyball, Ping-Pong and soccer.

COLEGIO BOLIVAR

Day — Coed Gr PS-12

Cali, Colombia. Apartado Aereo 26300. Tel: 57-2-555-2039. Fax: 57-2-555-2041. EST.
www.colegiobolivar.edu.co   E-mail: cbinfo@colegiobolivar.edu.co
Martin Felton, Dir. MA, PhD.

> **Col Prep. Curr**—Nat US. **Supp Lang**—Span. **Exams**—ACT CEEB TOEFL. **Feat**—Studio_Art Music.
> **Enr 1200.**
> **Fac 250.**
> **Est 1947.** Nonprofit. Sem (Sept-June). Assoc: ACCAS SACS.

COLEGIO COLOMBO BRITANICO

Day — Coed Gr PS-12

Cali, Colombia. Ave La Maria 69, Pance, Apartado Aereo 5774. Tel: 57-2-555-5385. Fax: 57-2-555-1191. EST.
www.colombobritanico.edu.co   E-mail: info@colombobritanico.edu.co
Pablo Grech Mayor, Head. Diana Velasquez, Adm.

> **Col Prep. IB PYP. IB Diploma. Curr**—Intl Nat UK. **Bilingual**—Span. **Exams**—CEEB TOEFL IGCSE. **Feat**—Stats Comp_Sci Econ Philos Relig Studio_Art. **Supp**—Rem_Math Rem_Read Tut.
> **Activities**—Arts Rec Service.
> **Enr 1172.** Avg class size: 19.
> **Fac 126.** M 34. F 92. US 3. Host 97. Other 26. Adv Deg: 7%.
> **Grad '05—73. US Col**—11. (Boston U, Brandeis, LA St-Baton Rouge, Loyola U-LA, U of NE-Lincoln, Purdue).
> **Summer:** Enrich Rec. 4 wks.
> Sci labs 8. Lang labs 3. Comp labs 4. Auds 1. Music studios 3. Dance studios 1. Gyms 1. Fields 2. Courts 2. Pools 2.
> **Est 1956.** Nonprofit. Tri (Aug-June).

Founded to provide a bilingual environment for elementary and secondary students, CCB enrolls children as young as age 2 into its prekindergarten program. Although most pupils are Colombian nationals, approximately five percent of the enrollment comes from other countries. Faculty devote significant attention to the cultures of both Colombia and England.

The integrated primary curriculum in grades 2-6 emphasizes inquiry and problem solving; as English is the main medium of instruction at this level, instructors encourage children to use English as their primary language of communication. The secondary school (grades 7-12) features programming leading to the Colombian Baccalaureate, the IGCSE and the International Baccalaureate Diploma. While pursuing the IB Diploma, students must take six courses, three at higher level and three at standard level.

Field trips, musical performances, dramatic productions and community service projects are integral to school life.

GEORGE WASHINGTON SCHOOL
(COLEGIO JORGE WASHINGTON)
Day — Coed Gr PS-12

Cartagena, Colombia. Apartado Aereo 2899. Tel: 57-5-665-3136. Fax: 57-5-665-6447. EST.
www.cojowa.edu.co   E-mail: director@cojowa.edu.co
Pete Nonnenkamp, Dir. BS, MAEd.

   Col Prep. Curr—US. **Bilingual**—Span. **Exams**—AP CEEB TOEFL. **AP**—Eng Calc World_Hist. **Feat**—Fr Comp_Sci Philos Relig Drama Music. **Supp**—LD.
   Sports Basket Baseball Soccer Softball Volley. **Activities**—Acad Arts Govt/Pol Media.
   Enr 608. US 30. Host 578. Accepted: 25%. Avg class size: 24.
   Fac 68. M 32. F 36. US 20. Host 40. Other 8. Adv Deg: 30%.
   Grad '05—44. Col—44. US Col—12. (Yale, Stanford, Wheaton-MA, TX Christian, U of Miami, FL Intl).
   Tul '05-'06: Bdg $7000 (+$500). **Day Col$734,000.**
   Endow Col$800,000,000. Plant val Col$10,000,000,000. Bldgs 8. Class rms 24. Lib 17,000 vols. Sci labs 1. Lang labs 1. Comp labs 3. Art studios 1. Music studios 1. Dance studios 1. Fields 1. Courts 2.
   Est 1952. Nonprofit. Quar (Aug-June). Assoc: ACCAS A/OPR/OS SACS.

Located on an oceanfront site, COJOWA enrolls students mainly from Colombia and the US. The bilingual curriculum corresponds to a general education in the US, and students prepare for both the US high school diploma and the Colombian Bachillerato.

ASOCIACION COLEGIO GRANADINO
Day — Coed Gr PS-12

Manizales, Colombia. Apartado Aereo 2138. Tel: 57-6-874-5774. Fax: 57-6-874-6066. EST.
www.granadino.edu.co   E-mail: colgranadino@granadino.edu.co
Michael Adams, Dir. BA, MA, EdD.

   Col Prep. Gen Acad. Curr—US. **Bilingual**—Span. **Exams**—CEEB. **Feat**—Comp_Sci Econ Govt Colombian_Stud Philos Visual_Arts Music. **Supp**—ESL LD.
   Sports—Basket Soccer Volley. **Activities**—Rec.
   Enr 600. B 275. G 325. Elem 475. Sec 125. Host 600. Avg class size: 22.
   Fac 65. M 21/5. F 38/1. US 22. Host 43. Adv Deg: 15%.
   Grad '05—35. Col—35. Avg SAT: M/V—927.
   Tui '05-'06: Day $2500.
   Bldgs 9. Class rms 40. Lib 10,000 vols. Comp labs 2. Auds 2. Athletic ctrs 1. Fields

2. Courts 3.
Est 1980. Nonprofit. Roman Catholic. (Aug-June). Assoc: ACCAS SACS.

Instruction at Colegio Granadino in the core subjects of English, math, science and social studies is in English. The school's parallel structure enables students to prepare for both the US diploma and the Colombian Bachillerato; most pupils at the high school level enroll in this dual program. Course work promotes the development of problem-solving, communicational, critical-thinking and computer skills. Assorted extracurricular activities and sports teams complement academics.

ACG is situated on the outskirts of Manizales, a city in a coffee-growing region near the Andes Mountains. Home to several universities, the area hosts an international theater festival, a poetry festival, concerts and a city fair. Accessible to the city are tropical recreational facilities, ecological parks and coffee farms.

COLUMBUS SCHOOL
Day — Coed Gr PS-12

Medellin, Colombia. Apartado Aereo 60562. Tel: 57-4-386-1122. Fax: 57-4-386-1133. EST.
www.columbus.edu.co   E-mail: superintendent@columbus.edu.co
David Cardenas, Supt.
  Col Prep. Curr—Nat US. **Bilingual**—Span. **Feat**—Shakespeare Comp_Sci Psych Studio_Art.
  Enr 1460. Elem 1099. Sec 361.
  Fac 147. US 30. Host 85. Other 32.
  Tui '05-'06: Day $3500-4000.
  Est 1947. Nonprofit. Quar (Aug-June). Assoc: ACCAS SACS.

ECUADOR

Sq. Miles: 98,985 (About the size of Colorado). **Country Pop:** 13,363,593 (2005). **Capital:** Quito, pop. 1,600,000. **Largest City:** Guayaquil, pop. 2,400,000. **Terrain:** Jungle east of the Andes, a rich agricultural coastal plain west of the Andes, high-elevation valleys through the mountainous center of the country and an archipelago of volcanic islands in the Pacific Ocean. **Ethnic Group(s):** Indigenous Mestizo Caucasian African. **Religion(s):** Roman_Catholic. **Official Language(s):** Spanish. **Other Language(s):** Quichua. **Government:** Republic. **Independence:** 1822 (from Spain). **GDP:** $30 billion (2004). Agriculture 7%. Industry 32%. Services 61%. **Currency:** US Dollar ($).

INTER-AMERICAN ACADEMY
Day — Coed Gr PS-12

Guayaquil, Ecuador. PO Box 0906-209U. Tel: 593-4-2871790. Fax: 593-4-2873358. EST.
Contact: 8424 NW 56th St, Ste GYE1096, Miami, FL 33166.
www.interamerican.edu.ec   E-mail: admin@interamerican.edu.ec
Maureen O'Shaughnessy, Exec Dir. PhD. **Abigail Ames, Adm.**

> **Col Prep. Curr**—US. **Exams**—ACT AP CEEB. **AP**—Eng Span Calc US_Hist. **Feat**—Fr Anat Comp_Sci Sociol Lat-Amer_Stud Studio_Art Music Bus Speech. **Supp**—ESL Tut.
> **Sports**—Basket Soccer Volley. **Activities**—Arts Govt/Pol Media.
> **Enr 208.** US 44. Host 85. Other 79. Accepted: 90%. Avg class size: 15.
> **Fac 25.** M 8/1. F 15/1. US 11. Host 9. Other 5. Adv Deg: 32%.
> **Grad '05—19. Col—16. US Col—14.** (USC 2, CA St Polytech-Pomona 1, U of AZ 1, Boston U 1, U of Miami 1, Emerson 1). Avg SAT: M/V—1085. Avg ACT: 25.
> **Tui '05-'06: Day $2900-9600** (+$2500). **Aid:** 23 pupils ($108,774).
> **Summer:** Enrich Rem Rec. Tui Day $633. 5 wks.
> Bldgs 9. Class rms 31. Lib 17,000 vols. Sci labs 1. Comp labs 1. Art studios 1. Music studios 1. Gyms 1. Fields 1. Courts 1. Pools 1.
> **Est 1979.** Nonprofit. Sem (Aug-June). Assoc: AASSA A/OPR/OS SACS.

Founded to serve Guayaquil's English-speaking community, IA offers a conventional US-style curriculum at all grade levels. The rigorous liberal arts curriculum places particular emphasis on the development of basic skills. Many members of the international student body are fluent in two or three languages. All pupils study Spanish, and English as a Second Language classes are available. Advanced Placement courses and preparation for the US College Boards are part of the high school curriculum.

ACADEMIA COTOPAXI
(AMERICAN INTERNATIONAL SCHOOL)
Day — Coed Gr PS-12

Quito, Ecuador. De Las Higuerillas y Alondras, Monteserrin, Casilla 17-11-6510. Tel: 593-2-246-7410. Fax: 593-2-244-5195. EST.
www.cotopaxi.k12.ec   E-mail: info@cotopaxi.k12.ec
William F. Johnston, Dir. EdD. **Paola de Pereira, Adm.**

> **Col Prep. IB PYP. IB Diploma. Curr**—Intl Nat US. **Supp Lang**—Span. **Exams**—CEEB. **Feat**—Comp_Sci Intl_Relations Psych Studio_Art Drama. **Supp**—ESL.
> **Sports**—Basket Soccer Swim Volley. **Activities**—Acad Arts Govt/Pol Rec.
> **Enr 475.** B 233. G 242. Elem 352. Sec 123. US 123. Host 201. Other 151. Accepted: 89%. Yield: 79%. Avg class size: 15.
> **Fac 67.** M 20/1. F 43/1. US 39. Host 16. Other 12. Adv Deg: 4%.
> **Grad '05—35. Col—32. US Col—23.** (Notre Dame 2, Loyola U-LA 2, U of New Orleans 2, Brown 1, NYU 1, Tulane 1). Avg SAT: M/V—1077.
> **Tui '05-'06: Day $5650-12,680** (+$4000). **Aid:** 25 pupils ($47,800).
> **Summer:** Acad Rem. 4 wks.
> Plant val $5,809,000. Bldgs 8. Class rms 64. 2 Libs 35,000 vols. Sci labs 1. Lang labs 1. Comp labs 4. Auds 1. Theaters 1. Art studios 2. Music studios 1. Gyms 1. Fields 3. Pools 1.

Est 1959. Nonprofit. Sem (Aug-June). Assoc: AASSA A/OPR/OS SACS.

Curriculum, community involvement, and pupil-teacher relationships similar to those found in contemporary US schools are featured at this school. The program is designed to provide a bicultural academic experience while simultaneously utilizing the most innovative educational practices. Although English is not the first language of most students, a majority of each year's graduates go on to colleges in the US.

ALLIANCE ACADEMY
Bdg — Coed Gr 1-12; Day — Coed PS-12

Quito, Ecuador. Casilla 17-11-06186. Tel: 593-2-226-6985. Fax: 593-2-226-4350. EST.
www.alliance.k12.ec   E-mail: alliance@alliance.k12.ec
Tim Wilbanks, Dir. MA.

> **Col Prep. Gen Acad. Curr**—US. **Supp Lang**—Span. **Exams**—CEEB. **AP**—Eng Span Calc Comp_Sci Bio US_Hist Music_Theory. **Feat**—Bible Studio_Art Journ Home_Ec. **Supp**—EFL ESL.
> **Enr 400.** Avg class size: 20.
> **Fac 49.** Adv Deg: 53%.
> **Grad '05—55. Col—55. US Col—5.** (Wheaton-MA, Nyack, John Brown, Crown, Messiah).
> **Tui '02-'03: Day $2940-6740.**
> **Summer:** Rem. 3 wks.
> Bldgs 14. Dorms 5. 2 Libs 35,000 vols. Gyms 1. Fields 2. Courts 2.
> **Est 1929.** Nonprofit. Nondenom Christian. Sem (Aug-May). Assoc: AASSA SACS.

Originally founded to educate missionaries' children, the school now accepts nonmissionary children into the day division and missionary-related students only into the boarding division. Many children come from American families, while others are from Canadian and Korean ones. English as a Second Language is offered in the special education department.

Extracurricular activities include band, orchestra, school newspaper and yearbook, drama and photography. The interscholastic sports program includes soccer, basketball, track and volleyball.

AMERICAN SCHOOL OF QUITO
Day — Coed Gr PS-12

Quito, Ecuador. Manuel Benigno Cueva 80-190, Urb Carcelen, PO Box 17-01-157. Tel: 593-2-2472-975. Fax: 593-2-2472-972. EST.
Contact: US Embassy Quito, Unit 5372, Box 004, APO, AA 34039.
www.fcaq.k12.ec   E-mail: dirgeneral@fcaq.k12.ec
Susan Barba, Dir. MA. Susan Montalvo, Intl Dir. MA.

> **Col Prep. IB MYP. IB Diploma. Curr**—Intl Nat US. **Bilingual**—Span. **Exams**—CEEB TOEFL. **Feat**—Comp_Sci Ecuadorian_Hist Econ Psych Studio_Art Bus. **Supp**—ESL LD.
> **Sports**—Basket F_Hockey Soccer Volley. **Activities**—Arts Govt/Pol Rec.
> **Enr 2240.** B 1000. G 1240. Elem 1440. Sec 800. US 70. Host 2050. Other 120. Accepted: 60%. Yield: 90%. Avg class size: 18.

Fac 232. M 30. F 202. US 55. Host 172. Other 5. Adv Deg: 10%.
Grad '05—160. Col—150. US Col—60. (Vassar 2, U of PA 2, Columbia 1, David-
son 1, Sarah Lawrence 1, Tulane 1). Avg SAT: M/V—1073.
Tui '05-'06: Day $7200. Aid: 115 pupils ($280,000).
Summer: Acad Rem Rec. Tui Day $175. 3 wks.
Bldgs 5. Class rms 125. 2 Libs 32,000 vols. Sci labs 9. Comp labs 7. Auds 1. Art
studios 6. Music studios 2. Gyms 1. Fields 5.
Est 1939. Nonprofit. (Sept-June). Assoc: AASSA ACCAS SACS.

Located in Ecuador's capital city, the American School enrolls students from
the international business and diplomatic community. The school's national section
follows a basic Ecuadorian curriculum with special emphasis on English, while the
international section, with a smaller student-teacher ratio to insure individualized
attention, follows a modified American curriculum that employs English as the
medium of instruction.

A junior college division features business administration and marketing programs.

THE BRITISH SCHOOL
QUITO

Day — Coed Gr PS-12

Quito, Ecuador. Casilla 17-21-52. Tel: 593-2-2374649. **Fax:** 593-2-2374650. **EST.**
www.bsq.edu.ec   **E-mail:** info@bsq.edu.ec
Daryl Barker, Dir. BA, MA, MEd. **Soledad Cordova, Adm.**
Col Prep. Gen Acad. IB Diploma. Curr—Intl UK. **Exams**—CEEB. **Feat**—Span
Comp_Sci Studio_Art. **Supp**—ESL LD.
Activities—Service.
Enr 240. Elem 202. Sec 38. US 16. Host 138. Other 86. Avg class size: 15.
Fac 32. M 6. F 26. US 2. Host 4. Other 26. Adv Deg: 18%.
Grad '05—14. US Col—3. (Boston U, Mesa St, U of OK).
Tui '05-'06: Day $4200-8880 (+$2000). **Aid:** 14 pupils ($56,000).
Plant val $750,000. Bldgs 6. Class rms 28. 2 Libs 8000 vols. Sci labs 2. Comp labs
1. Art studios 1. Music studios 1. Fields 1. Courts 2. Pools 1.
Est 1995. Nonprofit. Tri (Sept-June).

The school follows the UK national curriculum and emphasizes core subjects
such as English, math and science. Students participate in a Spanish and humanities
program that includes courses in language, history, geography, culture and customs.
Secondary schoolers continue to study Spanish and prepare for the International
Baccalaureate Diploma.

GUYANA

Sq. Miles: 82,980 (About the size of Idaho). **Country Pop:** 765,283
(2005). **Capital:** Georgetown, pop. 250,000. **Terrain:** Coastal plain,
inland highlands, rainforest, savanna. **Ethnic Group(s):** East_Indian
African Amerindian Caucasian Chinese. **Religion(s):** Christian Hindu

Muslim. **Other Language(s):** English Guyanese_Creole Carib Arawak. **Government:** Republic. **Independence:** 1966 (from United Kingdom). **GDP:** $658 million (2004). Agriculture 37%. Industry 20%. Services 43%. **Currency:** Guyanese Dollar (G$).

GEORGETOWN INTERNATIONAL ACADEMY
Day — Coed Gr PS-12

Georgetown, Guyana. 9-10 Delhi St. Tel: 592-226-1595. Fax: 592-226-1459. EST+1.
Contact: Dept of State, 3170 Georgetown Pl, Washington, DC 20521.
www.amschoolguyana.net   E-mail: admin@amschoolguyana.net
Rev. Canon Thurston Riehl, Dir. BA, MEd.
   Col Prep. Curr—US. Exams—AP CEEB. AP—Eng Fr Bio Environ_Sci Psych.
      Feat—Span Comp_Sci Studio_Art Music.
   Enr 66. Accepted: 95%. Yield: 99%. Avg class size: 10.
   Fac 15. Adv Deg: 86%.
   Grad '05—8. Col—8. US Col—5. (Cornell, Syracuse, Notre Dame, NYU).
   Tui '05-'06: Day $7779-7920 (+$3400). Aid: 19 pupils ($25,394).
   Plant val $837,000. Bldgs 2. Libs 1. Sci labs 1. Comp labs 1. Art studios 1. Gyms
      2. Fields 2.
   Est 1971. Nonprofit. Quar (Sept-June). Assoc: A/OPR/OS SACS.

Offering a curriculum compatible with US elementary and secondary schools, the school also helps students understand the history and geography of Guyana and the Caribbean. A range of minicourse options provides after-school enrichment.

PARAGUAY

Sq. Miles: 157,047 (About the size of California). **Country Pop:** 5,500,000. **Capital:** Asuncion, pop. 539,000. **Terrain:** East of the Paraguay River: grassy plains, wooded hills, tropical forests; west of the Paraguay River: low, flat, marshy plain. **Ethnic Group(s):** Mestizo. **Religion(s):** Roman_Catholic Mennonite Protestant. **Other Language(s):** Spanish Guarani. **Government:** Constitutional Republic. **Independence:** 1811 (from Spain). **GDP:** $7.98 billion (2004). Agriculture 28%. Industry 24%. Services 48%. **Currency:** Paraguayan Guarani (PG).

AMERICAN SCHOOL OF ASUNCION
Day — Coed Gr PS-12

Asuncion, Paraguay. Avenida Espana 1175. Tel: 595-21-600-479. Fax: 595-21-603-518. EST+1.
www.asa.edu.py   E-mail: asagator@asa.edu.py
Dennis M. Klumpp, Dir Gen.

Col Prep. Curr—Nat US. **Supp Lang**—Span. **Exams**—CEEB. **AP**—Span Calc Eur_Hist US_Hist Comp_Govt & Pol Psych. **Feat**—Fr Port Anat & Physiol Environ_Sci Econ Studio_Art Music Accounting. **Supp**—ESL.
Enr 583.
Fac 59.
Tui '05-'06: Day $3902-4390 (+$5500).
Est 1955. Nonprofit. Sem (Aug-July). Assoc: AASSA A/OPR/OS SACS.

PERU

Sq. Miles: 496,225 (About three times larger than California). **Country Pop:** 27,925,628 (2005). **Capital:** Lima, pop. 8,270,000 (2000). **Terrain:** Western coastal plains, central rugged mountains, eastern lowlands with tropical forests. **Ethnic Group(s):** Indian Mestizo. **Religion(s):** Roman_ Catholic. **Official Language(s):** Spanish Quechua Aymara. **Government:** Constitutional Republic. **Independence:** 1821 (from Spain). **GDP:** $67.1 billion (2004). Agriculture 4%. Industry 12%. Manufacturing 15%. Services 65%. **Currency:** Peruvian Sol (S/.).

HUASCARAN INTERNATIONAL SCHOOL
Day — Coed Gr K-8

Huaraz, Ancash, Peru. Casilla Postal 347. Tel: 51-43-452126. Fax: 51-43-452126. EST.
www.geocities.com/colegio_huascaran   E-mail: fjohnston@hisperu.edu.pe
Frank Johnston, Dir. BSS, MA.
  Gen Acad. Curr—Intl. **Feat**—Span Comp_Sci. **Supp**—Dev_Read ESL.
  Sports—Basket.
  Enr 37. B 16. G 21. Elem 37. US 2. Host 28. Other 7. Accepted: 100%. Avg class size: 10.
  Fac 5. M 3. F 2. US 2. Other 3.
  Grad '05—2.
  Tui '05-'06: Day $2700.
  Class rms 4. Libs 1. Sci labs 1. Comp labs 1. Dance studios 1. Fields 2. Courts 1.
  Est 2000. Nonprofit. Sem (Aug-June).

Located in the midst of the Andes Mountains, HIS shares its campus with Colegio Huascaran, a traditional Peruvian school. The two schools operate independently, although they share certain resources and occasionally compete with each other athletically. This small elementary school offers a program featuring characteristics found in Canadian, American, Australian and British schools.

In addition to its international pupils, HIS enrolls some Peruvian students who typically display some facility with English and who must complete home study to meet national curricular requirements. Expatriate pupils whose parents work for the Antamina Mine Company pay no tuition fees.

AMERICAN SCHOOL OF LIMA
(COLEGIO FRANKLIN DELANO ROOSEVELT)
Day — Coed Gr PS-12

18 Lima, Peru. Apartado 18-0977. Tel: 51-1-435-0890. Fax: 51-1-702-4500. EST.
www.amersol.edu.pe   E-mail: fdr@amersol.edu.pe
Carol Kloznik, Supt. BA, MA, PhD. **Guadalupe Mendez, Dir.** BA, MA, PhD. **Nora Marquez, Adm.**

> Col Prep. IB PYP. IB MYP. IB Diploma. Curr—Intl US. Supp Lang—Span. Exams—ACT CEEB. Feat—Creative_Writing Fr Comp_Sci Web_Design Econ Photog Studio_Art Theater_Arts Band Journ Outdoor_Ed. Supp—ESL LD Rem_Math.
>
> Sports—Basket Rugby Soccer Softball Swim Track Volley. Activities—Acad Arts Govt/Pol.
>
> Enr 1266. Elem 887. Sec 379. US 263. Host 744. Other 259. Accepted: 97%. Avg class size: 22.
>
> Fac 124. M 27. F 90/7. US 46. Host 64. Other 14. Adv Deg: 46%.
>
> Grad '05—103. Avg SAT: M/V—1032. Avg ACT: 22.
>
> Tui '05-'06: Day $8850-9900 (+$1050). Aid: 6 pupils ($11,252).
>
> Summer: Acad Enrich Rec. 4 wks.
>
> Bldgs 11. Class rms 105. Lib 58,000 vols. Sci labs 7. Comp labs 5. Theaters 2. Art studios 3. Music studios 4. Gyms 2. Fields 4. Courts 5.
>
> Est 1946. Nonprofit. Sem (Aug-June). Assoc: AASSA A/OPR/OS SACS.

Peruvians account for over half of the enrollment at this school, with American students making up the next largest group. Both American and Peruvian college preparatory curricula are offered, with nearly all instruction in English. Emphasis is placed on Latin American studies courses, which are taught in Spanish. In addition to the American and Peruvian curricula, the school conducts a full International Baccalaureate program (culminating in the IB Diploma).

Most American students prepare for the US College Boards and go on to colleges in the United States. Assistance for pupils with learning differences is available.

MARKHAM COLLEGE
Day — Coed Gr PS-12

Lima, Peru. Apartado 18-1048, Miraflores. Tel: 51-1-241-7677. Fax: 51-1-241-7678. EST.
www.markham.edu.pe   E-mail: headmaster@markham.edu.pe
Trevor S. McKinlay, Prin. BD, DipEd, MA.

> Col Prep. IB Diploma. Curr—Intl Nat UK. Bilingual—Span. Exams—IGCSE. Feat—Fr Comp_Sci Relig Studio_Art Music. Supp—Dev_Read ESL Rem_Math Rem_Read.
>
> Enr 1865. B 1296. G 569. US 22. Host 1809. Other 34. Avg class size: 25.
>
> Fac 127. M 56. F 71. Host 86. Other 41.
>
> Grad '05—124. Col—104. US Col—10. (MIT, Boston U, Lafayette, Notre Dame, Purdue, U of Rochester).
>
> Tui '05-'06: Day $3400-6800 (+$2000-6000).
>
> Summer: Acad Rev Rem Rec. Tui Day $200. 6 wks.
>
> Bldgs 20. Class rms 100. 2 Libs 21,000 vols. Sci labs 14. Comp labs 8. Auds 1.

Theaters 1. Art studios 5. Music studios 2. Gyms 2. Fields 5. Courts 5. Tennis courts 2. Squash courts 2. Pools 1.
Est 1945. Nonprofit. Sem (Mar-Dec).

Founded to meet the educational needs of sons of Anglo-Peruvians and British expatriates working in Peru, the school has experienced a change in student population over the years and now serves a coeducational, largely native enrollment. Markham's bilingual programming, however, continues to blend British and Peruvian systems. Overall, just over half of the curriculum is delivered in English, with this proportion rising as high as 70 percent in some sections of the upper school. Pupils prepare for the IGCSE examinations, then engage in the two-year International Baccalaureate program. Boys and girls may opt not to pursue the IB Diploma, in which case they follow the Peruvian national program. University preparation is of paramount importance in both sections.

To facilitate an understanding of the country among its students, Markham schedules expeditions and excursions to all parts of Peru. In a typical year, about half of the pupils engage in a trip outside the city limits. Options, which vary according to age, include outings to coastal areas; tours of regional cities and the jungle; extended community service projects in remote areas; and adventure treks to sites such as the Amazonian Rain Forest and sections of the Andes Mountains in Huascaran National Park.

An activity period is scheduled daily; each student takes part in at least two activities per week. In addition, pupils may participate in interscholastic or intramural athletics.

SURINAME

Sq. Miles: 63,037 (Slightly larger than Georgia). **Country Pop:** 438,144 (2005). **Capital:** Paramaribo, pop. 243,556. **Terrain:** Varies from coastal swamps to savanna to hills. **Ethnic Group(s):** Hindustani Creole Javanese Maroon Amerindians Chinese. **Religion(s):** Hindu Muslim Roman_Catholic Dutch_Reformed Moravian Jewish Baha'I. **Official Language(s):** Dutch. **Other Language(s):** English Sranan_Tongo Hindustani Javanese. **Government:** Constitutional Democracy. **Independence:** 1975 (from The Netherlands). **GDP:** $1.89 billion (2004). Agriculture 13%. Industry 22%. Services 65%. **Currency:** Surinamese Guilder (Sf.).

AMERICAN COOPERATIVE SCHOOL
Day — Coed Gr PS-12

Paramaribo, Suriname. Lawtonlaan 20. Tel: 597-499-806. Fax: 597-427-188. EST+2.
Contact: 8105 NW 74th St, Miami, FL 33116.
E-mail: acssuriname@yahoo.com

Avery M. Stewart, Dir. BEd, MEd.
  Col Prep. Curr—US. **Exams**—ACT CEEB TOEFL. **Feat**—Dutch Span Comp_Sci
    Studio_Art Drama Music. **Supp**—ESL.
  Sports—Basket Soccer Swim Volley. **Activities**—Govt/Pol Rec.
  Enr 101. B 53. G 48. Elem 62. Sec 39. US 17. Host 16. Other 68. Accepted: 90%.
    Yield: 98%. Avg class size: 8.
  Fac 17. M 5/1. F 9/2. US 10. Host 1. Other 6. Adv Deg: 23%.
  Grad '05—14. Col—3. US Col—1. (Georgetown).
  Tui '05-'06: Day $3500-6000 (+$750).
  Plant val $3,300,000. Bldgs 1. Class rms 15. Lib 8500 vols. Sci labs 1. Comp labs
    1. Gym/auds 1. Fields 1.
  Est 1965. Nonprofit. Nondenom Christian. Quar (Sept-June). Assoc: SACS.

Taught from a Christian perspective, ACS' program follows the US model in
preparing students for admission to US and international colleges. Performing arts
activities supplement academics. Intramural and interscholastics athletics are also
available.

URUGUAY

Sq. Miles: 68,000 (Slightly smaller than Oklahoma). **Country Pop:**
3,415,920 (2005). **Capital:** Montevideo, pop. 1,400,000. **Terrain:** Plains
and low hills **Ethnic Group(s):** European African Mestizo. **Religion(s):**
Roman_Catholic Protestant Jewish. **Official Language(s):** Spanish.
Government: Republic. **Independence:** 1825 (from Brazil). **GDP:** $13.2
billion (2004). Agriculture 7%. Industry 28%. Services 65%. **Currency:**
Uruguayan Peso ($U).

URUGUAYAN AMERICAN SCHOOL
Day — Coed Gr PS-12

Montevideo, Uruguay. Saldun de Rodriguez 2375, CP 11500. Tel: 5982-600-7681.
  Fax: 5982-606-1935. EST+2.
www.uas.edu.uy   E-mail: contact@uas.edu.uy
David E. Deuel, Dir. MS.
  Col Prep. Curr—Nat US. **Exams**—AP CEEB. **AP**—Eng Span Calc Bio Studio_Art.
    Feat—Fr Port Comp_Sci Music Indus_Arts Home_Ec. **Supp**—Dev_Read ESL
    Makeup Rem_Math Rem_Read Rev Tut.
  Sports—Basket Fencing F_Hockey Soccer Softball Volley. **Activities**—Acad
    Govt/Pol Rec.
  Enr 272. B 136. G 136. Elem 205. Sec 67. US 65. Host 90. Other 117. Accepted:
    100%. Avg class size: 17.
  Fac 42. M 7/3. F 20/12. US 8. Host 31. Other 3.
  Grad '05—7.
  Tui '05-'06: Day $U3000-9500 (+$U4000).
  Summer: Ages 6-14. Acad Enrich Rev Rec. Tui Day $U3000. 2 wks.
  Plant val $4,250,000. Bldgs 4. Class rms 26. Lib 16,000 vols. Sci labs 2. Comp

labs 1. Auds 1. Theaters 1. Art studios 1. Music studios 1. Gyms 1. Fields 1. Courts 1.

Est 1958. Nonprofit. Sem (Aug-June). Assoc: AASSA A/OPR/OS SACS.

Following US guidelines, the elementary program at UAS bases its grade-level organization on achievement. The dual program in the elementary years prepares students for secondary education either locally or abroad. The secondary school curriculum features Advanced Placement courses and an integrated Uruguayan studies program. Students prepare for the US College Boards and subsequent entry into colleges in the US.

ST. CLARE'S COLLEGE
URUGUAY
Day — Coed Gr K-12

Punta del Este, Uruguay. California y Los Medanos, San Rafael. Tel: 5984-249-0200. Fax: 5984-249-0200. EST+2.
www.stclares.edu.uy   E-mail: info@stclares.edu.uy
Dilamar Larrosa, Dir.

Col Prep. IB Diploma. Curr—Intl. **Bilingual**—Span. **Exams**—IGCSE. **Feat**—Comp_Sci Econ Studio_Art. **Supp**—ESL.

Sports—F_Hockey Hand Rugby Soccer. **Activities**—Arts Rec Service.

Enr 256. B 115. G 141. Accepted: 10%. Yield: 95%. Avg class size: 18.

Fac 62. M 6/18. F 12/26. US 2. Host 51. Other 9. Adv Deg: 14%.

Tui '05-'06: Day $U200-300 (+$U80).

Bldgs 2. Class rms 19. 3 Libs 2100 vols. Sci labs 1. Comp labs 1. Art studios 1. Music studios 1. Dance studios 1. Fields 2. Courts 1.

Est 2004. Inc. (Mar-Dec).

This bilingual school leads a largely Uruguayan student body through a college preparatory program that progresses from the IGCSE exams to the IB Diploma. During the school day, pupils fulfill a 160-hour community service requirement that includes such options as reading to special-needs children, workshop collaboration and recreation organization for other schools. Boys and girls engage in sports (which may include interscholastic competition) three times weekly, both during and after school hours.

VENEZUELA

Sq. Miles: 352,143 (Slightly more than twice the size of California). **Country Pop:** 25,375,281 (2005). **Capital:** Caracas, pop. 3,600,000 (2004). **Terrain:** Andes Mountains and Maracaibo Lowlands in northwest; central plains; Guiana Highlands in southeast. **Ethnic Group(s):** Spanish Italian Portuguese Arab German African. **Religion(s):** Roman_Catholic Protestant. **Official Language(s):** Spanish. **Government:** Federal Republic. **Independence:** 1811 (from Spain). **GDP:** $115 billion (2004). Agriculture 5%. Industry 48%. Services 47%. **Currency:** Venezuelan Bolivar (VBs).

ESCUELA CAMPO ALEGRE
Day — Coed Gr PS-12

Caracas, Venezuela. Apartado del Este 30382, Final Calle La Cinta, Las Mercedes. Tel: 58-212-993-5446. Fax: 58-212-993-0219. EST+1.
Contact: 8424 NW 56th St, Ste CCS 00007, Miami, FL 33166.
www.eca.com.ve   E-mail: info@eca.com.ve
Jean K. Vahey, Supt. BA, MS. **Joan Bastianini, Adm.**
  Col Prep. IB Diploma. Curr—Intl US. **Exams**—CEEB. **Feat**—Fr Span Environ_Sci Comp_Sci Venezuelan_Hist Econ Psych Studio_Art Theater_Arts Band. **Supp**—ESL LD Rem_Read.
  Sports—Basket Soccer Softball Swim Tennis Volley. **Activities**—Acad Arts Govt/Pol Rec Service.
  Enr 635. B 321. G 314. Elem 443. Sec 192. US 183. Host 112. Other 340. Accepted: 90%. Yield: 100%. Avg class size: 16.
  Fac 91. M 33. F 55/3. US 39. Host 31. Other 21. Adv Deg: 37%.
  Grad '05—54. Col—50. US Col—31. (Boston U 3, U of Miami 2, Swarthmore 2, Suffolk 2, Brown 1, Wesleyan U 1). Avg SAT: M/V—1105.
  Tui '05-'06: Day $6990-18,220 (+$2200-7200).
  Bldgs 7. Class rms 77. Lib 40,000 vols. Sci labs 3. Comp labs 5. Auds 2. Theaters 1. Art studios 3. Music studios 3. Dance studios 1. Gyms 1. Fields 1. Courts 6. Pools 1.
  Est 1937. Nonprofit. Sem (Aug-June). Assoc: AASSA ACCAS A/OPR/OS CIS SACS.

Serving American expatriate children and English-speaking pupils from many other nations, Escuela Campo Alegre follows a US-style curriculum that places particular emphasis on both the Spanish language and the history and culture of Venezuela (and Latin America in general). Spanish classes begin in kindergarten, while French courses commence in grade 7. The International Baccalaureate Diploma Program is an integral aspect of the high school curriculum.

An agreeable climate allows for year-round outdoor physical activities, as well as extensive field trips.

INTERNATIONAL SCHOOL OF CARACAS
(COLEGIO INTERNACIONAL DE CARACAS)
Day — Coed Gr PS-12

Caracas, Venezuela. Tel: 58-212-945-0444. Fax: 58-212-945-0533. EST+1.
Contact: Pakmail 6030, PO Box 025304, Miami, FL 33102.
www.cic-caracas.org   E-mail: cic@cic-caracas.org
Winthrop W. Sargent, Jr., Supt. BA, MEd.
  Col Prep. IB MYP. IB Diploma. Curr—Intl US. **Exams**—CEEB. **Feat**—Fr Span Econ Geog Visual_Arts Drama Music. **Supp**—EFL.
  Enr 225. B 120. G 105.
  Tui '05-'06: Day $12,631-17,630.

Est 1956. Nonprofit. Sem (Aug-June). Assoc: AASSA A/OPR/OS SACS.

ESCUELA BELLA VISTA
Day — Coed Gr K-12

Maracaibo, Venezuela. Ave Cecilio Acosta Calle 67, Sector La Lago 4001. Tel: 58-261-791-1674. Fax: 58-261-793-9417. EST+1.
Contact: Buzoom C-Mar-P-1815, PO Box 02-8537, Miami, FL 33102.
www.ebv.org.ve
Stephen Sibley, Supt. MA.
> **Col Prep. IB Diploma. Curr**—Intl US. **Feat**—Fr Comp_Sci Studio_Art Music.
> **Enr 430.**
> **Tui '02-'03: Day $7715-10,825** (+$270-1870).
> **Est 1948.** Sem (Aug-June). Assoc: AASSA SACS.

INTERNATIONAL SCHOOL OF MONAGAS
Day — Coed Gr PS-12

Maturin, Monagas, Venezuela. Km 1, Carretera via a La Toscana, Sector Costo Abajo. Tel: 58-414-992-1392. Fax: 58-414-764-4354. EST+1.
Contact: MUN 39, PO Box 02-5352, Miami, FL 33102.
www.ismonagas.com   E-mail: ism97@telcel.net.ve
Eric Spindler, Head. EdD.
> **Col Prep. Curr**—US. **Exams**—CEEB. **Supp**—Dev_Read EFL ESL Makeup Rem_Math Rem_Read Rev Tut.
> **Enr 110.** B 54. G 56. Elem 78. Sec 32. US 24. Host 50. Other 36. Accepted: 90%. Avg class size: 8.
> **Fac 20.** M 8. F 12. US 14. Host 5. Other 1. Adv Deg: 60%.
> **Grad '05—1. Col—1.** Avg SAT: M/V—1100.
> **Tui '02-'03: Day $6360.**
> Plant val $3,500,000. Bldgs 6. Class rms 33. Lib 8400 vols. Sci labs 2. Comp labs 1. Art studios 1. Music studios 1. Gyms 1. Fields 2.
> **Est 1997.** Nonprofit. Quar (Aug-June). Assoc: AASSA SACS.

Founded to meet the educational needs of elementary and secondary students of its corporate sponsors (various oil companies), other members of the area expatriate community and local families attracted to the school's international program, ISM bases its college preparatory curriculum on the US educational model. All instruction is in English, with the exception of Spanish language classes (which convene one or two periods daily). SAT preparation is part of the curriculum.

Soccer, volleyball, basketball and softball constitute the sports program, while Model UN, student council and forensics represent other extracurricular options. Company-sponsored pupils incur a higher tuition fee.

MORROCOY INTERNATIONAL SCHOOL
Day — Coed Gr PS-10

Puerto Ordaz, Bolivar, Venezuela. Calle Yuruani, Manz 131-01. Tel: 58-286-952-00-16. Fax: 58-286-952-18-61. EST+1.
Contact: MUN 4051, PO Box 025352, Miami, FL 33102.
E-mail: mischool@cantv.net
Howard Robertson, Head. BA, MEd.
   Gen Acad. Curr—Intl. Supp—ESL.
   Est 1990. Quar (Aug-June).

COLEGIO INTERNACIONAL DE CARABOBO
Day — Coed Gr PS-12

Valencia, Venezuela. Apartado 103. Tel: 58-241-842-65-51. Fax: 58-241-842-65-10. EST+1.
Contact: VLN 1010, PO Box 025685, Miami, FL 33102.
www.cic-valencia.org.ve   E-mail: admin@cic-valencia.org.ve
Joe Houston Walker, Dir. MA.
   Col Prep. Curr—US. Exams—ACT AP CEEB TOEFL. AP—Fr Span Calc Chem Eur_Hist US_Hist Psych Studio_Art. Feat—Comp_Sci Web_Design. Supp—ESL LD.
   Sports—Basket Soccer Softball Volley. Activities—Acad Arts Govt/Pol Media Rec Service.
   Enr 322. B 188. G 134. Avg class size: 15.
   Fac 53. M 11. F 33/9. US 24. Host 23. Other 6.
   Grad '05—18. Col—18. US Col—11. (Boston Col 2, Bentley 1, SUNY-Stony Brook 1, U of CA-Berkeley 1, Duke 1, Johnson & Wales 1). Avg SAT: M/V—1135.
   Tui '05-'06: Day $7700-13,000 (+$5000-6000).
   Summer: Gr 1-6. Acad Rev Rem. Tui Day $410. 5 wks.
   Bldgs 8. Class rms 48. 2 Libs 16,200 vols. Sci labs 3. Comp labs 4. Auds 1. Gyms 1. Fields 2.
   Est 1955. Nonprofit. Sem (Aug-June). Assoc: AASSA A/OPR/OS SACS.

Founded by four North American companies—Celanese, Firestone, Goodyear and US Rubber—this school provides a US-style college preparatory program. Instruction is in English, although pupils take daily Spanish courses. Most students enroll from either Venezuela or the US; the rest of the boys and girls come from approximately two dozen other nations. Graduates typically matriculate at competitive universities in the US.

ILLUSTRATED
ANNOUNCEMENTS

INDEX TO
ILLUSTRATED ANNOUNCEMENTS

In Your Own Words

Educators and parents have long trusted Porter Sargent for independent, objective school profiles available nowhere else.

Your program's Illustrated Announcement can support this mission, and it will be seen daily by:

- Parents
- Headmasters, and admissions and guidance counselors
- Consultants and vendors
- A worldwide network of educational professionals

Each reference-quality title is the book of record for its field, with a long shelf-life and high per-copy readership.

Please call 617-523-1670 or E-mail announcements@portersargent.com for details on joining the next edition.

The Handbook of Private Schools * The Directory for Exceptional Children
Schools Abroad of Interest to Americans * Guide to Summer Camps and Schools

AMERICAN OVERSEAS SCHOOL OF ROME

Via Cassia 811
00189 Rome, ITALY
Tel: +39 06 334381
Fax: +39 06 3326 2608
Web: www.aosr.org

The American Overseas School of Rome is an independent, non-denominational, non-profit, college preparatory, coeducational day and boarding school serving Italian, American, and foreign communities in Rome. The school was founded in 1946 by a group of English-speaking families, under the sponsorship of the United States and British ambassadors and the Director-General of the United Nations Food and Agricultural Organization. Located northwest of the center of Rome, the school is easily accessible to the international community.

The mission of the American Overseas School of Rome is to offer an excellent academic program and to create a harmonious atmosphere within which an international student body learns to live and work together in an American educational system. We are committed to teaching the students in our multi-cultural, mulit-lingual environment the best from the past, while giving them the thinking and technological skills required for the future.

Advanced Placement courses are available in English, Math, Science, Social Studies, Foreign Languages, Music and Art. The school also offers the IB Diploma Programme. A supervised boarding facility is available for high school girls and boys with good to excellent academic records and character recommendations.

On its present site, modern elementary and high school wings, each containing a library, were constructed around the original Roman villa. A full size gymnasium was added, and a playing field purchased, which more than doubled the area of the campus to over ten thousand square meters.

Accredited by the Middle States Association of Colleges and Secondary Schools, American Overseas School of Rome is a member of College Board, ECIS, NACAC, AAIE, MAIS, and RISA, and it is an associate member of NESA.

PATANA

Bangkok Patana School
The British International School in Thailand

2/38 Soi Lasalle, Sukhumvit 105, Bangkok 10260, THAILAND
Tel: 662 398-0200   Fax: 662 399-3179
E-mail: reception@patana.ac.th   Website: www.patana.ac.th

Mr. Andy Homden, Head of School

Bangkok Patana School was founded in 1957 to provide a British-style education for the children of expatriates living in Thailand. A not-for-profit foundation, the school currently has an enrolment of 2,140 students representing 50 nationalities. Some 9% of the students are US citizens and the school is recognised by the US State Department as suitable for Government employees. Other major national groups are UK (22%), Thai (21%) and Australian (8%). The school is accredited by the New England Association of Schools and Colleges (NEASC) as well as by the Council of International Schools (CIS). Bangkok Patana is also a member of the International Baccalaureate Organisation (IBO).

The Elementary and Secondary Divisions, on one campus, enrol students from two and a half to eighteen years of age. The school follows the UK National Curriculum adapted for its international student body and position in Thailand, and Secondary examination courses: General Certificate of Secondary Education/IGCSE at age sixteen and the International Baccalaureate/Patana Graduate Diploma at eighteen. Patana is also a testing centre for PSAT, SAT(I) and SAT(II). Over 90% of graduating students are accepted into leading colleges and universities worldwide including Yale, Cambridge and the London School of Economics (LSE).

The 44 acre campus in South East Bangkok provides excellent purpose-built facilities for the academic, extra-curricular and sports programmes which Bangkok Patana offers.

SAINT MAUR
INTERNATIONAL SCHOOL
83 Yamate-Cho, Naka-ku
Yokohama-Shi, Kanagawa-ken
JAPAN 231-8654
Tel: +81-45-641-5751   Fax: +81-45-641-6688
E-mail: office@stmaur.ac.jp   Web: www.stmaur.ac.jp

Saint Maur International School, established in 1872, continues its pioneering spirit and commitment to providing students of all nationalities, genders and beliefs with a quality international education within a caring family environment.

The school, noted as a leader in educational excellence and innovation, was the first school in Japan to introduce the International Montessori Program, the International General Certificate of Secondary Education (IGCSE) and International Primary Curriculum (IPC), as well as the Lions Quest values program, the Associated Board of the Royal Schools of Music (ABRSM), and the Trinity College of Music examinations. The school also offers the International Baccalaureate as well as the Advanced Placement courses and examinations.

Situated in the residential and historical area of Yokohama within well-maintained, earthquake reinforced, and air-conditioned/heated buildings, members of the school community are assured a safe and pleasant environment. The range of excellent facilities, combined with careful scheduling enables students of all ages to participate in a variety of clubs, extracurricular activities, and support programs which further enhance the development of each student's mental, physical, spiritual, creative and social well-being.

On graduating, 95-100% of students enter fine universities and colleges throughout the world.

ST. STEPHEN'S SCHOOL
ROME, ITALY

Philip Allen, *Headmaster*

Located in the historic center of Rome, St. Stephen's School is a nondenominational, co-educational college preparatory school which has served the American and international communities in Rome and Italy since 1964. The boarding and day program offered spans grades 9 through 12, with a postgraduate year option. In addition to its regular 4 year program, St. Stephen's welcomes a limited number of students, usually in their junior year, from respected American preparatory schools who wish to take advantage of our curriculum, especially with regard to our Classical Studies, Art History, Latin and Italian classes for one or two semesters.

The curriculum adapts a traditional independent school model to its unique Roman setting and fosters rigorous learning in an atmosphere of international fellowship, harmony and trust. St. Stephen's School is accredited by the New England Association of Schools and Colleges and the European Council of International Schools. Since 1975, it has offered the International Baccalaureate program, which is now a recognized entrance qualification for universities throughout the world. The school's early recognition of the potential importance of the IB attests to its pioneering spirit in the world of international education.

Enrollment is maintained at around 210 pupils because St. Stephen's believes that students are best served by keeping the student body small, thus allowing each student wider access to our first-rate faculty and campus resources. These resources include new chemistry and physics laboratories; a renovated library and the newly renovated performing arts/assembly hall and tennis, volleyball, and basketball courts; new art studios; and a photography lab, dance studio, and landscaped courtyard and terrace. In further pursuit of its educational mission, St. Stephen's maintains a selective admissions procedure. Students are chosen on the basis of personal promise and their potential to benefit from the school's curriculum. St. Stephen's welcomes students of all races, nationalities, religions and persuasions.

With students from approximately 40 nations, St. Stephen's is truly international in character. Students who have elected to follow the traditional American high school curriculum, many of whom have also participated in our AP program, have recently enrolled in North American universities such as Columbia, Cornell, Dartmouth, Swarthmore, Princeton, Yale, Wesleyan, Stanford, and the Universities of California and Chicago. About 1/2 of the graduates of 2005 entered universities in the UK.

The two and one half acre campus—just a ten minute walk from the Colosseum and the Roman Forum—offers students unique cultural, educational, and recreational advantages as well as frequent school-sponsored travel opportunities to other cities in Italy and the Mediterranean area. Life at St. Stephen's is intense and enjoyable with a happy blend of relaxation and rigor.

Contact: Admissions Office, St. Stephen's School, Via Aventina 3, 00153 Rome, Italy. Tel: (3906) 575.0605. Fax: (3906) 574.1941. E-mail: ststephens@ststephens-rome.com. Website: www.ststephens-rome.com.

WESLEY COLLEGE

577 St. Kilda Rd.
Melbourne, Victoria, AUSTRALIA 3004

Tel: 61 3 81026375
Fax: 61 3 95109150
Web: www.wesleycollege.net

Wesley was established in 1866 and is Registered School No. 1 in Victoria. Wesley is a diverse, dynamic learning community, committed to the care and flourishing of the whole person.

Catering for girls and boys from Kindergarten to Year 12 of whatever faith, race or ability, Wesley has three campuses in Elsternwick, Glen Waverley and Prahran, each having its own distinctive environment and character.

Wesley offers International Baccalaureate and has an enviable track record in academic, arts and sporting achievements as it prepares students for life beyond the classroom.

THE PORTER SARGENT HANDBOOK SERIES

11 Beacon St. Ste. 1400 Boston, MA 02108-3099 USA
Tel: 617-523-1670 Fax: 617-523-1021
info@portersargent.com www.portersargent.com

Tools for Independent Evaluation

In 1914, educator and writer Porter Sargent introduced *The Handbook of Private Schools* because he felt educators, administrators and parents needed an objective guide to quality schools and programs emphasizing the needs of the individual student.

The development of the Porter Sargent Handbook Series followed that very simple aim. Each publication is a source book of information for those who need—and ought—to know about the advantage of independent instruction, providing the most up-to-date narrative and statistical information on schools and programs serving those who seek out the best education worldwide.

The Handbook of Private Schools * The Directory for Exceptional Children
Schools Abroad of Interest to Americans * Guide to Summer Camps and Schools

ASSOCIATIONS AND ORGANIZATIONS

The list that follows comprises organizations and associations that offer information or services pertinent to nonpublic elementary or secondary education. Accrediting Associations conduct formal evaluations of schools interested in gaining accreditation; in some cases, accredited institutions are eligible for membership benefits. Advocacy Organizations provide assistance and active support for members of a specified population. Professional Organizations offer membership and benefits to specified professionals. School Membership Associations provide benefits for member schools, but do not have a formal accreditation process. Student Exchange Organizations provide intercultural learning opportunities around the world for students, young adults and teachers.

ACCREDITING ASSOCIATIONS

COUNCIL OF INTERNATIONAL SCHOOLS
21A Lavant St, Petersfield, Hampshire, GU32 3EL.
Tel: 44-1730-263131. Fax: 44-1730-268913.
E-mail: cois@cois.org. Web: www.cois.org.

**MIDDLE STATES ASSOCIATION OF COLLEGES
AND SCHOOLS**
3624 Market St, Philadelphia, PA 19104.
Tel: 215-662-5603. Fax: 215-662-0957.
E-mail: info@css-msa.org. Web: www.css-msa.org.

**NEW ENGLAND ASSOCIATION OF SCHOOLS
AND COLLEGES**
209 Burlington Rd, Bedford, MA 01730.
Tel: 781-271-0022. Fax: 781-271-0950.
E-mail: wbennett@neasc.org. Web: www.neasc.org.

**SOUTHERN ASSOCIATION OF COLLEGES AND SCHOOLS
COUNCIL ON ACCREDITATION
AND SCHOOL IMPROVEMENT**
1866 Southern Ln, Decatur, GA 30033.
Tel: 404-679-4500. Fax: 404-679-4541.
Web: www.sacscasi.org.

WESTERN ASSOCIATION OF SCHOOLS AND COLLEGES
533 Airport Blvd, Ste 200, Burlingame, CA 94010.
Tel: 650-696-1060. Fax: 650-696-1867.
E-mail: mail@acswasc.org. Web: www.acswasc.org.

ADVOCACY ORGANIZATIONS
GENERAL

FOREIGN SERVICE YOUTH FOUNDATION
PO Box 39185, Washington, DC 20016.
Tel: 301-404-6655.
E-mail: fsyf@fsyf.org. Web: www.fsyf.org.

ADVOCACY ORGANIZATIONS
PRIVATE EDUCATION

AMERICAN-SCANDINAVIAN FOUNDATION
58 Park Ave, New York, NY 10016.
Tel: 212-879-9779. Fax: 212-249-3444.
E-mail: info@amscan.org. Web: www.amscan.org.

PROFESSIONAL ASSOCIATIONS

**ASSOCIATION FOR THE ADVANCEMENT OF
INTERNATIONAL EDUCATION**
Sheridan College, PO Box 1500, Sheridan, WY 82801.
Tel: 307-674-6446. Fax: 307-674-7205.
E-mail: aaie@sheridan.edu. Web: www.aaie.org.

**COUNCIL ON INTERNATIONAL EDUCATIONAL
EXCHANGE**
7 Custom House St, Ste 3, Portland, ME 04101.
Tel: 207-553-7600. Fax: 207-553-7699.
E-mail: info@ciee.org. Web: www.ciee.org.

ENGLISH-SPEAKING UNION
Dartmouth House, 37 Charles St, London, W1J 5ED.
Tel: 44-20-7529-1550. Fax: 44-20-7495-6108.
E-mail: esu@esu.org. Web: www.esu.org.

**INTERNATIONAL COUNCIL ON EDUCATION
FOR TEACHING**
c/o National-Louis Univ, 1000 Capitol Dr, Wheeling, IL 60090.
Tel: 847-465-0191. Fax: 847-465-5617.
E-mail: icet@nl.edu. Web: http://myclass.nl.edu/icet.

INTERNATIONAL SCHOOLS SERVICES
15 Roszel Rd, PO Box 5910, Princeton, NJ 08543.
Tel: 609-452-0990. Fax: 609-452-2690.
E-mail: iss@iss.edu. Web: www.iss.edu.

STUDENT YOUTH TRAVEL ASSOCIATION
936 S Baldwin Rd, Ste 104, Clarkston, MI 48348.
Tel: 248-814-7982. Fax: 248-814-7150.
E-mail: info@syta.org. Web: www.syta.org.

SCHOOL MEMBERSHIP ASSOCIATIONS

ASSOCIATION OF AMERICAN SCHOOLS IN MEXICO
c/o US Embassy Quito, Unit 5372, Box 004, APO, AA 34039.
Tel: 593-2-224-2996. Fax: 593-2-243-4985.
E-mail: marysanc@uio.satnet.net. Web: www.tri-association.org.

**ASSOCIATION OF AMERICAN SCHOOLS IN
SOUTH AMERICA**
14750 NW 77th Ct, Ste 210, Miami Lakes, FL 33016.
Tel: 305-821-0345. Fax: 305-821-4244.
E-mail: info@aassa.com. Web: www.aassa.com.

**ASSOCIATION OF AMERICAN SCHOOLS OF
CENTRAL AMERICA**
c/o US Embassy Quito, Unit 5372, Box 004, APO, AA 34039.
Tel: 593-2-224-2996. Fax: 593-2-244-9141.
E-mail: marysanc@uio.satnet.net. Web: www.tri-association.org.

ASSOCIATION OF COLOMBIAN-CARIBBEAN AMERICAN SCHOOLS
c/o US Embassy Quito, Unit 5372, Box 004, APO, AA 34039.
Tel: 593-2-224-2996. Fax: 593-2-243-4985.
E-mail: marysanc@uio.satnet.net. Web: www.tri-association.org.

ASSOCIATION OF INTERNATIONAL SCHOOLS IN AFRICA
c/o International School of Kenya, PO Box 14103, Nairobi, 00800.
Tel: 254-20-418-1658. Fax: 254-20-418-0596.
E-mail: aisa@isk.ac.ke. Web: www.aisa.or.ke.

CANADIAN ASSOCIATION OF INDEPENDENT SCHOOLS
202-12 Bannockburn Ave, Toronto, Ontario, M5M 2M8.
Tel: 416-780-1779. 416-780-9301. Fax: 905-833-1296.
E-mail: admin@cais.ca. Web: www.cais.ca.

DEPARTMENT OF DEFENSE EDUCATION ACTIVITY
4040 N Fairfax Dr, Arlington, VA 22203.
Tel: 703-588-3116.
E-mail: edwebpoc@hq.dodea.edu. Web: www.dodea.edu.

EAST ASIA REGIONAL COUNCIL OF OVERSEAS SCHOOLS
Brentville Subdivision, Barangay Mamplasan, Binan, Laguna, 4024.
Tel: 63-49-511-5993. Fax: 63-49-511-4694.
E-mail: info@earcos.org. Web: www.earcos.org.

EUROPEAN COUNCIL ON INTERNATIONAL SCHOOLS
21B Lavant St, Petersfield, Hampshire, GU32 3 EL.
Tel: 44-1730-268244. Fax: 44-1730-267914.
E-mail: ecis@ecis.org. Web: www.ecis.org.

INDEPENDENT SCHOOLS COUNCIL INFORMATION SERVICE
Grosvenor Gardens House, 35-37 Grosvenor Gardens, London, SW1W 0BS.
Tel: 44-20-7798-1560. Fax: 44-20-7798-1561.
E-mail: iscislse@iscislse.co.uk. Web: www.isc.co.uk.

INTERNATIONAL BACCALAUREATE ORGANIZATION
475 Riverside Dr, 16th Fl, New York, NY 10115.
Tel: 212-696-4464. Fax: 212-889-9242.
E-mail: ibna@ibo.org. Web: www.ibo.org.

INTERNATIONAL SCHOOLS ASSOCIATION
c/o SEK Preparatory School, 10333 Diego Dr S, Boca Raton, FL 33428.
Tel: 561-883-3854. Fax: 561-483-2004.
E-mail: info@isaschools.org. Web: www.isaschools.org.

MEDITERRANEAN ASSOCIATION OF INTERNATIONAL SCHOOLS
Apartado 80-28080, Madrid, 28080.
Fax: 34-91-357-2678.
E-mail: rohale@mais-web.org. Web: www.mais-web.org.

NATIONAL ASSOCIATION OF INDEPENDENT SCHOOLS
1620 L St NW, Ste 1100, Washington, DC 20036.
Tel: 202-973-9700. Fax: 202-973-9790.
Web: www.nais.org.

NEAR EAST SOUTH ASIA COUNCIL OF OVERSEAS SCHOOLS
c/o American College of Greece, Gravias 6, Aghia Paraskevi, Athens, 15342.
Tel: 30-210-600-9821. Fax: 30-210-600-9928.
E-mail: nesa@nesacenter.org. Web: www.nesacenter.org.

OFFICE OF OVERSEAS SCHOOLS
US Dept of State, Rm H328, SA-1, Washington, DC 20522.
Tel: 202-261-8200. Fax: 202-261-8224.
E-mail: overseasschools@state.gov. Web: www.state.gov/m/a/os.

SWISS FEDERATION OF PRIVATE SCHOOLS
Hotelgasse 1, PO Box 316, Bern 7, 3000.
Tel: 41-31-328-40-50. Fax: 41-31-328-40-55.
E-mail: info@swiss-schools.ch. Web: www.swiss-schools.ch.

STUDENT EXCHANGE ORGANIZATIONS

AFS INTERNATIONAL PROGRAMS
71 W 23rd St, 17th Fl, New York, NY 10010.
Tel: 212-807-8686. Fax: 212-807-1001.
E-mail: info@afs.org. Web: www.afs.org.

INDEX OF SCHOOLS

INDEX OF SCHOOLS

Schools are referenced by page number. Boldface page numbers refer to the optional Illustrated Announcements of schools that subscribe for space. To facilitate the use of Illustrated Announcements, refer to the separate index preceding that section.

In Your Own Words

Educators and parents have long trusted Porter Sargent for independent, objective school profiles available nowhere else.

Your program's Illustrated Announcement can support this mission, and it will be seen daily by:

- Parents
- Headmasters, and admissions and guidance counselors
- Consultants and vendors
- A worldwide network of educational professionals

Each reference-quality title is the book of record for its field, with a long shelf-life and high per-copy readership.

Please call 617-523-1670 or E-mail announcements@portersargent.com for details on joining the next edition.

The Handbook of Private Schools * The Directory for Exceptional Children
Schools Abroad of Interest to Americans * Guide to Summer Camps and Schools

THE PORTER SARGENT HANDBOOK SERIES

11 Beacon St. Ste. 1400 Boston, MA 02108-3099 USA
Tel: 617-523-1670 Fax: 617-523-1021
info@portersargent.com www.portersargent.com

Tools for Independent Evaluation

In 1914, educator and writer Porter Sargent introduced *The Handbook of Private Schools* because he felt educators, administrators and parents needed an objective guide to quality schools and programs emphasizing the needs of the individual student.

The development of the Porter Sargent Handbook Series followed that very simple aim. Each publication is a source book of information for those who need—and ought—to know about the advantage of independent instruction, providing the most up-to-date narrative and statistical information on schools and programs serving those who seek out the best education worldwide.

Yes, send me the most recent editions of:

Title	Price	Qty	Total
The Handbook of Private Schools	$99.00		
The Directory for Exceptional Children	$75.00		
Guide to Summer Camps and Summer Schools	$45.00		
Schools Abroad of Interest to Americans	$45.00		

Domestic shipping is $7.00, plus $1.50 for each additional book. Non-US shipping quoted on request.

All prices in $US.

Subtotal	
MA addresses add 5% sales tax	
US shipping	$7.00
$1.50/add'l book	
TOTAL	

☐ Check or money order enclosed (payable on a US bank)

☐ Bill me (organizations only)

☐ Visa   ☐ MasterCard   ☐ American Express   ☐ Discover

Card # _____ Exp. Date _____

Card Holder_____

Signature _____

_____

First Name   Last Name

_____

Company Name

_____

Street Address (no P.O. Boxes, please)

_____

City   State   Zip

_____

Country   Postal Code

E-mail _____

Daytime phone _____   SAB06

PORTER SARGENT PUBLISHERS, INC.
400 Bedford St   Ste 322   Manchester, NH 03101   USA
Tel: 800-342-7470   Fax: 603-669-7945
orders@portersargent.com   www.portersargent.com